PROCESS AND PROCEDURE
EU ADMINISTRATION

This book is about the administrative procedures of the European Union, which we see as the 'super glue' holding in place the sprawling structures of the EU governance system. The early chapters deal with the structures expansively defined, the diverse functions of administrative procedures in the EU and the values that underpin them, concentrating on the respective contributions of the legislature and administration. A separate chapter deals with the important procedural function of rights protection through the two Community Courts and the contribution of the European Ombudsman. We then turn to 'horizontal' or general procedures, dealing with executive law-making, transparency and the regulation of government contracting. A study of Commission enforcement procedure ends the section. 'Vertical' or sector-specific studies in significant areas of EU administration follow, including competition policy, cohesion policy (structural funds) and financial services regulation. Separate chapters deal with policing cooperation through Europol and with the interplay of international and EU institutions in the fields of environmental procedure and human rights. The final chapter contains the authors' reflections on current proposals for codification but ends with a general evaluation of the role and contribution of administrative procedure in the construction of the EU.

Process and Procedure in EU Administration

Carol Harlow and Richard Rawlings

·HART·
PUBLISHING
OXFORD AND PORTLAND, OREGON
2014

Published in the United Kingdom by Hart Publishing Ltd
16C Worcester Place, Oxford, OX1 2JW
Telephone: +44 (0)1865 517530
Fax: +44 (0)1865 510710
E-mail: mail@hartpub.co.uk
Website: http://www.hartpub.co.uk

Published in North America (US and Canada) by
Hart Publishing
c/o International Specialized Book Services
920 NE 58th Avenue, Suite 300
Portland, OR 97213-3786
USA
Tel: +1 503 287 3093 or toll-free: (1) 800 944 6190
Fax: +1 503 280 8832
E-mail: orders@isbs.com
Website: http://www.isbs.com

© Carol Harlow and Richard Rawlings 2014

Carol Harlow and Richard Rawlings have asserted their right under the Copyright, Designs and Patents Act 1988, to be identified as the authors of this work.

Hart Publishing is an imprint of Bloomsbury Publishing plc.

All rights reserved. No part of this publication may be reproduced, stored in a retrieval system, or transmitted, in any form or by any means, without the prior permission of Hart Publishing, or as expressly permitted by law or under the terms agreed with the appropriate reprographic rights organisation. Enquiries concerning reproduction which may not be covered by the above should be addressed to Hart Publishing Ltd at the address above.

British Library Cataloguing in Publication Data
Data Available

ISBN: 978-1-84946-298-3

Typeset by Hope Services Ltd, Abingdon
Printed and bound in Great Britain by
CPI Group (UK) Ltd, Croydon CR0 4YY

Acknowledgements

We would like to thank all those who have helped us in writing this book. First and foremost our thanks go to Christopher Anderson, our research assistant, for his invaluable assistance in navigating the many complexities of the official websites and for the excellence of his briefings and literature searches. Individual chapters have been inflicted on many friends, in particular Darius Adamski, Elspeth Guild, Jane Jenkins, Paivi Leino, Ed Page, Melanie Smith, Keith Vincent and members of the ReNEUAL network. Some chapters were tested at or developed from conferences and workshops, notably at the Amsterdam Centre for European Law and Governance and the Cambridge Centre for Public Law. We would also like to thank those at Hart Publishing for their patience and support, particularly Rachel Turner. Last but not least, this book originated in our joint postgraduate course taught at the London School of Economics and University College London and we thank the many students who helped with it over the years.

Carol Harlow,
Richard Rawlings
April 2014

Table of Contents

Acknowledgements v
Table of Cases xiii
Table of Treaties, Agreements, etc xxi
Table of EU Laws xxvii

Introduction 1
   Administrative Procedure: A Functionalist Approach 1
      Definitions 2
      'Horizontal' and 'Vertical' 4
      Sharing the Space 5
      Some Parameters 6

1: A Fragmented Framework 9
   In Search of EU Administration 9
   Member States and Enlargement 13
      National Procedural Autonomy 13
      Import–Export 14
      Growing the Union 16
   The Commission in EU Administration 18
      Breaking the Mould 18
      Public Service and Bureaucratic Culture 20
      Disgrace and Reform 22
      The Secretariat-General (SG) 24
      Outcome: A Managerial Administrative Style 24
      E-Governance: A Brave New World 25
   Committees as Network Structures 27
      Committees: Opaque or Transparent? 29
   Agencies and Networking 31
      Gaining Acceptance 32
      Gathering Momentum 34
   Conclusion 36

2: Into the Office: Tenets, Values and Objectives 38
   Principles and Standards 39
      Rationality: Reasoned Decision-Making 39
      More 'Glue': Sincere Cooperation 40
      Subsidiarity Matters 42

viii *Table of Contents*

Administrative Manifesto: 'Good Governance'		45
Tough Love: Conditionality		46
Audit and Managerialism		48
'Soft Law', 'Soft Governance' and the OMC		51
Soft Governance Lisbon Fashion		53
Regulation *à la mode*: 'Better' and 'Smart'		55
IA Abounding		56
Regulatory Fitness and Performance Programme (REFIT)		58
'Administrator's Toolkit'		60
Conclusion		62

3: Firefighting and Fire-Watching: Courts and Ombudsmen ... 64
   The Functions of Courts ... 65
   The Courts and Administrative Procedure ... 68
      Proportionality Testing ... 68
   Intensity of Review ... 71
      Reason-Giving to Rationality ... 73
      Reasons and Due Process ... 74
      Rationality and Risk Assessment ... 75
   Prioritising People: The European Ombudsman (EO) ... 79
      Redress and Reform ... 80
      Values and Principles ... 82
   Complaints Handling and Networks ... 84
      Problem-Solving through SOLVIT ... 84
      The European Network of Ombudsmen (ENO) ... 85
   Good Administration and Fundamental Rights ... 87
      Procedure as a Human Right ... 89
   Conclusion ... 91

4: Input and Output Values: Executive Law-Making ... 93
   Law-Making and Delegation ... 94
      Scientific Knowledge and Technocratic Rule-Making:
         Output Legitimacy ... 96
   An EU Innovation: Law-Making by Committee ... 97
      Comitology and Transparency ... 101
   The Lisbon Treaty Reforms ... 102
      Delegated Acts: Article 290 ... 103
      Post-Lisbon Implementing Procedure: Article 291 ... 104
   Constructing a Civil Society? ... 106
      Committee Corporatism: The European Economic and

Social Committee	106
Tending the Roots	108
Registration and Representativeness	110
Consultation – and Beyond?	112
Enforceability?	113
Judicial Abstention	114
Lisbon – Towards Partnership?	116
Conclusion	117
5: Transparency: Building Administrative Procedures	**119**
Transparency or Openness?	119
Market Transparency	119
Freedom of Information – A Political Right	121
The Codes of Conduct: Administrative Procedures	123
Classification, Secrecy and the 'Summertime Coup'	126
Regulation: Open Government or Official Secrecy?	127
Law-Making: An Openness Principle	128
Openness Trumped	131
The EU and National Information Laws	133
The Statutory Procedures	134
Ombudsmen for Openness	135
Towards Reform?	139
Conclusion	140
6: The Pathways Model and Steering: Public Procurement	**142**
Coordinating National Procedures	144
Rationales in Context	144
Waves of Legislation	146
Procedures, Procedures, Procedures	148
Judicial Multitasking	149
Transparency and Scope	150
Social and Environmental Objectives	152
Step By Step	154
Review and Remedy	158
Recodification	161
Process: Assessment	162
Scope and Proportionality	164
Changed Pathways	165
Governance	167
Conclusion	168

x Table of Contents

7: Procedural Development, Institutional Tensions: Commission
   Infringement Process ... 170
   Basic Constitutional Parameters: Four Corners ... 170
       Policy Dynamics: Institutional Tensions ... 172
   Commission Fire-Watching ... 173
       Challenge and Opportunity ... 173
       Expanded Toolkit ... 175
   Deep Roots: Infringement Procedure ... 179
       An Elongated Decision-Making Chain ... 179
       Elaborating Priorities ... 181
       Frontloading: 'EU Pilot' ... 182
   Competing Conceptions ... 184
       Judicial Policy ... 184
       Access to Documents ... 185
       Citizens' Advocate ... 187
   The EP's Challenge ... 190
   Sanctions Procedure ... 191
       Commission and Court ... 191
       Snakes and Ladders ... 193
   Conclusion ... 195

8: Modernisation, Cooperation, Enforcement: Competition ... 196
   Modernisation ... 198
       Continuity 198
       ... And Change ... 199
       'Economic Turn' ... 201
       Interplay: Modernisation and the CJEU ... 202
   Cooperation ... 205
       Network Design ... 205
       Maturation ... 206
       Flanking Developments ... 208
       Good Governance Principles ... 209
   Enforcement ... 210
       Stages, Tracks and Steps ... 211
       In-House Check: The Hearing Officer ... 214
       Sanctioning Toolkit: Guidelines ... 216
       Soft Law and Fundamental Rights ... 217
   Conclusion ... 220

9:	**Programming, Partnership and Audit: Cohesion Policy**	221
	Programming: Policy and Principles	224
	Rise and Rise	224
	Administrative Vehicle	226
	Retrenchment: More Union Strategy	228
	Micro and Macro Conditionality	229
	Article of Faith: Partnership	231
	Rhetoric and Reality	232
	Partnership Agreements	234
	Code of Conduct	235
	Management and Financial Supervision: Audit	236
	Decentralised Management: Supervisory Growth	236
	Targeting?	238
	Blight on the System	239
	In Search of Results	241
	Conclusion	242
10:	**Agencies, Networks and Accountability: The Case of Europol**	244
	Early Days and Evolution	245
	Mission Creep: The Europol Convention	246
	The Convention Model of Rule-Making	248
	The Europol Decision: A Substantive Transformation	250
	Loyal Cooperation	251
	Europol as Rule-Maker	252
	Good Governance	253
	Europol and Data Protection	254
	Supervision and Control: The Joint Supervisory Body	257
	Re-Ordering the Blocks: The Europol Regulation	258
	Management and Administration	259
	A Robust Data Protection Regime?	263
	Democratic Accountability	265
	Conclusion	266
11:	**Integration and Crisis: Financial Services Regulation**	268
	Elite Conception	269
	The Four-Level Model	269
	Better Regulation	272
	External Dimension	273
	Regulatory Network	274
	Before the Fall: Evaluation	276
	Agencification: Fourth Wave	277

xii   Table of Contents

Market Turmoil: Re-Evaluation and Reform	277
Formal Network	279
ESA Template	281
Standards and Guidelines	282
Decisions, Decisions	284
Going On	286
New Frontier	287
Architectural Issues	288
Inside the SSM: Tasks, Powers and Division of Labour	290
Inside the Bank: Separation and Autonomy	291
Variable Geometry	292
Due Process and Accountability	294
Conclusion	295
12: Procedural Trading: An International Market	297
Aarhus: Ensconcing Environmental Democracy	299
First Steps: Walking Alone	299
Working with Friends	302
The Aarhus Model	305
Implementation and Transposition	306
Aarhus and Enforceability	307
The Aarhus Convention Compliance Committee	309
Creative Courts: UN Sanctions and Due Process	311
Courts and Due Process – Again	311
Smart Sanctions and Asset Freezing	312
Judicial Intervention	314
Intensity of Review	315
Due Process Rights	316
Conflicting Obligations: A Houdini Approach	319
Conclusion	321
13: Conclusion: A Regulatory Bureaucracy	322
The 'Three Cs' of EU Administration	323
Communication and E-Governance	324
Administration Under Law	325
Clashing Values	328
Evolving Structures, Changing Governance Modes	329
Enlargement: Problem or Opportunity?	330
Procedural Codification?	331
A Regulatory Bureaucracy	335
Index	341

Table of Cases

Aannemersbedrijf PK Kraaijeveld BV v Gedeputeerde Staten van Zuid-Holland
(Case C–72/95) [1996] ECR I–5403 308
Abdulrahim v Council and Commission (Case T–127/09) (judgment of
9 September 2010) 317
Access Info Europe v Council (Case T–233/09) [2011] ECR II–0073.....................130
Airtours v Commission (Case T–342/99) [2002] ECR II–2585 ....72, 202
Al–Aqsa v Council (Joined Cases C–539 and 550/10) (judgment of 15 November
2012)..316
Alcatel (Case C–81/98) [1999] ECR I–7671...159
Alvis v Council (Case 32/62) [1963] ECR 99..20
API and Sweden v Commission (Case C–514/07) [2010] ECR I–8533 186
API v Commission (Case T–36/04) [2007] ECR II–03207 131
ArcelorMittal v Commission (Case C–201/09 P) [2011] ECR I–2239....................204
Archer Daniels v Commission (Case C-397/03 P) [2006] ECR I–4429 216
Artegodan GmbH v Commission (Case T–74/00) [2002] ECR II–4945...................76
Asia Motor France and others v Commission (Asia Motor II) (Case T–7/92) [1993]
ECR II–669... 72–73
Association belge des consommateurs test–achats v Commission (Case T–224/10)
(judgment of 12 October 2011) 115
Asteris and Others v Commission (Joined Cases 97, 99, 193, 215/86) [1988]
ECR 2181..317
Atlanta AG and others v Council and Commission (Case T–521/93) [1996]
ECR II–1707...115
Atlanta AG v European Community (Case C–104/97) [1999] ECR I–6983 115
Automec (Case T–64/89T) [1990] ECR II–367..74
Ayadi v Council (Case T- 253/02) [2006] ECR II–2139 318
Azko Nobel Chemicals v Commission (Case C–550/07 P) [2010] ECR 1–08301 212
BAT and Reynolds v Commission (Joined Cases 142/94, 156/84) [1987] ECR 4487 72
BAT v Commission (Case T–111/00) [2001] ECR II–2997......................................102
Bavarian Lager Company v Commission (Case T–309/97) [1999] ECR II–3217 186
Bavarian Lager v Commission (Case T–194/04) [2007] ECR II–04523...... 131, 139, 213, 333
Bavarian Lager v Commission (Case C–28/08) [2010] ECR I–6055 .... 102, 131, 139,
186, 213, 333
Belgische Radio en Televisie v SV Sabam (Case C–127/73) [1974] ECR 51 198
Besselink v Council (Case T–331/11) (judgment of 12 September 2013)............................122
Borax Europe v Commission (Case T–121/05) [2009] ECR II–27..102
Borax Europe v Commission (Case T–166/05) [2009] ECR II–28..132
Bosphorus Hava Yollari Turizm ve Ticaret Anonim Sirket v Ireland (2006) 42 EHRR 1 90
Boxus and others v Région Wallonie (Joined Cases C-128/09, C-131, C-134, C-135/09)
[2011] ECR I–09711 310

xiv Table of Cases

Bund für Umwelt und Naturschutz Deutschland, Landesverband Nordrhein-Westfalen eV v Bezirksregierung Arnsberg (Case C–115/09) [2011] ECR I–03673 309
Bund Naturschutz in Bayern v Freistaat Bayern (Case C–396/92) [1994] ECR I–3717.....308
Carbotermo SpA v Commune di Busto Arsizio (Case C–340/04) [2006] ECR I–4137........151
Carvel and Guardian Newspapers v Council (Case T–194/94) [1995] ECR II–2769 125
Cemex v Commission (Case T–292/11) (judgment of 14 March 2014)...............................212
CEVA Santé Animale and Pharmacia Enterprises v Commission (Joined Cases T–344 and 345/00) [2003] ECR II–229..75
Chalkor v Commission (Case C–386/10 P) [2011] ECR I–13085...219
ClientEarth v Commission (Case T–111/11) (judgment of 13 September 2013).......187, 190, 309–310
Coditel Brabant SA v Commune d'Uccle (Case C–324/07) [2009] ECR I–8457 151
Commission and Council v Kadi (Joined Cases C–584, 593, 595/10 P) (Judgment of 18 July 2013) 318
Commission v Agrofert Holding (Case C–477/10P) (judgment of 28 June 2012) 132
Commission v Alrosa (Case C–441/07 P) [2010] ECR I–5949 213
Commission v Austria (Case C–212/02) (judgment of 24 June 2004)..................................159
Commission v Austria (Case C–614/10) (judgment of 16 October 2012)...........................257
Commission v Belgium (Case C–85/85) [1986] ECR 1149...184
Commission v Belgium (Case C–533/11) (judgment of 17 October 2013) 194
Commission v CAS Succhi di Frutta SpA (Case C–496/99) [2004] ECR I–3801 150
Commission v Council (AETR) (Case 22/70) [1971] ECR 263 73
Commission v Council (CITES) (Case C–370/07) [2009] ECR I–08917 73
Commission v Czech Republic, Slovenia and Luxembourg (Joined Cases C–545/10, 627/10, 412/11) (judgments of 11 July 2013)..182
Commission v Denmark (Case 211/81) [1982] ECR 4507...174
Commission v Éditions Odile Jacob (Case C–404/10 P) (judgment of 28 June 2012)........132
Commission v Estonia (Case C–505/09) (judgment of 29 March 2012)................................44
Commission v France (Calais Nord) (Case C–225/98) [2000] ECR I–7455..........................153
Commission v France (Case C–1/00) [2001] ECR I–9989...185
Commission v France (Case C–304/02) [2005] ECR I–6263 ....34, 192–193
Commission v France (Case C–340/02) [2004] ECR I–9845..150
Commission v France (Case C–419/03) (judgment of 15 July 2004) 76
Commission v France (Case C–121/07) [2008] ECR I–9159..76, 193
Commission v Germany (Case C–317/92) [1994] ECR I–2039..184
Commission v Germany (Case C–431/92) [1995] ECR I–02189..308
Commission v Germany (Joined Cases C–20/01 and 28/01) [2003] ECR I–03609 160
Commission v Germany (Case C–518/07) [2010] ECR I–1885..257
Commission v Greece (Case C–329/88) [1989] ECR 4159..184
Commission v Greece (Case C–387/97) [2000] ECR I–5047 192
Commission v Greece (Case C–112/06) (order of 2 October 2008) 192
Commission v Ireland (Case 45/87) [1988] ECR 4035...147
Commission v Ireland (Irish Waste) (Case C–494/01) [2005] ECR–I 3331 185
Commission v Ireland (Case C–427/07) [2009] ECR I–6277 178
Commission v Ireland (Case C–279/11) (judgment of 19 December 2012).......................194
Commission v Ireland (Case C–374/11) (judgment of 19 December 2012).......................194
Commission v Italy (Case 35/84) [1986] ECR 545..73–74
Commission v Italy (Case C–456/03) [2005] ECR I–5335 173

Table of Cases xv

Commission v Kadi (Joined Cases C–584, 593 and 595/10 P) (judgment of
  18 July 2013) 316
Commission v Luxembourg (Case C–576/11) (judgment of 28 November 2013) 194
Commission v Netherlands (Case 96/81) [1982] ECR 1791 ....40, 141
Commission v Netherlands (Case C–350/02) [2004] ECR I–6213 185
Commission v Netherlands (Dutch Coffee) (Case C–368/10) [2012] ECR I–000 153
Commission v Planet AE (Case C–314/11 P) (judgment of 19 December 2012) 82
Commission v Poland (Case C–504) (judgment of 29 March 2012) 44
Commission v Portugal (Case C–292/11 P) (judgment of 15 January 2014) 193–194
Commission v Solvay (Solvay 1) (Joined Cases C–287 and 288/95 P) [2000]
  ECR I–2391 204
Commission v Spain (Case C–71/92) [1993] ECR I–5923 155
Commission v Spain (Case C–278/01) [2003] ECR I–14141 192
Commission v Spain (Case C–562/07) [2009] ECR I–9553 184
Commission v Spain (Case C–88/07) [2009] ECR I–01353 185
Commission v Sytravel and Brink's France SARL (Case C–367/95P) [1998] ECR I–179 74
Commission v Sweden (Case C-270/11) (judgment of 30 May 2013) 194
Commission v Technische Glaswerke Ilmenau GmbH (Case C–139/07 P) [2010]
  ECR I–05883 ....132, 186
Commission v Tetra Laval (Case C–12/03 P) [2005] ECR I–987 ....78, 202–203, 219
Commission v T–Mobile Austria GmbH (Case C–141/02 P) [2005] ECR I–1283 89
Commission v United Kingdom (Case C–530/11) (judgment of 13 February 2014) 307
Concordia Bus Finland v Helsinki (Case C–513/99) [2002] ECR I–7213 ....153, 157
Conserve Italia Soc Coop v Commission (Case C–500/99 P) [2002] ECR I–867 238
Consten and Grundig v Commission (Joined Cases C–56 and 58/64) 198
Consumer Detergents (Case COMP/39579 (2011)) 213
Continental Can v Commission (Case C–6/72) [1973] ECR 215 198
Council v Access Info Europe (Case C–280/11) (judgment of 17 October 2013) 131
Council v Bamba (Case C–417/11 P) (judgment of 15 November 2012) 313
Delacre v Commission (Case C–350/88) [1990] ECR I–395 73
Dennekamp v Parliament (Case T–82/09) (2011) ECR II–418 71
Digital Rights Ireland and Seitlinger (Joined Cases C–293/12 and 594/12)
  (judgment of 8 April 2014) 67, 70, 90
Egan and Hackett v Parliament (Case T–190/10) (judgment of 28 March 2012) 122
Einfuhr– und Vorratsstelle für Getreide und Futtermittel v Köster, Berodt & Co
  (Case 25/70) [1970] ECR 1161 95
European Commission v Germany (Case C–480/06) [2009] ECR I–4747 151
EVN & Weinstrom v Austria (Case C–448/01) [2003] ECR I–14527 153
Fedesa and others (Case C–331/88) [1990] ECR I–4023 69
Fish Legal, Emily Shirley v Information Commissioner and others (Case C–279/12)
  (judgment of 19 December 2013) 306
*Fitzwilliam Executive Search Ltd v Bestuur van het Landelijk Instituut Sociale
  Verzekeringen* (Case C–202/97) [2000] ECR I–883 41
France Telecom v Commission (Case T–339/04) [2007] ECR II–521 ....206, 210
France v Commission (Case T–139/06) [2011] ECR II–07315 34
Francovich and Bonifaci v Italy (Joined Cases C–6/90 and 9/90) [1991]
  ECR I–5357 ....159, 192
Funke v France (1993) 15 EHRR 297 91

xvi *Table of Cases*

Gbago and others v Council (Case C–478/11) (judgment of 19 December 2012)..............316
Gebroeders Beentjes BV v Netherlands (Case 31/87) [1989] ECR 4365...............................152
General Electric v Commission (Case T–201/01) [2005] ECR II–5575 204
Germany v Commission (Case 24/62) [1963] ECR 63 73
Germany v Commission (Case T–59/09) (judgment of 14 February 2012) 186–187
Gestetner Holdings v Council and Commission (Case C–156/87) [1990] ECR I–781...........71
Girish Ojha v Commission (Case C–294/95) [1996] ECR I–5863...21
Guerra v Italy [1998] 26 EHRR 357 302
Hassan and Ayadi (Joined Cases C–399 and 403/06) [2009] ECR I–11393.......................319
Hassan v Council and Commission (Case T–49/04) [2006] ECR II–32 318
Hautala v Council (Case T–14/98) [1999] ECR II–2489..125
Hautala v Council (No 2) (Case C–353/99P) [2001] ECR I–9565..124
Hecq v Commission (Joined Cases C–116 and 149/88) [1990] ECR I–599 20
Hercules Chemicals NV v Commission (Case T–7/89) [1991] ECR II–1711.......................214
Hercules Chemicals NV v Commission (Case C–51/92 P) [1999] ECR I–4235...................214
Hoechst v Commission (Joined Cases 46/87 and 227/88) [1989] ECR 2859........................91
Holcim v Commission (Case T–296/11) (judgment of 14 March 2014).............................212
Hortiplant SAT v Commission (Case C–330/01) [2004] ECR I–1763 238
Humblet v Belgium (Case 6/60) [1960] ECR 559 20
Hungary v Commission (Case T–240/10) (judgment of 13 December 2013) 76
IBP v Commission (Case T–384/06) (judgment of 24 March 2011)....................................216
IFAW Internationaler Tierschutz–Fonds v Commission (Case T–168/02) [2004]
  ECR II–4135..133
*International Transport Workers' Federation and the Finnish Seamen's Union v
  Viking Line APB* (Case C–438/05) [2007] ECR I–10779 53
Internationale Handelsgesellschaft mbh BVerfGE 37, 271 (1974) 91
Internationale Handelsgesellschaft v Einfuhr– und Vorratsstelle Getreide (Case 11/70)
  [1970] ECR 1125..68
Internationaler Tierschutz–Fonds v Commission (Sweden intervening) (Case C–64/05 P)
  [2007] ECR I–11389 133
Inuit Tapiriit Kanatami and Others v Parliament and Council (Case C–583/11 P)
  (judgment of 3 October 2013) 115
Italy v Commission (Case C–566/10 P) (judgment of 27 November 2012) 89
Jussila v Finland (2007) 45 EHRR 39 219
Kadi and Al Barakaat International Foundation v Council and Commission
  (Joined Cases C–402 P and C–415/05 P) [2008] ECR I–6351 .... 7, 85, 314–315, 317,
                                                                                                                    319–320
KME and Others v Commission (Case C–389/10 P) [2011] ECR I–13125 219
KME v Commission (Case C–272/09 P) [2011] ECR I–12789 219
Kone Oyj v Commission (Case C–510/11 P) (judgment of 24 October 2013) 219
Križan v Slovenská inšpekcia životného prostredia (Case C–416/10)
  (judgment of 15 January 2013)..307
Kühne & Heitz NV v Produktschap voor Pluimvee en Eieren (Case C–453/00)
  [2004] ECR I–00837 41
Küster v Parliament (Case 79/74) [1975] ECR 725 89
*Landelijke Vereniging tot Behoud van de Waddenzee v Staatssecrtaris van Landhouw,
  Natuurhebeer en Visserij* (Case C–127/02) [2004] ECR I–7405.......................................78
Laval v Svenska Byggnadsarbetareforbundet (Case C–341/05) [2007] ECR I–11767 53

Table of Cases xvii

Lesoochranárske zoskupenie VLK v Ministerstvo životného prostredia Slovenskej republiky
  (Case C–240/09) [2011] ECR I–01255 308
Lianakis AE v Alexandroupolis (Case C–532/06) [2008] ECR I–251 ....150, 154, 159
Liga para a Protecção da Natureza (LPN) and Finland v Commission (Joined Cases
  C–514/11 P and 605/11 P) (judgment of 14 November 2013)...............................186, 309
Long term electricity contracts in France (Case COMP/39386 (2010)) 211
Lopez Ostra v Spain [1995] 20 EHRR 277..302
Mara Messina v Commission (Case T–76/02) [2003] ECR II–3203..................................133
Masterfoods v HB Ice Cream (Case C–344/98) [2000] ECR I–11369 208
Matra v Commission (Case C–225/91) [1993] ECR I–3203..72
Mattila v Council and Commission (Case T–204/99) [2001] ECR II–2265......................126
Mattila v Council and Commission (Case C–353/01P) [2004] ECR I–1073.....................126
Maxmobil Telekommunikation Service GmbH v Commission (Case T–54/99)
  [2002] ECR II–0313 88
Mecklenburg v Kreiss Pinneberg der Landrat (Case C–321/96) [1998] ECR I–3809 306
Menarini Diagnostics v Italy (App no 43509/08) (judgment of 27 September 2011)........219
Meroni v High Authority (Case 9/56) [1957/58] ECR 133 ....32, 36, 95, 252,
                                                                                          282, 285, 289, 327
Microsoft Corpn v Commission (Case T–201/04) [2007] ECR II–3601 204
Microsoft (tying) (Case COMP/39530 (2009)) 213
Mohamed El Morabit v Council (Joined Cases T–37 and 323/07) [2009] ECR II–131......318
Monsanto Agricoltora Italia SpA v Presidenza del Consiglio dei Ministro
  (Case C–236/01) [2003] ECR I–8105 76
Monsanto and others (Joined Cases C–58 to 68/10) [2011] ECR I–07763..........................76
Muñiz v Commission (Case T–144/05) [2008] ECR II–0335...101
Netherlands v Council (Case C–58/94) [1996] ECR I–2169..124
NS and others v SSHD (Joined Cases C–411 and 493/10) [2011] ECR I–13905 90
Omega Air and others (Joined Cases C–27 and 122/00) [2000] ECR I–2560ˇ...............72, 74
Organisation des Modjahedines des peuples d'Iran (OMPI) v Council (Case T–228/02)
  [2006] ECR II–4665 316–319
Organisation des Modjahedines des peuples d'Iran v Council (Case T–256/07)
  [2008] ECR II–3019 315
Orkem v Commission (Case 374/87) [1989] ECR 3283...91, 212
Osman v United Kingdom [1998] EHRR 101..90
Parking Brixen (Case C–458/03) [2005] ECR I–8612 140
Parliament v Council (Case C–133/06) [2008] ECRI–3189 95
Parliament v Council (Case C–355/10) (judgment of 5 September 2012) 100
Parliament v Council (Chernobyl) (Case 70/88) [1990] ECR I–2041 98
Parliament v Council (Comitology) (Case 302/87) [1988] ECR 5615................................98
Petrie and Others v Commission (Case T–191/99) [2001] ECR II–3677 186
Pfizer Animal Health v Council (Case T–13//99) [2002] ECR II–3305..............................76
Pressetext v Austria (Case C–454/06) [2008] ECR I–4401 ....151–152, 165
Pringle v Government of Ireland (Case C–370/12) (judgment of 27 November 2012)........47
R (Law Society) v Legal Services Commission [2007] EWCA Civ 1264 150
R v Environment Secretary ex p Omega Air and others (Joined Cases C–27 and 122/00)
  [2000] ECR I–2560 69
R v Health Secretary ex p British American Tobacco (Investments) and Imperial Tobacco
  (Case C–491/01) [2002] ECR I–11453 ....44, 69

xviii Table of Cases

R v MAFF and Commissioners of Customs and Excise ex p NFU (Case C–157/96)
[1998] ECR I–2211 76
R v Secretary of State for Transport ex p Factortame (Case C–213/89) [1990]
ECR I–2433 159
Rey Soda v Cassa Conguaglio Zucchero (Case 23/75) [1975] ECR 1279 95
Schindler Holding and Others v Commission (Case C–501/11 P) (judgment of
18 July 2013)..217, 219
Schneider Electric v Commission (Case T–310/01) [2002] ECR II–4071 202
Segi, Izaga, Galarraga v Council (Case C–355/04 P) [2007] ECR I–1657) 313
Sison v Council (Case T–47/03) [2007] ECR II–73...................................... 313, 317
Sison v Council (Joined Cases T–110, T–150 and T–405/03) [2005] ECR II–1429 315
Sison v Council (Case C–266/05 P) [2007] ECR I–1233 .... 315, 317
Solvay & Cie v Commission (Case 27/88) [1989] ECR 3355 212
Solvay v Commission (Solvay 2) (Joined Cases C–109 and 110/10) [2011]
ECR I–10329 204
Sonito v Commission (Case C–87/89) [1990] ECR I–1981....................................185
Sophie in't Veld v Council (Case T–529/09) (judgment of 4 May 2012)..............130
Sophie in't Veld v Commission (Case T–310/10) (judgment of 19 March 2013)................130
Stadt Halle (Case C–26/03) [2005] ECR I–1 151–160
Star Fruit v Commission (Case 247/87) [1989] ECR 291 185
Svenska Journalistforbundet v Council (Case T–174/95) [1998] ECR II–2289 121
Sweden and API v Commission (Joined Cases C–514/07 P, C–528/07 P, C–532/07 P)
[2010] ECR I–8533 131
Sweden and Turco v Council (Joined Cases C–39/05 and 52/05) [2008]
ECR I–4723 ....130, 189
Sweden v Commission (Case T–229/04) (2007) ECR II–2437...........................75, 77
Sweden v Commission and MyTravel Group plc (Case C–506/08 P) (judgment of
21 July 2011)...132
Swedish Interconnectors (Case COMP/39351 (2010)) 211
Tagaras v Court of Justice (Case T–18/89) [1991] ECR II–53..................................20
Társaság a Szabadságjogokért v Hungary (App 37374/05) [2009] ECHR 618...............132
Technische Glaswerke Ilmenau v Commission (Case T–237/02) [2006]
ECR II–5131..132, 186
Teckal Srl v Comune di Viano (Case C–107/98) [1999] ECR I–8121.............. 151, 165
Telaustria (Case C–324/98) [2000] ECR I–10745 150
Telekomunikacja Polska (Case COMP/39525 (2011)) 211
Terre Wallonie and Inter–Environment v Région Wallonie (Joined Cases C–105
and 110/09) [2010] ECR I–05611 306
Tetra Laval v Commission (Case T–5/02) [2002] ECR II–4381 ....72, 202, 219
Thesing and Bloomberg Finance v European Central Bank (Case T–590/10)
(judgment of 29 November 2012) 132
ThyssenKrupp v Commission (Case C–352/09 P) [2011] ECR I–2359 204
Toland v Parliament (Case T–471/08) (2011) ECR II–271 122
Transocean Marine Paint Association v Commission (Case 17/74) [1974]
ECR 1063..74, 312
Turco v Council (Case T–84/03) [2004] ECR II–4061 ....129–130, 189
UEAPME v Council (Case T–135/96) [1998] ECR II–2335...................................115
United Kingdom v Commission (Case C–180/96) [1998] ECR I–2265 76

UNECTEF v Heylens (Case 222/86) [1987] ECR 4097..317
United Kingdom v Council (Case C–84/94) [1996] ECR I–5755 44
United Kingdom v Council (Case C–150/94) [1998] ECR–I–7235 71
United Kingdom v Parliament and Council (*ESMA* case) (Case C–270/12)
  (judgment of 22 January 2014)..35, 66
Universale–Bau (Case C–470/99) [2002] ECR I–11617..151
Verein fur Konsumenteninformation v Commission (Case T–2/03) [2005]
  ECR II–1121..123
Vodafone Ltd v Secretary of State for Business, Enterprise and Regulatory Reform
  (Case C–58/8) [2010] ECR I–4999 45
WWF UK v Commission (Case T–105/95) [1997] ECR II–313 186
Yassin Abdullah Kadi v Commission (Case T–85/09) [2010] ECR II–5177 ....316, 320
Yassin Abdullah Kadi v Council and Commission (Case T–315/01) [2005]
  ECR II–3649..314

Decisions of the European Ombudsman

EO, Inv 132/21.9.95/AH/EN *Newbury Bypass* 188, 308
EO, Inv 1288/99/OV *Parga* 191
EO, Inv 146/2005/GG *German Waste Oils* 189
EO, Inv 97/2008/(BEH)JF 29
EO, Inv 111/2008/TS 257
EO, Inv 1935/2008/FOR *Intel* 213
EO, Inv 297/2010/(ELB)GG..218
EO, Inv 1260/2010/RT 189
EO, Inv 2591/2010/GG...81, 308
EO, Inv 0875/2011/JF 57
EO, Inv 1966/2011/(EIS)LP 284
EO, Inv 2510/2011/CK 71
EO, Inv 2166/2012/BEH...260
EO, Inv 2167/2012/BEH...260
EO, Inv 2168/2012/BEH...260

Rulings of the Aarhus Convention Compliance Committee

ACCC /C/2008/32 *ClientEarth*...310
ACCC /C/2010/54 *Irish Feed–In Tariffs*...310
ACCC/C/2011/61 *Crossrail Decision* 310

Table of Treaties, Agreements, etc

Amsterdam Treaty1997 126
    Art 255 123
    Declaration 12 300
Anti–Piracy Treaty 130
Charter of the Committee of European Securities Regulators 2001 275–276
    Art 4 275
    Art 5 275–276
    Art 6 276
Charter of the United Nations 314
    Art 47 316
Convention on Access to Information, Public Participation in Decision–Making and Access to Justice in Environmental Matters (Aarhus Convention) 6, 112, 127, 1
86, 299, 302–311, 321, 326–327
    Art 3 305
    Art 4 305
    Art 5 305
    Art 6 305
    Art 7 305
    Art 8 305
    Art 9(3) 308
    Art 9(5) 305
Convention on Mutual Assistance between Customs Administrations 1967 41
Council Common Position (CP) 2001/931 on the application of specific measures to
    combat terrorism [2001] OJ L344/93 .... 313, 315, 317
    Art 1(4)–(5) 314
Council of Europe Convention on Access to Official Documents 2009 298
Council of Europe Convention on cybercrime 31
Council of Europe Convention for the Protection of Individuals with regard to
    Automatic Processing of Personal Data 1981 256
EC Treaty. *See* Treaty establishing the European Community
EEC Treaty. *See* Treaty establishing the European Economic Community 1957
EP and ECB Inter–Institutional Agreement on the cooperation on procedures
    related to the Single Supervisory Mechanism 2013 .... 288, 295
    recital D 295
EU–US agreement on the processing and transfer of Financial Messaging Data for the
    purposes of the Terrorist Finance Tracking Program [2010] OJ 2010 L195/5 262
European Charter of Fundamental Rights 21, 26, 85, 88, 90–91, 136, 197,
219, 256, 300, 319–320, 325–326, 333
    Art 4 90

xxii *Table of Treaties, Agreements, etc*

Art 7..67, 90
Art 8..67, 90, 259
Art 37...300
Art 41... 40, 87–91, 191, 203, 325–326, 333
Art 41(1)..87
Art 41(2)..87
Art 41(2)(a)..87
Art 41(2)(b)..87
Art 41(2)(c)..87
Art 41(3)..87
Art 41(4)...87, 89
Art 42..203, 214
Art 47...218–219, 319
European Convention on Human Rights........ 90–91, 182, 197–198, 219, 298, 319, 325–326
   Art 3...319
   Art 5...90
   Art 6...90, 218–219, 320
   Art 6(1)...310
   Art 8..302, 319
   Art 10..132
   Art 13..90, 320
   Protocol 1 ....
      Art 1..319
Europol Convention 1995 ....246, 248, 266
   Art 2(1)... 246–247
   Art 4(4)..248
   Art 34..248
   Art 43(3)...247
   Protocol 1 247
   Protocol 2 ....247, 248
      Art 43(3)..247
   Protocol 3 248
Europol–Eurojust agreement 2008 261
International Convention for the Conservation of Atlantic Tunas......................298
Joint Action 95/73/JHA adopted by the Council on the basis of Art K.3 of the Treaty on European Union concerning the Europol Drugs Unit [1995] OJ L 62/1.......................245
Joint Action 2008/124/CFSP on the European Union Rule of Law Mission in Kosovo [2008] OJ L42/92 298
Lisbon Treaty 2007 ....11, 13–14, 27, 67, 89, 91, 94–95, 102–103, 116, 140, 182, 193, 219, 223, 229, 253, 267, 298, 309, 332, 338
   Art 88..258
Maastricht Treaty 1992 ....3, 18, 42, 79, 108, 191, 225, 329
   Art K1...245
   Art K3...245
   Declaration 17...120
   Declaration 23...108

Table of Treaties, Agreements, etc xxiii

Merger Treaty 1965. See Treaty of Brussels 1965
Prüm Convention on the stepping up of cross–border cooperation, particularly in combating terrorism, cross border crime and illegal migration 2005 (Schengen III) ...30, 245, 256
Single European Act 1985 (SEA) 97, 300
Sweden and Finland Accession Treaty 1995 121
    Declaration No 45 121
    Declaration No 47 121
Treaty of Brussels 1965 (Merger Treaty 1965) 18
    Art 5 40
Treaty establishing the European Community (TEC) 40, 311
    Art 3c 300
    Art 6 300
    Art 10 (ex EC Art 5) 323
    Art 21 87
    Art 155 ....13, 19
    Art 226 188
    Art 230 114
    Art 255 127
    Art 255(2) 127
    Art 257 107
    Art 258(3) 106
    Art 262 106
    Art 288 87
    Art 308 332
Treaty establishing the European Economic Community 1957 (EEC Treaty)
    Art 130R 300
    Art 130S 300
    Art 130T 300
Treaty Establishing the European Stability Mechanism 47, 288
    Art 12 47
Treaty on European Union 39, 120
    Preamble 9
    Art 2 182
    Art 4(3) 40, 170
    Art 5 43
    Art 5(3) 43
    Art 5(4) 68
    Art 6(2) 91
    Art 7 9
    Art 9 43
    Art 10(3) 116
    Art 11 ....94, 116
    Art 11(4) 94
    Art 13 40
    Art 17(1) 170
    Art 17(2) 93

xxiv   *Table of Treaties, Agreements, etc*

Art 19(1) (ex TEC Art 164) 66, 171, 326–327
Art 34 124
Art 35 .... 124, 313
Art 36 124
Protocol (No 2) on the Application of the Principles of Subsidiarity and
    Proportionality 43
    Art 3 43
    Art 7 44
    Art 8 44
Treaty on the Functioning of the European Union 145
    Art 3(1) 196
    Art 11 153
    Art 16 259
    Art 24 .... 89, 116
    Art 53 266
    Art 75 313
    Art 101 (ex EEC Art 85) 198, 207
    Art 102 (ex EEC Art 86) 198, 207
    Art 114 .... 45, 67
    Art 118 89
    Art 127(6) 288–289
    Art 129(1) 292
    Art 130 291
    Art 174 221
    Art 175 221
    Art 282 289
    Art 283 289
    Art 191 76
    Art 195 (ex TEC Art 228) 79
    Art 197 .... 14, 172, 331–332
    Art 197(1) 170, 176
    Art 197(2) 332
    Art 258 .... 171–173, 179–180, 183–184, 191–194, 285
    Art 259 173
    Art 260 .... 171, 173–174, 181, 192–194, 216
    Art 260(3) 193
    Art 261 198
    Art 263 .... 66, 115
    Art 275 313
    Art 288 94
    Art 289(1) 94
    Art 290 .... 94–95, 101, 103, 282
    Art 290(1) 217
    Art 291 .... 95, 104, 282
    Art 296 .... 40, 73, 319
    Art 298 .... 14, 140, 191, 332
Treaty of Rome 171, 191

UN S/RES/1267 (1999) Afghanistan 312–313, 319
UN S/RES/1373 (2001) Threats to international peace and security caused
  by terrorist acts 312–313
UN S/RES/1535 (2004) Threats to international peace and security caused by
  terrorist acts 320
UN S/RES/1730 (2006) General issues relating to sanctions 313, 320
UN S/RES/1735 (2006) Threats to international peace and security caused by
  terrorist acts 320
UN S/RES/1822 (2008) Threats to international peace and security caused by
  terrorist acts 320
UN S/RES/1904 (2009) Threats to international peace and security caused by
  terrorist acts 320
World Trade Organization Government Procurement Agreement 151

Table of EU Laws

Regulations

Regulation 17/EEC: First Regulation implementing Arts 85 and 86 of the Treaty [1962] OJ L13/204 .... 196, 198–200
Regulation (EEC) 31/62 laying down the Staff Regulations of Officials and the Conditions of Employment of Other Servants of the European Economic Community [1962] OJ 45/1385 20
Regulation (EEC) 2052/1988 on the tasks of the Structural Funds and their effectiveness [1988] OJ L185/9 224
Regulation (EEC) 1210/90 on the establishment of the European Environment Agency and the European Environment Information and Observation Network [1990] OJ L120/1 301
Regulation (EC) 659/1999 laying down detailed rules for the application of Art 93 of the EC Treaty 32
Regulation (EC) 1260/1999 laying down general provisions on the Structural Funds [1999] OJ L161/1
   Arts 14–19 227
Regulation (EC) 45/2001 on the protection of individuals with regard to the processing of personal data by the Community institutions and bodies and on the free movement of such data [2001] OJ L8/1 .... 139, 256
Regulation (EC) 1049/2001 regarding public access to European Parliament, Council and Commission documents [2001] OJ L145/43 ...... 82, 101, 127, 129–134, 136, 138–139, 186–187, 258, 260, 306, 310
   recitals, para 6 128
   Art 2(1) 135
   Art 2(4) 134
   Art 3(1)–(2) 135
   Art 4(1) 128, 131–132, 134, 187
   Art 4(2) 128–129, 134, 187
   Art 4(3) 128, 134
   Art 4(4)–(5) 133
   Art 4(6) 134
   Art 5 133
   Art 6 134
   Art 8 134
   Art 9 127
   Art 10 134
Regulation (EC) 881/2002 imposing certain specific restrictive measures directed against certain persons and entities associated with the Al–Qaida network 313–314
Regulation (EC, Euratom) 1605/2002 on the Financial Regulation applicable to the general budget of the European Communities [2002] OJ L248/1 .... 17, 48–50, 61, 84, 221, 224, 236–237, 241, 243, 337

xxviii Table of EU Laws

Regulation (EC) 1/2003 on the Implementation of the Rules on Competition
Laid Down in Arts 81 and 82 of the Treaty [2003] OJ L1/1 (Modernisation
Regulation) 196, 200, 203, 205, 207–208, 210, 213, 216, 220
   recital 15 .... 200, 205
   recital 18 205
   Art 9 213
   Art 11 205
   Art 11(1) 200
   Art 11(6) 205
   Art 12 205–206
   Art 14 214
   Arts 15–16 208
   Arts 17–21 212
   Art 23(2) 216
   Art 27(1) 214
   Art 27(2) 203, 210
   Art 28 210
Regulation (EC) 58/2003 laying down the statute for executive agencies to be
entrusted with certain tasks in the management of Community programmes
[2003] OJ L11/1 49
   Art 53 49
Regulation (EC) 1059/2003 on the establishment of a common classification of
territorial units for statistics (NUTS) [2003] OJ L154/1
   recital 7 226
Regulation (EC) 139/2004 on the control of concentrations between undertakings
[2004] OJ L 24/1 (Merger Regulation) 201
Regulation (EC) 725/2004 on enhancing ship and port facility security [2004]
OJ L129/6
   Art 9 177
Regulation (EC) 773/2004 Relating to the Conduct of Proceedings by the
Commission Pursuant to Arts 81 and 82 of the EC Treaty [2004] OJ L123/18 201
   Art 6(2) 214
   Arts 12–13 214
Regulation (EC) 882/2004 on official controls performed to ensure the verification
of compliance with feed and food law, animal health and animal welfare rules
[2004] OJ L165/1
   Art 45 177
Regulation (EC) 2007/2004 Frontex Regulation [2004] OJ L349/1 99
Regulation (EC) 560/2005 imposing certain specific restrictive measures directed
against certain persons and entities in view of the situation in Côte d'Ivoire
[2005] OJ L95/1 313
Regulation (EC) 768/2005 establishing a Community Fisheries Control Agency
and amending Regulation (EEC) No 2847/93 establishing a control system
applicable to the common fisheries policy [2005] OJ L128/1
   Art 3 34
Regulation (EC) 1083/2006 laying down general provisions on the European
Regional Development Fund, the European Social Fund and the Cohesion Fund
and repealing Regulation (EC) No 1260/199 [2006] OJ L210/25 226–227

Table of EU Laws xxix

recital 27 227
recital 65 227
Art 9..226
Art 13..227
Arts 25–28 228
Arts 29–30 227
Art 32..228
Art 37..228
Art 62..239
Art 73..239
Regulation (EC) 1085/2006 establishing an Instrument for Pre–Accession [2006]
  OJ L210/82 17
Regulation (EC) 1907/2006 concerning the Regulation, Evaluation, Authorisation
  and Restriction of Chemicals and Establishing a European Chemicals Agency
  [2006] OJ L396/1 (REACH Regulation)... 176, 306
  Arts 76–77 176
Regulation (EC) 1367/2006 on the application of the provisions of the Aarhus
  Convention on Access to Information, Public Participation in Decision–making
  and Access to Justice in Environmental Matters to Community institutions and
  bodies [2006] OJ L264/13.. 186, 310
Regulation (EC) 1987/2006 on the establishment, operation and use of the second
  generation Schengen Information System (SIS II) [2006] OJ L381/4 255
Regulation (EC) 168/2007 establishing a European Union Agency for Fundamental
  Rights [2007] OJ L53/1...88
Regulation (EC) 662/2008 as regards the conduct of settlement procedures in cartel
  cases [2008] OJ L171/3 213
Regulation (EC) 302/2009 concerning a multiannual recovery plan for bluefin tuna
  [2009] OJ L96/1 298
Regulation (EC) 401/2009 on the European Environment Agency and the European
  Environment Information and Observation Network [2009] OJ L 126/13 301
Regulation (EC) 1224/2009 establishing a Community control system for ensuring
  compliance with the rules of the common fisheries policy, etc [2009] OJ L343/1
  Art 7(d)...34
Regulation (EC) 904/2010 on administrative cooperation and combating fraud in
  the field of value added tax (recast) [2010] OJ L268/1 42
  recital 14 42
  recital 18 42
  Art 4..42
  Art 28..42
  Art 49..42
Regulation (EU) 1092/2010 on European Union macro–prudential oversight of the
  financial system and establishing a European Systemic Risk Board [2010] OJ L331/1
  Arts 3–5 280
  Arts 15–18 280
Regulation (EU) 1093/2010 establishing a European Supervisory Authority
  (European Banking Authority) [2010] OJ L331/12 (EBA Regulation)..........269, 281, 293
  recital 23 283
  Art 8(1)–(2)..281

xxx Table of EU Laws

Art 9 281
Art 10 282–283
Art 10(1) 282–284
Arts 11–12 283
Art 14 283
Art 15 282
Art 15(1) 283–284
Art 16 283
Art 16(2) 284
Art 16(3)–(4) 283
Art 17 285
Art 17(6) 285
Art 18 286
Art 19 285
Arts 21–23 281
Arts 29–35 281
Art 37 284
Art 38 286
Art 40 282
Art 41 285
Arts 42–55 282
Arts 58–61 282
Regulation (EU) 1094/2010 establishing a European Supervisory Authority
  (European Insurance and Occupational Pensions Authority) [2010]
  OJ L331/48 281
Regulation (EU) 1095/2010 establishing a European Supervisory Authority
  (European Securities and Markets Authority) [2010] OJ L331/84 281
Regulation (EU) 182/2011 laying down the rules and general principles concerning
  mechanisms for control by Member States of the Commission's exercise of
  implementing powers [2011] OJ L55/13 104–105
  Art 6(3) 105
Regulation (EU) 211/2011 on the citizens' initiative [2011] OJ L65/1 116
Regulation (EU) 1077/2011 establishing a European Agency for the operational
  management of large–scale IT systems in the area of freedom, security and justice
  [2011] OJ L286/1 255
Regulation (EU) 236/2012 on short selling and certain aspects of credit default swaps
  [2012] OJ L86/1 103
Regulation (EU) 826/2012 supplementing Regulation (EU) 236/2012 with regard to
  regulatory technical standards on notification and disclosure requirements with
  regard to net short positions, the details of the information to be provided to the
  European Securities and Markets Authority in relation to net short positions and
  the method for calculating turnover to determine exempted shares [2012]
  OJ L251/1 103
Regulation (EU) 827/2012 laying down implementing technical standards with
  regard to the means for public disclosure of net position in shares, etc
  [2012] OJ L251/11 103
Regulation (EU) 918/2012 supplementing Regulation (EU) 236/2012 on short selling
  and certain aspects of credit default swaps [2012] OJ L274/1 103

Regulation (EU) 919/2012 supplementing Regulation (EU) 236/2012 on short selling and certain aspects of credit default swaps with regard to regulatory technical standards for the method of calculation of the fall in value for liquid shares and other financial instruments [2012] OJ L274/16 103

Regulation (EU, Euratom) 966/2012 on the financial rules applicable to the general budget of the Union and repealing Council Regulation (EC, Euratom) 1605/2002 [2012] OJ L298/1 49

Regulation (EU) 462/2013 amending Regulation (EC) 1060/2009 on credit rating agencies [2013] OJ L146/1..279

Regulation (EU) 575/2013 on prudential requirements for credit institutions and investment firms [2013] OJ L176/1 279

Regulation (EU, Euratom) 883/2013 concerning investigations conducted by the European Anti–Fraud Office (OLAF) and repealing Regulation (EC) 1073/1999 and Regulation (Euratom) 1074/1999 [2013] OJ L248/1.......................49, 239

Regulation (EU) 1022/2013 amending Regulation 1093/2010 establishing the European Banking Authority as regards the conferral of specific tasks on the European Central Bank [2013] OJ L287/5
recital 7 284
recital 12 293
Art 1..283
Art 1(2)...293
Art 1(24)...294
Art 2..294

Regulation (EU) 1023/2013 amending the Staff Regulations of Officials of the European Union and the Conditions of Employment of other Servants of the European Union [2013] OJ L287/15............................. 20–21, 23, 49, 60, 84, 332
Title VI..20
Title VII 20
recitals 4–5...21
recital 7 21
Annex IX 20

Regulation (EU) 1024/2013 conferring specific tasks on the European Central Bank concerning policies relating to the prudential supervision of credit institutions [2013] OJ L287/63 ....269, 290–291, 293–294
recital 30 293
Art 3(6)...293
Art 4..289
Art 4(1)...290
Art 5..289
Art 6.. 290–291
Art 6(7)...291
Art 7(2)...292
Art 7(5)–(9)..293
Arts 9–13 290
Art 16...290
Art 18...290
Art 20...294
Art 21...295

xxxii Table of EU Laws

Art 22 294
Art 24 294
Art 25 292
Art 25(2) 291
Art 25(5) 292
Art 26 ....292, 294
Art 26(8) 292
Regulation (EU) 1303/2013 laying down common provisions on the European Regional Development Fund [2013] OJ L347/289
recital 2 228
recital 11 231
recital 87 227
recitals 124–125 237
Art 2(2) 234
Art 2(20) 235
Art 4 ....223, 228–230, 234, 236–238
Art 5 ....229, 231
Art 5(3) 235
Art 5(5) 235
Art 9 229
Arts 10–11 228
Art 14 235
Art 15 234
Art 16(2) 235
Art 16(4) 235
Arts 18–19 229
Art 20 ....229, 242
Arts 21–22 229
Art 23 230
Art 23(9) 231
Art 23(15) 231
Art 27 ....227, 229
Art 29 229
Art 47 223
Art 48 232
Arts 54–57 242
Art 72 236
Art 75 238
Arts 84–85 238
Arts 86–88 236
Art 89 229
Art 95 227–228
Art 122 238
Art 123 ....223, 238
Art 125 236
Art 125(4) 237
Arts 126–127 237

Table of EU Laws xxxiii

    Art 136...236
    Arts 138–139...238
    Art 143...236
    Art 148...239
    Arts 149–150...237
    Annex 1..228
    Annex III..230
    Annex XI..230
Regulation (EU) 240/2014 on the European code of conduct in the framework of the
    European Structural and Investment Funds [2014] OJ L74/1.......................................235
    Art 4...236
    Art 13...236
    Art 18...236
Regulation (EU) 468/2014 establishing the framework for cooperation within the Single
    Supervisory Mechanism between the European Central Bank and national competent
    authorities and with national designated authorities [2014] OJ L141/1
    (SSM Framework Regulation) 291, 294
    Arts 3–6...291
    Arts 8–10...291
    Arts 31–33...294
    Arts 39–66...291
    Arts 106–117...292
    Arts 118–119...293
    Arts 120–137...291

Directives

Directive 71/305/EEC coordinating public procurement procedures for works
    (Works Directive) [1971] OJ L185/15...147
Directive 76/160/EEC concerning the quality of bathing water [1976] OJ L31/1
    (Bathing Water Directive) 177
Directive 76/308/EEC on mutual assistance for the recovery of claims resulting from
    operations forming part of the system of financing the European Agricultural
    Guidance and Guarantee Fund, and of the agricultural levies and customs
    duties [1976] OJ L73/18...41
Directive 77/62/EEC coordinating procedures for the award of public supply
    contracts [1977] OJ L13/1...147
Directive 79/1071/EEC amending Directive 76/308/EEC on mutual assistance for
    the recovery of claims resulting from operations forming part of the system of
    financing of the European Agricultural Guidance and Guarantee Fund, and of
    agricultural levies and customs duties [1979] OJ L331/10................................41
Directive 85/337/EEC Environmental Impact Assessment Directive [1985] OJ L175/40 as
    later amended by Directive 2003/35/EC of 26 May 2003 on the assessment of
    the effects of certain public and private projects on the environment [2003]
    OJ L156/17 ....55, 300–301, 303, 308–309
    Art 1(2)...309

xxxiv *Table of EU Laws*

Directive 89/105/EEC relating to the transparency of measures regulating the pricing of medicinal products for human use and their inclusion within the scope of national health insurance systems [1989] OJ L40/08 (Transparency Directive) 120
Directive 89/665/EEC on the coordination of the laws, regulations and administrative provisions relating to the application of review procedures to the award of public supply and public works contracts [1989] OJ L395/33 .... 147, 158–160
    Art 1 158
Directive 90/313/EEC on the freedom of access to information on the environment [1990] OJ L158/56 .... 301–303, 305–306
    Art 3 302
Directive 91/271/EEC concerning urban waste–water treatment [1991] OJ L135/40 (Urban Waste–Water Directive) 194
Directive 91/414/EEC concerning the placing of plant protection products on the market [1991] OJ L230/1 (Plant Protection Products Directive) 77
Directive 92/13/EEC coordinating the laws, regulations and administrative provisions relating to the application of Community rules on the procurement procedures of entities operating in the water, energy, transport and telecommunications sectors [1992] OJ L76/14 (Utilities Remedies Directive) 147
Directive 92/43/EEC on the conservation of natural habitats and of wild fauna and flora [1992] OJ L206/7 (Habitats Directive), as amended by Council Directive 2006/105/EC [2006] OJ L363 .... 133, 186, 308
Directive 92/50/EEC relating to the coordination of procedures for the award of public service contracts [1992] OJ L209/1 .... 147, 154
Directive 92/108/EEC amending Directive 92/12/EEC on the general arrangements for products subject to excise duty and on the holding, movement and monitoring of such products and amending Directive 92/81/EEC [1992] OJ L390/124 41
Directive 93/36/EEC coordinating procedures for the award of public supply contracts [1993] OJ L199/1 147
Directive 93/37/EEC concerning the coordination of procedures for the award of public works contracts [1993] OJ L199/54 147
Directive 93/38/EEC coordinating the procurement procedures of entities operating in the water, energy, transport and telecommunications sectors [1993] OJ L199/84 .... 147, 154
Directive 95/46/EC on the protection of individuals with regard to the processing of personal data and on the free movement of such data [1995] OJ L281/31 (Data Protection Directive) 131, 256
    Arts 29–30 30
Directive 96/34/EC on the framework agreement on parental leave [1996] OJ 145/4
    Arts 3–4 115
Directive 96/61/EC concerning integrated pollution prevention and control [1996] OJ L257/26 (IPPC Directive) 304
Directive 2000/60/EC establishing a framework for Community action in the field of water policy [2000] OJ L327/1 (Water Framework Directive) 176, 305
    Art 21 176
Directive 2001/16 EC on the interoperability of the trans–European conventional rail system [2001] OJ L110/1 41

Directive 2001/42/EC on the assessment of the effects of certain plans and
  programmes on the environment [2001] OJ L197/30 (Strategic Environmental
  Assessment Directive)...302, 30
Directive 2001/44/EC amending Directive 76/308/EEC on mutual assistance for the
  recovery of claims resulting from operations forming part of the system of financing
  the European Agricultural Guidance and Guarantee Fund, and of agricultural levies
  and customs duties and in respect of value added tax and certain excise duties
  [2001] OJ L175/17 41
Directive 2003/4 on public access to environmental information and repealing
  Directive 90/313/EEC [2003] OJ L41/26 306–307
Directive 2003/6/EC on Insider Dealing and Market Manipulation [2003] OJ L94/16
  (Market Abuse Directive) 271
Directive 2003/35/EC providing for public participation in respect of the drawing up
of certain plans and programmes relating to the environment and amending with
  regard to public participation and access to justice Directives 85/337/EEC and
  96/61/EC [2003] OJ L156/17... 304–307
  Recital 3 307
Directive 2004/17/EC coordinating the procurement procedures of entities operating
  in the water, energy, transport and postal services sectors [2004] OJ L134/1 148
  recital 16 306
Directive 2004/18/EC on the co–ordination of procedures for the award of public
  works contracts, public supply contracts and public service contracts [2004] OJ
  L134/114...148, 154–157
  Ch IV 156
  Ch V..155
  recital 1 152
  Art 1(2)(a)..151
  Art 2..154
  Art 23..156
  Art 26..156
  Art 29..155
  Arts 32–33 155
  Art 41..158
  Art 43..158
  Arts 45–50 156
  Art 53(1)... 156–157
  Art 53(1)(a).. 156–157
  Art 53(1)(b)...157
  Art 53(2)..157
  Arts 75–76 158
  Art 81..158
Directive 2004/39/EC on Markets in Financial Instruments [2004] OJ L145/1
  (MIFID)..271
Directive 2005/85/EC on minimum standards on procedures in Member States for
  granting and withdrawing refugee status [2005] OJ L326/13 90
Directive 2006/7/EC concerning the management of bathing water quality and
  repealing Directive 76/160/EEC [2006] OJ L64/37 (Bathing Water Directive) 177

Directive 2006/24/EC on the retention of data generated or processed in connection with the provision of publicly available electronic communications services or of public communications networks and amending Directive 2002/58/EC (Data Retention Directive) 67, 194
Directive 2007/60/ EC on the assessment and management of flood risks [2007] OJ L288/27 (Floods Directive)..176
Directive 2007/66/EC amending Directives 89/665/EEC and 92/13/EEC with regard to improving the effectiveness of review procedures concerning the award of public contracts [2007] OJ L335/31 148
    Art 2a..160
    Art 2d..160
    Art 9..158
Directive 2008/50/EC on ambient air quality and cleaner air for Europe [2008] OJ L152/1 (Air Quality Directive) 176
    Arts 23–24 178
    Art 29..176
Directive 2008/98/EC on waste and repealing certain Directives [2008] OJ L312/3 (Waste Framework Directive) 176
    Arts 28–33 178
    Art 39..176
Directive 2009/29/EC amending Directive 2003/87/EC so as to improve and extend the greenhouse gas emission allowance trading scheme of the Community [2009] OJ L140/63 44
Directive 2009/81/EC on the coordination of procedures for the award of certain works contracts, supply contracts and service contracts in the fields of defence and security [2009] OJ L216/76 148
Directive 2010/24/EU concerning mutual assistance for the recovery of claims relating to taxes, duties and other measures [2010] OJ L84/1 41
Directive 2010/78/EU amending Directives 98/26/EC, 2002/87/EC, 2003/6/EC, 2003/41/EC, 2003/71/EC, 2004/39/EC, 2004/109/EC, 2005/60/EC, 2006/48/EC, 2006/49/EC and 2009/65/EC in respect of the powers of the European Supervisory Authority (European Banking Authority), the European Supervisory Authority (European Insurance and Occupational Pensions Authority) and the European Supervisory Authority (European Securities and Markets Authority) [2010] OJ L331/120 (Omnibus I) 286
Directive 2011/83/EU on consumer rights, amending Directive 93/13/EEC and Directive 1999/44/EC and repealing Directive 85/577/EEC and Directive 97/7/EC [2011] OJ L304/64 119
Directive 2011/92/EU on the assessment of the effects of certain public and private projects on the environment [2012] OJ L26/1 (Environmental Impact Assessment Directive)..55, 81, 307–308
Directive 2012/18/EU on the control of major–accident hazards involving dangerous substances, amending and subsequently repealing Directive 96/82/EC [2012] OJ L197/1
    recital 31 178
Directive 2012/27/EU on energy efficiency, amending Directives 2009/125/EC and 2010/30/EU and repealing Directives 2004/8/EC and 2006/32/EC [2012] OJ L315/1
    recital 66 178

Table of EU Laws   xxxvii

Directive 2013/36/EU on access to the activity of credit institutions and the prudential supervision of credit institutions and investment firms, amending Directive 2002/87/EC and repealing Directives 2006/48/EC and 2006/49/EC [2013] [2013] OJ L176/338 279
 recital 36 280
 recital 50 280
 Art 4 280
 Arts 6–7 280
 Arts 49–72 280
Directive 2014/23/EU on the award of concession contracts [2014] OJ L94/1 161
Directive 2014/24/EU on public procurement and repealing Directive 2004/18/EC [2014] OJ L94/65 ....154, 161, 164–168
 recital 1 ....142, 145
 recital 52 166
 recital 78 167
 recital 114 164
 Art 2 164
 Art 12 165
 Art 24 166
 Art 26 165
 Arts 29–31 165
 Arts 42–43 167
 Art 46 167
 Art 57 166
 Arts 58–59 167
 Art 67 166–167
 Art 68 166
 Art 70 167
 Art 72 165
 Art 83 168
 Arts 85–86 168
 Arts 90–91 154
Directive 2014/25/EU on procurement by entities operating in the water, energy, transport and postal services sectors [2014] OJ L 94/243 161

Decisions

Decision 87/373/EEC laying down the procedures for the exercise of implementing powers conferred on the Commission [1987] OJ L19/87 (First Comitology Decision) 97
Decision 93/731/EC on public access to Council documents [1993] OJ L340/43 124–126
 Art 4(2) 125
Decision 94/90/ECSC, EC, Euratom on public access to Commission documents [1994] OJ L46/58 ....101, 124, 126
Decision 94/262/ECSC, EC, Euratom on the regulations and general conditions governing the performance of the Ombudsman's duties [1994] OJ L113/15 79

xxxviii Table of EU Laws

Art 6(2)..79
Art 9..79
Decision 24/95 on measures for the protection of classified information applicable
  to the Secretariat General of the Council..126
Decision 97/632/EC, ECSC, Euratom on public access to European Parliament
  documents [1997] OJ L263/27..124
Decision 1999/468/EC laying down the procedures for the exercise of implementing
  powers conferred on the Commission [1999] OJ L184/23 (Second Comitology
  Decision)...98, 101–102
Decision 2001/527/EC establishing the Committee of European Securities Regulators
  [2001] OJ L191/43
  Arts 1–2..270
Decision 2001/973/EC, ECSC, Euratom amending the rules of procedure of the
  Commission [2001] OJ L345/94..124
Decision 2002/465/JHA on joint investigation teams [2002] OJ L162/1..................248
Decision 2004/5/EC establishing the Committee of European Banking Supervisors
  [2004] OJ L3/28..272
Decision 2004/6/EC establishing the Committee of European Insurance and
  Occupational Pensions Supervisors [2004] OJ L3/30..272
Decision 2004/9/EC establishing the European Insurance and Occupational Pensions
  Committee [2004] OJ L3/34..272
Decision 2004/10/EC establishing the European Banking Committee [2004]
  OJ L3/36..272
Decision 2006/83 EC, Euratom adopting the Rules of Procedure of the Council
  [2006] OJ L285/47
  Arts 7–8..83
Decision 2006/512/EC amending Decision 1999/468/EC laying down the procedures
  for the exercise of implementing powers conferred on the Commission [2006]
  OJ L200/11 (Third Comitology Decision)..99–100
Decision 2008/615/JHA on the stepping up of cross–border cooperation, particularly
  in combating terrorism and cross–border crime [2008] OJ L210/12 252
Decision 2008/616/JHA [2008] OJ L210/12...252
Decision 2008/617/JHA on the improvement of cooperation between the special
  intervention units of the Member States of the European Union in crisis
  situations [2008] OJ L210/73..252
Decision 2008/721/EC establishing Scientific Committees on Consumer Safety,
  Health and Environmental Risks and Emerging and Newly Identified Health Risks
  [2008] OJ L241/21..29
Decision 2008/977/JHA on the protection of personal data processed in the
  framework of police and judicial cooperation in criminal matters [2008]
  OJ L350/60..256
Decision 2009/371/JHA establishing the European Police Office [2009] OJ L121/37
  (Europol Decision)...244, 250–251, 253–257, 261
  Art 7(4)...251
  Art 10(1)...255
Decision 2009/882/EU adopting the Rules of Procedure of the European Council
  [2009] OJ L315/51..124

Council Decision 2009/934/JHA adopting the implementing rules governing
  Europol's relations with partners, including the exchange of personal data and
  classified information [2009] OJ L325/6 253
    Art 6...249
    Art 11...249
Decision 2009/935/JHA determining the list of third States and organisations with
  which Europol shall conclude agreements [2009] OJ L325/12 253
Decision 2009/937/EU adopting the Rules of Procedure of the Council [2009]
  OJ L325/35 124
Decision 2010/138/EU amending the Rules of Procedure of the Commission [2010]
  OJ L55/60
    Art 23...21
Decision 2010/252/EU supplementing the Schengen Borders Code as regards the
  surveillance of the sea external borders in the context of operational cooperation
  coordinated by the European Agency for the Management of Operational
  Cooperation at the External Borders of the Member States of the European
  Union [2010] OJ L111/20..100
Decision 2011/695/EU on the function and terms of reference of the Hearing Officer
  in competition proceedings [2011] OJ L275/29
    recital 3 215
    Art 1...215
    Art 3(2)...215
    Art 4...215
    Arts 10–12 215
    Art 14(2)...215
Decision 2012/504/EU on Eurostat [2012] OJ L251/49..226

Introduction

ADMINISTRATIVE PROCEDURE: A FUNCTIONALIST APPROACH

THIS BOOK IS about the administrative procedures of the European Union. We use this term capaciously to cover all administration executed by EU institutions and bodies at Union level or carried out by Member States or national bodies in the name of the Union. Our primary objectives are to show how the various entities engaged in public administration share out and coordinate their functions and to explore the procedures that have been developed to cope with inherent structural problems.

We would describe ourselves as functionalists. Our interest has always been in the role played by law in the design and working of administration and administrative processes.[1] We approach administrative law primarily as a complex web of laws, rules and procedures that determine the organisation, powers and duties of administrative authorities and govern the way that policy is implemented in specific areas. In this book we have tried to carry this functionalist approach over into the study of administrative procedures, generally seen as constituting the heartland of administrative law. We have tried to adopt an official's perspective on administrative procedure, approaching it as an administrator does through the body of law, rules, policies and practices that go to make up the procedural law of the administration.

In the first section of the book, we approach these questions at a general level. We focus in chapter one on the fragmented governance structures in the framework of which EU administrators have had from time to time to operate and the implications of this for process and procedure. In chapter two, we consider the administrative tenets and values that infuse the administrative process and the way in which administrative styles and priorities have varied over the years. Chapter three signifies a change of standpoint to one more characteristic of lawyers. We turn to consider the external actors whose values and principles have been influential in shaping the administrative process, focusing on the Court of Justice (CoJ) and General Court (GC, an acronym we use throughout the book to cover its previous existence as the CFI) and the European Ombudsman (EO). We are not simply interested, however, in the retrospective or 'firefighting' qualities

---

[1] See C Harlow and R Rawlings, *Law and Administration*, 3rd edn (Cambridge: CUP, 2009).

2 *Introduction*

of judicial review as an instrument of control, accountability or dispute resolution, but also in proactive or 'fire-watching' techniques, such as the procedural codes adopted by the administration and used by ombudsmen to promote good governance. Our general objective in this section has been to provide an overview of the main administrative procedures in use in the EU, together with an indication of the functions for which they are intended, a consideration of the values they express and a critical analysis of their use within the EU governance system. Subsequent chapters provide a series of case studies drilling down to the uses to which administrative procedures are put in practice and which point to a wide variance in practice and priorities in different administrative contexts.

Definitions

We have deliberately defined administrative procedure loosely, to mean no more than a course of action, or steps in implementing a policy, or part of an administrative process. And we have not sought to distinguish 'procedure' from 'process' or 'structure', terms involving much overlap. This point emerges very clearly in chapter one where, in discussing the governance structures that form the framework for EU administrative procedures, we treat committees as both a 'structure' and a 'procedure' since both fall within the dictionary definition of a procedure as 'a proceeding, a way of proceeding, a mode of conducting business or performing a task or a series of actions conducted in a certain order or manner'. Again, while 'procedures' necessarily form 'part of an administrative process', the two terms may also be used synonymously. In later chapters we have used our case studies to show how administrative 'procedures' operate within a specific administrative 'process'.

Those who look for a more elaborate definition will find one in an OECD conference paper:

> An administrative procedure is the formal path, established in legislation, which an administrative action should follow. Usually, an administrative action has to be carried out through a number of steps, which should be known in advance. A pre-established decision-making procedure is essential to any complex organisations if their activities have to be controlled internally and externally, which is particularly crucial if the organisation deals with public interests. At the same time, the procedure has to guarantee the rights of those dealing with the administration. The double guarantee, of the public interest and of the private interest of the citizens, is the crucible of the public administration of any democratic State ruled by law.[2]

Although useful, this definition contains value judgements, which in this book we may want to question, such as the assertion that procedures 'should be known in advance' or 'pre-established' and 'established in legislation'. These are rule of law

---

[2] W Rusch, 'Administrative Procedures in EU Member States' paper for the OECD/EU SIGMA Conference on Public Administration Reform and European Integration (OECD, 2009).

requirements rather than essential elements of an administrative procedure. Likewise, in the authors' view, the definition represents only the most visible part of the field. We look in chapter two at the uses of 'soft law' and other techniques of 'soft governance' and throughout the book many examples of procedures embedded in soft law instruments will be found. It is hard not to see these soft governance tools and techniques used widely in EU administration as 'procedures'. Sometimes locking-up together with formal law and sometimes not, soft law serves a number of different purposes. It may be used, for example, to encourage 'best practice' or to promote procedural convergence, two objectives that may overlap; equally, soft governance can be a way of preserving the diversity and pluralism that we see as a valuable feature of EU governance. Furthermore, this book takes seriously the phenomenon of 'proceduralisation' or the danger that formalisation will end by stultifying administrative and regulatory processes. Soft law as a halfway stage between diversity and legal uniformity is a theme that emerges clearly in many of our case studies and the wisdom of a possible move to codification of administrative procedure – a topical theme – is questioned in the final chapter.

In common with many administrative law texts, our book takes as a starting point that 'administration' is an executive function, executive and administration being largely undifferentiated in classical constitutional theory. In our national systems of government we know roughly what the terms 'executive' and 'administration' mean. In the EU, which lacks a government properly so called, it is not so easy to identify the executive. The founding Treaties authorised the Commission 'to act as the central administration of the EC' but this is by no means the whole story. The Commission shares its very considerable executive authority with other bodies. After the Maastricht Treaty in 1992, the Council had oversight of the new area of freedom, security and justice, effectively creating a secondary executive,[3] the outcome being a dual administration with differing cultures and different procedures. To complicate matters further, the EU is a multi-level system of 'governance' if not of 'government'[4] and it has followed national governments in a process of 'agencification'. As we show in chapter one, the unique and complex governance structure inevitably shapes administrative practice at Union level.

We have not sought here sharply to distinguish the policymaking and decision-making (executive) functions of the Commission – on which the literature tends to focus – from administration in the day to day sense of 'the performance of delegated, defined tasks, the taking of routine, programmed decisions, and the maintenance of organisational codes and practices to provide continuity and consistency'.[5] In this book, however, we have chosen to bring the three together. As we shall see, there is much routine administration within the Commission. Equally, much of the administrative procedure is policy laden.

[3] D Curtin, *Executive Power of the European Union* (Oxford: OUP, 2009).
[4] For the distinction, see R Rhodes, 'The New Governance: Governing without Government' (1996) 44 *Political Studies* 652.
[5] D Coombes, *Politics and Bureaucracy in the European Community* (London: Allen & Unwin, 1970) 114.

4 *Introduction*

Today, the collection of information is greatly facilitated by the excellent ICT system through which information is exchanged and recorded and the well-organised EUROPA website used to communicate with the public. The EU has had a communications policy, known as 'Communicating Europe', from the mid-1990s and rapid technological advances in the last decade help to explain the different phases of EU administration, though they are not, of course, a total explanation. But without ICT, EU administration would certainly look rather different and the EU administration would have to operate very differently. Without ICT too, the EU would have great difficulty in fulfilling its commitment to transparency, an important principle of good governance. These are the positive aspects of technological advance. Less positively, the installation at Union level of large databanks and the accumulation of vast quantities of personal data has caused both legal and administrative problems. These are considered in chapter ten in the context of a case study of Europol, the EU agency responsible for limited coordination of Member State police services. Problems of access to information at Union level in a growing climate of public expectation of transparency are treated in chapter five.

'Horizontal' and 'Vertical'

In the 'split-level' analyses common in early political science writing, functions were characteristically presented as divided between two levels: above, the Community and its institutions; below, national systems of government. In this analysis, rules and procedures would be described as 'horizontally applicable' if they referred to the Community and its institutions or 'vertically applicable' when they bound Member States. In this book, the terminology of 'horizontal' and 'vertical' is also used in a second sense. Procedures are termed horizontal when they apply generally to all administrative activity (subject to specific exceptions) and vertical when procedures are 'sector-specific' or applicable to a single policy area. Thus, the EU Regulation governing access to information discussed in chapter five is a horizontal law in the double sense of applying to EU institutions and agencies but not inside Member States and also because it is applicable across the whole field (with limited exceptions) of EU activity. In contrast, in our terminology, the financial services regulation described in chapter eleven is vertical in the double sense that it applies inside the Member States but only in a single generic field. Public procurement law is vertical in being applicable to the contracts of Member States and also because it contains specific provisions tailored to particular sectors such as public utilities; but it also contains general requirements applicable across the board and is hence partly horizontal (see further chapter six). Again, EU agencies possess powers to regulate their own, agency-specific procedures; increasingly, however, these have to conform to a horizontal EU paradigm. As we shall see, the exact relationship between horizontal and vertical administrative procedures is often a question of considerable difficulty. Double standards often apply. And which is to take priority, the general or the specific?

Sharing the Space

The basic two-tier structure has survived subsequent enlargements and Treaty changes, although the modus operandi has often changed radically. Initially – as further discussed in chapter one – EU administration tended to be characterised as 'direct' when carried out by the Commission but 'indirect' when Member States were responsible for implementing policy settled at EU level. Both direct and indirect administration is often now characterised as 'mixed' or 'shared'. This has created a need for shared administration in the slightly different sense of somehow bonding different national administrative paradigms and cultures, a recurrent problem throughout the book.

The EU is a major vehicle for procedural approximation and convergence. Member States, acting through the Commission, Council and European Parliament (EP), may choose to align their procedural practices through the formal EU machinery of governance and its law-making process, a process illustrated in chapter six where stages in the alignment of public procurement procedures are traced. Occasionally, the procedures of a single Member State may be seen to represent 'best practice' and be adopted as the EU model; more often minimum standards leaving room for divergence are adopted in the hope that these can be ratcheted up at a later date. Alternatively, standardisation may be achieved through a process of informal cooperation between the Commission and national officials, a soft governance process already mentioned. In short, procedural law and administration in EU Member States are undergoing a process of 'Europeanisation' and convergence in many different ways.[6] This fact is naturally recognised here and our case studies offer examples of variant processes of convergence and, occasionally, integration, which share the field with respect for divergence and subsidiarity. Nor should we too easily make the assumption that approximation means 'levelling up'; for some Member States, it may result in a considerable 'levelling down', as in the struggle over open government described in chapter five.

Not only has the process of gradual convergence made it harder to distinguish the horizontal from the vertical, but recent times have also seen a trend to fragmentation or disaggregation. At national level, administrative functions have been delegated downwards to regional and local government; sideways to regulatory agencies, often with substantial legislative or adjudicative powers; sideways to the private sector; upwards to international organisations such as the United Nations (UN) or World Trade Organization (WTO). The EU is a supranational regime operating a system of administrative governance of just this kind.[7] As this book shows very clearly, it has followed the trend to disaggregation. It is no longer merely an

---

[6] See C Harlow and R Rawlings, 'National Administrative Procedures in a European Perspective: Pathways to a Slow Convergence?' (2010) 2 *Italian Journal of Public Law* 215.
[7] M Flinders, 'Distributed Public Governance in the European Union' (2004) 11 *Journal of European Public Policy* 520; P Lindseth, *Power and Legitimacy: Reconciling Europe and the Nation-State* (Oxford: OUP, 2010).

incipient federation; it has become a sprawling system of network governance crisscrossed by a multitude of committees, working parties and other groups. In this context, the terminology of direct/indirect, with its implication of sharp distinction and separation, is no longer generally appropriate. It is increasingly replaced by new terminology of 'network governance', 'distributed public governance', 'multilevel governance and 'composite decision-making', more appropriate for the looser and more open structures that are continuing to develop.

Technically linked to the Commission and part of the EU governance network, agencies are an increasingly significant feature of the administrative landscape. Their contours are changing; they are starting to gain regulatory and executive functions, as illustrated by the studies of Europol in chapter ten and more dramatically with the new financial services agencies described in chapter eleven. Externally, the EU is a major player in wider globalised networks. It is a participating member of international organisations such as the WTO and UN. As we show in chapter twelve, it both imports and exports administrative procedures.

Some Parameters

Our deliberately broad definition contains two internal limitations. First, we attempt to draw the customary line between legislative and administrative processes, familiar from separation of powers theory. It has not always been easy to do this, due in part to the particular nature of EU law and rule-making. Thus, we have left to one side the consultation and conciliation procedures within the co-decision procedure, classifying them as clearly part of the cumbersome EU legislative process. On the other hand, chapter four covers formal executive rule-making at Union level in some detail. We include the arcane series of committees or 'comitology' set in place to help and advise or control and supervise – according to one's point of view – the Commission in making implementing acts, though whether these committees constitute 'structures' or 'procedures' we are disinclined to say. The book also covers administrative procedures that lead up to law-making, such as impact assessment, consultation procedures and the 'Better Regulation' programme.

Second, our account stops short at the doors of the court and does not extend to judicial procedures such as rules of court or the mundane rules as to registration of cases and exchange of documents between the parties to litigation, clearly administrative though the latter are. In examining environmental procedures prescribed by the Aarhus Convention, we do not dwell on the requirements for accessing the courts. Nor do we deal with the rules of standing to sue – something of a preoccupation for lawyers, especially private practitioners, who view administrative procedures through the prism of rights and the courts through which rights are established. Indeed, our functionalist approach has meant that courts and jurisprudence do not form the centrepiece of our account as they do of many other accounts by lawyers. Why would we seek to replicate inadequately the seminal and voluminous work by Jürgen Schwarze,[8] the doyen of EU administrative law? Or the later and more strictly focused discussion of judicial principles of administrative procedure by Hanns-Pieter Nehl?[9] Or the excellent contemporary analyses by Paul Craig[10] and Takis Tridimas[11] of the vast case law of the two Luxembourg Courts that bears more or less closely on our field?

In taking this line, we are not to be understood as dismissive of the judicial contribution. Courts fulfil three essential functions in the formation of administrative procedures: they interpret law and regulation; they recognise and sometimes generate general principles – though they are not the only actors who do this; and they test administrative procedure against values and standards that are acceptable to them. Not to recognise the important contribution of courts would be particularly futile in an era when courts, and especially transnational courts like CoJ and its assistant GC have been gaining power at the expense of governments and legislatures.[12] Courts are today widely viewed as the primary, if not the sole, guardian of human rights. They are also the arbiters of constitutions. It follows from this that, once procedural rights become accepted as constitutional rights or fundamental human rights, courts can legitimately lay claim to a principal role in establishing general principles of administrative procedure – as they did in the celebrated *Kadi* decisions challenging counterterrorism measures before EU courts highlighted in chapter twelve. Otherwise, we have selected certain key principles, such as the proportionality principle or due process requirements, with a view to illustrating the impact of courts on administrative procedure. We have also highlighted several values which to us typify EU administrative procedural law, notably the obligation to make reasoned decisions and the innovative duty of loyal or sincere cooperation, both treaty rights to which jurisprudence has made a significant contribution. In the case of the EO, we have focused on his efforts to embed good governance principles into Union administration, his contribution to greater administrative transparency and his role as 'Citizens' Advocate'.

Even within these limits our definition is a wide one which, if taken literally, would call for an encyclopaedia rather than the short book we planned; competition procedures alone, the subject of chapter eight, are the subject of many massive tomes. It follows too from what has been said that national administrative procedures will often form part of EU administrative law. To attempt a comprehensive comparative survey of this sort is beyond the scope of this short book and the ability of its authors. This does not mean that national administrative law will receive no further mention: far from it! Many of the most important principles of EU administrative law – such as the proportionality and due process principles already mentioned – have been borrowed more or less directly from national legal systems. No

---

[8] J Schwarze, *Europäisches Verwaltungsrecht* (1988) trans as *European Administrative Law* (London: Sweet and Maxwell, 1992; rev edn, 2006).
[9] H-P Nehl, *Principles of Administrative Procedure in EC Law* (Oxford: Hart Publishing, 1999).
[10] P Craig, *EU Administrative Law*, 2nd edn (Oxford: OUP, 2012).
[11] T Tridimas, *The General Principles of EU Law*, 2nd edn (Oxford: OUP, 2006).
[12] M Shapiro and A Stone Sweet, *On Law, Politics and Judicialization* (Oxford: OUP, 2002).

account can be all inclusive and this short book is neither a study in comparative law nor a practitioners' text for those who need to know in detail what rules and practices operate vertically in any specific sector.

To summarise, our aim has been to combine a general discussion of the role and contribution of administrative procedures with a carefully selected set of case studies designed to cast light on the way in which procedural rules develop and how they are used by administrators, economic actors and to a limited extent by civil society. Pursuing a functionalist approach, our concern has been with the plurality of bodies and institutions that enunciate and develop the content of administrative procedures and the way in which they help to further 'the European project' in their respective fields. Legislators, officials and courts all contribute to the process of elaborating principles and values as do other external firefighters such as auditors and ombudsmen. In ranging more broadly across the field, this book brings to the fore an aspect easily glossed over: the place of institutional politics, divergent attitudes and value systems in the development of process and procedure in EU administration. A comparison of judicial and ombudsmen interventions in respect of freedom of information (chapter five) and Commission enforcement process (chapter seven) serves to underwrite this fundamental if sometimes inconvenient truth.

Constitutionally, the EU may be an emergent polity built on shaky foundations but it has a developed and sophisticated bureaucracy, using this term in its institutional, Weberian sense. Yes, its administrative procedures are often faulty. Audit is insufficient or too rigid, communications break down, policies remain unimplemented, there is too much regulation and implementation is, in the negative sense of the word, bureaucratic. Yet the procedures are at their best remarkable not only for their innovation, but also for combining sturdiness with flexibility. In our view, administrative procedures stand at the heart of the European project, grounding a substantial part of its legitimacy. They are, to put this differently, a distinctive source of legitimation for the 'European project', for which we borrow Schmidt's useful term of 'throughput legitimacy'.[13] EU administrative procedure has been developed in the context of an innovative regulatory regime and in a framework of 'composite' decision-making, in which there is a multiplicity of decision-taking points and legally separate bureaucratic actors. In the course of writing the book, we have come to see it as the 'super glue' that holds the sprawling, unwieldy structures of the EU governance system in place. Law, customarily seen as the primary integrative mechanism,[14] has limits. Law is not self-implementing. What would the force of law be without an administration?

---

[13] V Schmidt, 'Democracy and Legitimacy in the European Union Revisited: Input, Output *and* "Throughput"' (2013) 61 *Political Studies* 2.

[14] eg, P Pescatore, *Law of Integration* (Leiden: Sijthoff, 1974); J Weiler, 'The Community System: The Dual Character of Supranationalism' (1981) 1 *Yearbook of European Law* 267; M Cappelletti, M Seccombe and J Weiler, *Integration Through Law: Europe and the American Federal Experience* (New York: de Gruyter, 1986) 15–57.

1

A Fragmented Framework

IN SEARCH OF EU ADMINISTRATION

EU GOVERNANCE STARTS with the Member States, whose governance systems vary greatly. Some are unitary states, others are federations or have devolved regional governments. Some are small, with centralised, unitary administrations, others large and decentralised. Most show a postmodern tendency to fragmentation, as governance functions are devolved to regulatory agencies, uploaded to international and transnational organisations (of which the EU is one) or shared with the private sector. As it stands today, the EU is best conceived as a confederation made up of 28 sovereign nation-states, equal in value[1] but with markedly different constitutional traditions and cultures, in the framework of which their respective administrative systems are rooted. Respect for these is jealously guarded by the founding Treaties, which promise 'to deepen the solidarity between [European] peoples while respecting their history, their culture and their traditions'. There are of course many common features.

Although, shaped by their historical experience, they are in many ways dissimilar, the governance systems of Member States must be based on democratic principles.[2] Democracy figures prominently with the rule of law, respect for human rights, freedom and equality in the Preamble to the Treaty on European Union (TEU), where the concepts are described as *universal* values derived from the 'cultural, religious and humanist inheritance of Europe', to which all Member States express their firm commitment. This is not to discount the push to convergence; much (though emphatically not all) in EU administrative procedure clearly reflects and reinforces the underlying dynamic of convergence. Yet the initial thrust towards 'ever closer union' has slackened somewhat and the framework of EU governance as it stands today is fragmented to an unusual degree; made up, as commentators have put it, of 'bits-and-pieces'[3] or 'opaque structures and

---

[1] A vast literature surrounds this proposition: see for an introduction to the pluralist argument, M Avbelj and J Komárek (eds), *Constitutional Pluralism in the European Union and Beyond* (Oxford: Hart Publishing, 2012).

[2] TEU Art 7 now provides a procedure to suspend the rights of a Member State against which a finding has been made of a serious and persistent breach of these values. At the time of writing, there is concern over the democratic status of Hungary.

[3] D Curtin, 'The Constitutional Structure of the Union: A Europe of Bits and Pieces' (1993) 30 *Common Market Law Review* 17.

procedures'.[4] It is not easy to map the EU administration. Coordination is achieved only through careful networking.

The EU governance system is hard to classify. The Treaties are not a constitution properly so-called, although the Court of Justice (CoJ) in particular often acts as though they were.[5] It is not a true federation, although for administrative purposes it has many federal characteristics;[6] it has a similar need, for example, to communicate with and work closely with its Member States. It has been described by Majone as a regulatory regime with the Commission as its motor.[7] Lindseth calls it an extension into transnational space of the twentieth-century 'administrative state', in which rule-making, adjudicatory and implementation powers are blocked up in a powerful executive; for practical purposes, the Commission.[8] Other writers view the EU as a system of 'network governance'[9] and the Commission as a 'network organisation' or 'coordinator of networks'.[10] It is of course all these things.

Although we do not wish to pursue the search for an appropriate, all-encompassing typology, each of these descriptions lends something to our study. The EU was and remains today a regulatory regime at least in the sense that its main output is regulation. This has meant the development of formal regulatory procedures, many vested in the Commission as executive: the 'Better Regulation' agenda, for example, impact assessment or the consultation procedures discussed in later chapters. Equally, the EU fits the model of Lindseth's administrative governance system, epitomised by a strong executive government in which a formidable combination of legislative and executive power is bestowed on the Commission, though the adjudicative power of the EU is vested in a forceful and independent policymaking judiciary. This has led in time to the much discussed legitimacy deficit and, as we shall see in later chapters, a search for administrative substitutes for representative democracy. The EU is also a paradigm system of 'network governance'. It is riddled with committees to represent the Member States, working groups and other advisory bodies, and has now embarked on a process of 'agencification' or 'distributed EU governance', as described in chapters ten and eleven. This puts a premium on what we see as the crucial 'three Cs of EU governance' – Communication, Cooperation and Coordination. Central to EU administration is the devising of procedures to assure them.

At this point it is best to abandon the never-ending search for a theory of EU governance to focus more narrowly on administration. In the early years, a 'split-

[4] K Lenaerts and D Gerard, 'The Structure of the Union according to the Constitution for Europe: The Emperor is Getting Dressed' (2004) 29 *European Law Review* 289.
[5] F Mancini, 'The Making of a Constitution for Europe' (1989) 26 *Common Market Law Review* 595; M Kumm, 'The Jurisprudence of Constitutional Conflict: Constitutional Supremacy in Europe before and after the Constitutional Treaty' (2005) 11 *European Law Journal* 262.
[6] R Schütze, *From Dual to Cooperative Federalism: The Changing Structure of European Law* (Oxford: OUP, 2009).
[7] G Majone, 'The Rise of the Regulatory State in Europe' (1994) 17 *West European Politics* 77.
[8] P Lindseth, *Power and Legitimacy: Reconciling Europe and the Nation-State* (Oxford: OUP, 2010).
[9] T Börzel, 'European Governance' (2010) 48 *Journal of Common Market Studies* 191.
[10] L Metcalfe, 'The European Commission as a Network Organization' (1996) 26 *Publius* 4.

level analysis' was generally applied to EU administration, in which administration was classified as 'direct' when carried out at Community level and 'indirect' when carried out by the Member States. Direct administration was exceptional, being largely confined to the core area of competition discussed in chapter eight and the internal administration of the Community institutions and civil service as described below. Programmes for which the Commission and now its executive agencies have responsibilities resembling direct administration still come into being, especially in matters like the multi-annual research programme[11] which involves multiple grants and subsidies. In general, however, administration was categorised as 'indirect' and it was more usual to provide the Commission with supervisory powers.

Well before the Lisbon Treaty, however, split-level analysis was being questioned. Craig indeed argues that the traditional pattern has always been one of 'shared' or 'mixed administration', instancing the Common Agricultural Policy (CAP)[12] and structural funding programmes, discussed at length in chapter nine. In shared management,

> [t]he Commission and the Member States have distinct administrative tasks which are inter-dependent and set down in legislation and where both the Commission and the national administrations need to discharge their respective tasks for the Community policy to be implemented successfully.[13]

Writing in 2006, Hofmann and Türk suggested a 'spectrum of joint administration', with 'pure direct administration by EU institutions at one end and pure indirect administration by Member State authorities at the other'.[14] Later studies suggest a more complex pattern. Chiti preferred the terminology of 'bottom-up' mechanisms of integration – where an EU objective is carried out through mutual cooperation between Member States – and 'top-down' or Commission inspired mechanisms of integration. Cassese initiated the terminology of 'composite decision-making'[15] or 'composite administration', a term defined inclusively by Schmidt-Aßmann to cover administration by 'co-dependent organisms':

> [T]he numerous interacting national and Community institutions, authorities, offices, bodies and other legal entities that are duly authorised to implement EC law as well as the laws of the individual Member States passed according to EC requirements. Although performing the latter task separately, according to their national

---

[11] See Commission, 'Horizon 2020 – The Framework Programme for Research and Innovation' (Communication) COM (2011) 808 final.

[12] P Craig, *EU Administrative Law*, 2nd edn (Oxford: OUP, 2012) 6–7.

[13] Committee of Independent Experts, 'Second Report on Reform of the Commission – analysis of current practice and proposals for tackling mismanagement, irregularities and fraud' (Brussels, 1999) [3.2.2].

[14] H Hofmann and A Türk, 'Policy Implementation' in H Hofmann and A Türk (eds), *EU Administrative Governance* (Cheltenham: Edward Elgar, 2006) 74.

[15] S Cassese, 'European Administrative Proceedings' (2004) 68 *Law and Contemporary Problems* 21; H Hofmann, 'Composite Decision Making Procedures in EU Administrative Law' in H Hofmann and A Türk (eds), *Legal Challenges in EU Administrative Law: Towards an Integrated Administration* (Cheltenham: Edward Elgar, 2009).

competency provisions, they are united by the common task of effective and uniform administration.[16]

In parallel, we find the conceptual vocabulary of 'multi-level governance' and 'network' emerging in the literature. Multi-level governance theory seriously undermined split-level analyses of EU administration by enhancing the role of regional actors and presenting EU policy formation as 'a process involving self-organizing, multi-level actors – and one which signalled a move away from "hierarchical steering" towards communication-based instruments'.[17] The term had originated in studies of EU structural funding[18] as an attempt to empower sub-national actors by enhancing their visibility and 'bringing them into decision-making arenas'.[19] Multi-level governance was conceived as an 'information society', reliant for its efficacy less on hierarchical formalities and more on collaborative information gathering and exchange, signalling in procedural terms a shift from legal formality to the soft governance techniques described in chapter two. The EU was being reconceptualised as a 'multi-level information environment' in which data exchange, benchmarking and best practice were encouraged both vertically and horizontally between and across the governance layers and the term 'governance' denoted the use of 'soft' policy instruments, encouraging coordination, benchmarking and best practice without threat of sanction.[20]

The interlock is clearly tight between multi-level or layered governance and 'network governance', loosely defined as a set of relatively stable relationships of a non-hierarchical and interdependent nature linking a variety of actors, who share common policy goals and exchange resources to pursue their shared interests through cooperation.[21] Perhaps inevitably, the multi-level EU, in which 'policy communities' and 'issue networks' now flourish, has come to be characterised as system of 'networked governance'. Whether or not the network concept really amounts to a new mode of European governance (or even of governance) may be disputed; the usefulness of the concept is that it reduces the importance of split-level analysis by drawing attention to the many separate but interdependent organisations that actually participate in EU administration and the ways in which they interact. The new structures generate problems. Multi-level decision-making can mean that the governance system is 'uncoupled from the democratic circuit'[22] with serious consequences for citizen-participation and democratic

[16] E Schmidt-Aßmann, 'Introduction: European Composite Administration and the Role of European Administrative Law' in O Jansen and B Schöndorf-Haubold (eds), *The European Composite Administration* (Antwerp: Intersentia, 2011) 1–2.

[17] P Stephenson, 'Twenty Years of Multi-Level Governance: Where Does it Come From? What is it? Where is it Going?' (2013) 20 *Journal of European Public Policy* 817, 820; M Egan, 'Governance and Learning in the Post-Maastricht Era?' (2009) 16 *Journal of European Public Policy* 1244.

[18] G Marks and L Hooghe, 'Contrasting Visions of Multi-Level Governance' in I Bache and M Flinders (eds), *Multi-Level Governance* (Oxford: OUP, 2004).

[19] Stephenson, above (n 17) 824.

[20] Ibid.

[21] T Börzel, 'What's So Special about Policy Networks? An Exploration of the Concept and its Usefulness in Studying European Governance' (1997) (16)1 *European Integration online Papers* 1.

[22] Stephenson, above (n 17) 826.

accountability,[23] matters addressed in chapter five. In such a framework certain types of administrative procedure gain a new importance. Schmidt-Aßmann has led the way in highlighting as special features of EU governance the joint information, support and coordination processes that are prerequisites for effective administration of the terrain.[24] Elegant models of 'shared' or 'composite' administration can, however, obscure as much as they reveal. As this book will amply demonstrate, notions of unity or interdependency, let alone 'uniform administration', should not be allowed to disguise the often ad hoc, piecemeal and sprawling nature of EU administration.

MEMBER STATES AND ENLARGEMENT

National Procedural Autonomy

Split-level analysis encourages a view of EU administration as a hierarchy with the Commission at its apex; from the standpoint of administrative procedures however, it is more logical to start from the Member States. Up until the Lisbon Treaty, there was no direct underpinning for EU administration – indeed, no direct provision for any administration. Everything rested on the slender basis of EC Article 155, which mandated the Commission to ensure that the provisions of the Treaty and the measures taken by the institutions pursuant to the Treaty were applied and empowered the Commission to take 'implementing' measures. How the provision should be interpreted is a moot point. Craig deduces from its breadth an inherent mandate for the construction of an administration based on Community agencies planted in each of the original six Member States to implant Community regulations. He intimates that this was not done 'largely because of practical considerations, rather than any formal limit on its powers'.[25] More plausibly, Schütze argues that the Community was based on the German model of 'executive federalism', according to which its executive and legislative powers were co-extensive and subsidiary to those of the Member States.[26] This formulation corresponds more closely with a general understanding that administration was 'strictly an area of national sovereignty [where] there cannot be any European policy since there is no Community competence in this area'.[27]

With very limited exceptions then, implementation of Community law and policy and the procedures used to implement them were understood to be the

---

[23] Y Papadopoulos, 'Problems of Democratic Accountability in Network and Multilevel Governance' in T Conzelmann and R Smith (eds), *Multi-level Governance in the European Union: Taking Stock and Looking Ahead* (Baden Baden: Nomos, 2008).

[24] Schmidt-Aßmann, above (n 16) 4.

[25] Craig, above (n 12) 4.

[26] R Schütze, 'From Rome to Lisbon: "Executive Federalism" in the (New) European Union' (2010) 47 *Common Market Law Review* 1385.

[27] M Mangenot, *Public Administrations and Services of General Interest: What Kind of Europeanisation?* (Maastricht: EIPA, 2005) 4.

responsibility of the Member States. The default position, which has survived several enlargements, treaty changes and administrative reforms, is one of national procedural autonomy. While today this receives additional support from the principle of subsidiarity, according to which action should not be taken at Union level unless it will be more effective than action taken at national, regional or local level (see chapter two), the position may course be modified by EU legislation. Increasingly, legislative provision bears directly on the national administrative system, exemplified by rafts of requirements to ensure the independence of domestic regulatory or supervisory bodies or to follow common procedures. Many illustrations will be found in this volume. The Lisbon Treaty changed this position by providing in TFEU Article 298 that 'an open, efficient and independent European administration' was a matter of 'common interest' to the Member States and by authorising the Union to support Member States' efforts 'to improve their administrative capacity to implement Union law' (TFEU Article 197). Detailed discussion of these somewhat ambiguous provisions is reserved for chapter thirteen.

Import–Export

The argument for procedural autonomy rather suggests that national administrative procedures differ significantly both from each other and from the Union administration. There is no doubt some truth in this. On the other hand, it is often suggested that pressure from the EU is driving national administrative systems and public services to converge. EU law is of course a strong integrative force and there certainly may be top-down pressure from EU institutions for approximation or harmonisation of administrative procedures, as this book will demonstrate. There may too be bottom-up convergence when Member States choose to align their procedural practices through the formal EU machinery. But, administrative convergence is not a one-way process, nor are convergence and 'Europeanisation' synonymous. The EU is not an island and nor are its Member States.

The Commission, the core EU administration, did not spring into being fully staffed and equipped with administrative know-how and a toolkit of procedures; its expertise came from national administrations, with which Community officials had also to work. The Community civil service was composed of officials of different nationalities, who brought with them variable practices drawn from different cultural traditions. The Communities were patterned on a French model and it has been suggested that even today the Commission 'bears distinct traces of the predominant French influence during its formative years', including a predominantly 'regulatory and legalistic cast of mind'.[28]

---

[28] C Pollitt and G Bouckaert, *New Public Management Reform, A Comparative Analysis*, 3rd edn (Oxford: OUP, 2011) 69–70.

There are other major examples of national cultural traditions being exported. Throughout this book we trace a preference for governance through rules that suggest the influence of the German *Rechtsstaat* ideal, according to which government should be closely regulated by law in the form of written rules. It is certainly possible that the *Rechtsstaat* ideal travelled to Brussels and Luxembourg with German civil servants and lawyers who staffed the new institutions[29] but the preference is shared by other Member States. The 1999 Finnish Constitution, for example, contains the provision that 'the exercise of public powers shall be based on an Act. In all public activity, the law shall be strictly observed'. The preference for rules underlies pressure at Union level for a unitary governance style with generally uniform procedures and also arguments for an Administrative Procedures Act discussed in chapter thirteen.

On the other hand, if the UK administrative model traditionally relies more on administrative practice and discretion, it has developed (together with certain other Member States)[30] a strong, managerial culture in recent years. This may be said to have influenced Commission management (see below). Again, the arrival of the Scandinavian bloc with a strong commitment to open government was very influential (as chapter five will show) in pushing the Union towards greater transparency; support from Jacob Söderman, the first European Ombudsman (EO) – an office itself borrowed from Scandinavia – was particularly helpful. Conversely, a strong commitment in other Member States to official secrecy helps to explain why access to information procedure has proved so impervious to reform. We should note too that legal principles are often uploaded. The principle of due process for individuals – a central procedural principle of EU administrative law – is based on English precedents; similarly, the celebrated proportionality principle is borrowed from German public law (see chapter three).

But just as unreal as the divide between direct and indirect administration is that between Union and national officialdom. Officials from national administrations are 'omnipresent' in the EU, participating at every level of decision-making and involved at all stages of the policy cycle.[31] They represent their Member States on multiple advisory committees and working groups and juggle to position their national administration favourably – arguing, for example, for a British as against a German model of environmental impact assessment or vice versa.[32] In Justice and Home Affairs policymaking after Maastricht, the power of national officialdom would be even greater. As Guild has cynically observed, the relevant 'third pillar' procedures 'permit senior officials to think the unthinkable and adopt the

---

[29] Today some 25% of Commission officials have legal qualifications: H Kassim et al, *The European Commission of the Twenty-First Century* (Oxford: OUP, 2013) 40.
[30] See G Hammerschmid et al, *Public Administration Reform in Europe* (Berlin: COCOPS, 2013).
[31] H Kassim, 'The European Administration: Between Europeanisation and Domestication' in J Hayward and A Menon (eds), *Governing Europe* (Oxford: OUP, 2003) 141.
[32] A Héritier, 'The Accommodation of Diversity in European Policymaking and the Outcomes: Regulatory Policy as a Patchwork' (1996) 3 *Journal of European Public Policy* 149.

unpalatable, far from the clamour of national parliaments and human rights organisations'.[33]

Horizontal communication between 'Europeanised' national administrations, perhaps via Union-supported channels, has also become commoner.[34] For example, French and British immigration services might collaborate over a problem at the Channel ports; national civil servants concerned over environmental policy might meet to establish a common position; neighbouring sub-state authorities might work together on a cross-border basis under the auspices of EU regional policy. Conditions may be ripe for particular clusters of national authorities to communicate and collaborate more closely. The European Network of Law Enforcement Technology Services (ENLETS) is an initiative started in France, comprising a 'core group' of police services in eight Member States, which cooperate on technological research and development. Soft law in the form of standard-setting then emerges from informal meetings, circulation of policy papers and consultation of stakeholders. This and similar initiatives are discussed in chapter ten, while chapter two shows more 'cooperation and coordination networks' coming into being for the purposes of sharing information or providing mutual assistance. Many will be products of soft governance, though these may in time mature into an EU process or be taken over by an EU agency. They too are a major force for convergence.

Growing the Union

Pursuing the theme, the development of EU administration largely reflects successive waves of enlargement. Union expansion from six to 28 Member States introduced greater variation in administrative systems and cultures. Today's Union clearly poses challenges of a different order from the club atmosphere of the foundational years. Multiplying demands have been placed on the centralised administrative apparatus generating continued pressure for structural and procedural reforms. From competition to cohesion policy and on to economic cooperation and policing: the fact of enlargement as a main driver of changing EU administrative arrangements is shown in this book across many subject matters. It has to be said: size – distance – matters.

The great Enlargement into central and eastern Europe at the beginning of the century has pride of place in the history of the Union. The accession of ex-Soviet bloc countries, young democracies with distinctive administrative cultures and some relatively new administrative structures, posed a huge administrative challenge. Not only did a vast body of regulation (the *acquis*) – covering a wide range

---

[33] E Guild, 'The Constitutional Consequences of Lawmaking in the Third Pillar of the European Union' in P Craig and C Harlow (eds), *Lawmaking in the European Union* (Dordrecht: Kluwer Law International, 1998) 81.

[34] F Lafarge, 'Administrative Cooperation between Member States and Implementation of EU Law' (2010) 16 *European Public Law* 597.

of subject matter from agricultural production through competition and consumer rights to environmental protection – have to be introduced into the many new Member States[35] but efforts also had to be made to see it actually implemented. A helpful factor here was the influx of a body of Commission personnel recruited from Enlargement states, typically highly qualified and with personal knowledge of the difficulties.[36] To offset the problems – or so it is suggested[37] – the notion of a 'European administrative space', postulating a common administrative framework and shared principles, was introduced. This was used to justify a supranational jurisdiction while, under the conditionality principle discussed in chapter two, administrative as well as economic capacity became a membership condition.

A 1995 Commission White Paper setting out a road map for approximation contained the warning that a merely formal transposition of legislation would not be enough to ensure that the internal market functioned effectively after further enlargement: 'Accordingly, equal importance is attached to the establishment of adequate structures for implementation and enforcement, which may be the more difficult task'.[38] The instrument by which this objective was to be achieved was the PHARE programme, originally designed to provide economic assistance to Poland and Hungary but later extended to the Balkan applicant states.[39] Among its objectives PHARE included helping national and regional administrations and the regulatory and supervisory bodies of candidate countries to acquire the capacity to implement the Community *acquis* and 'familiarise themselves with Community objectives and procedures'. The programme operated through the classic 'carrot' of funding and through institutional cooperation or 'twinning', whereby candidate states allied themselves with institutions in a Member State of their choosing. Implementation of national programmes was decentralised insofar as this was permitted by the EU Financial Regulation. Today the legacy of PHARE includes the read-across of administrative techniques into the Instrument for Pre-Accession Assistance (IPA), which has effectively grounded the EU's ongoing engagement with candidate members such as Albania or Bosnia and Herzegovina.[40] For the period from 2007 to 2013, the overall budget was some €11.5 billion; a similarly sized budget has been set for 'IPA II' (2014–20) – 'carrots' indeed!

---

[35] See M Jozon, 'The Enlarged European Union and the Mandatory Requirements' (2005) 11 *European Law Journal* 549; P Hille and C Knill, '"It's the Bureaucracy, Stupid": The Implementation of the Acquis Communautaire in EU Candidate Countries 1999–2003' (2006) 7 *European Union Politics* 531.

[36] See Kassim et al, *The European Commission of the Twenty-First Century*, above (n 29) ch 2.

[37] E Heidbreder, 'Structuring the European Administrative Space: Policy Instruments of Multi-Level Administration' (2011) 18 *Journal of European Public Policy* 709, 715.

[38] Commision, 'Preparation of the Associated Countries of Central and Eastern Europe for Integration into the Internal Market of the Union' (White Paper) COM (95) 163 final.

[39] D Bailey and L De Propris, 'A Bridge Too Phare? EU Pre-Accession Aid and Capacity-Building in the Candidate Countries' (2004) 42 *Journal of Common Market Studies* 77.

[40] Council Regulation (EC) 1085/2006 of 17 July 2006 establishing an Instrument for Pre-Accession (IPA) [2006] OJ L210/82.

THE COMMISSION IN EU ADMINISTRATION

Breaking the Mould

We should always bear in mind that, even at Union level, the Commission is not the sole EU executive or even the whole of the Union level administration. The Council of Ministers, which meets in 10 distinct formations, is serviced by its own General Secretariat, tasked with providing its administrative services.[41] After the Maastricht Treaty created the second and third pillars – Common and Foreign Security Policy (CFSP) and Justice and Home Affairs (JHA) – the Council Secretariat expanded exponentially to emerge as virtually a parallel executive; around 3500 EU officials currently work there.[42] Coreper, the major configuration of senior Member State officials, is seen as developing a strong collective identity and ethos, methods of working and procedures.[43] Again, EU structures are notably unsettled and new bodies with administrative functions may emerge: the European Council has, for example, recently gained a President and a High Representative for Foreign Affairs has been appointed, both with independent offices staffed by EU officials. Recently too there has been a substantial growth in the number of EU agencies staffed by EU officials. Curtin, who deplores the complex structures and lack of transparency, describes the EU executive power as made up of 'many unseen layers', which include floating perimeters of working groups and committees.[44] It is nonetheless fair to see the Commission, made up of around 40 directorates and specialised units, as the core of the Union's public service, consuming up to 50 per cent of the administrative budget.

When the modern day Commission came into being in 1967,[45] it had two main functions. It was first and foremost a powerful policymaking agency (*administration de mission*). Key tasks included developing a system to regulate competition, creating procedures for coordination of Member State economic policies and, so far as was necessary, working towards an approximation of Member State laws. In the long view, this would help ground the formal 'Community method' of proceeding, whereby the Commission formulates policy and makes a legislative proposal to the Council and EP, which adopt legislative and budgetary acts, with the Court of Justice of the European Union (CJEU) acting as guardian of the rule of

---

[41] T Christiansen, 'Out of the Shadows: The General Secretariat of the Council of Ministers' (2002) 8 *Journal of Legislative Studies* 80.

[42] Secretariat staffing rose from 30 posts in 1953 to 2290 in 1995 and 3173 in 2012: Commission, 'Definitive adoption of the EU's general budget for the financial year 2012' [2012] OJ L56/1.

[43] J Lewis, 'Institutional Environments and Everyday EU Decision Making' (2003) 36 *Comparative Political Studies* 97; J Lempp, '"Coreper Enlarged": How Enlargement affected the Functioning of the Committee of Permanent Representatives' (2007) 6 *European Political Economy Review* 31.

[44] D Curtin, *Executive Power of the European Union* (Oxford: OUP, 2009) 3 and D Curtin, 'Challenging Executive Dominance in European Democracy' (2014) 77 *Modern Law Review* 1.

[45] The 1965 Treaty of Brussels merged the Euratom Commission and ECSC High Authority and also provided for a unified Community budget.

law.[46] But the Commission was also a workaday public service (*administration de gestion*).[47] As such, routine administrative activity in the sense of 'the performance of delegated, defined tasks, the taking of routine, programmed decisions, and the maintenance of organisational codes and practices to provide continuity and consistency',[48] was part of a bureaucratic DNA.

EC Article 155 conferred on the Commission some major powers and functions in relation to the common market:

- To ensure that the provisions of this Treaty and the measures taken by the institutions pursuant thereto are applied.
- To formulate recommendations or deliver opinions on matters dealt with in this Treaty, if it expressly so provides or if the Commission considers it necessary.
- To exercise the powers conferred on it by the Council for the implementation of the rules laid down by the latter.
- [To] have its own power of decision and participate in the shaping of measures taken by the Council and by the Parliament in the manner provided for in the Treaty.

The Commission was not a conventional executive, however; in Majone's powerful analysis, it was an agenda setting agency with 'no analogue either in parliamentary or presidential democracies'. Significantly for our subject, control of the Commission would largely be achieved through procedural tools and techniques:

> There are two main forms of control of agency decisions: oversight – monitoring, hearings, investigations, budgetary reviews, sanctions – and procedural constraints. The received view on procedures is that they are primarily a means of assuring fairness and legitimacy in regulatory decision-making. This is of course a very important function of procedures, but ... procedures also serve control purposes.[49]

Supervisory procedures involving oversight and monitoring, information sharing and reports are key tools for the Commission to steer and control implementation of EU policy by Member States. Risk regulation, a central EU function in areas of food and products safety, furnishes myriad examples.[50] Again, 'procedural constraints' such as consultation or impact assessment are at the heart of the 'Better Regulation' agenda now enthusiastically adopted and pursued by the Commission (see chapter two).

---

[46] For a Commission definition of the Community method, see Commission, 'European Governance – A White Paper' COM (2001) 428 final, 8 (hereafter WPEG).

[47] E Pisani, 'Administration de gestion, administration de mission' (1956) 2 *Revue française de science politique* 315.

[48] D Coombes, *Politics and Bureaucracy in the European Community* (London: Allen & Unwin, 1970) 114.

[49] G Majone, 'Agenda Setting' in M Moran, M Rein and R Goodin (eds), *The Oxford Handbook of Public Policy* (Oxford: OUP, 2008) 231, 235.

[50] See below, ch 2 pp 57; ch 3 pp 75. And see E Vos (ed), *European Risk Governance: Its Science, Its Inclusiveness and Its Effectiveness* (Mannheim: Connex, 2008).

Public Service and Bureaucratic Culture

It is said that in its early days the Commission worked as a group of 'convinced Europeans ... in a markedly un-hierarchical and informal way';[51] it was a 'porous' or 'trust' organisation, operating through informal relationships, mutual trust and intensely-shared objectives.[52] In this context, the decision to endow the young Community with its own, independent public service rather than rely on officials seconded from Member State administrations was significant. The Staff Regulations adopted for Community officials in 1962[53] set in place a permanent, centrally organised, hierarchical, public service based on rules. The paradigm was bureaucratic with recruitment and promotion based on merit and a lengthy and detailed code: the reality was a culture of patronage and national quotas.[54] The Staff Regulations now cover all EU institutions and bodies including EU agencies. They provide a career structure and procedures for recruitment, appointment and promotion, conditions of service, pay and benefits and retirement. Crucially, officials possess a right of legal challenge to the Luxembourg Courts.[55]

In practice there were many gaps and ambiguities in the regulations, opening the way for much legal wrangling; some of the most important principles of EU administrative law have been established in staff disciplinary proceedings. In 1963, for example, the Court insisted on the right to a hearing in disciplinary proceedings not provided in the regulations, reasoning that it was 'a generally accepted principle of administrative law in force in the Member States ... which meets the requirements of sound justice and good administration [and] must be followed by Community institutions'.[56] Later cases firmed up the procedures: a decision to reassign an official against his will must, for example, be reasoned, state the grounds on which it is based and be taken with 'necessary diligence, particular care and regard to the personal interests of the official concerned'.[57] Legal certainty was another fundamental administrative law principle to make an early appearance: 'every measure of the administration having legal effects', including the date of appointment, must be clearly recorded, so that the official was clear as to his rights and remedies.[58] Typically, however, it was far from clear when the Courts would impose stringent procedural requirements and when they would

---

[51] Coombes, above (n 48) ch 11.
[52] A Stevens with H Stevens, *Brussels Bureaucrats? The Administration of the European Union* (Basingstoke: Palgrave Macmillan, 2001) 27.
[53] Regulation (EEC) 31/62 [1962] OJ 45/1385. The Regulation has been regularly updated: see now Regulation 1023/2013/EU amending the Staff Regulations of Officials of the European Union and the Conditions of Employment of other Servants of the European Union [2013] OJ L287/15.
[54] M Cini, *The European Commission: Leadership, Organisation and Culture in the EU Administration* (Manchester: Manchester University Press, 1996).
[55] Titles VI and VII and Annex IX; Case 6/60 *Humblet v Belgium* [1960] ECR 559. Staff proceedings were transferred to the Court of First Instance (CFI), now the General Court (GC) in 1988, then to the Civil Service Tribunal in 2004.
[56] Case 32/62 *Alvis v Council* [1963] ECR 99.
[57] Joined Cases C-116 and 149/88 *Hecq v Commission* [1990] ECR I-599.
[58] Case T-18/89 *Tagaras v Court of Justice* [1991] ECR II-53.

uphold the wide discretion of the institutions to 'organize their departments to suit the task entrusted to them'.[59] Redolent with fine distinctions, a complex case law highlights a significant disadvantage of procedural development through legal process.[60]

Today, the Staff Regulations constitute a useful repository of values: 'the European civil service is expected to live up to the highest standards of professional ethics and to remain independent at all times'; 'the value of the European civil service lies equally in its cultural and linguistic diversity'.[61] Premised on classic bureaucratic principles of 'competence' 'impartiality' and 'stability',[62] they link today to guarantees of objectivity and equal treatment in the European Charter of Fundamental Rights (ECFR) and the EO's 'Code of Good Administrative Behaviour' (see chapter three). Nevertheless, the heavy reliance on formal rule-making and adjudication raises the problem of bureaucracy in its most negative sense of stasis and, perhaps surprisingly, research suggests that this how the Staff Regulations are viewed internally.[63]

Bureaucratic culture is often institutional in character. In the case of the Commission however, with its internationally recruited bureaucracy reflecting disparate cultural traditions and public service practices, research has tended to downplay the idea of a homogenous culture.[64] The Commission's own procedural rules provide that 'departments shall work in close cooperation and in coordinated fashion from the outset in the preparation and implementation of Commission decisions'.[65] But silo mentality – internal fragmentation – is a familiar bureaucratic vice and at the beginning of the century, Kassim described each Directorate-General (DG) as possessing 'its own functional responsibilities, operating procedures and culture' and as 'interacting with a particular constituency'. Inter-service consultation was 'beset by difficulties' and procedures were 'not always followed or enforced'.[66] As the next section shows, managerial reforms introduced early in the twenty-first century aimed to professionalise through standardisation. Yet a decade later, a major survey confirmed that the DGs remain 'powerful, introspective, and traditionally resistant to cooperation'; each 'has its own mission, networks, and culture', reinforced by 'a concentration of policy expertise and experience in each department'.[67] Inevitably, this has procedural

---

[59] Case C-294/95 *Girish Ojha v Commission* [1996] ECR I-5863.
[60] See S Pappas, 'Case Law of the European Civil Service Tribunal: Re-starting or Continuation? (2010) 31 *Human Rights Law Journal* 1.
[61] See M Cini, *From Integration to Integrity, Administrative Ethics and Reform in the European Commission* (Manchester: Manchester University Press, 2007).
[62] Regulation (EU, Euratom) 1023/2013, recitals 4–5, 7.
[63] Only 18% of 243 officials recently surveyed thought the Regulations helpful, while 28% thought them 'not at all helpful' and 27% found them 'something of a hindrance' Kassim et al, *The European Commission of the Twenty-First Century*, above (n 29) 229.
[64] M Abélès, I Bellier and M McDonald, *An Anthropological Approach to the European Commission* (Brussels: European Commission, 1993).
[65] Commission Decision amending its Rules of Procedure 2010/138/EU [2010] OJ L 55/60, Art 23.
[66] Kassim, 'The European Administration', above (n 31) 159.
[67] Kassim et al, *The European Commission of the Twenty-First Century*, above (n 29) 184.

consequences: DG Environment, for example, looks kindly on citizen participation, DG Competition (DG Comp) is more circumspect.[68]

Disgrace and Reform

Commission structural and procedural inadequacies, accentuated by staffing problems and an overly relaxed Commission culture, precipitated the fall of the Santer Commission in 1999. The steady rise in EU competences had led to a serious mismatch between activities, programmes and staffing and a growing number of projects were outsourced to outside contractors. A system of 'mini-budgets' came into being whereby project budgets were used to fund temporary recruitment; 'technical assistance offices' (TAOs) were set up and engaged on a contractual basis to provide expertise that the Commission lacked. These practices created problems of control, exposing the inadequacy of the Commission's management capacity, already the subject of previous internal inquiries.[69] Eventually, the European Court of Auditor's refusal to sign off the Community accounts precipitated the appointment by the EP of an investigatory committee of independent experts 'to examine the way in which the Commission deals with fraud, mismanagement and nepotism, including a fundamental review of Commission practices in the awarding of all financial contracts'.[70] The Experts, who focused their attention on four typical programmes overseen by the Commission, found serious procedural irregularity and laxity in Commission oversight of the operation of the programmes. There had been unsupervised delegation, inappropriate contracting-out, fraud and other irregularities and failure to take necessary action. The Experts identified within the Commission a 'dysfunctional organisational climate and structure', 'weaknesses of the information channels and control mechanisms', 'a reactive culture', the lack of 'a guiding philosophy' and 'overall view of the situation'. The long chains of responsibility involved in EU administration demanded robust supervisory procedures of report-back, monitoring, spot checks, etc that were plainly lacking or ignored.[71] Financial procedures were sub-standard; there was a dearth of contractual expertise and effective supervision and the financial regulations, audit and anti-fraud procedures were all in need of overhaul.[72] The

---

[68] M Cini, 'Administrative Culture in the European Commission: The Cases of Competition and Environment' in N Nugent (ed), *At the Heart of the Union* (Basingstoke: Palgrave Macmillan, 1997).

[69] Notably the Spierenburg Report (1979) and the Schmidhuber Memo on Financial Management (1995); and see Stevens and Stevens, above (n 52) 181–94; E Schön-Quinlivan, *Reforming the European Commission* (Basingstoke: Palgrave Macmillan, 2012) ch 3.

[70] Committee of Independent Experts, 'First Report on Allegations regarding fraud, mismanagement and nepotism in the European Commission' (1999); 'Second Report on Reform of the Commission – analysis of current practice and proposals for tackling mismanagement, irregularities and fraud' (1999).

[71] Vol 1 [5.8.3].

[72] Ibid, [9.4.9–10].

scathing report ended with the famous comment that 'it was becoming difficult to find anyone who had even the slightest sense of responsibility'.[73]

Administrative reform was clearly urgent. The new Prodi Commission targeted three main areas of administrative activity: strategic priority setting and resource allocation; human resources management, resulting in overhaul and reform of the Staff Regulations; and financial management and control, considered in chapter two. Handed direct responsibility, Vice-President Kinnock pushed a badly shaken Commission to focus on output functions, adopt a more managerial culture and experiment with a raft of managerial practices, basing his reform programme explicitly on fashionable 'new public management' (NPM) principles of economy, efficiency and output effectiveness.[74] Perhaps this was not surprising. Commonly characterised by rules, accountability and quantitative audit procedures and using a methodology of targeted goals, standard-setting, performance indicators, measurement and control and 'value for money' (VFM) audit,[75] NPM as a broad managerial style of administration had swept through the English speaking world in the 1990s.

Power has described NPM as a 'process by which environments are made auditable, structured to conform to the need to be monitored ex post . . . The standards of performance themselves are shaped by the need to be auditable'.[76] In this sense, NPM undoubtedly left its mark on the Commission: on the methodology of financial management; on the increased homogeneity of policy formation and management; and on the recent focus on transparency evidenced in the Transparency Initiative (see chapter five). Under the capacious heading of 'Activity Based Management' more effort would now go into strategic planning and budgeting, with operational programming and management matched to strategic priorities. Each DG was to design monitoring arrangements that ensured regular information gathering. This would be aggregated into an Annual Activity Report, evaluated and fed back into planning and programming for subsequent years. 'Performance-oriented working methods' and procedures were introduced: standards and codes of good administrative behaviour were adopted, decision-making and administrative procedures were simplified, archives and record-keeping modified. There was much stress in NPM on systematic ex ante and ex post evaluation and the Commission has steadily stepped up its use of evaluative tools such as impact assessment and performance indicators, independent validation and audit.[77]

---

[73] Ibid, [5.2.3], [5.8.3–7], [9.4.25].
[74] Commission, 'Reforming the Commission – White Paper. Vol II: Action Plan' COM (2000) 200 final. See also, Schön-Quinlivan, above (n 69) ch 5.
[75] P Hoggett, 'New Modes of Control in the Public Service' (1996) 74 *Public Administration* 9. The precise contours of NPM are open to debate: see Hammerschmid et al, above (n 30). Our use of the acronym is purely for convenience.
[76] M Power, *The Audit Society, Rituals of Verification* (Oxford: OUP, 1997) 8.
[77] COM (2000) 200 final, 13–18.

The Secretariat-General (SG)

Structurally, this meant a significant boost for the SG, the President's department in charge of policy priorities, resource allocation and performance management throughout the Commission. A Deputy Secretary-General was duly mandated to promote improved working methods across the Commission; meanwhile, a new Internal Audit Service reporting to an Audit Progress Committee would contribute independent appraisals of internal risk management, control and governance processes (now an established feature).[78] As Radaelli and Meuwese point out, procedure has morphed in EU administration from a means of policy implementation into a substantive policy objective 'with its own actors, resources, tools, processes, and outcomes'.[79] The Commission now abounds with new categories of consultant, project officers, central regulatory quality units, technical committees, internal audit capacities and other managerial posts – cloned no doubt in national administration. The whole is supported by the Secretariat-General which, in the words of its online 'mission statement', 'ensures the overall coherence of the Commission's work – both in shaping new policies, and in steering them through the other EU institutions'.

Today, the Secretariat-General, with 600 staff, is the hub of the Commission, tasked with assisting the 'smooth and effective functioning' of, and providing 'strategic direction' to its sprawling structures. Not only does the SG help in shaping new policies and 'steering them through the other EU institutions', but it has the increasingly important external role of 'interface' with EU institutions, national parliaments and civil society, as when the Commission work programme is presented to the EP or discussed annually by national parliaments. Despite its additional policy functions, however, the SG remains focused on administration; it has 'a narrow conception of its coordination role' and – in true hierarchical fashion – remains 'primarily concerned with enforcing the observance of procedure and the working of Commission machinery'.[80]

Outcome: A Managerial Administrative Style

How far the reform package – the most comprehensive in the Commission's life to date – was attributable to the influence of NPM is debateable; it is hard to distinguish a characteristic bureaucratic tendency to favour 'very detailed rules' and a 'regulatory and legalistic cast of mind'[81] from proceduralism induced by NPM techniques. Without joining the debate, all that we need to say is that the reforms

---

[78] Commission, 'Mission Charter of the Internal Audit Service' (Communication) C (2013) 3317 final.
[79] C Radaelli and A Meuwese, 'Better Regulation in Europe: Between Public Management and Regulatory Reform' (2009) 87 *Public Administration* 639, 640.
[80] Kassim et al, *The European Commission of the Twenty-First Century*, above (n 29) 186.
[81] Pollitt and Bouckaert, above (n 28) 257.

introduced a style of managerial administration that prevails within the Commission to the present day. Paradoxically, a managerial style, typically introduced to counter a supposedly bureaucratic mindset, is itself a form of proceduralism that, administered in heavy doses is apt to have a dulling effect. Expanding this theme, the Commission has increasingly emerged in middle age as a hierarchical bureaucracy. On the other hand, it may be seen today as pointing in several different directions. Pollitt and Bouckaert indeed suggest that the Commission style of administrative proceduralism has mostly been promoted by the Commission 'for use elsewhere'.[82] Amid much concern about internal control in an otherwise fragmented framework, it has acted as a conduit for NPM-style procedural forms across the so-called 'European administrative space' in Member States' own administrations or in EU programmes administered on a decentralised basis. Among many instances noted in this volume we would single out for mention the PHARE programme with twinning arrangements partly inspired by the managerialist methodology of establishing policy goals, evaluation and peer review.[83]

E-Governance: A Brave New World

The importance of the ICT revolution to EU administration can scarcely be exaggerated. Imagine officials trying to pursue the European project on the basis of old-fashioned card indexes. The majority of routine tasks, such as answering enquiries or maintaining document registers, are today performed electronically. Bureaucratic rule-making is today increasingly dependent on ICT. ICT systems have also played a central role in buttressing the Commission's special position as a 'leader in network construction'.[84] It is indeed fair to describe the path of European integration as grounded in the mass use of intranets.

Early experiments with ICT were limited in scope and designed for the provision of technical information necessary for policymaking, a process rendered more efficient by the establishment of Eurostat as the Commission's Statistical Office in 1959 and still a core element in 'Better Regulation'. But the Commission has always shown special interest in the Single Market potential of ICT, not only as a main driver of economic growth under the flagship 'Digital Agenda for Europe',[85] but also as an aid to opening up markets and as a tool for closer regulatory 'steering' in systems of indirect administration (see chapter six on public procurement). By

---

[82] Ibid.
[83] E Tulmets, 'The Management of New Forms of Governance by Former Accession Countries of the European Union: Institutional Twinning in Estonia and Hungary' (2005) 11 *European Law Journal* 656.
[84] S Bartolini, 'New Modes of European Governance: An Introduction' in A Héritier and M Rhodes (eds), *New Modes of Governance in Europe* (Basingstoke: Palgrave Macmillan, 2011) 5.
[85] Commission, 'A Digital Agenda for Europe' (Communication) COM (2010) 245 final, 2; D van Welsum, W Overmeer and B van Ark, *Unlocking the ICT Growth Potential in Europe: Enabling People and Businesses* (Brussels: European Commission, 2013).

2006, initial efforts at something called an 'e-Commission'[86] were clearly in need of a revamp. The institution had 'on average' reached the level of 'online government', meaning email as well as the (excellent) external website. 'Integrated government' whereby some but not all parts of administrative activity are automated, was notable by its absence. A little known but bureaucratically significant DG Informatics (DG DIGIT) was mandated to pursue a four-year plan with a view to 'enabling efficiency and transparency' by means of ICT.[87] Today DIGIT's vision statement has it leading a 'digital transformation' of the Commission in decidedly managerialist fashion: creating 'new ways of working and collaboration for staff' and delivering 'information systems supporting rationalised business processes within the framework of the corporate IT Governance strategy'.[88] DIGIT also looks outwards, promoting the Commission programme for ICT inter-operability across Union and national administrations, aimed at effective cross-border e-Government services and the establishment of 'trusted information exchange'.[89]

Adopted in 2012, the current 'e-Commission' strategy represents another step change: 'social, economic and technical landscapes' have changed considerably over the course of the previous plan.[90] The talk now is of 'user-centric digital services' delivered to Member States, business and citizens through multiple channels. Perhaps hinting at resistance, the strategy emphasises the importance to implementation of 'a partnership between the policy, administration and IT communities'. Attention is drawn to the rationalising potential inside the Commission from so-called 'cloud computing'; planned 'external dimension actions' also reference the idea of 'complete end-to-end automation of processes'.[91] Yet more faceless bureaucracy beckons at the heart of the Union.

Alongside, the less positive effects of 'e-governance' were beginning to cause concern. Initially, information remained essentially the property of Member States and EU institutions. Before it became the subject of general EU legislation, access to documents was subject to institutional rules of procedure or Member State discretion; document registers (if they existed), agendas and minutes of committees and even of the Council were not widely available to the public (see chapter five); equally, bureaucratic rules or 'soft law', the chief way in which officialdom develops and delivers policies were by no means always publicly available. Data processing and retention, with the accumulation of personal data in Europe-wide data banks, raised significant legal and political issues of privacy and human rights and of accountability (see chapter ten). The implications are profound. We take these significant issues up later in the context of the ECFR, the expanding EU criminal justice policy and the struggle for open government.

[86] Commission Memorandum, 'Towards the e-Commission: Implementation Strategy 2001–2005'.
[87] Communication to the Commission, 'e-Commission 2006–2010: enabling efficiency and transparency'.
[88] See for details, DG Informatics, *Annual Activity Report 2012*.
[89] Commission, 'Towards interoperability for European public services' (Communication) COM (2010) 744 final.
[90] Commission, 'e-Commission 2012–2015' (Communication) SEC (2012) 492 final, 5.
[91] Ibid, 10, 12.

COMMITTEES AS NETWORK STRUCTURES

If the appetite for internal reform and pace of change within the Commission has slowed in recent years,[92] it may simply be that the Commission has other things on its mind. The EU political agenda has passed through at least three widely differing phases: huge enlargement of the Union's territory; a phase of constitutionalism marked by the unsuccessful movement for an EU constitution, culminating in 2009 with the entry into force of the Lisbon Treaty; and the eurozone crisis, the regulatory fallout of which is considered in chapter eleven. Christensen discerns a new, post-managerial style in governance: 'post-NPM reforms are mainly inter-organizationally oriented. They seek to improve the horizontal coordination of governmental organisations and also to enhance coordination between the government and other actors'.[93] This certainly captures the recent Commission interest in soft governance techniques, further explored in chapter two.

By the start of the new millennium, the chains of administration with which the Commission was increasingly working at different levels had grown longer and more complex. As the EU struggled to produce an effective common fisheries policy or deal with energy problems and climate change, for example, policy networks extended both inside the EU and externally. The Commission cooperated not only with EU Member States and agencies, but also with international organisations, powerful international NGOs, commercial corporations, voluntary organisations and so on. There was a need, as Metcalfe argued in a percipient paper,[94] to strengthen the Commission's effectiveness by the construction of efficient policy regimes and administrative partnerships, and for development of its coordination capacities. Yet a decade later Bartolini was calling the EU 'a leader' in network construction and coordination and 'probably the most innovative producer of new types of decision-making arrangements'.[95] How had this been achieved?

Part of the answer lies in 'EU governance by committee'. The Commission has long had a raft of advisory bodies and working groups at its disposal. Some are highly formal like the European Economic and Social Committee (EESC) or Committee of the Regions (CoR), with a treaty basis and prescribed consultation function. The several hundred 'comitology' committees and scientific committees are established in secondary legislation and primarily concerned in law-making (see chapter five). In addition, there are myriad advisory committees, expert groups and working groups advising the Commission and Council committees. A figure of around 1500 is suggested but the general opacity makes it hard to be sure.

---

[92] Pollitt and Bouckaert, above (n 28) 68.
[93] T Christensen, 'Post-NPM and Changing Public Governance' (2012) 1 *Meiji Journal of Political Science and Economics* 1.
[94] Metcalfe, above (n 10) 43.
[95] Bartolini, above (n 84) 5.

From a networking perspective, EU committees are invaluable, acting as machinery for information gathering and a conduit to carry information into and out of the EU. They are 'important arenas where national and supranational decision-makers meet, interact, persuade, argue, bargain, adapt, learn and re-socialise'.[96] The Commission relies heavily on Member State representatives to anticipate problems with implementation in particular legal orders. Committees are ubiquitous. They are 'active at every stage of the political process within the EU machinery – assisting the Commission in drafting legislation, preparing the dossiers on which the Council takes decisions, supervising the implementation of EC law by the Commission'.[97] They open doors for officials from Member States and candidate countries into EU affairs and may also afford an opportunity for civil society and external actors to participate. The doors also open outwards, facilitating EU participation in international affairs and establishing the position of the Union as a main player in globalised networks, which may themselves have a direct impact on EU administrative procedures (see chapter twelve).

EU committees are difficult to classify. Whether they are strictly speaking procedures or rather governance structures is a moot point; they are probably both. Certainly the term 'committee procedure' is understood to mean a core modus operandi of meetings, agendas, minutes and votes. Originating in the agricultural sector,[98] committees rapidly expanded to meet demands for scientific and technical expertise sufficient to enable the regulation of the internal market.[99] A wide range of expertise is needed, from setting targets for air quality, authorising cosmetic products, establishing automobile safety standards and determining sustainable fish catches, to developing strategies to tackle unemployment and designing European research programmes. (Some of this expertise is now supplied by agencies.) Composition varies according to function; some committees are representative of Member State interests, others are purely expert.[100] Complaints have been heard about quality and independence. A recent complaint[101] from an animal rights organisation that an expert working group lacked the necessary expertise to give a valid opinion provoked a draft recommendation from the EO that a public trawl for experts should have been made. The Commission responded that it had adopted a new procedure for selecting experts

---

[96] Kassim, 'The European Administration', above (n 31) 142.

[97] M Egeberg, G Schaefer and J Trondal, 'The Many Faces of EU Committee Governance' (2003) 26 *West European Politics* 19. And see J Trondal, 'EU Committee Governance and the Multilevel Community Administration' in H Hofmann and A Türk (eds), *EU Administrative Governance* (Cheltenham: Edward Elgar, 2006).

[98] C Bertram, 'Decision-making in the EEC: The Management Committee Procedure' (1967) 5 *Common Market Law Review* 246.

[99] E Vos, 'EU Committees' in C Joerges and E Vos (eds), *EU Committees: Social Regulation, Law and Politics* (Oxford: Hart Publishing, 1999).

[100] See Å Gornitzka and U Sverdrup, 'Who Consults? Expert Groups in the European Union' (2007) Arena Working Paper 12; M Field, 'The Anatomy of EU Policy-Making: Appointing the Experts' in R Servent and A Busby (eds), 'Agency and Influence inside the EU Institutions' (2013) 17 *European Integration online Papers*.

[101] Inv 2558/2009/(TN)DK.

for working groups, starting with a search in its pool of scientific advisers on risk assessment and database of external experts and leading on to a web-based call for outside experts. This may lessen the chance of bias – an improvement on the situation at the time of the BSE crisis, when the extent to which the relevant scientific committee was dominated by its UK members was unexpectedly revealed by an EP inquiry,[102] sparking off reform.

The three main Scientific Committees on Consumer Safety (SCCS), Health and Environmental Risks (SCHER) and Emerging and Newly Identified Health Risks (SCENIHR)[103] are structured and relatively highly proceduralised. Composed so far as is possible of independent and objective scientific experts, and supported by a secretariat in DG Health and Consumers (DG SANCO), they are essentially tasked with advising the Commission on policy and legislative proposals in their respective policy domains. They may meet singly or interact through workshops and can call on additional expertise from a pool of scientific advisers, a database of experts and open consultations. There are extensive common procedures covering independence, transparency, communication with stakeholders and scientific principles and standards.[104] In addition, the Commission has set out general principles and guidelines covering the collection of advice through all expert groups and external consultants, ad hoc or permanent.[105] This is important, as procedure in scientific cases is closely scrutinised by the GC (see chapter three).

Committees: Opaque or Transparent?

An EO investigation into the Standing Committee on the Food Chain and Animal Health (SCFCAH) sheds much needed light on the way committees operate.[106] A complaint from a non-profit organisation alleged that SCFCAH procedure during consultations on changes to the law on baby milk formulae had been insufficiently transparent and that evidence was improperly recorded; full records of the meetings should be made available to the public and observers allowed to attend meetings. In its response, DG SANCO distinguished comitology committees like SCFCAH, where 'standards similar to those of other decision-making processes' obtained and a document register contained agendas of committee meetings, draft implementing measures, summaries of meetings and voting results of opinions delivered by a given committee, from expert groups, where a provisional schedule of draft agendas and summary records was published annually. Even so, the Commission said it had 'put a lot of effort' into increasing the transparency

[102] EP, 'Report on alleged contraventions or maladministration in the implementation of Community law in relation to BSE' A4-0020/97/A (7 February 1997) [5], [6].
[103] Established by Commission Decision 2008/721/EC, [2008] OJ L241/21.
[104] Commission, 'Rules of Procedure of the SCCS, SCHER and SCENIHR', Document SCs/01/04 final (C7 (2004) D/370235).
[105] Commission, 'The Collection and Use of Expertise by the Commission: Principles and Guidelines' (Communication) COM (2002) 713 final.
[106] Inv 97/2008/(BEH)JF.

30 *A Fragmented Framework*

and accountability of expert groups; the Transparency Register contained information on objectives and the membership of every group. The EO found no maladministration. Surprisingly, he professed himself satisfied with the Comitology Register, which afforded sufficient information on the discussions, their outcome and the voting, and noted that citizens might apply for access to the short and rapid 'back to office reports' on matters relevant for Commission policies. He also considered the available information on expert groups was 'sufficient for the general public to get sufficiently acquainted with the sort of expert advice the Commission receives from the groups it establishes'.

Assuming this is so, it is decidedly less true of the many smaller, informal and often ad hoc committees or working groups operating in the area of the secretive third pillar. From the outset, a practice obtained here of using such bodies to formulate policy, to be taken up later in more formal arrangements. Notable for their lack of transparency and accountability, these heterogeneous bodies have been used by the Council in sensitive areas such as those covered by the Prüm Convention (Schengen III),[107] which provides for the establishment of DNA profile databases and allows access to partner countries' fingerprint databases. In contrast, the Article 29 Data Protection Working Party stands out as adviser to the Commission as a relatively open and conventional 'independent' body of representatives of all EU data supervisory bodies plus one Commission representative. It has advisory status, informs the Commission on discrepancies in Member States' data protection provisions and issues opinions on proposed new regulation. It has adopted its own short but formal rules of procedure, committing it to publish agendas, opinions, recommendations and any documents adopted on its website – though minutes and draft documents are perhaps understandably restricted and there is no duty to consult.[108]

Compare the European Cooperation Group on Undercover Activities, apparently started in 2001 at the suggestion of national agencies using undercover investigators, including agencies from Albania, Macedonia, Norway, Russia, Serbia, Switzerland, Turkey and Ukraine. This group has engaged in an embryonic form of rule-making, circulating a private memorandum of understanding drafted by some of the members that sets out standards and criteria for undercover policing.[109] This activity clearly impinges on civil liberties, yet its existence was apparently unknown until a civil society organisation revealed its existence to the EP.[110] Again, the joint EU–US Working Group on cyber security and cybercrime was announced in a memorandum and press statement at a joint EU–US

---

[107] Convention on the stepping up of cross-border cooperation, particularly in combating terrorism, cross border crime and illegal migration, signed 27 May 2005.

[108] Arts 29 and 30 of Directive 95/46/EC on the protection of individuals with regard to the processing of personal data and on the free movement of such data [1995] OJ L281/31; Rules of Procedure (15 February 2010).

[109] European Cooperation Group on Undercover Activities, Memorandum of Understanding for the use of UC Officers (17 February 2004).

[110] Statewatch News Online, 'EU: State guidelines for the exchange of undercover police officers revealed' (17 May 2013).

summit in 2010. The Group is tasked to develop collaborative approaches and encourage Member States to accede to the Council of Europe Convention on cybercrime. It can also, however, assist states outside the region to meet its standards and become parties; engage with the private sector and encourage the sharing of 'good practice' with industry and stands as a model for outreach to other countries or organisations that address similar cyber issues in order to share approaches and related activities. There are no published procedures and no apparent duties of consultation or publication.[111]

Not before time, the Commission moved in 2010 to establish a new institutional framework for its own expert groups.[112] The declared aim was to strengthen transparency by including them on the public register of expert advisers now available on the Commission website and by publishing members' names. Horizontal rules, applicable to the setting up of all Commission expert groups whether formally or informally established, would now provide a procedure and template for consultation by all DGs. The Commission believes that expert groups' own rules of procedure should conform to the standard published by the SG unless specific requirements dictate otherwise. This is a step, but only a step, in the direction of much needed procedural standardisation in the committee world.[113]

AGENCIES AND NETWORKING

In recent times there has been a rapid rise in the practice of delegating governmental functions to 'arm's-length public bodies'.[114] The EU is no exception. EU agencies in the accepted sense of a public body with legal personality, a distinct, formal identity and internal hierarchy, with functional capacities and a degree of organisational and financial autonomy, have arrived in EU administrative space in successive waves. The first was no more than a ripple and attracted little attention; a more intense wave of agencification was noted between 1990 and 1995;[115] since 2000, EU agencies have proliferated and gained new powers; recently, development has surged again, driven by the global financial crisis.[116]

---

[111] See Commission Memorandum 10/597 (20 November 2010); Memorandum 11/246 (14 April 2011).

[112] Communication from the President to the Commission, 'Framework for Commission expert groups: Horizontal rules and public register' C (2010) 7649 final.

[113] As demanded by E Vos, 'The Rise of Committees' (1997) 3 *European Law Journal* 210.

[114] OECD, *Distributed Public Governance: Agencies, Authorities and Other Autonomous Bodies* (London: OECD, 2002); M Flinders, 'Distributed Public Governance in the European Union' (2004) 11 *Journal of European Public Policy* 520.

[115] E Chiti, 'The Emergence of a Community Administration: The Case of European Agencies' (2000) 37 *Common Market Law Review* 309.

[116] See D Geradin, R Munoz and N Petit (eds), *Regulation through Agencies in the EU. A New Paradigm for European Governance* (Cheltenham: Edward Elgar, 2005); M Busuioc, M Groenleer and J Trondal (eds), *The Agency Phenomenon in the European Union* (Manchester: Manchester University Press (2010).

Gaining Acceptance

In Anglo-American terminology, regulatory agencies have delegated authority to perform clearly specified tasks, including regulation.[117] In the Community, delegation was at first recognised only within very narrow limits because of the influential *Meroni* doctrine laid down long ago in the era of the Coal and Steel Community. In *Meroni*,[118] the CoJ insisted that delegated power could never exceed the limits of the powers granted by the Treaty to the delegator, and that powers involving 'a wide margin of discretion' could never be delegated because they bring about an 'actual transfer of responsibility'. Thus, the first ten agencies were largely devoted to information gathering and were, with the exception of the Office for Harmonization in the Internal Market (OHIM), the European patents office, which had adjudicative functions, purely advisory to the Commission.[119] The European Environment Agency (EEA), for example, was envisaged by the Commission as 'a technical body with a basic mission to collect information and data on the environment and provide this to the Community and Member States for framing and implementing sound and effective environment policies'.[120] Significantly, the EP at the time favoured a full-blown power of inspection located in an autonomous agency, something for which Member States show scant enthusiasm.

By 2000, EU agencies were beginning to be accepted as part of the institutional landscape and a Commission liking for what the Commission classified as 'regulatory agencies' was appearing. The WPEG stated that the advantage of agencies lay in

> their ability to draw on highly technical, sectoral know-how, the increased visibility they give for the sectors concerned (and sometimes the public) and the cost-savings that they offer to business. For the Commission, the creation of agencies is also a useful way of ensuring it focuses resources on core tasks.[121]

However, the WPEG stressed the limitations supposedly imposed by the Treaties such that, in Anglo-American eyes, 'regulatory agencies' were scarcely that.[122] Such bodies, it was said, 'cannot adopt general regulatory measures' and 'cannot be granted decision-making power in areas in which they would have to arbitrate

---

[117] M Shapiro, 'The Problems of Independent Agencies in the United States and European Union' (1997) 4 *Journal of European Public Policy* 276.

[118] Case 9/56 *Meroni v High Authority* [1957/58] ECR 133. For the view that *Meroni* has been widely misinterpreted, see M Chamon, 'EU Agencies between *Meroni* and *Romano* or the Devil and the Deep Blue Sea' (2011) 48 *Common Market Law Review* 1055.

[119] A Kreher, 'Agencies in the EC –A Step Towards Administrative Integration in Europe' (1997) 4 *Journal of European Public Policy* 225.

[120] E Murillo-Mastilla, 'The European Environmental Agency: Political, Managerial, Financial and Legal Accountability' in A Kreher (ed), *The EC Agencies Between Community Institutions and Constituents: Autonomy, Control and Accountability* (Florence: EUI, 1997) 21.

[121] COM (2001) 428 final, 24.

[122] See Craig (n 12), ch 6.

between conflicting public interests, exercise political discretion or carry out complex economic assessments'.[123]

Agency structure was beginning to show an identifiable common framework, and in 2002 the Commission came forward with an 'operating framework for regulatory agencies'.[124] Regulatory agencies should each have a Management Board (MB) representative of the Member States with responsibility for defining the agency's general operating guidelines within parameters set by the governing legal framework, which might be contained in Commission implementing measures. Clearly concerned for its own position, the Commission suggested a standardised 15-member administrative board comprising six Commission representatives with six appointed by the Council to represent national authorities plus three non-voting members to represent other stakeholders. The Board would be responsible for adopting the agency's work programme and rules of procedure and 'be involved in' the appointment of the Executive Director and other appointments. The Executive Director was responsible for implementing the programme of activities and proper management of the agency. Staff and financial regulations were based on standard Commission models and finance was included in the general EU budget with supervision by the Commission's financial controller and audit by the ECA. Yataganas, noting that agencies were in principle responsible for their own rules of procedure, highlighted the function of administrative procedures in ensuring compliance and facilitating oversight and control.[125] Little was heard of this operating framework however; in 2005, the Commission proposed an inter-institutional agreement[126] but without success.

According to Rittberger and Wonka, who analyse EU agencies specifically in terms of networking,[127] agencies promote 'horizontal cross-fertilisation among national administrations'. They are important players in pan-European networks, helping to bring together relevant regulatory players, public and private, national, sub-national and transnational. Typifying the evolution of EU agencies, the EEA today has significant network functions. Its first Director listed its clientele as the EU institutions (especially DG Environment), Member States, regional and local government associations, private sector organisations representing trade and industry and unions and environmental NGOs.[128] In 2012, the EEA was networking with

---

[123] COM (2001) 428 final, 24.
[124] Commission, 'The operating framework for the European regulatory agencies' (Communication) COM (2002) 718 final.
[125] X Yataganas, 'Delegation of Regulatory Authority in the European Union' (2001) Jean Monnet Working Paper 03/01.
[126] Commission, 'Draft Interinstitutional Agreement on the operating framework for the European regulatory agencies' COM (2005) 59 final.
[127] B Rittberger and A Wonka, 'Introduction: Agency Governance in the European Union' (2011) 18 *Journal of European Public Policy* 780, 781. And see D Levi-Faur, 'Regulatory Networks and Regulatory Agencification: Towards a Single European Regulatory Space' (2011) 18 *Journal of European Public Policy* 810.
[128] D Jíménez-Beltràn, 'The European Environmental Agency' in A Kreher (ed), *The EC Agencies Between Community Institutions and Constituents: Autonomy, Control and Accountability* (Florence: EUI, 1997) 60.

32 member countries. It is responsible for coordinating the European Environment Information and Observation Network (EIONET), a 'partnership network' set up by the EEA, its member countries and cooperating bodies. EIONET processes and disseminates information from a further network of around 1500 experts from some 40 countries and up to 400 national bodies dealing with environmental information. As well as supporting IMPEL (EU Network for the Implementation and Enforcement of Environmental Law), a specialist enforcement network, the EEA has links, inter alia, with the European Network of Heads of Environmental Protection Agencies and the European Network of Heads of Nature Conservation Agencies. It also has close contacts with Green Force, a network of conservation practitioners, and the Green Spider Network of Environmental Information Officers, both primarily dependent on DG Environment.[129]

Gathering Momentum

The later waves of agencification have added more than 20 agencies, some classifiable as 'regulatory' in the Anglo-American sense. There were at the time of writing 33 EU 'decentralised' agencies plus three under the European Health Committee (CDSP); over 5000 administrative posts had been assigned to them and the cost to the EU budget was some €750 million. More significantly, agencies were beginning to acquire a considerable agglomeration of functions and powers. The initial brief of the fisheries agency (EFCA), for example, had been information gathering,[130] with enforcement of fishing policy left – in a classic example of indirect administration – to national administrations and agencies. As the case law described in chapter seven testifies, however, 'loyal cooperation' was notably lacking in the case of fishing;[131] consequently, the Member States in Council agreed to give EFCA supervisory and indirect enforcement powers. It is now able to draw up joint operational procedures in relation to joint control and inspection activities undertaken by two or more Member States;[132] to authorise individuals to carry out an inspection and assign them to international waters as Community inspectors; and, at the request of the Commission, to establish joint deployment plans to coordinate Member States' control and inspection activities on the basis of international control and inspection programmes. This begins to look much like a regulatory agency as that term is commonly understood – a development that raises serious questions about accountability by no means yet resolved (see chapter ten).

---

[129] See further Final Report of the EEA Evaluation (2012) available at: http://www.eea.europa.eu/about-us/governance/eea-evaluations/eea-evaluation-2013/evaluation-of-the-european-environment/view.
[130] Regulation (EC) 768/2005 [2005] OJ L128/1, Art 3.
[131] Notably, Case C-304/02 *Commission v France* [2005] ECR I-6263; Case T-139/06 *France v Commission* [2011] ECR II-07315, discussed in chapter 7. The principle of 'loyal cooperation' is discussed in chapter 2.
[132] Regulation (EC) 1224/2009 [2009] OJ L343/1, Art 7(d). cp Europol, below p 251.

Reflecting the changes, the Commission issued a new Communication in 2008, calling on the Council and EP to join it in developing 'a clear and coherent vision for the future place of agencies in the Union's governance'.[133] A new, four-fold classification was suggested to distinguish agencies that were merely advisory and networking agencies from agencies able to adopt legally binding individual decisions or 'in charge of operational activities'. Once again the Commission moved to standardise the rules governing appointments and governance and also suggested a standard approach for evaluation of agency performance.[134] This time the work bore fruit with the agreement of a Common Approach based on the work of an inter-institutional working group.[135] Decidedly managerial in method, the Common Approach includes provision for impact assessment before a new agency is established plus ex ante and ex post evaluations of the agencies' programmes and activities based on performance indicators. Five-yearly evaluations of overall agency performance linked to sunset clauses in the governing legislation give reinforcement.

The Common Approach has now been concretised in a Commission road map,[136] which sees the Commission working with agencies to map existing rules and standards and develop guidelines and best practices; governing legislation is in the course of being revised in accordance with a detailed action plan. Raising potentially tricky issues of independence and autonomy, the road map also contains a novel 'alert-warning system' authorising the Commission to notify the EP and Council in a 'carefully motivated decision' of any proposed agency action or decision likely to be illegal or ultra vires. In the face of an essentially pragmatic, instrumentalist and increasingly forceful set of institutional developments, the Commission considers the Common Approach 'a very important step for defining a more coherent and efficient framework for the functioning of agencies' – more standardisation and reassertion of Commission control. Yet its first progress report also speaks darkly of ongoing institutional tensions: 'The Commission would welcome a more coherent and reform-minded approach on the side of the co-legislator when discussing issues stemming from the Common Approach'.[137]

The Court's very latest word on the subject is cautious adaptation in a changed administrative milieu. At issue in the *ESMA* case[138] were the powers of the European Securities and Markets Authority, one of the new breed of European Supervisory Authorities operative in financial services regulation to adopt emergency measures restricting or prohibiting 'short selling' and hence to protect

---

[133] Commission, 'The European Agencies – The Way Forward', Communication COM (2008) 135 final, SEC (2008) 323.

[134] Ibid, 7.

[135] Joint Statement of the EP, Council and Commission on decentralised agencies (19 July 2012); see Commission Press Release at IP/12/604 (13 June 2012).

[136] Road map on the follow-up to the Common Approach on EU decentralised agencies (December 2012).

[137] Commission, 'Progress report on the implementation of the Common Approach' (December 2013) 1.

[138] Case C-270/12 *United Kingdom v Parliament and Council* (judgment of 22 January 2014).

36 A Fragmented Framework

against volatility in stocks and shares in national financial markets (see chapter eleven). Among the matters raised by the United Kingdom was *Meroni*; would not ESMA have 'a very large measure of discretion' of the kind previously discountenanced in the WPEG?[139] Rejecting the challenge, the CoJ went some way to laying a ghost. *Meroni* had involved delegation to 'entities governed by private law'; ESMA 'is a European Union entity, created by the EU legislature'. Further, the agency's discretionary – regulatory – powers were substantively and procedurally structured and confined. Attention was here drawn to the threat based and secondary nature of the intervention powers, allowing agency intervention only if the national authorities had not taken adequate measures, as also to legal duties to consult and periodically to review the intervention. In the Court's view, all this added up to the powers being 'precisely delineated and amenable to judicial review in the light of the objectives established by the delegated authority' – hence sufficient for *Meroni*.[140] The judgment neither rules in all-powerful EU agencies, nor rules out distributed governance at Union level. The Court instead gives agencification the 'amber light' to proceed.

CONCLUSION

In this chapter we set about linking administrative procedures with the fragmented institutional framework of the EU, one which is almost permanently in a state of change. We looked first at the significant role played by national administration at every stage of the implementation process, paying particular attention to the traffic in concepts and practices both horizontally and vertically across Europe. Stress was laid on Enlargement as providing an enrichment of, and successive set of challenges for, EU administrative styles and procedures. Moving on to consider the role of the EU Commission as the core EU executive, we observed a mature and increasingly professional bureaucracy greatly concerned with procedure – indeed, with a managerial style which verges on proceduralisation. Largely driven by the demands of a bigger and more complex Union, the Commission was also viewed in the role of a 'network organisation': the hub of a complex set of policy networks and networks of institutional actors, with largely supervisory functions. Committees and latterly agencies were placed at the heart of this development: a pointer to future organisational change. The picture that emerges is of a cluttered and confused EU administrative or regulatory 'space' in which leading actors are working towards modest standardisation.

The heavy premium placed on administrative procedural techniques of communication, cooperation and coordination has been highlighted. Without highly developed tools and techniques for producing and sharing information, the sprawling system of EU administration simply cannot be efficacious. Denied

---
[139] Ibid, [28]–[29].
[140] Ibid, [43]–[54].

intense forms of administrative cooperation across the regulatory cycle of rule formulation, application and enforcement, the Single Market would be far less than the sum of its parts, an aspect pursued in later chapters. As for coordination, attention is drawn to the major potential of administrative procedure for 'steering' the work of others through more or less sophisticated 'wiring systems'. Ranging from the blandly routine to the carefully principled, and on to the heavily policy laden, these steering mechanisms are a common theme of this volume.

2

Into the Office: Tenets, Values and Objectives

ATRUISM YES, but the fact that EU administrative process is commonly shaped from within by the bureaucracy, as well as by the lawgiver from without, has not always been given the prominence it deserves. In adopting an administration-centred stance familiarly associated with a functionalist approach, this chapter looks more closely at the administrative tenets and values, including those expressed by the treaty makers and legislature, which influence the design and operation of procedures. The chapter establishes a taxonomy of procedural functions or objects – an 'administrator's toolkit' – helpful for navigating the many vagaries of EU administration. This links forward to the discussion in chapter three of the important procedural purpose of rights protection and the major external contribution of courts and ombudsmen.

Expanding on the earlier discussion of 'new public management' (NPM), this chapter highlights the changing administrative styles – or as we prefer, fashions – exhibited at Union level, which are frequently rooted in national and/or international practice. As already indicated, the rise of audit technique can scarcely be exaggerated: a necessary response to endemic problems of corruption[1] but also, as previously indicated, reflecting and reinforcing a particular set of attitudes to problem solving. Epitomising soft governance – and its propensity to formalise – is the 'Open Method of Coordination' (OMC), of which much was heard in the early years of this century. So-called 'better' or 'smart' regulation now dominates the field, in large measure through the voguish administrative procedure of 'impact assessment' (IA).

It is appropriate to begin with some overarching administrative principles and standards. We first sketch in two foundational features: the treaty-based obligations of reason-giving and sincere cooperation. Reference to subsidiarity as a political and administrative precept builds on the 'bottom-up' perspective introduced in the previous chapter. Principles of good governance adopted in the Commission's 'White Paper on European Governance' (WPEG) will suitably illustrate the executive's role as a source of administrative values. Serving as a useful reminder that relevant principles and standards may themselves be contested,

---

[1] Commission, 'EU Anti-Corruption Report' COM (2014) 38 final.

the strong – coercive – potential for 'steering' associated with conditionality as a principle of Union assistance also commands attention.

Whether 'principles' are really distinguishable from 'procedures' is itself debatable: is reasoned decision-making, for example, a 'principle' or a 'procedure'? Both are correct. Here we have chosen to treat it as a principle, primarily because of its basis in the Treaties and its primary importance in shaping the EU administrative process.

PRINCIPLES AND STANDARDS

Rationality: Reasoned Decision-Making

The EU is a polity committed to the rule of law, described in the Treaty on European Union (TEU) as a 'universal value' to which Member States are 'attached'. As we have suggested, the *Rechtsstaat* idea of a state where administrative activity is 'assigned to predictable legal forms'[2] and which functions through rules is highly influential in EU administration. The point is underlined by Schwarze, who observes that, having submitted itself in principle to the rule of law, the EU had 'as a consequence thereof, the obligation to provide impartial and fair administrative procedures'.[3] Schwarze goes on to say that administrative discretion – a special target of twentieth-century administrative law systems – is 'nowadays justifiable only if discretion is exercised under strict observance of procedural guarantees'.[4]

As Weber stated in his seminal treatise on bureaucracy, administrative behaviour should be based on the 'weighing of ends and means' or 'rationally debatable reasons'.[5] Thus, reason-giving is a core value of rational administration. Simon too has argued in his influential theory of 'bounded rationality' that forcing decision-makers to spell out the steps in their argument helps them to focus on key issues and lessens the risk of capricious choices and arbitrariness.[6] For Friedrich, the very concept of authority implies the capacity to give reasons.[7] Mashaw spells out the dignitary implications of reason-giving, maintaining that 'to be subject to administrative authority that is unreasoned is to be treated as a mere object of the law or political power, not a subject with independent rational capacities'.[8] From

---

[2] M Stolleis, *A History of Public Law in Germany, 1914-45*, trans Dunlap (Oxford: OUP, 2004) 9; F van Dun 'Political Liberalism and the Formal *Rechtsstaat*' (2004) available at: philpapers.org.

[3] See G Nolte, 'General Principles of German and European Administrative Law – A Comparison in Historical Perspective' (1994) 57 *Modern Law Review* 191.

[4] J Schwarze, 'Judicial Review of European Administrative Procedure' [2004] *Public Law* 146, 156.

[5] M Weber, *Economy and Society: An Outline of Interpretive Sociology*, trans Wittich (Berkeley, CA: University of California Press, 1978) 41.

[6] H Simon, *Reason in Human Affairs* (Oxford: Blackwell, 1983) 19–23.

[7] C Friedrich, 'Authority, Reason and Discretion' in C Friedrich (ed), *Authority* (Cambridge, MA: Harvard University Press, 1958) 28.

[8] J Mashaw, 'Reasoned Administration: The European Union, the United States, and the Project of Democratic Governance' (2007) 76 *George Washington Law Review* 99, 105.

40 *Tenets, Values and Objectives*

this it is only a step to the deduction that the requirement of reasons is a fundamental right as it has now become in ECFR Article 41 (see chapter three).

Reasoned decision-making has always been a central tenet of EU administration, first established in the EC Treaty, which provided that every 'legal act', and specifically regulations, directives, decisions, must state the reasons on which they are based. As articulated in TFEU Article 296, the duty now reads that 'Legal acts shall state the reasons on which they are based and shall refer to any proposals, initiatives, recommendations, requests or opinions required by the Treaties'. This is a clear commitment to rationality and legality, locking together bureaucratic practice and rationality in a single legal provision redolent of the *Rechtsstaat* ideal. It is, however, one thing to establish a duty to give reasons and quite another to formulate the content of that duty. As we shall see in chapter three, much of the time and energy of the Court of Justice of the European Union (CJEU) has been directed towards this.

More 'Glue': Sincere Cooperation

Like reason-giving, the principle of cooperation has been recognised in the Treaties from the beginning. As one of our designated 'three Cs' of EU governance', which has special resonance in multi-level decision-making and composite administrative process, it represents in our view another core value of EU administration and reflects its most important political functions. Established by EEC Article 5, the duty of sincere cooperation is now set out in TEU Article 4(3):

> Pursuant to the principle of sincere co-operation, the Union and the Member States shall, in full mutual respect, assist each other in carrying out tasks which flow from the Treaties.
>
> The Member States shall take any appropriate measure, general or particular, to ensure fulfilment of the obligations arising out of the Treaties or resulting from the acts of the institutions of the Union.
>
> The Member States shall facilitate the achievement of the Union's tasks and refrain from any measure which could jeopardise the attainment of the Union's objectives.

Again, usefully underwriting such practices as inter-institutional agreements and joint declarations, TEU Article 13 provides that 'the institutions shall practice mutual sincere cooperation'.

The principle of sincere cooperation often surfaces in case law. In the early case of *Commission v Netherlands*,[9] the CJEU relied on the principle not only to underwrite a duty to provide information about implementation of a directive, but also by specifying that the information 'must be clear and precise', to define its parameters. As a fallback provision on which the Commission can rely to underpin its supervisory functions, Article 4(3) effectively grounds a category of infringement action (see chapter seven). Again, the Court has from time to time conjured obli-

---

[9] Case 96/81 *Commission v Netherlands* [1982] ECR 1791.

gations of administrative cooperation – acceptance of documentation etc – in support of the mutual recognition of regulatory activity in other Member States.[10] The principle has likewise been used to buttress individual protection at the national level, as in *Kühne & Heitz*,[11] where it was held that an authority with power to reopen a final decision must in certain circumstances do so if it is necessary in order to give effect to EU law.

As a source of inspiration in legislative and administrative development, the influence of the principle is far-reaching. It features prominently in the recitals to EU regulations or directives concerning the internal market, effectively heralding provision on mutual assistance, and in particular information exchange,[12] across all or part of the policy and regulatory cycles. Perhaps hopefully, cooperation between national administrations should 'promote the adoption of decisions that are lawful and consistent throughout Europe', 'facilitate the action of the administrations when dealing with "cross-border issues"' and 'reduce the national-based regulation of economic activities with a view to creating a common economic space'.[13]

Widening and deepening over time, in some fields the relevant provision on administrative cooperation is particularly intense. Perhaps not surprisingly given recent economic travails, the new legislation on a single supervisory mechanism for eurozone banks provides a striking illustration (see chapter eleven). Another good example is the modernised – decentralised – competition procedures, where the development involves much in the form of formalised soft law (see chapter eight). Cooperation cannot be lightly assumed, however. Set in the context of police cooperation, the new Europol Regulation points to deficiencies caused by failure of network members to cooperate (chapter ten). Structural and cultural differences between national administrations, lack of clearly identified 'partners' and language problems, elements of Member State competition and/or mistrust: all – and more – must be factored in.[14]

Mutual assistance between Member States in the fields of market, customs and tax goes back many years.[15] Targeted especially on recovery of monies,[16] it was slowly extended to VAT, excise duties and taxes on some investments.[17] In the light of the greatly enlarged internal market and rise of electronic transactions,

---

[10] See eg, Case C-202/97 *Fitzwilliam Executive Search Ltd v Bestuur van het Landelijk Instituut Sociale Verzekeringen* [2000] ECR I-883.
[11] Case C-453/00 *Kühne & Heitz NV v Produktschap voor Pluimvee en Eieren* [2004] ECR I-00837.
[12] D Galetta, H Hofmann and J Schneider, 'Information Exchange in the European Administrative Union' (2014) 20 *European Public Law* 89.
[13] M Lottini, 'From "Administrative Cooperation" in the Application of European Union Law to "Administrative Cooperation" in the Protection of European Rights and Liberties' (2012) 18 *European Public Law* 127, 128.
[14] See F Lafarge, 'Administrative Cooperation between Member States and the Implementation of EU Law' (2010) 16 *European Public Law* 597.
[15] Convention of the Member States of the EEC on the provision of mutual assistance by their customs authorities (Rome, 1967).
[16] Directive 76/308/EEC [1976] OJ L73/18. See also Directive 2010/24/EU [2010] OJ L84/1 and Directive 16/2001 [2001] OJ L110/1.
[17] See Directive 79/1071/EEC [1979] OJ L331/10; Directive 92/108/EEC [1992] OJ L390/124; and Directive 2001/44/EC [2001] OJ L175/17, respectively.

however, the last few years have seen a welter of EU legislation designed to make cooperation between tax administrations more efficient and effective. Take the revamped Regulation on administrative cooperation and combating fraud in the field of VAT,[18] where – putting in issue the political willingness of governments to act – a Commission review had found that 'the level of administrative cooperation [was] not commensurate with the size of intra-Community trade' and that 'a lot of problems' needed addressing at management level in the Member States, 'such as the priority to be given within the tax administration to provide assistance to other Member States'.[19] The Commission proceeded to highlight the need for 'a much faster mechanism for the exchange of information, covering much more, and better targeted, information'. Tellingly, it pinpointed the importance of interstate feedback as a means of improving (and checking on) the quality of the information provided.[20] The new recast Regulation establishes, among other things, enhanced general duties to cooperate, a clearer definition of the information to be collected and exchanged via automated access to databases and minimum standards for the registration and deregistration of taxable persons. Some of the provision is very detailed, covering such matters as single central liaison offices for contacts with other Member States, involvement in administrative enquiries in other countries and pooling of Member States' experiences by the Commission.[21]

The wider development serves to illustrate a chief feature of EU cooperative administration: mutually reinforcing elements of hard law and soft governance (see further below). In the meantime, two specialist EU programmes had been established, CUSTOMS 2013 and FISCALIS 2013, with a joint budget of some €480m.[22] Filled out through the usual panoply of steering and working groups, they have operated as forums – personal contact – for national officials at different levels of seniority. Clearly, it helps to talk.

Subsidiarity Matters

It has to be said that subsidiarity or the idea that decision-making should take place at the lowest possible level,[23] is not a tenet or value that one associates primarily with the Court or Commission. It is rather a concept introduced in the Maastricht Treaty by the Member States in response to concerns about the EU's

[18] Regulation (EC) 904/2010 of 7 October 2010 on administrative cooperation and combating fraud in the field of value added tax (recast) [2010] OJ L 268/1.
[19] Commission, 'Report on the application of Council Regulation (EC) 1798/2003' COM (2009) 428 final, 4, 9.
[20] Council Regulation (EC) 904/2010, recs 14 and 18; Commission, 'On a coordinated strategy to improve the fight against VAT fraud in the European Union' (Communication) COM (2008) 807 final.
[21] Council Regulation (EC) 904/2010, Arts 4, 28, 49.
[22] Commission, DG for Taxation and the Customs Union, *Participating in Customs and Fiscalis Cooperation Programmes* (2009).
[23] See N Barber, 'The Limited Modesty of Subsidiarity' (2005) 11 *European Law Journal* 308.

expansionist – perhaps even federalist – tendencies[24] and subsequently affirmed and considerably strengthened at Lisbon. Effectively establishing a twin test of (a) necessity and (b) 'added value', TEU Article 5(3) states that Union level action in areas that do not fall within its exclusive competence shall be taken

> only if and insofar as the objectives of the proposed action cannot be sufficiently achieved by the Member States, either at central level or at regional and local level, but can rather, by reason of the scale or effects of the proposed action, be better achieved at Union level.

Symbolic of enhanced constitutional sensitivities in a greatly enlarged Europe and highlighting an increased interest in the potential for legal pluralism,[25] Article 5(3) further provides first, that the institutions 'shall apply the principle of subsidiarity' as laid down in the accompanying Protocol on the principles of subsidiarity and proportionality and second, that 'national parliaments ensure compliance with the principle of subsidiarity in accordance with the procedure set out in that Protocol'.[26] Any draft legislative act must contain a detailed statement making it possible to appraise compliance with the principles of subsidiarity and proportionality and TEU Article 9 requires the Commission to report annually on its application and submit annual reports to the Council, the EP and national parliaments.

At the heart of Commission policy development today is IA, a mainline administrative procedure suitably equipped with its own internal guidelines (see further below). These have latterly included a list of specific questions that services should address with a view to 'respecting the subsidiarity principle'.[27] Denoted by 'scale' and/or 'effectiveness', evidence of 'clear benefits' of Union over Member State level action is asked for. The analysis produced by this historically integrationist institution may, of course, be eminently contestable but the development does suggest that legislators are starting to take subsidiarity seriously enough for it to impinge on the consciousness of the Commission.[28] Indeed, to the extent that the Commission has to provide reasons for concluding that a Union objective can be better achieved at Union level and, wherever possible, to substantiate these by 'qualitative and quantitative indicators', TEU Article 5 effectively puts IA on a constitutional footing.

Ex ante control by national parliaments is the primary accountability machinery in matters of subsidiarity. The Protocol set in place the so-called 'yellow card' and 'orange card' procedures improving the position of national parliaments

---

[24] N Emiliou, 'Subsidiarity: An Effective Barrier against the "Enterprises of Ambition"?' (1992) 17 *European Law Review* 383; A Estella, *The EU Principle of Subsidiarity and its Critique* (Oxford: OUP, 2002).

[25] N Barber, 'Legal Pluralism and the European Union' (2006) 12 *European Law Journal* 306.

[26] Protocol (No 2) on the Application of the Principles of Subsidiarity and Proportionality. The main provisions of the Protocol only apply to (draft) legislative acts, though these are given a wide meaning (Art 3).

[27] Commission, 'Impact Assessment Guidelines' SEC (2009) 92, 22–23.

[28] See further, Commission, 'Annual Report on Subsidiarity and Proportionality for 2012' COM (2013) 566 final. And see European Scrutiny Committee, *12th Report for 2013–14* (HC 83-xii) para 19.

(Article 7). This has begun to prompt more networking between legislatures on a pan-European basis. IPEX, 'the platform for EU Interparliamentary Exchange' is suddenly awash with discussion of possible non-compliance of legislative proposals with the principle of subsidiarity[29] and, led by the Committee of the Regions (CoR), exceptionally empowered by Article 8 of the Protocol to challenge legislative acts on grounds of subsidiarity,[30] numerous sub-state authorities have been clubbing together in the 'Subsidiarity Monitoring Network' (SMN). These are institutional developments of some significance for political accountability in EU governance. However, in the case of one of the two yellow cards to date – on controversial proposals for a new 'decentralised agency' in the form of the European Public Prosecutor's Office – the Commission has been happy to press on.[31]

Much the same can be said of Commission conduct in the matter of greenhouse gas emissions. National authorities in Estonia and Poland had calculated their emission allowances under the relevant directive, following which the Commission, using a different method of calculation, exercised supervisory powers to disallow the national plans. The two Member States successfully argued before the Luxembourg Courts that this procedure allowed the Commission de facto to take over the allocation of allowances from the Member States, effectively centralising emissions trading procedure. In achieving its subsidiarity-like result, the Court of Justice (CoJ) held that the Commission must respect the Member States' 'margin for manoeuvre' in transposing the directive.[32] The Commission undoubtedly overstepped the mark in the *Estonia* and *Poland* cases by seeking (in Osborne and Gaebler's celebrated metaphor)[33] to 'row' when it was only entitled to 'steer'. Typically, however, it fought back with a more harmonised scheme for trading greenhouse gas emission allowances.[34]

The *Estonia* and *Poland* cases are perhaps the closest the CJEU has come to invoking subsidiarity. CJEU decisions upholding the principle of subsidiarity against EU legislation are notable by their absence and, although Article 8 of the Protocol specifically affords jurisdiction, the historically integrationist CoJ has tended to treat subsidiarity as a non-justiciable political principle thus affording the Union authorities considerable leeway in their exercise of policy discretion.[35]

---

[29] See further, COSAC, *Eighteenth Bi-annual Report: Developments in European Union Procedures and Practices Relevant to Parliamentary Scrutiny* (September 2012).

[30] Art 8 also allows national parliaments (chambers) to take subsidiarity cases to the CJEU.

[31] Commission Review of the proposal for a Council Regulation on the establishment of the European Public Prosecutor's Office with regard to the principle of subsidiarity, Communication COM (2013) 851.

[32] Case C-504 *Commission v Poland* (judgment of 29 March 2012) [51], [66]; Case C-505/09 *Commission v Estonia* (judgment of 29 March 2012) [53], [66], [68].

[33] D Osborne and T Gaebler, *Reinventing Government* (New York: Addison Wesley, 1992).

[34] Council Directive 2009/29/EC of 23 April 2009 amending Directive 2003/87/EC so as to improve and extend the greenhouse gas emission allowance trading scheme of the Community [2009] OJ L140/63.

[35] See eg, Case C-84/94 *United Kingdom v Council* [1996] ECR I-5755; Case C-491/01 *R v Health Secretary ex p British American Tobacco (Investments) and Imperial Tobacco* [2002] ECR I-11453.

In *Vodaphone*,[36] for example, controversial legislation on roaming charges on mobile phone networks was challenged on the grounds that the changes were disproportionate and violated the subsidiarity principle. The CoJ confirmed that subsidiarity must be taken into account when TFEU Article 114, which establishes criteria for harmonisation measures, is used as a basis for legislation and it carried out its own subsidiarity assessment, seemingly more thoroughly than in the past. Nevertheless, the Court upheld the validity of the provisions: 'the Community legislature could legitimately take the view that it had'.[37]

Administrative Manifesto: 'Good Governance'

In 2001, the Commission published its thinking on good governance in the EU in its 'White Paper on European Governance' (WPEG).[38] Its reasons for this move, which took place in the aftermath of the Santer Commission's resignation, are debateable: they reflect a general concern over legitimacy of the governance system but also a debate instigated by academics over the need for a more deliberative method of decision-making[39] and pressure from civil society for a more open style of governance in the EU (see chapters four and five).

The WPEG identified openness, participation, accountability, effectiveness and coherence as the five principles that should underpin good governance at every level of government from global to regional and local. A noticeably administration-centred meaning was given to these principles:

1. **Openness:** The Institutions should work in a more open manner. Together with the Member States, they should actively communicate about what the EU does and the decisions it takes. They should use language that is accessible and understandable for the general public. This is of particular importance in order to improve the confidence in complex institutions.
2. **Participation:** The quality, relevance and effectiveness of EU policies depend on ensuring wide participation throughout the policy chain – from conception to implementation. Improved participation is likely to create more confidence in the end result and in the Institutions which deliver policies. Participation crucially depends on central governments following an inclusive approach when developing and implementing EU policies.
3. **Accountability:** Roles in the legislative and executive processes need to be clearer. Each of the EU Institutions must explain and take responsibility for

---

[36] Case C-58/8 *Vodafone Ltd v Secretary of State for Business, Enterprise and Regulatory Reform* [2010] ECR I-4999.
[37] Ibid, [78].
[38] Commission, 'European Governance – A White Paper' COM (2001) 428 final, 1, 10.
[39] C Joerges and J Neyer, 'From Intergovernmental Bargaining to Deliberative Political Processes: The Constitutionalisation of Comitology' (1997) 3 *European Law Journal* 273; O Gerstenberg and C Sabel, 'Directly-Deliberative Polyarchy: An Institutional Ideal for Europe?' in C Joerges and R Dehousse (eds), *Good Governance in Europe's Integrated Market* (Oxford: OUP, 2002).

what it does in Europe. But there is also a need for greater clarity and responsibility from Member States and all those involved in developing and implementing EU policy at whatever level.
4. **Effectiveness:** Policies must be effective and timely, delivering what is needed on the basis of clear objectives, an evaluation of future impact and, where available, of past experience. Effectiveness also depends on implementing EU policies in a proportionate manner and on taking decisions at the most appropriate level.
5. **Coherence:** Policies and action must be coherent and easily understood ... Coherence requires political leadership and a strong responsibility on the part of the Institutions to ensure a consistent approach within a complex system ... Policies can no longer be effective unless they are prepared, implemented and enforced in a more inclusive way.

In subsequent chapters, we shall follow the unsteady progress of these five principles – which have never been withdrawn – within the Union public service and across 'EU administrative space'. They are dear to the EO, who persists with a generous interpretation; the Council by way of contrast has been infinitely slow in sincerely adopting the principle of openness, especially where security can be invoked. The principles are sufficiently general to be easily accepted, like motherhood and apple pie, as a general public good but, as we shall see, there is ample scope for disagreement over their application.

Tough Love: Conditionality

A cynical observer might also note a connection with the conditionality principle imposed on candidate states at around the same time. The conditionality principle required an applicant state to show it had satisfactorily 'adjusted its administrative structures' to EU membership, necessitating a guarantee of regulatory and managerial capacity and quality of staff and standards across all public administration settings.[40] As articulated in a joint Commission/OECD paper,[41] the conditionality principle required reliability, predictability, openness, transparency and accountability, common principles said to be applicable throughout 'the EU administrative space'. The paper stressed the need for professionalism and NPM values of efficiency and effectiveness; a competent civil service should target 'mechanisms of control and accountability' in order to prevent abuse of public powers and mismanagement of public resources and it should also seek to foster an appropriate administrative culture and pattern of conduct. The aim was to 'give legitimacy to the public administration in the eyes of citizens and taxpayers

[40] Presidency Conclusion, *EU Bulletin* No 12 (1995) 18.
[41] F Cardona, 'European principles for public administration' (1999) SIGMA Paper No 27, CCNM/SIGMA/PUMA(99)44/REV1. And see K Smith, 'The Evolution and Application of EU Membership Conditionality' in M Cremona (ed), *The Enlargement of the European Union* (Oxford: Hart Publishing, 2004).

in order to build up public confidence in the administration'.[42] This mirrors the objective of the WPEG.

As commentators were quick to observe, the conditionality principle stood for extensive penetration of the Accession States' internal structures in defiance of the basic principle of national administrative autonomy.[43] The development also followed the example of interventionist international practices – external leverage or 'carrots and sticks' – pioneered by the IMF and World Bank. Likewise, the Union has often utilised the principle in bilateral trade agreements and association and cooperation agreements with third countries around the globe, most obviously with a view to promoting democratic structures and human rights.[44]

Yet an important seed had been planted in the internal world of EU governance. Established Member States like Greece, Ireland and Spain would be made grimly aware of the full potential of conditionality in the subsequent global financial and eurozone crisis.[45] Recognised by treaty provision as capable of ranging 'from a macro-economic adjustment programme to continuous respect of pre-established eligibility conditions',[46] conditionality now lies at the heart of the European Stability Mechanism (ESM), launched in 2012 with a mandate to provide assistance to those eurozone countries facing financial difficulties. This in turn connects to the tellingly titled 'Treaty on Stability, Coordination and Governance in the EMU', which – chiefly promoted by Germany – requires self-correcting budget disciplines.[47] Again, the principle has been reworked and increasingly vigorously applied as part of the Union's 'Europe 2020' strategy for 'smart, sustainable and inclusive growth' both in the form of a set of contract-like terms (ex ante conditionalities) and performance benchmarks for further funding or support (ex post conditionalities).[48] Completing the circle, conditionality will be seen in chapter nine taking on a new lease of life in structural funding: the EU's much vaunted cohesion policy of which Enlargement countries in central and eastern Europe are today the chief beneficiaries. Such is the pace and intensity of the development that conditionality may be described as an emergent 'fourth C' of EU governance. Grounding huge sets of administrative procedures under the broad functional rubrics of planning, funding and supervision, conditionality shows the Union both spreading its tentacles – more Europeanisation – and

---

[42] Cardona, above (n 41). And see, T Böhmelt and T Freyburg, 'The Temporal Dimension of the Credibility of EU Conditionality and Candidate States' Compliance with the *acquis communautaire*, 1998–2009' (2013) 14 *European Union Politics* 250.

[43] R Biebr and M Vaerini, 'Implementation and Compliance: Stimulus for New Governance Structures in the Accession Countries' in G Bermann and K Pistor (eds), *Law and Governance in an Enlarged European Union* (Oxford: Hart Publishing, 2004).

[44] L Bartels, *The Application of Human Rights Conditionality in the EU's Bilateral Trade Agreements* (Brussels: 2008).

[45] B de Witte, A Héritier and A Treschel (eds), *The Euro Crisis and the State of European Democracy* (Florence: EUI, 2012).

[46] Treaty Establishing the European Stability Mechanism, Art 12. And see Case C-370/12 *Pringle v Government of Ireland* (judgment of 27 November 2012).

[47] P Craig, 'The Stability, Coordination and Governance Treaty: Principle, Politics and Pragmatism' (2012) 37 *European Law Review* 231.

[48] Commission, 'Taking stock of the Europe 2020 strategy' (Communication) COM (2014) 130 final.

taking on a distinctly harder, more coercive edge.[49] In this regard all Member States are equal – but some are more equal than others.

AUDIT AND MANAGERIALISM

A sound public service is dependent on a robust system of audit in its oldest sense of financial accountability and responsibility. In the case of the Community budget, however, financial management and audit has always been a problem. This was partly because Member State and Union interests did not always coincide; partly because it was some years before an elected EP was able to assume control of budgetary matters; partly because of variable standards and audit techniques in Member States and their different understandings of audit.[50]

The independent experts dealt at length with reform of 'the old-fashioned procedures of financial control' but although there was general agreement that the Financial Regulation which contains the procedures for the establishment and implementation of the general EU budget was unsuited to the requirements of modern management and in need of fundamental revision, replacing it took several years. The new Financial Regulation,[51] which closely mirrored the Experts' recommendations, was made subject to post-legislative audit and triennial review. It would cover centralised management of the budget through Commission Directorates-General (DGs); situations of shared management as in the Common Agricultural Policy (CAP); and decentralised management of funds intended to benefit third countries or bodies. In other words, all EU operations – direct and indirect administration, shared and decentralised management, grants and subsidy – would now be covered by the Regulation and its procedures, which also extend to agencies. For the first time, legislation contained 'over-arching principles that frame the entirety of Community administration' an evolution hailed by Craig as a 'constitutionalisation' of Community administration.[52]

The Prodi–Kinnock reforms[53] focused on rationalising internal audit procedures. A central financial service, independent internal audit service and audit progress committee were installed, thus drawing a clear line between officers who authorise expenditure and audit officials and procedures. Accountancy procedures were standardised by internal control templates built on a common format for the audit unit of every DG. Responsibility was delegated to authorising officers and spelled out in guidance and procedural rules, which extend to content and

---

[49] M Dawson and F de Witte, 'Constitutional Balance in the EU after the Euro-Crisis' (2013) 76 *Modern Law Review* 817.

[50] Ernst and Young, 'Overview and comparison of public accounting and auditing practices in the 27 EU Member States' prepared for Eurostat (December 2012).

[51] Regulation (EC, Euratom) 1605/2002 on the Financial Regulation applicable to the general budget of the European Communities [2002] OJ L248/1.

[52] P Craig, 'The Constitutionalisation of Community Administration' (2003) 28 *European Law Review* 840.

[53] See above, ch 1, p 24.

scope of reports, declarations of assurance and annual activity reports. The package was made enforceable against individuals through the disciplinary procedures of the (reformed) Staff Regulations. Constitutional oversight was supplied by the EP and CoJ. Direct financial management of projects was entrusted to a new breed of executive agency: either a public body (including national and international entities) or a private body with a public interest mission; delegation of wide discretion was expressly forbidden. Executive agencies, listed by the Commission, are regulated by EU secondary law, established for a fixed period and geared to the management of Community programmes.[54] This standardises structure, firmly establishes Commission control and provides for financial supervision. The sums involved can be huge; among the six bodies currently listed, the Innovation and Networks Executive Agency (INEA) leads the way with a budget of €37bn for 2014–20.

The revamped Financial Regulation also strengthened supervisory procedure. Where shared or decentralised management was involved, the Commission was authorised to 'assume final responsibility for the implementation of the budget' and to 'conduct regular checks to ensure that the actions to be financed from the Community budget have been implemented correctly'.[55] In the latest post-Lisbon and post-financial crisis modification, national fund managers for structural and other EU funds under shared management will have to issue annual management declarations that will be subject to independent audit.[56] Ex ante and ex post evaluations are to be conducted according to guidance provided by the Commission in every programme or activity that entails significant spending and results disseminated to all spending, legislative and budgetary authorities. OLAF, the EU anti-fraud unit, is also empowered to conduct external on-the-spot inspections and checks in Member States and occasionally even in non-EU countries.[57]

The new Regulation would also inaugurate an ongoing wave of audit reform in EU administration. The primary concern of the European Court of Auditors (ECA), the central Community audit authority, modelled on the French Cour des comptes, had always been strictly with legality. The ECA gave (and still gives) a Declaration of Assurance to the EP that the EU budget has been implemented 'correctly' in the limited sense that expenditure has been compliant with applicable laws and regulations. Today, however, the ECA has assumed the function of 'value for money' (VFM) auditing or the assessment and evaluation of EU processes and procedures in terms of value for money. VFM language infuses ECA reports. A report on co-financed road projects,[58] to take a single example, makes

[54] Regulation (EC) 58/2003 laying down the statute for executive agencies to be entrusted with certain tasks in the management of Community programmes [2003] OJ L11/1.
[55] Ibid, Art 53.
[56] Regulation (EU, Euratom) 966/2012on the financial rules applicable to the general budget of the Union and repealing Council Regulation (EC, Euratom) 1605/2002 [2012] OJ L298/1. See further ch 9.
[57] Regulation (EU, Euratom) 883/2013 concerning investigations conducted by the European Anti-Fraud Office (OLAF) and repealing Regulation (EC) No 1073/1999 of the European Parliament and of the Council and Council Regulation (Euratom) 1074/1999 [2013] OJ L248/1.
[58] ECA, Special Report 5/203, 'Are EU Cohesion Policy Funds well spent on roads?' (16 July 2013).

50 Tenets, Values and Objectives

three main recommendations: (i) EU co-financing of road projects should depend on clear objectives with targets for travel time, gains in road safety, capacity improvements and economic effects; (ii) payments should be linked to the use of cost-effective road building techniques in line with best practice; (iii) Member States should ensure international competition on construction projects and focus their procurement systems on delivering the most economical offers. These recommendations move far from the mere demarcation of legality; they emerge as policy issues with implications for Commission practice as the Commission noted in its reply with a detailed defence of its IA procedures. The EU is, in sum, no longer 'an outlier in regard to its budgeting and auditing procedures'.[59]

EU financial arrangements are replete with NPM values and methodology as is the latest ECA practice. The same NPM values infused the Barroso Commission's plans for financial management, taken forward in the later era of austerity or retrenchment. These went a step further in 'integrated internal control', not only covering Commission management and audit practices, but touching more controversially on those of Member States. In typical fashion, the Barroso plan started with a road map or description of the planned Commission initiative together with an estimated timetable for the proposal, which also indicated how any necessary IAs would be planned and taken forward. The road map was followed up in a complex Action Plan covering an administrative network that included Commission services, national administration and agencies but also an 'accountability network' composed of the ECA, supreme audit institutions and OLAF. It is no exaggeration to speak of a veritable 'audit explosion'[60] or thoroughgoing attempt to assert a distinctive mentality of administrative control (see chapter one).

Effectively building on the initial reform of the proceduralised 'hard law' model of the Financial Regulation, this ambitious plan for integrated audit illustrates the 'soft governance' methods favoured by the Commission as a technique for organising networks and integration. To kick-start the road map and Action Plan, the Commission issued a Communication, technically binding only on itself,[61] tying the Member States in with guidance – all soft law instruments. Implementation of the programme would be through communication, dialogue and gradual development of 'agreed upon procedures', with the evaluative methodology of studies, estimates and pilot projects coupled with cost–benefit analysis, sharing of results, management declarations and audit assurance much in evidence. In this way, the legal obligation to provide annual audit summaries to the Commission could gradually be supplemented by voluntary disclosures and declarations of certification from national audit authorities.[62] Of course, this did this not close the door to

[59] H Kassim et al, *The European Commission of the Twenty-First Century* (Oxford: OUP, 2013) 222.
[60] M Power, *The Audit Explosion* (London: Demos, 1994).
[61] Commission, 'Action Plan towards an Integrated Internal Control Framework (Communication) COM (2006) 9 final and 'Report on Commission Action Plan' COM (2008) 110 final.
[62] P Levy, M Barzelay and A-M Porras-Gomez, 'The Reform of Financial Management in the European Commission: A Public Management Policy Cycle Case Study' (2011) 89 *Public Administration* 1546.

further 'hard law' intervention: quite the reverse. Indeed, at the time of writing, the EU legislature is on the point of agreeing a new regulatory framework designed to promote the quality of audit across the EU.[63]

'SOFT LAW', 'SOFT GOVERNANCE' AND THE OMC

The terminology of 'soft law', generously defined as 'rules of conduct which, in principle, have no legally binding force but which nevertheless may have practical effects'[64] or as rules intended to 'influence bureaucratic decision-making in a non-trivial fashion',[65] usefully conveys a prevailing sense of ambiguity. By the early 1990s, the phenomenon of soft law with its capacity for aiding the process of integration had begun to be noticed but its regular use in the wider framework of a 'new governance method' only began to attract academic attention at the turn of the millennium.[66] Just as bureaucrats operate through 'soft' rule-making so 'soft governance' is in many ways a natural starting point for administrative projects, using this term in the broadest sense of all forms of governance that depend on voluntariness, social interaction and socially shared rules.[67]

The EU abounds in soft law instruments, ranging from the relatively formal declarations attached to treaties, inter-institutional agreements, Commission communications and proposals for legislation to the much 'softer' mass of internal advice recommendations, guidelines and instructions that clutter our footnotes. Soft law is used for a multiplicity of purposes, most obviously perhaps for sidestepping political obstacles, as where the institutions are not in agreement or legislative progress is blocked by opposition from Member States. In other words, soft governance operating through informal processes is used to bypass the official 'Community method', with its emphasis on formal procedures and institutional balance.[68] Again, soft law may be adopted as a soft governance tool in areas of joint or limited or even disputed competence. In this type of scenario indeed, encouraging 'best practice' or promoting procedural convergence may be the most the Commission and Council can hope to achieve, at least in the short term. A further use is to inform stakeholders or the public at large about administrative

---

[63] See Commission, Proposal COM (2011) 778 final; Commission ,Proposal COM (2011) 779 final.
[64] F Snyder, 'Soft Law and Institutional Practice in the European Community' in S Martin (ed), *The Construction of Europe* (Dordrecht: Kluwer Academic, 1994) 198.
[65] L Sossin and C Smith, 'Hard Choices and Soft Law: Ethical Codes, Policy Guidelines and the Role of Courts in Regulating Government' (2003) 40 *Alberta Law Review* 867, 871.
[66] Notably, A Héritier 'New Modes of Governance in Europe: Policy Making without Legislating?' in A Héritier (ed), *Common Goods: Reinventing European and International Governance* (Lanham, MD: Rowman and Littlefield, 2001); J Scott and D Trubek (eds), 'Special Issue on Law and New Approaches to Governance in Europe' (2002) 8(1) *European Law Journal* 1.
[67] See T Christiansen and C Neuhold (eds), *International Handbook on Informal Governance* (Cheltenham: Edward Elgar, 2012).
[68] G della Cananea, 'Administration by Guidelines: The Policy Guidelines of the Commission in the Field of State Aids' in I Harden (ed), *State Aid: Community Law and Policy* (Trier: Schriftenreihe der Europaischen Rechtsakademie Trier*, 1993).

practice and procedure: taxation and customs duty furnish many illustrations in the shape of codes of practice or guidelines, as does competition policy described in chapter eight. Soft law further serves as a vital medium for the 'three Cs' of communication, cooperation and coordination in EU governance; as such, it is part of the 'hidden wiring' helping to hold a piecemeal system together.

Some soft law is 'harder' than others. To depart from an inter-institutional agreement would normally produce political repercussions, while in the realm of EU grants and subsidies there may be sufficient leverage to command obedience (see chapter nine on structural funding). Equally, national authorities may carry out non-binding reporting requirements voluntarily in the knowledge that, if they fail to do so, their position in a European network will suffer. There may nonetheless be a place for formal law, not least when soft law 'obligations' are honoured in the breach rather than the observance, as was the case in the context of the recent financial crisis (see chapter eleven). In practice, soft governance techniques are routinely used in conjunction with hard law,[69] as with the Commission action plans and roadmaps that are followed up in the implementation of new legislation (see chapter seven). And despite their determinedly informal character, soft law provisions may on occasion be recognised and enforced by courts.[70]

There is much reliance in soft governance on 'benchmarking' whereby targeted issues such as environmental pollution or gender discrimination can be singled out for consideration at every stage in decision-making. In the multi-level EU governance system, this form of 'composite decision-making has commonly required the creation of new organisational channels and procedures – networks – to facilitate dialogue and exchange between different policy arenas and actors'.[71] The soft governance paradigm may therefore be partly responsible for the fragmented nature of the governance structures described in chapter one. This is epitomised in the convoluted networks engaged with Europol in coordinating cross-border policing (see chapter ten).

Much is positive about soft governance, especially in terms of innate respect for diversity and pluralism among the Member States. Deliberately flexible and not overly-constraining norms also reflect and reinforce the important administrative value of responsiveness. As for particular institutional contexts, soft governance is especially useful in capacity building through guidance, assistance and training as illustrated by the pioneering PHARE programme; it is, for example, a valuable way of actively familiarising candidate countries with EU goals and procedures.[72]

---

[69] D Trubek and L Trubek, 'Hard and Soft Law in the Construction of Social Europe: The Role of the Open Method of Coordination' (2005) 11 *European Law Journal* 343; M Dawson, 'Three Waves of New Governance in the European Union' (2011) 36 *European Law Review* 208.

[70] Classically through the doctrine of legitimate expectation: see P Craig, *EU Administrative Law*, 2nd edn (Oxford: OUP, 2012) ch 18.

[71] A Lenschow, 'New Regulatory Approaches in "Greening" EU Policies' (2002) 8 *European Law Journal* 19.

[72] S de la Rosa, 'The Open Method of Coordination in the New Member States – The Perspectives for its Use as a Tool of Soft Law' (2005) 11 *European Law Journal* 618.

Especially in view of their limited legal powers, soft governance also provides valuable tools for EU agencies, used in the construction of voluntary policy networks and to persuade non-EU parties to engage with EU policies.

To its adversaries on the other hand, soft governance is a deliberately shadowy construct, exploited to disguise EU expansionism. It is to be regarded warily as 'a soft framework for hard law interventions'[73] – a stepping stone on the road to detailed legislative policies. Soft law is also perceived as undemocratic, a theme naturally trumpeted by the European Parliament.[74] It insulates both policymaking and rule-making from the scrutiny of representative institutions and from civil society, generating major concerns over accountability, transparency and the protection of individual rights. From time to time, therefore, pressure is generated for greater proceduralisation through the addition of techniques that are becoming standard in other areas of EU administration, especially consultation and transparency requirements. Equally questionable is the transfer of power that may result to the juristocracy in Luxembourg with its natural preference for filling gaps with norms favourable to its integrationist agenda. This was exemplified in the controversial *Viking* and *Laval* cases[75] concerning collective industrial action in Scandinavia, criticised on the basis that a national system of labour relations based on soft governance methods was overridden by the 'hard law' of the CJEU.[76] Yet, with all its faults, soft governance in the EU is inevitable; it is an essential means for progress across the cycle of policy development, implementation and supervision.

Soft Governance Lisbon Fashion

Soft governance techniques were taken to new heights in the 'Open Method of Coordination' (OMC), which originated in the European Economic and Monetary Union (EMU)[77] but was formally authorised by the European Council in 2000 and became the major procedural innovation of the Lisbon Strategy (a 10-year action and development plan for the EU economy, aimed at social and environmental progress through sustainable growth and employment). The Lisbon Presidency Conclusions characterised OMC as 'a means of spreading best practice and achieving greater convergence towards the main EU goals'. Today, the social OMC is made an integral component of the ongoing Europe 2020 strategy.

---

[73] S Regent, 'The Open Method of Coordination: A New Supranational Form of Governance' (2003) 9 *European Law Journal* 190, 191.

[74] See EP Resolution of 4 September 2007 on institutional and legal implications of the use of 'soft law' instruments (2007/2028(INI)) recital Y.

[75] Case C-341/05 *Laval v Svenska Byggnadsarbetareforbundet* [2007] ECR I-11767; Case C-438/05 *International Transport Workers' Federation and the Finnish Seamen's Union v Viking Line APB* [2007] ECR I-10779.

[76] eg, J Malmberg and T Sigeman, 'Industrial Action and the EU Economic Freedoms – The Autonomous Collective Bargaining Model Curtailed by the European Court of Justice' (2008) 45 *Common Market Law Review* 111. EU law would in any event trump national law here.

[77] D Hodson and I Maher, 'The Open Method as a New Mode of Governance' (2001) 39 *Journal of Common Market Studies* 719.

A 'fully decentralised approach' was envisaged in line with the principle of subsidiarity, with national, regional and local administrations working in variable forms of partnership with the social partners, companies and NGOs.[78] The Commission would 'network' with the different providers and users and help Member States 'progressively to develop their own policies' through the benchmarking of best practices. Yet, notably echoing the managerial methods of NPM, the suddenly very fashionable style of OMC would entail:

- Fixing guidelines for the Union combined with specific timetables for achieving the goals which they set in the short, medium and long terms.
- Establishing, where appropriate, quantitative and qualitative indicators and benchmarks against the best in the world and tailored to the needs of different Member States and sectors as a means of comparing best practice.
- Translating these European guidelines into national and regional policies by setting specific targets and adopting measures, taking into account national and regional differences.
- Periodic monitoring, evaluation and peer review organised as mutual learning processes.[79]

An essential element of OMC is Member State consent and close cooperation. So target setting would see national experts participating in committee structures that ultimately feed into the Council[80] and enforcement is typically through soft measures of peer review and peer pressure, though these may be strengthened by withholding the 'carrot' of subsidies and by the slender 'stick' of 'naming and shaming'.

The performance of OMC in specific areas, such as labour market regulation, employment and pensions and social inclusion, has been charted in some detail.[81] General studies tackle the question of whether OMC produces policy convergence and/or Europeanisation.[82] Empirical studies tend to suggest that Member States are still in the driving seat; a study of welfare reform concludes, for example, that EU policy is 'translated and mediated differently in each country according to the domestic institutional and historic context' and, perhaps more significantly, that the dominant influence is that of national politics.[83] Member States are most supportive when successful in exporting national policy to Union level; otherwise

---

[78] See M Dawson, 'EU Law "Transformed"? Evaluating Accountability and Subsidiarity in the "Streamlined" OMC for Social Inclusion and Social Protection' (2009) 13 *European Integration online Papers* 8.

[79] Lisbon Presidency Conclusions (23–24 March 2000) [37], [38].

[80] C de la Porte, 'Is the Open Method of Coordination Appropriate for Organizing Activities at European Level in Sensitive Policy Areas?' (2002) 8 *European Law Journal* 38.

[81] E Barcevicus, J Weishaupt and J Zeitlin (eds), *Assessing the Open Method of Coordination: Institutional Design and National Influence of EU Social Policy Coordination* (Basingstoke: Palgrave Macmillan, 2014).

[82] C Radaelli, 'Europeanization, Policy Learning and New Modes of Governance' (2008) 10 *Journal of Comparative Policy Analysis* 239.

[83] P Graziano, S Jacquot and P Paller, *The EU and the Domestic Politics of Welfare State Reforms* (Basingstoke: Palgrave Macmillan, 2011) 316. But see above, n 26.

they follow their own lines and 'rarely [move] beyond national priorities'.[84] There is much research too – with decidedly variable opinions – on whether the OMC facilitates participation and, if so, whether this is genuine 'bottom-up' participation or controlled and structured by the Commission.[85] A decade on, OMC has lost some of its sheen.

REGULATION À LA MODE: 'BETTER' AND 'SMART'

The movement for regulatory reform is famously a global rather than a solely European initiative.[86] It reflects both the dominant scientific ideology of the late twentieth and twenty-first centuries that underlies acceptance of 'governance by experts' and a heavy managerial reliance on regulatory tools. In the Community, a 'Better Regulation' project, which aimed to improve the quality of legislation in the interests of business in particular, was formally a response to the need expressed at the Edinburgh, Gothenburg and Laeken European Councils to simplify and improve the Community regulatory environment and consider the possible economic, social and environmental effects of policy proposals – colloquially, 'to cut red tape'. Given the scale of inter-penetration of regulatory law and practice in the EU, Member States already pursuing better regulation principles were naturally keen to export them to Brussels.[87]

The project was effectively launched by the Mandelkern Group, a high level group of regulatory experts who recommended, in 2001, that the Commission should develop a general tool for assessing the economic, social and environmental impacts of proposed legislation.[88] The basic idea was hardly new, even in EC law; the Environmental Impact Assessment Directive[89] had applied to national projects likely to have significant environmental effects since the 1980s (see chapter twelve). Testimony to the international allure of a 'rational policy process', the use of regulatory impact analysis had become widespread in OECD countries, aided by the active dissemination of 'best practice'.[90] Now there would be a thoroughgoing quest for more targeted, proportionate and consistent regulatory

---

[84] P Copeland and B ter Haar, 'A Toothless Bite? The Effectiveness of the European Employment Strategy as a Governance Tool' (2013) 23 *Journal of European Social Policy* 21, 33.

[85] See for concise literature reviews, A Harcourt, 'Participatory Gains and Policy Effectiveness' (2013) 51 *Journal of Common Market Studies* 667; Radaelli, 'Europeanization', above (n 82).

[86] J Braithwaite and P Drahos, *Global Business Regulation* (Cambridge: CUP, 2000); R Baldwin, M Cave and M Lodge, *Understanding Regulation: Theory, Strategy and Practice*, 2nd edn (Oxford: OUP, 2012).

[87] See the joint statement by the Irish, Dutch, Luxembourg, UK, Austrian and Finnish Presidencies, *Advancing regulatory reform in Europe* (2004).

[88] Final Report of the EU High Level Consultative Group on Regulatory Quality (November 2001).

[89] Council Directive 85/337/EEC (several times amended and subsequently codified as Council Directive 2011/92/EU [2012] OJ L26/1). And see ch 12.

[90] OECD, *Building an Institutional Framework for Regulatory Impact Analysis (RIA): Guidance for Policy Makers* (2008).

interventions at Union level using IA, beginning with Commission IA procedures for all major policy proposals raising issues of sustainable development.[91]

'Better Regulation in Europe' is self-evidently a broad genus, and one which is inextricably linked with NPM.[92] It is usefully visualised as having a core mix of substantive and procedural purposes: to increase competitiveness by minimising regulatory burdens; to promote so-called 'evidence-based decision-making'; and to address legitimacy concerns by reflecting good governance values of transparency and participation by affected interests.[93] Further, in the extravagant version of Commission policy and practice, a series of processes and procedures locks up together in a single coherent package: IA; more or less open consultation procedures; legislative simplification via (re-)codification; screening and withdrawal of pending proposals; and monitoring and reducing of administrative burdens.[94]

IA Abounding

Typical of Union governance, the sudden fashion for IA rested on the soft law basis of a Commission Action Plan[95] and internal guidelines.[96] Targeted directly on legislative proposals as laid out in the Commission's work programmes, it was 'to contribute to the decision-making processes by systematically collecting and analysing information on planned interventions and estimating their likely impact'.[97] In other words, the intention was (or so it was said) to assist the legislator in decision-making and to supplement rather than replace political judgement. The Guidelines establish a basic template. Officials learn of four prospective procedural steps designed to test the possible consequences of new regulation: identification of the problem; identification of the objectives; exploration of the likely impact of different policy options; and comparison of the options, which are generally laid out in any subsequent proposal. There are two retrospective steps: monitoring and evaluation and the demand to specify the analytical basis for the IA. Periodically updated, the Guidelines have fleshed out the process in increasing detail. As well as subsidiarity, particular attention is paid to the underlying and notably heavily litigated principle of proportionality (see chapter three).[98]

[91] Commission, 'A Sustainable Europe for a Better World: A European Union Strategy for Sustainable Development' (Communication) COM (2001) 264 final.
[92] S Weatherill (ed), *Better Regulation* (Oxford: Hart Publishing, 2007).
[93] C Radaelli and A Meuwese, 'Better Regulation in Europe: Between Public Management and Regulatory Reform' (2009) 87 *Public Administration* 639.
[94] A Alemanno, 'The Better Regulation Initiative at the Judicial Gate: A Trojan Horse within the Commission's Wall or the Way Forward?' (2009) 15 *European Law Journal* 382, 391.
[95] Commission, 'Simplifying and Improving the Regulatory Environment' (Communication) COM (2001) 726.
[96] Commission, 'Impact Assessment' (Communication) COM (2002) 276 final; Commission, 'Impact Assessment Guidelines' SEC (2005) 791.
[97] ECA, Special Report 3, 'Impact assessments in the EU institutions: do they support decision-making?' (2010) 6.
[98] Commission, 'Impact Assessment Guidelines' SEC (2009) 92, 28–29. For further details, see A Meuwese, *Impact Assessment in EU Lawmaking* (Dordrecht: Kluwer Law International, 2008).

As the Guidelines make abundantly clear, there is a close connection to the many risk assessment processes conducted for the Commission. For example, part of the mandate of the main scientific committees has been to collect, coordinate and offer their opinion on the best scientific evidence available in a given area;[99] 'risk assessment dialogues' with international experts designed to identify best practice in risk assessment methodology are par for the course. A different but related point, the Commission would eventually move to extend IA beyond the legislative work programme into the realm of implementing measures and comitology proceedings.[100] Risk regulation in financial services has also been an important laboratory for this – not always, it must be said, with gratifying results (see chapter eleven).

The pursuit of IA has necessitated a degree of structural change inside the Commission. As well as the machinery to support inter-service consultation and normally a public consultation at least of designated stakeholders, a substantial internal quality control system has grown up. As well as IA units in the DGs, ad hoc inter-service steering groups, and general oversight by the Secretariat-General, an arm's length Impact Assessment Board (IAB) was established in 2006. Testimony to the heavy premium placed on IA as an analytical tool, the IAB is tasked with examining and issuing opinions on all the Commission's IAs. Published on the Commission's website after the Commission has adopted the corresponding proposal, they contain repeated calls for improvement.[101]

A recent EO investigation gives a useful insight into the process in action. A citizen disputed the conclusions in an IA on a Commission proposal for new road safety legislation.[102] The Commission explained its 'strict and rigorous' procedure. It had drafted its questions in close cooperation with an external consultant and then used its Internet-based consultation mechanism, designed to receive and rapidly store reactions to new initiatives in a structured way, to promulgate them. A 'fully-fledged IA' had then been conducted with a view to estimating

> the potential societal, environmental and safety advantages and disadvantages, as well as the associated costs and benefits to European citizens, national authorities in the Member States and to industry stakeholders, based upon the best available evidence available at the time of writing.

The Commission had organised workshops for experts and stakeholders during the consultation phase. It had posted the complainant's critical views on the relevant website together with other contributions. It had followed 'a procedure' to guarantee the quality of the IA, working with its IAB. The options finally chosen represented 'a balance between the assessed aspects' and had at every stage been

---

[99] Commission, 'Rules of Procedure of the SCCS, SCHER and SCENIHR', Document SCs/01/04 final (C7 (2004)D/370235).
[100] Commission, 'Second strategic review of Better Regulation in the European Union' (Communication) COM (2008) 32 final; A Alemanno and A Meuwese, 'Impact Assessment of EU Non-Legislative Rulemaking: The Missing Link in "New Comitology"' (2013) 19 *European Law Journal* 76.
[101] See also, IAB, *AR 2012*, 15–22.
[102] Inv 0875/2011/JF.

58 *Tenets, Values and Objectives*

shared with stakeholders. Fortunately for the Commission, this was enough broadly to satisfy the EO.

Notwithstanding internal efforts to prescribe a 'proportionate level of analysis',[103] the IA system represents a considerable procedural burden, which the Commission has voluntarily undertaken to carry. Among the various explanations,[104] the most probable is the Commission's concern to legitimate its policymaking in terms of output efficiency. But like many pseudo-scientific procedures, it is hard to say how effective the IA process really is. An inconclusive VFM audit carried out by the ECA between 2003 and 2008 found that IA 'generally provided a sound description of the problem at stake and the objectives pursued'. It had been used by the Commission to improve the design of its initiatives, although evaluation reports were often difficult to understand and compare.[105] A less complacent academic study from the same period pointed up methodological problems, lack of adequate training and insufficient exchange of information between stakeholders; evidently, a supposedly rational process had far to go in ensuring the quality and consistency of decision-making.[106]

Regulatory Fitness and Performance Programme (REFIT)

Undaunted, the Commission would soon be speaking of so-called 'smart regulation', another appealing moniker coined by regulatory theorists with a view to promoting the use of multiple policy instruments as part of a determinedly flexible and holistic approach to regulation.[107] Again following in the footsteps of the worldwide search for a regulatory 'third way' between traditional forms of 'command and control' regulation and over-reliance on market disciplines, a 'stakeholder consultation' explained that 'smart regulation is not about more or less legislation, it is about delivering results in the least burdensome way'.[108] A 2010 Communication duly proclaimed that it was 'time to step up a gear . . . better regulation must become smart regulation and be further embedded in the Commission's working culture'.[109] From the standpoint of process and procedure, the Commission saw smart regulation in the EU as having three main characteristics:

1. It concerns the whole policy cycle – from the design of a piece of legislation, to implementation, enforcement, evaluation and revision.

---

[103] Commission, 'Impact Assessment Guidelines' SEC (2009) 92, 12–16.
[104] See C Radaelli, 'Regulating Rule-Making via Impact Assessment' (2010) 23 *Governance* 89.
[105] ECA, Special Report 3, above (n 97) 7.
[106] C Radaelli and F de Francesco, *Regulatory Quality in Europe* (Manchester: Manchester University Press, 2007).
[107] N Gunningham and P Grabosky, *Smart Regulation: Designing Environmental Policy* (Oxford: Clarendon Press, 1998).
[108] Commission, Stakeholder consultation on smart regulation (April 2010) [1].
[109] Commission, 'Smart Regulation in the European Union' (Communication) COM (2010) 543 final, 1. And see R Baldwin, 'Is Better Regulation Smarter Regulation?' [2005] *Public Law* 485.

2. It must be a shared responsibility of the European institutions and of Member States.
3. The views of those most affected by regulation have a key role to play.

The development serves further to illustrate the place of overarching administrative and legal principles.

The Communication thus explained that 'the aim of smart regulation is to design and deliver regulation that respects the principles of subsidiarity and proportionality and is of the highest quality possible'.[110] Many Member States had been pressing the Commission 'to advance the agenda on smart regulation ... in particular by reducing the overall EU regulatory burden as part of the EU's agenda for growth and competitiveness'.[111] In 2012 therefore, the Commission issued a further Communication, committing itself to strengthening its main smart regulation tools (IA, stakeholder consultation, evaluation) and launching the Regulatory Fitness and Performance Programme (REFIT). REFIT committed the Commission services to mapping the entire EU legislative stock with a view to identifying unnecessary burdens, gaps and inefficient or ineffective measures including possibilities for simplification or repeal.[112] The Commission signalled a range of ongoing or proposed legislative measures aimed at simplification and burden reduction and also the publication of a REFIT scoreboard to track progress at Union and national level.

The follow-up Communication in late 2013 avers that 'from start to finish Smart Regulatory principles and practices motivate Commission action'.[113] Today almost all Commission proposals likely to have significant impacts are accompanied by an IA and 'increasing attention is being paid' to ex-post policy evaluation';[114] between 2010 and 2012, the Commission had conducted some 340 public consultations and 'a number of social partner consultations' in the process of policy development and review.[115] According to this official evaluation, administrative burdens associated with EU legislation had been reduced by a quarter in 13 main priority areas between 2007 and 2012, to the particular benefit of small and medium-sized enterprises (SMEs). The review conceded however that, over 50 years of EU activity later, there remain 'many challenges on the path to regulatory fitness'. The Commission had apparently gleaned, for example, that 'there are methodological difficulties regarding the assessment of costs and benefits and the cumulative impact of regulation', as also that 'a variety of regulatory impacts

[110] COM (2010) 543 final, 2.
[111] Memorandum to the Commission from 13 national governments, '10 point plan for smart regulation' (November 2012).
[112] Commission, 'EU Regulatory Fitness' (Communication) COM (2012) 746.
[113] Commission, 'Regulatory Fitness and Performance (REFIT): Results and Next Steps' (Communication) COM (2013) 685 final, 2.
[114] See further, Commission, 'Strengthening the foundations of Smart Regulation – improving evaluation' (Communication) COM (2013) 686 final.
[115] COM (2013) 685 final, 3.

60   *Tenets, Values and Objectives*

. . . may reinforce, oppose or contradict each other'.[116] Emphasising that smart regulation is a continuous process not an event, the Commission talks of 'constant reinvigoration to keep up the momentum'.[117] Time will tell.

'ADMINISTRATOR'S TOOLKIT'

In the course of the first two chapters, we have referred to numerous functions for which administrative procedures are used, singling out for special attention certain administrative techniques of general importance that underlie all modern administration and particularly so in the fragmented framework of EU governance. The ordering of the following taxonomy of procedural objects and instruments reflects this. For the convenience of the reader, we have added some cross-references to our case studies.

- **Communication:** in a hierarchy, rules and procedures are used to communicate and exchange information; in the multi-level decision-making processes of the EU, communication holds administrative networks together. (Multiple illustrations are given in this volume.)
- **Information gathering and retention:** vital components of the EU administrative process, delivered today via sophisticated forms of ICT management and a strong e-governance system. Freedom of information and data protection are particular concerns with major procedural implications (see chapter four on transparency and chapter ten on Europol).
- **Cooperation:** the raison d'être of so much in the multi-level EU administration, reflecting its most important political functions; very intense in certain policy domains and commonly increasing under the broad rubric of 'administrative cooperation'. Burgeoning 'soft law' techniques help to underwrite collaborative activity, especially in new fields (see chapter eleven on financial services).
- **Coordination of networks and regulatory steering:** emerging as another chief theme as EU governance became ever more complex; frequently associated with governance by committee and 'agencification' at Union and/or national level. Familiarly associated in 'soft governance' terms with OMC, while being powerfully illustrated in policy domains like competition (chapter eight) as well as scientifically challenging areas of risk regulation (see chapter one).
- **Hierarchical control:** officials at the top of a bureaucracy use rules and procedures as a way to control subordinates and manage the amount of discretion at their disposal. (See the Staff Regulations in chapter one.)

---

[116] Ibid, 8, 11. The Commission has commissioned a major study: A Renda, L Schrefler, G Luchetta and R Zavatta, *Assessing the Costs and Benefits of Regulation* (Brussels: CEPS, 2013).
[117] COM (2013) 685 final, 2.

- **Contracting and outsourcing:** today given much greater prominence as a pillar of governance and vehicle for public–private endeavours in the Member States; in the guise of 'public procurement', a major subject of Single Market policy (see chapter six).
- **Policy development and planning:** a *sine qua non* of public administration in the guise of agenda and priority setting, and development of programmes and projects; frequently overlooked by lawyers (but included in chapter nine on structural funds and also chapter twelve with regard to environmental decision-making).
- **Rule-making and standard-setting:** another core technique of modern administration that promotes uniformity and consistency in decision-making and hence key bureaucratic values of objectivity and equal treatment. A chief arena for IA but also for competing output values (efficiency and effectiveness) and input values (openness and participation) (as discussed in chapter five on executive law-making).
- **Implementation** [of programmes and regulatory policies]: illuminated in EU governance by systems of 'shared management' involving the Commission and national and sub-national administrations; apt to involve highly detailed legislative provision and commonly the realm also of Commission guidelines, opinions and recommendations (see chapter nine on structural funding).
- **Individualised or single-case decision-making:** a general practice that is the classic area of concern for lawyers in terms of control of discretion and measured against juridical tests such as proportionality (sketched in chapter three and further examined in chapter twelve with regard to 'asset-freezing').
- **Disbursement of funds, financial regulation and audit:** important fields of both direct and composite administration; a central area of responsibility for the Commission and the Court of Auditors, governed by the Financial Regulation (chapter one) and the genesis, not least with a view to combating corruption, of much specialist administrative machinery (as described in chapter nine on structural funding).
- **Supervision via monitoring and evaluation:** nothing less than an industry in EU composite administration and taking on further impetus in the context of Enlargement. Characterised by a welter of duties to report (accountability) and much use by the Commission of 'independent' studies (commonly appearing in the footnotes to this volume).
- **Enforcement and sanctioning:** a variable mix of preventive, negotiatory and court-oriented techniques of legal accountability; encompassing both general or horizontal forms of infringement procedure (chapter seven) and sectoral or vertical regimes of administrative sanctions, for example in competition (chapter eight).
- **Complaints handling:** internal administrative review and also alternative dispute resolution operationalised on a cross-border and pan-European basis; a subject matter of growing interest to the Commission, EO – and citizens (see chapter three).

Although the listing is intended to be indicative rather than exhaustive, this taxonomy usefully points up the sheer scale and variety of procedural functions. Underwritten by the great expansion of EU competences over the years, there are variable demands for particular functions in different policy domains. To cope with this, much by the way of *lex specialis* is demanded: irrespective of whether, as some now advocate, some kind of general law on EU administrative procedure is introduced, as discussed in our concluding chapter. The overlapping and fluid or elastic nature of the functions is another main feature of administrative procedure. Where, for example, does 'coordination' or 'implementation' end, or 'supervision' or 'enforcement' begin?[118]

The high degree of interlock between different techniques needs special emphasis in the light of the changing administrative tenets and styles examined in this chapter. Enough has been said to illustrate how NPM ideology, strong in contemporary EU governance, sets in place a standardised administrative process consisting of policy identification, planning, performance indicators, impact assessment, evaluation and audit. Again, as every EU official worth his salt should know, there is far more to regulation than simply passing a law: 'full-blown' regulation was once described as combining 'three basic elements: rule formulation; monitoring and inspection; enforcement and sanctions'.[119] The current fashion for 'better' and/or 'smart' regulation exemplifies this obvious point.

CONCLUSION

Building on the discussion in chapter one of the development of administrative procedures within a complex and rapidly changing structural framework, this chapter has highlighted the importance of overarching administrative principles in their shaping and design. The good governance trio of transparency, accountability and participation are seen today as great arbiters of legitimacy and appear in this light in EU administration. In this chapter, we have highlighted reason-giving as the original great pillar of accountability, subsidiarity as a main driver of cooperative and coordinating techniques and, reinforcing the traditional EU concern for 'output legitimacy',[120] with efficiency and effectiveness. However, the chapter has pointed up the contested nature of many of the principles over time and space and in terms of their operationalisation in EU governance – a chief theme of this volume. The rise of conditionality is enough to dispel overly comfortable notions of administrative and political harmony.

---

[118] For alternative typologies, see M Chiti, 'Forms of European Administrative Action' (2004) 68 *Law and Contemporary Problems* 37; H Hofmann, G Rowe and A Türk, *Administrative Law and Policy of the European Union* (Oxford: OUP, 2011) ch 4.

[119] C Hood and C Scott, 'Bureaucratic Regulation and New Public Management in the United Kingdom: Mirror-image developments?' (1996) 23 *Journal of Law and Society* 321, 336.

[120] A concept borrowed from F Scharpf, *Governing in Europe: Effective and Democratic?* (Oxford: OUP, 1999).

Conclusion 63

In focusing on the role of the bureaucracy as generator of administrative tenets and values, we have naturally highlighted the central place of the Commission as executive and organiser of networks; indeed, much in our 'administrator's toolkit' reflects its favoured administrative practices. The Commission – or at least the Secretariat-General – might also be described as a dedicated follower of fashion. Another key theme has been the influence of domestic and international movements in administrative and regulatory ideology on EU administrative process and procedure. Much effort has gone into promoting the managerial NPM ideology inside the Commission, which has in turn done much to promote audit-style techniques more broadly in EU administration. The canon of 'better' or 'smart' regulation has been pursued with an almost religious fervour, with impact assessment chief among the rituals. Soft governance, of which the OMC is but one example, recurs in determinedly understated fashion.

Enough has also been said to point up the role of, and interplay between, multiple sources in grounding and shaping EU administrative process and procedure. The notion of procedures as 'guaranteeing rights', something which like most lawyers we accept unhesitatingly, represents a new angle of approach in which administrative procedural developments and the celebrated EU 'general principles of law' are shown to be closely interwoven. With this in mind, we now turn to the vital contribution of courts and valuable role of the ombudsman technique in developing and upholding procedural values and principles.

3

Firefighting and Fire-Watching: Courts and Ombudsmen

CLASSICAL WESTERN CONSTITUTIONAL theory allocates the main functions of control and accountability to courts and parliaments, exercising parallel scrutiny functions. In common with other parliaments the European Parliament (EP) possesses considerable scrutiny powers, derived from and built up in the context of its budgetary powers. In chapter one, we saw these powers used as the basis for an investigation by experts into the Commission's administrative capacities, inaugurating a new phase of administrative reform, new financial procedures, stronger audit and a new style of administrative management. Parliaments also speak – or purport to speak – as the *vox populi*. In exercising this important representative function, we shall find the EP fighting for greater transparency and access to information (chapter five) and advocating a possible codification of administrative procedure (chapter thirteen). In this chapter however we focus on the considerable influence of the two Luxembourg Courts, comparing their approach with that of the European Ombudsman (EO), a Scandinavian addition to the EU accountability machinery. Often their respective contributions will lock up together in the protection of the individual, as powerfully illustrated in the development of a right to good administration. But the values that the two types of scrutineer seek to inculcate and the methods used to inculcate them are by no means identical.

Because it is set in motion by individual litigants and ends with a decision in individual cases, judicial review is in essence a firefighting function. In this chapter, however, we focus on the fire-watching elements in judicial decision-making, which take the form of establishing parameters inside which the administration has to operate. The judiciary tends to possess a well-established and decided set of values, extracted over the years from judicial decisions and formulated as 'general principles' or principles that are applied consistently in a series of judicial decisions and possess in addition some universal quality deserving of general recognition.[1] The general principles of EU law are wide-ranging and operate at several levels. Deservedly they are the subject of many important texts, which we cannot hope to emulate. We have instead selected as illustrative of the judicial approach

---

[1] A Lorenz, 'General Principles of Law: Their Elaboration in the Court of Justice of the European Communities' (1964) *American Journal of Comparative Law* 12.

to procedure a mere handful of examples. We have focused narrowly on areas where judges have had the greatest influence on procedure, as in the formulation of due process principles (discussed at greater length in chapter twelve). We have considered the influential doctrine of proportionality, a principle accepted so widely today that it has been called a global constitutional law principle.[2]

We turn then to the EO's fire-watching style in formulating and promoting principles of good administration. An ombudsman's capacity to affect administrative procedure differs significantly from that of courts. Courts have the last word on legal issues and their judgments are final and binding; ombudsmen make recommendations. In some ways, however, their influence is more direct, since their investigative method, access to files and power to institute 'Own Initiative Investigations' (OII) give them direct access to the administration. In recent years too there has been a shift of emphasis in the ombudsman world.[3] Ombudsmen have become 'fire-watchers', promoting good administration. We look in this context at the EO's contribution to complaints handling, an important input function of administration in consumer-oriented modern societies and one that the Commission actively promotes. We look too at the emergence of the European Network of Ombudsmen (ENO), established by the EO and coordinated by his office. We see this as the beginning of an 'accountability network' of ombudsmen, designed not only to facilitate the processing of complaints in a multi-level, network governance system, but also to provide a measure of accountability for composite decision-making.[4]

THE FUNCTIONS OF COURTS

The OECD definition cited in our introduction[5] tells us that administrative procedure must 'guarantee the rights of those dealing with the administration'. It adds that the guarantee must be proportionate in the sense of containing a 'double guarantee' of individual versus public interest. This inbuilt tension within administration is reflected in the judicial review process. On the one hand, courts act as protectors of the rights of the individuals and a control on executive excess; on the other, they act as arbiter of the legality of executive action and sometimes as protector of its privileges. Both judges and administrators are, in other words, under a duty to 'balance' the public interest against the rights of those who have dealings with the administration. They often balance the competing interests differently; judicial review may be more concerned with rights, administration with the collective public interest; this is, however, by no means inevitable.

---

[2] A Stone Sweet and J Mathews, 'Proportionality Balancing and Global Constitutionalism' (2008) 47 *Columbia Journal of Transnational Law* 73.

[3] P Bonnor, 'Ombudsmen and the Development of Public Law' (2003) 9 *European Public Law* 237.

[4] C Harlow and R Rawlings, 'Promoting Accountability in Multi-Level Governance: A Network Approach' (2007) 13 *European Law Journal* 542.

[5] See above, Introduction, p 2.

Equally, different administrative law systems may draw the lines differently. Thus Kadelbach contrasts German administrative law, which he describes as focused on judicial protection of the individual, with the French system, concerned with legality of administrative process[6] while Bell contrasts the state-centred French system with rights-oriented, common law systems of judicial review.[7] These different stances are reflected in the EU system. Here it is important to emphasise the very particular mandate of the Court of Justice of the European Union (CJEU). Its mission as set out in the Treaties is to ensure that 'in the interpretation and application of the Treaties the law is observed' (TEU Article 19(1), ex TEC Article 164). This fundamental obligation, once described by a judge as 'a genetic code transmitted to the Court of Justice by the founding fathers',[8] pushes the Courts in the view of some observers to exercise their powers in a consistently integrative fashion.[9]

Based on classical separation of powers theory, many Western constitutional systems restrain the judiciary from substantive review of administrative decisions. The role of the judge is to declare the law and not to substitute judicial decisions for that of the appointed decision-maker.[10] In line with this principle, the judicial review process permits a court to consider the legality of an administrative decision but not to come to a conclusion on its merits – though it has to be said that courts often tread very near the line. The grounds for review by the CJEU, which are laid down in TFEU Article 263, broadly follow this pattern. The CJEU is competent to review acts of the administration on grounds of: lack of competence; infringement of an essential procedural requirement; infringement of the Treaties and of any rule of law relating to their application and misuse of powers. Cautiously, we would describe this as a broadly procedural mandate in the sense of being clearly focused not on correctness but on legality.

There are, however, other factors to be taken into consideration. These start with the overall mission of the CJEU (cited above), which gives the Court of Justice (CoJ) powers of constitutional review over the EU legislator, hence much of the status of a constitutional court.[11] When, for example, the CoJ was asked to rule in the short selling case[12] on the controversial question whether powers delegated to the European Securities and Markets Authority (ESMA) by a regulation made in

---

[6] S Kadelbach, 'Administrative Law' in C Joerges and R Dehousse (eds), *Good Governance in Europe's Integrated Market* (Oxford: OUP, 2002) 186.

[7] J Bell, 'Mechanisms for Cross-fertilisation of Administrative Law in Europe' in J Beatson and T Tridimas (eds), *New Directions in European Public Law* (Oxford: Hart Publishing, 1998) 149–51.

[8] F Mancini and D Keeling, 'Democracy and the European Court of Justice' (1994) 57 *Modern Law Review* 175, 186.

[9] M Shapiro, 'The European Court of Justice' in P Craig and G de Burca (eds), *The Evolution of EU Law* (Oxford: OUP, 1999); M Pollack, *The Engines of Integration* (Oxford: OUP, 2003) ch 3. The most notorious critique is by H Rasmussen, *European Court of Justice* (Copenhagen: Gadjura, 1998).

[10] See M Vile, *Constitutionalism and Separation of Powers*, 2nd edn (Indianapolis: Liberty Fund, 1998).

[11] Shapiro, 'The European Court of Justice', above (n 9).

[12] Case C-270/12 *United Kingdom v Parliament and Council* (judgment of 22 January 2014); and see above, ch 1, p 35.

terms of Article 114 TFEU went beyond the treaty powers, this was not technically a substantive question. It did not require the Court to decide whether short selling ought to be regulated; that question was for the regulator. It fell within the definition of a procedural ruling in the sense that it involved questions of competence. Clearly, however, the ruling went much further. In deciding that the powers delegated to ESMA did not in fact go beyond the ambit of the regulation, the Court was making a judgement about the nature of the powers, while the ruling that the regulation came within the boundaries of TFEU Article 114 was a significant constitutional ruling, the effects of which were highly political.

A second recent case referred to the CoJ the question of the validity of the Data Retention Directive, passed with a view to harmonising Member State provisions concerning data retention by publicly available electronic communications services or public communications networks and in force since 2006. The Court had been asked to test the validity of the directive against two fundamental Charter rights: the right to respect for private life (ECFR Article 7) and the right to the protection of personal data (ECFR Article 8). It came to the conclusion that the directive 'interferes in a particularly serious manner with the fundamental rights to respect for private life and to the protection of personal data', adding the rider that 'the fact that data are retained and subsequently used without the subscriber or registered user being informed is likely to generate in the persons concerned a feeling that their private lives are the subject of constant surveillance'.[13] Once again this is technically a procedural judgment based on the standard test of proportionality and the fact that there were no procedures governing access to the data retained. Once again it goes much further. Indeed, this case epitomises the changing role of courts that are endowed with authority to test legislation against the standards of human rights. So although both decisions can correctly be described as procedural to do so is greatly to diminish them.

Some constitutions, such as that of Finland, contain a right to good administration though they do not usually go into great detail about the ingredients of that right. In many cases, the details will be fleshed out, as they are in a majority of EU Member States, in a general Administrative Procedures Act (APA). This may be more or less complete and extensive. The case of the EU is rather different. Before the Lisbon Treaty, there was no treaty right to good administration,[14] though there was provision for reason-giving.[15] It was left to the legislator, administration and courts to fill procedural gaps. No general right to due process was provided by the Treaties and the EU has no APA. Instead, the CJEU stepped in to establish general principles, starting with the idea that rights of natural justice existed in competition cases. This left significant gaps; there were, for example, statutory rules providing for a fair hearing in competition, mergers and anti-dumping cases

---

[13] Joined Cases C-293/12 and 594/12 *Digital Rights Ireland and Seitlinger* (judgment of 8 April 2014).
[14] But see below, p 87.
[15] See below, p 73.

68 *Courts and Ombudsmen*

but none for the common customs tariff.[16] To rely entirely on judges for procedural protection is not entirely satisfactory; courts are not always willing to fill gaps and their judgments are ex post facto and unpredictable. One of the arguments put forward for a general horizontal EU APA that will enumerate general procedural requirements is that it will lend the legitimacy of the EU legislator to the general principles of EU administrative procedure. We pick this argument up in our final chapter.

THE COURTS AND ADMINISTRATIVE PROCEDURE

Today, when procedural rule-making has proliferated and expanded to cover much of the ground, it has become harder to maintain Schwarze's initial view of the Luxembourg Courts as 'the primary source of all administrative procedure'.[17] Rather, their position is one of filling in gaps. It remains true, however, that procedural requirements are regularly 'developed and concretised by case law' and that the general principles of review have been developed on the basis of 'unwritten general principles of law common to the constitutional traditions of the Member States'.[18] There is often a process of judicial exchange or 'dialogue', when general principles recognised in a Member State legal order are adopted by the CJEU, which has the effect of giving the principle vertical effect in every national legal order or 'constitutionalising' it. Of the three most commonly applied general principles, proportionality was famously borrowed from German law, reason-giving was a treaty obligation and the Courts' due process rules derive from the English concept of natural justice. Occasionally too the CJEU has added to the common stock its own original principles, as with the duty of fidelity, which we described in chapter two as a primary principle of EU administrative law and administration.

Proportionality Testing

As it found its way into the EU Treaties, proportionality had the limited meaning that Union action 'shall not exceed what is necessary to achieve the objectives of the Treaties' (TEU Article 5(4)). This formulation equates broadly with the concept as it was introduced to EU law in the *Internationale Handelsgesellschaft* case.[19] Here the Advocate General said only that 'the individual should not have his free-

---

[16] K Lenaerts and L Vanhamme, 'Procedural Rights of Private Parties in the Community Administrative Process' (1997) 34 *Common Market Law Review* 531, 533; I Forrester, 'Due Process in EC Competition Cases: A Distinguished Institution with Flawed Procedures' (2009) 34 *European Law Review* 817.
[17] J Schwarze, 'Developing Principles of European Administrative Law' [1993] *Public Law* 229.
[18] Ibid.
[19] Case 11/70 *Internationale Handelsgesellschaft v Einfuhr- und Vorratsstelle Getreide* [1970] ECR 1125.

dom of action limited beyond the degree necessary in the public interest',[20] a test applied by the CJEU to justify a legislative provision that was 'appropriate for ensuring the normal functioning of the organization of the market in cereals in the general interest' without imposing an 'undue burden on importers or exporters'.[21] This simple formula, which allows much discretion to the decision-maker, is less strict than the three-stage test used in German public law, from which the principle derives.[22] This involves a decision-maker asking three closely-linked and admittedly overlapping questions:

1. Is the measure/decision **appropriate** for obtaining the objective?
2. Is it **necessary**, in the sense that no other measure is available which is less restrictive of freedom?
3. Is it **proportionate** to its aim?

In *Fedesa*,[23] dealing with an outright ban on the use of hormones in livestock farming, this was indeed the test applied by the Court, which said that:

> [T]he lawfulness of the prohibition of an economic activity is subject to the condition that the prohibitory measures are appropriate and necessary in order to achieve the objectives legitimately pursued by the legislation in question; when there is a choice between several appropriate measures recourse must be had to the least onerous, and the disadvantages caused must not be disproportionate to the aims pursued.

The test actually applied in recent EU case law is most often a two-stage test to the effect that a measure must be 'appropriate and necessary for achieving its objective'. And the Court in the *Omega Air* case[24] further weakened the proportionality test by ruling first, that the measure 'clearly disclosed the essential objective pursued by the institution' so that 'it would be excessive to require a specific statement of reasons for the various technical choices made'[25] and second, by applying only a 'light touch' standard of review. A wide measure of discretion was, in short, left to the administration.

Craig and Tridimas conclude after a detailed survey of the case law that proportionality testing by the CJEU tends in practice to involve the two-stage test applied differently in different areas of Community activity.[26] Intensity of review varies widely but generally entails only 'light touch review' when the area is one of special expertise, such as banking or scientific risk assessment. The test has, in other

---

[20] Ibid, 1147.
[21] Ibid, [25]. And see Case C-491/01 *R v Health Secretary ex p British American Tobacco (Investments) and Imperial Tobacco* [2002] ECR I-11453, [123]; F Jacobs, 'Recent Developments in the Principle of Proportionality in European Community Law' in E Ellis (ed), *The Principle of Proportionality in the Laws of Europe* (Oxford: Hart Publishing, 1999).
[22] R Alexy, *A Theory of Constitutional Rights*, trans Rivers (Oxford: OUP, 2002).
[23] Case C-331/88 *Fedesa and others* [1990] ECR I-4023.
[24] Joined Cases C-27 and 122/00 *R v Environment Secretary ex p Omega Air and others* [2000] ECR I-2560, [63].
[25] Ibid, [67].
[26] P Craig, *EU Administrative Law*, 2nd edn (Oxford: OUP, 2012); T Tridimas, *The General Principles of EC Law*, 2nd edn (Oxford: OUP, 2006) 'Overview' [3.10].

words, been adapted to the needs of the regulatory, economic Community, where it has assumed the characteristics of 'a flexible principle which is used in different contexts to protect different interests and entails varying degrees of judicial scrutiny'.[27] In reviewing national measures, however, testing may be much stricter, especially in cases affecting the four freedoms, where a double proportionality test is applicable, first to evaluate the national measure as an appropriate implementation of EU law and second, to evaluate any exceptional circumstances or defences (such as public policy or *ordre public*) put forward by the Member State. In this way, proportionality may have a 'Europeanising effect' on national administrations and legal orders,[28] requiring national policymakers and judges to consider the appropriateness of their measures in the light of a potential evaluation by the CJEU.

It could be said of the proportionality principle as used by the judiciary that it operates to lend an impression of objectivity and scientific rationality to a judicial process that is essentially discretionary in character and often borders on a policy choice. But institutions other than judges apply the principle; indeed, it is today so widely accepted in EU law that it is fair to call it a 'fundamental principle' of all administrative decision-making. In the *Data Retention* case cited earlier, for example, the directive itself employed the principle, providing that the access provisions were to be defined by each Member State 'in accordance with necessity and proportionality requirements'. The Austrian court asked a specific question as to proportionality and the CoJ made its assessment on the basis of the following formulation:

> [A]ccording to the settled case-law of the Court, the principle of proportionality requires that acts of the EU institutions be appropriate for attaining the legitimate objectives pursued by the legislation at issue and do not exceed the limits of what is appropriate and necessary in order to achieve those objectives.[29]

The Commission reports regularly in its Better Lawmaking Reports on the use of the treaty requirement that the content and form of Union action must not exceed what is necessary to achieve the objectives of the Treaties: any decision must therefore favour 'the least restrictive option'.[30] It also applies both principles in preparing Road Maps and Action Plans (above, chapter two) and reports annually on the process. The Commission Impact Assessment Board has been known to criticise an IA proposal on the ground that it should have more clearly presented 'the necessity and value-added of EU action'.[31]

---

[27] Tridimas, above (n 26) 137.

[28] J Schwarze, 'The Role of General Principles of Administrative Law in the Process of Europeanization of National Law: The Case of Proportionality' in L Ortega (ed), *Studies on European Public Law* (Madrid: Lex Nova, 2005).

[29] Joined Cases C-293/12 and 594/12 *Digital Rights Ireland and Seitlinger* (judgment of 8 April 2014), above (n 13) [46].

[30] Commission, 'Report from the Commission on Subsidiarity and Proportionality: 18th report on Better Lawmaking for 2010' COM (2011) 344 final, 2.

[31] Commission, 'Annual Report on Subsidiarity and Proportionality for 2012' COM (2013) 566 final, 2.

Proportionality finds a place too in the EO's 'Code of Good Administrative Behaviour' (below), where it is said that 'measures taken are proportional to the aim pursued' and officials are urged to 'respect the fair balance between the interests of private persons and the general public interest'. It makes an occasional appearance in ombudsman investigations. For example, in a complaint against the European Investment Bank (EIB), the EO sought advice from the European Data Protection Supervisor, who replied that, in considering its response to a request for information containing personal data, the EIB would need 'to take into account the approach of the GC'. When the EIB interpreted the jurisprudence so as to lay the burden of proof on the applicant to 'demonstrate the necessity and proportionality of having public access to personal data', the EO concluded that it had failed to proceed 'to the balancing exercise' required by the Data Protection Regulation.[32] The EO seems to expect of the administration that it will carefully apply a simple balancing test of public versus private interest. One could argue therefore that the proportionality test as applied by all EU institutions amounts to little more than a replication of the balancing test that administrative lawyers view as the core function of administrative law.

INTENSITY OF REVIEW

The efficacy of any court as machinery for the protection of rights or accountability lies in the intensity of its review. How far a court will wish to go in scrutinising administrative decision-making is essentially a discretionary matter and the flexibility of the principles at their disposal adds to the discretion. Just as courts can bend the proportionality principle to create a sliding scale of administrative discretion, so they can vary the intensity of their review without openly changing the standard.[33]

In acknowledgment of the technical nature and complexity of the decisions that the Commission is asked to make in the area of economic regulation, the CoJ first adopted a 'light touch' standard of review for manifest error (*erreur manifeste d'appréciation*) borrowed from French administrative law. To quote the CoJ:

> In a situation . . . which involves an appraisal of complex economic situations, judicial review must be limited to verifying whether the relevant procedural rules have been complied with, whether the facts on which the contested choice is based have been accurately stated, and whether there has been a manifest error in the appraisal of those facts or a misuse of powers.[34]

---

[32] Inv 2510/2011/CK with Opinion of European Data Protection Supervisor (EDPS) and citing Case T-82/09 *Dennekamp v Parliament* (2011) ECR II-418.
[33] M Shapiro, 'The Giving Reasons Requirement' in M Shapiro and A Stone Sweet, *On Law, Politics and Judicialization* (Oxford: OUP, 2002) 228.
[34] Case C-150/94 *United Kingdom v Council* [1998] ECR-I-7235, [54]; Case C-156/87 *Gestetner Holdings v Council and Commission* [1990] ECR I-781, [63].

But as from the 1990s, commentators began to suggest a change in attitude. Courts were deepening the intensity of review without openly changing the standard and the grant of major discretionary power to the administration was now made only in return for a corresponding 'respect for extended procedural guarantees'.[35] This may partly reflect the arrival of the Court of First Instance (CFI), ambitious to ensconce itself as the EU Administrative Court.

This conclusion is underpinned by cases like *Asia Motor France II*, where the General Court (GC) stated its function as being 'limited to verifying whether the relevant rules on procedure and on the statement of reasons have been complied with, whether the facts have been accurately stated and whether there has been any manifest error of appraisal or a misuse of powers'.[36] Yet it went on to conduct an intense scrutiny of the proceedings before annulling the contested decision on the ground that it was 'vitiated by a manifest error in the assessment of the facts which led [the Commission] to err in law'.[37] In the later *Airtours*[38] and *Tetra Laval*[39] cases, the GC again 'crawled all over' the Commission merger procedures without overtly deviating from the principle of manifest error; instead, it manipulated the burden of proof. Scrutinising every step of the process and carefully comparing the evidence of the parties, it concluded in each case that the Commission had not 'proved to the requisite legal standard' the reasons for its decision. In neither case could this be said to be 'light touch' review; in *Airtours*, indeed, after a scrutiny described by one practitioner as 'rigorous', the GC, while reiterating the guiding principle that the 'judicature must take account of the discretionary margin implicit in . . . provisions of an economic nature', effectively substituted its own decision for that of the Commission in a merger case that it clearly thought wrong.[40]

Contrariwise, in *Omega Air*, which concerned a legislative act, the CoJ stated that where a policy involved a 'complex economic situation', the Council's discretion extended

> not only in relation to[sic] the nature and scope of the provisions which are to be adopted but also, to a certain extent, to the findings as to the basic facts, especially in the sense that it is free to base its assessment, if necessary, on findings of a general nature.[41]

Does this merely demonstrate the traditional reluctance of courts to challenge the legislator? Does it reflect disagreement between the two Courts? Or does it reflect

---

[35] L Azoulay, 'The Judge and the Community's Administrative Governance' (2001) 7 *European Law Journal* 425, 429.

[36] Case T-7/92 *Asia Motor France and others v Commission (Asia Motor II)* [1993] ECR II-669 [33] citing joined Cases 142/94, 156/84 *BAT and Reynolds v Commission* [1987] ECR 4487; Case C-225/91 *Matra v Commission* [1993] ECR I-3203.

[37] Case T-7/92 *Asia Motor France and others v Commission (Asia Motor II)* [1993] ECR II-669, [55].

[38] Case T-342/99 *Airtours v Commission* [2002] ECR II-2585.

[39] Case T-5/02 *Tetra Laval v Commission* [2002] ECR II-4381.

[40] See B Vesterdorf, 'Certain Reflections on Recent Judgments Reviewing Commission Merger Control Decisions' in M Hoskins and W Robinson (eds), *A True European. Essays for Judge David Edward* (Oxford: Hart Publishing, 2003).

[41] Joined Cases C-27 and 122/00 *Omega Air and others* [2000] ECR I-2560, [65].

divergent views in the chambers and panels of the two Courts that are today the standard method of adjudication? The opacity of CJEU reason-giving makes it difficult to say.[42]

Reason-Giving to Rationality

For Shapiro, 'requiring an agency to give reasons in order for a court to review the agency's decision allows the court to decide whether the agency was justified in reaching the decision it reached'.[43] In other words, review of reasons opens the way to substantive judicial review. If correct, this places the Luxembourg Courts in an advantageous position, since reason-giving is a right embedded in the Treaties (see TFEU Article 296), giving it a very special position in EU administrative law. For the CJEU, reason-giving has a threefold purpose: it allows interested parties to defend their rights; it allows the Court to exercise its supervisory functions; and, at a constitutional level, it allows Member States and 'all interested nationals' to check the way in which the Commission has applied the Treaty.[44] This formula underscores the constitutional dimension of reason-giving.

The Court was quick to adopt the right to reasons in *Commission v Italy*[45] as a general principle of law but, as Bignami observed, 'knowing the grounds for a Commission decision is one thing, obtaining a reply on every objection of fact, policy, and law is another thing altogether'[46] and the lengths to which the Court will expect the Commission to go are highly unpredictable. Take *Asia Motor France II* (above). Here the GC ruled that the Commission need *not* deal with every argument advanced by the applicant. Yet not only did the Court scrutinise the Commission's reasons with great care, but it also demanded answers to its own extra questions and came to a different conclusion from the appointed decision-maker. It added to the confusion by ruling that the reasons, though 'sufficient' in the sense that they allowed the facts and legal considerations on which the Commission had relied to be identified, were 'insufficient' in the sense that reasons must 'not only be full but also rational'.[47] To put this differently, the GC had expanded the meaning of the word 'reasons' to cover 'reasoning'. Nehl justifiably characterises this as a paradigm example of substantive under the guise of procedural review.[48]

---

[42] But see D Kelemen and M Malecki, 'Do ECJ judges all speak with the Same Voice? Evidence of Divergent Preferences from the Judgments of Chambers (2012) 19 *Journal of Economic Public Policy* 59.
[43] Shapiro, 'The Giving Reasons Requirement', above (n 33) 241.
[44] eg, Case 24/62 *Germany v Commission* [1963] ECR 63; Case 22/70 *Commission v Council* (AETR) [1971] ECR 263, [42]; Case C-350/88 *Delacre v Commission* [1990] ECR I-395; Case C-370/07 *Commission v Council* (CITES) [2009] ECR I-08917, [42].
[45] Opinion of AG Lenz in Case 35/84 *Commission v Italy* [1986] ECR 545.
[46] F Bignami, 'Creating European Rights: National Values and Supranational Interests' (2005) 11 *Columbia Journal of European Law* 241, 345.
[47] Case T-7/92 *Asia Motor France and others v Commission (Asia Motor II)* [1993] ECR II-669, [35], [55], [65].
[48] H-P Nehl, *Principles of Administrative Procedure in EC Law* (Oxford: Hart Publishing, 1999) 142.

74 *Courts and Ombudsmen*

The standard formula of the modern case law underlines the conceptual link between reasons and rationality. A statement of reasons must 'disclose in a clear and unequivocal fashion the reasoning followed by the institution which adopted the measure in question in such a way as to enable the persons concerned to ascertain the reasons for the measure and to enable the competent Community court to exercise its power of review'.[49] In Omega Air, the CJEU designated this 'settled case-law'. Yet on this occasion, the Court ruled that it was 'not necessary for details of all relevant factual and legal aspects to be given' and that 'if the contested measure clearly discloses the essential objective pursued by the institution, it would be excessive to require a specific statement of reasons for the various technical choices made'.[50] The beauty of the giving reasons requirement is, in short, that just as it can be 'converted from a very mild, essentially procedural requirement into a very draconian, substantive one',[51] so it can just as easily be returned to its former mildness.

Reasons and Due Process

Advocate General Lenz in *Commission v Italy* treated the right to reasons as a due process right, linking it to the need to inform the subject of an administrative decision of the decision 'immediately and in writing'.[52] In *Transocean Paint*,[53] a competition case generally seen as the foundation of due process in EU law, the CoJ greatly extended its requirements, ruling that the Commission must not only give prior notice of conditions to which it intended to subject the applicant, but also an opportunity to submit observations to the Commission.[54] In *Automec*,[55] the GC classified due process in competition cases as a three-stage procedure: (i) an information-gathering stage, which may include an informal exchange of views between the parties; (ii) a reason-giving stage, which includes rights to notice in terms both of statutory requirements and a fair hearing; (iii) a decision-making stage at which the Commission must consider the complainant's observations. But even within this framework, due process rights are almost infinitely adjustable. Craig, who believes that such matters are a question for individual legal systems, lists ten or more variable items of content.[56] Most often contested in EU competition cases are the right to notice and full information concerning the decision; the right to access the Commission file; the question whether the right to make representations is documentary or extends to an oral hearing and, if the latter, whether the parties can be legally represented; whether a right to cross-examination is included; how detailed the reasons for the decision must be; and

[49] Case C-367/95P *Commission v Sytravel and Brink's France SARL* [1998] ECR I-179, [63].
[50] Joined Cases C-27 and 122/00 *Omega Air and others* [2000] ECR I-2560, [45]–[46].
[51] Shapiro, 'The Giving Reasons Requirement', above (n 33) 235.
[52] Above (n 45).
[53] Case 17/74 *Transocean Marine Paint Association v Commission* [1974] ECR 1063.
[54] Ibid, [15].
[55] Case T-64/89T *Automec* [1990] ECR II-367.
[56] Craig, above (n 26) 322.

how and when it must be notified. Every sub-rule seems to have manifold exceptions that no one has ever succeeded in listing or classifying.[57] Moreover, as with proportionality testing, courts adopt different attitudes to due process rights in different situations. In chapter twelve, for example, we shall see how they have modelled due process in cases involving terrorism and human rights.

Whether the Luxembourg Courts have been too protective or not protective enough in imposing due process rights in complex competition cases is a hotly contested question, which turns on the Commission's position as 'prosecutor and judge' in the proceedings and the application of criminal procedure to administrative cases (see chapter eight). Without taking sides in the dispute, we note that competition lawyers, concerned with the heavy concentration of regulatory and adjudicative power in the Commission, are inclined to deplore the insufficiency of judicial intervention, while at the other end of the spectrum commentators complain of excessive judicial proceduralism that undercuts the Commission's regulatory functions. Nehl, for example, attributes to the CJEU a 'deep metamorphosis' of the EU administrative process and 'ongoing process of "constitutionalisation" with respect to procedural requirements'.[58]

Rationality and Risk Assessment

Risk regulation is, as we noted in chapter one, a central function of EU administration with its own complex and well-established comitology procedures. Equally, it is an area in which the review process is difficult and delicate. Sensitive and contentious political issues are involved in risk assessment cases; climate change;[59] the use of antibiotics or hormones for veterinary purposes;[60] food scares;[61] are all issues on which the public feels strongly. Member States differ over environmental protection and on measures necessary to protect the environment and cherish their rights to legislate in the national interest.[62] Commission and Courts may find themselves squeezed between well-resourced environmental protection groups, transnational corporations determined to protect their manufacturing interest and Member States challenging institutional refusal to take action.[63] Take the prohibition of genetically modified organisms. France was fined €10 million by the CJEU for its six-year refusal to implement EU laws authorising

---

[57] See E de La Serre, 'Procedural Justice in the European Community Case-law Concerning the Rights of the Defence: Essentialist and Instrumental Trends' (2006) 12 *European Public Law* 225.
[58] Nehl, above (n 48) 11; Lenaerts and Vanhamme, above (n 16).
[59] See V Heyvaert, 'Governing Climate Change: Towards a New Paradigm for Risk Regulation' (2011) 74 *Modern Law Review* 817.
[60] Joined Cases T-344 and 345/00 *CEVA Santé Animale and Pharmacia Enterprises v Commission* [2003] ECR II-229.
[61] See A Szajkowska, 'The Impact of the Definition of the Precautionary Principle in EU Food Law' (2010) 47 *Common Market Law Review* 173.
[62] G Skogstad, 'Legitimacy and/or Policy Effectiveness?: Network Governance and GMO Regulation in the European Union' (2003) 10 *Journal of European Public Policy* 321.
[63] Case T-229/04 *Sweden v Commission* (2007) ECR II-2437.

76 Courts and Ombudsmen

cultivation of GMO crops despite which France subsequently used the safeguard clause for a further ban.[64] Attempts to get a genetically modified potato authorised met resistance, both in Council and the relevant scientific committee. This led the Commission to grant authority without resubmitting its modified draft decision to a scientific committee for consideration. The decision was, however, annulled, requiring the process to be reopened.[65]

No one likes to take responsibility for disasters and it is therefore understandable that during the notorious scare over 'mad cow disease' (BSE) the CJEU was happy to validate pre-emptive action by the Commission to ban British exports of beef and beef products.[66] But scientific evidence is often contested and uncertain; arguably, Commission officials lack the degree of specialist scientific knowledge necessary for evaluation, making the Commission heavily reliant on the advice of its scientific committees and expert agencies.[67] Inevitably, the Courts too are driven back on administrative procedure. They are inclined to focus on procedural questions: Has an appropriate IA been conducted? Was a general or a focused consultation required? Were the requisite scientific authorities consulted and were their qualifications adequate?

Two interpretative principles are especially relevant to review of risk assessment measures. Under the rationality principle discussed above, the Courts have sometimes been willing to review the legality and the reasoning of a scientific committee and their case law, based overtly on 'manifest error of assessment', in practice holds the Commission strictly to the letter of its procedures – especially where these are laid down (as they usually are) in sector-specific legislation.[68] The second ground of review is the novel precautionary principle now incorporated in TFEU Article 191, which commits the EU to 'a high level of protection' in environmental policy to be 'based on the precautionary principle'. Article 191 leaves room for considerable disagreement over the meaning and application of the term and also creates ambiguity as to the field of application. Does the precautionary principle primarily bind the legislator? Or does it also govern the process and procedures by which public authorities take risk assessment decisions in the absence of conclusive evidence of likely harm?

It was the celebrated *Pfizer* case[69] that established the place of scientific expertise in decision-making. Here the GC ruled first, that it would be 'exceptional' for the

---

[64] C-419/03 *Commission v France* (judgment of 15 July 2004); Case C-121/07 *Commission v France* [2008] ECR I-9159; Joined Cases C-58 to 68/10 *Monsanto and others* [2011] ECR I-07763. See also Case C-236/01 *Monsanto Agricoltora Italia SpA v Presidenza del Consiglio dei Ministro* [2003] ECR I-8105; M Weimer, 'Applying Precaution in EU Authorization of Genetically Modified Products – Challenges and Suggestions of Reform' (2010) 16 *European Law Journal* 624.

[65] Case T-240/10 *Hungary v Commission* (judgment of 13 December 2013).

[66] Case C-180/96 *UK v Commission* [1998] ECR I-2265, [99]; Case C-157/96 *R v MAFF and Commissioners of Customs and Excise ex p NFU* [1998] ECR I-2211, [62]–[64].

[67] The Commission is probably on stronger ground than the Courts; 26% of senior Commission officials have qualifications in science: see H Kassim et al, *The European Commission of the Twenty-First Century* (Oxford: OUP, 2013) 40.

[68] eg, Case T-74/00 *Artegodan GmbH v Commission* [2002] ECR II-4945.

[69] Case T-13//99 *Pfizer Animal Health v Council* [2002] ECR II-3305.

Commission to proceed to assess complex scientific evidence without obtaining an opinion from the appropriate scientific committee[70] and second, that decisions must be based on 'the best available data and the most recent results of international research'.[71] The Court ruled that where a scientific committee was consulted the Commission must not ignore its findings but stopped short at holding it bound by committee conclusions. The characteristic Commission response was to structure its discretion, setting out its proposed procedures in guidelines.[72] These specified that an IA and cost–benefit analysis would be conducted; that procedures would be open; that space would be made to accommodate interested parties; and that measures would be regularly monitored and modified where change was justified by new scientific evidence. Where action was deemed necessary, measures based on the precautionary principle should be:

- *Proportional* to the chosen level of protection.
- *Non-discriminatory* in their application.
- *Consistent* with similar measures already taken.
- *Based on an examination of the potential benefits and costs* of action or lack of action (including where appropriate and feasible, an economic cost–benefit analysis).
- *Subject to review*, in the light of new scientific data.
- *Capable of assigning responsibility* for producing the scientific evidence necessary for a more comprehensive risk assessment.

The Guidelines also stated that the precautionary principle might in some situations imply a 'presupposition' that potentially dangerous effects deriving from a phenomenon, product or process had been identified, hinting at a reversal of the burden of proof.[73]

Commentators were generally disappointed with the application of the precautionary principle in early cases.[74] The GC seemed to be using it to police the framework of the regulatory process but stopping short at deeper penetration. Some see *Sweden v Commission*[75] as a turning point. The case involved a dispute over Paraquat, a weedkiller that some Member States wished to see banned. The Commission, after consulting two scientific committees, decided to authorise the product. Sweden attacked this decision, pointing first to failure to comply with the very precise and complex procedural steps laid down in the Plant Protection Products Directive and the way the dossier had been handled in respect of the scientific studies. Second, Sweden argued that, in terms of the directive, the

---

[70] Ibid, [270].
[71] Ibid, [149]–[63].
[72] Commission, 'Communication on the precautionary principle' (COM (2000) 1 final, 4, 6.
[73] Ibid, 6.4.
[74] eg, K-H Ladeur, 'The Introduction of the Precautionary Principle into EU Law. A Pyrrhic Victory' (2003) 40 *Common Market Law Review* 1455; V Heyvaert, 'Facing the Consequences of the Precautionary Principle in EC Law' (2006) 31 *European Law Review* 186; A Alemanno, 'The Shaping of European Risk Regulation by Community Courts' (2008) Jean Monnet Working Paper 18/08.
[75] Case T-229/04 *Sweden v Commission* (2007) ECR II-2437.

Commission could authorise a potentially toxic product only if it has been shown *beyond reasonable doubt* that the product was 'completely safe in at least one representative type of use'.[76] The Court, having carefully scrutinised the evidence, concluded that this standard had not been reached and both claims were upheld.[77]

The effect on administrative procedure of a jurisprudence in which courts steadily ratchet up the standard of procedural review by requiring more evidence, further and better reasons, access to files and opportunities to make representations must necessarily be considerable. The CJEU requires that evidence relied on by the Commission be 'factually accurate, reliable and consistent'; it must 'contain all the information which must be taken into account in order to assess a complex situation and whether it is capable of substantiating the conclusions drawn from it'[78] – Shapiro's synoptic decision-making. This involves the decision-maker, usually the Commission in complex anti-dumping, merger, state aids and competition cases, in assembling a mass of evidence. Officials must also take the utmost care to record the minutiae of complex economic investigations in the knowledge that the way is open for corporate bodies to dispute every stage of the procedure, demanding more reasons; greater access to the administrative file; the right to make representations; the right to be represented; and so on through multiple judicial review applications and appeals. In cases involving risk assessment, where regulation usually prescribes the evaluative procedure, every step in fact-finding, choice of scientific advisers, production of evidence, consultation of committees and evaluation – must all be carried out to near perfection. It is impossible to sidestep these obstacles by granting unlimited discretion to the administration because discretion is also challengeable by judicial review. Officials are pushed towards compromise and negotiated solutions, the preferred position of transnational corporations. The ambivalence of the case law means that officials cannot foresee which procedural irregularities or omissions will seem to the court to be trivial or irrelevant. Rulings on procedural questions delay unfavourable outcomes, allow further opportunities to present a case. Kelemen calls this phenomenon 'Eurolegalism', a process in which proceduralism sets the framework for law games and courts lay the groundwork for proceduralism.[79] A radical judicialisation of the policymaking process, it is seen by some as the future of governance in the globalised capitalist world.

---

[76] Ibid, [140]. See similarly Case C-127/02 *Landelijke Vereniging tot Behoud van de Waddenzee v Staatssecrtaris van Landhouw, Natuurhebeer en Visserij* [2004] ECR I-7405.

[77] See further C Anderson, 'Contrasting Models of EU Administration in Judicial Review of Risk Regulation' (2014) 51 *Common Market Law Review* 1, 18–23.

[78] Case C-12/03 P *Commission v Tetra Laval* [2005] ECR I-987, [39], [48].

[79] D Kelemen, 'Suing for Europe: Adversarial Legalism and European Governance' (2006) 39 *Comparative Political Studies* 101; D Kelemen, *Eurolegalism: The Transformation of Law and Regulation in the European Union* (Cambridge, MA: Harvard University Press, 2011).

PRIORITISING PEOPLE: THE EUROPEAN OMBUDSMAN (EO)

The Office of EO was established by the 1992 Maastricht Treaty. She or he is appointed by the EP and reports to its Petitions Committee.[80] The EO Statute highlights the quality of independence. The appointee must either meet the 'conditions for the exercise of the highest judicial office' or possess the 'acknowledged competence and experience to undertake the duties of Ombudsman'; she or he must 'offer every guarantee of independence' and give a solemn undertaking before the CJEU that he will perform his duties with 'complete independence and impartiality'.[81] It is unthinkable that the EO should be appointed from inside the EU public service; equally, no EO has been a judge; indeed, all three appointees to date have been national ombudsmen.[82]

The EO's official function is to 'help uncover maladministration . . . and make recommendations with a view to putting an end to it' (TFEU Article 195, ex TEC Article 228). Maladministration is said to occur when a public body fails to act in accordance with a rule or principle which is binding upon it, an embryonic definition later amplified to cover 'administrative irregularities, unfairness, discrimination, abuse of power, failure to reply, refusal of and unnecessary delay'.[83] In the EO's view, 'illegality necessarily implies maladministration but maladministration does not automatically entail illegality'[84] – at least in the sense of conduct that could be sanctioned by a court. Recently, however, the EO has turned his attention to fire-watching. Nikiforos Diamandorous openly asserted that his role was to 'serve the general public interest by helping to improve the quality of administration and of service rendered to citizens by the EU institutions'. He also told officials that they were 'not only to respect their legal obligations, but also to be service-minded and to ensure that members of the public are properly treated and enjoy their rights fully'.[85] The 'further remarks' sometimes appended to his inquiries 'have a single purpose: to serve the public interest by helping the institution concerned to raise the quality of its administration in the future'; his 'critical remarks' also have 'an educative dimension'.[86]

The EO has competence in all cases involving a 'Community institution or body', excluding the CJEU in its judicial capacity but including EU agencies, and can accept complaints from any citizen or resident of a Member State or corporate body

---

[80] Decision of the EP on the regulations and general conditions governing the performance of the Ombudsman's duties [1994] OJ L113/15, as amended by Decisions of 14 March and 18 June 2008.

[81] Arts 6(2) and 9.

[82] Jacob Söderman (1995–2003) previously the Finnish ombudsman; Nikiforos Diamandorous (2003–13) previously the Greek ombudsman; Emily O'Reilly (2013–) previously the Irish ombudsman.

[83] EO, *The European Ombudsman, What does he do?*, All EO documents are available on the EO website at: http://www.ombudsman.europa.eu/start.faces

[84] EO, *AR 2009*, 27.

[85] Citations from the website of the EO under 'resources'.

[86] EO, 'Follow-up to critical and further remarks – How the EU institutions responded to the Ombudsman's recommendations in 2011'. And see Bonnor, 'Ombudsmen and the Development of Public Law', above (n 3).

with an office within EU territory.[87] In contrast to the CJEU, the majority of ombudsman complaints come from individuals; in 2012, for example, 85.3 per cent were from individuals and only 14.7 per cent from corporations. According to the *Annual Report for 2012*, the office handled 2442 complaints and enquiries, of which only 740 were within competence, leading to 450 investigations. This low recurrent figure is a cause for concern to the EO and is one of the main reasons for the establishment of the ENO (below); in 2012, for example, 1467 complaints were transferred to a national ombudsman or other competent network member. The EO has recently taken decisive action to remedy the systemic defect. He has streamlined his own procedures to deal speedily with complaints falling outside his mandate by allowing the Registry to handle them subject to a reasoned request for the EO to review the determination. The Registry explains simply why a given complaint falls outside the mandate and either transfers it to a competent body or advises the complainant where to turn. These procedures have significantly reduced delay.

If the starting point for an investigation is normally a complaint, the power under Article 2 of the EO Statute to undertake own initiative investigations gives the EO something of the quality of a 'government inspector', standing halfway between administration and adjudication. This investigative character is underlined by the primarily documentary and investigatory procedure used in ombudsman investigations, typically with access to official files and offices.[88] Officials are under an obligation to supply the investigator with any information or documentary evidence that she or he requests and public servants are obliged to testify at the EO's request.[89] A finding of maladministration results in recommendations for reform and/or redress and, even where there is no maladministration, the EO may attach critical remarks coupled with suggestions for improvement. OIIs end in a special report to the EP; they are relatively frequent; in 2012, for example, there were 10 OIIs.[90]

Redress and Reform

An ombudsman's capacity to affect administrative procedure differs considerably from that of courts. The impact of an ombudsman is direct and if – as lawyers like to protest – his recommendations are not *legally* binding, they are certainly not ineffective. Indeed, two in-depth surveys of compliance conducted in 2012 showed a compliance rate of around 82 per cent; statistics will now be published annually.[91]

[87] Statute, Art 2.
[88] See for an account of EO procedure, I Harden, 'When Europeans Complain: The Work of the European Ombudsman' (2000) 3 *Cambridge Yearbook of European Law* 199; A Tsadiras, 'Unravelling Ariadne's Thread: The European Ombudsman's Investigative Powers' (2008) 45 *Common Market Law Review* 757.
[89] Statute, Art 3.
[90] EO, *AR 2012*, 6.
[91] Ibid, 7.

Where an institution rejects a friendly solution or draft recommendation, the EO may send a special report to the EP, as he did in a disturbing case where OLAF (the EU anti-fraud unit) put up on its website a press release accusing a journalist of bribery, which it refused to remove. The EO judged the allegations to be neither necessary nor proportionate and recommended that they be withdrawn, adding the following rider:

> It is good administrative practice to ensure, when taking decisions, that the measures adopted are proportional to the aim pursued. In particular, the administration ought to avoid restricting the rights of citizens when those restrictions are not in a reasonable relation with the purpose pursued by the action. These standards ought to apply not only to decisions, but to the activity of administrations in general.[92]

After taking advice from the EO, OLAF made the necessary corrections. Nonetheless, the EO felt the issue sufficiently important to warrant a special report.[93]

In a similar inquiry involving a Commission refusal to instigate infringement proceedings in respect of failure to conduct an environmental impact assessment (EIA) before the expansion of Vienna Airport,[94] the EO closed his first investigation after the Commission agreed to keep its infringement file open pending an assurance from the Austrian authorities that a retrospective EIA had been conducted in accordance with EU law. The Commission later stalled, generating further complaints and a second investigation. The EO concluded that the Commission had failed to comply with the principles of good administration properly to address the complainants' arguments over a manifest conflict of interest; to take appropriate action when faced with a clear infringement of EU law; and to accept the EO's advice. A special report asking for EP support in persuading the Commission to correct its approach produced a resolution in which the EP asked for changes to a proposal for a new directive.[95]

Unlike a court, an ombudsman can monitor recommendations to see them implemented. The *Annual Reports* of the EO record follow-up on investigations and a practice has been introduced of highlighting 'star cases', where the institutional response has been particularly satisfactory. Investigations often produce rapid procedural change. In a complaint concerning Commission failure to deal properly with a request for access to documents, involving a year's delay in replying to the initial request, the EO stated that the Commission had clearly not handled the request for access promptly. As it had apologised, he would normally take no further action but in this case that would not be enough. He questioned the Commission about the efficacy of its staff training courses on implementing

---

[92] Inv 1840/2002/GG.
[93] Inv 2485/2004/GG; Inv 3446/2004/GG.
[94] Inv 1532/2008/(WP)GG; Inv 2591/2010/GG; Special Report concerning the inquiry into complaint 2591/2010/GG.
[95] EP Resolution of 12 March 2013 on the Special Report of the European Ombudsman concerning his inquiry into complaint 2591/2010/GG against the European Commission (Vienna Airport) (2012/2264(INI)). Following negotiations over amendment, the EP adopted its first reading position to the revised EIA Directive in March 2014; the Council will consider this in April 2014.

Regulation 1049/2001. The Commission replied that the Directorate-General (DG) at fault (DG Justice) had taken a number of steps to raise awareness of Regulation 1049/2001 among staff and management. It had distributed internal guidelines, to be published on its intranet website, on how to handle requests for access. These set the rules out in plain terms and explained the procedure to be followed from the registration of the request to the final drafting of the reply. Many staff had also participated in an in-house training session with training materials circulated after the session. DG Justice also encouraged its staff to participate in training sessions organised by the Secretariat-General and regularly distributed information on such sessions. This detailed response was duly starred by the EO in his *Annual Report*.[96]

After a visit to the European Systematic Risk Board, the EO made suggestions for tackling potential conflicts of interest, improving recruitment procedures, increasing general transparency and handling access to documents requests. A year later he recorded receipt of a follow-up action plan confirming that most of his suggestions had been adopted and that 'measures in the right direction' were in hand to implement the rest.[97] Again, the receipt of multiple complaints concerning the computerised 'Early Warning System' (EWS), which blacklists tenderers, contractors and other parties considered to pose a threat to the EU's financial interests, triggered an OII and public consultation. The EO issued a draft recommendation calling on the Commission 'to guarantee the rights of those targeted to be heard before they are listed, and also both to respect their right of access to their file and to ensure that it informs them of their rights to complain to the Ombudsman or to go to court'. The Commission replied that it intended to make changes, taking into account the EO's findings and litigation then in preliminary stages before the GC. On this basis, the EO closed his inquiry but not without calling for interim measures to ensure respect for fundamental rights in the period leading to the EWS review; the Commission should inform him about those measures.[98]

These examples nicely illustrate some different functions of courts and ombudsmen. Ombudsmen are usually easy to access; the CJEU has restrictive rules of standing and admissibility. Courts make authoritative rulings on the law containing, as we saw earlier, a measure of legal values, for which the administration usually shows a healthy respect. Ombudsmen exercise a valuable follow-up function, stipulating and monitoring implementation of appropriate procedures.

Values and Principles

The values on which Jacob Söderman, the first EO, would concentrate became evident in the first OII opened shortly after his installation, questioning Community

---

[96] Inv 849/2010/KM; Inv 3163/2007/(BEH)KM; *AR 2012*, 36.
[97] Inv OI/10/2012/EIS.
[98] Inv OI/3/2008/FOR; PR 13/2012. In Case C-314/11 P *Commission v Planet AE* (judgment of 19 December 2012), which mainly concerned admissibility, the Commission lost on all points.

institutions and bodies on their procedures for access to documents. The EO persuaded those that had no rules to introduce them, though he did not pronounce on the adequacy of existing rules[99] – perhaps because this was a very new office and its relations with the institutions were not yet clarified. There was certainly less reticence in the finding by Nikiforos Diamandorous that the Council's refusal to open its legislative proceedings to the public constituted maladministration – a finding that arguably took him to the very edge of his mandate.[100] Perhaps coincidentally, the finding pre-empted a change in the Council's procedural rules to allow Council deliberations, now held largely in public, to be broadcast on the Internet.[101] Both EOs have lobbied consistently for more generous access to information (see chapter five).[102]

Jacob Söderman was deeply committed to the idea that administration should be open, accountable, efficient and service-minded. Openness facilitated accountability and encouraged participation; it also acted as a deterrent against corruption. 'Service-mindedness' implied that the administration exists to serve citizens and not vice versa.[103] His first attempt to instil these values inside the EU administration was through the 'European Code of Good Administrative Behaviour',[104] a soft law instrument that requires officials to be objective, impartial, service-minded, correct, courteous and accessible to the public. They should 'try to be helpful', provide information to the public on request and reply as completely and accurately as possible to questions in the recipient's chosen language. Where necessary, they should apologise. In the Commission's own Code the points are made somewhat differently:

> The Commission and its staff have a duty to serve the Community interest and, in so doing, the public interest.
> The public legitimately expects quality service and an administration that is open, accessible and properly run.
> Quality service calls for the Commission and its staff to be courteous, objective and impartial.[105]

---

[99] Special Report and Decision by the EO following the Own-Initiative Inquiry into Public Access to Documents held by Community Institutions and Bodies (1997). And see R Rawlings, 'Engaged Elites: Citizen Action and Institutional Attitudes in Commission Enforcement' (2000) 6 *European Law Journal* 4.

[100] EO, Special Report following the draft recommendation to the Council in complaint 2395/2003/GG (2005); PR 12/2005, PR 13/2006 welcoming moves from the Austrian Presidency for greater transparency in the Council.

[101] Arts 7 and 8 of Council Decision 2006/83 [2006] OJ L285/47.

[102] See J Söderman, 'The role and impact of the EO in access to documentation and the transparency of decision-making' (EIPA seminar, Maastricht, 1997); N Diamandouros, 'Contribution of the EO to the public hearing on the Revision of Regulation 1049/2001' (LIBE, 2008).

[103] EO, *AR 2001*, 19.

[104] EO, 'The European Code of Good Administrative Behaviour', as approved by the European Parliament in September 2001. And see P Bonnor, 'The European Ombudsman: A Novel Source of Soft Law in the European Union' (2000) 25 *European Law Review* 39; M De Leeuw, 'The European Ombudsman's Role as a Developer of Norms of Good Administration' (2011) 17 *European Public Law* 349.

[105] Commission, 'Code of Good Administrative Behaviour. Relations with the Public' [2000] OJ L/267.

84 *Courts and Ombudsmen*

The EO is always mindful of his clientele, which has strongly influenced his attitude to Commission services.[106] Thus, when in 2009 he launched a statement of public service principles for EU civil servants, specific mention was made of contacts with citizens and civil society organisations and to the benefit that would accrue to the general public from a straightforward and concise statement of principle. A public consultation on the draft followed shortly after.[107] In 2012, following another public consultation, 'a high-level distillation of the ethical standards to which the EU public administration adheres' was added to the Code. Five important public service principles drawn from the Staff Regulations, Financial Regulation and Code of Good Administrative Behaviour – commitment, integrity, objectivity, respect for others and transparency – were singled out as the hallmarks of a good administration to be used as benchmarks for future investigations.[108]

COMPLAINTS HANDLING AND NETWORKS

The EO's fire-watching function extends to complaints handling. The Code requires officials to point out appeal and complaint rights and direct the citizen where necessary to the appropriate organisation. There are direct links too on the EO website to the Commission's informal complaints handling procedures. The 'Exercise your rights' section of the Commission website encourages citizens to 'exercise their rights', registers and promotes the informal pursuit of complaints.[109]

Problem-Solving through SOLVIT

SOLVIT, a Commission complaints handling service, was launched in a 2001 Communication as a 'problem-solving network'[110] in which Member States would work with the Commission to solve problems caused by the misapplication of internal market law by public authorities. SOLVIT provides a simple, informal online service. Anyone may lodge a complaint with the Commission against a Member State for any measure (law, regulation or administrative action) or practice attributable to a Member State that they consider incompatible with a provision or principle of EU law. The Commission will then take the matter up with SOLVIT centres in the Member States concerned. To exemplify, SOLVIT intervened successfully to obtain the registration in Belgium of a French student

---

[106] See N Diamandouros, 'The European Ombudsman: serving citizens' (23 September 2009).

[107] Results of the public consultation – Public service principles for EU civil servants (2011). There were only 56 responses.

[108] EO, *Public Service Principles for the EU Civil Service* (2012).

[109] See Commission, 'Updating the handling of relations with the complainant in respect of the application of Union law' (Communication) COM (2012) 154 final.

[110] Commission, 'Effective problem solving in the internal market (SOLVIT)' (Communication) COM (2001) 702 final.

entitled to register as a student under EU law but refused registration because the educational establishment in question was not recognised by the Belgian authorities. Redress would normally require litigation.

SOLVIT may secure change in administrative practices. When customers of a Swedish company marketing in Denmark could not obtain a customary government rebate because the requisite registration number was available only to companies registered in Denmark, the Danish authorities announced after SOLVIT's intervention that the number was no longer needed for the subsidy.[111] In 'SOLVIT plus' cases, where non-compliant national regulation is applied by a national public authority, SOLVIT centres can ask relevant national authorities to have the regulation amended, avoiding time-consuming and often ineffective calls for infringement proceedings. Dissatisfied complainants are advised how to go further – perhaps to an ombudsman. SOLVIT works on a purely voluntary basis, using informal, 'soft governance' techniques, though calls for formalisation have recently been heard, pointing to proceduralisation and the possibility of attracting questions over vires.

The EO tends to see a simple and accessible complaints system as a necessity for a well-functioning public authority. In 2012, he opened an OII to investigate concerns that Frontex, the EU borders agency, was failing to comply with the human rights obligations required by its governing regulation. This expressly stipulates compliance with the European Charter of Fundamental Rights (ECFR) and mandates codes of conduct for Frontex operations with administrative arrangements to promote and monitor compliance. The findings drew attention to the lack of internal complaints machinery to deal with violations of fundamental rights, an omission that the EO insisted should be rectified immediately, arguing that the gap meant not only that complainants would have no opportunity to have their complaints dealt with directly by Frontex, but also that Frontex would be less aware of concerns about the manner in which it operated. When Frontex refused to comply, arguing that complaints were 'ultimately the responsibility of the particular Member State on whose territory the incident occurred', the EO (now Emily O'Reilly) duly issued a special report asking for parliamentary support to secure compliance.[112]

The European Network of Ombudsmen (ENO)

In a multi-level governance system, complaints handling is complex and victims tend to fall through gaps, as illustrated in the paradigm case of *Kadi*, discussed in chapter twelve. The present authors have argued that such cases can only be

---

[111] Examples from 'SOLVIT, solutions to problems with your EU rights', available at http://ec.europa.eu/solvit/: And see M Lottini, 'From "Administrative Cooperation" in the Application of European Union Law to "Administrative Cooperation" in the Protection of European Rights and Liberties' (2012) 18 *European Public Law* 127.

[112] Inv OI/5/2012/BEH-MHZ.

resolved by cooperation between 'accountability agencies' specialising in accountability or dispute resolution, such as courts, parliaments or auditors.[113] SOLVIT marks the start of one such network; the ENO, set up in 1996 to link the 'European family of ombudsmen' through a network of liaison officers,[114] is another. To quote the Deputy EO: 'if citizens are to be protected against maladministration, co-operation among administrations needs to be matched by co-operation among ombudsmen through the European Network of Ombudsmen'.[115]

All but two of the 28 Member States have national ombudsmen and several have more, with regional and local ombudsmen or ombudsmen for particular services, each with limited competence. Even inside a single state, substantial differences exist between public sector ombudsmen in terms of functions, powers and orientations.[116] This makes complaining a difficult and not very user-friendly proposition. Like SOLVIT, the ENO works informally to resolve problems through voluntary cooperation. It shares experience and best practice via biannual seminars and meetings, a regular newsletter, an electronic discussion forum and a daily electronic news service. When, for example, Spanish citizens complained to the EO that the Commission was pushing the Spanish authorities to end free public libraries, the EO learned that the Spanish Ombudsman was handling similar complaints. The two ombudsmen agreed to share information and the EO requested information from other ENO ombudsmen on alternative ways of implementing EU law. No fewer than ten members of the network responded, providing information against which the Commission's decision to bring infringement proceedings against Spain could be measured.[117] More recently, when an Austrian citizen raised the issue of bee mortality through neonicotinoids with the Austrian Ombudsman Board, the Board registered a complaint with the EO, asking whether the Commission had conducted the requisite statutory review procedure as it should have done in view of new scientific evidence presented. Satisfied that the Commission was in the course of conducting a full review, the EO closed his inquiry after passing the information back to the Austrian Ombudsman.[118] In time, these straws in the wind might point the way to an effective supranational network of grievance handlers.

---

[113] Harlow and Rawlings, above (n 4).
[114] EO, *AR 1996*, 92–93; N Diamandouros, 'The role of the Ombudsman in future Europe and the mandates of Ombudsmen in future Europe' (31 March 2005). And see C Nassis, *Good Administration in the EU: The Role of the European Ombudsman and the European Network of Ombudsmen* (QUB: Esperia Publications, 2009).
[115] I Harden, 'The Ombudsman as a Remedy for the Protection of the Right to Good Administration', speech made at Vilnius, 14–15 April 2005).
[116] See R Lawson, *General report to the fifth seminar of the National Ombudsmen of EU Member States* (The Hague: European Ombudsman, 2005).
[117] Inv 3452/2004/JMA.
[118] Inv 512/2012/BEH.

GOOD ADMINISTRATION AND FUNDAMENTAL RIGHTS

We have so far been discussing the work of administrators, legislators, judges and ombudsmen in building EU administrative procedure. After the 1999 Cologne Council, however, when drafting of a human rights charter was under consideration, Jacob Söderman argued strongly in his opening speech to the Convention for a Charter right to good administration.[119] The time was ripe to acknowledge 'at the level of principle' a citizen's right to have his or her affairs dealt with 'properly, fairly and promptly by an open, accountable and service-minded public administration'. Such a right would 'have a broad impact on Member States' and help 'to make the twenty-first century the century of good administration'. Practical implementation should be assured in regulations.

The eventual outcome was ECFR Article 41, which reads:

1. Every person has the right to have his or her affairs handled impartially, fairly and within a reasonable time by the institutions, bodies, offices and agencies of the Union.
2. This right includes:
    (a) the right of every person to be heard, before any individual measure which would affect him or her adversely is taken;
    (b) the right of every person to have access to his or her file, while respecting the legitimate interests of confidentiality and of professional and business secrecy;
    (c) the obligation of the administration to give reasons for its decisions.
3. Every person has the right to have the Union make good any damage caused by its institutions or by its servants in the performance of their duties, in accordance with the general principles common to the laws of the Member States.
4. Every person may write to the institutions of the Union in one of the languages of the Treaties and must have an answer in the same language.

Article 41 is an attempt, albeit limited, at a positive delineation of good administration but it is narrow – narrower than the European Code of Good Administrative Behaviour or even the EO's distillation of Public Service Principles. Most of its provisions are picked up without amplification from EU sources: paragraph (1) is a general principle recognised by all institutions; paragraph (2) fastens on a limited number of judicially-pronounced due process rights; paragraph (3) replicates TEC Article 288; paragraph (4) repeats TEC Article 21. It is in short, 'merely a non-exhaustive list of pre-existing rights ... which all seem to be part more intuitively than demonstrably of good administration'.[120] Moreover, the right is applicable only to 'the institutions, bodies, offices and agencies of the Union' and is

---

[119] EO, speech at the public hearing on the draft Charter of Fundamental Rights of the European Union: preliminary remarks (2 February 2000); 'The Struggle for Openness in the EU' (speech to ECAS, 21 March 2001).

[120] R Bhousa, 'Who Said there is a "Right to Good Administration"? A Critical Analysis of Article 41 of the Charter of Fundamental Rights of the European Union' (2013) 19 *European Public Law* 481, 482.

therefore ill-equipped to deal with joint and shared administration and composite decision-making.

This does not mean that we should discount the symbolic value of Article 41 insofar as it ensconces the EU citizen at the forefront of EU public administration and installs 'service-mindedness' as its primary value.[121] In this respect it has recently been invoked by the EP in pressing the argument for a 'European Law of Administrative Procedure' (see chapter thirteen). Mainstream commitment to the Charter by the Union institutions at a practical level has, however, been described as negligible.[122] The Commission's response to the Charter was generally muted. It undertook to promote a 'fundamental rights culture' by publishing a human rights checklist and providing training to its staff. It guaranteed to mainstream Charter rights at all stages of administrative procedure, 'from the initial drafting of a proposal within the Commission to the impact analysis, and right up to the checks on the legality of the final text' and to report annually on implementation of these policies.[123] The letter of the law is in this respect observed. An EU Fundamental Rights Agency (FRA) set up in 2007 and tasked with providing 'independent, evidence-based advice on fundamental rights', is expected to provide backup to the institutions and 'to play an active role in clarifying the scope of the Charter to citizens'.[124] Perhaps good administration does not figure high on the list of human rights seen by the agency as fundamental; certainly, references to Article 41 do not figure prominently in its publications.

Article 41 could in time be moulded by the Courts into a principle of considerable significance. In his 1999 analysis of the economic case law, Nehl believed that he was 'watching the birth of a judicial general principle of sound administration', as references to 'due diligence' or 'duty of care' began to appear in the case law.[125] In the *Maxmobil* case, the GC expressly associated the principle with ECFR Article 41, stating that

> diligent and impartial treatment of a complaint is associated with the right to sound administration, which is one of the general principles that are observed in a State governed by the rule of law and are common to the constitutional traditions of the Member States.[126]

---

[121] See K Kanska, 'Towards Administrative Human Rights in the EU: Impact of the Charter of Fundamental Rights' (2004) 10 *European Law Journal* 296.

[122] S Smismans, 'The European Union's Fundamental Rights Myth' (2010) 48 *Journal of Common Market Studies* 45.

[123] Commission, 'Strategy for the effective implementation of the Charter of Fundamental Rights by the European Union' (Communication) COM (2010) 573 final, 1.1.

[124] See Council Regulation (EC) 168/2007 of 15 February 2007 establishing a European Union Agency for Fundamental Rights [2007] OJ L53/1. And see FRA, External Evaluation of the Agency (2012), 5, 7.

[125] Nehl, above (n 48) ch 9.

[126] Case T-54/99 *Maxmobil Telekommunikation Service GmbH v Commission* [2002] ECR II-0313, [48].

But this reasoning met a cold reception in the CoJ, which pushed the GC back onto traditional grounds: checking the facts and statement of reasons to a standard of manifest error.[127] There are as yet no signs of repentance.[128] At the practical level then, Article 41 has not achieved its full potential.

In the context of administrative procedure, Article 41(4), which highlights the administrative importance of language as the primary means of communication in a multilingual community, deserves a mention.[129] Language has always played an important part in the development of the EU. A specialised DG is responsible for translation into the 24 official languages at high cost to the budget. Linguistic rights are protected by Articles 24 and 118 of the Treaty on the Functioning of the European Union and occasionally recognised by the Courts, though usually only in staff cases.[130] Article 13 of the EO's 'Code of Good Administrative Behaviour' introduces a new note. It mentions the need to correspond with citizens in their chosen language and the EO has underlined the 'paramount importance for citizens to be able to access information in a language they can understand'. It would be 'ideal' for material intended for external communication with citizens to be published in *all* official languages and for documents directed to persons outside the EU institutions to be available in as many languages as possible.[131] He has also criticised the Commission for publishing a consultation paper only in English.[132] Not only does this reflect the intention to promote citizen interest and participation in EU affairs expressed in the Lisbon treaty but it may also point to a new period in the life of the EU in which greater recognition is given to the principle of subsidiarity, pluralism and the wish of people to preserve their characteristic cultures. This would have the effect of prioritising democratic input values over the administrative output values of efficiency.

Procedure as a Human Right

Although human rights texts characteristically prioritise substantive rights, procedural issues have come to figure increasingly on the human rights agenda, as chapter twelve of this book amply demonstrates.[133] Chapter twelve also illustrates the point that the Luxembourg Courts preferred – at least until recently – to base their judgments in human rights cases on the general principles of EU law rather

---

[127] Case C-141/02 P *Commission v T-Mobile Austria GmbH* [2005] ECR I-1283, [16]–[21].
[128] H-P Nehl, 'Good Administration as a Procedural Right or General Principle' in H Hofmann and A Türk (eds), *Legal Challenges in Administrative Law: Towards an Integrated Administration* (Cheltenham: Edward Elgar, 2009).
[129] M Aziz, 'Mainstreaming the Duty of Clarity and Transparency as part of Good Administrative Practice in the EU' (2004) 10 *European Law Journal* 282.
[130] eg Case 79/74 *Küster v Parliament* [1975] ECR 725; Case C-566/10 P *Italy v Commission* (judgment of 27 November 2012).
[131] Inv 2876/2008/(VL)BEH.
[132] Inv 0640/2011/AN.
[133] See further, C Harlow, 'Global Administrative Law: The Quest for Principles and Values' (2006) 17 *European Journal of International Law* 187.

than on the Charter or other human rights texts.[134] Since the Charter has acquired treaty status, they have, however, begun to refer to it more frequently.[135] It could be said that the CoJ is as yet a relative novice in human rights issues, though we see this position as likely to change swiftly with the increased authority of the Charter and the extended jurisdiction of the CJEU over the area of justice and home affairs. In *NS and others v SSHD*,[136] for example, the applicants challenged a decision by the UK Government to return them to Greece for determination of their asylum claims in terms of the governing 'Member State responsible' policy. Their case against *refoulement* was that the Greek asylum system did not comply with the common standards of EU law, including the directive on minimum procedural standards.[137] Basing itself on the substantive right in ECFR Article 4, the CoJ ruled that Member States may not transfer an asylum seeker to a state where 'systemic deficiencies in the asylum procedure' give substantial grounds for believing that she or he would face a real risk of inhuman or degrading treatment. Arguably, systematic procedural deficiencies point also to violations of Article 41, though this was not mentioned. Again, in the *Digital Rights Ireland* case mentioned earlier,[138] the challenge was mounted on ECFR Articles 7 and 8. The CoJ stated that interference with these rights was 'particularly serious' and merited 'strict' application of the proportionality principle.

Although the Council of Europe has a considerable record of work on public administration,[139] no general right to good administration was contained in its Convention on Human Rights (ECHR). ECHR Articles 5 and 6 do, however, give specific protection to due process rights and procedures and Article 13, which deals with the question of effective remedy, may sometimes have an impact on cases of maladministration.[140] Despite strenuous efforts to prevent differing or even conflicting interpretations of human rights law,[141] the two supreme European Courts have clashed on these issues, notably in the area of competition

---

[134] See H Hofmann and C Mihaescu, 'The Relation between the Charter's Fundamental Rights and the Unwritten General Principles of EU Law: Good Administration as the Test Case' (2013) 9 *European Constitutional Law Review* 73.

[135] According to G de Búrca, 'After the EU Charter of Fundamental Rights: The Court of Justice as a Human Rights Adjudicator?' (2013) 20 *Maastricht Journal of European and Comparative Law* 168, 169, between 2009 and 2012, the CoJ 'engaged substantially' with the ECFR in 27 of 122 references and the GC did so in 7 of 37.

[136] Joined Cases C-411 and 493/10 *NS and others v SSHD* [2011] ECR I-13905.

[137] Council Directive 2005/85/EC OJ L 326, 13.12.2005.

[138] Joined Cases C-293 and 594/12 *Digital Rights Ireland and Seitlinger and Others* (judgment of 8 April 2014), above (n 13).

[139] See, eg, Council of Europe, Resolution (77) 31 (28 September 1977); Council of Europe, *The Administration and You* (Council of Europe Publications, 1996).

[140] eg, *Osman v United Kingdom* [1998] EHRR 101.

[141] Notably *Bosphorus Hava Yollari Turizm ve Ticaret Anonim Sirket v Ireland* (2006) 42 EHRR 1; O De Schutter, 'The Two Lives of *Bosphorus*: Redefining the Relationships between the European Court of Human Rights and the Parties to the Convention' (2013) 4 *European Journal of Human Rights* 584.

procedure.[142] References to the ECHR in the CoJ case law are as yet relatively infrequent,[143] a position that may have to change if the EU accedes to the ECHR. Accession, authorised by the Lisbon Treaty (TEU Article 6(2)), is currently under negotiation and awaits ratification by the Council of Europe Assembly – which should not be too easily assumed.[144] On accession, the EU institutions will for the first time be directly bound by the ECHR and the CJEU, as an EU institution, will have to pay much greater deference to ECtHR rulings in cases to which the EU is a party. This radical change will open the CoJ to a welcome degree of external scrutiny by a powerful judicial competitor.[145]

CONCLUSION

The title of this long chapter is 'Firefighting and Fire-Watching' and we have used our space to focus primarily on fire-watching. We first examined the way in which the Luxembourg Courts and EO have used their fire-watching functions to influence EU administrative procedure. We looked at the values that they try to inculcate and considered the impact on administrators and administration. Both institutions engage in procedural standard-setting and both have helped to shape EU administration yet they stand in somewhat different positions and their style and techniques differ. Courts operate through the evolution of general principles embodied in judgments that technically bind administration; ombudsmen operate through soft law recommendations and monitoring.

The firefighting mission of the CJEU to see EU law enforced is executed at two different levels. At Union level, it reviews the processes and decisions of EU institutions and agencies, working through the limited grounds for review to enunciate general principle. These, as we have tried to show, reflect established judicial values drawn in the first instance from the administrative law of Member States. While the Courts have no direct access to the administrative process, their indirect impact has been very considerable. At Member State level, the Courts' relationship with national administration is doubly indirect, being based on national

---

[142] Case 374/87 *Orkem v Commission* [1989] ECR. 3283; Joined Cases 46/87 and 227/88 *Hoechst v Commission* [1989] ECR 2859; *Funke v France* (1993) 15 EHRR 297. And see C Dautricourt, 'A Strasbourg Perspective on the Autonomous Development of Fundamental Rights in EU Law: Trends and Implications' (2010) Jean Monnet Working Paper 10/10.

[143] Of 122 cases in which the CoJ referred to the ECFR there were 20 ECHR references: De Búrca, above (n 125) 7.

[144] For the negotiated text at the time of writing, see European Council, *Accession of the European Union to the European Convention for the protection of Human Rights and Fundamental Freedoms (ECHR): State of play* (November 2012). And see J-P Jacqué, 'The Accession of the European Union to the European Convention on Human Rights and Fundamental Freedoms' (2011) 48 *Common Market Law Review* 995.

[145] Though the German Constitutional Court has contested both competence and performance of the CoJ in human rights cases since the celebrated decision in *Internationale Handel gesellschaft mbh* BVerfGE 37, 271 (1974). On the current relationship, see Special Issue, 'The OMT Decision of the German Federal Constitutional Court' (2014) 15(2) *German Law Journal* 107–382.

courts and through them with national administration. As later chapters show, this process tends to attract charges of intrusiveness and bias towards integration.

The EO avoids this dilemma, his primary function being to investigate complaints of maladministration by Union institutions and agencies. His investigatory method gives him direct access to administration, allowing him to working directly to promote good governance. We have seen the EO transform a primarily firefighting mandate into a vehicle for standard-setting and fire-watching, a quasi-political function that we shall follow later in the area of freedom of information (see chapter five). Unlike the CJEU, the EO has no 'binding' powers of enforcement but, as we have tried to show, his interventions are nonetheless effective. The EO has no direct relationship with national administrations but has used his fire-watching function efffectively to build a 'soft governance' complaints handling network that may in time do much to spread good governance principles across EU administration.

Finally, we have traced the progression of good governance principles into a constitutionalised fundamental right. Article 41 of the EU Charter, to which both Courts and Ombudsman have contributed, provides EU citizens with a right to good administration. This right is at present underdeveloped and much of what we say is therefore speculative. Interpreted widely, Article 41 could act as an important and badly needed stimulant for good administration throughout the common 'European administrative space'. It could come to be valued as an important fundamental right of citizenship, as is certainly not the case as present. This would, however, entail a shift in priorities between input and output values of good administration. This important question is further addressed in chapter thirteen.

4

Input and Output Values: Executive Law-Making

NO BOOK ON administrative process could sensibly omit materials on executive law-making and this book is no exception. In chapter two, we looked briefly at the role of 'soft law' or informal bureaucratic rule-making in the 'soft governance' methods used by the Commission to forward cooperation between the actors in its many policy networks. This chapter provides a study of formal executive law-making in the EU – a term that we use with caution. The concern of administrative law with law-making is normally limited to law-making by the executive, leaving law-making by the legislature as the terrain of constitutional law. Executive legislation takes two main forms: some constitutions, such as that of France, recognise an inherent executive power to legislate in matters affecting its functions; in contrast, in the common law world, executive legislation is seen as a 'delegated' power authorised by the legislature.

Legislation has never in practice been the sole responsibility of a legislature, however; it is an output function of government, shared by legislature, executive and administration. Increasingly, officials play a large part in law-making, drafting legislation, filling in the details, often procedural, of 'framework laws' made by the legislature and completing complex legislative schemes.[1] The vogue for 'evidence-based' law and 'better regulation' has heightened the role of administrators, who carry out and shape the pre-legislative impact assessment (IA) and consultation exercises on which law and regulation is increasingly founded and also the post-legislative evaluation that often follows. In the EU, the fuzzy divide is further blurred by the character of the law-making process. TEU Article 17(2) allows legislative acts to be adopted only on the basis of a Commission proposal unless the Treaties provide otherwise; and 'other acts' may be adopted on the basis of a Commission proposal if the Treaties so provide (as they often do). This puts the Commission in a uniquely powerful position as combined policymaker and lawmaker – and indeed makes the cut-off point between legislative and administrative process chosen in our introduction somewhat hard to maintain.

In national governance systems, the chief justifications for delegated legislation are functional in character: executive legislation saves parliamentary time; it deals

---

[1] See E Page, *Governing by Numbers: Delegated Legislation and Everyday Policymaking* (Oxford: Hart Publishing, 2001).

with detailed, procedural elements of administrative process; it is essential to cater for the increasingly technical nature of much modern regulation, etc. In recent years, however, a wider movement for democratic governance and participatory input has taken root, reflecting a conception of the EU as a polity based on democratic values. This has led to demands for 'input values' to be expressed in rule-making. In this chapter, we chart the growing movement for citizen participation in executive rule-making and try to evaluate the effectiveness of new administrative procedures evolving to meet this demand. Reflecting the debate over 'democratic deficit', the struggle for input values is keenest in respect of the comitology process described below, where we visit the struggle for 'government in the sunshine' in the specific context of law-making.

The argument for democracy has now moved on to demand participation rights for civil society in policymaking and rule-making. In this regard, the Lisbon Treaty, which underscored input values in TEU Article 11, is often seen to mark a new beginning. Article 11(4) introduced the European Citizens' Initiative (ECI), which purports to involve citizens directly in the initiation of European legislative proposals. We critically consider the administrative procedures deemed necessary to implement (or perhaps impede) this innovation. We also evaluate Commission efforts to encourage a more vigorous European civil society, resulting in a heavy proceduralisation of consultation procedures. The chapter reflects an assumed progression from output values of efficiency and effectiveness with the executive firmly in the driving seat to democratic input values of openness and participation. The reality is, we shall suggest, somewhat different.

LAW-MAKING AND DELEGATION

In the EU, a creature of delegation, it would seem logical that *all* its regulatory powers, based on the 'pooled sovereignty' of Member States, were delegated in character. Such a conclusion would, however, certainly surprise and probably annoy most EU lawyers and is hardly consonant with the Lisbon Treaty, which speaks throughout of 'Union law', prescribes co-decision as 'the ordinary legislative procedure' and describes 'legal acts adopted by legislative procedure' in the form of regulation, directives and decisions, as 'legislative acts' (Articles 288, 289(1)).[2] For the first time, the Treaty also distinguishes 'delegated' from 'implementing' legislation, specifically designating delegated acts made in terms of Article 290 as 'non-legislative acts' and requiring the word 'implementing' to be inserted in the title of implementing acts.

---

[2] Where possible we have avoided the legal technicalities of this terminology. But see J-C Piris, *The Lisbon Treaty, A Legal and Political Analysis* (Cambridge: CUP, 2010) ch 11; H Hofmann, 'Legislation, Delegation and Implementation under the Treaty of Lisbon: Typology meets Reality' (2009) 15 *European Law Journal* 482; H Hofmann, G Rowe and A Türk, *Administrative Law and Policy of the European Union* (Oxford: OUP, 2011) 524–35.

As we have explained, the Court of Justice (CoJ) in its *Meroni*[3] jurisprudence recognised delegation only within very narrow limits and confirmed in an important case,[4] decided shortly before the Lisbon Treaty, that no implicit power to make delegated legislation could be assumed. The Council, in the course of negotiating a regulation on asylum procedure required by the Treaties, had failed to agree a list of safe countries. Unwilling to lose control in this sensitive area, it took new powers to establish a list, specifying consultation procedure rather than the co-decision stipulated in the Treaty, which gives much greater power to the European Parliament (EP). Before the Court, the Council advanced the argument that a power to make delegated legislation was inherent in the Treaty. The CoJ was unconvinced; law-making and decision-making procedures were established by the Treaties and were 'not at the disposal of the Member States or of the institutions themselves'; to rule otherwise would 'undermine the principle of institutional balance'. Delegation can take place therefore only within the parameters of TFEU Articles 290 and 291.

Although the Court left the Commission without power to make delegated legislation, it did validate the rule-making powers needed for expanding Community programmes. In *Köster*,[5] procedure used to introduce licensing of cereals in the common agricultural market was challenged on the basis that the licensing scheme ought to have been the subject of a Commission proposal voted through by the Council (then the Community legislator). The CoJ, however, confirmed the legality of the delegation, while once more insisting that the delegator must retain control. In providing for 'implementing regulations', the Council must set out 'the basic elements of the matter to be dealt with' and authorise the mode of proceeding, in this case by 'management committee' procedure, explained below. Again in *Rey Soda* the CoJ upheld the conferral on the Commission of 'wide powers of discretion and action', ruling that they should be exercised under the 'so-called management committee procedure, a mechanism which allows the Council to give the Commission an appreciably wide power of implementation whilst reserving where necessary its own right to intervene'.[6] These decisions opened the door to the wide use of implementing powers to regulate markets, in agricultural policy and in areas of scientific and technological complexity, such as food safety, pharmaceuticals or biotechnology. If, in the context of agencies, the *Meroni* doctrine may seem an anachronistic hindrance,[7] in the law-making context, it provides a very necessary control.

---

[3] Case 9/56 *Meroni v High Authority* [1957/58] ECR 133; see above, ch 1, p 32.
[4] Case C133/06 *Parliament v Council* [2008] ECR.I-3189 noted by Craig (2009) 46 *Common Market Law Review* 193.
[5] Case 25/70 *Einfuhr- und Vorratsstelle für Getreide und Futtermittel v Köster, Berodt & Co* [1970] ECR 1161.
[6] Case 23/75 *Rey Soda v Cassa Conguaglio Zucchero* [1975] ECR 1279, [12], [13].
[7] See below, ch 10, pp 32–4.

Scientific Knowledge and Technocratic Rule-Making: Output Legitimacy

Traditional justifications for delegation developed in the early nineteenth-century blend with the late twentieth-century case for regulation by experts. In the EU, where risk regulation is a central function and difficult economic issues predominate, the output values encapsulated in the managerial adage of economy, efficiency and effectiveness are important. However, even technical regulation is not without some input values, notably the due process requirements that safeguard the interests of those affected by regulation, as discussed in chapter three.

The argument from expertise, used initially to justify transfers of rule-making power from inexpert legislators to a professional administration, was later turned against generalist administrators, who had to cede power to 'experts', seated on committees or based in agencies supposedly staffed by experts. Thus, the White Paper on European Governance (WPEG) conceded that agencies, initially purely advisory, might be authorised to take individual decisions in specific areas, notably where 'a single public interest predominates and the tasks to be carried out require particular technical expertise (eg air safety)'. They should not, however, adopt general regulatory measures.[8] The White Paper on Food Safety, which served as a basis for the European Food Safety Authority (EFSA), reflected this pattern, saying that 'the drafting and making of legislation will remain the responsibility of the Commission, the Parliament and the Council'. This was carried over into the governing legislation, which authorises the EFSA to 'provide scientific advice and scientific and technical support for the Community's legislation and policies in all fields which have a direct or indirect impact on food and feed safety'.[9] Hesitantly, however, EU agencies are being entrusted with rule-making powers (see chapter eleven).

The argument for expertise leads also to a further transfer of rule-making and standard-setting powers: to transnational networks in which EU bodies and agencies may participate. This may involve private cooperation in norm-formation, usually within a specific public policy area, as in the case of the European Committee for Standardization (CEN), the European Committee for Electrotechnical Standardization (CENELEC) and the EU Emissions Trading System (ETS). These are semi-public bodies set up as private international non-profit organisations. They exist to coordinate and draft technical standards relating to products, services and telecommunication systems applicable within the EU and globally.[10] Initially, rules made by such networks are 'soft law', which may be consensually adopted by

---

[8] Commission, 'European Governance – A White Paper' COM (2001) 428 final, 24 (hereafter WPEG).

[9] Commission, 'White Paper on Food Safety' COM (1999) 719 final, 63; Art 22 of Regulation (EC) 178/2002 of 28 January 2002 laying down the general principles and requirements of food law, establishing the European Food Safety Authority and laying down procedures in matters of food safety [2002] OJ L31/1.

[10] H Schepel, *The Constitution of Private Governance – Product Standards in the Regulation of Integrating Markets* (Oxford: Hart Publishing, 2005) 241–46.

the network participants; alternatively, it may be made enforceable by the Council as legislature or Commission as executive authority. Technically not a subdelegation, the process raises similar issues of participation, transparency and access.

AN EU INNOVATION: LAW-MAKING BY COMMITTEE

The Council's attitude to EU law-making and – perhaps more important – that of the diplomats who serve the Council in Coreper (the Permanent Representatives Committee) derives in many ways from international practice and procedure. The Council has tended to cling to diplomatic practice, resisting attempts to open up the legislative process to public scrutiny and jealous of the rising European Parliament (EP). Thus, reflecting standard practice in treaty negotiation, comitology committees are representative of Member States; scientific committees, for example, are composed of independent experts but the experts are nominated by the Member States. This standard representative model was later taken forward into agency management boards.[11]

Securing institutional agreement over comitology procedure proved more than usually difficult. The First Comitology Decision[12] took effect just before the Single European Act (SEA) entered into force in 1987. Procedurally it was formal and legalistic. Four fixed models of committee procedure were provided from which the Council could choose when conferring implementing powers on the Commission:[13]

- **Advisory committee procedure** required the Commission to take 'the utmost account' of the committee's opinion, but did not formally bind it.
- **Management committee procedure** allowed the Commission to adopt an implementing measure before referring it to the committee. In case of a negative opinion, the Commission was obliged under the strictest form of the procedure to suspend the measure; in a looser variant, it could choose whether or not to suspend. The measure was referred back to the Council, which could annul or amend it within a three-month period. Only if it did not do this could the Commission proceed.
- **Regulatory committee procedure** allowed the committee to consider a text in draft form. A positive opinion entitled the Commission to proceed 'in accordance with the opinion of the committee'; a negative opinion, or no opinion, meant that the Commission had to submit a proposal without delay to the Council, which at least in the *contre-filet* procedure, possessed a right of veto.

---

[11] E Vos, '50 Years of European Integration, 45 Years of Comitology' (2009) 3 *Maastricht online Working Papers* 4.

[12] Council Decision 87/373/EEC of 13 July 1987, laying down the procedures for the exercise of implementing powers conferred on the Commission [1987] OJ L19/87.

[13] See for a detailed account, F Bergstrom, *Comitology: Delegation of Powers in the European Union and the Committee System* (Oxford: OUP, 2005) 195–207.

98   *Executive Law-making*

- **'Safeguard procedure'**, used mainly in the area of international trade, provided that committee procedure might be dispensed with or an ad hoc committee used. It gave the last word sometimes to the Commission, sometimes to the Council.

The Decision also regulated committee voting procedure; where a vote became necessary, it closely mirrored Council voting procedure.

These procedures satisfied no one. They were rigid yet uncertain and complex. They did not guarantee the Council's place as 'master of the Treaties' and left no place for the EP, which immediately challenged them in court.[14] A destructive inter-institutional battle ensued in which the procedures were systematically manipulated – as procedures tend to be – for political ends. To the Commission's annoyance, the Council adopted the 'unhelpful practice' of regularly attaching to legislation 'a blocking mechanism whereby it can prevent a decision being taken'.[15] The EP was equally obstructive. It steadily rejected Commission proposals for joint EP–Council harmonisation measures, arguing that comitology procedure was inapplicable to legislation passed by co-decision. It inserted 'sunset clauses' into legislation and passed amendments substituting the less onerous for the more restrictive comitology procedures preferred by the Council. It blocked funding. The EP was thus able to secure through the soft law tool of inter-institutional agreement concessions that significantly modified the governing statutory procedures. The Plumb–Delors agreement, for example, committed the Commission to supply the EP with draft measures at the same time as the comitology committee, while the *modus vivendi* provided that the EP should be given prior notice of and information about proposed measures together with an opportunity to express its views.[16]

The Second Comitology Decision,[17] enacted in 1999 after prolonged and difficult negotiations, had three avowed objectives: (i) to issue guidance on the selection of comitology committees; (ii) to clarify and simplify management procedure; and (iii) to standardise criteria for their use. Management procedure should be used for 'management measures', especially for implementing common agricultural and fisheries policy and programmes with substantial budgetary implications; regulatory procedure for 'measures of general scope designed to apply essential provisions of basic instruments' or 'designed to adapt or update certain non-essential provisions of a basic instrument'. The general fallback position was an advisory committee, leaving the Commission with maximum discretion.

---

[14] Ruled inadmissible in Case 302/87 *Parliament v Council (Comitology)* [1988] ECR 5615. Comitology procedure was later validated in Case 70/88 *Parliament v Council (Chernobyl)* [1990] ECR I-2041.

[15] Commission, 'Conferment of implementing powers on the Commission' (Communication) (SEC (90) 2589 final) 10–11.

[16] See A Maurer et al, *'Inter-institutional Agreements in the CFSP: Parliamentarisation through the Backdoor?'* (Pittsburgh University Archive of European Integration, 2005). The full story is told by K St John Bradley at (1992) 29 *Common Market Law Review* 693; (1997) 3 *European Law Journal* 230; (2008) 31 *West European Politics* 837.

[17] Council Decision 1999/468/EC of 28 June 1999 laying down the procedures for the exercise of implementing powers conferred on the Commission [1999] OJ L184/23.

The key difference between management and regulatory procedure now lay in the degree of Council control: in regulatory procedure, the Council became involved whenever the committee failed to vote in favour; in management committee procedure only when the committee voted against the measure. Simplified management procedure allowed the Commission to introduce measures immediately, though negative opinions had to be reported to the Council, which had three months to take a different decision. The EP gained from regulatory procedure where, in the event of disagreement with the committee, the Commission had without delay to submit to the Council a proposal relating to the measures to be taken and notify the EP; if the proposal seemed to the EP to be ultra vires, it could say so to the Commission. Only if the Council failed to react or voted against the proposal could it be adopted by the Commission as it stood.

The Commission expressed its dissatisfaction not only to the Constitutional Convention (where it led in time to a true power of delegation) but also in the WPEG, which questioned 'the need to maintain existing committees, notably regulatory and management committees'.[18] Stressing the need for clarity in the legislative process, the Commission argued for 'a simple legal mechanism' allowing its implementation functions to be tested by the Council and EP against the empowering legislation. Arguably, the 2006 revisions moved in precisely the opposite direction with **regulatory committee procedure with scrutiny**.[19] This introduced a scrutiny committee composed of Member State representatives and chaired by the Commission to vote on draft texts. The Council and EP gained a veto power, exercisable within certain complicated time limits *whether or not* the scrutiny committee approved the draft text, while implementing measures could only be maintained in force provisionally on health protection, safety or environmental grounds. However, the new scrutiny powers were not as substantial as they seemed. They applied only to legislation enacted by co-decision when it authorised implementing measures 'of general scope' designed to amend 'non-essential elements' of the basic legislation. Moreover, the legislators could intervene only when draft measures seemed to exceed the powers granted in the governing legislation.

The nebulous terminology of 'essential' and 'non-essential' elements of legislation, taken up at Lisbon, was always likely to require frequent judicial interpretation and has in fact already been litigated. The 'Frontex Regulation',[20] made in the context of the Schengen Borders Code, establishes a new borders agency, Frontex, empowering it in urgent cases to draw up an operational plan and deploy a Rapid Border Intervention Team at the request of a Member State. The Regulation stipulates 'Comitology 3 procedure' in making implementing rules. A Commission draft decision, designed to deal with a steadily rising death toll caused by mari-

---

[18] WPEG, 31.

[19] Council Decision 2006/512/EC of 17 July 2006 amending Decision 1999/468/EC laying down the procedures for the exercise of implementing powers conferred on the Commission [2006] OJ L200/11 (the Third Comitology Decision).

[20] Council Regulation (EC) 2007/2004 [2004] OJ L349/1, as amended.

time 'people trafficking', stated that the 'rules and the non-binding guidelines . . . shall form part of the operational plan drawn up for each operation coordinated by the Agency', effectively fettering the discretion of Member States. When the appropriate comitology committee failed to deliver an opinion, the Commission sent the draft to the Council and EP. The EP did not veto the decision, giving the somewhat curious reason that, given the urgency of the situation, an imperfect legal instrument was better than none; later, however, the EP did challenge the decision as ultra vires.[21]

The Council and Commission argued first that the action was inadmissible because the EP had failed to exercise its right of veto. The CoJ responded that 'administrative procedures' could not be a substitute for judicial review nor could labelling the relevant rules 'non-binding guidelines' disguise their essential quality as rules. Disputing the meaning of the term 'essential elements', the Council next presented the audacious argument that it was for the legislature to 'fix the limits of the delegation, define what the essential aims of the basic legislation are and also decide the essential elements which cannot be delegated to the Commission'. It was therefore enough 'to define the general objectives and basic methods by granting the Commission the authorisation to adopt, in case of need, supplementary measures which are relevant to surveillance, and extensive implementing powers'. Not unnaturally the Court rejected this contention. Determining whether 'essential elements' had been delegated was not – contrary to the Council and Commission's claim – a question solely for the legislature, but 'must be based on objective factors amenable to judicial review'. In this case, the conferral of enforcement powers on border guards was a policy matter requiring the attention of the legislature.

What followed is a paradigm example of reasons why administration may seek to bypass formal legislative processes. The Commission duly presented a proposal for new legislation in line with the Court's requirements[22] but progress was blocked by six Mediterranean Member States, arguing – apparently contrary to the Court's conclusions – that the proposal fell outside the EU competence.

Comitology 3 had by no means ended pressure for reform. Little had been done to reduce the complexity of the system; it could indeed be said to have been significantly increased. The time normally taken to make implementing regulations had potentially been lengthened.[23] Moreover, by involving the EP in the comitology system[24] and incorporating the two legislative bodies into the regulatory procedure, Comitology 3 had arguably produced an unfortunate hybrid executive–legislative

---

[21] Decision 2010/252/EU [2010] OJ L111/20; Case C-355/10 *Parliament v Council* (judgment of 5 September 2012).

[22] Commission, Proposal, COM (2013) 197 final. And see S Peers, 'EU Rules on Maritime Rescue: Member States Quibble while Migrants Drown' *Statewatch Analysis* (22 October 2013).

[23] T Christiansen and B Vaccari, 'The 2006 Reform of Comitology', EIPA Scope 2006/39, 13.

[24] G Schusterschitz and S Kotz, 'The Comitology Reform of 2006. Increasing the Powers of the European Parliament without Changing the Treaties' (2007) 3 *European Constitutional Law Review* 68.

process, undercutting the output rationale for executive regulation while doing little to enhance democratic input processes.[25]

Comitology and Transparency

A year before Comitology 2, an influential committee of the UK Parliament insisted that:

> A full and authoritative list of comitology committees, their functions and activities should be readily available to the public. In addition, it should be possible to obtain precise details of the remit of each committee, membership and agendas. Rules of procedure should be published. All comitology proposals and working documents should be accessible on the same terms as other Commission or Council documents. Opinions of the committees should be made public. Full use should be made of the Internet to ensure rapid publication of information and facilitate consultation of interested parties.[26]

If Comitology 2 did not go this far, it did take tentative steps towards greater transparency. It made the principles of public access to Commission documents[27] applicable to comitology committees. It required the Commission to list every comitology committee together with its legal basis and publish the information in the *Official Journal* (OJ); to present an annual report about committee proceedings; and to report regularly to the EP on the basis of a Comitology Register. This had to include data on committee meetings, agendas, draft texts of implementing measures, lists of authorities representing the Member States, voting results and summary records of meetings, all of which are theoretically now available online.[28]

We should not assume, however, that the transparency of comitology committees is thereby assured. Studies of the Register have found serious defects. Only documents labelled 'publicly accessible' are available on the Register; others are listed by name and date and can be accessed only by a formal request in terms of Regulation 1049/2001.[29] *Muñiz*[30] exemplifies common complaints of poor quality and minimal information in comitology proceedings. The Commission had published the formal decision of a management committee based on earlier proceedings in a working group to which access was refused. The familiar arguments were rehearsed that to disclose the working group's advice before a final decision had

---

[25] Regulations requiring RPS are gradually being transferred to Art 290 procedure; see COM (2013) 451 final [3–4].
[26] UK House of Lords EU Committee, *Delegation of Powers to the Commission: Reforming Comitology* (HL 1998–99, 23) 22.
[27] Adopted as Commission Decision 94/90/EC on public access to Commission documents ([1994] OJ L46/58).
[28] Available in an improved version at: ec.europa.eu/transparency/regcomitology/index.cfm. And see COM (2010) 67 final recast of 2007/0286 (COD).
[29] G Brandsma et al, 'How Transparent are EU "Comitology" Committees in Practice?' (2008) 14 *European Law Journal* 819. For the regulation, see below ch 5.
[30] Case T-144/05 *Muñiz v Commission* [2008] ECR II-0335.

been taken might expose committee members to undue pressure; and that a 'space to think' for Commission officials was 'fundamental in safeguarding the Commission's decision-making process, which would be seriously undermined if that institution could no longer rely on full and frank advice from its services'. Finding that the committee minutes made no reference to the advice or even to 'the main points of [its] assessments', the General Court (GC) pinned comitology to the 'higher' standards of openness required of legislative proceedings,[31] ruling that access to the committee minutes was insufficient in proceedings of a legislative nature to satisfy the public's right to the widest measure of access to documents and of openness.

Comitology 2 also required every committee to adopt rules of procedure based on standardised rules published in the OJ.[32] But although all committees keep minutes, a recent study found that there was no standard template; that the Commission often listed decisions only briefly; and that the only full reports, made by committee members for their principals, were generally unavailable.[33] The Commission shows a particular unwillingness to reveal Member States' voting records or the identity of their representatives. In *Borax Europe v Commission*,[34] the Commission called together 'a group of experts' to advise on the toxicity of certain chemicals. Industry representatives participated in the first stage of a meeting but then withdrew to allow deliberation. Borax contested the accuracy of the summary published on the website of the European Chemicals Bureau and applied to access the full record. It was met with the standard Commission argument against disclosing identities because 'the economic interests at stake' risked exposing experts to external pressure. Unconvinced, the GC annulled the refusal on the ground that the Commission had shown no serious threat to its decision-making process. As judgment was delivered only on 11 March 2009 concerning a meeting held on 5 June 2004, its utility to the applicants is, however, questionable.

THE LISBON TREATY REFORMS

The new dispositions of the Lisbon Treaty are said more clearly to demarcate the institutional division of functions and to put the co-legislators 'on an equal footing in relation to the conferral of delegated and implementing powers'.[35] They have, however, done little to simplify executive law-making procedures.

---

[31] See below, ch 5, p 128.

[32] 'Standard Rules of Procedure for Committees' OJ C [2011] C 206/06:

[33] G Brandsma, *Backstage Europe: Comitology, Accountability, and Democracy in the European Union* (PhD thesis, Utrecht University, 2010) ch 5.

[34] Case T-121/05 *Borax Europe v Commission* [2009] ECR II-0027. See also Case T-111/00 *BAT v Commission* [2001] ECR II-2997. Note that these GC cases antedate Case C-28/08 *Bavarian Lager v Commission* [2010] ECR I-6055 (see below, ch 5, p 131).

[35] See Commision, 'Proposal for a Regulation laying down the rules and general principles concerning mechanisms for control by Member States of the Commission's exercise of implementing powers' COM (2010) 83 final, 2010/0051.

Delegated Acts: Article 290

TFEU Article 290 grants a true power of delegated legislation in a framework set by the legislators. The Commission can now adopt 'non-legislative acts of general application' to supplement or amend 'non-essential elements' of the legislative act; 'essential elements' may not be delegated and the 'objectives, content, scope and duration' must be 'explicitly defined' in the legislative act.[36] The Commission can present draft measures simultaneously to the Council and EP, each of which may 'object' and revoke the delegation. Comitology committees are replaced by advisory committees, which are to have a 'consultative' rather than an 'institutional' role[37] – an escape from the procedural burdens of comitology justified on the ground that the legislators both control the exercise of delegated powers and may also object on any grounds.[38] In the first three years since entry into force of the Lisbon Treaty, more than 50 delegated acts were adopted, in areas ranging from securities law to fisheries, food and energy.

Does this imply that important or controversial policies will be dealt with under Article 290? In practice, it is more likely that a combination of legislative techniques will make up a package. When the EU moved to regulate credit short selling, for example, the governing legislation was fleshed out in three delegated regulations and an implementing regulation dealing with technical and procedural matters such as the exact format of the information to be provided to the European Securities and Markets Authority (ESMA).[39] These are now available on the Europa website together with the proposal, impact assessment (IA), consultation, the request for technical advice from ESMA that led up to the legislation and the press releases announcing it. ESMA's draft technical advice and final reports are available on the ESMA website.[40]

As for advisory committees, Christiansen and Dobbels feel that the Commission has been able to take advantage of 'a fairly non-proceduralised way of adopting delegated acts [to] maintain a large degree of leeway in the way that it runs the process and prepares [them]'.[41] There are no formal requirements for committees to be listed nor does the Commission Communication contain specific procedural requirements, though a Common Understanding does commit the Commission to

---

[36] See further B Riessen, 'Delegated Legislation after the Treaty of Lisbon: An Analysis of Article 290 TFEU' (2010) 35 *European Law Review* 837. For the Parliament's view, see the József Szájer Report 2010/2021(INI), adopted 5 May 2010.

[37] COM (2010) 83 final, 2010/0051 (COD) 4; P Craig, *EU Administrative Law* 126–28.

[38] COM (2010) 83 final, 2010/0051 (COD) 5.

[39] Respectively Regulation (EU) 236/2012 [2012] OJ L86/1; Commission Delegated Regulation (EU) 918/2012, [2012] OJ L274/1; Commission Delegated Regulation (EU) 919/2012 , [2012] OJ L274/16; Commission Delegated Regulation (EU) 826/2012 [2012] OJ L251/1; Commission Implementing Regulation (EU) 827/2012 [2012] OJ L251/11.

[40] ESMA's technical advice on possible Delegated Acts concerning the regulation on short selling and certain aspects of credit default swaps ((EC) No 236/2012 (19 April 2012).

[41] T Christiansen and M Dobbels, 'Non-Legislative Rule Making after the Lisbon Treaty: Implementing the New System of Comitology and Delegated Acts' (2013) 19 *European Law Journal* 42, 54.

'timely', 'appropriate' and 'transparent' consultation.[42] The Commission clearly cannot operate without advisory committees – to do so would undercut the major justification for delegation: expertise in the face of the technocratic nature of the subject matter. Whether it will be able to maintain the informality is perhaps doubtful. Denmark, Germany and the UK have taken the lead in demanding clarification of consultation procedures and the Commission's attitude is said to be 'conciliatory'.[43] Craig too has predicted a rapid proceduralisation of advisory committees; statutory comitology-style procedures in specific legislation or even greater reliance on implementing procedure.[44]

Post-Lisbon Implementing Procedure: Article 291

TFEU Article 291 authorises the use of implementing powers by the Commission where 'uniform conditions for implementing legally binding Union acts are needed'. The Council and EP gain a 'right of scrutiny' to scan draft implementing measures for ultra vires, though their decision is not final. EU legislation is to lay down rules and general principles 'concerning mechanisms for control by Member States of the Commission's exercise of implementing powers'. Regulation 182/2011[45] simplifies and rationalises comitology procedure by rolling up management and regulatory committees into a new 'examination procedure'; advisory procedure, which requires the Commission only to 'take utmost account' of the committee's views, is to become the norm. This potential relaxation is, however, undercut by the lengthy list of matters reserved for examination procedure[46] and – as Craig points out in a close textual analysis[47] – by the fact that examination procedure contains two tracks decidedly reminiscent of previous management and regulatory procedures.

The composition and procedure of committees is standardised. A new written procedure is introduced and, in a steady move to proceduralisation, detailed rules now cover:

> [T]he choice of procedure under which a committee is consulted, the length of time before a meeting is convened, the kinds of documents that need to be shared in advance of the meeting, the number of days before the meeting that draft measures and support-

---

[42] European Council, Common Understanding, 8753/11, PE/64 INST 195 [4].
[43] R Watson and M Malère, 'Council Clawing Back Power' *Europolitics* (8 February 2012).
[44] P Craig, *The Lisbon Treaty: Law, Politics and Treaty Reform* (Oxford: OUP, 2010) 58–59.
[45] Regulation 182/2011 (EU) of 16 February 2011 laying down the rules and general principles concerning mechanisms for control by Member States of the Commission's exercise of implementing powers [2011] OJ L55/13.
[46] It covers acts of general scope designed to implement basic acts; specific implementing acts with a potentially important impact; programmes with substantial implications; common agricultural and common fisheries policies; the environment, security and safety, or protection of the health or safety of humans, animals or plants; the common commercial policy; taxation.
[47] P Craig, 'Delegated Acts, Implementing Acts and the New Comitology Regulation' (2011) *European Law Review* 671, 684–85.

ing documents are distributed to committee members, the majority required when the committee votes on a draft implementing act, the summary record of the meetings that are uploaded in the public register, and the actions required by the Commission in carrying out its mandate after the meeting. Even greater proceduralisation is the result of Commission internal rules and guidelines about how to manage comitology committee meetings, how to slot opinions from comitology committees into the Commission's inter-service consultation mechanism, and the growing practice of also submitting draft implementing measures to regulatory impact assessment.[48]

Negative committee decisions are for the first time referred to an Appeals Committee composed of Member State representatives (in practice from Coreper), a procedure designed to ensure that only in very exceptional circumstances could implementing acts be adopted that are not in accordance with a committee's opinion and then only for a limited period of time. If the Appeals Committee rules against the Commission's proposed action, the Commission must abide by this decision. According to the online Comitology Register, the Appeals Committee is not a permanent body but rather 'a procedural tool which gives EU countries the opportunity to have a second discussion at a higher level of representation'; higher perhaps but also less expert and possibly more complaisant. Rules of procedure have nonetheless been adopted, which the Commission can evaluate and propose amendment to.[49]

Appeals machinery came into play when the Commission, in reliance on advice from the EFSA, proposed a two-year ban on three neonicotinoid pesticides said to pose 'high acute risks' to honeybees. The Standing Committee on the Food Chain and Animal Health failed to reach a qualified majority and the proposal was referred to the Appeals Committee, which also failed to agree. The Commission had the last word; Article 6(3) of the Regulation leaves it free to go forward in case of a non-decision, which it has duly done.[50] But this may not be the end of the story. The European Ombudsman (EO) has been asked to investigate a complaint of procedural shortcomings in preparing the Regulation and an action for annulment has been registered with the GC.[51]

The Lisbon restructuring modifies rather than rectifying the structural complexities of comitology, while the system of advisory committees intended largely to replace it may represent a procedural step backwards to an undesirable degree of informality. There is heavy reliance on parliamentary watchfulness and potential for review by the Courts. Hardacre and Kaeding predict[52] that the heightened transparency and accessibility will slow down the adoption of delegated acts and

---

[48] Christiansen and Dobbels, above (n 41) 47.
[49] Appeal Committee Rules of Procedure, adopted 29 March 2011 [2011] OJ C183/05, 13.
[50] See 'Europe Restricts 3 Commonly Used Pesticides in Effort to Protect Honeybees' *Scientific American* (29 April 2013); 'EU to ban fipronil to protect honeybees' *The Guardian* (16 July 2013).
[51] Inv 1047/2013/BEH was abandoned on the ground of the pending litigation.
[52] M Hardacre and A Kaeding, 'The Execution of Delegated Powers after Lisbon. A Timely Analysis of the Regulatory Procedure with Scrutiny and its Lessons for Delegated Acts' (2010) EUI Working Paper RSCAS 2010/85.

increasingly politicise the process, opening the way to an increased number of challenges – an apparent victory for output over input values. But all this leaves a crucial question of democratic deficit unanswered: is the regulatory process sufficiently open to civil society participation?

CONSTRUCTING A CIVIL SOCIETY?

Committee Corporatism: The European Economic and Social Committee

In the early years of the Community, a French corporatist model governed consultation. The Treaties installed the Committee of the Regions[53] and the Economic and Social Committee (ESC, now EESC) as corporatist substitutes for popular consultation in regional and social policy. Consultation was mandatory where the Treaty so provided (as it frequently did), otherwise it was discretionary (TEC Article 262). The EESC had advisory status and it was questionable how influential its opinions were in the face of competition from a host of advisory committees and the maturing EP. According to Lodge and Herman:

> The ESC was mainly consulted on draft proposals, when policy choices and guidelines had already been established. Indeed the consulting institutions were frequently criticized for denying the ESC any right of initiative, while at the same time encouraging the proliferation of expert committees which brought representatives of economic and social forces into the formative stages of the policy-making process. This had the effect of making the [Community] consultative machinery more complicated, while reducing the effectiveness of its institutionalized consultative body.[54]

Smismans admits that the EESC has only 'occasionally' put an issue on the policy agenda but sees it as 'able to yield valuable expertise which led to technical amendments of the Commission proposals',[55] a generally pessimistic conclusion confirmed by a more recent study.[56]

Representativeness was not at first an issue; it was either assumed or more probably ignored. Mainly representing employers' organisations and trade unions, EESC members were nominated by Member States subject to unanimous ratification by the Council (in practice Coreper). Moreover TEC Article 258(3) included the mantra – hardly consonant with representativeness – that 'the members of the Committee may not be bound by any mandatory instructions. They shall be

---

[53] See T Cole, 'The Committee of the Regions and Subnational Representation to the European Union' (2005) 12 *Maastricht Journal* 49.
[54] J Lodge and V Herman, 'The Economic and Social Committee in EEC Decision-making' (1980) 34 *International Organisations* 265, 272.
[55] S Smismans, 'The Economic and Social Committee: Towards Deliberative Democracy via a Functional Assembly' (2000) 4 *European Integration online Papers* 1.
[56] C Hönnige and D Panke, 'The Committee of the Regions and the European Economic and Social Committee: How Influential are Consultative Committees in the European Union?' (2013) 51 *Journal of Common Market Studies* 452.

completely independent in the performance of their duties, in the general interest of the Community'. There was no obligation for the EESC to consult 'grass roots' organisations. But it also had power to adopt its own procedures,[57] and could issue own-initiative opinions. Seeking to re-brand itself as 'a bridge between Europe and organised civil society', it used the power in 1992 to adopt an Opinion on 'The Citizens' Europe', following this up with an own-initiative opinion on the contribution of civil society organisations in building Europe.[58] A liaison committee was established to strengthen cooperation with civil society **organisations** and bolster the EESC role as chosen intermediary between the EU institutions and **organised** civil society. The emphasised words are significant: the EESC had become a 'functional assembly',[59] where organised interests, more especially management and labour, met and debated with selected civil society organisations. Its formal Opinions, voted in plenary sessions, are drawn up in a process which is 'geared to achieving a consensus' so that they 'accurately reflect the views of **organised** civil society'.[60]

As amended at Nice, TEC Article 257 provided that the EESC should consist of 'representatives of the various economic and social components of organised civil society and, in particular, representatives of producers, farmers, carriers, workers, dealers, craftsmen, professional occupations, consumers and the general public' – the latter something of a catch-all constituency. At the time of writing, the EESC has some 344 members divided into three groups: employers, employees and 'various interests' – the latter said to include 'other representatives and stakeholders of civil society, particularly in the economic, civic, professional and cultural field', in practice always a minority, often overlapping with Groups I and II and holding public posts. The 'diverse groupings' are said to be bound together 'by their sense of duty towards the large proportion of the EU population whose interests they represent'.[61] But in what sense are they representative? They are after all still nominated by national governments in a notably untransparent process that bears little relation to the way civil society actually operates.[62]

In 2005, the Commission moved to formalise its relations with the EESC by signing a Protocol of Cooperation.[63] This supported a stronger advisory role for the EESC with input into pre-legislative and post-legislative impact analyses (to put this differently, the EESC became a selected consultee). It was also charged

[57] Most recently codified in Rules of Procedure, CESE 1083/2010 FR/GW/DS/NT.
[58] EESC, 'The Citizens' Europe' (27 May 1992); Opinion on the role and contribution of civil society organisations in the building of Europe' CES 851/1999, OJ C329. And see S Smismans, 'An Economic and Social Committee for the Citizen, or a Citizen for the Economic and Social Committee?' (1999) 5 *European Public Law* 557.
[59] Smismans, 'The Economic and Social Committee', above (n 55) 3–5.
[60] EESC, 'Opinion on Organized Civil Society and European Governance: The Committee's Contribution to the Drafting of the White Paper' CES 535/2001 254, [2001] OJ C95.
[61] EESC, Mission Statement, available at: http://www.eesc.europa.eu/?i=portal.en.about-the-committee.
[62] D Curtin, 'Private Interest *Representation* or Civil Society *Deliberation*? A Contemporary Dilemma for European Union Governance' (2003) 12 *Social & Legal Studies* 56.
[63] CESE 1391/2005 FR/HR/CAT/hn.

with the ambiguous task of drafting 'exploratory opinions in areas of particular importance to organised civil society' with a view to presenting 'an integrated approach which allows the views of all stakeholders in civil society to be taken into account as widely as possible'. There was a price tag. The EESC was to work closely with the Commission, which would decide when exploratory opinions were appropriate; there would be regular annual meetings 'on the initiative of the Commission' to identify questions of common interest and examine and evaluate implementation of 'priorities'. This inevitably raises the question whether the EESC is a bridge to civil society or a Commission agent.[64]

Tending the Roots

The Commission's direct relationship with civil society is also highly regulated. This has not always been so. In the early years, the Commission was considered accessible and informal. Its relationships with the public were of two main kinds. First, Brussels was – and is today –widely known as the European lobbyist's capital and the Commission, with its key policymaking functions, has always been targeted by interest groups and lobbyists.[65] After several budgetary scandals and accusations of cronyism (see chapter one), the 'European Transparency Initiative' launched in 2005 introduced a measure of necessary regulation of interest group lobbying. An online register of interests and code of conduct is now maintained,[66] agreed after some difficulty with the EP, which jealously guards its role as the prime forum for articulation of civil society views[67] and is hence a target for heavy lobbying.

Second, the Commission has worked since the 1970s to bring into being and support through funding European 'peak associations' or networks of NGOs working at European level on issues of public interest. Declaration 23 attached to the Maastricht Treaty stressed the importance of relationships with 'the voluntary sector', leading to the creation of a new budget line in 1997 'to promote co-operation with NGOs and other voluntary sector organisations and to strengthen

---

[64] S Smismans, 'An Economic and Social Committee for the Citizen', above (n 58).
[65] C Harlow, 'A Community of Interests? Making Use of European Law' (1992) 55 *Modern Law Review* 33; J Greenwood, *Representing Interests in the European Union*, 2nd edn (Basingstoke: Macmillan, 2007).
[66] Commission, 'A Framework for relations with interest representatives by the Commission (Register and Code of Conduct)' (Communication) COM (2008) 323 final; Agreement between the European Parliament and the European Commission on the establishment of a transparency register [2011] *OJ L191/29*. Two registers are now available on the Europa website: the Transparency Register, available at: http://ec.europa.eu/transparencyregister/info/homePage.do; and the Register of Commission Expert Groups and Other Similar Entities, available at: http://www.eesc.europa.eu/?i=portal.en.about-the-committee.
[67] B Kohler-Koch, 'Organized Interests in the EC and the European Parliament' (1997) 1 *European Integration online Papers* 9: E Heidbreder, 'Civil Society Participation in EU Governance' (2012) 7(2) *Living Reviews in European Governance*.

the capacity of these organisations to engage in civil dialogue at European level'.[68] A prime example is the European Citizens Advisory Service (ECAS), set up in 1991 under Belgian law as an international non-profit organisation. Membership is open to all non-profit organisations that are 'independent of government, party politics and economic interests', including public authorities with an engagement towards the development of civil society, but excluding all commercial interests.

The core ECAS mission is to enable NGOs and individuals 'to make their voice heard within the EU' and provide advice on 'how to lobby, fundraise, and defend European citizenship rights'. It claims to have enlarged NGO representation at European level, presents itself 'as catalyst and presenter of new ideas' and is involved in an ambitious, overarching project funded by the Nuffield Foundation to create a 'European civil society house', accessible physically and online. Since 2002, ECAS has been running the 'Your Europe Advice Service' for Directorate-General Internal Market and Services (DG Markt), a Europe wide service with a giant database, manned by a multilingual legal team, which affords advice to EU citizens on their rights under internal market rules or on alternative ways to resolve their problems. It has strong links with Solvit, the non-legal complaints handling service described in chapter three. In 2012, ECAS received a grant of €523,481 towards its budget of €1081,473 to run this service, with an additional grant of €174,857 from the Commission Education, Audiovisual and Culture Executive Agency (EACEA). In the same year, ECAS income from members was €28,107 and 'other revenue' amounted to €184,701. Thus, ECAS is undeniably heavily dependent on Commission funding.

The same is true of CONCORD, the European Confederation of Relief and Development NGOs, founded in 2003 by development NGOs to act as the 'main interlocutor with the EU institutions' on development policy. CONCORD comprises 27 national associations and 18 international networks and claims support from 'millions of citizens across Europe'; all board members represent NGOs. CONCORD works through a 'structured dialogue' with EU institutions, its main objective being to encourage 'further and deeper engagement from the European Commission' with development projects throughout the world and, with this in mind, to strengthen civil society organisations or NGOs. The two main elements of CONCORD's income for 2011 were €576,000 from members and NGOs and €700,000 by Commission grant. Subvention has not deterred CONCORD from being on occasion highly critical. It publishes a reader to pilot NGOs through the 'large body of rules and regulations' that govern EU contracting procedure and has gone on record as saying that the EU bureaucracy 'must be shaped in such a way to ensure the smooth delivery of helpful development projects, rather than serve as a complex and energy-intensive obstacle'; to let NGOs know what is expected of them, greater transparency about outcomes is needed, together with greater standardisation, consistent modes of working and the establishment of a

---

[68] Commission, 'Promoting the Role of Voluntary Organisations and Foundations in Europe' (Communication) COM (97) 241 final, [9.8].

code of good practice.[69] Undoubtedly, however, CONCORD has common interests with the Commission and is highly dependent on Commission funding.

The EESC has expressed concern about NGO dependence on public funding, suggesting that NGOs should enhance their financial independence by boosting income from their membership and external sources – easier said than done. Somewhat contradictorily, it has also argued that the voluntary sector should have better access to structural funds.[70] Not all NGOs are prepared to adopt a Commission agenda in exchange for funding – an independent attitude that is said to explain gaps in the human rights network[71]- but when they do, their independence is necessarily thrown into question. There may be a modicum of truth in the extreme accusation that CSOs are 'sock puppet charities ... hand-picked and financed by the European Commission', programmed to lobby for closer European integration, bigger budgets and more EU regulation.[72]

Registration and Representativeness

The Commission explicitly rejected the international law model of official consultative status for NGOs on the basis that in the EU, the decision-making process 'is first and foremost legitimised by the elected representatives of the European peoples'.[73] Registration began simply as a register of groups with which the Commission had contacts. The justifications were fairness – to reduce the risk of policymakers listening to one side of the argument or of particular groups getting privileged access – and transparency – to provide the general public with information about 'NGOs which belong to them'.[74] But a managerial note quickly crept in as the Commission insisted that relevant 'target groups' would need to be identified on the basis of clear criteria. These now include: the wider impact of the policy on other policy areas; the need for specific experience, expertise or technical knowledge; the need to involve non-organised interests where appropriate; and the track record of participants in previous consultations.[75] The Commission claims the right to refuse registration – Statewatch, for example, has had an application rejected on the basis that it was not a 'representative' organisation and did not have 'members'.[76] This does not mean

[69] CONCORD website at: http://www.concordeurope.org/ 'Funding for NGOs'.
[70] CES 535/2001254, [5.6[–[5.7].
[71] R Sánchez-Salgado 'Giving a European Dimension to Civil Society Organizations' (2007) 3 *Journal of Civil Society* 253, 264.
[72] C Snowdon, 'Europuppets: The European Commission's Remaking of Civil Society' (2013) Institute for Economic Affairs, Discussion Paper 45.
[73] Commission, 'Towards a reinforced culture of consultation and dialogue-General Principles and Minimum Standards for Consultation of Interested Parties by the Commission' (Communication) COM (2002) 704 final, [2.2].
[74] Undated discussion paper presented by President Prodi and Vice-President Kinock 'The Commission and NGOs: Building a stronger partnership', [3.2.4].
[75] Commission, 'General principles and minimum standards for consulting non-institutional interested parties' (Communication) COM (2002) 277.
[76] Curtin, above (n 62) 60.

that Statewatch has not got considerable expertise to offer. There have also been protests that the register is unbalanced in favour of business[77] and that registration risks closing the doors to less established organisations,[78] while Greenpeace – an NGO that does not accept EU or governmental funding – claims that the register is unfit for purpose:

> A credible EU lobbying transparency register should include names of individual lobbyists and the issues that they try to influence, provide precise and comparable financial information on lobbying, and have effective sanctions to ensure the accuracy and completeness of the information disclosed.[79]

More fundamental is the claim that registration is an inappropriate 'neo-liberal' restriction of the democratic political process:

> Many CSOs do not claim any exclusive 'representation' of the interests they pursue: after all, anybody can start a new civil society organization ... One can thus discern the beginnings of an effort to strap civil society into an institutional straitjacket, such as that harnessing already represented functional (largely private) interests such as social partners and professional associations.[80]

Concern has also been expressed at the use of the concept of 'representativity' as 'a tool to structure interest intermediation'.[81] This was originally justified on the ground of balance: the Commission should take care in the composition of a formal or structured consultation to ensure that bodies properly reflect the sector they purport to represent and, where this was not the case, to use other forms of consultation to ensure balance.[82] This may be relevant to consultation but is less so in the context of relationships with civil society, which should surely not be selective. Later, the Commission, while firmly disavowing any intention of interfering with their internal arrangements, transferred the onus of showing representativity to NGOs. Controversially arguing that 'with better involvement comes greater responsibility', it explicitly linked additional consultation privileges to 'more guarantees of openness and representativity'.[83] This type of bureaucratic regulation of civil society by officialdom not only undercuts the drive for rights of citizen participation but can also be seen as a negation of the very concept of civil society.

---

[77] D Obradovic and J Vizcarino, 'Good Governance Requirements concerning the Participation of Interest Groups on EU Consultation' (2006) 43 *Common Market Law Review* 1049, 1053 state that around 1732 of 2600 special interest groups with which the Commission then had contacts represented business and only around 520 represented citizens' interests. This replicates the position with the EESC.
[78] N Perez-Solorzano Borragán and S Smismans, 'Representativeness: A Tool to Structure Interest Intermediation in the European Union?' (2012) 50 *Journal of Common Market Studies* 403, instancing CSO answers to the EESC consultation on representativeness of European CSOs in June 2006.
[79] Greenpeace entry on the Transparency Register, above (n 66).
[80] Curtin, above (n 62) 57.
[81] Borragán and Smismans, above (n 79) 416–17.
[82] COM (2002) 704 final, 19–20.
[83] WPEG 4, 15.

CONSULTATION – AND BEYOND?

Arguably, Commission relationships with civil society reflect a confusion between participation by civil society in politics and established administrative practices of consultation in policymaking and law-making. Consultation has long been obligatory in sector-specific EU legislation; it figures prominently in the Commission's 'Better Regulation' agenda and is compulsory in environmental matters under the Aarhus Convention (see chapter twelve). But a new period began with a 1997 Commission Communication that asserted 'a high level of political commitment' to more systematic consultation with the voluntary sector.[84] The WPEG chose 'participation' – a stronger word than consultation – as a good governance principle requiring 'wide participation throughout the policy chain from conception to implementation'. Typically, the obligation fell on national governments to 'follow an inclusive approach when developing and implementing EU policies'[85] but from this time on the case for direct citizen participation in policymaking and rule-making (urged by ECAS) has climbed steadily up the EU political agenda.

As already indicated, a series of soft law instruments was used to structure and proceduralise Commission relationships with civil society in order to ensure 'an adequate and equitable treatment of participants in consultation processes'.[86] Describing consultation as 'a win-win option for all actors', the Commission in 2002 laid claim to a long tradition of consulting outside interest parties in the formulation of its policies; it had incorporated external consultation into the development of almost all its policy areas but practice was variable. It was therefore proposing a more transparent consultation process to promote accountability and inculcate mutual learning and exchange of good practices within the Commission. General principles and standards for consultation would be provided to help the Commission rationalise its consultation procedures and carry them out in a meaningful and systematic way, together with a coherent but flexible framework for consultation.[87]

The Commission today operates three separate forms of consultation, two of which are distinctly bureaucratic. First, the corporate consultation machinery of the EESC, the Committee of the Regions, the confusing network of comitology committees, working groups and EU agencies, all remain in place. Second, where the Commission seriously wishes to obtain further expert advice or feel the pulse of public opinion, it is likely to select 'target groups' and set up a formal, time-limited, written consultation exercise, based on documentation available online. This may involve expert working groups or groups registered on the Commission Transparency Register. In third place comes open consultation, usually conducted

[84] COM (97) 241 final, [9.7].
[85] WPEG, 10.
[86] Commission, 'Consultation document: Towards a reinforced culture of consultation and dialogue – Proposal for general principles and minimum standards for consultation of interested parties by the Commission (Communication) COM/ 2002/0277 final.
[87] Ibid.

online, where a dedicated information website, 'Your Voice in Europe', lists all open consultations and allows citizens to express their views. New structures have recently been emerging; policy forums, 'citizens' conferences', 'civil dialogue' and European round tables have all been tried. Some of this machinery is aimed at informing – in involving citizens generally in EU affairs or bringing new policies to their attention; some is designed genuinely to encourage input from stakeholders. A complaint that many consultation documents intended for the public at large were only available in English or in a limited number of EU languages earned a critical remark from the EO on the ground that citizens cannot participate effectively in a consultation if they do not understand it. There was only a limited change in practice.[88]

A recent survey suggests that open online consultation has been successful in involving a wider range of different actors; it tends, however, to be restricted to less technical issues and limited by the standardised questionnaires that are used.[89] There is generally a self-selection of participants, largely dominated by stakeholders; in other words, the outcomes of open consultation are often similar to those obtained by targeting. When, for example, the Commission was contemplating a change in the highly controversial policy of undersize fish discard, it published online IAs[90] together with a set of specific questions. It then conducted an open online consultation directed at citizens, organisations and public authorities. This produced 394 contributions, which were synthesised and again published.[91] The result was used as the basis for discussion with the warring Member States and apparently contributed to an overwhelming positive vote in the EP – which had itself responded to the consultation – forcing a change of heart in the Council and a change in the Common Fisheries Policy. Or did it? Was this just a further example of Kohler-Koch's nominal 'Astroturf' representation'?[92]

Enforceability?

Extremely protective of its consultation procedures, the Commission has been careful to articulate its practices in soft law instruments, explicitly expressing the hope that they would not prove justiciable: 'An over-legalistic approach would be

[88] Inv 640/2011/AN.
[89] C Quittkat, 'The European Commission's Online Consultations: A Success Story?' (2011) 49 *Journal of Common Market Studies* 653.
[90] Commission, 'Studies in the Field of the Common Fisheries Policy and Maritime Affairs Lot 4: Impact Assessment Studies related to the CFP and Impact Assessment of Discard Reducing Policies' (March and June 2011).
[91] Commission Staff Working Document, 'Synthesis of the Consultation on the Reform of the Common Fisheries Policy' SEC (2010) 428 final (16 April 2010). There were 117 replies from 'stakeholder organisations'; 63 from (mainly environmental) CSOs; 16 from academia; 30 from public bodies; 8 from EU advisory bodies, including the EESC; 11 from third countries, notably Norway; and 114 from the general public; 1329 responses indicating pressure group lobbying were not included.
[92] B Kohler-Koch, 'Civil Society and EU Democracy: "Astroturf" Representation' (2010) 17 *Journal of European Public Policy* 100.

114 *Executive Law-making*

incompatible with the need for timely delivery of policy, and with the expectations of the citizens that the European Institutions should deliver on substance rather than concentrating on procedures'.[93] And it tried to quiet demands for a 'legally-binding instrument' with the assurance that 'when the Commission decides to apply the principles and guidelines, its departments have to act accordingly'.[94]

Perhaps surprisingly, this approach was endorsed by the EO when ECAS complained of Commission failure to consult NGOs on the future of the structural funds. ECAS questioned the minimum consultation standards on the grounds of lack of clarity and asked whether the sectoral approach to consultation should be supplemented by horizontal default provisions. This was an approach for which the EO, in the light of his 'Code of Good Administrative Behaviour', ought to have had some sympathy. Instead, he cleared the Commission of maladministration, accepting an assurance that it had set up a special area for debate on the future of cohesion policy on its Internet site, giving all interested parties an opportunity to express their views. ECAS was advised to approach the Commission with suggestions for improvement: 'it would be good administration for the Commission to give serious consideration to any such suggestions'.[95] A later investigation from Friends of the Earth (FoE) echoed the doubts of Greenpeace concerning the Transparency Register (above). FoE complained of the Commission's failure to deal properly with complaints that the Transparency Register contained inaccurate information. Here the EO took a stronger line, emphasising that complaints make a valuable contribution to effective implementation of the Register and should be welcomed as an opportunity to enhance the accuracy of the information it contains. Complaints should be thoroughly investigated and the responses should deal in sufficient detail with complainants' arguments. Stronger measures have nonetheless been demanded, most obviously a general codification of European administrative procedure or an EU equivalent of the American Administrative Procedures Act (see chapter twelve).

Judicial Abstention

Whether oversight by the Luxembourg Courts would live up to expectations is in fact very questionable. Such precedents as exist are not very encouraging. For 50 years, the narrow definition of individual standing to sue contained in TEC Article 230, which required both direct and individual interest [96] was interpreted with such severity by the CJEU as virtually to shut the door to judge-made participa-

---

[93] COM (2002) 704 final.
[94] Ibid.
[95] Inv 948/2004/OV; Inv 406/2008/(WP)VIK.
[96] The enormous literature is sufficiently summarised by Craig, *EU Administrative Law* 306–18; S Peers and M Costa, 'Judicial Review of EU Acts after the Treaty of Lisbon' (2012) 8 *European Constitutional Law Review* 82, 82–86.

tion rights for private parties. TFEU Article 263 marginally improved the situation by granting standing 'against a regulatory act which is of direct concern to them and does not entail implementing measures'.[97] It was hoped by some that this might ease the position of groups.[98] But only a generous interpretation of the provision could assist the many public interest groups which might wish to participate in an EU rule-making process and the most significant test case so far, brought by Canadian representative groups to challenge an EU regulation on trade in seal products, shows no signs of a judicial thaw. Refusing to construe the provision generously, the CoJ interpreted 'regulatory' to exclude 'legislative' acts.[99]

Interest to sue is not the only barrier raised by the CJEU in consultation cases. In the notorious *Atlanta* case,[100] the applicants, severely disadvantaged by a change in EU policy, complained that they had a 'legitimate expectation' that their established trade in bananas would continue, amounting to a sufficient interest to justify a pre-regulatory hearing before the Commission. But in line with its customary attitude, the Commission had 'made it a precondition of a hearing that all traders speak "with one voice"', a condition that we have met before, in practice impossible to fulfil because of the traders' divergent interests. Consequently the applicants' views were not heard and their particular situation was ignored. Rejecting their claim, the GC endorsed the classical doctrine that 'the right to be heard in an administrative procedure affecting a specific person cannot be transposed to the context of a legislative process leading to the adoption of general laws' and flatly refused to extend to the collective legislative process case law on the right to make representations in cases involving sanctions on individuals. 'The only obligations of consultation incumbent on the Community legislature, other than the duty to consult the EP, [are] those specified in primary or secondary legislation'.

Statutory consultation rights figured in the *UEAPME* case.[101] In the framework of a complex legislative scheme for implementing the Framework Agreement on parental leave, Articles 3 and 4 of Directive 96/34 provided for agreements between management and labour that could be implemented either contractually or by adoption as a Council decision. The Commission was obliged 'to consult management and labour' in two distinct rounds of consultation – a mandatory requirement that contains wide discretion. A Communication set out criteria for consultation based on representativeness and listed those bodies that the Commission saw as fulfilling them. UEAPME and other small unions were invited

---

[97] SUS Balthasar, 'Locus Standi Rules for Challenges to Regulatory Acts by Private Applicants: The New Article 263(4) TFEU' (2010) *European Law Review* 542.

[98] On which see C Harlow, 'Towards a Theory of Access for the European Court of Justice' (1992) 12 *Yearbook of European Law* 213.

[99] C-583/11 P *Inuit Tapiriit Kanatami and Others v Parliament and Council* (judgment of 3 October 2013). And see Case T-224/10 *Association belge des consommateurs test-achats v Commission* (judgment of 12 October 2011).

[100] Case T-521/93 *Atlanta AG and others v Council and Commission* [1996] ECR II-1707 approved on appeal as Case C-104/97 *Atlanta AG v European Community* [1999] ECR I-6983.

[101] Case T-135/96 *UEAPME v Council* [1998] ECR II-2335.

116 *Executive Law-making*

to the first round but at the second, negotiatory stage designed to lead to regulation, the Commission confined consultation to those bodies that had agreed on further action, arguing that, as masters of the regulatory process, they were also masters of the procedure.

Accepting a sort of provisional admissibility, the GC went on (as is its practice) to scrutinise the procedure in great detail before ruling the action inadmissible. In the absence of legislative provision for parliamentary – democratic – participation, the GC accepted that the Council and Commission were under a duty to verify that the signatories to the agreement were truly representative; this had been done. UEAPME, on the other hand, had failed to show 'distinctive representativeness' – a very high burden of proof and threshold for standing. This leaves the Commission in an advantageous position; at the first stage, it shapes the legislation; at the second stage, it designs the procedures; at a third stage, it is able to pick and choose its contributors, subject only to light review by the Courts.

Lisbon – Towards Partnership?

The Lisbon Treaty seemed to promise a new deal for civil society[102] with a guaranteed right for all citizens to participate in the democratic life of the Union underpinned by an obligation for the institutions to 'maintain an open, transparent and regular dialogue with representative associations and civil society', to give 'citizens and representative associations' an opportunity to publicly exchange views and 'carry out broad consultations with parties concerned' in all policy areas (TEU Articles 10(3) and 11). This promised something more than the carefully controlled consultation that had previously been the norm. The Treaty also introduced the citizens' initiative (ECI), which seemed to offer citizen participation in agenda setting. The ECI, which closely resembles a regulated version of a parliamentary petition, can only be initiated by a 'citizens' committee' of seven or more organisers resident in at least seven different Member States who must be EU citizens entitled to vote in EP elections other than MEPs (TFEU Article 24).

Typically, the ECI has now been taken over and heavily proceduralised by the Commission. The governing Regulation[103] adds that a proposal must be registered with the Commission and accompanied by itemised documentation. It must include detailed accounts of funding and its sources, which must be updated regularly. If the procedures are not correctly followed, the Commission must refuse registration, giving its reasons in a written decision that advises petitioners of the remedies available (generally complaint to the EO and judicial review). If accepted, the ECI must be supported by statements made in a specified format, verified and

---

[102] See D Curtin, H Hofmann and J Mendes, 'Constitutionalising EU Executive Rule Making Procedures: A Research Agenda' (2013) 19 *European Law Journal* 1, 4.

[103] Council Regulation (EU) 211/2011 of 16 February 2011 on the citizens' initiative [2011] OJ L65/1. And see Commission, 'Green Paper' COM (2009) 622 final; Commission, Proposal COM (2010) 119 final.

certified by national authorities and registered with the Commission. A hearing will then be held before the EP. Perhaps it is hardly surprising that, of 14 ECIs registered since the procedure opened in May 2012, only two have at the time of writing reached the final stages. The 'Right2Water' initiative is organised by a coalition of trade unions to halt the privatisation of water authorities; the 'One of us' campaign, organised by a coalition of well-known 'right to life' campaigners, demands that the EU should ban and end the financing of activities which presuppose the destruction of human embryos.[104]

ECI procedure has followed the model of the Transparency Register closely in that it is both highly controlled and also maintains a high degree of Commission discretion. Because it is contained in a legally binding regulation, however, it is subject to judicial oversight. This is the reform for which CSOs and academic commentators have long been campaigning. Nonetheless, this deeply bureaucratic process, designed no doubt to deter lobbying by powerful commercial entities, is hardly the clear, simple, user-friendly and proportionate procedure hoped for by the EP![105]

CONCLUSION

In a system of representative government in which an elected legislature empowers and controls the executive, the standard justification for delegated legislation is speed, efficiency and expertise: output values. At national level, there may or may not be pressure for direct input from civil society (though it has to be said that pressure for citizen input is growing). Not unnaturally, output values are strongly represented in EU administrative procedure, where they seem justifiable in terms of the regulatory context and technical aspect of EU regulation. They are reflected in the expert comitology and myriad advisory committees and working groups that underpin Commission policymaking. They are reflected in the 'Better Regulation' agenda, which has introduced new administrative procedures such as impact assessment, post-legislative evaluation and targeted consultation. They are reflected again in the introduction at Lisbon of a truly delegated legislative process. These procedures are designed to speed up the lengthy EU law-making process and improve quality while at the same time increasing effectiveness by nurturing a process of gradual harmonisation.

Rooted in treaty-making and diplomatic practice, transnational rule-making is effected through committees, working parties and ad hoc groupings that purport to represent the parties to rule-making but are by no means always representative. Opaque networks evolve, composed of stakeholders and commercial interests to

---

[104] Commission website, Official Register of the Citizens' Initiative.

[105] EP Resolution of 7 May 2009 requesting the Commission to submit a proposal for a regulation of the European Parliament and of the Council on the implementation of the citizens' initiative (2008/2169(INI). And see M Dougan, 'What are we to Make of the Citizens' Initiative?' (2011) *Common Market Law Review* 1807.

which standard-setting powers may be delegated and pressure groups posing as representative of civil society may play a part. This is a context in which simple administrative procedures, such as formal appointment procedures, publication of agendas, minutes, lists of attendance and other standard committee procedures go some way – but not far enough – to open up rule-making processes and provide the transparency on which legal accountability can be based. The Commission has, however, taken the procedural path in another direction, attempting to regulate civil society through a raft of highly proceduralised consultation and anti-lobbying procedures.

In this chapter, we have tried to assess how far administrative procedures can help to resolve major problems of transparency, accountability and legitimacy caused by the transfer of law-making outside the nation state to transnational bodies and institutions. We have not attempted to settle the question whether the rising number of increasingly vocal pressure groups can claim truly to represent civil society, though we have noted with concern the Commission's attempt to stimulate networking by funding 'peak associations' and supporting NGO networks working at EU level. We have also criticised its attempts to contain civil society organisations within a bureaucratic framework epitomised in its growing interest in representativity. We see these measures as at the same time bureaucratic and anti-democratic.

We are not to be understood, however, as saying that the Commission has deliberately manipulated administrative procedures so as to repress negative opinion or frustrate civil society; it is rather that it has routed civil society into bureaucratic channels with which it is comfortable. The role of administrative procedures in creating stability, enhancing efficiency and effectiveness, contributing to transparency and accountability is well understood. It can be and is beginning to be measured by social science techniques and evaluated by scholars. Whether administrative procedures can bring a civil society into being is another question altogether!

5

Transparency: Building Administrative Procedures

THIS CHAPTER IS about transparency, its place in the EU governance system and more particularly the procedures that support it. Together with accountability, transparency heads the list of good governance principles that characterise the systems of popular democracy in which most Europeans live – or aspire to live – today. Transparency in the sense of open government or 'government in the sunshine' is a constitutional and political concept and right of democratic citizenship, which enables citizens to participate in policymaking and renders public authorities accountable. But it is, as this chapter will show, a contestable concept and a highly divisive issue on which the 28 Member States and EU institutions have differing views. The chapter therefore illustrates the very real problems of designing administrative procedures in an area of considerable divergence of opinion and practice. These problems are heightened in a context where the main stakeholders are sovereign Member States and by the ideal of consensus that characterises EU policymaking

TRANSPARENCY OR OPENNESS?

Market Transparency

Transparency is a portmanteau word into which different ideas have been packed. Economists value transparency as a market principle rooted in rational decision-making theory: they believe that 'policies are more likely to be rational if they are transparent than if they are opaque', and this means 'making it clear who is taking the decisions, what the measures are, who is gaining from them, and who is paying for them'.[1] In the market context of the EU, this is a key understanding on which EU consumer law, for example, is based; consumer legislation tends to specify in considerable detail precisely what information must be made available to consumers.[2] The same market-oriented concept of transparency is found in the

---

[1] J Black, 'Transparent Policy Measures' in *Oxford Dictionary of Economics* (Oxford: OUP, 1997) 476.
[2] eg, Directive 2011/83/EU, [2011] OJ L304/64.

1989 Transparency Directive,[3] which is designed to regulate Member State systems for pricing medicinal products in the interest of a coordinated market. This lays out in some detail a set of procedural requirements designed to enable interested parties to verify that national pricing and reimbursement decisions do not create obstacles to trade. Where, for example, an application is made at national level to market a pharmaceutical product or increase its price, Directive 89/105 requires a decision to be adopted and **communicated** to the applicant within 90 days of receipt of the application; if supplementary **information** is needed, the applicant must be **notified** in detail what additional **information** is required; the final decision must be taken within 90 days of its receipt. If the application is turned down, the decision must contain a **statement of reasons** based on objective and verifiable criteria; the applicant shall be **informed** of the remedies available to him; and so on. Characteristically, these provisions, which typify EU regulatory procedure, are aimed at Member States. So too is the final provision that the 'competent authorities' shall annually **publish** in an appropriate publication and **communicate** to the Commission a list of prices fixed in the period (emphasis ours). Report back to the Commission has always been a feature of EU administrative procedure, designed to underpin the Commission's supervisory function.

The economic concept of transparency has from the first been highly influential in building the Community [4] – it is, after all, an *economic* community with all that this implies – and this initial view of transparency as a tool for market efficiency and rationality has shaped the debate over open government, which is the primary subject of this chapter. Significantly, the debate in the EU is not framed, as it has been elsewhere, around freedom of information, open government or 'government in the sunshine'. It is, as Héritier reminds us, a debate heavily influenced by the economic concept of transparency and framed around the narrow concept of access to information:

> [The debate] came about because of the perceived lack of transparency and openness in the complicated European decision-making processes, and its tendency to intensify problems of control and accountability. Because of the opacity of the decision-making processes of the Community bureaucracy and its innumerable informal committees and opaque policy networks as well as that of Council meetings, an attempt was made to secure a right to information in these areas.[5]

In Declaration 17 of the Maastricht Treaty, transparency appears for the first time as a process linked intimately to democracy – a foundational value protected in the Treaty on European Union (TEU) as a universal and inviolable human right:

---

[3] Council Directive 89/105/EEC relating to the transparency of measures regulating the pricing of medicinal products for human use and their inclusion within the scope of national health insurance systems [1989] OJ L040/08.

[4] See A Menon and S Weatherill, 'Legitimacy, Accountability and Delegation in the European Union' in A Arnull and D Wincott (eds), *Accountability and Legitimacy in the European Union* (Oxford: OUP, 2002).

[5] A Héritier, 'Composite Democracy in Europe: The Role of Transparency and Access to Information' (2003) 10 *Journal of European Public Policy* 814, 821.

'Transparency of the decision-making process strengthens the democratic nature of the institutions and the public's confidence in the administration'.[6]

Prior to Maastricht, transparency in this sense had not been a high priority. In many Member States it was neither a fundamental value nor a constitutional right[7] nor did every Member State possess freedom of information legislation. France, which did, and the UK, which did not, leant heavily towards official secrecy; Denmark and the Netherlands, which did, took openness very seriously. Swedish and Finnish accession greatly strengthened the campaign for freedom of information in the EU. In their 1995 Accession Treaty, Sweden and Finland welcomed developments taking place in the EU towards greater openness and open government:

> Open government and, in particular, public access to official records as well as the constitutional protection afforded to those who give information to the media are and remain fundamental principles which form part of Sweden's constitutional, political and cultural heritage.[8]

The response of the 11 existing Member States, that they 'take it for granted that, as a member of the European Union, Sweden will fully comply with Community law in this respect', indicated the shape of things to come.

Freedom of Information – A Political Right

Shortly afterwards, the Swedish Journalists Union (SJU) deliberately put matters to the test. It applied in parallel to the Council and 46 Swedish public authorities to access 20 EU documents in their possession. In Sweden, 18 documents (with some deletions) were forthcoming; the Council, standing on the exceptions in its procedural rules for security and confidentiality, ultimately delivered four. In a test case brought by the SJU,[9] the General Court (GC) arrived at two important conclusions. First, it held the application admissible on the ground that it was enough when access to information was in issue to be the addressee of a refusal to release a document; no reason need be given for requesting access; no 'individual and direct' interest need be shown; and the fact that the documents were already in the public domain was irrelevant. Second, it ruled that the access rules applied in the third pillar. The significance of this lay in the fact that it opened a window on policy-making and law-making across the notably untransparent and unaccountable

---

[6] See D Curtin, 'Citizens' Fundamental Right of Access to EU Information: An Evolving Digital *passepartout*?' (2000) 37 *Common Market Law Review* 7, 8.

[7] For the reasons, see J Ziller, 'European Models of Government: Towards a Patchwork with Missing Pieces' (2001) 54 *Parliamentary Affairs* 102.

[8] Declarations No 45 and 47 of the Final Act [of accession] OJ C241/0397. And see I Österdahl, 'Openness v Secrecy: Public Access to Documents in Sweden and the European Union' (1998) 23 *European Law Review* 336.

[9] Case T-174/95 *Svenska Journalistforbundet v Council* [1998] ECR II-2289. Sweden, Denmark and the Netherlands supported the Union; France and the UK supported the Council.

fields of justice and home affairs. Less auspicious was the fact that the Court gave no real answer to the applicant's claim that the 'fundamental principle' of openness had been breached. The case was decided on purely procedural grounds: the Council must not only consider each document individually, but must also show that it had done so, giving specific reasons for any refusal to disclose. Moreover, the judicial attitude to openness was revealed as somewhat suspect when it refused to produce research prepared by its research and documentation service and penalised the SJU in a costs order for publishing documents in the pending case on the Internet.

Two sides were now confronting each other. On one side stood Sweden, Denmark, Finland and the Netherlands, with strong support from the two European Ombudsmen (Jacob Söderman and Nikiforos Diamandouros), both deeply committed to open government. The European Parliament (EP), which has always posed as the mouthpiece of citizens, largely supported transparency (except where its own self-interest was in issue).[10] Strong support has come too from individual MEPs such as Heidi Hautala and Michael Cashman, installed in strategic EP committees as rapporteur. Civil society has also been strongly represented. Statewatch, Access Info, the European Citizens Advisory Service (ECAS) and other civil society organisations (CSOs) working for civil liberties and transparency, have campaigned consistently and hard, using test cases and complaints to the European Ombudsman (EO) to good effect.

On the side of secrecy there has been a shifting majority in the Council, often headed by France, Germany, Spain and the UK. But the EU institutions, whose interests tend to differ, are by no means unanimous.[11] As diplomatic bodies, dealing with powerful international actors, especially the United States, over contentious subjects such as counterterrorism, cybercrime, policing and defence, the Council and European Council tend to prioritise security and international relations and incline naturally towards secrecy.[12] And strong support came at a crucial point from Javier Solana as Secretary General of the European Council and former Secretary General of NATO for an amendment that introduced a classification system.[13] The Council has also consistently stressed its diplomatic character, refusing to acknowledge the parliamentary character of its role.

The Commission's main concerns seem slightly different. Its primary concern has been the 'space to think' – its ability, in other words, to exchange ideas, opinions and information in the absence of lobbyists and pressure groups. This ground to

---

[10] eg, Case T-471/08 *Toland v Parliament* (2011) ECR II-271; Case T-190/10 *Egan and Hackett v Parliament* (judgment of 28 March 2012).

[11] See B Bjurulf and O Elgstrom 'Negotiating Transparency' (2004) 42 *Journal of Common Market Studies* 249.

[12] See notably Case T-331/11 *Besselink v Council* (judgment of 12 September 2013).

[13] Statewatch News Online, 'Solana plans for the security state agreed, an end to EU openness?' (July 2000). And see D Galloway, 'Classifying Secrets in the EU' (2014) 52 *Journal of Common Market Studies* 668; D Curtin, 'Overseeing Secrets in the EU: A Democratic Perspective' (2014) 52 *Journal of Common Market Studies* 684.

refuse access is employed in over 25 per cent of responses to requests; the protection of investigations – a ground that covers competition and mergers, state aids, fraud and infringement proceedings – is most frequently invoked (45.10 per cent). The Commission is also concerned with the administrative costs of openness, by no means negligible as recent reports tend to show. In 2012, for example, 17,940 new documents had to be added to the register of Commission documents. There were 6014 first-stage requests for access – a sharp decrease from 6447 in 2011 – involving 5274 replies and 229 new confirmatory applications with 160 negative replies. Full disclosure was given in 74.48 per cent of cases and partial disclosure in 8.61 per cent; 16.91 per cent of requests were fully refused.[14] Figures for the Council are similarly heavy. In 2012 its public register reached two million documents online with around 75 per cent publicly available and directly downloadable and 15 per cent partially available. It received 1871 initial requests for access to a total of 6166 documents from 847 individual applicants; 544 documents were classified. There were 23 confirmatory requests for access to 78 previously refused documents.[15] Even with the help of ICT and the Internet, this is a substantial administrative burden.

The task of redaction imposed by jurisprudence can also be heavy; in the *IFAW* case,[16] for example, a consumer group, which wanted information on a possible cartel, requested access to the Commission file. The Commission refused point blank on the ground that the effort involved in examining the papers would be wholly disproportionate; more than 47,000 pages were involved. Perhaps surprisingly, the GC adhered strictly to the principle that the Commission must examine every document to see that refusal of access was justifiable. Departure from this principle must be quite exceptional and all other options must be carefully considered and explained in detail in a reasoned decision. As this had not been done, the refusal of access was annulled.

THE CODES OF CONDUCT: ADMINISTRATIVE PROCEDURES

At Edinburgh in 1992 the European Council had decided to leave freedom of information to the Member States; it did, however, ask the Commission to work on ways and means to bring the Community 'closer to its citizens'.[17] At Amsterdam in 1997 a new Article 255 was inserted in the Treaty, establishing a right of access to 'documents' of the Council, Commission and EP for 'any natural or legal person residing or having its registered office in a Member State'. The Council as legislator should determine the 'general principles and limits' of the new right and the three institutions must each incorporate in their rules of procedure specific provisions regarding access to documents. These took the form of Codes of

---

[14] Commission, 'Report on the application in 2012 of Regulation (EC) No 1049/2001 regarding public access to European Parliament, Council and Commission documents' COM (2013) 515 final.
[15] Council, *AR 2013*.
[16] Case T-2/03 *Verein fur Konsumenteninformation v Commission* [2005] ECR II-1121, [94]–[131].
[17] See Bull EC 10-1992, 9; Bull EC 12-1992, 7.

124 *Transparency*

Conduct issued as institutional decisions[18] an inherently restrictive way of proceeding unsuccessfully challenged by the Netherlands in court. The Court of Justice (CoJ) chose, however, to interpret the contested provisions narrowly, assigning to the legislature the right to establish general principles and limiting judicial control to procedure:

> So long as the Community legislature has not adopted general rules on the right of public access to documents held by the Community institutions, the institutions must take measures as to the processing of such requests by virtue of their power of internal organization, which authorizes them to take appropriate measures in order to ensure their internal operation in conformity with the interests of good administration.[19]

The Codes which, because of the judgment in this case, applied only to documents created by the institutions, nonetheless promised that the public would have 'the widest possible access' to 'documents'. This term was defined relatively widely and construed by the Courts as a right to 'information', with the consequence that the institutions had to consider 'redacting' a document to issue any unexceptional parts.[20] The Codes encouraged the institutions to develop best practice, train their personnel, provide information and assistance to citizens and publish their principles, practice and procedural rules[21] and they set out the application process in considerable detail. Applications had to be written and precise and a written 'confirmatory application' asking for reconsideration could be presented in case of refusal. Applications must be processed within one month; negative decisions must be reasoned and the avenues of appeal notified. Documents could be consulted on the spot or copied at a reasonable fee, leaving administrative discretion in the case of repeat applications and very large documents. The Codes also saw the start of document registers in the institutions. The procedures and the list of privileged documents were sufficiently restrictive, however, to be the subject of much litigation and many ombudsman complaints.

The Council was the first target, perhaps because it is a legislative body whose procedures ought to be open, perhaps because the intergovernmental procedures of the 'third pillar' were peculiarly opaque. Policy was formulated in informal meetings of officials, the Council legislated by adopting 'common positions' and 'framework decisions', parliamentary input was confined to consultation (TEU Articles 34, 36) and the Luxembourg Courts had minimal competence (TEU Article 35). This was a substantial motive to demand access via the Codes. Perhaps

---

[18] Council Decision 93/731/EC of 20 December 1993 on public access to Council documents [1993] OJ L340/43; Commission Decision of 94/90/ECSC of 8 February 1994 on public access to Commission documents [1994] OJ L46/58; EP Decision on public access [1997] OJ L263/27.

[19] Case C-58/94 *Netherlands v Council* [1996] ECR I-2169, [26], [37]. The EP supported the Netherlands; the Commission and France supported the Council.

[20] See Case C-353/99P *Hautala v Council (No 2)* [2001] ECR I-9565, [11] and [22]–[23].

[21] Commission Decision 2001/973/EC of 5 December 2001 amending its rules of procedure [2001] OJ L345/94, now available on the Commission website as *Access to European Commission Documents, A Citizen's Guide*. And see Council Decision 2009/937/EU of 1 December 2009 adopting the Council's Rules of Procedure [2009] OJ L325/35; European Council Decision 2009/882/EU of 1 December 2009 adopting its Rules of Procedure [2009] OJ L315/51.

surprisingly, numbers of applications remained low[22] but early in 1994 John Carvel, *The Guardian's* reporter on EU affairs, brought a significant test case. Learning through a press release of a Justice Council meeting, Carvel applied for the minutes, attendance and voting records and decisions. The Council replied that its proceedings were confidential and a confirmatory application met with a negative response.

Before the GC, Carvel argued that a 'blanket refusal' to disclose documents violated Article 4(2) of Decision 93/731, which implied that a balancing test was necessary before the Council decided to refuse access. Denmark and the Netherlands intervened to give evidence that this had not been done and the Council conceded that, due to need to meet a deadline, the decision had been taken by A-item procedure without discussion. It insisted, however, that all confirmatory applications were now regularly examined by its Information Working Party. In a path-breaking judgment, the GC annulled the decisions, introducing what would become the standard proportionality test: the Council must 'genuinely balance the interest of citizens in gaining access to its documents against any interest of its own in maintaining the confidentiality of its deliberations'. This it manifestly had not done. But *The Guardian* had to register a second action before the Council reluctantly complied.[23]

In *Hautala*, a Green MEP followed up a parliamentary question on EU arms policy by requesting a confidential report made for the Council by its Working Group on Conventional Arms Exports. Given the political nature of the subject matter, the GC was probably wise to underline the limited nature of its jurisdiction. Review was said to be

> limited to verifying whether the procedural rules have been complied with, the contested decision is properly reasoned, and the facts have been accurately stated, and whether there has been a manifest error of assessment of the facts or a misuse of powers.[24]

Staying strictly within these guidelines, the Court reasoned that exceptions must be 'construed and applied strictly, in a manner which does not defeat the application of the general rule' and that the proportionality principle required derogations to remain 'within the limits of what is appropriate and necessary for achieving the aim in view'.

Although Decision 93/731 did not expressly require the Council to consider the question of partial access (redaction), it did not expressly prohibit such a possibility. Conceding that the institutions might, in the interests of good administration, balance the interest in limited public access against the administrative burden

---

[22] From 1994 to 1996, 142 applicants requested access to 443 Council documents, of which 19% (28) concerned institutional affairs and information policy: *First Report on the Implementation of the Council Decision on Public Access to Council Documents* (July 1996). The first overview of the regulatory regime (COM 2004/45) suggested that requests for access were increasing by about 50% annually.

[23] Case T-194/94 *Carvel and Guardian Newspapers v Council* [1995] ECR II-2769, [65]. Denmark, the Netherlands and EP supported Carvel.

[24] Written Question P-3219/96 [1997] OJ C186/48; Case T-14/98 *Hautala v Council* [1999] ECR II-2489, [72], [84]–[86]. Finland and Sweden supported Hautala; France supported the Council.

126 *Transparency*

caused by excessively lengthy files or the work of redaction, the Court nonetheless annulled the decision since redaction had not even been considered. In *Mattila*[25] the GC was more lenient, declining to annul a decision vitiated by procedural error when assured by the Council and Commission that the final outcome had not been affected. It was rightly reprimanded by the CoJ, which emphasised the function of procedures in guaranteeing due process rights:

> [P]ermitting the Council and the Commission to communicate to the appellant the reasons for the refusal to grant partial access to a document for the first time before the Community courts would render redundant the procedural guarantees expressly laid down in Decisions 93/731 and 94/90 and seriously affect the appellant's rights, which require that, except in exceptional cases, any decisions adversely affecting a person must state the reasons on which it is based, in order to provide the person concerned with details sufficient to allow him to ascertain whether the decision is well founded or whether it is vitiated by an error which will allow its legality to be contested.

These strong judicial decisions were heartening for proponents of open government.

Classification, Secrecy and the 'Summertime Coup'

The Amsterdam Treaty committed the Council to legislate within two years but agreement proved extremely difficult, creating space for an unexpected move by Javier Solana, previous Secretary General to NATO. Under the existing classification procedure introduced in 1995, documents were classified either as 'Secret', 'Confidential' or 'Restricted', highly protected at every stage, or as internal institutional documents (such as in-house notes and correspondence), classified as 'limité' or 'SN' and less strictly protected. Both categories needed the authorisation of the Secretary General or a Director General before release and the implementing decision set in place a detailed internal management system for classified documents.[26] In response to a request from NATO, Solana now initiated proceedings in the Council to harden these procedures, involving changes to the draft regulatory proposal then under consideration.

Against fierce opposition from Sweden, Finland and the Netherlands and without wider consultation, changes to the Code of Conduct were rushed through the Council by written procedure in August 2000. These effectively constructed a class exception for documents classified 'Top Secret', 'Secret' and 'Confidential'.[27] The provisions, which amount to de facto official secrets legislation, drafted by

---

[25] Case T-204/99 *Mattila v Council and Commission* [2001] ECR II-2265; Case C-353/01P *Mattila v Council and Commission* [2004] ECR I-1073, [32].

[26] Decision 24/95 of the Secretary General to the Council on measures for the protection of classified information applicable to the Secretariat General of the Council (30 Jan 1995). And see, D Curtin, *Top Secret Europe* (University of Amsterdam, 2011) 12–16.

[27] Council Decision, LIMITE, INF 93 JUR 268 (31 July 2000). And see Statewatch News Online, 'Solana plans for the security state agreed, an end to EU openness?' (30 October 2000).

officials in terms of an administrative procedure and adopted by the legislature with no democratic input, would now find their way into already contested proposals for a new general regulation. Article 9 of Regulation 1049/2001 (below) now provides that 'sensitive documents', more particularly those dealing with security, defence and military matters and classified as 'Top Secret', 'Secret' and 'Confidential' by the institution which classified them 'shall be recorded in the register or released only with the consent of the originator'. This may be a Member State, a third country or international organisation, clearly leaving much scope for variant practice.

REGULATION: OPEN GOVERNMENT OR OFFICIAL SECRECY?

After many disagreements, caused partly by a Commission draft proposal classifying 'internal working documents' as inaccessible, a proposal for a new regulation was finally agreed by the Commission and Council.[28] An 'Open Letter from civil society to the EP', objecting to the undemocratic nature of the legislative proceedings, urged further amendments to a text said to reduce citizens' rights under the Code of Conduct; violate the commitment in Article 255 TEC by derogating from the baseline of the existing Codes; widen the exception for sensitive documents; and disregard the Aarhus Convention.[29] The EP, however, asked for only minor amendments, leaving in place a compromise text that veers perplexingly between openness and secrecy.

Regulation 1049/2001 opens grandly with commitments to the principles of openness and transparency as expressed in the conclusions of the Birmingham, Edinburgh and Copenhagen Councils. It purports 'to give the fullest possible effect to the right of public access to documents and to lay down the general principles and limits in accordance with TEC Article 255(2)'. Its principal objective is to establish a *right* of access to documents extending to 'any citizen of the Union or natural or legal person residing or having its registered office in a Member State' and to define the principles and conditions of access and limits to the right. Taken together with the statement that 'all rules concerning access to documents of the institutions should be in conformity with this Regulation', the recitals create an expectation that openness will become the general rule, applicable horizontally to all EU activities, to which other regulation would be subordinate.[30]

---

[28] Commission Proposal COM (2000) 0030 final, [2000] OJ C177E/70; M Cashman and H Maij-Weggen, *Report of the EP on Public Access to Documents of the EP, Council and Commission*, A5-0318/2000. And see Statewatch, 'Secret Europe' (4 February 2000); T Bunyan, *Secrecy and openness in the EU – the ongoing struggle for freedom of information* ch 7 (available on the Statewatch website at: http://www.statewatch.org/secret/freeinfo/

[29] Statewatch News Online, 'Open Letter from civil society on the new code of access to documents of the EU institutions' (May 2001).

[30] See M de Leeuw, 'The Regulation on the Public Access to European Parliament, Council, and Commission Documents in the European Union: Are Citizens Better Off?' (2003) 28 *European Law Review* 324, 330–32.

Yet the regulation contains an unusually wide set of exemptions. These combine mandatory and discretionary procedures unhappily and are arranged in three categories. Article 4(1) makes it **mandatory** to refuse access to documents that would undermine the protection of the public interest in security, defence and military matters, international relations, financial, monetary and economic policy of the Community or a Member State and the privacy and integrity of individuals, with special reference to EU data laws. This leaves a little space for discretion. Article 4(2) slightly widens this space for cases involving individual commercial interests, court proceedings and legal advice, inspections, investigations and audits, where refusal is **mandatory subject to an 'overriding public interest' in disclosure**. Article 4(3), designed to protect the so-called 'space to think', deals with internal documents and decisions that have not yet been taken. It imposes a three-stage test that includes a double dose of discretion: (i) access **shall** be refused; (ii) if disclosure would seriously undermine the institution's decision-making process; (iii) **unless** there is an overriding public interest in disclosure. Redolent of institutional and official discretion, these are tough exceptions, which in some cases extend after the decision has been taken. It is hardly surprising to find them regularly referred for interpretation to the Courts and EO.[31]

Law-Making: An Openness Principle

Paragraph 6 of the recitals to Regulation 1049/2001 asserts the important democratic principle of public access to the law-making process. The wording is perhaps unhappy: 'wider access' is to be granted in cases where the institutions are 'acting in their legislative capacity, including under delegated powers'. It is perhaps unfortunate also that documents which should 'to the greatest possible extent' be directly accessible to the public are to be balanced against 'the effectiveness of the institution's decision-making process'. This opens the way for the argument, dear to the Council, that bargaining and negotiation 'requires closed doors'.

While the EP presented itself as deeply committed to transparency and in 1999 revised its Rules of Procedure to reflect this commitment,[32] the Council was slow to respond. The catalyst was the EO, acting on a complaint from a German MEP and political party about the Council practice of holding closed meetings in some

---

[31] For full analysis of the case law, see J Heliskosi and P Leino, 'Darkness at the Break of Noon: The Case Law on Regulation No 1049/2001 on Access to Documents' (2006) 43 *Common Market Law Review* 735; P Leino, 'Just a Little Sunshine in the Rain: The 2010 Case Law of the European Court of Justice on Access to Documents' (2011) 48 *Common Market Law Review* 1215; D Adamski, 'How Wide is "the Widest Possible"? Judicial Interpretation of the Exceptions to the Right of Access to Official Documents Revisited' (2009) 46 *Common Market Law Review* 521 and D Adamski, 'Approximating a Workable Compromise on Access to Official Documents: The 2011 Developments in the European Court of Justice' (2012) 49 *Common Market Law Review* 559.

[32] EP, 'Rules of Procedure' [1999] OJ L202/1 now Rules 103, 104 of the Rules of Procedure (2013).

legislative proceedings. The Secretary General's explanation that 'a substantial part' of Council legislative activity was in practice already public and 'nearly all documents' relating to it could be accessed via Regulation 1049/2001 was not enough for the EO. Treating this as an administrative procedure, he concluded that the Council's failure to make appropriate amendments to its Rules of Procedure and to give good reasons for refusing to meet publicly were instances of maladministration and duly sent a special report to the EP.[33] In 2005, the Council amended its Rules of Procedure 'to improve the openness and transparency of its formal meetings and to reach the widest public possible' by debating both legislative and non-legislative matters in public[34] and agreed to open proceedings under co-decision procedure to the public; a year later it opened up some important policy debates.[35]

An exception contained in Article 4(2) imposes a mandatory exemption for court proceedings and legal advice. With some justification, the Council interpreted this strictly, refusing access to two documents containing opinions from its legal service as to the validity of draft legislation. When a complaint reached the EO, he found the refusal 'particularly surprising', since it concerned an opinion drawn up in relation to the draft for Regulation 1049/2001. He went on to distinguish opinions given in the context of (possible) court proceedings, for which lawyer–client privilege should normally be available, from opinions on draft legislation, which should normally become available to the public when the legislative process has concluded. It was then up to the institution to show that disclosure would seriously undermine its decision-making process and that there was no overriding public interest in disclosure. Conceding that only the Courts were competent finally to answer the question, the EO rejected the Council's view that the issue lay outside his mandate and sent the case on to the EP in a special report, asking it to support his call for the Council to reconsider the application.[36]

The issue reached the Courts in *Turco*, concerning access to an opinion from the Council's legal service concerning the legality of a proposed directive on asylum procedures. The Council refused access, arguing that legal advice was an important instrument to ensure compatibility of new legislation with EU law so that disclosure might create legal uncertainty. The GC construed the exception widely so as to privilege legal service opinions and also held that no overriding public interest had been shown.[37] The case was considered of such strategic importance that Sweden took it over on appeal to the CoJ, which drew a line similar to that drawn by the EO. The Court underlined the obligation to examine the requested documents carefully to ensure (i) that they were in fact legal opinions and (ii) that disclosure would create a 'reasonably foreseeable risk' that the

---

[33] Inv 2395/2003/GG.
[34] Council Secretariat Information Sheet, 'Openness and Transparency of Council Proceedings' (December 2005).
[35] M de Leeuw, 'Openness in the Legislative Process in the EU' (2007) 32 *European Law Review* 295.
[36] Inv 1542/2000/(PB)SM. Whether this investigation was *intra vires* is surely a moot point.
[37] Case T-84/03 *Turco* v *Council* [2004] ECR II-4061. Finland, Denmark and Sweden supported Turco; the UK and Commission supported the Council.

Council's ability to obtain 'frank, objective and comprehensive advice' would be undermined. The obligation was not absolute; it did not preclude refusal but a detailed statement of reasons for refusal was necessary. The CoJ then disallowed as specious both limbs of the Council's defence to the effect first, that disclosure would create a risk from pressure or lobbying and second, that it might raise doubts in the minds of citizens and undermine the legitimacy of the decision-making process. The Court retorted briskly that it was secrecy rather than openness that would undermine legitimacy; openness could only help to reinforce the quality of the reasoning.[38]

The seminal victory for openness in *Turco* was followed up in *In'tVeld*,[39] where an MEP asked for access to advice from the Council's legal service in the context of confidential negotiations with the US on the Anti-Counterfeiting Trade Agreement (ACTA) – the Anti-Piracy Treaty. The GC drew on *Turco* to hold the Council strictly to the procedure of individual consideration of each document and to proof of overriding public interest. The Court ruled that too many documents had been classified as 'confidential' but the Dutch MEP remained dissatisfied, commenting that the ruling upheld the culture of discretion and diplomatic confidentiality of the 1950s. In *Access Info Europe*,[40] which involved highly contested proposals for reform of Regulation 1049/2001, AIE wanted access to a note to the Council's Working Party on Information, which detailed amendments tabled by named Member States. The Council had granted only partial access, in reliance on the argument that disclosure of information relating to the identity of those who made the proposals would seriously undermine the Council's decision-making process. The GC, which asked several penetrating questions, was unconvinced by the Council's detailed reasons. Once again discounting arguments based on the risk of pressure from lobbyists, the Court opined that it was 'specifically the principle of democratic legitimacy which requires those responsible for the proposals contained in the requested document to be publicly accountable for their actions'. Proposals were by their very nature, 'designed to be discussed' and 'public opinion [was] perfectly capable of understanding that the author of a proposal is likely to amend its content subsequently'.[41] On appeal, the Council argued for a 'negotiating space' on account of the peculiar character of the EU legislative process; it was 'very fluid and requires a high level of flexibility on the part of Member States so that they can modify their initial position, thus maximising the chances of reaching an agreement'. The GC had got the balance wrong, attributing 'undue and excessive weight to the transparency of the decision-making process, without taking any account of the needs associated with the effectiveness of that process'. In an unusually forceful judgment, the CoJ upheld the reasoning of

---

[38] Joined Cases C-39/05 and 52/05 *Sweden and Turco v Council* [2008] ECR I-4723 noted by Arnull at (2009) 46 *Common Market Law Review* 1219. The Netherlands, Finland and Denmark supported Sweden and Turco; the Commission and UK supported the Council.

[39] Case T-529/09 *Sophie in't Veld v Council* (judgment of 4 May 2012). ; Case T-310/10 *Sophie in't Veld v Commission* (judgment of 19 March 2013).

[40] Case T-233/09 *Access Info Europe v Council* [2011] ECR II-0073.

[41] Ibid, [69]–[74].

the GC in every particular, adding for good measure that the document requested did not fall into any exception specifically listed in the Regulation but formed 'part of the legislative process'.[42]

The *API* case[43] brought by the International Press Association to obtain access to the Commission's pleadings in cases brought before the Luxembourg Courts is somewhat different. The Commission refused access to documents in all pending cases and pleaded the right to protect the general EU infringement procedures (see chapter seven). The GC accepted the argument that pleadings are covered in their entirety until the proceedings have reached the hearing stage, yet partially annulled the Commission decision. On appeal, the Grand Chamber endorsed its own case law, which had created 'general presumptions applicable to certain categories of document' to which access can be refused without specific consideration of each case. Yet it somewhat confusingly ruled that documents must be examined individually to ensure that a real risk of prejudice was involved. Adding tartly that a non-specific 'public right to know' about important legal and political issues was not sufficient to outweigh the statutory exceptions, the Court stood on the fact that Regulation 1049/2001 did not apply to the Courts; the nature of the judicial process; and the principle of 'equality of arms' between the parties.[44] This leaves the legislative process as a special category where exceptionally there is a presumption of full openness.

Openness Trumped

After a period seen generally as liberal, the *Bavarian Lager* case came as a shock.[45] Bavarian Lager wanted full disclosure of particulars of a meeting held between the Commission and UK representatives, which it had not been permitted to attend. The Commission granted partial access but redacted the names of those who had attended, claiming that disclosure would compromise its ability to conduct inquiries. The GC annulled this decision. The CoJ, on the other hand, chose to stick closely to the letter of Article 4(1), ruling that openness must give way before a justifiable claim based on the Data Protection Directive[46] that disclosure would undermine 'the privacy and integrity of the individual'. Ironically, the decision was taken in defiance of a strong intervention from the European Data Protection

---

[42] Case C-280/11 *Council v Access Info Europe* (judgment of 17 October 2013) [62]. Spain, the Czech Republic and France supported the Council; the EP, the UK and Greece supported Access Info.

[43] Case T-36/04 *API v Commission* [2007] ECR II-03207.

[44] Joined Cases C-514/07 P, C-528/07 P, C-532/07 P *Sweden and API v Commission* [2010] ECR I-8533. *Denmark and Finland supported Sweden and API; the UK supported the Commission.* The case is singled out for criticism in EP Resolution of 14 September 2011 on public access to documents (Rule 104(7)) for the years 2009–10 (2010/2294(INI)) point 22.

[45] Case T-194/04 *Bavarian Lager v Commission* [2007] ECR II-04523; Case C-28/08 *Bavarian Lager v Commission* [2010] ECR I-6055; Denmark, Sweden and Finland supported Bavarian Lager; the UK and Council supported the Commission.

[46] Directive 95/46/EC on the protection of individuals with regard to the processing of personal data and on the free movement of such data [1995] OJ *L281/31*.

Supervisor, who wished to see openness confirmed as the general principle to which other legislation must cede.[47] In *Thesing*,[48] where the applicant was a journalist wanting access to internal policy papers of the European Central Bank on financing deficit and government debt management with special reference to Greece, the GC confidently denied access, overriding a claim under ECHR Article 10, which protects access to documents under the rubric of freedom of opinion.[49] The Article 4(1) exception for financial, monetary and economic policy was allowed to trump the Article 10 right on the ground that the market environment had been very vulnerable; that disclosure would affect the proper functioning of the financial markets; and that Eurostat had around the same time published a report on the Greek situation.

The tighter attitude was confirmed, perhaps more justifiably, in a cluster of commercial cases where sector-specific regulations clashed with the horizontal general principles of openness. In *Technische Glaswerkel Ilmenau*,[50] the applicant, which was involved in state aid proceedings, sought access to a non-confidential version of Commission files together with an opportunity to submit observations. The Commission refused access on the ground that the files were part of a current formal investigation procedure. Overruling the GC, which had required individual examination of the documents, the CoJ held that the absence of specific rights of access in the sectoral legislation must be taken into account in interpreting Regulation 1049/2001; if interested parties were able to obtain access to the Commission's administrative file indirectly, the system for review of state aid would be called into question. The same reasoning permeates case law on mergers where, in reliance on the exception for commercial interests and the purpose of investigations, third parties were refused access to Commission documents relating to merger control proceedings. Here the Court allowed the Commission to refuse access without individual examination, creating a virtual class exception.[51] Yet in *Mytravel*[52] the CoJ, again overruling the GC, ruled in a complex dispute over concentrations that the Commission could not simply claim blanket protection for the documents of a working group set up to consider appealing a case that it had lost, but must consider the individual documents. In contrast, in *Borax Europe*,[53] the GC ruled that the Commission had failed to prove any serious risk from releasing the report of a working party of experts advisory to a comitology committee. Such inconsistent case law is quite simply unacceptable.

[47] See EDPS, 'Public access to documents containing personal data after the *Bavarian Lager* ruling', available on the EDPS website. The CoJ also largely disregarded the elegant Opinion of AG Sharpston.
[48] Case T-590/10 *Thesing and Bloomberg Finance v European Central Bank* (judgment of 29 November 2012).
[49] See notably App 37374/05 *Társaság a Szabadságjogokért v Hungary* [2009] ECHR 618.
[50] Case T-237/02 *Technische Glaswerke Ilmenau v Commission* [2006] ECR II-5131; Case C-139/07 P *Commission v Technische Glaswerke IlmenauGmbH* [2010] ECR I-05883. Denmark, Finland and Sweden supported TG. The sectoral legislation was Council Regulation (EC) 659/1999.
[51] Case C-404/10 P *Commission v Éditions Odile Jacob* (judgment of 28 June 2012); Case C- 477/10 P *Commission v Agrofert Holding* (judgment of 28 June 2012).
[52] Case C-506/08 P *Sweden v Commission and MyTravel Group plc* (judgment of 21 July 2011).
[53] Case T-166/05 *Borax Europe v Commission* [2009] ECR II-28.

Yet the case law shows the two Luxembourg Courts – by no means always in agreement – struggling to reconcile a set of highly inconsistent principles. In treaties and declarations, the Council speaks strongly in favour of openness, democracy and transparency. This is not, however, how it behaves. Similarly, Regulation 1049/2001 purports 'to give the fullest possible effect to the right of public access to documents' yet the long list of exceptions to disclosure and the mandatory nature of many of the exceptions makes the regulation look more like official secrets legislation than a freedom of information Act. Balancing the different interests and strongly held views is thus no easy task.

The EU and National Information Laws

The Birmingham Council expressly reserved freedom of information as a national competence, a restriction reflected in the Codes of Conduct by the 'authorship rule', according to which documents held by an institution but originating from a third party could be accessed only via the author. Regulation 1049/2001 changed the balance. Member States were warned that they should observe the 'principle of loyal cooperation', should 'take care not to hamper' the proper application of the regulation and should 'respect the security rules of the institutions'. Under Article 4(4), an institution faced with a request to disclose a third party document was to 'consult' the third party with a view to assessing whether an exception was applicable 'unless it is clear that the document shall or shall not be disclosed'. This gave the institution the first and last chance to evaluate the request. Article 4(5) allowed a Member State to 'request' an institution not to disclose a document originating from it 'without its prior agreement'. Article 5 effectively undid the Swedish journalists' victory by providing that a Member State asked for an EU document 'shall consult with the institution concerned in order to take a decision that does not jeopardize the attainment of the objectives of this Regulation'.

At first these procedures were construed loosely, for example, by accepting signatures from regional governments or junior officials as representing a Member State.[54] Member State rights were severely weakened, however, by the important *IFAW* decision. IFAW, an environmental pressure group, had requested access to documents received by the Commission in connection with Commission approval of an industrial project on a German site protected by the Habitats Directive. Germany refused permission to disclose. The GC construed the term 'request' in Article 4(5) to mean 'instruct': the Member State need give no reasons and Commission refusal to disclose without further examination or consideration of the documents was therefore justified.[55] The CoJ felt differently.[56] It ruled that to

---

[54] Case T-76/02 *Mara Messina v Commission* [2003] ECR II-3203; P Cabral, 'Access to Member State Documents in EC Law' (2006) 31 *European Law Review* 378.

[55] Case T-168/02 *IFAW Internationaler Tierschutz-Fonds v Commission* [2004] ECR II-4135. Sweden, Denmark and Finland supported IFAW; the UK and Spain supported the Commission.

[56] Case C-64/05 P *Internationaler Tierschutz-Fonds v Commission (Sweden intervening)* [2007] ECR I-11389.

construct a 'discretionary right of veto' with potential effect to exclude from public scrutiny an especially important class of documents that could form the basis of and cast light upon the EU decision-making process, would be incompatible with the objectives of the Regulation. The Court went on to analyse the procedural implications in some detail. The Regulation created a 'joint decision-making process' dependent on 'dialogue' to be carried on in accordance with the duty of loyal cooperation. Where an institution receives a request for access to a Member State document it must rapidly, and in line with the statutory time limits, open a dialogue with the Member State; if the Member State objects, it must give reasons for refusing access; in the absence of reasons, the institution must make its own decision and, if it considers none of the statutory exceptions applicable, grant access. Its decision must

> not merely record the fact that the Member State concerned has objected to disclosure of the document asked for, but also set out the reasons relied on by that Member State to show that one of the exceptions to the right of access in Article 4(1) to (3) of the regulation applies. That information will allow the person who has asked for the document to understand the origin and grounds of the refusal of his request and the competent court to exercise, if need be, its power of review.[57]

Once again, the CoJ had lifted decision-making to Union level with a ruling likely to impinge on the national administrative practice of Member States.

The Statutory Procedures

The procedures ordained by the Regulation mirror those set in place by the Codes of Conduct. A wide definition of 'document' covers all texts, whether written or stored electronically, and sound, visual and audiovisual recordings. Applications may be written or electronic but must be 'sufficiently precise' and a very long or large number of document(s) should be the subject of a negotiated fair solution (Article 6). Applications must be promptly acknowledged and processed within 15 working days; a written and reasoned reply is necessary in case of whole or partial refusal with details of the right to make a 'confirmatory application'; failure to reply also activates this right. A refusal can generate a 'confirmatory application' and a further refusal must specifically inform the applicant of his right to institute court proceedings or complain to the EO (Article 8). Article 2(4) provides that documents are to be made accessible to the public in response to a written application directly in electronic form or through a register. Article 4(6) provides for redaction. Access can be provided on the spot, online or by written copy, according to the applicant's preference but if the copy exceeds 20 pages, he may be charged (Article 10).

[57] Ibid, [89].

According to Statewatch, a CSO accustomed routinely to making applications, the institutions are well capable of manipulating the procedures. Statewatch describes some 'covert means of refusing access':

> Article 2.1 says that the request must be 'sufficiently precise'. Thus a general request, for example for documents concerning 'migration', would be refused. To get a response it is necessary to either give the exact title or better still to give the reference number (eg: 11237/98 ASIM 22). Although the Council Decision says that 'Where necessary, the applicant shall be asked for further details' this is rarely if ever used.
>
> Article 3.1 says applicants should either be sent copies of documents with a bill for the cost (introduced in February 1996) or by 'consulting it on the spot' – this means granting access but requiring the applicant to go to Brussels to 'consult it' . . . Article 3.2 says that 'the General Secretariat shall endeavour to find a fair solution to deal with repeat applications and/or those which relate to very large documents'. The Council interpretation of this Article has been highly restrictive. For example, many applications from Statewatch have been treated as 'repeat applications' on the grounds that our requests all concern justice and home affairs – they are never for the same document. They have also chosen to hold that requests for a very large *number* of documents means the same thing as very large documents. The key phrase in this Article is 'fair solution'. In practice this means that the Council having decided that a request say for documents from four different meetings requires a 'fair solution' then only provide documents from the third and fourth meetings and refuse to consider meetings one and two.[58]

Statewatch has used the EO with some success to complain about such problems.

OMBUDSMEN FOR OPENNESS

Both European Ombudsmen have been staunch supporters of open government and have manifested their support in several ways. The ombudsman's principal tools are citizens' complaints and own-initiative investigations (OII). Complaints on access to documents began to appear in the EO's earliest reports. In 1996, when the Council had questioned his competence, Jacob Söderman retorted that 'the purpose of creating the office of Ombudsman was to emphasize the Union's commitment to transparency. It is therefore clear that transparency and the right of access to documents are matters of great concern to the Ombudsman'.[59] As already indicated, the EO was active in pressing the Council to open up legislative proceedings and has taken a firm line over registers.

The online public register of Council documents (operational since January 1999) automatically lists in the register 'all non-sensitive documents submitted to the Council or to one of its preparatory bodies which are to serve as a basis for deliberations, could influence the decision-making process or reflect the progress

---

[58] Bunyan, above (n 28). Allegedly, the Commission has considered blacklisting Statewatch.
[59] Inv 45/26.7.95/JPB/PD/B.

made on a given subject'.[60] But when Statewatch applied for some unnumbered documents, the Council claimed that it was unable to identify the documents concerned – if, indeed, they existed. Statewatch also complained over the exclusion of 'Confidential', 'Restreint' and 'SN' documents and 'non-papers' from the register. The EO found maladministration on both counts, justifying the additional administrative work on the grounds both of the principles of good administration and also because of 'the fundamental importance which the right of citizens to have access to documents held by the Council has in order to guarantee openness and transparency in the latter's decision-making'. A special report to the EP followed, censuring the Council for failure to release the relevant documents and failure to provide the necessary assurances that the draft recommendations had been fully complied with.[61]

Statewatch has also complained about Commission failure to produce its annual report on access to documents on time and about its online documents register, which covers only legislative texts and adopted Commission reports thus excluding the majority of Commission documents. The EO discounted the Commission response that it was not legally committed to register *all* its documents and was working to extend its registers, and found maladministration. His decision recorded that the Commission had not bothered to dispute the fact that 'only a fraction' of its documents were on its register and he recommended a 'comprehensive register'.[62]

Annual Reports confirm that complaints over access to information form a consistently high proportion of the EO's workload.[63] This fact alone enables the EO to make an important contribution to openness. Investigative procedure allows staff to access files and talk to officials, providing a good picture of what is actually happening and allowing the EO to assess whether claims of privilege are really justified. Friendly settlements are often achieved, as in a recent complaint from ECAS over failure to release documents involving the UK opt out from the European Charter of Fundamental Rights (ECFR), where the Commission reconsidered its position and released requested documents after an initial approach from the EO.[64] An ombudsman is also well placed to see whether recommendations are implemented; as indicated in chapter three, they can be

---

[60] Council Rules of Procedure Annex II, made applicable to the European Council by Art 10 of its Rules of Procedure. In 2011, 1,729,944 documents were listed, with 77.3% public and downloadable. Of 26, 219 documents classified partially accessible 4858 were accessible online.

[61] Inv 917/2000/GG with special report to the EP.

[62] Inv 668/2007/MHZ; Decision of the EO closing his inquiry into complaint 3208/2006/GG. The recommendations were endorsed by the EP Committee on Civil Liberties: see INI/2007/2154 (A6-0459/2008).

[63] In 2002, as Regulation 1049/2001 became effective, 2511 complaints were registered: 653 fell within the mandate; of these 27% involved lack of transparency, including refusal of information. In 2005, shortly after Enlargement, 4416 complaints were registered: 1184 fell within the mandate; of these 24% involved lack of transparency, including refusal of information. In 2011, 2510 complaints were registered: 698 fell within the mandate; of these 16.2% were requests for information and 7.1% involved public access to documents.

[64] Inv 2293/2008/(BB)(FOR)TN; PR 5/2013 (04 March 2013); ECAS Press Release (4 March 2013).

monitored regularly to check the outcome. A follow-up on the Statewatch complaint reports that:

> During the Ombudsman's inquiry, the Commission consistently argued that it was going to expand the scope of its registers and led the Ombudsman to believe that the problem was mainly a technical one. The Ombudsman regrets that the Commission's response to the critical remark in this case suggests that it has no intention of trying to complete its register.[65]

The Commission website confirms that this remains the case.

Reports can also be backed up by special reports to the EP Petitions Committee. Eight of the 12 special reports submitted in the last ten years concerned transparency. In 2010, a special report criticised the Commission's handling of a request for access to letters from Porsche written during discussions with manufacturers over carbon dioxide emissions. It was not on this occasion the lack of transparency that was in issue – the Commission had decided to release the letters – but its treatment of Porsche, which had not consented to the release. The Commission had disregarded the procedural rules by failing to inform Porsche of its intentions or of the legal remedies available to it. It had also delayed writing to Porsche for 15 months after the EO's draft recommendation was issued. With regret the EO concluded that the Commission was guilty not only of maladministration, but also of failure to cooperate with him sincerely and in good faith; its attitude was detrimental both to inter-institutional dialogue and to the public image of the EU. He asked the EP to consider inviting the Commission to acknowledge breach of its duty of sincere cooperation, and to give an undertaking to the EP that it would in future respect this duty.[66]

OIIs are appropriate to establish principle or tackle endemic problems. In his first report, Jacob Söderman announced that, although he expected to utilise the power sparingly, he would use it where multiple complaints suggested that a more general inquiry would be appropriate.[67] Soon afterwards he opened an OII into the rules of access of 15 EU bodies, other than the Council and Commission, which had such rules already. Finding that only one agency, the Office for Harmonization in the Internal Market (OHIM) had adopted such rules though others 'intended to do so', the EO recommended them to 'adopt, and make easily available to the public, rules governing public access to all documents not already covered by existing legal provisions allowing access or requiring confidentiality'.[68]

---

[65] 'Follow-up to critical and further remarks– How the EU institutions responded to the Ombudsman's recommendations in 2008'. The Commission website at: http://ec.europa.eu/transparency/regdoc/index.cfm?language=en&CFID=253020354&CFTOKEN=e32e842815e5d7de-B3A3604E-0D53-7532-F52C1B BEA04FF7DF&jsessionid=95049c869cac33df88414f3e1150383d5146TR (visited April 2014) suggests that the recommendations are not yet fully implemented.
[66] 'Special Report concerning lack of cooperation by the European Commission in complaint 676/2008/RT' (24 February 2010, 7 July 2010).
[67] EO, AR 1995, 22.
[68] Own-Initiative Inquiry into Public Access to Documents held by Community Institutions and Bodies (616/PUBAC/F/IJH, December 1997).

138 *Transparency*

A year later, the EO was able to report to the EP that all but the CoJ had conformed to his procedural recommendations. On content, he merely observed:

> Compared to the provisions governing some national administrations ... the rules on public access to documents held by Community institutions and bodies are generally quite limited. In particular, they give no right of access to documents held by one body, but originating in another. Nor do they require the establishment of registers of documents which could both facilitate citizens' use of their right of access and promote good administration by preventing the loss of documents.[69]

He hinted that the EP might both 'encourage institutions and bodies which have not already made their rules available in all the official languages of the Communities to do so' and consider 'whether the rules that have been adopted ensure the degree of transparency that European citizens expect of the Union'.

Transparency is one of five core principles selected by the EO as essential for the EU public service – namely, commitment to the EU and its citizens, integrity, objectivity, respect for others and transparency – and it is interpreted as meaning that civil servants should be willing to explain their activities and give reasons for their actions. They should keep proper records and welcome public scrutiny of their conduct, including their compliance with these public service principles.[70] The EO's 'Code of Good Administrative Behaviour' reflects the need to foster a culture of openness within the public service, which should infuse all its proceedings. The Code underlines the need to correspond with citizens in their chosen language; to provide members of the public with the information that they request and, when appropriate, advise them on how to initiate an administrative procedure in a clear and understandable manner. Records are to be kept of incoming and outgoing mail, documents received and so forth (Article 24). Any refusal to disclose information on grounds of confidentiality must be reasoned (Articles 18, 22) and direct requests for access to documents must be dealt with 'in accordance with the rules adopted by the Institution and in accordance with the general principles and limits laid down in Regulation (EC) No 1049/2001'; where necessary, the applicant shall be advised to apply in writing (Article 23).

It is hard to evaluate the EO's effectiveness in promoting open government in the EU. As already emphasised, ombudsmen have certain advantages; they can inspect administrative behaviour and monitor implementation but, in the absence of an empirical study, one cannot know what the impact of ombudsman rulings really is. The EO also has to operate within a framework of judicial principle and needs to tread carefully in this respect. Both EOs have consistently expressed commitment to open government and this commitment has been reflected both in the 'Code of Good Administrative Behaviour' and in active campaigning for

---

[69] 'Special Report to the EP following the Own-Initiative Inquiry into Public Access to Documents' OI/1/98/OV (2002). And see R Rawlings, 'Engaged Elites: Citizen Action and Institutional Attitudes in Commission Enforcement' (2000) 6 *European Law Journal* 4.

[70] 'Public Service Principles for the EU Civil Service', available on the EO website.

law reform.[71] Jacob Söderman openly canvassed for Regulation 1049/2001 and Nikiforos Diamandorous has played a substantial role in the present campaign for reform – a complex and acrimonious process, which has yet to achieve results.[72] All we can do is to register continued ombudsman support for openness; we are not in a position to evaluate the effects.

TOWARDS REFORM?

Talk of greater openness permeated debate on the European Constitution and was taken up in the Commission's Transparency Initiative. A review was announced and a Green Paper published pointing to a number of areas where the law seemed confused or defective.[73] The Commission pointed to the need to iron out procedural inconsistencies between the general regime of Regulation 1049/2001, the more generous access available in environmental matters (see chapter twelve) and the more restrictive data protection regime of Regulation 45/2001 considered in the *Bavarian Lager* case (above). There was also a need to clarify the law on documents originating in Member States or obtained from third parties.

A public consultation followed, in which a majority of the 81 respondents agreed on the need for greater openness and complained of difficulty in finding information on the limited registers and websites. The corporate sector, however, was strongly hostile, fearful over uncontrolled access to confidential business information and inadequate data protection.[74] Claiming to increase transparency, the Commission then issued its proposal.[75] The reaction from civil society groups was general dismay. Particularly contentious was a definition of 'document' as a document 'drawn-up by an institution and formally transmitted to one or more recipients or otherwise registered, or received by an institution'. As CSOs pointed out at an EP hearing, this would significantly restrict access and encourage abuse by officials, who could avoid publication simply by deciding not to transmit

---

[71] J Söderman, 'The Role and Impact of the EO in Access to Documentation and the Transparency of Decision-Making' in V Deckmyn and I Thomson (eds), *Openness and Transparency in the European Union* (Maastricht: EIPA, 1998).

[72] EO, 'Response to the Green Paper' (29 October 2007); 'Contribution of the EO, P Nikiforos Diamandouros, to the public hearing on the Revision of Regulation 1049/2001 on public access to Documents: LIBE (2008)'.

[73] See H Kranenborg, 'Is it Time to Revise the European Regulation on Public Access to Documents?' (2006) 12 *European Public Law* 251; Commission Green Paper, 'Public Access to Documents held by Institutions of the European Community: A Review' (COM (2007) 185 final.

[74] Staff Working Paper, 'Report on the Outcome of the Public Consultation on the Review of Regulation (EC) No 1049/2001' SEC (2008) 29/2.

[75] Commission Press Release, 'The European Commission proposes to improve access to documents of the EU institutions', IP/08/661 (30 April 2008); Commission 'Proposal for a Regulation of the EP and Council regarding public access to EP, Council and Commission documents' COM (2008) 229 final. The texts are compared by the EP legislative observatory, 2008/0090/COD/Access to Documents.

140 *Transparency*

or register documents formally.[76] Further restrictions included strengthened protection where decisions had not yet been taken and of Member State documents. Statewatch drew attention to the fact that the Commission proposed tweaking the provision for registers so as to avoid compliance with the EO's recommendations.[77]

A stalemate ensued, as CSOs and the EP came together to push for more transparency, while the Council and Member States were unable to agree.[78] To break the deadlock, the Commission proposed an alternative regulation, which would make only minimal changes, a tactic heavily criticised in the Cashman Report for the Civil Liberties, Justice and Home Affairs Committee of the EP (LIBE), which pushed for sweeping amendments.[79] In plenary, the EP passed a major resolution, outlining the history of the debate over transparency and referencing the major judicial decisions and the EO's work.[80] It called on the Council to review its rules and increase transparency regarding legislative procedures, making detailed suggestions for improvement; on the Commission to open up committee and comitology proceedings; on the EP itself to adopt more transparent and open procedures; and finally, on the Inter-institutional Committee to 'address as a matter of urgency the issues mentioned in this resolution'. There the matter rests at the time of writing.

CONCLUSION

In its Resolution, the EP asserted that the EU should stand at the forefront, providing a model of institutional transparency and modern democracy for the Member States and, indeed, for the world at large. With Article 298 TFEU the Lisbon Treaty had 'introduced a new constitutional framework of EU institutional transparency, with a view to an open, efficient and independent European administration . . . by establishing a firm fundamental right of access to documents of EU institutions, bodies, offices and agencies'.[81] This is far from the truth. At treaty level, transparency is lauded as an overarching principle, to which EU officials must conform. At other, more practical levels, statutory exceptions are treated as creating 'general presumptions' justifying refusal to adhere to the principle of openness. The case law is variable and has arguably never recovered

---

[76] Statewatch Presentation at EP hearing on proposed amendments to Regulation 1049/2001 SEC (2008) 29/2 And see Corporate Europe Observatory, 'Open Letter to Commissioner Ashton re DG Trade's Vademecum' (14 May 2009); EuObserver, 'EU officials warned to be careful about email content' (6 May 2009).

[77] Statewatch Presentation, above (n 76).

[78] See Note from the Danish Presidency on the final state of play, Inter-institutional File:2008/0090 (COD) 10698/12 (22 June 2012).

[79] The Cashman Report on the Commission Proposal for a recast regulation (COM (2008)) PE 439.989v02-00 (1 September 2011) is available at 2008/0090 (COD).

[80] Resolution of 14 September 2011 on public access to documents (Rule 104(7)) for the years 2009–2010 (2010/2294(INI)).

[81] Ibid.

from the refusal of the CoJ in the early *Netherlands* case to refrain from creating a clear 'public right to know'. Opinion in the Council is sharply divided. New legislation is blocked. In circumstances where officials are left with no clear signals, they are likely to feel justified in either following the rulebook very closely or in interpreting the rules to their own advantage. Open government is expensive in so many ways.

6
The Pathways Model and Steering: Public Procurement

NOWHERE IS THE rich interplay between domestic administrative process and EU law procedural requirements better illustrated than in public contracting for works, supplies and services. In the words of a recent comparative survey, 'the creation of a common European law on public procurement is one of the most ambitious objectives for the transformation of public law that the European Union has undertaken'.[1] Continued convergence via 'rules [that] exist to bring some common disciplines to regulation of this critical government function'[2] is the Commission's resounding message. As such, with the internal contractual processes of Member State authorities being framed in 'vertical' fashion according to EU prescriptions, public procurement is a chief example both of Europeanised public administration on the frontline and of the 'horizontal' or non-sector specific codification of administrative procedures on a pan-European basis. The evolving regulatory regime is characterised by successive waves of legislation going back some 40 years, extending to some notable innovation in the realm of remedies.[3]

On the other hand, as the comparative survey promptly concedes, 'the harmonisation process of European law on public procurement can also be seen as a significant example of the actual European unification process: slow, irregular, imperfect, complex'.[4] Conceptually speaking, the codification is a step down on the ladder of supranational intervention from 'pure' harmonisation or legal demands for uniformity. It is the realm of provisions 'coordinating national procedures': 'a common framework within which the nationally defined procedure must be kept' (and allowed to operate).[5] Typically the EU legislation, in the form here of directives, not only drives but is also driven by national developments in law and administration. Further, the EU codification only regulates certain aspects

---

[1] M Morón (ed), *Public Procurement in the European Union and its Member States* (Valladolid: Lex Nova, 2012) 8.
[2] Commission Staff Working Paper, 'Evaluation Report: Impact and Effectiveness of EU Public Procurement Legislation' SEC (2011) 853 final, iv.
[3] Public procurement by EU institutions and bodies lies outside the scope of this chapter.
[4] Morón, above (n 1) 9.
[5] Directive 2014/24/EU on public procurement and repealing Directive 2004/18/EC [2014] OJ L94/65, recital 1; 'Evaluation Report', above (n 2) 21.

of public procurement, leaving large areas to be regulated (or not) by national legislation.

Public procurement also merits a chapter in this volume as an administrative process of great practical importance and one that references the familiar visualisation of administrative procedure as 'the formal path, established in legislation', whereby 'an administrative action has to be carried out through a number of steps'.[6] Involving stress on transparency of decision-making and the use of objective criteria specified in advance, the basic model reflects the familiar *Rechtsstaat*-style assumption that whenever there is broad administrative discretion, arbitrariness or discrimination follows automatically. Rule-making through directives with a view to structuring or guiding, confining or circumscribing and checking or reviewing[7] the exercise of administrative discretion in successive parts of the decision-making process is at the heart of the EU's 'common framework'. Further however, in the light of demands for competition and manageability in routine transactions, and for more flexibility in complex (large-scale) contracts, public purchasers are presented with a set of alternative procedural routings to follow: in the Commission's words, 'a menu of common procedures';[8] or, as we prefer, 'the pathways model'.

This regulatory regime illuminates the major instrumental dimension to administrative procedure – what Schmidt-Aßmann calls the 'particular steering potential ... in terms of reaching substantive targets'.[9] Viewed as a 'wiring system' for coordination (see chapter one), the EU procedural requirements are often dry and technical but also heavily policy laden. The touchstone is repeated recourse to the classic administrative law concept of relevancy, with certain considerations being factored in, and others factored out, as our public contract-maker proceeds step by step along a pathway. At times the procedures convey strong commands, especially in the cause of market transparency; on other occasions a light touch on the tiller.

There is steering, and there is steering. Whereas the EU rules are not intended to force public authorities to go to the commercial market ('compulsory competitive tendering'), their practical workings reflect the fashion in many national systems for 'contractual governance' and especially for outsourcing or contracting out.[10] To recall the metaphor: 'the state steers, it does not row'. Attention is drawn to the place of public contract as a policy lever and, more particularly, as a repository for rules, principles and standards and hence as an alternative source of

---

[6] See above, Introduction, p 2.

[7] Techniques associated in the Anglo-American administrative law tradition with KC Davis, *Discretionary Justice* (Westport, CT: Greenwood Press, 1969).

[8] 'Evaluation Report', above (n 2) iv.

[9] E Schmidt-Aßmann, 'Structures and Functions of Administrative Procedures in German, European and International Law' in J Barnes (ed), *Transforming Administrative Procedure* (Seville: Global Law Press, 2008) 62.

[10] J-B Auby, 'Comparative Approaches to the Rise of Contract in the Public Sphere' [2007] *Public Law* 40; also, R De Hoog and L Salamon, 'Purchase-of-Service Contracting' in L Salamon (ed), *The Tools of Government: A Guide to the New Governance* (Oxford: OUP, 2002).

regulation.[11] Recent trends in public administration serve to highlight the tension at the heart of the public procurement regime between *imperium* or the command of law (in the form of the EU procedural codification and national implementing legislation), and the *dominium* power of Member States (the deployment of wealth in aid of domestic policy objectives (fuelled by the great public power of taxation)). Referencing the functional limitations of contractual specification and/or rule-bound techniques for 'controlling' discretion, the effectiveness of costly administrative procedures is at stake here.

COORDINATING NATIONAL PROCEDURES

Rationales in Context

From the standpoint of the Single Market, public contracting is an obvious target for legislative intervention. A significant and influential factor in the economy, it is estimated to account for around one-fifth of EU GDP.[12] About a fifth of that total – some €450 billion – is spent on purchases above the value thresholds set out in the directives such that the EU procedural models apply. While individual works contracts – construction projects perhaps – usually involve the highest sums, recent statistics on the total value of contract award notices published in the *Official Journal* show contracts for services as the frontrunner (42 per cent), followed by works (36 per cent) and goods (22 per cent). Reflecting both different levels of economic activity and diverse approaches to contractual governance the situation is however marked by wide variation across Member States. In 2010 for example, three countries (France (26 per cent), Poland (14 per cent) and Germany (13 per cent)) accounted for half of all the advertised contract awards, while two others (UK (27 per cent) and Italy (13 per cent)) accounted for much of the total value.[13]

From an economic perspective, the regulatory regime has classically been about combatting entrenched domestic preference in public purchasing, and so, with a view to efficiency or cost savings and European competitiveness in global markets, of promoting the effective operation of the Single Market.[14] Burgeoning procedural requirements in the cause of market liberalisation was the resulting paradox.[15] It is worth pausing however to unpack the notion of 'domestic preference'. Relevant 'pull factors' may range from the personal (corruption) and consciously national ('Buy British') to the local (unemployment), and on through

---

[11] C Harlow and R Rawlings, *Law and Administration*, 3rd edn (Cambridge: CUP, 2009) chs 8–9.
[12] Commission, 'Annual Public Procurement Implementation Review' SWD (2012) 342 final, 6.
[13] Ibid, 11.
[14] Commission, 'White Paper – Completing the Internal Market' COM (85) 310.
[15] M Chiti, 'Regulation and Market in the Public Procurement Sector' (1995) 7 *European Review of Public Law* 373; S Arrowsmith, 'The Past and Future Evolution of EC Procurement Law: From Framework to Common Code?' (2006) 35 *Public Contract Law Journal* 337.

bureaucratic inertia and convenience (shared language) to the virtues of reputation, mutual understanding and responsiveness associated with 'repeat' contracting. We touch here on some famous contract theory concerning two different forms of exchange:[16]

- '*Discrete*' or individuated model of contracting – typically, short-term arrangements to purchase standardised goods and services. The model reflects and reinforces the desideratum of highly competitive markets.
- '*Relational*' model of contracting – typically involving the purchase of complex goods and services over extended periods of time. The model underwrites the importance to smooth and effective contractual workings of core elements of cooperation, continuity and trust.

Signalled by the demand for repeated bouts of competitive bidding, and fitting the policy objective of a well integrated Single Market, EU procedures have commonly pressed domestic practice in the direction of the discrete model of contracting. Yet relational contract theory points up some functional limitations to this process – domestic preference may not be so easily overpowered and sometimes for good reason.

From a legal perspective, the procedural framework gives tangible expression to the basic rights and freedoms of market operators in the EU's 'economic constitution', more especially through an associated cascade of general principle. As well as featuring prominently in the case law, this theme is highlighted in the first recital to Directive 2014/24, the newly revamped 'classic' public sector directive covering works, services and supplies contracts:[17]

> The award of public contracts by or on behalf of Member States' authorities has to comply with the principles of the Treaty on the Functioning of the European Union (TFEU), and in particular the free movement of goods, freedom of establishment and the freedom to provide services, as well as the principles deriving therefrom, such as equal treatment, non-discrimination, mutual recognition, proportionality and transparency. However, for public contracts above a certain value, provisions should be drawn up coordinating national procurement procedures so as to ensure that those principles are given practical effect and public procurement is opened up to competition.

EU policies on public procurement have become more elaborate over the years. While market integration and protection against trade barriers remain core goals, other aims and objectives are increasingly pressed or at least more clearly accommodated by the regulatory regime. A prime example is 'value for money' (VFM) for public purchasers, an objective naturally gaining prominence amid the fiscal consolidation and entrenchment associated with the eurozone crisis, but one which also raises concerns about EU interference in the realm of Member State

---

[16] I Macneil, 'Relational Contract Theory: Challenges and Queries' (2000) 94 *Northwestern University Law Review* 877. See also D Campbell, H Collins and J Wightman (eds), *Implicit Dimensions of Contract: Discrete, Relational and Network Contracts* (Oxford: Hart Publishing, 2003).

[17] See further, B Drijber and H Stergiou, 'Public Procurement Law and Internal Market Law' (2009) 46 *Common Market Law Review* 805.

responsibilities.[18] Other laudable aims featuring in recent Commission documentation include fighting corruption, support for small and medium-sized enterprises (SMEs) and promoting technological innovation.[19] The development is linked to attempts at a more joined-up approach to EU policies as expounded in the Commission's 'Europe 2020' strategy for 'smart, sustainable and inclusive growth'.[20] Reform of public procurement is visualised boldly here as a key lever for 'strengthening citizens' confidence in their internal market'.[21]

When it comes to the exercise of *dominium* power to achieve industrial, social and environmental objectives, the design and workings of the regulatory framework naturally prove politically contentious. Going directly to the role and functions of the state in modern society, this is familiar territory for administrative lawyers – under the broad rubric of 'contract compliance'.[22] In the case of EU public procurement law, the many technical procedural requirements should not be allowed to obscure a significant swing in the ideological pendulum. Whereas in the 1980s especially there was a pervasive interest in market disciplines, recent years bear witness to the search for a more rounded – less economically bracing – approach. So it is that what in the official discourse used to be 'secondary' objectives became 'horizontal' objectives and latterly 'strategic' objectives.[23] Facilitated as we shall see by the evolving jurisprudence, the development is most powerfully shown in the rise of so-called 'green procurement': from a Commission interpretative communication in 2001[24] mentioning some opportunities to what today is virtually the default position.[25]

Waves of Legislation

As evidenced by very low rates of import penetration, early efforts at breaking the stranglehold of domestic preference in public purchasing achieved very little. Relevant directives lacked an effective enforcement mechanism and in practice

---

[18] See S Arrowsmith and P Kunzlik, 'Public Procurement and Horizontal Policies in EC Law: General Principles' in S Arrowsmith and P Kunzlik (eds), *Social and Environmental Policies in EC Procurement Law – New Directives and New Challenges* (Cambridge, CUP, 2009).

[19] For an accessible overview, see 'Evaluation Report', above (n 2) ch 2.

[20] Commission, 'Europe 2020: A strategy for smart, sustainable and inclusive growth' (Communication) COM (2010) 2020 final.

[21] Commission, 'Single Market Act: Twelve levers to boost growth and strengthen confidence' (Communication) SEC(2011) 467 final, 3.

[22] C McCrudden, *Buying Social Justice: Equality, Government Procurement, and Legal Change* (Oxford: OUP, 2007).

[23] See generally, R Caranta and M Trybus (eds), *The Law of Green and Social Procurement in Europe* (Copenhagen: Djøf Publishing, 2010).

[24] Commission, 'The Community law applicable to public procurement and the possibilities for integrating environmental considerations into public procurement' (Communication) COM (2001) 274 final.

[25] P Kunzlik, 'From Suspect Practice to Market-based Instrument: Policy Alignment and the Evolution of EU Law's Approach to "Green" Public Procurement' (2013) 22 *Public Procurement Law Review* 97.

Coordinating National Procedures 147

were largely ignored;[26] application of basic treaty articles by the Court of Justice (CoJ) remained sporadic and peripheral.[27] A second wave of legislative reform initiated in the mid-1980s as part of the then vibrant Single Market Programme involved widening the regulatory framework by bringing in the utilities[28] and deepening it by strengthened procedural requirements and a special regime of remedies for use in the national systems. Different activities – works, supplies, services – were each made the subject of a specific directive,[29] which received general underpinning from a compliance directive on remedies and domestic review procedures.[30] 'Contracting authorities' were broadly defined to include central government, local government and public agencies: thresholds were used to exempt minor contracts.

Reviewing the scheme in the late 1990s, the Commission initially suggested little change: although the economic impact had been relatively limited, with public purchasing continuing to operate overwhelmingly along national lines, the existing framework should be given more time to bite.[31] As the consultation process made clear however, this meant skating over a series of difficulties with formal legal ordering shown by the directives.[32] Whereas the Commission had spoken of 'a few rules based on common sense',[33] there were multiple complaints about the over-rigidity and the unreadability of a fragmented and often highly technical legal framework. Rather than improving the efficiency of purchasing, too much emphasis on individuated contracting risked undermining the important relational values of collaboration and coordination; considerable compliance costs were being imposed, hard to justify. For those purchasers determined to discriminate and/or avoid legal sanction, there was, in the language of Anglo-American administrative law, ample scope for cynical 'games with rules' and for impenetrable 'boiler plate' reasons. The legislative framework also looked increasingly dated in the face of contractual modalities such as electronic auctions and framework agreements (establishing generic terms for future contracts). Indeed, the revolution in ICT had begun, opening up new horizons of pan-European public purchasing.[34]

---

[26] Directive 71/305/EEC (Works) [1971] OJ L185/15); Directive 77/62/EEC (Supplies) [1977] OJ L13/1. And see generally F Weiss, *Public Procurement in European Community Law* (London: Athlone Press, 1992).

[27] For an exception that proves the rule, see Case 45/87 *Commission v Ireland* [1988] ECR 4035.

[28] Which were given their own, rather more flexible regime: Directive 93/38/EEC (Utilities) OJ L199/84; Directive 92/13/EEC (Utilities Remedies) OJ L76/14.

[29] Directives 93/37/EEC (Works) [1993] OJ L199/54; 93/36/EEC (Supplies) [1993] OJ L199/1; 92/50/EEC (Services) [1992] OJ L209/1.

[30] Directive 89/665/EEC on the coordination of the laws, regulations and administrative provisions relating to the application of review procedures to the award of public supply and public works contracts) [1989] OJ L395/33.

[31] Commission, Green Paper, 'Public Procurement in the European Union: Exploring the Way Forward' COM (96) 583.

[32] Commission, 'Public Procurement and the European Union' (Communication) COM (98) 143.

[33] Commission, *Public Procurement in Europe: The Directives* (1994) 3.

[34] Commission, 'Action Plan for the Implementation of the Legal Framework for Electronic Public Procurement' (Communication) (2004).

A third wave of legislation eventually resulted, with the Commission now proclaiming the virtues of simplification, modernisation and flexibility.[35] This codification has boasted a consolidated ('classic') public sector directive;[36] a revised directive on utilities;[37] a later directive on defence procurement (previously the chief subject matter exclusion);[38] and a significantly strengthened compliance directive.[39] In the course of the drafting, various technical distinctions were ironed out and relevant court rulings 'cut and pasted' into the legislation with the aim of greater clarity. Yet the legislation sent out mixed messages.[40] Better to accommodate more collaborative forms of government contracting, the regulatory framework was loosened in certain respects, as through the provision of an extra pathway ('competitive dialogue procedure'). Meanwhile, a distinction was drawn between so-called 'priority' services, subject to the full regulatory disciplines by reason of the potential for cross-border trade, and 'non-priority' or community-oriented ones, for example social services, where contracting authorities would be allowed more flexibility. In certain other respects, the regulatory screw was tightened against administrative discretion, for example through detailed provisions on framework agreements and e-auctions.

At the time of writing, the EU public procurement regime is once again in transition as a new legislative package is made the subject of mass legislative implementation in Member States. Equally however, history appears to be repeating itself. As we shall see, criticisms of the existing regime closely echo the criticisms of the scheme it replaced. Again, the official rhetoric is one of simplification, burden lifting and greater flexibility, while the substance of the reform is more confused.[41]

Procedures, Procedures, Procedures

We should beware an overly 'top-down' perspective: more particularly one which treats Member States as if they are monoliths. To the contrary, and notwithstanding efforts at centralisation and aggregation of demand in the last few years, public purchasing in the EU is highly fragmented. The Commission's own evaluation

---

[35] 'Public Procurement and the European Union', above (n 32) 3.
[36] Directive 2004/18/EC on the co-ordination of procedures for the award of public works contracts, public supply contracts and public service contracts [2004] OJ L134/114.
[37] Directive 2004/17/EC coordinating the procurement procedures of entities operating in the water, energy, transport and postal services sectors [2004] OJ L134/1.
[38] Directive 2009/81/EC on the coordination of procedures for the award of certain works contracts, supply contracts and service contracts in the fields of defence and security [2009] OJ L216/76.
[39] Directive 2007/66/EC amending Council Directives 89/665/EEC and 92/13/EEC with regard to improving the effectiveness of review procedures concerning the award of public contracts [2007] OJ L335/31.
[40] See generally, S Arrowsmith, *The Law of Public and Utilities Procurement*, 2nd edn (London: Sweet & Maxwell, 2005).
[41] For a useful comparative perspective, see H-J Pries (ed), *Public Procurement: An Overview of Regulation in 40 Jurisdictions Worldwide* (London: Global Competition Review, 2012).

speaks of a very large and heterogeneous population of public authorities – over 250,000 contracting authorities in the Single Market managing procurement budgets of different sizes and possessing very different administrative capacities, of which some 35,000 publish an award notice in the *Official Journal* in any one year. Further, in terms of this mass exercise of *dominium* power, 'the money is spent in a wide variety of ways and disbursed via an enormous number of distinct procedures (over two million procedures for the award of public contracts per year)'.[42]

The limits to EU-centred institutional capacity are further highlighted. The Commission laments that 'feedback from Member States shows . . . significant discrepancies in terms of availability of information on various aspects of procurement, its depth and comprehensiveness.' Showing the complementarity of techniques of 'soft governance' with formal regulatory methods, the Commission envisages – none too soon – taking 'the lead in exchanging information, experience and best practice in partnership with the Member States'.[43] At the same time, conditions have been ripe for EU public procurement to generate an active legal advice market – in part funded from the public purse. Complex regulation, after all, connotes many opportunities for clarifying, exploring and testing legal problems and uncertainties in the rules and hence the absorption of substantial lawyerly resources. An inconvenient truth perhaps, but the spectre of so-called 'eurolegalism' – a multiplying cycle of juridification[44] – has loomed large in this sector.

JUDICIAL MULTITASKING

A fast moving jurisprudence has done much to shape the regulatory framework and associated administrative procedures in recent years.[45] At one and the same time, this sees the courts elaborating general principles in the cause of market integration and protection of fundamental freedoms; determining the broad parameters of the legislative framework; interpreting and filling gaps in the directives; specifying relevant factors and links in the decision-making chain; and developing and imposing remedies and sanctions. Typical of a decentralised and privately policed system in which Member State authorities bear primary responsibility for correct implementation of the rules, it is the domestic court judges who do most of the 'heavy lifting'. As far as the Court of Justice of the European Union (CJEU) is concerned, this is a classic field for preliminary reference procedure, which serves in conjunction with Commission infringement proceedings to produce a steady

---

[42] 'Evaluation Report', above (n 2) iii, vi.
[43] Ibid, 4, 37.
[44] See above, ch 3, p 78.
[45] C Bovis, 'Developing Public Procurement Regulation: Jurisprudence and its Influence on Law Making' (2006) 43 *Common Market Law Review* 461 and C Bovis, 'Public Procurement in the EU: Jurisprudence and Conceptual Directions' (2012) 49 *Common Market Law Review* 247.

150 *Public Procurement*

stream of new public procurement cases. Analysis of the Court's docket reveals a diverse set of complaints of wrongful application of the rules: from discrimination and evasion of the administrative procedures to lack of transparency, and on through unfair exclusion from competitions to the undue use of legislative exemptions.[46] The case law reflects the law games of eurolegalism.

Transparency and Scope

Take the principle of transparency. In support of equal treatment ('a level playing field') the CJEU has in this context afforded it an expansive meaning to the extent, confirmed in *Lianakis*,[47] of requiring elements of rule-based decision-making in accordance with a *Rechtsstaat* philosophy. Potential bidders should know 'all the elements' to be taken into account by the contracting authority in identifying the economically most advantageous offer, and their relative importance. Likewise, for compliance with the principle and also with the general terms of the directives, national court judges may find it necessary to insist on clear definition of the subject matter of the contract and on certainty of terms.[48] Again, in the 'breakthrough' case of *Telaustria*,[49] the Court produced the idea of positive obligations of transparency arising outside the ambit of the detailed provisions of the directives. So, for example, contracts below the value thresholds but of cross-border interest should be sufficiently advertised to allow for competition and for the impartiality of the process to be reviewed.

All this has major implications in terms of the broader administrative process. First, from the perspective of EU law, the regulatory framework takes on a dual character: an inner 'core' of codified text bearing ample testimony to the interplay of courts and legislators; and, inevitably occasioning complaints about uncertainty and associated administrative costs especially in small contracts, a 'periphery' of floating principles.[50] Matters are however less clear-cut on the frontline, where the demands of best practice and/or defensive administration mean that conditions are ripe for spillover. Commission research highlights a thriving export of requirements from the core to the periphery in the domestic law and practice of various Member States.[51] Second, the issue is raised of the functional limitations of contract as a means of planning for the future ('presentation'). Detailed information and specification are all very well but, set in terms of the relational

---

[46] 'Annual Public Procurement Implementation Review 2012', above (n 12) 29–30.
[47] Case C-532/06 *Lianakis AE v Alexandroupolis* [2008] ECR I-251, [36].
[48] See in the British context, *R (Law Society) v Legal Services Commission* [2007] EWCA Civ 1264. Relevant CJEU authorities include Case C-496/99 *Commission v CAS Succhi di Frutta SpA* [2004] ECR I-3801; Case C-340/02 *Commission v France* [2004] ECR I-9845.
[49] Case C-324/98 *Telaustria* [2000] ECR I-10745; see also Case C-458/03 *Parking Brixen* [2005] ECR I-8612.
[50] D Dragos and R Caranta (eds), *Outside the Procurement Directives – Inside the Treaty?* (Copenhagen: Djøf Publishing, 2012).
[51] 'Evaluation Report', above (n 2) 47–50.

attributes of responsiveness and fine-tuning, bleeding out contractual discretion in the name of transparency can mean too much rigidity. From the standpoint of efficient and effective procedures, more 'front-end' work is also apt to be associated with administrative delay and expense. Third, in so framing the regulatory regime, the accumulated jurisprudence of the CJEU acts as a straitjacket on reform: even more than the international requirements on public procurement arising under the World Trade Organization's (WTO) Government Procurement Agreement (requirements which, with the major exception of value thresholds, are commonly loose or open-ended).[52]

As for the scope of the legislative framework, the CJEU has rightly adopted a functional, not a formalist, approach to the basic conceptual requirement of a 'public contract . . . for pecuniary interest concluded in writing between one or more economic operators and one or more contracting authorities'.[53] In particular, the Court has recognised contemporary developments in contractual governance involving vertical and horizontal forms of institutional cooperation ('in-house' procurement and 'spin-out' companies and shared service structures or pooling arrangements). Such is the realm of the '*Teckal* exemption', whereby transactions with a distinct legal entity are protected from the exigencies of formal tendering process provided that this vehicle is both under the 'decisive influence' of, and carries out the 'essential' part of its activities in partnership with, the purchaser or joint purchasers.[54] Demonstrating a common concern in public procurement law about loopholes being exploited, the exception to the exception is part-ownership of the contractor by the private sector.[55]

Conversely, in the leading case of *Pressetext*,[56] the CoJ significantly expanded the traction of the legislative code. At issue was the proper scope of managerial discretion to make changes after the award of a contract under the procurement rules. An unfettered discretion could make a mockery of the regulatory framework to the detriment of other, more realistic, tenderers. Yet the limits to presentiation cannot be ignored: as any experienced commercial practitioner knows, there will be situations, for example involving technological difficulties in long and complex contracts, where the parties' reasonable assumptions are not realised and renegotiation is the obvious and most cost-effective way forward. *Pressetext* has made this administrative routing a hazardous one however. A materially varied contract might thus be classified as a new contractual award within the meaning of the legislation where it would (i) have resulted in different firms

---

[52] S Arrowsmith and R Anderson (eds), *The World Trade Organisation Regime on Government Procurement: Challenge and Reform* (Cambridge: CUP, 2011).

[53] Council Directive 2004/18/EC, Art 1(2)(a). For a classic illustration, see Case C-470/99 *Universale-Bau* [2002] ECR I-11617.

[54] Case C-107/98 *Teckal Srl v Comune di Viano* [1999] ECR I-8121; Case C-340/04 *Carbotermo SpA v Commune di Busto Arsizio* [2006] ECR I-4137. On cooperative (municipal) arrangements, see Case C-324/07 *Coditel Brabant SA v Commune d'Uccle* [2009] ECR I-8457; Case C-480/06 *European Commission v Germany* [2009] ECR I-4747.

[55] Case C-26/03 *Stadt Halle* [2005] ECR I-1.

[56] Case C-454/06 *Pressetext v Austria* [2008] ECR I-4401.

bidding or a different outcome, or (ii) extends the contract to include additional services, or (iii) changes 'the economic balance of the contract' in favour of the contractor.[57] The further twist is that, by reason of prior reforms to the enforcement system, the new award might be held 'ineffective' (see further below). *Pressetext* has constituted a major flashpoint in EU public procurement law: one which we will see the legislature concerned to address.

Social and Environmental Objectives

And then there is the multifaceted question of contract compliance. From the standpoint of administrative procedures, a recital to the currently applicable directive on public works etc points up the historically close interplay of legislative with judicial technique and the overarching constraints placed on the use of contract as a policy lever via the exercise of purchaser discretion:

> This Directive is based on Court of Justice case-law, in particular case-law on award criteria, which clarifies the possibilities for the contracting authorities to meet the needs of the public concerned, including in the environmental and/or social area, provided that such criteria are linked to the subject-matter of the contract, do not confer an unrestricted freedom of choice on the contracting authority, are expressly mentioned and comply with the fundamental principles.[58]

An element of institutional conflict must be factored into the equation. As regards permissible considerations, there is a considerable history of the Commission urging market purity – from the regulatory perspective, a determinedly narrow form of pathway(s) model – and the Court, if cautiously, mitigating this at the suit of contracting authorities interested to secure, or at least accommodate, social and/or environmental desiderata. Further highlighting the complexity of the administrative procedures, the secondary issue is raised of the stage or stages at which such considerations might operate: qualifications for possible suppliers; contract performance conditions; the award criteria.

The early benchmark case is *Beentjes*,[59] in which the Court recognised that the standard test of 'most economically advantageous offer' afforded contracting authorities a modicum of discretion to specify relevant award criteria. So whereas in accordance with the legislation the initial selection of tenderers had to be based on an exhaustive list of technical and financial requirements, a contractual condition relating to the employment of long-term unemployed persons was permissible provided that – in accordance with fundamental principle – it had no discriminatory effect on tenders from other Member States. While showing no sympathy for a plea of local inexperience of the detailed procedural framework,

---

[57] Ibid, [34]–[37].
[58] Council Directive 18/2004/EC, recital 1. See further, Drijber and Stergiou, above (n 17).
[59] Case 31/87 *Gebroeders Beentjes BV v Netherlands* [1989] ECR 4365.

a not insignificant feature in view of the highly fragmented character of procurement administration, the Court would hold to this line at the beginning of the century in *Calais Nord*,[60] another case concerning a local project to combat unemployment.

A few years more, and the Court adjusted position in the light of the growing demands for 'green' procurement (underwritten by the treaty requirement that environmental protection requirements be integrated into the definition and implementation of Community policies and activities (TFEU Article 11)). So in the famous case of *Concordia Bus*[61] the administrative law curb of relevancy was again relaxed, with the city of Helsinki being allowed to favour the local bus company on the basis of low emissions and noise levels. These environmentally-friendly factors were permissible 'additional criteria' for an authority choosing the most economically advantageous offer. The judgment did however make clear that such considerations must relate to the subject matter of the contract, a limitation taken up in later cases.[62] Although this may sound dry and technical, it has been a proverbial 'red-line' for the Commission, one that operates to preclude general or free-standing policies of contract compliance.

The latest leading authority is '*Dutch Coffee*'.[63] An infringement case, it concerned the labelling of 'fair trade' and organic agricultural products of the ingredients in coffee machines. In finding that the Netherlands had failed to fulfil its obligations, the judgment underscores the strong constraining effects of the principle of transparency on the flexible exercise of policy choice. Recalling that 'all the conditions and detailed rules of the award procedure must be drawn up in a clear, precise and unequivocal manner in the notice or contract documents', the CoJ ruled that open textured contractual requirements to comply with the 'criteria of sustainable purchases and socially responsible business' and to contribute 'to improving the sustainability of the coffee market and to environmentally, socially and economically responsible coffee production' were out of order.[64] On the other hand, the judgment makes clear that EU law does not, in principle, preclude a public contract grounded in social elements such as fair trade. Provided that there is the requisite specificity, liberally-minded contracting authorities might incorporate in the award criteria considerations of a social nature that not only 'concern the persons using or receiving the works, supplies or services which are the object of the contract, but also other persons'. While the precise ramifications require working out in subsequent cases, new vistas are opened up in terms of the classic administrative law discretion to make rules. Irrespective of legislative codification, this matter will run and run.

---

[60] Case C-225/98 *Commission v France ('Calais Nord')* [2000] ECR I-7455.
[61] Case C-513/99 *Concordia Bus Finland v Helsinki* [2002] ECR I-7213.
[62] See further Case C-448/01 *EVN & Weinstrom v Austria* [2003] ECR I-14527.
[63] Case C-368/10 *Commission v Netherlands* [2012] ECR I-000.
[64] Ibid, [109]–[111].

STEP BY STEP

Now let us follow the pathway(s) model, better to illuminate both the steering potential and the functional limitations of this type of regulatory procedural framework; and, more particularly, the role of proactive or rule-bound techniques for confining, structuring and checking discretion, reflecting and reinforcing in turn the dictates of transparency. By this is meant more or less detailed legislative provision at successive stages of the public purchasing process about bounded elements of choice (as by minima and maxima), about mandatory and permissible and irrelevant considerations, and about opportunities for scrutiny by stakeholders; with all this being underwritten by the general regulatory principle of pre-announcement – specification in advance – of the chosen routing and criteria by the individual contracting authority. That is to say, a double dose of rules: statutory and mandated administrative/contractual ones.

Conceptually speaking, the model can be visualised in terms of five main stages: (1) initiation and choice of procedural routings; (2) preparation and publication of tender documents; (3) selection (and exclusion) of bidders; (4) tender evaluation and award; (5) post-decisional procedures. Directive 2004/18, which has governed the vast majority (90 per cent) of award notices in the *Official Journal*,[65] affords good illustration. Although in the course of being replaced by Directive 2014/24, it will continue to operate as the 'classic' public sector directive until April 2016.[66]

The departure point is the ringing statement of principle in Article 2 of Directive 2004/18 that 'contracting authorities shall treat economic operators equally and non-discriminatorily and shall act in a transparent way'. With a view to implementation in national legislation, the directive has then fleshed out multiple series of steps along the pathway(s), as for example at the early stages through the rules on determining applicability and requirements to advertise electronically in the *Official Journal*. Statistics show that, as between Member States, the entirety of the regulated process could typically take between 60 and 240 days to complete.[67]

That the model is both determinedly logical and complex was underscored in *Lianakis*. The issue was raised of the relationship between the assessment of firms (stage 3) and the evaluation of bids (stage 4). Giving due weight to administrative practicalities, the CoJ confirmed that the two sets of reviews could take place simultaneously. The Court emphasised however that the two links in the decision-making chain are distinct and governed by separate rules. A criterion such as proven experience that was 'essentially linked' to the suitability of a bidder could not (also) be specified as an award criterion for the determination of the most economically advantageous tender.[68]

---

[65] With the Utilities Directive accounting for 10%: 'Annual Public Procurement Implementation Review 2012', above (n 12) 10.
[66] Council Directive 2014/24/EU, Arts 90–91.
[67] 'Evaluation Report', above (n 2) 118.
[68] *Lianakis* [30]–[32]. The case involved the earlier (Services) Directive 92/50.

Directive 2004/18 having added competitive dialogue, the 'menu of common procedures' available at the preliminary stage now consisted of four alternative pathways for contracting authorities to follow:[69]

- *Open procedure*, all interested firms being allowed to tender.
- *Restricted procedure*, tenders being invited from a list of firms drawn up by the authority.
- *Negotiated procedure*, the contractual terms being negotiated with chosen contractors.
- *Competitive dialogue procedure*, providing space for discussions with suppliers to develop suitable solutions, on which chosen bidders are then invited to tender.

Typically however, gradations of purchaser discretion are involved. Signifying that the open and restricted procedures are the standard options (as befits their conjuring of competitive disciplines), the legislation has afforded contracting authorities a free choice between them. Conversely, use of the negotiated procedure, which sits comfortably with the relational desiderata of cooperation and mutual learning, has been strictly confined precisely because of the informality and opacity.[70] Competitive dialogue, tied under Directive 2004/18 to 'particularly complex contracts', represents a complicated compromise.[71] Under the legislation, efficient techniques like framework agreements or (for repetitive purchases) dynamic purchasing systems could also be adopted at this stage, for use in the context of one or more of the main pathways.[72]

The general patterns of use have been eminently predictable. The traditional open call has accounted for three-quarters of award notices and (as it is commonly used for smaller contracts) for half of their total value. With restricted procedure the situation is reversed: roughly 10 per cent of notices and 25 per cent of value.[73] A reminder however of the diverse approaches and attitudes to contractual governance, the overall pattern is marked by considerable variation across Member States; the UK for instance, a veritable world leader in outsourcing and public–private partnership, etc, has seen much use of competitive dialogue.[74] A prescriptive regulatory design has also tended to generate new pressure points. That in the face of highly detailed requirements competitive dialogue can also be slow, expensive and resource intensive, has naturally generated demands for greater flexibility.[75]

As regards the invitation to tender, it is a key legislative principle that the subject matter of the purchase should be defined through non-discriminatory technical specifications, thereby limiting foreclosure of markets by reference, in

[69] Directive 2004/18/EC, ch V.
[70] See Case C-71/92 *Commission v Spain* [1993] ECR I-5923.
[71] Directive 2004/18/EC, Art 29.
[72] Ibid, Arts 32–33.
[73] 'Evaluation Report', above (n 2) 111–22.
[74] HM Treasury, *Review of Competitive Dialogue* (November 2010).
[75] S Arrowsmith and S Treumer (eds), *Competitive Dialogue in EU Procurement* (Cambridge, CUP, 2012).

the Commission's words, 'to proprietary or idiosyncratic specifications'.[76] Requirements on the use of European technical specifications (or a properly designated substitute) represent a natural starting point.[77] Such specifications could be defined 'in terms of performance or functional requirements'; however, in a clear echo of the case law on transparency, 'such parameters must be sufficiently precise to allow tenderers to determine the subject-matter of the contract and to allow contracting authorities to award the contract'.[78] Again, as in the case of permissible considerations recognised for the purposes of contract compliance, we read that 'the conditions governing the performance of a contract may, in particular, concern social and economic considerations'.[79]

The close interplay of technical with policy-laden elements is further highlighted in the choice of participants according to qualitative selection criteria. The legislation has included an exhaustive battery of tests for suitability on the basis of standing and competence: from proof of a firm's economic and financial capacity to carefully prescribed evidence of technical ability, including statements about past projects, and on through certification of quality assurance and environmental management standards.[80] While this sounds good (not least when public money is involved), there exists the restrictive potential of 'red tape' on competition and, as regards the broad strategic objective of promoting SMEs, the disproportionate effects on them of strongly risk-averse requirements concerning economic and financial capacity and, further, of the administrative burden of heavy documentation requirements. As to the flipside, the exclusion of economic operators from participation in a public contract, Directive 2004/18 stiffened the regulatory framework in view of the never-ending fight against criminality in lucrative government contracts. Under the broad rubric of 'sound procedures', the legislation declared that firms 'shall be excluded' in the light of fraud or corruption and 'may be excluded' for other relevant offences, for example environmental crime.[81]

The crucial award stage shows 'steering' writ large. Article 53(1) of the Directive not only specifies a commercial outlook, but also incorporates flanking measures to curb administrative discretion accordingly:

The criteria on which the contracting authorities shall base the award of public contracts shall be either:

> (a) when the award is made to the tender most economically advantageous from the point of view of the contracting authority, various criteria linked to the subject-matter of the public contract in question, for example, quality, price, technical merit, aesthetic and functional characteristics, environmental characteristics,

---

[76] 'Evaluation Report', above (n 2) iv.
[77] Directive 2004/18/EC, ch 4.
[78] Ibid, Art 23.
[79] Ibid, Art 26.
[80] Ibid, Arts 46–50.
[81] Ibid, Art 45; see further, S Williams-Elegbe, *Fighting Corruption in Public Procurement* (Oxford, Hart Publishing, 2012).

> running costs, cost-effectiveness, after-sales service and technical assistance, delivery date and delivery period or period of completion, or
> (b) the lowest price only.
>
> 2. Without prejudice to the provisions of the third subparagraph, in the case referred to in paragraph 1(a) the contracting authority shall specify . . . the relative weighting which it gives to each of the criteria chosen to determine the most economically advantageous tender.
>
> Those weightings can be expressed by providing for a range with an appropriate maximum spread.
>
> Where, in the opinion of the contracting authority, weighting is not possible for demonstrable reasons, the contracting authority shall indicate . . . the criteria in descending order of importance.

It is no surprise to learn that, of the two basic options in Article 53(1), the blunt instrument of lowest price has been largely confined to smaller and simpler transactions.[82] As regards determination of the most economically advantageous offer, sub-paragraph (a) represents a typical example of structuring discretion with a checklist of relevant factors. The influence of case law (*Concordia Bus*) is again clearly visible. Article 53(2), which shows an invasive attempt at confining discretion, is especially noteworthy. Underpinned by developments in ICT, and linking with audit technique, public purchasing was now to be formally shaped in terms of mathematical formulae. The get-out clause is in turn limited by enhanced provision for checking discretion ('demonstrable reasons').

The demand in Directive 2004/18 to specify weightings was a novel one. The Commission championed it on the basis that the previous stipulation, to list the criteria 'where possible' in descending order of importance, had undercut the pathway(s) model by preserving too much discretion.[83] But what, it may be asked, of the distorting effects of treating public purchasing less as an exercise of continuous and skilful judgement and more as a mechanical exercise of advanced calculations and spreadsheets?[84] Increased administrative cost must also be factored in, a feature heavily underlined by the case law requirement to disclose 'all the elements'. Err on the side of caution, and specify in advance the weighting of any sub and sub-sub factors, has been the considered advice of leading practitioners.[85]

The pathway(s) model needs searchlights. Directive 2004/18 further involved, under the broad rubric of checking discretion, an injection of transparency at the post-decisional stage. As well as public notice of the contract award, strengthened reasons-giving requirements were specified, extending at the request of a rival

---

[82] 'Evaluation Report', above (n 2) xix.
[83] Commission, 'Explanatory Memorandum to Proposal for a Directive on the Co-ordination of Public Sector Award Procedures' COM (2000) 275, 12.
[84] R Boyle, 'EU Procurement Green Paper on the Modernisation of EU Public Procurement Policy: A Personal Response' (2011) 20 *Public Procurement Law Review* 171.
[85] S Hannaford and J Thompson, 'Procurement Problems in the Credit Crunch' (2009) *Construction Law Review* 32.

bidder to 'the characteristics and relative advantages of the tender selected'.[86] Linkage with a specially enhanced private law model of enforcement is immediately apparent. A raft of informational and statistical obligations on contracting authorities and Member States has also buttressed the monitoring role of the Commission.[87]

The legislation stopped short of prescribing the arrangements for monitoring and supervision at the domestic level. It would instead be a matter of general duty and organisational discretion: 'Member States shall ensure implementation of this directive by effective, available and transparent mechanisms. For this purpose they may, among other things, appoint or establish an independent body'.[88] Comparative analysis duly reveals the wide panoply of such arrangements: centralised and decentralised administrative machinery; particular examples of guidance bodies and knowledge centres; general and specialist supervisory bodies; some systems of control ex ante; internal and external audit offices.[89] The Commission, we shall see, has not been best pleased.

REVIEW AND REMEDY

An essential element of the system, individual review procedures at national level further reflect the rich diversity of legal and administrative cultures across Europe. Left free to choose their own arrangements, subject to minimum requirements in the Compliance Directive to provide aggrieved bidders with rapid and effective means of redress,[90] the Member States have used a wide variety of mechanisms. These start with internal review by the contracting authority, move on through specialised review boards or offices to arbitration panels and tribunals and, finally, ordinary courts.[91] This domestic institutional development neatly illustrates the many shades of Europeanised public administration. On the one hand, the pathway(s) model is more or less elongated. Different Member States have adopted one, two or three tiers of external review,[92] though all are topped by some form of judicial process (judicial review perhaps).[93] On the other hand, the review and remedies framework is incorporated at the domestic level to a greater or lesser degree: a majority of Member States have applied the directive equally to contracts above and below the EU thresholds, while others (Germany for example) have resisted this form of 'regulatory creep'.[94]

---

[86] Directive 2004/18/EC, Art 41.
[87] Ibid, Arts 43, 75–76.
[88] Ibid, Art 81.
[89] 'Evaluation Report', above (n 2) 57–65.
[90] Directive 89/665/EEC, Art 1.
[91] OECD, 'Public Procurement Review and Remedies Systems in the European Union' (2007) Sigma Papers, No 41.
[92] 'Evaluation Report', above (n 2) 69.
[93] As required by Directive 2007/66/EC, Art 9.
[94] 'Evaluation Report', above (n 2) 67.

Perhaps hopefully the Commission sees the framework as 'crucial to making sure contracts ultimately go to the company which has made the best offer, and therefore to building confidence among businesses and the public that public procurement procedures are fair'.[95] Great reliance has been placed on private legal action to police the disparate domestic practice; the Commission, after all, can only do so much by way of infringement proceedings (see chapter seven). The special legal remedies afforded by the Compliance Directive are designed both to incentivise litigation by market operators and ratchet up the potential costs for contracting authorities of non-compliance; they represent, in other words, 'regulation in the shadow of the law'.[96]

Whereas the original design was typically skeletal, the CoJ has done much to fill out the rules using the general principle of 'effectiveness'.[97] As with the famous cases of *Factortame*[98] and *Francovich*,[99] the remedies operate to erode the procedural autonomy of national law in order to establish the means for the vindication of EU law rights. Starkly illustrating the penetration of the EU regulatory framework into domestic systems, a discernible feature in many EU public procurement law cases is the shared nationality of the participants. In *Lianakis*, for example, Greek operators challenged the award of a contract by a Greek authority to a Greek competitor before – of course – a Greek court.

The pre-contractual remedies are wide-ranging. The national court thus has powers to make an interim order halting progress, to set aside a decision or amend any document and to award damages to firms for breach of duty. Under the first Compliance Directive however, once a contract was made, damages were typically the only available remedy. Aggrieved suppliers had little incentive to make a claim in this situation. National systems were commonly ill-equipped to assess the chance of winning the contract; essentially a contribution to company costs, the remedy had no real corrective effect.[100]

Pre-contractual remedies sound well, but they may be defeated by a 'race to signature' by awarding authorities. The CoJ held in *Alcatel* that where a national system of remedies did not allow a supplier to overturn a concluded contract, and failed to guarantee the possibility of challenging an award decision pre-contractually, it was non-compliant.[101] Bringing much needed clarity to the situation, and designed to ensure that participants have a proper opportunity to consider seeking review, the amended Compliance Directive prescribes minimum standstill periods (10–15 days) between the award decision and the making of the

---

[95] Ibid, 26.
[96] See generally, S Treumer and F Lichère (eds), *Enforcement of the EU Public Procurement Rules* (Copenhagen: Djøf Publishing, 2011); D Fairgrieve and F Lichère (eds), *Public Procurement Law: Damages as an Effective Remedy* (Oxford: Hart Publishing, 2011).
[97] Not least in Case C-81/98 *Alcatel* [1999] ECR I-7671.
[98] Case C-213/89 *R v Secretary of State for Transport ex p Factortame* [1990] ECR I-2433.
[99] Joined Cases 6, 9/90 *Francovich and Bonafaci v Italy* [1991] ECR I-5357.
[100] Commission, 'Impact Assessment Report – Remedies in the Field of Public Procurement' SEC (2006) 557.
[101] *Alcatel* [1999] ECR I-7671. And see Case C-212/02 *Commission v Austria* (judgment of 24 June 2004).

160 *Public Procurement*

contract. From the standpoint of this volume, it is a striking example of administrative procedures being reordered in order to facilitate legal challenge against the administration. Again, cases from Germany had drawn attention to what the CoJ termed 'the most serious breach of Community law in the field of public procurement on the part of a contracting authority':[102] the direct award of a contract that should have been subject to a transparent and competitive award procedure. Local favouritism, shared ownership, corruption: all might be reasons, mused the Commission.[103] The revised Compliance Directive accordingly provides for the remedy of 'ineffectiveness'.[104] Indicative of the never-ending tension over national procedural autonomy, Member States are however allowed to choose whether this powerful remedy entails retrospective cancellation (of all contractual obligations) or, coupled with powers to impose fines and shorten the contract period, prospective cancellation (of those obligations yet to be performed).[105]

The revamp has significantly changed the regulatory terms of engagement. For suppliers, there are clearly more opportunities and incentives to bring legal claims; conversely, for buyers, the potential consequences are now much more serious, not least in terms of administrative and contractual disruption. Wider 'ripple effects' in terms of formal and informal complaints direct to contracting authorities are part of this; increased pressure may be put on public purchasers to settle cases. Equally however, it does not do to gloss over underlying difficulties with the private enforcement model. Formal legal disputing with prospective major customers carries its own risks!

Commission research points up major differences in the scale of the litigation in national systems. While a low ratio of review proceedings to procurements is apparent in many Member States (5 per cent or less), in others it approaches 20 per cent. The rates of successful challenge are said to be substantial, hovering around one-third of the total number of cases in the jurisdictions analysed. Tellingly however, despite many years of experience, officials in Brussels think it 'difficult to judge the "attractiveness" of the review procedures in a given Member State'. Certain factors suggest themselves: very speedy procedures or conversely, as in the UK, high litigation costs. Against the backdrop of multiple litigation cultures however, the best the Commission can muster is that a low percentage of reviewed decisions may mean that

> procurement procedures are generally in order and there is no need to turn to a review body or that trust in the review procedure in the Member State is low and tenderers do not use the system in spite of infringements being committed.[106]

---

[102] Case C-26/03 *Stadt Halle* [2005] ECR I-1 [37]. See also Joined Cases C-20/01 and 28/01 *Commission v Germany* [2003] ECR I-03609.

[103] 'Impact Assessment Report', above (n 99) 8.

[104] As also to sanction breaches of the standstill period: Directive 2007/66/EC, Art 2a.

[105] Ibid, Art 2d; see further, J Golding and P Henty, 'The New Remedies Directive of the EC: Standstill and Ineffectiveness' (2008) 17 *Public Procurement Law Review* 146.

[106] 'Annual Public Procurement Implementation Review 2012', above (n 12) 31–32. See further, K Gelderman, P Ghijsen and J Schoonen, 'Explaining Non-Compliance with European Union Procurement Directives: A Multidisciplinary Perspective' (2010) 48 *Journal of Common Market Studies* 243.

The issue is raised of pan-European forms of alternative dispute resolution. Placed on a permanent footing in 2003 by agreement of the Member States, the Public Procurement Network (PPN) is one of the species of cooperative administrative arrangements emerging in the EU in recent years focused on providing non-judicial means of individual protection (see chapter three). Operated through designated contact points and official channels (with a view to operator anonymity), the PPN deals specifically with cross-border cases,[107] while also providing a collaborative outlet for the exchange of information and best practice. The lack of visibility has, however, proved a major hindrance: to date firms have made little use of this informal facility and only a few disputes have been resolved.[108] The Network's considerable potential is yet to be realised.

RECODIFICATION

A fourth wave of legislation is now upon us in the form of revised public sector and utilities directives[109] and, effectively playing 'catch-up' with the rise of public–private partnerships, a new directive on works and service concessions.[110] Far from the idea of simply coordinating national procedures to avoid discrimination and obstacles to cross-border trade, the Commission conveys the impression of a basic redesign of the regulatory framework in the wider service of Union economic and industrial policy:[111]

> Public procurement ... is one of the market-based instruments to be used to achieve the Europe 2020 objectives by improving the conditions for business to innovate and by encouraging the wider use of green procurement supporting the shift towards a resource efficient and low-carbon economy. At the same time, the Europe 2020 strategy stresses that public procurement policy must ensure the most efficient use of public funds and that procurement markets must be kept open Union-wide (all the more in times of financial crisis).

In the real world, however, underlying tensions between different policy aims are not so easily glossed over. The Commission's own consultation graphically illustrates this. Most businesses and contracting authorities believed that the existing rules allowed sufficient space for societal policy objectives; most NGOs did not.[112] Nonetheless, the Communication on the Single Market Act specified as a key action:

---

[107] PPN, *Guidance for companies prevented from competing in foreign markets because of discriminatory public procurement practices* (2005).
[108] M Lottini, 'From "Administrative Cooperation" in the Application of European Union Law to "Administrative Cooperation" in the Protection of European Rights and Liberties' (2012)18 *European Public Law* 127.
[109] Directive 2014/24/EU on public procurement and Directive 2014/25/EU on procurement by entities operating in the water, energy, transport and postal services sectors [2014] OJ L 94/243.
[110] Directive 2014/23/EU on the award of concession contracts [2014] OJ L94/1.
[111] Commission Memorandum 11/931, 'Proposals to modernise the European public procurement market' (December 2011).
[112] Commission Consultation on the modernisation of EU public procurement policy (2011).

Revised and modernised public procurement legislative framework, with a view to underpinning a balanced policy which fosters demand for environmentally sustainable, socially responsible and innovative goods, services and works. This revision should also result in simpler and more flexible procurement procedures for contracting authorities and provide easier access for companies, especially SMEs.[113]

In seeking to square the policy circle, the Commission has sought to combine leaner or more user-friendly procedures with enhanced opportunities for strategic usage through a more generous regulatory framework. Yet the picture is muddied, with doses of permissive provision, to a greater or lesser extent animating in character, being mixed together with some new mandatory requirements. The specialist legal advice market will be further boosted! An additional twist is provided by options for national systems to insist on certain procedures: a noteworthy element of diversity or discretion to make rules in the context of Europeanised public administration.

Process: Assessment

According to the Commission, the approach to reform was the very model of a modern set of pre-legislative procedures (see chapter four). Published in January 2011, a Green Paper on modernisation[114] launched a public consultation covering the main issues of strategic usage, simplification and flexibility, and combating favouritism and corruption. Trumpeted as 'a high response', 623 replies were received from a variety of stakeholders, including Member State governments and regional and local purchasers (29 per cent), industry associations and undertakings (40 per cent), as well as Civil Society Organisations (CSOs) (17 per cent), academics and individual citizens; the input was then summarised by officials in a 'synthesis' paper and discussed at a public conference.[115] Meanwhile, DG Internal Market and Services (DG Markt) had been coordinating 'a comprehensive evaluation of the impact and effectiveness' of the EU legislation; a project which included some specially commissioned economic research. According to the Commission:

> The findings of the evaluation showed clearly that the public procurement Directives ... have helped to establish a culture of transparency and outcome-driven procurement, generating savings and improvements in the quality of procurement outcomes that far exceed the costs, for public purchasers and suppliers, of running those procedures. The evaluation has also found that differences in implementation and application of the Directives have led to different outcomes in different Member States. The

---

[113] 'Single Market Act: Twelve levers', above (n 21) 19.
[114] Commission, 'Green Paper on the modernisation of EU public procurement policy: Towards a more efficient European Procurement Market' COM (2011) 15/47.
[115] Commission, 'Green Paper on the modernization of EU public procurement policy: synthesis of replies' (June 2011).

time taken to complete procedures and the cost to public purchasers vary widely across Member States.[116]

And then there is the 'better' or 'smart' regulation process of impact assessment (IA) (see chapter two). Showing the lengths to which this can go, 'a package of preferred options was identified that should optimise the synergies between the different solutions allowing savings due to one type of action to neutralise related costs caused by another', or so it was claimed.[117] Following scrutiny by the Commission's high-level Impact Assessment Board, amendments were made in accordance with the standard internal procedure for quality assurance. The proposal for new legislation was published in December 2011, accompanied by the final IA report.[118] According to the Explanatory Memorandum, the process had served to distil the policy into five main legislative objectives:

1. Simpler, more flexible procedures.
2. More scope for strategic usage in support of common societal goals.
3. Better access for SMEs.
4. Sounder procedures.
5. Improved governance.

In fact, the legislative stage of the reform exposes the limitations of the Commission's technocratic pre-legislative procedures. Raw politics could not be and – if democratic principle means anything in the EU – should not be excluded in a matter as important and, especially as regards contract compliance, as contested as this one. Hundreds upon hundreds of amendments were proposed to the Commission's draft and some major changes were made, for example about governance. Consequently, directives originally intended for adoption by the end of 2012 were eventually finalised in early 2014.

The paper trail underwrites some awkward questions about efficacy or fitness for purpose of the regulatory 'menu of common procedures'. Take the chief starting point of the regulatory intervention: low rates of import penetration. Direct cross-border procurement has accounted for 3.5 per cent of the value of contracts advertised at EU level (1.6 per cent of awards): an underwhelming achievement. SMEs appear to have done poorly in the face of the complex framework, as might also have been expected.[119] From the standpoint of contract theory, the multiple pull-factors and/or relational considerations cannot be wished away. Pointing up the importance of local connections, the official evaluation found that almost 40 per cent of regulated contracts were awarded to suppliers located within a radius of 50 km, rising to 50 per cent for those within 100 km.[120] The greater impact has

[116] Commission, 'Proposal for a Directive on public procurement' COM (2011) 896 final, 5.
[117] Ibid.
[118] Commission Staff Working Paper, 'Impact Assessment of Proposals for Directives on Public Procurement and Utilities Procurement' SEC (2011) 1585 final.
[119] 'Evaluation Report', above (n 2) xiii, 108–09. The Commission had previously called for a change in procurement culture in this regard: 'European Code of Best Practices Facilitating Access by SMEs to Public Procurement Contracts' SEC (2008) 2193.
[120] 'Evaluation Report', above (n 2) 139.

been in indirect cross-border procurement via subsidiaries or affiliates (13.4 per cent by value).[121]

The annual budgetary savings for contracting authorities from increased competition were estimated to be in the order of €20 billion. However, the evaluation also pointed up the hefty costs for suppliers and contracting authorities of compliance with the legislation: a yearly estimate of €5.2 billion or 1.3 per cent of the value of the procurements.[122] Concerns about the cumbersome and expensive nature of the regime, as characterised by lengthy procedures and complicated rules and associated risks, have additional credence when ventilated from the front line. The public consultation had – once again – produced a litany of complaint about the design and workings of the regulatory framework. The need for simplification and flexibility was the chief thread, as epitomised in criticisms of 'excessive formalisation' and 'the level of detail'; and, more generally, of heavy administrative burdens and lack of proportionality. 'A large majority of respondents consider that the procedures provided under the current directives do not allow contracting authorities to obtain the best possible procurement outcomes'.[123] In the trademark terms of cost–benefit analysis, the evaluation concluded that there was 'scope for efforts to strike a better balance'.[124]

Scope and Proportionality

Once more focusing on public sector procurement, we see significant changes being made to the coverage and bite of the regulatory regime.[125] Directive 2014/24 brings more services within the full rules, so abolishing the distinction between so-called priority and non-priority ones. On the other hand, in recognition both of the evident sensitivities at Member State level and of an especially limited cross-border dimension, it establishes a lesser regime (centred on observance of the basic principles) for 'services to the person' in sectors such as health and education.[126] Greater discernment – proportionality – is also evident in new provisions regarding 'sub-central' government purchasers.[127] Sitting more comfortably with the heterogeneous character of contracting authorities, these involve higher thresholds and less onerous advertising requirements and time limits. A litigation 'hotspot' is readily envisaged as these reduced legislative requirements for compliance are tested against the general principles.

---

[121] Ibid, xiii.
[122] Ibid, xvii–xviii.
[123] 'Synthesis of replies', above (n 114) 10. See further, S Arrowsmith, 'Modernising the EU's Public Procurement Regime: a Blueprint for Real Simplicity and Flexibility' (2012) 21 *Public Procurement Law Review* 71.
[124] 'Evaluation Report', above (n 2) 156.
[125] For further details, see (2014) 23 *Public Procurement Law Review* special issue – The New EU Procurement Directives.
[126] Directive 2014/24, recital 114.
[127] As defined in Directive 2014/24, Art 2.

Directive 2014/24 contains textbook examples of attempts to codify court rulings in the context of administrative process. Article 12, for example, aims to inject greater legal certainty into *Teckal*-type arrangements by using percentages (which, reflecting more or less hawkish approaches, were much haggled about in the legislative process). As regards the vexed issue of contractual modification, Article 72 tackles *Pressetext* by reading across the operative part of the judgment and then glossing it with some highly specified exemptions including on corporate restructuring or insolvency and unforeseen circumstances. And so back again to the never-ending 'juridification cycle' of judicial and legislative interaction: no doubt the CoJ will soon be called upon to interpret these provisions.

Changed Pathways

In the light of the widespread demand for greater flexibility, new routings are made available at the discretion of the Member State.[128] Largely replacing negotiated procedure, the 'Competitive Procedure with Negotiation' allows for revised bids once a negotiation is formally ended, subject to tighter safeguards against discrimination, as for example a ban on changes to the qualification criteria.[129] Meanwhile, as the nomenclature indicates, the 'Innovation Partnership' supports the Single Market Act policy of facilitating cutting edge technological developments; supplier and purchaser may jointly explore the possibilities on condition that the resulting supplies, services or works correspond to the agreed performance levels and maximum costs.[130] The competitive dialogue procedure is also made more accessible,[131] so further demonstrating a tilt away from the simplistic 'discrete' model of contracting. Whether their highly detailed nature renders the provisions fit for purpose however remains to be seen.

From the standpoint of administrative procedures, a firm push in favour of e-procurement on grounds of economy, simplification and better access commands attention. To put this in perspective, a series of useful electronic resources have appeared over the years on the Commission's website: most notably TED (daily updates on tender notices); SIMAP (general information and resources); and eCERTIS (database of certificates and attestations commonly requested at national level). But with an uptake in only 5 to 10 per cent of procurement procedures, the EU regime has signally failed to meet ambitious political targets on the use of electronic means of communication and information exchange. Flanked by standard non-legislative measures such as dissemination of best practice as part of a broad-ranging Commission strategy on digitisation,[132] Directive 2014/24 envisages

---

[128] Ibid, Art 26.
[129] Ibid, Art 29.
[130] Ibid, Art 31.
[131] Ibid, Art 30.
[132] Commission, 'A strategy for e-procurement' (Communication) COM (2012) 179 final; Commission, 'End-to-end e-procurement to modernise public administration' (Communication) COM (2013) 453 final.

a mandatory and rapid transition towards fully electronic communication across key stages of the pathways model up to and including the electronic submission of bids.[133] Draft legislation was recently published on electronic invoicing.[134]

Looking more closely, we see how particular steps along the pathways are reordered so as to accommodate different 'steers'. Take the problem of corruption. Against a backdrop of concern, more especially in certain Member States in southern and eastern Europe,[135] it is solemnly declared that 'the financial interests at stake and close interaction between the public and the private sector make public procurement a risk area for unsound business practices'.[136] Directive 2014/24 now includes a general legislative requirement founded on general jurisprudential principle:

> Member States shall ensure that contracting authorities take appropriate measures to effectively prevent, identify and remedy conflicts of interests arising in the conduct of procurement procedures so as to avoid any distortion of competition and ensure equal treatment of all economic operators.[137]

In other words, in the face of national administrative autonomy, firm rules are intended on (for example) disclosure of private interests and, if conflicts cannot otherwise be avoided, exclusion of firms. Then again, the directive provides some corporate incentive in the form of 'self-cleansing'. By taking 'concrete technical, organisational and personnel measures that are appropriate to prevent further criminal offences or misconduct', barred contractors may be permitted to start bidding again.[138]

Further illustrating the element of Member State discretion to make rules, domestic systems may provide that the award of certain types of contract must be based on the 'most economically advantageous tender'.[139] A different but related point, contracting authorities can now base their decisions on a sophisticated cost-effectiveness approach known as 'life-cycle costing'. As well as the direct or internal costs across all the successive stages of acquisition and production, use and maintenance and disposal and/or recycling of the purchase, this may include external environmental costs (pollution) if verifiable and able to be monetised. While this suitably animating provision sits well with the Europe 2020 objectives, some standardisation is called for to curb procedural discretion. Effectively enabling a sector-by-sector development, purchasers must adhere to a common EU methodology for the calculation of life cycle costs where adopted by a legislative or delegated act.[140]

---

[133] Directive 24/2014, recital 52.
[134] Commission, 'Proposal for a Directive on electronic invoicing in public procurement' COM (2013) 449 final.
[135] As evidenced in international 'league tables': see Transparency International, Corruption Index 2013.
[136] COM (2013) 449 final, 11.
[137] Directive 2014/24, Art 24.
[138] Ibid, Art 57.
[139] Ibid, Art 67.
[140] Ibid, Arts 67–68.

Meanwhile, the treatment of SMEs shows a more holistic approach across different stages of the pathways model.[141] The Commission believes that they will 'greatly benefit' from a more streamlined approach to documentation requirements, not least in the form of self-declarations as prima facie evidence for selection purposes.[142] Again, notwithstanding the associated financial risk, turnover requirements for firms are now generally capped by reference – proportionality – to the estimated contract value. Purchaser discretion is also checked by a requirement to justify why high value procurement is not divided into 'bite-sized' lots. Putting aside concerns about administrative cost and efficiency, national rules may go further by making divisions into lots compulsory.[143]

According to the Commission, the broader dispensation on the strategic use of public procurement represents an 'enabling approach' for contracting authorities in 'response to new challenges'.[144] More precisely, the reworked regulatory regime demonstrates a less assertive approach to the structuring and confining of discretion under the stern rubric of a commercial outlook and, conversely, pays greater heed in the legislative drafting to the creative role of government contract as an important policy lever in the broad context of the Europe 2020 strategy. Typically happening in the shadow of the case law development, this is well illustrated in a softening of approach as regards the early stages in the life cycle of a product. Directive 2014/24 thus confirms that relevant environmental and social/ethical criteria may be used both in the technical specifications or contract performance conditions and in the award stage, 'including factors involved in the specific process of production'.[145] Conversely, by reference to linkage with the subject matter of the contract, generalised corporate responsibility requirements remain excluded. In the language of steering, the revision is no '90 per cent turn' but rather the proverbial 'light touch on the tiller'.

Governance

Under the original Commission proposal, each Member State would have been required to have a single oversight body in charge of monitoring, implementation and control of public procurement. As boldly envisioned by DG Markt, the governance framework would thus have moved closer to the decentralised but highly integrated model now established in competition law (chapter eight). Suggested regulatory tasks included own-initiative opinions and guidance, examining complaints and receiving reports on individual procedures and annual and detailed statistical reporting. Naturally it was said that the great diversity of existing governance arrangements 'compromises the efficient and uniform application' of EU

---

[141] Ibid, recital 78.
[142] COM (2013) 449 final, 11; Directive 2014/24, Art 59.
[143] Directive 2014/24, Arts 46 and 58.
[144] COM (2013) 449 final, 9.
[145] Directive 2014/24, Arts 42, 67, 70. See also Art 43 (labelling).

public procurement law. The Commission further envisaged a rigorous form of administrative cooperation between Member States, extending to designated liaison points and electronic dialogue via the fast-growing Internal Market Information System (IMI).[146]

Notably however, the Commission was seen by the Council to have overstepped the mark in this core area of state activity.[147] A case of national administrative autonomy reasserted and burdensome change avoided at a time of austerity, Directive 2014/24 leaves national systems free to take their own view of how to organise the necessary monitoring, advice and reporting functions.[148] While the original proposals on administrative cooperation have largely been accepted, the national reporting obligations are substantially watered down.[149] In short, what has not happened in terms of governance is the more significant.

CONCLUSION

In the typically bland words of Brussels officialdom, 'the correct, efficient and effective application of EU public procurement rules across the Union remains a constant challenge'.[150] Yet the Commission and CoJ in particular could scarcely be accused of a lack of effort. Legislation has been piled on legislation and jurisprudence has proliferated in the attempt to impose 'some common disciplines' across the Member States. This chapter has shown how, largely driven and justified via the appealing principle of 'transparency', the important administrative law strategy of structuring, confining and checking discretion along decision-making pathways is of the essence of this. Close examination further highlights myriad micro-developments taking place over many years and voluntary elements of 'spillover' in the form of Europeanised public administration. Currently illustrated in another wave of reform, the EU regulatory regime even appears self-generating, so possessing a momentum of its own.

Emblematic of so much in EU administrative procedure, the potent mix in the regulatory regime of the policy-laden with dry and technical provision is a major theme. It finds tangible expression, at one level, in inter-institutional disputes between Commission and CoJ on techniques of contract compliance; at another level, in changing regulatory fashion on the use of those techniques; and at yet another level, in the constitutional sub-text of more or less integration, as in the disagreement over governance. The efficacy of a cross-cutting 'horizontal' codification targeted 'vertically' on Member States is rightly questioned. The Commission's own evaluation of this flagship policy could identify only a limited

---

[146] COM (2013) 449 final, 12–13, 101–03.
[147] As made evident in a 'Presidency compromise text' of 30 November 2012.
[148] Directive 2014/24, Art 83.
[149] Ibid, Arts 85–86.
[150] 'Annual Public Procurement Implementation Review 2012', above (n 12) 4.

cost–benefit achievement, including startlingly low levels of import penetration. Even an innovative system of legal remedies has had limited impact.

Amid multiplying policy rationales, hence legislative 'steering' pointing in various directions, and with never-ending attempts at fine-tuning and gap-filling, the internal wiring of the regulatory system has become increasingly complicated. From the standpoint of professional procurement practice, 'juridification' in the shape of detailed procedural provision may be seen as part of the problem. Likewise, it appears that insufficient attention has been paid in the regulatory design to contract theory, with the twin results of understandable resistance associated with, and undermining of the cooperative-style benefits of, the relational model of contracting. The new legislation tackles some important pressure points, so injecting welcome doses of flexibility and proportionality into the administrative procedures. Even so, the picture is decidedly mixed, not least in the contested area of contract compliance. Enough has been said to highlight the powerful mediating effects in the regulatory regime of fragmented arrangements and diverse practices inside the Member States. 'Steering' on a pan-European basis is far more easily said than done.

7

Procedural Development, Institutional Tensions: Commission Infringement Process

P ASSING EU LAWS is all very well, but law is not self-enforcing. Policy objectives risk not being attained, benefits to citizens and market actors may be only partially realised, expenditure is liable to be compromised and ultimately the Union's foundations may be threatened, unless arrangements are made to secure their effective application. The performance of requisite enforcement roles – to demonstrate the rule of EU law (essential for market credibility and institutional legitimacy), to contribute to efficient and effective Union policies in instrumentalist fashion and to help vindicate rights and freedoms and mediate between different interests – lies at the very heart of the European construction. Yet perfect enforcement is a chimera: simply too great and intrusive a task in the face of a burgeoning *acquis*. Enforcement raises important issues of administrative policy and process, or discretion, procedural design and trade-off.

BASIC CONSTITUTIONAL PARAMETERS: FOUR CORNERS

Let us recall the four corners within which EU enforcement policy and practice must be framed. First comes the division of labour, or primary responsibility of Member States for implementing and ensuring compliance with Union law matched with the Commission's exclusive role of 'guardian of the Treaties'. That is to say, on the one hand, the all-embracing duty to 'take any appropriate measures, general or particular, to ensure fulfilment of the obligations' stemming from the Treaties or acts of the institutions (TEU Article 4(3)); on the other, the double duty to 'ensure the application' of those obligations and 'oversee the application of Union law under the control' of the Court of Justice of the European Union (CJEU) (TEU Article 17(1)). Second is the concomitant element of shared and mutual responsibility, which post-Lisbon finds expression in the Treaties not only in the overarching principle of sincere cooperation, but also in the substantial constitutional statement in TFEU Article 197(1) that 'effective implementation of

Union law by the Member States, which is essential for the proper functioning of the Union, shall be regarded as a matter of common interest'.

Third, we note the Commission's generic or 'horizontal' powers of formal legal action against Member State infringements, which famously go back to the Treaty of Rome and which have been buttressed in recent times by powers to request financial sanctions in the face of continued non-compliance (now TFEU Articles 258, 260). Flanked by the special legal and administrative regimes found in competition and state aids, for example, the resulting centralised procedures constitute the ultimate 'hard core'[1] of EU enforcement practice.[2] The classic illustration in EU governance of administrative procedures grafted onto or fleshing out skeletal legal provision, the design is that of an elongated decision-making chain in which Member States should be given ample opportunity and encouragement to achieve voluntary compliance. Historically an article of faith for the Commission, a particular conception of infringement procedure as elite, bipolar, discretionary and closed has informed this.[3]

Fourth is the role and contribution of law enforcement by private actors in the national systems, which finds ringing endorsement in the constitutional demand that Member States 'provide remedies sufficient to ensure effective legal protection in the fields covered by Union law' (TEU Article 19(1)). Fuelling references to the Court of Justice (CoJ), today's mass routing of individual legal action to 28 sets of domestic courts was simply unimaginable when infringement procedure was conceived by the 'Founding Fathers'.[4] One option for the EU legislator is reinforced mechanisms of national redress (as illustrated in the previous chapter on public procurement); conversely, avenues of private enforcement may be used to justify restricting outside involvement in the elite model of public advocacy. Then again, contemporary concerns about 'eurolegalism' (see chapter three) cannot obscure some painful facts of life: deep-seated problems of access to justice for many individuals and groups; procedural complications and cost and delay associated with a diverse and multi-level EU legal system; complex and challenging subject matters of EU regulation. Given the Commission's unique capacities as a strategic and repeat player to fill enforcement gaps, complementarity between public and private advocacy has an important place in EU governance.[5]

---

[1] J Pelkmans and A de Britto, *Enforcement in the EU Single Market* (Brussels: Centre for European Policy Studies, 2012) 16.

[2] For successive overviews, see H Audretsch, *Supervision in European Community Law*, 2nd edn (Amsterdam: Elsevier, 1986); A Ibanez, *The Administrative Supervision and Enforcement of EC Law: Powers, Procedures and Limits* (Oxford: Hart Publishing, 1999); M Cremona (ed), *Compliance and Enforcement of EU Law* (Oxford: OUP, 2012).

[3] For early accounts, see A Evans, 'The Enforcement Procedure of Article 169 EEC: Commission Discretion' (1979) 6 *European Law Review* 442; A Dashwood and R White, 'Enforcement Actions under Articles 169 and 170 EEC' (1989) 14 *European Law Review* 388.

[4] See further, M Claes, *The National Courts' Mandate in the European Constitution* (Oxford: Hart Publishing, 2006).

[5] R Rawlings, 'Engaged Elites: Citizen Action and Institutional Attitudes in Commission Enforcement' (2000) 6 *European Law Journal* 4.

Policy Dynamics: Institutional Tensions

Enforcement issues have moved steadily up the EU agenda since the turn of the century. Enlargement has undoubtedly been a factor, while difficult economic climes have also brought to the fore countervailing demands for leniency and for firm protection of EU law and policy, and for more targeted approaches. Meanwhile, an evolving EU enforcement policy has featured prominently in the pressing quest for more efficient and effective market governance. The Commission has kept matters on the boil through a series of major communications, tellingly titled (in more traditional style) 'Better Monitoring of the Application of Community Law' (2002); (in the language of new public management) 'A Europe of Results – Applying Community Law' (2007); and (in determinedly holistic terms) 'Better Governance for the Single Market' (2012).[6] Different but related policy thrusts will be highlighted in the course of this chapter: wider deployment of compliance-promoting instruments; early resolution of enforcement issues; less recourse to formal infringement proceedings; and more targeted and sharper use of financial sanctions.

'Fire-watching', we are reminded, is of the essence of enforcement (in the suitably broad sense of all activities designed to ensure appropriate compliance with legal norms). In this regard the Commission's guardianship role should be generously conceived and particularly so in the light of TFEU Article 197. While general monitoring of compliance has long been practised, executive strategies of effective prevention had been stunted, together with alternative forms of dispute resolution prior to SOLVIT (chapter three). Today's more rounded – proactive – enforcement policy is multifaceted: general and specific arrangements; hard and soft forms of intervention; application at different points in the regulatory cycle; more or less opaque. In the particular administrative context of TFEU Article 258, a new form of 'frontloading' designed to facilitate early settlement of potential infringement proceedings calls for special attention: the so-called 'EU Pilot', which is officially visualised in terms of 'partnership' with Member States.[7]

A maturing EU polity, or at least one in which much is heard of good governance values, naturally raises the issue of 'guarding the guardian'.[8] One way to see this is in terms of a double accountability system involving multiple actors: as well as the primary legal accountability of Member States to Commission and Court implied by Article 258, a secondary set of legal, administrative and political accountabilities owed by the Commission to the Court, the European Ombudsman

---

[6] Respectively: Commission, 'Better Monitoring of the Application of Community Law' (Communication) COM (2002) 725 final; Commission, 'A Europe of Results – Applying Community Law' (Communication) COM (2007) 502 final; 'Commission, Better Governance for the Single Market'(Communication) COM (2012) 259 final.

[7] Commission, '30th Annual Report on monitoring the application of EU Law (2012)' COM (2013) 726 final, 10.

[8] M Smith, *Centralised Enforcement, Legitimacy and Good Governance in the EU* (Abingdon: Routledge, 2009).

(EO), and the European Parliament (EP).[9] Conditions have once again been ripe for some institutional games of tug of war over administrative procedure: competing perspectives on the value of transparency in enforcement practice or the degree of involvement of citizens infuse the relationship between the various actors. Nonetheless, the chapter will show how the traditional model of Article 258 founded on strong administrative discretion remains largely intact, though subject to modest procedural change and continuing pressure for more radical reform. Meanwhile, the CoJ is seen asserting a firm control over sanction procedures under Article 260, at the expense of both Commission and Member States.

COMMISSION FIRE-WATCHING

Challenge and Opportunity

Much is heard today of the 'compliance deficit'. But how could multiple governance systems ever keep abreast of an *acquis* that now consists, together with the primary law of the Treaties, of some 10,000 regulations and 2000 directives?[10] The full extent of non-compliance in the official sense of failure by a Member State 'to fulfil an obligation under the Treaties' (Articles 258–60) is one of those famous 'known-unknowns'. A continuing flow of cases through the formal infringement procedure both demonstrates that Commission 'fire-watching' is incomplete and familiarly represents the 'tip of the iceberg'.

In the face of an awesome challenge, the Commission is seen falling back on a standard five-fold classification of infringements:

(a) violation of directly applicable provisions (in treaties, regulations and decisions);
(b) non-transposition of directives into national law, or more accurately failure to notify implementing measures;
(c) incomplete or incorrect transposition of directives;
(d) improper application of directives; and
(e) non-compliance with CoJ judgments;

to which may be added:

(f) failure to cooperate with 'the guardian of the Treaties'.[11]

Two related features are immediately apparent. First, some of these are truly tough nuts, whereas others are – or at least should be – easier to crack; second, for tackling the different types of infringement, some very different forms of administrative procedure are required at Union level. Perhaps then it is not surprising

---

[9] C Harlow and R Rawlings, 'Accountability and Law Enforcement: The Centralised EU Enforcement Procedure' (2006) 31 *European Law Review* 447.
[10] '30th Annual Monitoring Report', above (n 7) 2.
[11] Case C-456/03 *Commission v Italy* [2005] ECR I-5335.

that the Commission has focused especially on (b). At this end of the spectrum, ICT can have a simple but effective role to play in pointing up infringements; at the other end of the spectrum, the laborious checking needed to establish persistent administrative infringements at ground level gobbles resources and may well require the assistance of market participants or NGOs.

The classification is but a basic template. Categories (a) and (d) in particular stand for an 'implementation deficit' in day-to-day administration which covers a multitude of sins. A 2008 Commission Communication on implementing environmental law makes the point admirably: the *acquis* 'needs to be applied to a wide range of natural conditions, under very varied national and regional administrative arrangements, and in situations that often have a cross-border dimension'.[12] Attention is directed to the deeper level of compliance familiarly characterised by the regulatory routines of monitoring and inspection which, in this broad policy domain, are typically in the hands of Member States. And hence not only to specific acts or omissions imperilling environmental protection, but also to systemic breaches of positive obligations to secure the effective functioning of EU law, which may be evidenced for example by lackadaisical administrative supervision and patchy application of sanctions (see further below).

Grounded in compliance theory, a series of research studies usefully points up the underlying whys and wherefores of infringement. They notably include the lack of clarity in much EU legislation associated with the need for political compromise in the supranational law-making process and with the commonly complex regulatory subject matter. For confirmation, one need only refer to public procurement (see chapter six). Predictably, however, Commission officials are less likely to identify this as a chief barrier to timely transposition than are their national counterparts.[13] A whole series of different but related country-level explanations is in play to explain 'saints and sinners' among Member States.[14] Legitimacy is naturally one, as broadly conceived in terms of cultural respect for the rule of law and for the EU as a source of rules. Indeed, it must be remembered that non-compliance may represent a stage in a power struggle over treaty competences or other constitutionally-oriented disagreement over interpretation.[15] Again, cases on sanctions procedure sometimes suggest determinedly rationalist explanations, namely that Member States are obstinate or even defiant by reason of the costs, economic or otherwise, of compliance. To the extent that sharper enforcement – financial penalties – can shift domestic calculations, TFEU Article 260 takes on special resonance. Clearly recognising an opportunity, the Commission has in the period following the 'White Paper on European Governance' (WPEG) gone much further, consistently empha-

---

[12] Commission, 'Implementing European Community Environmental Law' (Communication) COM (2008) 773 final, 3.
[13] M Ballesteros et al, *Tools for Ensuring Implementation and Application of EU Law and Evaluation of their Effectiveness* (Brussels: EP, 2013) 33–34.
[14] J Tallberg, 'Paths to Compliance: Enforcement, Management, and the European Union' (2002) 56 *International Organization* 609; T Börzel et al, 'Obstinate and Inefficient: Why Member States do not comply with European Law' (2010) 43 *Comparative Political Studies* 1363.
[15] See Case 211/81 *Commission v Denmark* [1982] ECR 4507.

sising more prosaic managerial factors. Non-compliance, we are reminded, will often be involuntary or the product of shortcomings in administrative capacities, knowledge and awareness in domestic systems. Grist to the mill of an expansive enforcement policy, political scientists have spoken in this context of the 'world of dead letters',[16] for which read 'law in the books' (compliant transposition) and not 'law in action'. All this places a premium on a facilitative, capacity-building role for the Commission and on preventive – fire-watching – activities.

Expanded Toolkit

In ranging beyond infringement procedure to include other kinds of compliance-promoting tools, the Commission has looked increasingly far and wide: from ex ante information strategies to various instruments for ongoing dialogue with Member States, and on via ICT to ex post disciplines of public accountability. With a view more particularly to avoiding formal legal action, emphasis is placed on 'more cooperation in preventing problems arising'.[17] So too, combinations of these multiplying techniques are successively directed, if in varying degrees, to issues of transposition, implementation and application. The Commission has effectively sustained the strategy through myriad provisions for compliance-promoting tools in legislative proposals and, with reference to its overarching competence as 'guardian of the Treaties', by a mass conjuring of soft governance methods.

The Commission's 2002 Communication heralded the step change, singling out as a key policy action 'to boost the preventive stage of monitoring'.[18] Officials would start by developing and promoting the tools which already existed. Originating in the early administrative phase of infringement action, informal and ad hoc 'package meetings' provide a convenient forum for discussing compliance or transposition issues emerging in a particular sector with national competent authorities. Geared to finding practical solutions, and also a way of managing complaints to the Commission (see below), these have come to be recognised as a key element of EU enforcement process, most obviously in the environmental field. The next step is flanking meetings with other stakeholders for informative and checking purposes.[19] Then comes the classic managerial technique of league tables. First published in 1997, the Internal Market Scoreboard benchmarks the transposition of directives country by country on a regular, updated basis. Officially designed 'to promote peer pressure between the Member States by creating a form

---

[16] G Falkner and O Treib, 'Three Worlds of Compliance or Four? The EU15 Compared to New Member States' (2008) 46 *Journal of Common Market Studies* 293, 309.
[17] COM (2007) 502 final, 2.
[18] COM (2002) 725 final, 6. And see S Andersen, *The Enforcement of EU Law: The Role of the European Commission* (Oxford: OUP, 2012).
[19] See further, P Koller and L Cashman, 'Implementing EC Environmental Law: Compliance Promotion and Enforcement by the European Commission' (2009) 6 *Journal for European Environmental and Planning Law* 1.

176 *Commission Infringement Process*

of mutual monitoring of efforts to apply European legislation',[20] this archetypal technique of soft governance fits neatly today with the constitutional expression in TFEU Article 197(1) of 'common interest'. Over the years the Scoreboard has given tangible expression to political decisions in the Council about targets, most obviously the degree of tolerance of non-communication (latterly a 'transposition deficit' rate of 1 per cent) and, in line with the revolution in ICT, has become more detailed and sector-sensitive.[21] Nonetheless, it is what it is: a statistical tool. The Scoreboard is easy to read – good for media engagement – but only scratches the surface of non-compliance. Indeed it is apt, if overly relied upon, to skew enforcement efforts towards what is easily measurable.

Many of the compliance-promoting instruments are in fact common features of EU governance: enforcement process effectively constitutes a chief node of their development. Sometimes legislatively mandated, sometimes not, guidelines – interpretative communications – are an obvious example. Likewise, for exchange of information and good practice, and more particularly for tackling issues of transposition and implementation, (legislatively mandated) expert committees and (informal enforcement) networks once again bring together Commission and/or Member State officials. Examples of legislation stipulating that the Commission will be assisted by a committee for the purposes of implementation include such basic instruments as the Water Framework Directive, the Air Quality Directive and the Waste Framework Directive.[22]

Alongside, IMPEL, the long-standing EU Network for the Implementation and Enforcement of Environmental Law, brings together the inspection authorities of EU Member States and adjacent countries for the collective purposes of improving monitoring both within and across national boundaries and for promoting cooperation with the Commission.[23] Access may sometimes be afforded to privileged stakeholders, as for example with the determinedly expert network for common implementation of the Water Framework and Floods Directives:[24] the dauntingly titled 'WFD CIRCA Interest Group', typically linked together through the Commission's Directorate-General (DG) Environment website. The strength of the general dynamic is difficult to overstate. In part helping to keep Member States' own enforcement efforts up to scratch, we have seen the rise of major multifunctional networks such as the 'vertical' and 'horizontal' European Competition Network (see chapter eight). Again, constituted under the auspices of the European Chemical Agency by the REACH Regulation,[25] the lesser-known Forum

---

[20] COM (2002) 725 final, 5.

[21] For the '15th anniversary edition', see Internal Market Scoreboard, 26 (February 2013).

[22] Directive 2000/60/EC (Water Framework Directive) [2000] OJ L327/1, Art 21); Directive 2008/50/EC (Air Quality Directive) [2008] OJ L152/1, Art 29; Directive 2008/98/EC (Waste Framework Directive) [2008] OJ L312/3, Art 39.

[23] Commission and IMPEL, Memorandum of Understanding on Core Elements of Future Co-operation (2009).

[24] Directive 2007/60/ EC (Floods Directive) [2007] OJ L288/27.

[25] Regulation (EC) 1907/2006 concerning the Regulation, Evaluation, Authorisation and Restriction of Chemicals and Establishing a European Chemicals Agency [2006] OJ L396/1, Arts 76–77.

for Exchange of Information on Enforcement (FEIE) coordinates the network of national authorities allocated enforcement functions in this policy area. Tasked among other things with advising on the enforceability of restrictions, with identifying enforcement strategies and with proposing, coordinating and evaluating harmonised enforcement projects and joint inspections, the Forum's title is misleadingly soft.

Much in the toolbox is double-edged, effectively functioning not only to help solve compliance problems, but also to glean information about them. In cohesion policy for example, EU legislation now routinely imposes inspectorial obligations on Member States, which must then designate and monitor the workings of the competent authorities (see chapter nine). The Commission's annual monitoring reports highlight the growth of inspectorial functions at Union level, ranging from collection of the Union's own resources from VAT to 'event-driven' reform as with BSE or oil spillage at sea (audit and inspection programmes delivered via the Commission's Food and Veterinary Office and the European Maritime Safety Agency respectively).[26] To these must now be added a raft of investigative powers associated with the great leap forward in European integration that is the move to 'Banking Union' (see chapter eleven).

Geared to correct and complete transposition, especially of legislation like the controversial Bathing Water Directives,[27] seen as almost incapable of implementation, so-called 'conformity-checking' studies involve at their fullest extent horizontal assessment and comparison for all Member States' implementing measures with a view to highlighting inconsistencies and possibly inviting peer pressure. DG Environment in particular has made copious reference to them on its website; typically undertaken by sub-contractors on behalf of the Commission, the studies are only occasionally published: a practical essay in confidentiality prior to formal infringement proceedings very recently approved by the General Court (see below).

From the procedural standpoint two further techniques are particularly noteworthy. The first, correlation tables prepared by Member States listing where each provision of a directive is transposed in domestic law, has special applicability in federal systems, providing central government and Commission officials alike with a clearer overview and control point. Conversely, however, the Council, in defence of national administrative autonomy, has pushed back Commission attempts to include mandatory requirements for correlation tables in directives, provoking the Commission and EP to include a policy statement in favour of compulsion in their 2010 inter-institutional Framework Agreement.[28] Solemnly recorded in joint political declarations, an uneasy compromise currently prevails, whereby the Member States will on a 'case-by-case basis' accede to reasoned

---

[26] Regulation 882/2004/EC] OJ L165/1, Art 45; Regulation 725/2004/EC [2004] OJ L129/6, Art 9.

[27] Directive 76/160/EEC concerning the quality of bathing water [1976] OJ L31/1 and (the replacement) Directive 2006/7/EC [2006] OJ L64/37.

[28] Framework Agreement on Relations between the EP and the Commission [2010] OJ L304/47, Art 44(1).

requests from the Commission for 'explanatory documents' which, if the national authorities consider it useful, 'can take the form of correlation tables'.[29] Building on previous practice and at one with the general requirement that information on transposition be 'clear and precise',[30] such arrangements are also recorded in (non-binding) recitals to individual directives.[31]

As the nomenclature suggests, transposition and implementation plans (TIPS) can penetrate more deeply into issues of compliance. Member States are commonly required to produce planning documents not least in EU environmental policy where major directives are apt to specify obligations to analyse, propose and evaluate in considerable detail.[32] Recently, however, the Commission as part of its 'Smart' Regulation agenda has moved to provide 'enhanced assistance' in the form of TIPS.[33] Perhaps hopefully, TIPS aim to identify all the key risks for the timely and correct implementation of a new directive and the appropriate actions to mitigate those risks. Initially rolled out for environmental legislation, the Commission now treats the technique as standard in health and consumer protection and is beginning to experiment with it more generally. Already committed to working with Member States to share best practice in implementation plans, the Commission also envisages coupling TIPS with proposed programming for the monitoring and evaluation of measures and prioritising support to Member States for building up the necessary capacity to monitor implementation.[34] In terms of enforcement policy, this is the Commission's facilitative role writ large.

Effectiveness is hard to assess, not least because these additional compliance-promoting instruments are themselves apt to entail opaque forms of elite negotiation. A recent study for the EP also points up the fact of competing perceptions: whereas Commission officials are generally pleased with their efforts, Member State officials are less sanguine. Indeed, with the single exception of package meetings, praised by domestic officials as providing a forum for dialogue that may include competent regional and local authorities, each separate preventive activity was accounted more effective when viewed from Brussels. Committees and networks were mostly commonly favoured, with the Commission's interest in maintaining satisfactory relations identified as sometimes leading to a softening of position 'for the greater good' when opposed by Member States in significant numbers. Conformity checking provoked the most disagreement, with Commission bureaucrats rating it highest of all and national officials regarding it as costly and overly formalistic.[35]

---

[29] Joint Political Declarations on explanatory documents of 28 September 2011 and 27 October 2011 [2011] OJ C369.
[30] Case C-427/07 *Commission v Ireland* [107].
[31] eg Directive 2012/27/EU (energy efficiency) [2012] OJ L315/1, recital 66; Directive 2012/18/EU (dangerous substances) [2012] OJ L197/1, recital 31.
[32] For specific provision, see Air Quality Directive , Arts 23–24 and Waste Framework Directive, Arts 28–33.
[33] '30th Annual Monitoring Report', above (n 7)10.
[34] Commission, 'Regulatory Fitness and Performance (REFIT): Results and Next Steps' (Communication) COM (2013) 685 final, 9.
[35] Ballesteros et al, above (n 13) 43–52.

From the standpoint of regulatory theory, the expanded toolkit of compliance-promoting instruments sits comfortably with the parallel development of financial sanctions under the Treaty: prevention in the shadow of the law or, though subject to long drawn-out procedures (see below), enhanced regulatory capacity to play a more forceful hand.[36] Not before time the Commission recently went further, summoning up the classical idea of the 'feedback loop': from rule design and implementation to infringements and back. Re-packaged as part of the governance cycle under the Regulatory Fitness and Performance Programme (REFIT) (see chapter two), there is talk of recurrent problems in the application of law as signified by complaints or court rulings being incorporated in systematic processes of post-legislative scrutiny led by the Commission's Impact Assessment Board.[37]

DEEP ROOTS: INFRINGEMENT PROCEDURE

An Elongated Decision-Making Chain

As is well known, Article 258 envisages – in the original wording – a two-stage process in cases of infringement: stage 1 'formal administrative' or 'pre-litigation' involving delivery of a reasoned opinion; stage 2 'judicial' involving application to the Court. The Article also insists that the Member State concerned 'shall have the opportunity to submit its observations', effectively meaning a frontwards extension of stage 1 to include the so-called 'Article 258 letter' sent formally to request these. Despite a mandatory wording in Article 258, the Commission resorts to a reasoned opinion only if no settlement can be reached and only at this point do the Commissioners take an explicit decision as to whether there has been non-compliance such as to warrant proceeding to the judicial stage.[38] In the absence of further instructions, the Commission possessed a wide discretion to devise administrative procedures. In practice, Commission services would often choose to initiate matters with an informal letter indicating reasons to suspect a violation and requesting further information and observations; today, this 'pre-infringement' or 'informal administrative' stage is the subject of more structured and centralised procedure in the form of 'EU Pilot'.

This elongated decision-making chain reflects and reinforces the idea of a *cooperative* enterprise culminating – hopefully – in voluntary compliance, as also the idea of an 'international procedure' incorporating techniques of elite diplomacy and intergovernmental relations.[39] This is a model with deep roots. Analysing the

---

[36] I Ayres and J Braithwaite, *Responsive Regulation: Transcending the Deregulation Debate* (Oxford: OUP, 1992).
[37] COM (2013) 685 final, 11.
[38] For a convenient summary, see T Hartley, *The Foundations of European Union Law*, 7th edn (Oxford: OUP, 2010) ch 10.
[39] R Grant and R Keohane, 'Accountability and Abuses of Power in World Politics' (2005) 99 *American Political Science Review* 1.

process as it operated around 1990, a leading commentator spoke of the 'administrative negotiation of effectiveness'; the 'main form of dispute settlement' was negotiation, with litigation a 'sometimes inevitable but nevertheless generally a minor part' of the process.[40] The Commission's reports consistently show a tapering structure: small proportions of court cases to infringement procedures resolved in bipolar fashion.[41] Proceedings drop off sharply after formal notice is served and at the point of reasoned opinion.

At first sight, the Commission has good reason to be pleased with the effectiveness of the elongated (formal administrative) procedure. But whether we would be right to draw this conclusion depends partly on the available information relating to negotiation and settlement, in practice sharply limited. Noteworthy also is the high (if reducing) proportion of investigations founded on citizens' complaints.[42] Notwithstanding the evident risks of skewing the enforcement process, the Commission cannot but proclaim 'the vital role'[43] played by multiple eyes and ears in helping it to detect infringements (and cover for limited resources). Environmental law continues to generate the most infringement proceedings (20 per cent in 2012), flanked today by transport, taxation and internal market regulation. Despite – or perhaps because of – the Commission's best efforts to promote compliance, the Article 258 list of chief 'sinners' – featuring Italy, Spain and Belgium – is also strikingly familiar.[44]

There has however been a big drop in the overall number of infringement procedures in recent years, a development all the more noteworthy in view of Enlargement. In the three years between 2004 and 2006 some 11,000 cases were opened under Article 258; in the equivalent period between 2009 and 2011 some 6500 cases; 2012 saw a further fall, with 1343 cases open at the end of the year. Perhaps the Commission's refocus on fire-watching strategies is having some desired effect? Further illuminating the practical significance of administrative procedures, the closer filtering of files through the 'EU Pilot' scheme – quiet accommodation with the Member State outside the Treaty framework – provides another, more tangible, explanation. A general increase in the number of late transposition infringement procedures also commands attention;[45] the number of new directives may be the chief driver but, as explained below, the fast-tracking of financial sanctions combined with electronic techniques for detection points in the same direction.

---

[40] F Snyder, 'The Effectiveness of European Community Law: Institutions, Processes, Tools and Techniques' (1993) 56 *Modern Law Review* 19, 27, 30.

[41] eg in 2012, 46 CoJ judgments were delivered and 1062 files were closed on the basis of Member State compliance: '30th Annual Monitoring Report', above (n 7) 8–9.

[42] In 2012, 44% of new pre-infringement files, compared with 54% own initiative investigations and 2% via EP petitions.

[43] Commission, 'Updating the handling of relations with the complainant in respect of the application of Union law' (Communication) COM (2012) 154 final, 2.

[44] '30th Annual Monitoring Report', above (n 7) 5–7.

[45] There were some 2500 such cases in the period 2010–2012.

Elaborating Priorities

Testimony to the historic pull of diplomacy style 'international procedure', it was only in the WPEG that the Commission began to elaborate a transparent set of enforcement priorities. Behind the novel criteria lay Enlargement and increased demands to husband resources. Geared to the classic guardianship role of securing the rule of EU law, three broad types of infringement were ranked in the 'serious' category, hence targeted for quicker and more intensive treatment: (i) those that undermined basic foundations, such as violations of the fundamental freedoms; (ii) those that undermined the smooth functioning of the EU legal system, for example repeated or cross-border infringements; and, specifically as a way of averting problems for individuals, (iii) failures in the transposition of directives. Signalling the increased emphasis on alternative dispute resolution (ADR) and on fire-watching more generally, the WPEG explained that in other types of case 'other forms of intervention could be explored before launching formal infringement proceedings'.[46]

The Commission appears a true convert to this way of structuring discretion. One major advantage is the periodic opportunity to revise or fine-tune in the light of changing institutional or market circumstances. In 'A Europe of Results' in 2007 the Commission evinced a slightly different approach, declaring as a priority those infringements which (a) present 'the greatest risks' (non-communication of national measures); (b) have 'widespread impact' for citizens and businesses; and, underwriting the constitutional importance of TFEU Article 260, (c) represent 'the most persistent infringements confirmed by the Court'. It recognised that (b) required a tailored or sectoral approach grounded in impact evaluations of specific issues.[47] Matters were soon followed up in an important Commission Communication on environmental law. Stressing 'the irreversible nature of the harm' as a prioritisation factor, the Commission singled out systemic breaches of environmental protection requirements threating human health or high value ecosystems; breaches of core, strategic or planning obligations on which fulfilment of other obligations depends; and with special resonance for cohesion policy, breaches concerning big infrastructure projects or interventions involving EU funding. Showing the valuable link with accountability, the Commission declared its willingness to discuss these criteria with the EP and 'interested parties', including how to apply them in specific subject areas like nature conservation, water and waste.[48]

Perhaps it is not surprising that in the wake of the global financial crisis enforcement priorities have become more instrumental or policy driven. The talk is of focusing scarce resources around 'core EU single market laws' selected by reference

---

[46] Commission, 'European Governance – A White Paper' COM (2001) 428 final, 25–26; COM (2002) 725 final, 11–12.
[47] COM (2007) 502 final, 9.
[48] COM (2008) 773 final, 8–9.

182 *Commission Infringement Process*

to key services sectors and network industries with the most potential for economic growth, such as retail and wholesale trade or transport. With the aim of accelerating Member States' full compliance, the Communication 'Better Governance for the Single Market' established new targets for handling infringements in these areas: zero tolerance as regards timely and correct transposition, reduction of the duration of infringement procedures to 18 months and achieving full compliance with the Court's judgments within 12 months. The Communication emphasised in bold type that where problems persisted the Commission would use its enforcement powers 'with the utmost vigour'.[49] This is likely to involve the repeat player in concerted forms of formal infringement action: regulatory 'packages' of individual procedures against multiple Member States. A recent spate of court cases concerning EU legislative demands for managerial independence in the railways sector well illustrates the strategy.[50]

Let us recall that the Lisbon Treaty not only founds the operation of the centralised enforcement procedures across the whole of EU law by speaking of failure to fulfil an obligation 'under the Treaties', but also promises accession of the Union to the European Convention on Human Rights (ECHR). A whole new vista is thereby opened up in respect of criminal law and policing measures, hitherto obscured by transitional provisions.[51] In the light of recent controversies ranging from France's treatment of Roma people to threats to judicial independence in Hungary and Romania, the Commission has also expressed concern about failure to respect fundamental constitutional values encapsulated in the Rule of Law (TEU Article 2).[52] Time will tell whether this heralds another targeted bout of enforcement action under the rubric of complementarity, with formal infringement procedure as a possible alternative to references to the CJEU in actions brought by private individuals.

Frontloading: 'EU Pilot'

'A Europe of Results' also signalled a major reworking of the centralised enforcement process. Taking the elite model to new heights, the talk was of 'increased commitment, co-operation and partnership between the Commission and Member States'.[53] At the heart of this lay the 'EU Pilot' project, a step on from general compliance-promoting tools that initially involved 15 Member States. In place of ad hoc and piecemeal arrangements, a carefully planned but determinedly

---

[49] COM (2012) 259 final, 4.
[50] See, eg, Joined Cases C-545/10, 627/10, 412/11 *Commission v Czech Republic, Slovenia and Luxembourg* (judgments of 11 July 2013).
[51] S Peers, 'Sanctions for Infringement of EU Law after the Treaty of Lisbon' (2012) 18 *European Public Law* 37.
[52] Commission, 'A New EU Framework to strengthen the Rule of Law' (Communication) COM (2014) 158 final. And see Editorial, 'A Revival of the Commission's Role as Guardian of the Treaties?' (2012) 49 *Common Market Law Review* 1553.
[53] Commission, 'EU Pilot Evaluation Report' COM (2010) 70 final, 2.

informal administrative stage would be grafted onto the decision-making chain ahead of the formal 'Article 258 letter'. Designed to ensure that problems are corrected as quickly and effectively as possible, to promote internal management control both in the Commission and among Member States, and to lessen the load on resource-intensive infringement proceedings,[54] this element of frontloading in the form of 'pre-infringement procedure' sits well with the primary responsibility of the 28 Member States to ensure compliance.

As first presented – Member States to deal directly with complainants and inform the Commission – the Pilot looked suspiciously like outsourcing (to the 'accused') of guardianship responsibilities.[55] As operationalised however, the working method underwrites the bipolar disciplines of dialogue and supervision, while hopefully leaving the Commission better placed to judge whether matters should be escalated to infringement procedure. Yet again the key is ICT. Linked respectively to CHAP, the Commission's electronic register of complaints and inquiries, and to NIF, its infringement database, the Pilot platform allows for the logging and tracking online of all relevant contacts with the Member State on a confidential basis. The standard procedure then involves an individual file with descriptive information and Commission interrogatories and benchmarks of ten weeks for answers including any proposed solutions and for Commission assessment. Behind this lies – yes – 'an active network'.[56] Echoing the role played inside the Commission by the Secretariat- General, Member States have each designated a central contact point tasked to ensure coordination between the various domestic authorities and Commission services. The Commission already speaks of a 'well-established working method' of general application.[57] On from the experimental phase, the framework has been successively rolled out to all Member States and, following in the footsteps of complaint-based cases, to the Commission's own initiative files. Applied in principle across the *acquis*, it is now also used for most types of possible infringement. The one major exception is non-notification of directives, the subject instead of fast track procedure under the Treaty (see below) and of automatic tracking via a separate database.

According to a 2011 Commission study, some 2100 case files were entered in the Pilot system in a three-and-a-half year period: judging the response 'acceptable', the Commission had closed the file in some 80 per cent of the pre-infringement procedures; only 300 or so files were subject to transfer into the pre-litigation stage of Article 258. The electronic framework had also delivered tangible benefits in speedier processing: on average, Member State answers were just below the 10-week benchmark, while Commission assessments were just above.[58] Momentum has

[54] COM (2007) 502 final, 7–8.
[55] Ibid, 7; M Smith, 'Enforcement, Monitoring, Verification, Outsourcing: The Decline and Decline of the Infringement Process' (2008) 33 *European Law Review* 777.
[56] COM (2010) 70 final, 7; for further details, see Commission Staff Working Paper, 'Functioning of the System – Accompanying Document to the Commission's Second Evaluation Report on EU Pilot' SEC (2011) 1626.
[57] Commission, 'Second Evaluation Report on EU Pilot' COM (2011) 930 final, 7.
[58] Ibid, 4–6.

continued to increase: in 2012, a further 1400 files were entered in the system and 1175 were closed.[59] It was left to a rival EP study to point up the different perceptions of insiders and outsiders: much praise from both Commission and Member State officials for the ease of process and sense of partnership built on trust; concern in civil society about the quality of solutions actually achieved.[60]

Although generally supportive of EU Pilot as an efficient way of dealing with complaints, the EO too has expressed unease. A number of his investigations have found unwarranted delay or a lack of diligence in the Commission assessment.[61] With a view to respect for citizens, the EO has tried through an Own-Initiative Investigation (OII) to have the Pilot procedures integrated in the Commission's soft law mini-code on relations with the complainant (see below), but with no real success.[62] The managerialist drive to a 'well-established working method' has also left the system facing demands from the EP, which typically seeks formalisation in the guise of legally binding procedures. So too, conscious of its own privilege, the EP wants entitlement 'to request information in anonymous form in order to be fully aware of all relevant aspects in the implementation and application of Union law'.[63]

COMPETING CONCEPTIONS

Judicial Policy

The judges have once again played an important role in the design and workings of administrative procedure. Confirming the Commission's position at the heart of the Article 258 process, the judicial policy has been one of sustaining and (latterly) further empowering the traditional model, while ensuring basic procedural protection for Member States. The CoJ long ago recognised the importance of giving the country concerned an opportunity either to comply of its own accord with treaty requirements or to justify its position;[64] though 'multiple opportunities' would be the more accurate description. Likewise, the Court has restated time and again the Commission's broad discretion as effective 'gatekeeper'[65] of the process: whether or not and when to commence infringement proceedings and whether or not and when to refer a case.[66] More particularly, the Court has in manifold declarations of inadmissibility held to the view that third parties –

[59] '30th Annual Monitoring Report', above (n 7) 7–8.
[60] Ballesteros et al, above (n 13) 69–73.
[61] Draft Recommendation in Inv 503/2012/RA (7 May 2013); Inv 332/2013/AN (13 January 2014).
[62] OI/2/2011/OV (28 March 2012).
[63] EP Resolution of 4 February 2014 on the 29th Annual Monitoring Report (2011) (P7-TA(2014)0051) [16]–[18], [22].
[64] See, eg, Case C-85/85 *Commission v Belgium* [1986] ECR 1149.
[65] B Steunenberg, 'Is Big Brother Watching? Commission Vversight of the National Implementation of EU Directives' (2010) 11 *European Union Politics* 359.
[66] As in Case C-329/88 *Commission v Greece* [1989] ECR 4159; Case C-317/92 *Commission v Germany* [1994] ECR I-2039; Case C-562/07 *Commission v Spain* [2009] ECR I-9553, respectively.

complainants to the Commission – can have no legally enforceable right to require it to adopt a specific position. This amounts to a 'judicial firewall' around Commission discretion.[67]

This is not to say that the two institutions have been at one. Historically, for the Commission, the Court was essentially an adjunct to a political and administrative procedure; in contrast, by elaborating 'essential guarantees' for Member States – clear specification of the allegations, reasonable time to prepare a defence, etc – the Court has effectively superimposed on the administrative stage the character of the pre-litigation stage of a judicial process.[68] The case law then effectively establishes the parameters of a rigorous, bipolar framework in which the accountability of, or protection from abuse by, the Commission is all one way. When did a Member State ever complain that in taking – or indeed in not taking – infringement proceedings against it, the Commission was taking its role as 'guardian of the Treaties' insufficiently seriously?

The Court is however seen rebalancing the bipolar model in the Commission's favour by relaxing procedural requirements in the case of 'general and persistent infringements' as in the *Irish Waste* case,[69] where the Court directly engaged with the difficulty of combating wrongful or lackadaisical application of EU norms at ground floor level, not least when, as is typically the scenario in environmental protection, the Commission lacks inspectorial powers. The Commission had eventually decided to take a more strategic approach to enforcement, using multiple complaints as compelling evidence of systemic regulatory failure. In ruling that a declaration could be granted on this general basis, the Court opened the way to the Commission adducing further evidence of a 'GAP infringement' during proceedings, while effectively putting the burden on the Member State to demonstrate that the problems are only isolated ones. The Commission meanwhile is freed from having to terminate enforcement action where specific breaches are remedied, and may subsequently request financial sanctions should the defective administrative practices and procedures not be made good. If still somewhat inchoate,[70] the development clearly has considerable potential.

Access to Documents

Perhaps, however, the judicial attitude to access to documents (see chapter four) constitutes the true litmus test. Faced with the argument that transparency

---

[67] Case 247/87 *Star Fruit v Commission* [1989] ECR 291 and Case C-87/89 *Sonito v Commission* [1990] ECR 1-1981, are classic authorities. In similar vein, a Commission decision not to proceed escapes non-contractual liability.

[68] See further, Harlow and Rawlings, above (n 9). Standard illustrations from a copious case law include Case C-1/00 *Commission v France* [2001] ECR I-9989 and Case C-350/02 *Commission v Netherlands* [2004] ECR I-6213.

[69] Case C-494/01 *Commission v Ireland* [2005] ECR-I 3331; P Wenneras, 'A New Dawn for Commission Enforcement' (2006) 43 *Common Market Law Review* 31.

[70] See Case C-88/07 *Commission v Spain* [2009] ECR I-01353.

promotes legitimacy and rationality in the exercise of discretionary powers, the CJEU has repeatedly underscored the importance to the elite, bipolar model of the wraparound of confidentiality. Two cases arising prior to Regulation 1049/2001 set the tone. In *Petrie*,[71] complainants to the Commission asked to examine the formal letter of notice and reasoned opinion. Accepting the Commission's plea of confidentiality as highly functional in enabling 'genuine cooperation and an atmosphere of mutual trust', the GC thought it right to preserve the possibility of 'an amicable resolution of the dispute' prior to judicial intervention. Access was refused.[72] In *Bavarian Lager*,[73] the GC came to the same conclusion, referencing 'a process of negotiation and compromise'.[74]

A trio of very recent cases shows the continuing tensions. In the *LPN* case,[75] an environmental NGO joined with Finland in an attack on the *Petrie* line of jurisprudence. Having complained to the Commission that a construction project infringed the Habitats Directive,[76] the group had unsuccessfully sought access to the file prior to the case being closed at the pre-litigation stage. Strenuously upholding a protective policy on secrecy and with it the discretionary, bipolar model of enforcement, the CoJ dismissed the challenge. It spoke of early disclosure of documents as changing 'the nature and progress' of infringement procedure because 'it could prove even more difficult to begin a process of negotiation and to reach an agreement'. Downplaying the standard obligation to consider releasing individual documents, it was but a small step to confirming the legal presumption that disclosure at the administrative stage is harmful.[77] The judgment lends credence to the view that 'overriding public interest' as justification for disclosure is mere window dressing. Finland's contention that information on environmental protection merits special treatment[78] was brusquely rejected and it was left to Sweden, intervening, to point up the catch-22 of requiring specific justification in the light of 'the fact that the institution concerned is the only party which is aware of the content of the documents of which disclosure is requested'.[79]

Germany v Commission[80] put a modest dent in the wraparound of confidentiality, so opening up some potential for subsequent political accountability. An infringement procedure having been closed, Germany objected to the Commission's release

---

[71] Case T-191/99 *Petrie and Others v Commission* [2001] ECR II-3677, drawing on Case T-105/95 *WWF UK v Commission* [1997] ECR II-313.

[72] Ibid, [67]–[68].

[73] Case T-309/97 *Bavarian Lager Company v Commission* [1999] ECR II-3217.

[74] Ibid, [40].

[75] Joined Cases C-514/11 P and 605/11 P *Liga para a Protecção da Natureza (LPN) and Finland v Commission* (judgment of 14 November 2013).

[76] Directive 92/43/EEC on the conservation of natural habitats and of wild fauna and flora [1992] OJ L206/7.

[77] *LPN* case [63]–[68], drawing in particular on the *Ilmenau* case on state aid; see above, ch 5, p 132.

[78] In terms of the Aarhus Convention, implemented by Council Regulation (EC) 1367/2006 [2006] OJ L264/13; see further, ch 12.

[79] *LPN* case, [88], [93].

[80] Case T-59/09 *Germany v Commission* (judgment of 14 February 2012); following in the footsteps of Case C- 28/08 *Bavarian Lager v Commission* [2010] ECR I-6055 and Case C-514/07 *API and Sweden v Commission* [2010] ECR I-8533.

under Regulation 1049 of documents including its reply to the letter of formal notice and minutes of a meeting with national officials on the basis that disclosure might harm 'international relations' (Article 4(1)) and disrupt the enforcement process by casting light on the 'negotiating tactics, compromises and strategies which could be used in future procedures'. The GC confirmed however that the general presumption of confidentiality ceases once compliance has been achieved; in accordance with the broader jurisprudence on public access, the Commission was entitled in these circumstances to disregard the Member State's concerns as 'abstract and purely hypothetical'.[81] *ClientEarth*,[82] on the other hand, shows the Article 4(2) mandatory exception on 'inspections, investigations and audits' being stretched forward to encompass generalised elements of 'fire-watching'. The NGO sought access to some 60 compliance-checking studies mentioned in a DG Environment plan. The Commission willingly provided access to those studies showing proper transposition but held back much of the rest on grounds of actual or possible future utility in infringement procedures. The GC ruled that as 'targeted instruments designed to detect specific infringements of EU law' they were subject to the general presumption of non-disclosure.[83] This blurs the conceptual distinction between infringement proceedings properly so-called and preventive compliance-promoting tools.

Citizens' Advocate

It would be strange if the EO had not received a steady stream of complaints about the workings of infringement procedure. The Commission's heavy reliance on complainants for the purpose of energising the elite bipolar model naturally generates pressure for a more assertive and timeous approach and for greater openness. With the court route blocked, discontent surfaces in a forum created explicitly in the service of 'citizens of the Union'. The EO has spoken of 'supervising the supervisor' by 'examining the Commission's behaviour in analysing and treating the infringement complaint' while 'fully respect[ing] the Commission's discretionary power recognised by the Treaties and the case-law'.[84] Closer inspection shows the EO becoming more demanding over the years but with only a modicum of success. There are four interwoven threads: (i) rudimentary administrative protections for complainants; (ii) diligence on the part of the Commission in taking complaints seriously; (iii) a Commission culture of justification; and (iv) the never-ending saga of access to documents.

Early complaints to the EO revealed a degree of arrogance in the Commission services. Far from buttressing the legitimacy of the process in the eyes of citizens,

---

[81] Case T-59/09 *Germany v Commission* [72], [78], [81].
[82] Case T-111/11 *ClientEarth v Commission* (judgment of 13 September 2013).
[83] Ibid, [49], [70], [75].
[84] EO, *AR 2012*, 43–44; and see N Diamandouros, 'The EU Administration and National Administrations: Making the Relationship Work for Citizens' (23 February 2011).

complainants were being treated as little more than information fodder. Take the *Newbury Bypass* case,[85] where the complainants first heard of closure of the file from a press release; the subsequent OII,[86] which highlighted the 'excessive time' taken to process complaints and 'lack of information' about progress; or the infamous affair of *Macedonian Metro*,[87] where the Commission misled the complainant into believing that the file was closed on legal grounds and not as an act of political discretion. Absent firm control by the Secretariat-General, a fragmented approach to infringement work in individual Commission services was itself a recipe for complaints, reflected and reinforced by the lack of clear procedures to regulate the Commission's relations with complainants.[88]

Seizing the high ground – 'discretionary power is not the same as dictatorial or arbitrary power'[89] – in the face of constitutional objections raised by the Commission's Legal Service, Jacob Söderman eventually wrung from the Commission the limited but nonetheless significant concession of a Communication on 'administrative measures for the benefit of the complainant with which it undertakes to comply'.[90] Basic procedural guarantees were introduced, such as registration of genuine complaints and protection of anonymity; a notional time limit of one year for deciding whether or not to initiate infringement procedure; periodic updates; reasons for closing a case and a last-ditch opportunity to persuade the Commission otherwise. This then is no 'contradictory procedure' of the kind which the EO operates, nor could it be without undercutting the traditional format of infringement procedure. Even so, it is a mistake to assume Commission compliance. The EO has repeatedly found breaches of this soft law mini-code, to the extent in one case of DG Employment completely ignoring it.[91] Nor does the subject of another OII,[92] a decade long failure to publish the mini-code in any EU official language introduced since 2002, suggest an outward-looking administrative culture. Only with a recent revising Communication[93] has this matter been rectified.

Highlighting an incipient challenge to the elite model, Nikiforos Diamandouros promoted 'due diligence' as a principle of good administrative behaviour. In this respect, the EO's assessment came to be two-pronged, based on both the general 'level of care which the Commission is expected to exercise when responding to infringement complaints' and the specific provisions of the Communication on relations with complainants.[94] That the EO's patience should not be regarded as

---

[85] Inv 206/1995/HS.
[86] Own-Initiative Inquiry into the Commission's administrative procedures for dealing with complainants under Art 226; *AR 1997*, 270.
[87] Inv 995/98/OV.
[88] Smith, 'Centralised Enforcement', above (n 8) ch 5.
[89] Inv 995/98/OV [1.7].
[90] Commission, 'Relations with the Complainant in respect of Infringements of Community Law' (Communication) COM (2002) 141 final.
[91] Inv 2403/2008/OV, [40].
[92] Inv OI/2/2012/VL.
[93] COM (2012) 154 final.
[94] Inv 1561/2010/(MB)FOR, [55].

inexhaustible was demonstrated in the *German Waste Oils* affair,[95] where the Commission failed for several years to follow up a scientific study relating to a dispute over recycling. Sending a clear message, the EO noted that for the purpose of ascertaining whether the Commission had acted diligently 'all the relevant facts of the case needed to be considered'.[96]

By the time he left office in 2013, Nikiforos Diamandouros had elaborated on familiar standards of review. Taking the guarantee of reason-giving as a starting point, explicit reference was now made to 'substantive' as well as 'procedural' aspects under an increasingly broad rubric of tackling maladministration. The EO would check whether 'the analyses and conclusions reached by the Commission were reasonable, well-argued and thoroughly explained' to complainants. Indeed, 'if the Ombudsman were fundamentally to disagree with the Commission's assessment, he would state so, while pointing out that the highest authority in interpreting EU law is the CoJ'.[97] Pressing the argument that by providing adequate explanation the Commission can improve relations with citizens, increase its legitimacy and strengthen its effectiveness as 'guardian of the Treaties', the EO went so far as to provide a template. A Commission reply when closing the file should clarify (a) why the matter complained about falls outside the scope of EU law; or (b) why otherwise there is no infringement; or (c) why it is unclear whether there is an infringement, which then demands adequate explanation for not investigating further; or (d) why there is considered to be an infringement, which then demands adequate explanation of the substantive decision to drop the case.[98] Nor is this nascent form of 'hard look review' without tangible effects. In one recent case, a finding of insufficient clarity of reasoning prompted the Commission to reopen informal discussions with the Member State under 'EU Pilot',[99] while in another the Commission launched new infringement proceedings when the EO escalated matters to a draft recommendation.[100] At one level, this challenge to the closed nature of bipolar process is about promoting a culture of justification in the Commission; more prosaically, it is about keeping the Commission on its toes – a not insignificant contribution in view of the judicial 'no-go area' for citizens.

A recent transparency investigation[101] has produced perhaps the clearest articulation of why, in the Commission's view, transparency is inherently inimical to the effective functioning of infringement procedure. Echoing the Council's unsuccessful defence in *Turco* concerning legislative process,[102] the Commission expresses particular concern about 'undue pressure' from third parties resulting from disclosure that 'could result in slowing down the process of achieving compliance.'[103]

---

[95] Inv 146/2005/GG.
[96] Ibid, draft recommendation [1].
[97] EO, *AR 2012*, 43–44.
[98] Inv 1623/2009/(BB)(TS)FOR, [28–29].
[99] Ibid.
[100] Inv 1260/2010/RT.
[101] Inv 1947/2010/PB.
[102] See above, ch 5, p 129.
[103] Inv 1947/2010/PB, [61].

Offering the Commission 'an opportunity to consider pursuing a more nuanced approach', the EO articulated the competing conception of a more open enforcement process attuned to efficiency and effectiveness. The Commission's position, he tartly observed, is 'not immediately evident or self-explanatory'; might not 'the robust involvement of public opinion and civil society' have a functional role to play in upholding the rule of law? Representing another high watermark in EO endeavours, his draft recommendations envisaged a new set of Commission procedures including 'systematic consultation' on whether a Member State wished to insist on confidentiality, as well as explanations to complainants of what was meant in individual cases by 'undue pressure'.[104] In the face of judicial decisions like *ClientEarth*, however, the EO felt unable to conclude that the Commission's refusal to budge constituted maladministration.

THE EP'S CHALLENGE

The EP has naturally sought to thicken the line of political accountability from the Commission; and the more so, in view of the greater premium placed on enforcement in recent times. Priorities, strategies and resources for infringement action and, more broadly, efficiency and effectiveness in EU enforcement process, clearly are appropriate subjects for scrutiny. In this respect the Commission's annual monitoring reports provide some but only some rendering of account in the form of general commentary and statistics and supplementary sector-specific information. As the EP committee tasked with the oversight, JURI has pressed hard for better data and also for closer cooperation or dialogue with the Secretariat-General.[105] In this it has been strongly supported by the Petitions Committee, in receipt of the EO's reports and duly articulating the complainant perspective.[106] Equally naturally the Commission has been reluctant to reveal more of the mysteries of infringement action.

An uneasy compromise exists under the 2010 inter-institutional agreement. The Commission is to make available to the EP 'summary information concerning all' infringement cases entering the pre-litigation stage, including, if the EP so requests, 'on a case-by-case basis and respecting the confidentiality rules, in particular those acknowledged by the CoJ, on the issues to which the infringement procedure relates'.[107] From the standpoint of the co-legislator, understandably concerned to share the benefits of the feedback loop, this allows for a modicum of tracking (beyond the ex post possibilities of freedom of information in individual

---

[104] Ibid, [61], [63].
[105] See, eg, JURI, Report on the 29th Annual Monitoring Report (2011) (A7-0055/2014).
[106] See, eg, the Weiland Report on the deliberations of the Committee on Petitions 2003–04 (2004/2090 (INI)).
[107] Framework Agreement on Relations between the EP and the Commission (2010), Art 44(2).

cases). Yet more squabbling has resulted, in part over the amount of detail the EP is entitled to receive.[108]

The argument that the citizen who complains should be formally recognised in legislation as a party in infringement procedure is hardly new. The first EO, evidently the more concerned the more he looked,[109] was ultimately willing to countenance the break-up of the elite model; in Jacob Söderman's vision, the Commission could serve as arbitrator between the individual and Member State.[110] Today, highlighting the deep-seated differences between the institutions, matters take the form of an annual ritual. The EP passes a motion calling for a hard law version of the Communication on relations with complainants amid much discourse on the importance of principles of good administration and, though the Commission's file is not the complainant's file in terms of ECFR Article 41,[111] of individual procedural protection. When the Commission carries on regardless, the EP 'deplores the fact that there has been no follow-up to its previous resolutions'.[112]

But this is only part of the jigsaw. Praying in aid the principles of legality and legitimacy, the EP envisages 'a legally binding act containing the rules governing the whole pre-infringement and infringement procedure'[113] to be made under TFEU Article 298. This might either take the form of a specific regulation or, as discussed in chapter thirteen, be one part of a general horizontal codification of administrative procedure. JURI has put 'binding time-limits' high on the agenda, together with the raft of procedural disciplines from which the Court has largely shielded the Commission under Article 258 (notification, access to the file, obligation to give reasons, etc). No doubt concerned by the potential for enervating and wasteful forms of 'satellite litigation', the Commission's ever resourceful Legal Service has set about deflecting the Parliament by questioning whether Article 298 can ground legislation regulating responsibilities which the Treaties directly confer on their 'guardian'.[114] Thoroughgoing legal reform of infringement procedure currently appears far off!

SANCTIONS PROCEDURE

Commission and Court

The long period prior to the Maastricht Treaty was that of the toothless watchdog. On the one hand, the Treaty of Rome proffered an image of legality; as and when

[108] EP Resolution of 4 February 2014, [21]–[22].
[109] See especially, Inv 1288/99/OV (the *Parga* case).
[110] J Söderman, 'The Citizen, the Rule of Law and Openness' (10 June 2001).
[111] See above, ch 3, p 87.
[112] See, eg, EP Resolution of 4 February 2014, [17], [20].
[113] Ibid, [16].
[114] See EP Resolution of 21 November 2012 on the 28th Annual Monitoring Report (2010) (P7-TA(2012)0442), [19].

192 *Commission Infringement Process*

failure to fulfil its obligations was established in a declaratory judgment, 'the State shall be required to take the necessary measures to comply'. On the other, as a burgeoning list of unimplemented judgments served to highlight, all the Commission could do if yet more negotiations failed to secure compliance was to return to the Court for a further declaratory ruling. Against the backdrop of the celebrated *Francovich* decision,[115] where the Court attempted to plug the gap by establishing an individual right to sue for damages, Member States at Maastricht finally agreed to support centralised enforcement with a measure of pecuniary incentive. Predictably however, they were not willing to unleash the Commission by giving it direct power to determine an infringement and levy a sanction as happens in competition procedure (see chapter eight). The reworked treaty provision signalled the close interplay of executive and judicial discretion. The Commission could now return to the CoJ, specifying the amount of financial sanction that it considered appropriate in the circumstances, whereupon the Court, if it found non-compliance with its first judgment, could choose to impose a lump sum or penalty payment on the Member State concerned; in formal terms, an order to pay into the account 'European Union own resources' operated by the Commission. Worse, the staged procedures of Article 258 were duplicated in Article 260 – a cumbersome model of enforcement entailing multiple small steps along a very long 'pathway'.

The Commission initially proceeded with extreme caution. It set about developing 'a more transparent and coherent policy' by issuing guidelines indicating how its new powers to recommend fines and penalty payments would be used. This involved structuring and confining administrative discretion by mathematical formulae: the application of coefficients based on seriousness of the breach, duration of the breach and ability to pay, calculated on the basis of Member States' GNP.[116] When eventually court cases began to surface, three well-known decisions set the tone. In *Commission v Greece*,[117] following five years' non-compliance with a judgment concerning an illegal landfill site, the CoJ imposed a daily penalty payment of €20,000. Yet, highlighting problems of forcing governments into remedial action, new infringement proceedings would prove necessary 14 years after the original judgment.[118] *Commission v Spain*[119] demonstrated Commission accountability to the Court when the CoJ set aside the Commission's proposal, substituting a comparatively small annual penalty of €625,000; the reasoning was opaque though, giving the sanctions procedure an air of unpredictability. *Commission v France*[120] was particularly helpful to the Commission for

---

[115] Joined Cases C-6/90 and 9/90 *Francovich and Bonifaci v Italy* [1991] ECR I-5357.
[116] Commission Memorandum 96/C 242/07 on applying Article 228 of the EC Treaty [1996] OJ C242/6; Commission Communication 97/C 63/02 on the method of calculating penalty payments [1997] OJ C63.
[117] Case C-387/97 *Commission v Greece* [2000] ECR I-5047.
[118] Case C-112/06 *Commission v Greece* (order of 2 October 2008). See further, B Jack, 'Enforcing Member State Compliance with EU Environmental Law' (2011) 23 *Journal of Environmental Law* 73.
[119] Case C-278/01 *Commission v Spain* [2003] ECR I-14141.
[120] Case C-304/02 *Commission v France* [2005] ECR I-6263.

dealing with 'GAP infringements'. Confronted with an endemic regulatory failure to tackle violations of EU fisheries policy in certain regions of France over many years, the CoJ determined that the phrase 'lump sum or penalty payment' in Article 260 need not be read disjunctively. France was ordered to pay €58 million for each six-month period of future non-compliance and – in the light of 'the public and private interests in issue' – a lump sum of €20 million.[121] An evident gap in the sanctions framework had been filled by bold teleological interpretation.

Conceptually speaking, Article 260 would now bear a dual character. From the regulatory standpoint, it makes up an integrated decision-making chain with Article 258: there is synergy between persuasion and sanction, shifting the elite bargaining model in favour of the Commission. On the other hand, in accordance with the Court's own view of a provision that bears directly on its authority, Article 260 provides 'a special judicial procedure for the enforcement of judgments',[122] tilting it towards 'second order compliance' with rulings of a supranational court. The aftermath of *Commission v France* further highlights the role of inter-institutional rivalry in shaping administrative procedure. The Commission reworked its guidelines to serve twin purposes: the penalty payment to induce the Member State to end a breach of obligations as soon as possible; the lump sum to encourage the recidivist Member State into general patterns of compliance.[123] Sharpening its claws, the Commission declared a policy of requesting both sanctions on the theory that, while the Member State could still choose to avoid periodic payments by late compliance, it would be stuck with paying a lump sum – a very public mark of disapproval. The CoJ's response was suitably subtle. In a case involving Member State defiance of EU policy on genetically modified organisms (GMOs),[124] it reasserted ownership of the formal proceedings: emphasising the need to consider the particular facts and echoing Commission criticism of the Member State's previous recalcitrance, it levied a lump sum.

Snakes and Ladders

The Lisbon Treaty provides two ladders for the Commission. First, there is fast-tracking of proceedings brought for failure to notify measures transposing a directive. TFEU Article 260(3) thus bypasses the procedural duplication in the Treaty provisions: the Commission can recommend financial sanctions when pleading an Article 258 case and the Court is confined to rejecting or reducing but not increasing the proposed tariff. The Commission has embraced this stronger

---

[121] Ibid, [113]–[15].
[122] Case C-292/11 P *Commission v Portugal* (judgment of 15 January 2014), [39]–[40]. And see L Prete and B Smulders, 'The Coming of Age of Infringement Proceedings' (2010) 47 *Common Market Law Review* 9.
[123] Commission , 'Application of Article 228 of the EC Treaty' (Communication) SEC (2005) 1658', [10]–[12]; M Smith, 'Inter-institutional Dialogue and the Establishment of Enforcement Norms: A Decade of Financial Penalties under Article 228 EC' (2010) 16 *European Public Law* 547.
[124] Case C-121/07 *Commission v France* [2008] ECR I-9159.

incentive to transpose timeously with enthusiasm:[125] in 2012, 35 such cases were referred to the Court.[126] Second, Lisbon saw a modest streamlining of what should now be called the standard track. The Commission need no longer issue a reasoned opinion in Article 260 cases: it can move directly from formal letter and Member State observations to Court referral. It would appear that the sanctions procedure at large has gained some momentum, noteworthy in light of the drop-off in Article 258 infringement procedures. At the beginning of 2013, the Commission had 128 open sanctions cases, 11 referred to the Court for the second time.[127]

The CoJ has continued fleshing out its view of what are relevant and irrelevant considerations for the imposition of financial sanctions and what is proportionate in financial terms. In *Commission v Sweden*,[128] which concerned delay in transposing the Data Retention Directive, Sweden was treated leniently as a first-time offender but – typically – internal political difficulties in implementation were not considered relevant. The CoJ has also taken on board the need to tailor financial sanctions to the scale of efforts being made; some EU environmental legislation, for example, demands substantial investment over many years. In *Commission v Belgium*,[129] where Belgium could point to slow but steady progress in meeting the demands of the Urban Waste-Water Directive, it was said that penalty payments would reduce progressively as implementation became more effective. Similarly, the Court will consider the economic background, as in *Commission v Ireland*,[130] where it was moved by the sharp fall in GDP.[131]

The recent case of *Commission v Portugal*[132] represents the sting in the tail. Portugal having failed to comply to the Commission's satisfaction with a CoJ judgment imposing daily penalty payments, the Commission tried out a competition-type model of in-house determination of sanction subject to review by the GC. Insisting that it had fully implemented the judgment by introducing a replacement law, Portugal appealed to the GC, which annulled the decision on grounds upheld by the CoJ on appeal. The CoJ reprimanded the Commission for straying beyond the narrow confines of the Article 260 judgment; allowing a greater margin of Commission discretion would undermine the rights of the defence; the Commission could not sidestep the jurisdiction of the CoJ to rule on

---

[125] See Commission, 'Implementation of Article 260(3) TFEU' (Communication) SEC (2010) 1371 final.

[126] '30th Annual Monitoring Report', above (n 7) 4–5.

[127] Ibid, 9-10. See further, P Wenneras, 'Sanctions against Member States under Article 260 TFEU: Alive, but not Kicking?' (2012) 49 *Common Market Law Review* 145.

[128] Case C-270/11 *Commission v Sweden* (judgment of 30 May 2013).

[129] Case C-533/11 *Commission v Belgium* (judgment of 17 October 2013); see also, Case C-576/11 *Commission v Luxembourg* (judgment of 28 November 2013).

[130] Case C-279/11 *Commission v Ireland* (judgment of 19 December 2012); see also Case C-374/11 *Commission v Ireland* (judgment of 19 December 2012).

[131] The Commission now regularly updates relevant economic data: see Commission, 'Updating of data used to calculate lump sum and penalty payments to be proposed by the Commission to the Court of Justice in infringement proceedings' (Communication) C (2013) 8101 final.

[132] Case C-292/11P *Commission v Portugal* (judgment of 15 January 2014).

the conformity of national legislation with EU law; nor could the GC rule on compliance when the national law in question had not previously been examined by the CoJ.[133] Back to square one!

CONCLUSION

The Commission was slow to grasp the huge potential of implementation through fire-watching measures but the early years of this century bear testimony to a more thoughtful approach based on partnership with the Member States and on managerial explanations of non-compliance. The chapter has thus focused on the place of compliance-promoting tools in a general package of hard and soft law reforms, while pointing up the strong role in EU governance of enforcement networks and the room for compliance through agency supervision. Informal package meetings have given way to correlation tables and transposition and implementation plans as well as the electronic wizardry of scoreboards. In general this wide-ranging procedural development is a progressive move; the more so, when viewed in the context of formal infringement procedures which – even post-Lisbon – are unwieldy. Fire-watching, however, needs to be carefully targeted and tailored so as not to substitute managerial 'box-ticking' for actual performance.

This case study also brings into sharp focus the importance of institutional preferences and value systems in the shaping of process and procedure in EU administration. The Commission is seen clinging tightly to an elite model of dialogue, informality and confidentiality, while also utilising its privileged position as core Union executive to promote more frontloading in the infringement process. Just as Court rulings have shaped the administrative process, by imposing for example the 'rights of the defence', so deep-rooted administrative practices and procedures have largely determined the patterns of judicial activity. The elite discretionary model has largely found favour with the CoJ, but the Court has also been careful to exercise firm control over the imposition of financial sanctions. From a different perspective, the EO has intervened to secure a foothold for individual complainants in infringement procedure, but – for understandable reasons – it has typically been an uphill struggle. There may be scope for greater political accountability, as the EP, at present an outsider, certainly hopes. But as matters stand, implementation primarily rests with the Member States and there is every sign that they wish to maintain their authority.

---

[133] Ibid, [46]–[56].

8

Modernisation, Cooperation, Enforcement: Competition

COMPETITION LAW AND practice is of the essence of the EU's 'economic constitution', an indispensable regulatory aspect of the Single Market. As demonstrated today in the work of the Directorate-General for Competition (DG Comp), the coverage is immense. It includes under the rubric of 'antitrust' the two main areas chosen for consideration in this case study, *cartels* (anti-competitive agreements) and *abusive market behaviour* (by dominant firms), as well as encompassing mergers (which could be harmful to the competitive process) and state aids (that could distort competition). Historically, functionally and latterly in terms of governance technique, competition occupies a prominent place in the design of EU administrative procedure. Rightly described as a 'most challenging [area] to traverse' in view of 'numerous regulations and notifications, a voluminous case law and an abundant economic literature',[1] it was nonetheless an easy choice for inclusion in this volume.

For some four decades, competition was the chief example of direct administration by the Commission affecting 'individuals' (legal persons or companies). This was the realm of the famous Regulation 17,[2] a strong power conferring but skeletal procedural framework for regulation. A veritable 'litigation hotspot', competition duly emerged as the chief forcing ground for Court of Justice of the European Union (CJEU) jurisprudence on the 'rights of the defence' via actions for annulment. Today, effectively confirming the Community's legislative monopoly, TFEU Article 3(1) specifies 'the establishing of the competition rules necessary for the functioning of the internal market' as one of the few areas of exclusive competence. However, in the early years of the new millennium both the administrative and adjudicative building blocks of the system underwent fundamental reform under the attractive banner of 'modernisation'.[3] The mantra now was 'decentralisation', whereby national governmental and legal systems

---

[1] U Aydin and K Thomas, 'The Challenges and Trajectories of EU Competition Policy in the Twenty-first Century' (2012) 34 *European Integration* 531.

[2] Council Regulation 17/EEC: First Regulation implementing Articles 85 and 86 of the Treaty [1962] OJ L13/204.

[3] Commission, 'White Paper on the Modernisation of the Rules Implementing Articles 81 and 82 of the Treaty' COM (1999) 101 final; Council Regulation 1/2003/EC on the Implementation of the Rules on Competition Laid Down in Articles 81 and 82 of the Treaty [2003] OJ L1/1.

would also have a chief role to play in the application and enforcement of EU competition law.

The European Competition Network (ECN), comprised of the Commission and the newly empowered national competition agencies, lies at the heart of this development. As such, the reform exemplifies the central role in EU governance of communication, cooperation, and coordination – our 'three Cs'. It reflects too the chief role of Enlargement as a driver of policy and administrative change, as well as the essential facilitative role of ICT in grounding novel operational arrangements on a pan-European basis. Today, the ECN's expansive development makes it a leader among EU multi-level networks. Largely grounded in soft law measures, it is described by the Commission as 'an innovative model of governance' for the implementation of EU law.[4] Questions are inevitably raised about internal network relations – the tendency to the hierarchical or 'flat' – and, in view of a design that prioritises information flows between agencies while largely respecting national administrative autonomy, about values of coherence, effectiveness and accountability.

A recurring theme of this volume is that substance and procedure go hand in hand: modernisation of the competition system is no exception.[5] The chequered history of external – transatlantic – influences in shaping EU administrative process and procedure is likewise illustrated,[6] predictably so in a policy domain increasingly dominated by multinationals. Reflecting a greater stress on consumer welfare in accordance with the globally successful discipline of neoclassical economics, the EU regulatory development bears testimony to what is loosely called a 'more economic approach' (emphasis on market impact over the form of the restrictive agreement or practice).[7] Economic analysis, we learn, now 'plays a central role in competition enforcement'.[8] From a functionalist perspective, decentralisation has the particular merit of allowing the Commission to concentrate on the proverbial 'tough nuts': large-scale and complex cases of a transnational nature including powerful and secretive cartels. Tougher sanctions tend however to fuel complaints of unfairness in the decision-making process and insufficient judicial scrutiny. Whereas powerful economic operators have been interested to explore the potential of the European Charter of Fundamental Rights (ECFR) and (in view of the EU's promised accession) the European

---

[4] Commission, 'Report on the functioning of Regulation 1/2003' (Communication) COM (2009) 206 final, 42.

[5] D Gerber, 'Two Forms of Modernisation in European Competition Law' (2007–08) 31 *Fordham International Law Journal* 1235; I Lianos and D Gerardin (eds), *Handbook on European Competition Law*, Vol 1 *Substantive Aspects* and Vol 2 *Enforcement and Procedure* (Cheltenham: Edward Elgar, 2013).

[6] See, eg, B Leucht and M Marquis, 'American Influences on EEC Competition Law: Two Paths, How Much Dependence?' in K Patel and H Schweitzer (eds), *The Historical Foundations of EU Competition Law* (Oxford: OUP, 2013).

[7] S Bishop and M Walker, *The Economics of EC Competition Law*, 3rd edn (London: Sweet & Maxwell, 2010).

[8] Commission Staff Working Paper, 'Best Practices for the Submission of Economic Evidence and Data Collection' SEC (2011) 1216 final, [1].

Convention on Human Rights (ECHR), the Commission will be seen utilising soft law tools in an ongoing reform of competition procedures.

MODERNISATION

Continuity ...

Showing the broad freedom of manoeuvre afforded by the Treaties, there has however been no material change in the two famous Articles grounding EU antitrust law: TFEU Article 101 (ex EEC Article 85) on cartels, prohibiting and rendering automatically void agreements and concerted practices that distort competition, subject to powers of exemption; and TFEU Article 102 (ex EEC Article 86) on monopolies and oligopolies, prohibiting abuse of a dominant position. Dating from 1962, Regulation 17 provided some very necessary infill, serving both as the blueprint for the institutional structure of the system and 'procedural bible'.[9] Standing for a powerful, integrated model of enforcement, it allowed the Commission to investigate cases, determine infringements and levy sanctions. As a form of 'fire-watching', it gave the Commission exclusive jurisdiction over exemptions for restrictive agreements as economically beneficial, which for operators meant notifying arrangements with a view to securing negative clearance. Conversely, the role of national systems was marginalised. National regulators might police their countries' own (diverse) competition laws, but were required to desist in cases affecting Member State trade once the Commission began an investigation; incentives for private enforcement were also lacking, notwithstanding direct effect.[10]

Providing a supplementary element of judicial supervision to the general review of legality, the constitutional quid pro quo would be 'unlimited jurisdiction' for the CJEU to review a penalty imposed by the long-toothed watchdog.[11] However, as well as fleshing out the procedural protection,[12] the judges were from the very beginning major contributors to the substantive design of the system. It was in the early years especially that the Court of Justice (CoJ) promoted an expansive approach to competition law,[13] one that fitted the then dominant view of unifying the market – economic integration – as the chief purpose of the regulatory framework.[14] In other words, the CJEU was accustomed to wearing two hats in this

---

[9] For the early development, see D Gerber, 'The Transformation of European Community Competition Law' (1994) 35 *Harvard International Law Journal* 97.

[10] Case C-127/73 *Belgische Radio en Televisie v SV Sabam* [1974] ECR 51.

[11] ie, to cancel, reduce or increase it: TFEU Art 261.

[12] K Lenaerts and L Vanhamme, 'Procedural Rights of Private Parties in the Community Administrative Process' (1997) 34 *Common Market Law Review* 531.

[13] Classic examples are Joined Cases C-56 and 58/64 *Consten and Grundig v Commission* (meaning of 'effect on Member State trade') and Case C-6/72 *Continental Can v Commission* [1973] ECR 215 (jurisdiction over mergers).

[14] B Hawk, 'Antitrust in the EEC – The First Decade' (1972) 41 *Fordham Law Review* 229.

chief field of EU market regulation: working cooperatively with the Commission to build the capacities of the system; and, especially after the General Court (GC) was created in 1989, functioning as an administrative court to scrutinise the Commission's enforcement activities.[15]

Lawyerly habits of mind were for many years a defining characteristic of DG Comp. This fitted with a strong German influence expressed in the ordo-liberal view of competition law as part of an economic constitution guaranteeing market freedoms and, further, of the importance of *Rechtsstaat* values over ad hoc political decision-making.[16] But centred on the form of conduct, the model could easily degenerate into an excessively formalist or technical approach to enforcement: much literal analysis of documents, little reference to economics.[17] Only slowly was this legalistic mindset eroded with the development of the Single Market and corresponding focus on 'consumer welfare', and an expansion of DG Comp. Nonetheless, from the standpoint of administrative procedure, the Regulation 17 framework had much to commend it. Centralisation helped with coherence and uniformity as the Commission sought to spread the gospel in a field at first undeveloped outside Germany. Especially valuable for developing experience, expertise and authority in a novel and sensitive supranational setting, the routines of notification and negative clearance meant secure information flows for the Commission. Firms, meanwhile, gained a measure of legal certainty from this safe-harbour approach to regulation.

... And Change

Even so, pressure for reform understandably grew, culminating in the late 1990s.[18] As the Single Market expanded, and with it the breadth and depth of the regulatory regime, the centralised administrative framework creaked ever more loudly. Confronted with burgeoning demands on its limited resources, the Commission increasingly had to use rationing devices such as *de minimis* and block exemptions. The Commission's White Paper on modernisation in 1999 recognised that more radical reforms were demanded.[19] The system was 'coming of age'[20] with a

---

[15] U Everling, 'The Court of Justice as a Decision-Making Authority' (1984) 82 *Michigan Law Review* 1294; H Nehl, *Principles of Administrative Procedure in EC Law* (Oxford: Hart Publishing, 1999).

[16] S Quack and M-L Djelic, 'Adaptation, Recombination and Reinforcement: The Story of Antitrust and Competition Law in Germany and Europe' in W Streek and K Thelen (eds), *Beyond Continuity: Institutional Change in Advanced Political Economies* (Oxford: OUP, 2005).

[17] V Korah, 'From Legal Form toward Economic Efficiency – Article 85(1) of the EEC Treaty in Contrast to US Antitrust' (1990) 35 *Antitrust Bulletin* 1009; B Hawk, 'System Failure: Vertical Restraints and EC Competition Law' (1995) 32 *Common Market Law Review* 973.

[18] F Montag, 'The Case for a Radical Reform of the Infringement Procedure under Regulation 17' (1996) 17 *European Competition Law Review* 428.

[19] C-D Ehlermann, 'The Modernisation of EC Antitrust Policy: A Legal and Cultural Revolution' (2000) 37 *Common Market Law Review* 537.

[20] A Weitbrecht, 'From Freiburg to Chicago and Beyond – The First 50 Years of European Competition Law' (2008) 29 *European Competition Law Review* 81, 84.

well-developed body of law and policy, yet the bureaucracy and compliance costs associated with the reactive routines of Regulation 17 were considerable. The case for the Commission redirecting resources to take stronger measures against the most harmful restrictive practices was a compelling one. There were too demands from industry for greater convergence in the light of diverse national systems and practices. Enlargement into central and eastern Europe beckoned and with it the particular challenge of fostering a competition culture in post-communist states.[21] Bound up with global shifts of power, an increasingly integrated world economy was generating further – competitive – pressures for reform. Increased emphasis on economic analysis might help ground a more proactive stance by the Commission and, in the guise of an established disciplinary framework, greater common understanding across Member States.[22]

Regulation 1/2003, the 'Modernisation Regulation' that replaced Regulation 17, is a formidable piece of legislation. It made a whole series of related changes to the regulatory framework, the most obvious being decentralisation, which produced a multiple enforcement system specifically intended to promote wider application of EU competition law and a more level playing field for cross-border businesses.[23] The Commission would operate its integrated model of enforcement in a more targeted manner, while national competition authorities (NCAs) and courts would be empowered and obliged to apply EU antitrust rules in their entirety. Conceptually speaking, the paradigm of direct or highly centralised administration was thus replaced with a model of extended parallel competence between the Union and Member State levels. In order to maximise the potential while avoiding the pitfalls of fragmentation, this demanded not only 'vertical' but also 'horizontal' cooperation between the NCAs.[24] The Modernisation Regulation duly declared that the Commission and the NCAs 'should form together a network of public authorities applying the Community competition rules in close cooperation'.[25] So was born the ECN.

The Modernisation Regulation gave tangible expression to the idea of 'less is more' in Commission enforcement. In freeing up resources for the fight against powerful cartels and large-scale abusive monopolies, it abolished the practice of notifying business agreements. Just as the potential for private enforcement was enhanced by decentralisation,[26] so firms were now expected to deal with the risk of non-compliance through self-assessment. The Commission would also be better equipped to detect and address serious infringements; enhanced enforcement

[21] For a useful retrospective, see K Cseres, 'The Impact of Regulation 1/2003 in the New Member States' (2010) 6 *Competition Law Review* 145.
[22] Gerber, 'Two Forms of Modernisation', above (n 5).
[23] 'Report on the Functioning of Regulation 1/2003', above (n 4) 2.
[24] S Brammer, *Co-operation between National Competition Agencies in the Enforcement of EC Competition Law* (Oxford: Hart Publishing, 2009).
[25] Regulation 1/2003, recital 15; see also Art 11(1).
[26] See D Kelemen, *Eurolegalism: The Transformation of Law and Regulation in the European Union* (Cambridge, MA: Harvard University Press, 2011) ch 5. Legislative reform is currently underway here: Commission, 'Proposal for a Directive on certain rules governing actions for damages under national law for infringements of the competition law provisions' COM(2013) 404 final.

tools for this 'super-regulator' were another important feature of the legislation (see below). Such major reform demands much in the way of executive and bureaucratic rule-making. Echoing the jurisprudence on the rights of the defence, matters such as initiating Commission proceedings or hearing the parties were made the subject of an implementing regulation.[27] Underwriting administrative values of flexibility and responsiveness, while perhaps helping to assuage concerns about a loss of legal certainty, a particular premium was however placed on soft law instruments. This fitted with the logic of the reform: 'a shift from giving comfort to individual agreements to a system in which the emphasis is on general guidance that can be helpful to numerous undertakings and other enforcers'.[28] A whole new package of notices and guidelines dealing with the substance and conduct of competition proceedings was adopted.[29] Space had opened up for consultation with stakeholders, a praiseworthy feature. Yet with paper piled on paper, transparency cannot be assumed; one leading competition lawyer reports having 'to hack my way through the thickets of guidance'.[30]

'Economic Turn'

The 'more economic approach' came increasingly to the fore as part of the wider modernisation process. Associated with intellectual developments in the United States,[31] and heralded in 1989 by a Merger Regulation[32] targeted on the risks for consumer welfare from a strengthening of dominant positions, it would be championed by successive Competition Commissioners, in particular economist Mario Monti who aimed 'to ensure that competition policy is fully compatible with economic learning'.[33] Today, made visible across the whole regulatory cycle of policy development, legislation and guidelines[34] and casework,[35] this is Commission orthodoxy. As a 'best practices' document puts it, 'economics as a discipline provides a framework [for] formulating the possible consequences of the practices

---

[27] Commission Regulation 773/2004/EC Relating to the Conduct of Proceedings by the Commission Pursuant to Articles 81 and 82 of the EC Treaty [2004] OJ L123/18.
[28] 'Report on the Functioning of Regulation 1/2003', above (n 4) 9.
[29] eg, Commission Notice on the Effect on Trade Concept Contained in Articles 81 and 82 of the Treaty [2004] OJ C101/81; Commission Notice on the Handling of Complaints by the Commission under Articles 81 and 82 of the EC Treaty [2004] OJ C101/65.
[30] R Whish, 'Preface' in *Competition Law*, 6th edn (Oxford: OUP, 2009).
[31] Most obviously the Chicago School, represented in works such as R Posner, *Antitrust Law*, 2nd edn (Chicago: University of Chicago Press, 2001).
[32] Regulation 139/2004/EC on the control of concentrations between undertakings, [2004] OJ L 24/1.
[33] M Monti, 'A Reformed Competition Policy: Achievements and Challenges for the Future' (Brussels, Centre for European Reform, 2004) 1.
[34] See, eg, 'Guidance on the Commission's enforcement priorities in applying Article 82 of the EC Treaty to abusive exclusionary conduct by dominant undertakings' [2009] OJ C45/2.
[35] N Forwood, 'The Commission's "More Economic Approach" – Implications for the Role of the EU Courts' in C-D Ehlermann and M Marquis (eds), *European Competition Law Annual 2009: Evaluation of Evidence and its Judicial Review in Competition Cases* (Oxford: Hart Publishing, 2010).

under review' and 'provides tools to identify the direction and magnitude of these effects empirically'.[36] Further, in the words of the current Commissioner, Joaquin Almunia, 'cases are not an end in themselves; they only have value if they allow us to improve the operation of markets and the benefits this implies for consumers'.[37]

Officials have on occasion rightly sounded a note of caution. Even assuming consumer welfare as the basic criterion, there is often room for reasonable differences of view in the treatment of individual cases. A memorandum on the submission of economic evidence preaches diligence: 'when alternative studies produce contradictory conclusions, their relative merits should be carefully investigated; the right approach cannot be to discard them as if they were incorrect or unscientific'.[38] The workload implications can also be considerable. For those complex cases where it is most demanded, economic analysis 'may involve the production, handling and assessment of voluminous sets of quantitative data, including, when appropriate, the development of econometric models'.[39]

Interplay: Modernisation and the CJEU

Classically illustrating the impact of judicial review on administrative procedure, the CJEU played a significant role in promoting the 'economic turn' as part of the wider modernisation process. Famously, matters came to a head in 2002 when the GC, ratcheting-up intensity of review under the principle of manifest error (see chapter three), annulled merger prohibition decisions for errors of assessment and lack of convincing economic analysis in *Airtours*,[40] *Tetra Laval*,[41] and *Schneider Electric*.[42] As a vehicle for judicial discretion the preferred formulation of the CoJ on appeal in *Tetra Laval*[43] could hardly be bettered. While the Commission had 'a margin of discretion with regard to economic matters', the CJEU need not refrain from reviewing its 'interpretation of information of an economic nature'. Not only must the judges establish whether the evidence relied on was 'factually accurate, reliable and consistent' but also whether it 'contains all the information which must be taken into account in order to assess a complex situation' and whether it was 'capable of substantiating the conclusions drawn'.[44] With the benefit of hindsight, DG Comp sees the imbroglio bringing 'long-term benefits in that the Commission decided to rapidly upgrade its capability to undertake more sophisticated economic analysis.'[45] Faced with such coruscating judicial language

---

[36] 'Best Practices for the Submission of Economic Evidence', above (n 8) 1.
[37] J Almunia, 'Staying ahead of the curve in EU competition policy' (19 April 2011).
[38] D Neven and R De Coninck, *Best Practices on the Submission of Economic Evidence and Data Collection* (Office of the Chief Competition Economist, 2010) 2.
[39] 'Best Practices for the Submission of Economic Evidence', above (n 8) 1.
[40] Case T-342/99 *Airtours v Commission* [2002] ECR II-2585.
[41] Case T-5/02 *Tetra Laval v Commission* [2002] ECR II-4381.
[42] Case T-310/01 *Schneider Electric v Commission* [2002] ECR II-4071.
[43] Case C-12/03 P *Commission v Tetra Laval* [2005] ECR I-987.
[44] Ibid, [39].
[45] Commission, 'Report on Competition Policy 2010' COM (2011) 328 final, 15.

as 'insufficient, incomplete, insignificant and inconsistent evidence',[46] it had little option.

The following year saw the creation of a dedicated team of specialists led by a Chief Competition Economist (CCE) tasked with providing independent guidance and generally promoting the development of economic expertise within DG Comp.[47] Reporting directly to the Director-General, the CCE helps in particular with methodological issues, liaising in turn with the Economic Advisory Group on Competition Policy (EAGCP), a repository of academic expertise. The remit includes both policy development and contribution to the soundness of individual decisions, which itself involves several roles. As well as supporting the case teams in compiling and assessing evidence and assisting the Legal Service in court cases, the CCE provides arm's length advice to the Competition Commissioner ahead of formal Commission decisions. Today, the CCE is a ket part of an in-house set of checks and balances designed to promote a requisite degree of 'challenge' within the enforcement process.[48]

Given the many incentives, opportunities and capacities for disputing in competition, continuing high volumes of litigation are only to be expected. The statistics testify to the scale of the burden placed on the Luxembourg Courts. Since 2000, over 800 completed court cases have been recorded on the official Curia website under the rubric of 'competition' (excluding state aids). Chiefly tasked with the twin roles of (a) hearing direct actions for annulment of Commission decisions, and (b) regulating fines via 'unlimited jurisdiction', the GC naturally takes most of the strain. Decentralisation however also affects the CoJ's caseload; to appeals from the GC are added increased demands for assistance from national courts through preliminary reference procedure. If there is one EU policy domain that merits the tag of 'adversarial legalism',[49] it is competition.

DG Comp must be ever mindful of due process requirements. Though hardly necessary, Regulation 1/2003 declares that the rights of the defence 'shall be fully respected'.[50] Today, the official documentation is replete with references to the general principles of procedural protection developed by the CJEU, and in particular to the individual rights of good administration and access to the file in ECFR Articles 41–42 (see chapter three). The touchstone is the *Antitrust Manual of Procedures*, the chief source of 'bureaucratic law' or internal guidance.[51] In documenting procedural minutiae against the backdrop of case law, it gives staff chapter and verse.

---

[46] Case C-12/03 P *Commission v Tetra Laval* [2005] ECR I-987, [48].
[47] L Röller and P Buigues, *The Office of the Chief Competition Economist* (OCCE, 2005).
[48] DG Comp, 'Proceedings for the application of Articles 101 and 102 TFEU: Key actors and checks and balances' (2011).
[49] Kelemen, *Eurolegalism*, above (n 26).
[50] Regulation 1/2003, Art 27(2).
[51] Commission, *Antitrust Manual of Procedures: Internal DG Competition working documents on procedures for the application of Articles 101 and 102 TFEU* (March, 2012). See also DG Comp, 'Best practices on the conduct of proceedings concerning Articles 101 and 102 TFEU' [2011] OJ C308/6.

Occasional procedural setbacks in the courts fuel a sense of 'enforcement in the shadow of the law',[52] though DG Comp is well versed in classic administrative tactics such as taking the same decision twice. In a number of recent cases the Commission has reopened administrative procedures and readopted decisions following an adverse ruling;[53] prospective litigants must understand that pleading 'procedural technicalities' may ultimately prove fruitless. Nor is it a surprise to learn that this regulatory domain is characterised by long-running 'litigation sagas' involving powerful multinational interests. The well-known Soda Ash affair, which further highlights the importance of proper procedural routines, provides an illustration. In 2000, the CoJ in *Solvay 1*[54] annulled decisions fining the companies for competition law breaches committed in the 1980s; there had been no proper authentication by signature. The Commission was again caught out when it readopted the decisions. In *Solvay 2*,[55] the CoJ held that the rights of the defence were infringed; documents had been mislaid, effectively denying full access to the file.

The greater emphasis on economic analysis successfully demanded by the CJEU raises a question mark over the exercise of 'judicial control' over substantive decision-making. In typical Anglo-American parlance, leading competition law practitioners complain of too much 'judicial deference' in the face of complex economic appraisals.[56] Pointing up low success rates in competition litigation against the Commission, reference is made to a 'luxurious growth of light judicial review' in recent years that should be 'pruned'.[57] Commission officials mount a stout defence, stressing the importance of not making enforcement disproportionately difficult in the face of the powerful multinational interests engaged. Improved administrative procedures that contribute to the Commission's many successes in Luxembourg deserve praise. Flexible judicial standards provide continuing potential for exacting scrutiny on law and facts; a somewhat messy application of judicial review[58] reflects the highly fact-specific nature of competition proceedings, the more so when oriented to economic effects.[59] As we shall see, there is an ongoing battle royal in the CJEU over all this.

---

[52] I Van Bael, *Due Process in EU Competition Proceedings* (The Hague: Kluwer International, 2011); C Kerse and N Khan, *EC Antitrust Procedure*, 6th edn (London: Sweet & Maxwell, 2012).

[53] eg Case C-352/09 P *ThyssenKrupp v Commission* [2011] ECR I-2359; Case C-201/09 P *ArcelorMittal v Commission* [2011] ECR I-2239.

[54] Joined Cases C-287 and 288/95 P *Commission v Solvay* [2000] ECR I-2391.

[55] Joined Cases C-109 and 110/10 *Solvay v Commission* [2011] ECR I-10329.

[56] B Adkins, 'A Question of Deference' (2014) 13 *Competition Law Insight* 1. And see I Lianos, '"Judging Economists": Economic Expertise in Competition Litigation: A European View' in I Lianos and I Kokkoris (eds), *Towards an Optimal Competition Law System* (The Hague: Kluwer International, 2009).

[57] I Forrester, 'A Bush in Need of Pruning: The Luxuriant Growth of Light Judicial Review' in C-D Ehlermann and M Marquis (eds), *European Competition Law Annual 2009: Evaluation of Evidence and its Judicial Review in Competition Cases* (Oxford: Hart Publishing, 2010).

[58] For varying degrees of scrutiny see, eg, Case T-201/01 *General Electric v Commission* [2005] ECR II-5575; Case T-201/04 *Microsoft Corpn v Commission* [2007] ECR II-3601.

[59] F Castillo de la Torre, 'Evidence, Proof and Judicial Review in Cartel Cases' in C-D Ehlermann and M Marquis (eds), *European Competition Law Annual 2009: Evaluation of Evidence and its Judicial Review in Competition Cases* (Oxford: Hart Publishing, 2010).

COOPERATION

Network Design

As an administrative framework for the multiple enforcement of EU competition law by 'close cooperation',[60] the ECN involves two vital elements: (a) case allocation between multiple NCAs and the Commission; and (b) confidential exchange of information and evidence between the members. To avoid inefficiencies, the aim according to the legislation is that each case should be handled by a single regulator.[61] The Commission's 'Notice on Cooperation within the Network'[62] then enumerates and structures the principles of allocation through a set of presumptions centred on the sensible concept of 'the well-placed authority': (a) the NCA first seised of the matter should be in a good position to proceed; (b) if not, the case will be transferred to another NCA in timely fashion; (c) if more than three Member States are involved, the Commission will assume jurisdiction on the basis of Union interest. Recalling the need for effective administrative procedures in Member States, an authority is said to be well placed if it can gather the necessary evidence and is empowered to end the violation, as also that there are market effects in its jurisdiction.[63] Regulation 1/2003 provides the hard law failsafe. Should cooperation ever break down amid a jostling for jurisdiction at national level, the Commission may take charge of a case.[64]

The ECN is a paradigm example of how information gathering and (electronic) exchange grease the wheels of EU governance. How could case allocation sensibly work if there was no requirement to notify investigations to the Commission and other NCAs? So too, the multiple enforcement system would be seriously impaired if there was no provision for information flows between authorities during investigations or on pending decisions.[65] This is the realm of 'ECN Interactive', a secure intranet and database connecting the members. Indeed, with no formal legal personality and only a small secretariat, the ECN is appropriately characterised as a 'virtual network'.[66]

A third element must be factored in: national procedural autonomy (see chapter one). Constituted in the light of diverse administrative law traditions, the NCAs designated by the Member States will have their own practices and procedures. Domestic court systems have taken different approaches to enforcement,

---

[60] Regulation 1/2003, recital 15 and Art 11.
[61] Ibid, recital 18; S Brammer, 'Concurrent Jurisdiction under Regulation 1/2003 and the Issue of Case Allocation' (2005) 42 *Common Market Law Review* 1383.
[62] Commission Notice on Cooperation within the Network of Competition Authorities [2004] OJ C101/43; buttressed by Joint Statement of the Council and the Commission on the Functioning of the Network of Competition Authorities (December 2002).
[63] Notice on Cooperation, above (n 62) 8.
[64] Regulation 1/2003, Art 11(6).
[65] Ibid, Arts 11, 12; K Dekeyser and E De Smijter, 'The Exchange of Evidence within the ECN' (2005) 32 *Legal Issues of Economic Integration* 161.
[66] See ECN Brief, 'A look inside the ECN, its members and its work' (Special Issue, December 2010).

with some but not all regarding competition law breaches as criminal in nature and having as a sanction imprisonment for company officers.[67] The design of the multiple enforcement framework goes some way to meeting inevitable concerns about inconsistency, conflicts of laws or gaps in legal protection. Using exchanged information to found sanctions against natural persons requires equivalency in the procedural protection and kinds of sanction available in the respective jurisdictions.[68]

The possibility of the CJEU second-guessing the internal workings of the network was tested in *France Telecom*,[69] where the company sought to invoke the principles of subsidiarity and sincere cooperation against a Commission decision to conduct an inspection when the national authorities were already dealing with the matter. Dismissing the application, the GC confirmed that the Commission remained free to act. Addressed to regulators and not firms, the Notice on Cooperation specifically excluded individual rights to have a particular authority handle a case.[70] Notably, at the time the network was created some critics considered the dispersion of power and authority to the national level trumped by the Commission's hand in the planning of the system and ongoing capacities for guidance, intervention and calling to account other members.[71] In practice however, a 'flatter' version of the network appears to have prevailed: DG Comp naturally in a leadership role, but subject to the containing influence of some powerful NCAs and labouring under the heavy demands of complex cases.[72]

Maturation

Neatly illustrating the propensity of networks to generate their own momentum, the ECN has rapidly outgrown its standard classification as an 'enforcement network'.[73] Officially designated as 'the basis for the creation and maintenance of a common competition culture in Europe',[74] it has seen a growing emphasis on policy development.[75] As so often, mutual learning and dissemination of best practices feature prominently, but with the added connotation of the network as

[67] T Möllers and A Heinemann (eds), *The Enforcement of Competition Law in Europe* (Cambridge: CUP, 2008).
[68] Regulation 1/2003, Art 12.
[69] Case T-339/04 *France Telecom v Commission* [2007] ECR II-521.
[70] Ibid, [79]–[80], [83]–86].
[71] See, eg, A Riley, 'EC Antitrust Modernisation: The Commission Does Very Nicely – Thank You' (2003) 24 *European Competition Law Review* 604, 657.
[72] F Cengiz, 'Multi-level Governance in Competition Policy: The European Competition Network' (2010) 35 *European Law Review* 660; D Gerardin, 'Public Enforcement: The ECN – Network Antitrust Enforcement in the European Union' in I Lianos and D Gerardin (eds), *Handbook on European Competition Law – Vol 2, Enforcement and Procedure* (Cheltenham: Edward Elgar, 2013).
[73] H Hofmann, G Rowe and A Türk, *Administrative Law and Policy of the European Union* (Oxford: OUP, 2011) 309.
[74] Notice on Cooperation, above (n 62) [1].
[75] I Maher, 'Competition Law Modernization: An Evolutionary Tale?' in P Craig and G de Búrca (eds), *The Evolution of EU Law*, 2nd edn (Oxford: OUP, 2011).

vehicle for, and subject to, the influence of neoclassical economics. Recalling the important adhesive role of epistemic communities, decentralisation and hence capacity-enhancement and greater local awareness have thus gone hand in hand with the vision of 'an intellectual framework for achieving consistency'.[76] Referring to the ECN's 'deeper significance' in generating 'the spirit of mutual trust and collaboration', Commissioner Almunia has even called it a 'family'.[77]

The network's caseload is considerable. By March 2014, members had notified 1717 investigations and 721 envisaged decisions.[78] Highlighting the significance of the decentralisation, NCAs are responsible for the great majority. While statistically speaking the competition authorities in France, Germany and Italy have led the way, the figures reveal a fair spread of regulatory activity across the EU, including in the E-12 Enlargement states. Cartels (Article 101) clearly continue to present particular problems, outscoring abuse of dominance cases (Article 102) by a proportion of over 2:1.

Perhaps however it is the sheer intensity of the contacts between officials – an 'extensive informal communication culture'[79] – that most merits the ECN's characterisation as 'a thick network'.[80] There are myriad meetings: from periodic meetings for the heads of authorities to regular plenaries for network liaison officers and on through a fluid set of working groups and sub-groups organised both horizontally in terms of common issues such as due process, and vertically by industry sector such as financial services, pharmaceuticals and food. Conditions are ripe for 'slop over' from EU law to domestic systems, another recurring theme of this volume. The Commission reports 'an unprecedented degree of voluntary convergence of the procedural rules' following the entry into force of Regulation 1/2003.[81] An example of this process of soft harmonisation is provided by the ECN's 'model leniency programme' begun in 2006.[82] As an effective means of cartel busting, developing protection for whistle-blowers has become a priority of EU competition policy, linked in turn to demands for greater consistency of treatment across jurisdictions. Founded on political and administrative commitments, the programme has had considerable success in encouraging Member States to align their practices with the model criteria for leniency prepared and agreed in the ECN.[83]

---

[76] Gerber, 'Two Forms of Modernisation', above (n 5) 1258.
[77] ECN Brief, above (n 66) Foreword.
[78] Source: DG Comp website: http://ec.europa.eu/dgs/competition/index_en.htm.
[79] Cengiz, above (n 72) 668.
[80] I Maher and O Stefan, 'Competition Law in Europe: The Challenge of a Network Constitution' in D Oliver, T Prosser and R Rawlings (eds), *The Regulatory State: Constitutional Implications* (Oxford: OUP, 2010).
[81] Commission Staff Working Paper Accompanying the Report on the Functioning of Regulation 1/2003 SEC (2009) 574 final, [201].
[82] ECN, Model Leniency Programme (revised version, 2012).
[83] ECN, Model Leniency Programme: Report on Assessment of the State of Convergence (2009).

Flanking Developments

The ECN's maturation should not be viewed in isolation. In the cause of coherence, decentralisation also requires elements of judicial cooperation both between courts and with the regulators. Building on the previously established principle that national courts should not rule contrary to Commission competition decisions,[84] Regulation 1/2003 further elaborates on the overarching principle of sincere cooperation; the Commission and NCAs may intervene in domestic proceedings and Member States must report court judgments.[85] But the basic constitutional principle of judicial independence militates against the creation of a formal court network parallel to the ECN;[86] instead, an informal forum is provided by the self-governing Association of European Competition Law Judges.

In view of increased global economic interdependence, it would be strange if the EU at large and the Commission in particular had not prioritised the international dimension of competition policy – the more so, it may be said, in the light of a proliferation of national competition regimes across the world, hence 'a complex global web of competition laws'.[87] Or, as the Commission puts it, 'the EU has a strategic interest in developing international rules and cooperation on competition policies to ensure European firms do not suffer in third countries'.[88] Much effort has gone into exporting EU competition law disciplines and modalities to other, especially neighbouring and/or developing, countries.[89] As well as the candidate countries, most states signing association agreements with the EU have been pressed to reform through the 'sticks and carrots' of the conditionality principle (see chapter two).

The EU has made increasing use of bilateral cooperation agreements on competition with major trading partners. Starting in the 1990s with the US, Canada and Japan, the strategy now extends to memorandums of understanding with Brazil, Russia, China and India. Reference is typically made 'to the importance of cooperation and coordination for the enhancement of the effective, transparent and non-discriminatory enforcement' of the competition laws in the two jurisdictions.[90] As one would expect, the measure of agreement varies considerably between countries, ranging from exchange of experience and policy dialogue to procedures for requesting enforcement action, and on up to sharing of informa-

---

[84] Case C-344/98 *Masterfoods v HB Ice Cream* [2000] ECR I-11369.
[85] Regulation 1/2003, Arts 15–16; Commission Notice on the Cooperation between the Commission and Courts of the EU Member States in the application of Articles 81 and 82 EC [2004] OJ C101/43.
[86] See to this effect, SEC (2009) 574 final, [276].
[87] Aydin and Thomas, above (n 1) 533; drawing on D Levi-Faur, 'The Global Diffusion of Regulatory Capitalism' (2005) 598 *Annals of the American Academy of Political and Social Science* 12.
[88] Commission, 'Global Europe – Competing in the World' (Communication) COM (2006) 567 final, 7.
[89] A Papadopoulos, *The International Dimension of EU Competition Law and Policy* (Cambridge: CUP, 2010).
[90] Memorandum of understanding on cooperation in the area of anti-monopoly law with China (2012).

tion on cases of mutual interest and coordination of enforcement actions. In our age of globalisation, such initiatives are liable to deepen over time, so producing further nests of administrative procedure.

Taking on the mantle of a global player, DG Comp is seen redoubling its efforts in multilateral forums.[91] With a view to shaping competition practice, UNCTAD (the UN Conference on Trade and Development), the World Trade Organization (WTO) and particularly in this field the Organisation for Economic Co-operation and Development (OECD), are obvious reference points. Exemplifying the rise of global networks in which the Union and/or Member States are actively involved (see further chapter twelve), the informal International Competition Network (ICN) deserves special mention. Founded in 2001 and today attracting authorities from some 100 jurisdictions, it exists 'to advocate the adoption of superior standards and procedures in competition policy around the world [and] to formulate proposals for procedural and substantive convergence'.[92] DG Comp, alongside ECN members from France, Germany, Italy, the Netherlands and the UK, is naturally on the steering group.

Good Governance Principles

Focused on effectiveness and coherence (two of the good governance principles listed in the 'White Paper on European Governance' (WPEG), a five-year Commission evaluation was understandably upbeat about the ECN. Behind the vast increase in the scale of EU enforcement activities lay major sector inquiries by ECN members, which led to many individual investigations especially in the liberalised utilities sectors.[93] The smaller and newer agencies had been able to tap into a deep pool of experience and expertise in suitably confidential fashion; in the shadow of the network, many Member States had 'reinforced or reviewed their enforcement structures to optimise their effectiveness', for example by adopting the institutionally integrated model. Constant dialogue had 'significantly contributed' to coherent application of the rules; there had been few disputes over case allocation and even fewer parallel investigations or reallocations.[94] Information gathering and exchange had 'proven to be one of the cornerstones of the modernisation package'. In short, the task of boosting enforcement while ensuring consistency and coherence had been 'largely achieved'; cooperation in the ECN had 'surpassed expectations'.[95]

The evaluation skated over other good governance principles: not surprisingly perhaps, in view of some intractable problems. Take transparency, where we find

[91] U Aydin, 'Promoting Competition: European Union and the Global Competition Order' (2012) 34 *European Integration* 663.
[92] ICN, Mission Statement (2001); Vision for the Second Decade (2011).
[93] Commission Staff Working Paper Accompanying the Report on the Functioning of Regulation 1/2003, above (n 81) [184].
[94] Ibid, [29]–[30].
[95] Ibid, [23], [183[, [242].

echoes of the debate over Commission infringement procedure (see chapter seven). The essential quid pro quo of determinedly open relations within the network is the wraparound of confidentiality to protect against firms' preying eyes. Placed firmly under professional secrecy rules, members are prohibited from disclosing outside the network any information received pursuant to Regulation 1/2003 save that required to prove an infringement.[96] Or take accountability. From an internal perspective the ECN scores highly. Given the major dispersal of regulatory authority and capacity and the strong mutual commitments to inform and collaborate, members are operating as a 'network of accountability'[97] in which they must account to each other on a regular and detailed basis; in other words, inter-agency accountability is enshrined in the day to day operation or interdependency of the multiple enforcement framework. The never-ending rounds of meetings militate against (national) agency capture and the Commission's powers exist to shore up and fill any gaps in the system. Conversely, the very thickness of the network militates against effective forms of external accountability. As *France Telecom* points up, courts and also legislatures inevitably struggle to get a grip on the multi-level network; the more so, in view of a determinedly soft governance framework. The dual position of NCAs as part of the EU and domestic administrative law systems is an added complication for oversight in Member States.

As for equal treatment, the evaluation naturally had national procedural autonomy in its sights.[98] It does not do however to overlook the continuing dynamics associated with this type of network, whereby such differences may be expected to flatten over time or otherwise take on the settled mantle of informed divergence. Exhibiting a potent mix of top-down, bottom-up and horizontal pressures, the ECN is properly credited with facilitating a gradual and pragmatic approach to the management of legal diversity in national jurisdictions.[99] This is exemplified by a series of ECN recommendations on investigative and decision-making powers, specifically intended as 'advocacy tools' for use inside Member State systems.[100]

ENFORCEMENT

The Commission has seized the opportunity presented by decentralisation to wield the big stick in big cases. In-house assessment is notably positive: the Commission has used its enhanced enforcement tools 'actively, and overall suc-

[96] Regulation 1/2003, Arts 27(2), 28.
[97] See on this concept, C Scott, 'Accountability in the regulatory state' (2000) 27 *Journal of Law and Society* 38.
[98] 'Report on the Functioning of Regulation 1/2003', above (n 4) 33. See further, A Andreangeli, 'The Public Enforcement of Articles 101 and 102 TFEU under Council Regulation No 1/2003: Due Process Considerations' in I Lianos and D Gerardin (eds), *Handbook on European Competition Law – Vol 2, Enforcement and Procedure* (Cheltenham: Edward Elgar, 2013).
[99] C Lemaire and J Gsalter, 'The Silent Revolution Beyond Regulation 1/2003' (2008) 8(2) *CPI Antitust Chronicle* 22.
[100] See, eg, ECN, Recommendation on investigative powers, enforcement measures and sanctions in the context of inspections and requests for information (December 2013).

cessfully', becoming 'more proactive' and 'tackling weaknesses in the competitiveness of key sectors of the economy in a focused way'.[101] The channelling of resources into economic analysis of abuse of dominance, and into investigative – 'police' – work on secretive cartels, underwrites what in truth is a never-ending struggle.

Some eye-watering sanctions have been imposed. Take cartels.[102] In the five years from 2008 to 2012, the Commission adopted some 30 decisions imposing fines totalling almost €8 billion on 200 undertakings; household names such as E.ON (gas), Pilkington (car glass) and ThyssenKrupp (elevators and escalators) were each fined over €300 million. Despite the many calls on the CJEU's 'unlimited jurisdiction', undertakings have had only limited success in contesting the scale of penalties.[103] More records were broken in 2013 when the Commission levied fines of €1.71 billion following the scandalous manipulation of interbanking lending rates (the LIBOR and EURIBOR cases). Showing the advantages of the Commission as a powerful repeat player, certain sectors are notable for sustained enforcement action against abuse of dominant position. A detailed inquiry into energy markets in 2007 was the prelude to a series of antitrust decisions involving binding commitments from dominant firms to ease market entry and so end potential infringements.[104] Again, the emphasis on consumer welfare as a regulatory goal was illustrated in firm enforcement action on Internet access. Low broadband penetration rates and high prices in Poland, for example, led the Commission to mount an investigation, which resulted in a fine of €127.5 million for the incumbent firm.[105]

Stages, Tracks and Steps

As the *Antitrust Manual of Procedures* makes abundantly clear, the Commission's enforcement process is complex. As a 'pathways model' of administrative procedure (see chapter six), it can be visualised in terms of (a) the main stages of decision-making; (b) the main tracks or choices of routing; and (c) the individual steps or links in the resulting decision-making chains. The design is largely the product of a slow micro-development, punctuated by bursts of procedural reform, most recently in 2011.[106] This well illustrates the way in which procedural

---

[101] 'Report on the Functioning of Regulation 1/2003', above (n 4) 10, 41.
[102] DG Comp, Cartel Statistics. See generally, C Harding and J Joshua, *Regulating Cartels in Europe*, 2nd edn (Oxford: OUP, 2011) and, for contextualisation, E Combe and C Monnier, 'Fines Against Hardcore Cartels in Europe: The Myth of Overenforcement' (2011) 56 *Antitrust Bulletin* 235.
[103] Ibid, Tables 1.2, 1.4.
[104] Commission, Inquiry into the European gas and electricity sectors (Communication) COM (2006) 851 final; Case COMP/39386 Long term electricity contracts in France (2010); Case COMP/39351 Swedish Interconnectors (2010); Case COMP/39317 E.ON Gas Foreclosure (2010); Case COMP/39316 Gaz de France Foreclosure (2010).
[105] Case COMP/39525 *Telekomunikacja Polska* (2011).
[106] On the system prior to the 2011 reform, see H Viaene, 'Administrative Proceedings in the Area of EU Competition Law' (EP, 2011).

protections are built up from a variety of sources: treaties, legislation, case law, soft law and EO decisions. The prominence given to the rights of the defence should not obscure the wider role of executive discretion in fashioning key internal modalities and disciplines; in particular, the way in which competition procedures may elaborate on court rulings. The self-description of the *Manual* as 'a practical working tool, which evolves through updates ... to reflect new experience gained in applying the competition rules',[107] reflects this point.

The three main stages of decision-making are the natural concomitant of an institutionally integrated model of enforcement:

1. *Preliminary stage*: initiation of proceedings (via Commission own initiative or complaint or whistle-blowing), initial assessment (filtering of cases for insufficient Union interest, prioritisation and reallocation of cases to NCAs via the ECN).
2. *Investigative stage*: either before or after the formal opening of proceedings.
3. *Formal decision-making stage*: including, where appropriate, the imposition of sanctions.

The design of the investigative phase reflects the difficulty of cracking serious market abuse. To enhance its chances, the Commission now has an important trio of powers in the armoury:

a. To require undertakings to provide it with all necessary information, either through simple request or binding (sanctioned) decision.
b. To take statements from company officers etc.
c. To conduct 'dawn raids' with the assistance of national authorities.[108]

But these powers cannot – should not – exist in a vacuum. They are governed by the overarching general principle of proportionality (which effectively limits so-called 'fishing expeditions')[109] and also cross-cut by (difficult) case law on two corollaries of the rights of the defence: the privilege against self-incrimination[110] and legal professional privilege.[111]

The Commission has moved to supplement the investigative phase with dialogue. At voluntary 'state of play' meetings, DG Comp endeavours to give undertakings 'ample opportunity for open and frank discussions' with a view to contributing 'to the quality and efficiency of the decision making process'.[112] Informal meetings may also be arranged with complainants and interested third

---

[107] DG Comp, *Antitrust Manual*, above (n 51) Preface.
[108] Regulation 1/2003, Arts 17–21.
[109] A recent set of GC decisions confirms that reasonable suspicion grounds exercise of powers to seek information: see, eg, Case T-292/11 *Cemex v Commission* and Case T-296/11 *Holcim v Commission* (judgments of 14 March 2014).
[110] eg, Case 374/87 *Orkem v Commission* [1989] ECR 3283; Case 27/88 *Solvay & Cie v Commission* [1989] ECR 3355.
[111] eg, Case C-550/07 P *Azko Nobel Chemicals v Commission* [2010] ECR I-08301.
[112] Commission Notice on Best Practices for the Conduct of Proceedings Concerning Articles 101 and 102 TFEU [2011] C308/06, [54]–[55].

parties, a practice which raises concerns familiar from the *Bavarian Lager* case.[113] In *Intel*,[114] the EO received a complaint that the case team had failed to take minutes of a discussion with a third party, which provided potentially exculpatory evidence. Recalling that any procedural irregularity may constitute maladministration, even if there is no breach of the rights of the defence, the EO made a 'further remark' about proper record-keeping, which now finds tangible expression in the official guidance.[115] The affair well illustrates the EO's self-description as an 'additional means of external control' that may be 'of assistance to the Commission in identifying and correcting weakness in its competition law procedures'.[116]

The formal decision-making stage features an expanded choice of routings:

- Prohibition and sanction.
- Commitments offered by the undertaking.
- Settlement: in cartel cases.
- Closure: as by rejection of a complaint.

As the CoJ has recognised,[117] considerations of procedural economy will feature prominently here. Take commitment decisions, whereby firms under investigation enter into legally-binding obligations regarding their future behaviour. Formally added to the armoury by Regulation 1/2003,[118] the procedure has obvious advantages for the Commission in terms of time and resources: the more so, in economically complex abuse of dominance cases.[119] The very fact that such commitments are voluntary limits litigation, while fines may be levied in the event of breach. Settlement procedure was introduced in 2008 for similar reasons.[120] Once apprised of the evidence in the file, the undertaking must acknowledge liability; in return, the putative fine is typically reduced by 10 per cent. DG Comp now regularly screens cartel cases for this alternative enforcement option, which can drastically reduce the duration of proceedings in big cases.[121]

As one would expect, procedural protection is highly developed in the formal decision-making stage. But illustrating the particularity of the rights of the defence, the scope for individual participation varies widely as between parties subject to proceedings, complainants and interested third parties. At certain points the

[113] See above, ch 5, p 131.
[114] Inv 1935/2008/FOR.
[115] Best Practices for the Conduct of Proceedings, above (n 112) [39]–[40].
[116] N Diamandouros, 'Improving EU Competition Law Procedures by Applying Principles of Good Administration: The Role of the Ombudsman' (2010) 1 *Journal of European Competition Law & Practice* 379, 380. See also, A Scordamaglia-Tousis, 'The Role of the European Ombudsman in Competition Proceedings: A Second Guardian of Procedural Guarantees?' (2012) 3 *Journal of European Competition Law & Practice* 29.
[117] Case C-441/07 P *Commission v Alrosa* [2010] ECR I-5949.
[118] Regulation 1/2003, Art 9.
[119] See, eg, Case COMP/39530 *Microsoft (tying)*(2009).
[120] Commission Regulation 662/2008/EC as regards the conduct of settlement procedures in cartel cases [2008] OJ L171/3; Commission Notice on the Conduct of Settlement Procedures in Cartel Cases [2008] OJ C167/1. See further, C-D Ehlermann and M Marquis (eds), *European Competition Law Annual 2008: Antitrust Settlements under EC Competition Law* (Oxford: Hart Publishing, 2010).
[121] See, eg, Case COMP/39579 *Consumer Detergents* (2011).

administrative procedures are firmly bipolar in character; however, in marked contrast to Commission infringement procedures against Member States (see chapter seven), at other times they are more inclusive. It is also in this critical and sensitive stage that the thickets of soft law in the form of guidance and best practices are most dense. Special care must be taken to blunt arguments of legitimate expectation by ensuring that stakeholders understand that 'the specificity of an individual case' may require 'an adaptation of, or deviation from' the best practices.[122] The *Antitrust Manual of Procedures* solemnly declares that placing the working documents in the public domain 'does not change their character as purely internal guidance to staff'; they 'do not create or alter any rights or obligations'.[123]

The steps involved in prohibition and sanction neatly illustrate the interplay between 'fire-watching' and 'firefighting' or ex ante and ex post control. Take the first step, the statement of objections. Setting out DG Comp's preliminary view of the facts, law and appropriate actions, it should satisfy the basic due process requirement that parties know the case against them.[124] The second step – access to the file for addressees of a statement of objections – is likewise mandated (and made subject to restrictions) under ECFR Article 42.[125] As the name suggests, a third step of 'written reply and expressions of view' represents the right to be heard with add-ons. In a variant on American-style notice and comment procedure, the Commission has thus adopted the practice of soliciting a written response from a party to the proceedings and circulating a redacted version to other parties, complainants and interested third parties and inviting their views. Last but not least, parties subject to proceedings have the right to an oral hearing.[126] Designed (somewhat optimistically) to guarantee that 'all attendees can express themselves freely',[127] this is not a public hearing. Senior managers in DG Comp and Member State representatives are likely to attend, together with the case team; complainants and other interested parties may also be allowed in to express a view.[128]

In-House Check: The Hearing Officer

The Commission has rightly gone further in prioritising the role of internal, supervisory control ahead of the final decision-making by the College of Commissioners. As well as the requirement to justify draft decisions to an advisory committee drawn from NCAs,[129] there is today peer review by panels comprised of other DG

---

[122] Best Practices for the Conduct of Proceedings, above (n 112) [5].
[123] DG Comp, *Antitrust Manual*, above (n 51) Preface.
[124] Regulation 1/2003, Art 27(1).
[125] As under previous case law: Case T-7/89 *Hercules Chemicals NV v Commission* [1991] ECR II-1711; Case C-51/92 P *Hercules Chemicals NV v Commission* [1999] ECR I-4235.
[126] Regulation 773/2004/EC, Art 12.
[127] Best Practices for the Conduct of Proceedings, above (n 112) [93].
[128] Regulation 773/2004/EC, Arts 6(2) and 13.
[129] Regulation 1/2003, Art 14.

Comp officials. Nor is the CCE the only designated arm's length officer in an in-house system of checks or balances that, by bolstering the administrative process, may also help with 'judge proofing' in this most litigious field. Attention is drawn to the dedicated role in procedural protection of the Hearing Officer (HO), an office first created in the 1980s and progressively expanded as the Commission sought to fend off criticism of excessive concentration of powers.[130] Reporting directly to the Competition Commissioner, though with a separate website, the HO should be 'an independent person experienced in competition matters' with 'the integrity necessary to contribute to the objectivity, transparency and efficiency' of proceedings.[131] There are today two HOs, supported by a team of advisers.

While DG Comp remains charged with the primary obligation of respecting procedural rights, the HO undertakes various tasks designed 'to safeguard [their] effective exercise'.[132] Chief among them is an arbiter function in procedural disputes between the parties and DG Comp. This function involves a mix of decisional and recommendatory powers: for example about access to the file and disclosure of business secrets or exercise of the privilege against self-incrimination. The HO operates ahead of the courts by accessing files, identifying and correcting errors and generally upholding legal doctrine – perhaps partly as a form of alternative dispute resolution. His second main task is the organisation and conduct of the oral hearing through a wide-ranging case-management function.[133] Reporting functions are another important part of the package: for example at the interim stage to ensure that 'due account is taken of all the relevant facts' in individual cases;[134] and, constituting an alternative source of soft law, generally to promote procedural best practices. Meanwhile, the Commission's broad regulatory discretion is carefully preserved. The HO may make observations to the Commissioner on policy matters raised by a competition proceeding, but the mandate does not include reviewing the merits of individual decisions. When exercising functions, the HO 'shall take account of the need for effective application of the competition rules'.[135]

Until recently the reach of the model was unduly restricted, formally encompassing only the formal decision-making stage of the administrative process. Today however the HO is mandated to act as a guardian of procedural rights 'throughout competition proceedings before the Commission'.[136] This sits comfortably with the Commission's expanded powers in the investigative phase and

---

[130] M Albers and J Jourdan, 'The Role of the Hearing Officers in EU Competition Proceedings: A Historical and Practical Perspective' (2011) 2 *Journal of European Competition Law & Practice* 185.

[131] Commission President, Decision 2011/695/EU on the function and terms of reference of the Hearing Officer in competition proceedings [2011] OJ L275/29, recital 3.

[132] Ibid, Art 4. See further, Hearing Office, Guidance on the Procedures of the Hearing Officers in Proceedings Relating to Articles 101 and 102 TFEU (2011).

[133] Ibid, Arts 10–12.

[134] Ibid, Art 14(2).

[135] Ibid, Art 3(2).

[136] Ibid, Art 1. See further, W Wils, 'The Role of the Hearing Officer in Competition Proceedings before the European Commission' (2012) 35 *World Competition* 431.

216 *Competition*

may also help to avoid unnecessary litigation. Take the vexed issue of legal professional privilege, where the HO may be asked to inspect documents and make a recommendation. Those disputing this experienced and independent person's view are likely to face an uphill struggle in the GC.

Sanctioning Toolkit: Guidelines

As heralded by Regulation 1/2003, the Commission has at its disposal a highly developed toolkit of sanctions in antitrust cases. Financial penalties, behavioural and structural remedies and interim measures are all available. Take fines, where the legislation duly specifies that in fixing the amount regard must be had both to the gravity and duration of the infringement, subject to a maximum level of 10 per cent of annual total turnover.[137] The Commission has yet again resorted to soft law with a view to enhancing the legitimacy of enforcement action. Fining guidelines operate to structure and confine discretion through a series of policy-based mathematical calculations;[138] case law confirms their status as 'rules of practice from which the administration may not depart in an individual case without giving reasons compatible with the principle of equal treatment'.[139] There is a clear parallel here with financial sanctions against Member States in infringement proceedings under TFEU Article 260 (see chapter seven).

Firms cannot say but that they have been warned. Revamped in 2006, the guidelines state that fines 'should have a sufficient deterrent effect' not only on the parties but also – general deterrence – on other operators tempted to act unlawfully.[140] They also point up the importance of the regulatory discretion to make rules. For the first step of calculating the basic amount of a fine, the Commission has understandably chosen to assign cartels a high percentage range for gravity of infringement (typically 15 to 30 per cent of the value of sales): enormous fines follow remorselessly. The second step of tailoring a fine better to reflect the particular circumstances predictably references a whole series of aggravating as well as mitigating factors, chief among them repeat infringements, cartel leadership and obstruction of the investigative process.[141] As part of the never-ending interplay between Commission and CJEU in competition, the GC has elaborated on the meanings of these concepts in cases concerning the application of the guidelines.[142] Other sections of the guidelines confirm the need for elements of flexibility in this fast-moving field. Amid the economic difficulties of recent times, for

---

[137] Regulation 1/2003, Art 23(2). See D Geradin, C Malamataris and J Wileur, 'The EU Competition Law Fining System' in I Lianos and D Gerardin (eds), *Handbook on European Competition Law – Vol 2, Enforcement and Procedure* (Cheltenham: Edward Elgar, 2013).
[138] Commission, Guidelines on the Method of Setting Fines Imposed Pursuant to Article 23(2)(a) of Regulation 1/2003 (2006).
[139] Case C-397/03 P *Archer Daniels v Commission* [2006] ECR I-4429, [91].
[140] Guidelines on the Method of Setting Fines, above (n 138) [4].
[141] Ibid [23], [28]–[29].
[142] See, eg, Case T-384/06 *IBP v Commission* (judgment of 24 March 2011).

example, there has been a small stream of cases concerning reduction of fines that would otherwise 'irretrievably jeopardise the economic viability of the undertaking'.[143] Mention should also be made of a separate leniency notice in cartel cases[144] heavily advertised on the Commission's website. Specifying full immunity from fines for the first telltale, and up to 50 per cent reductions for firms providing additional evidence, it is a peculiarly strong (and naturally controversial) instance of soft law technique.

The recent *Schindler* case saw the fining guidelines attacked head-on.[145] The Commission had imposed fines of €143 million for participation in a cartel, a decision challenged on the ground that the breadth of the Commission discretion violated the principle of legality. Recalling ECtHR jurisprudence, the CoJ explained that 'the fact that a law confers a discretion is not in itself inconsistent with the requirement of foreseeability' provided that the scope and manner of its exercise 'are indicated with sufficient clarity'; here the compendium of maximum limit, Commission guidelines and settled case law on the concepts involved was enough.[146] Schindler claimed also that guidelines 'in practice . . . decisive for the setting of fines' should have been adopted by the EU legislature. Falling back on a conventional legal classification, the Court confirmed the status of the guidelines as 'rules of practice' that merely described the Commission's methodology and chosen criteria; they were neither legislation nor delegated legislation for the purpose of TFEU Article 290(1). Nor did they provide the legal basis for fines; this lay in the regulation. In the Court's words, 'no provision of the Treaties prohibits an institution from adopting such rules of practice'.[147] Had the Court not validated this informal process of administrative rule-making, the outcome would have been of potentially great consequence in EU governance.

Soft Law and Fundamental Rights

In re-emphasising the standard administrative values of flexibility and responsiveness, DG Comp's continuing pursuit of a soft law policy is determinedly pragmatic. The most recent package of procedural reforms in 2011 made much of 'best practices'. Often going beyond what is legally required, the general notice on conduct of proceedings aimed 'to increase understanding of the Commission's investigation process and thereby enhance the efficiency of investigations and ensure a high degree of transparency and predictability in the process'.[148] As well as expanding the dialogic role of statements of objection and state of play meetings, practices such as early access for parties to the key submissions of complainants

---

[143] Guidelines on the Method of Setting Fines, above (n 138) [35].
[144] Commission Notice on Immunity from Fines and Reduction of Fines in Cartel Cases (2006).
[145] Case C-501/11 P *Schindler Holding and Others v Commission* (judgment of 18 July 2013).
[146] Ibid, [57]–[59].
[147] Ibid, [61], [66]–[68]. A battery of pleas concerning particular applications of the guidelines and of the leniency notice also failed.
[148] Best Practices for the Conduct of Proceedings, above (n 138) [1].

were established. In fact, DG Comp is more transparent than it might like to be; the *Antitrust Manual of Procedures* was only published following an EO investigation.[149] The Commission having refused a request for access on the ground that disclosure would be highly detrimental to the decision-making process, the EO successfully counselled a more proportionate response. While some sensitive operational details rightly remain confidential, making many of the internal rules available for public information and comment was appropriately achieved by friendly settlement.

The Commission is naturally concerned to see off demands for more thoroughgoing procedural reform. Some critics, especially in private legal practice, will not be assuaged however. The concentration – 'non-separation' – of investigative, determinative and sanctioning powers in the Commission is said to be constitutionally awkward, even monstrous.[150] As well as the potential for prosecutorial bias, particular bones of contention include the fact that the HO hears but does not decide cases and that final decision-making is by (political appointees in) the College of Commissioners.[151] In its fullest extent, this is a call to break up the integrated model of enforcement in favour of prosecution by the Commission and decision-making by a specialist court.[152] The Commission is able to mount a strong defence. From the viewpoint of regulatory efficiency and effectiveness, the integrated model of enforcement stands for a sustained and focused control of market activities[153] – especially, it may be said, given the demands for elaborate information management and sophisticated economic analysis in complex cases.[154] Director-General Italianer has been robust: 'the EU enforcement system ... is an excellent system and we have made it even better'; it is 'anchored in the rule of law and fundamental rights'.[155]

The question then is sharply posed: can basic reform of the system be forced on the Commission by cleverly advised undertakings successfully invoking human rights?[156] Post-Lisbon, the entitlements to 'a fair and public hearing ... by an independent and impartial tribunal' in both ECFR Article 47 and ECHR Article 6

---

[149] Inv 297/2010/(ELB)GG.

[150] See, eg, M Karayanidi, 'Does the European Commission have too much Power Enforcing European Competition Law?' (2011) 12 *German Law Journal* 1446.

[151] I Forrester, 'Due Process in EC Competition Cases: A Distinguished Institution with Flawed Procedures' (2009) 34 *European Law Review* 817.

[152] See further, A Andreangeli et al, 'Enforcement by the Commission – The Decisional and Enforcement Structure in Antitrust Cases and the Commission's Fining System' in M Merola and D Waelbroeck (eds), *Towards an Optimal Enforcement of Competition Rules in Europe* (Brussels: Bruylant, 2010).

[153] W Wils, *Efficiency and Justice in European Antitrust Enforcement* (Oxford: Hart Publishing, 2008).

[154] P Lowe, 'Reflections on the Past Seven Years – "Competition Policy Challenges in Europe"' (Brussels, Commission, 2009).

[155] A Italianer, 'Recent developments regarding the Commission's cartel enforcement' (14 March 2012).

[156] I Forrester, 'A Challenge for Europe's Judges: The Review of Fines in Competition Cases' (2011) 36 *European Law Review* 185; R Wesseling and M Van der Woude, 'The Lawfulness and Acceptability of Enforcement of European Cartel Law' (2012) 35 *World Competition* 573. And see generally, A Andreangeli, *EU Competition Enforcement and Human Rights* (Cheltenham: Edward Elgar, 2008).

have proved something of a magnet, heightened perhaps by pending EU accession to the ECHR. The Commission could take heart however from a trio of cases decided in 2011. In *Menarini*,[157] where the Italian ECN member had imposed a large fine, the ECtHR confirmed the fact that the procedures fell within the definition of a 'criminal proceeding' under the Convention but they were not of the 'hard core' variety requiring determination by an independent tribunal.[158] Rejecting the notion that an integrated enforcement model contravened the right to a fair hearing, the ECtHR ruled that, with judicial review on grounds of proportionality available, the national courts had the requisite 'full jurisdiction'.[159] The *KME* and *Chalkor* cases,[160] which also concerned large fines, saw the CoJ reach not dissimilar conclusions in the context of the Charter. In an apparent check on 'light-touch' review in areas giving rise to complex economic assessments, the CoJ rehearsed the potent *Tetra Laval* formula, so highlighting the importance of the general principle of effective judicial protection to which Article 47 gives expression. It was, however, made clear that the GC, when exercising the 'unlimited jurisdiction' over fines, was not required to conduct a fresh and comprehensive investigation of the file on its own initiative.[161]

At the time of writing, the *Schindler* and *Kone* cases[162] represent the latest bout in what will no doubt be a continuing struggle. Invoking ECHR Article 6, Schindler argued in terms that the Commission's procedure infringed the principle of separation of powers and also rule of law principles applicable to criminal law procedures. The CoJ would have none of it. While noting that the contested decisions pre-dated the Lisbon Treaty, the Court recognised that 'in any event' the fact that the Commission imposes fines is not in the light of *Menarini* 'in itself contrary to Article 6'.[163] Referencing *Chalkor*, the Court confirmed that the GC cannot use the Commission's margin of discretion in complex economic cases as a basis for not undertaking an in-depth review of law and facts, but also that such review, supplemented by the special 'unlimited jurisdiction', should be sufficient for compliance with Article 47.[164] This was reiterated in *Kone*, where the CoJ said that judicial review in an action for annulment 'has neither the object nor the effect of replacing a full investigation of the case in the context of an administrative procedure'.[165] In sum, the cases suggest that in the post-Lisbon era the Charter, coupled with ECtHR jurisprudence, may well produce greater intensity of judicial review in competition proceedings; but the basic administrative framework is preserved.

---

[157] *Menarini Diagnostics v Italy* App no 43509/08 (judgment of 27 September 2011).
[158] *Jussila v Finland* (2007) 45 EHRR 39; see further, W Wils, 'The Increased Level of EU Antitrust Fines, Judicial Review, and the ECHR' (2010) 33 *World Competition* 5.
[159] *Menarini v Italy* [38]–[33], [57]–61].
[160] Cases C-272/09 P *KME v Commission* [2011] ECR I-12789; C-386/10 P *Chalkor v Commission* [2011] ECR I-13085; and C-389/10 P *KME and Others v Commission* [2011] ECR I-13125.
[161] C-386/10 P *Chalkor v Commission* [2011] ECR I-13085 [54], [64].
[162] Case C-501/11 P *Schindler Holding*; Case C-510/11 P *Kone Oyj v Commission* (judgment of 24 October 2013).
[163] Ibid, [33].
[164] Ibid, [36]–[38].
[165] Case C-510/11 P *Kone Oyj v Commission* [26].

CONCLUSION

Competition remains at the cutting edge of process and procedure in EU administration. Effectively re-launched through the Modernisation Regulation, the regulatory framework has continued to evolve, in large measure by in-house – executive – creativity. An abundant application of neoclassical economics, increasingly underscored by an international trade in regulatory tools and techniques, is at the heart of this. Decentralisation as carried forward in the burgeoning soft governance modalities of the ECN is a particularly striking development. Output values, in terms of scale and speed of processing, and more broadly the diffusion of disciplinary techniques, feature prominently; other values of transparency, participation and accountability suffer accordingly. Enough has been said to identify an essential paradox of the competition modernisation process founded on 'close cooperation'. The complex dynamics denoted by the 'Europeanisation' of national administrative process through the revamped enforcement framework exemplifies not 'decentralisation versus convergence' but rather 'decentralisation plus convergence' – perhaps even 'decentralisation aiding convergence'.

Competition sees administrative procedures under pressure in a uniquely litigious environment. Evolving under the long shadow of 'eurolegalism' but with a view to promoting regulatory legitimacy, the Commission's use of soft law recognises the need for proceduralisation, crucially however from within rather than without. Among an increasingly sophisticated system of internal checks and balances in DG Comp, the HO role may be singled out as a development worthy of more general application in single-case decision-making. If burdensome and technically challenging, the 'more economic approach' also suggests a certain freedom of manoeuvre for the Commission to deliver effective competition enforcement. Time will tell whether the European judges will remain resolute in resisting the temptation to redesign the institutional framework. Associated at one level with constitutional change, and at another with muscular approaches to sanctioning, the Commission may expect to endure more stringent forms of judicial scrutiny. An excessively legalistic focus however should not be allowed to hide the importance of procedural reform under the broader rubric of good administration.

9

Programming, Partnership and Audit: Cohesion Policy

THIS BOOK WOULD not be complete without a chapter devoted to the exercise of *dominium* power in the form of EU expenditure, the realm of that most important EU administrative law instrument, the Financial Regulation (see chapter two). The regional – sub-state – dimension also commands attention as a major feature of the European landscape, not least in terms of the implementation of EU law and policy at grass roots level. Straddling them is a cohesion policy boldly intended to promote the 'overall harmonious development' of the Union (TFEU Article 174); and, in particular, to reduce 'disparities between the levels of development of the various regions and the backwardness of the least favoured regions' (TFEU Article 175). Further, as developed under successive Union strategies, the policy is meant to contribute to the competitive position of the EU as a whole amid the increased pressures of globalisation.[1]

At its best, this is the EU making a positive difference to lots of peoples' lives through what are commonly called the structural funds. According to an official evaluation in 2010, 'the policy has created new jobs, increased human capital, built critical infrastructure and improved environmental protection... undoubtedly, without cohesion policy, disparities would be greater'.[2] The glossy pages on the Commission's website that outline many fine projects should not however divert attention from important and challenging issues of administrative process and governance. According to the same evaluation, 'the pace of reform over the past decade has been relatively slow and this has affected the impact of the policy "on the ground"'.[3] The structural funds are a prime example of, in the official lexicon of EU governance, 'shared management': the by now familiar categorisation of distinct but interdependent administrative tasks set down in legislation, which the Commission and the national administrations must respectively perform for successful delivery of a policy (see chapter one). As this chapter will

---

[1] On the shifting and expanding rationales, see W Molle, *European Cohesion Policy* (Abingdon: Routledge, 2007); I Begg, 'Cohesion or Confusion: A Policy Searching for Objectives' (2010) 32 *European Integration* 77.
[2] Commission, 'Investing in Europe's Future: Fifth report on economic, social and territorial cohesion' (2010) xxii.
[3] Ibid, xix.

demonstrate, the innate difficulties of designing and operating such a system are not to be gainsaid.

Another conceptualisation grounded in the German tradition sees the structural funds as 'Common European Administration'.[4] In view of the tapestry of federal, devolved and unitary systems of government in Member States,[5] this is valuable in helping to showcase the elements of cooperation and coordination so necessary for effective policy development and implementation. Equally however, the evident tensions that exist in varying degrees both between the collective Union interest and the interests of individual Member States, and between central and regional and/or local interests in the different national constitutional systems, cannot be glossed over. Much ink has been spilt under the competing banners of 'multi-level governance' and 'liberal inter-governmentalism' on the extent to which pre-existing core government authority has been effectively challenged in cohesion policy by Commission discretion and the involvement of sub-state actors.[6] Ebbs and flows in the power relations are naturally reflected and reinforced in the design and workings of the administrative process.

Some general features deserve emphasis. At Union level the Commission, and more particularly the Directorate-General for Regional and Urban Policy (DG Regio), takes on a broad multitasking role. It is naturally responsible, at the one end of the administrative process, for making the budgetary commitments to Member States that effectively fuel programmes and, at the other, for making payments covering certified expenditure and clearing accounts in accordance with the principle, enshrined in the Financial Regulation, of sound financial management. But far more than this, DG Regio will be actively engaged cooperating and collaborating with, supporting and supervising and encouraging, cajoling and sometimes sanctioning, Member State authorities. Sub-divided into two chief parts – Policy, Performance and Compliance, and Implementation – the DG currently boasts eight directorates with titles ranging from 'Administrative Capacity Building' to 'Operational Efficiency' and some 35 units ordered both functionally and by Member State.[7]

Correspondingly heavy demands are placed on domestic governance structures in what constitutes a largely decentralised system. From trans-regional initiatives and big infrastructure development to technology transfer, business training and new premises for particular types of regional enterprise, and on through multiple forms of community-based regeneration and social and environmental schemes:

[4] B Schondorf-Habold, 'Common European Administration: The European Structural Funds' in O Jansen and B Schondorf-Habold (eds), *The European Composite Administration* (Oxford: Hart Publishing, 2011).

[5] For a useful introduction, see R Scully and R Wyn Jones (eds), *Europe, Regions and Regionalism* (Basingstoke: Palgrave Macmillan, 2010).

[6] Beginning with G Marks, 'Structural Policy and Multi-level Governance in the EC' in A Cafruny and G Rosenthal (eds), *The State of the EC, Vol 2: The Maastricht Debate and Beyond* (Boulder, CO: Lynne Rienner: 1993) 391; M Pollack, 'Regional Actors in an Intergovernmental Play: The Making and Implementation of EC Structural Policy' in C Rhodes and S Mazey (eds), *The State of the EU, Vol 3: Building a European Polity?* (Boulder, CO: Lynne Rienner: 1995).

[7] Further details are available in the DG's annual management plan.

the sheer scale and differentiated nature of the front line activity is hard to exaggerate. Forms of support have become increasingly mixed: not simply grants to enterprise, but also with the aid of the European Investment Bank (EIB), innovative forms of 'financial engineering' that may involve venture capital, as well as advice and guidance and support for networking between all and sundry.[8] A touchstone is the series of specially designed bodies which Member States are required to establish or designate for each operational programme.[9] Pride of place goes to the managing authority, which has the main responsibility for the effective and efficient implementation of the funds and, more particularly, for devising and applying proper selection procedures and ensuring compliance with the principle of sound financial management. The more broadly-based monitoring committee, established with the agreement of the managing authority and supported by it, is tasked with reviewing implementation and progress. The certifying authority is charged with drawing up and submitting to the Commission payment applications and statements of expenditure; the audit authority is tasked with verifying the effective functioning of the management and control system.

Lengthy and often highly technical legal provision underwrites all this. In the Commission's experience, the rules governing spending programmes are 'often perceived as unnecessarily complicated and difficult to implement'. Echoing initiatives like the Regulatory Fitness and Performance Programme (REFIT) (see chapter two), there has been much talk of 'simplification': the Commission would like to reduce the 'heavy administrative burden' on all parties, which can have 'the unintended effect of discouraging participation, increasing error rates and delaying implementation'.[10] While some more targeted approaches are in prospect, the problem is deep-rooted. Consider the official hierarchy of rules in the recently 'simplified' policy framework.[11] Factoring in the Lisbon Treaty arrangements on executive law-making (see chapter five), this has six main layers: general provisions, common provisions, fund-specific provisions, delegated acts, implementing acts and Commission guidelines; to which, in the intricate system of 'shared management', must be added a cornucopia of domestic legal provision.

In sum, conditions have been ripe for a thick development of administrative procedure. Linked to the general themes of steering, close cooperation and accountability in EU administration, we will concentrate on three main aspects. We look first at programming, whereby, across successive EU budgetary cycles, cohesion policy themes and priorities have been established, national and regional programmes elaborated, projects developed and so on. At the time of writing, arrangements for the programming period 2014–20 proceed apace in a framework expressly conceived in terms of the Union's broader agenda on competitiveness

---

[8] *Investing in Europe's Future*, above (n 2) especially ch IV.
[9] Council Regulation 1303/2013/EU laying down common provisions on the European Regional Development Fund, etc [2013] OJ L347/320, Arts 47, 123.
[10] Commission, 'Proposal for a Regulation laying down general and common provisions for the ERDF, etc' COM (2011) 615 final, 2.
[11] Centred on Regulation 1303/2013.

and growth and also, underwriting the Council's role, sound economic governance. Enhanced tools and techniques for steering domestic policy and administration are of the essence of this more prescriptive approach: to the extent, it may be said, of 'harnessing' less well off states and regions. Long hovering in the wings, but now giving cohesion policy a more stringent feel, the conditionality principle is brought centre stage (see chapter two).

Intimately bound up with ideas of multi-level governance, 'partnership' is perhaps the best known organisational principle in this policy domain. It has found institutional expression in a multiplicity of arrangements involving the DG, national authorities at central, regional and local governmental levels and an array of public, private and civil society actors within the regions. The Commission has consistently championed the principle on grounds of good governance and, in particular, of policy effectiveness. The reality may be far from the rhetoric, in part a reflection of constitutional and cultural diversity among Member States, but DG Regio appears undaunted. Efforts are made to embellish 'partnership' for the new programming period.

In the words of the famous instruction, 'follow the money'. To do so is to appreciate the elongated, complex and multifaceted nature of the 'shared management' system. In the light of deep-seated concerns about fraud and error in the structural funds, attention is naturally drawn to the role of audit. Reform of the Financial Regulation underwrites the importance of effective supervisory systems for securing regularity. However, at one with broader managerialist developments in EU administration (see chapter two), audit-style technique ranges much wider. From the concept of 'value for money' (VFM) to complex methodologies for evaluating performance, the revamped framework for the 2014–20 programming period is seen taking the search for substantive results to new heights.

PROGRAMMING: POLICY AND PRINCIPLES

Rise and Rise

Community regional policy had begun in fits and starts in the early 1970s, but a watershed moment came in 1988 with the inauguration of a five-year programming period.[12] Addressing concerns about the economic and social effects of increased competitive disciplines in those less well off parts of Member States already struggling to compete, the development was clearly linked to the drive to complete the Single Market. While the sums involved remained comparatively modest (some ECU 64 billion), this 'mark I' programming period cemented a process of budgetary growth largely driven by accession or enlargement. In the long view, it also entrenched some governing features of regional policy, which

---

[12] Regulation 2052/1988/EEC on the tasks of the Structural Funds and their effectiveness [1988] OJ L185/9.

would be tweaked and/or supplemented in subsequent programming periods. The centrepiece would be the European Regional Development Fund (ERDF), designed to promote investment and correct major regional imbalances, flanked by smaller funds including the European Social Fund (ESF) targeted on unemployment.[13]

In view of the path-breaking provisions on European Economic and Monetary Union (EMU) in the Maastricht Treaty, the pressure was again on for a concrete expression of solidarity in the form of stronger distributive policies. With the addition of a Cohesion Fund specifically for the protection of the poorer (Mediterranean) Member States, the total for the 'mark II' period (1993–99) was some ECU 168 billion. Sitting comfortably with establishment of the subsidiarity principle, and in particular of a Committee of the Regions (CoR) that would naturally prove a staunch advocate of structural funding, it was in this period that expansive views of multi-level governance in Europe began to flower.[14] Coupled with what the official history describes as 'a paradigm shift' in cohesion policy in favour of Union objectives of competitiveness and growth,[15] a further step change in funding took place at the beginning of the century: for the 'mark III' period (2000–06), some €210 billion was initially allocated. In the light of the telling statistics that the 10 states joining in 2004 brought a 20 per cent increase in EU population but only a 5 per cent increase in GDP, it was too a case with Enlargement of building on the pre-accession financial instruments (see chapter one) with an extra two-year allocation of €22 billion.

The 'mark IV' period (2007–13) has seen the structural funds continuing to move east, and rightly so, in view of huge challenges of economic and industrial restructuring.[16] An official map of cohesion policy showed Poland as leading recipient, followed by a mix of older (Spain and Italy) and newer (Hungary and the Czech Republic) Member States.[17] Accounting for over one-third of the expanded Union budget, and having finally overtaken CAP expenditure as the lead item, the total allocation was €347 billion. In short, cohesion policy had become a flagship policy of European integration. But the appealing official mantra of growth and jobs would soon be horribly underscored by economic recession.

---

[13] On the early periodic development, see J Scott, 'Regional Policy: An Evolutionary Perspective' in P Craig and G de Búrca, *The Evolution of EU Law* (Oxford: OUP, 1999).

[14] L Hooghe (ed), *Cohesion Policy and European Integration: Building Multi-Level Governance* (Oxford: OUP, 1996). There was even talk of something called a 'Europe of the Regions': see C Jeffrey (ed), *The Regional Dimension of the European Union: Towards a Third Level in Europe?* (London: Frank Cass, 1997).

[15] Commission, 'EU Cohesion Policy 1988–2008: Investing in Europe's Future' (2008) 19.

[16] M Baun and D Marek (eds), *EU Cohesion Policy after Enlargement* (Basingstoke: Palgrave Macmillan, 2008); J Bachtler, C Mendez and H Oraze, 'From Conditionality to Europeanization in Central and Eastern Europe: Administrative Performance and Capacity in Cohesion Policy' (2014) 22 *European Planning Studies* 735.

[17] Commission, 'Cohesion Policy 2007–2013: Commentaries and Official Texts' (2007) 24.

Administrative Vehicle

The 1988 reforms constituted a system replete with principles. Intended to secure the sustained and concerted intervention which is the hallmark of cohesion policy, programming is a key management principle in its own right. As the basic administrative vehicle for planning, that most expansive bureaucratic activity, it further serves to ground other main principles shaping the policy development and implementation. As well as partnership, the 'mark I' programming model emphasised two particular principles designed to (be seen to) make a difference.

'Concentration' has a dual meaning in this context. In the geographical sense of allocating funds to those areas in greatest need, the principle has been a defining feature of the ERDF. Variously branded in terms of 'Objective 1' or the 'convergence objective', the development and structural adjustment of 'lagging regions' (with GDP less than 75 per cent of the EU average) accounted for over 80 per cent of available funds in the recently completed programming period. Application of the principle has demanded a rich growth of statistical procedures. Originally worked up by Eurostat[18] in cooperation with national counterparts, a common classification of territorial units ('NUTS') has been enshrined in legislation. Intended to provide 'objective criteria . . . in order to ensure impartiality when regional statistics are compiled and used',[19] it is largely constructed by reference to size of population and political and administrative arrangements. This technocratic element should be kept in perspective however. The importance of political bargaining in the broader process of allocation not only at intergovernmental level, but also between central and regional authorities, is well attested.[20]

'Concentration' is also about themed objectives or priorities. This has taken various forms over the years, commonly in relation to employment. The approach gained increased impetus in the 2000 to 2006 and 2007 to 2013 programming periods through the strategic use of the dominium power in support of Union industrial and economic aims. Cohesion policy was thus presented as 'the major instrument at Community level for the modernisation of the Union's economy',[21] with much of the spending on the convergence objective being earmarked for technological development and innovation.[22] The development entailed a dose of Lisbon-style forms of soft governance (see chapter two) founded on special

---

[18] For Eurostat, see Commission Decision 2012/504/EU.

[19] Regulation 1059/2003/EC on the establishment of a common classification of territorial units for statistics (NUTS) [2003] OJ L154/1, recital 7.

[20] See, eg, F Bouvet and S Dall'erba, 'European Regional Structural Funds: How Large is the Influence of Politics on the Allocation Process?' (2010) 48 Journal of Common Market Studies 501; T Bodenstein and A Kemmerling, 'Ripples in a Rising Tide: Why Some EU Regions Receive More Structural Funds than Others' (2011) 16 *European Integration online Papers* 1, available at: http://eiop.or.at/eiop/index.php/eiop.

[21] 'Cohesion Policy 2007–2013', above (n 17) 3.

[22] Regulation1083/2006/EC laying down general provisions on the ERDF, the ESF and the Cohesion Fund [2006] OJ L210/25, Art 9; Annex IV.

arrangements for dialogue with the Council and regular reporting and review of strategic performance.[23]

'Additionality', meaning that Member States should not replace their own structural aid with support from Union funds,[24] is a principle easy to state and difficult to secure. At one and the same time, it sits comfortably with requirements of co-financing from public and/or private resources[25] and is a natural source of friction between the Commission and individual Member States. Successive legislative frameworks have sent out mixed messages. For example, better to accommodate diverse practices of national budgeting and accounting, but conversely making it more difficult for the Commission to impose discipline, later programming models would incorporate flexibilities relating to particular developments like privatisations. Conversely, armed with a specific power of financial correction, the Commission is now tasked with undertaking more regular and targeted statistical verification.[26]

As for the interior design of the programming vehicle, the marks I, II and III models saw the growth of a sophisticated set of administrative procedures, at the heart of which lay a wide-ranging management instrument, the Community Support Framework (CSF). This enabled inputs from the wider national partnership, grounded dialogue between the Commission and Member State and structured the elaboration and implementation of operational programmes at sub-state levels. Drawn up by the Commission on the basis of a development plan drafted by the competent domestic authorities and with the agreement of the Member State, the CSF thus established the priorities and forms of assistance for a region. Illustrating the periodic fine-tuning, a streamlined variant was introduced in 1993, whereby the CSF could be combined with operational programmes in a 'Single Programming Document', while in 1999 the 'Programme Complement' was introduced, in which proposed measures and potential beneficiaries were specified.[27]

Much in the design appeared outdated however in the light of Enlargement and the Union's stated preference for a more strategic policy constructed in terms of the updated Lisbon agenda centred on economic growth.[28] The programming vehicle for 2007–13 highlighted the role of both subsidiarity and proportionality as overarching principles.[29] Connoting a greater decentralisation of cohesion policy, the legislation underlined Member State responsibilities for the management

---

[23] Ibid, Arts 29–30; Commission, 'Cohesion Policy: Strategic report on programme implementation 2007–2013' SWD (2013) 129 final. See further, C Mendez, 'The Lisbonization of EU Cohesion Policy: A Successful Case of Experimentalist Governance?' (2011) 19 *European Planning Studies* 519.

[24] Regulation 1303/2013, Art 95.

[25] Ibid, Art 27.

[26] Ibid, recital 87; and see Annex X.

[27] See on the mark III period, Regulation 1260/1999/EC OJ L161/1, Arts 14–19; and for discussion, Schondorf-Habold, 'Common European Administration', above (n 4).

[28] Communication from the Commission President, 'Working together for growth and jobs: A new start for the Lisbon Strategy' COM (2005) 24 final.

[29] Regulation 1083/2006, especially recitals 27 and 65, and Art 13.

and oversight of operational programmes.[30] A new scheme of programming was introduced, which saw the CSF replaced by the tellingly titled National Strategic Reference Framework (NSRF).[31] Member States would define and justify their policy priorities in a single overall strategy; the Commission would check this for consistency with Council guidelines fleshing out the demands of the Lisbon strategy.[32] The Commission, it was officially stated, would be 'the guarantor' of strategic implementation, with 'more confidence placed in the Member States'.[33]

Retrenchment: More Union Strategy

As indicated, there has been another swing in the pendulum. The design of the 'mark V' programming vehicle for 2014–20 reflects a time, in the Commission's words, 'when public money is scarce and when growth enhancing investment is more needed than ever'.[34] Pegged at €352 billion, the funds did not escape demands for Union budgetary restraint against the backdrop of a thoroughgoing financial and economic crisis which has seen hitherto shrinking regional disparities in GDP and unemployment grow again.[35] Fiscal consolidation across the EU also promises to increase the role of cohesion policy as an important source of public investment; it currently represents over half of this in many of the less developed Member States and regions.[36] Concentration is again a major theme; a firmer set of priorities goes hand in hand with support for lagging regions (€182 billion) and for a new category of slightly better off 'transition regions' (€35 billion). The Commission has been particularly concerned to improve synergies for growth through complementary policy objectives in different funds.[37] Labelled 'European Structural and Investment Funds' (ESI Funds) and operationalised through a 'Common Strategic Framework',[38] the ERDF, the ESF and the Cohesion Fund are now more closely aligned with the sector-specific European Agricultural Fund for Rural Development and the European Maritime and Fisheries Fund.

At one with developments, for example, in public procurement (see chapter six), cohesion policy is presented as an essential means for delivering the Union's Europe 2020 strategy. With an eye to international competitiveness, the general Regulation 1303/2013 formally recognises 'smart, sustainable and inclusive growth' as a chief

---

[30] Ibid, Arts 32, 37; see further, J Bachtler and C Mendez, 'Who Governs Cohesion Policy? Deconstructing the Reforms of the Structural Funds' (2007) 45 *Journal of Common Market Studies* 535.
[31] For practical details, see R Smail, L Broos and E Kuijpers, *Managing Structural Funds* (Maastricht: EIPA, 2008).
[32] Regulation 1083/2006, Arts 25–28
[33] 'Cohesion Policy 2007–2013', above (n 17) 6–7.
[34] Commission, 'Proposal for a Regulation on specific provisions concerning the ERDF' COM (2011) 614 final, 1.
[35] See Commission, 'Eighth Progress Report on Economic, Social and Territorial Cohesion' COM (2013) 463 final.
[36] Ibid, 16.
[37] COM (2011) 615 final, 2–5.
[38] Regulation 1303/2013, recital 2, Arts 10–11 and Annex 1.

goal, together with strengthening economic, social and territorial cohesion in accordance with the Treaties.[39] It specifies a list of thematic objectives derived from the 2020 strategy such as strengthening research and innovation, supporting the shift towards a low-carbon economy, combating poverty and promoting social inclusion, as well as enhancing institutional capacity and efficient public administration.[40] There is a firm legislative emphasis on Member States using the funds for types of development valued by the Union and in ways that promote Union economic and industrial goals. Domestic programmes receiving CSF funding must relate to one of the thematic objectives;[41] high percentages of Member State funding allocations are earmarked for the three core themes of research and innovation, competiveness of small and medium size enterprises (SMEs) and sustainable energy, though there is more flexibility for lagging regions given their broader range of needs.[42] The fund-specific legislation further structures and confines Member State discretion through detailed listing of 'investment priorities within the thematic objectives', for example support for SMEs by developing new business models.[43]

Micro and Macro Conditionality

One conundrum of structural funding in terms of effectiveness is the likelihood of poor administrative capacities coupled with an adverse economic environment in those areas where it is chiefly deployed. In preparing for the 2014–20 period, the Commission's 'Fifth Cohesion Report' focused on this issue, observing that 'sound macroeconomic policies, a favourable microeconomic environment and strong institutional frameworks are preconditions for creating jobs, stimulating growth, reducing social exclusion and bringing about structural changes'.[44] 'To ensure that EU funding creates strong incentives for Member States to deliver Europe 2020 objectives and targets', the mark V programming vehicle uses the conditionality principle to give matters a harder edge, hence up-playing the qualifications for access to, and use of, the funds. 'Ex ante conditionalities' are commonly targeted on what the Commission calls 'bottlenecks in policy, regulatory and institutional frameworks',[45] while 'ex post conditionalities' make the release of additional funding more closely attuned to mid-term performance.[46]

Public procurement procedures steer the (Member States') use of *dominium* power; here (Union) *dominium* power is used in order to steer. Depending on how firmly they are applied, ex ante conditionalities have the potential significantly to

---

[39] Ibid, Arts 4 and 89. The reference to territorial cohesion was added by the Lisbon Treaty.
[40] Ibid, Art 9.
[41] Ibid, Arts 18, 27, 29.
[42] Regulation 1301/2013/EU on the European Regional Development Fund [2013] OJ L347/289, Art 4.
[43] Ibid, Art 5.
[44] 'Fifth Cohesion Report', above (n 2) xxv. See further, Commission Conditionality Task Force, Structural Reform Conditionality in Cohesion Policy (April 2011).
[45] COM (2011) 615 final, 8; Regulation 1303/2013, Art 19.
[46] Ibid, Arts 20–22.

increase the policy importance of structural funding. Each of the listed thematic objectives comes with conditionalities attached.[47] A first bundle of requirements concerns implementation of EU law, especially the correct transposition of directives in related subject matters such as energy efficiency and environmental protection. Providing an additional tool with which to press for the recipients' compliance, this particular 'carrot' has obvious advantages for the Commission over the reactive 'stick' of infringement proceedings (see chapter seven).

A second bundle of conditionalities goes further, effectively operating as a 'tin opener' on national plans and strategies not otherwise subject to EU mandatory requirements. Some elements, for example in education, reflect recommendations or guidance at EU level, so giving the Commission enhanced capacity to influence Member State behaviour in the realm of soft law. Other elements are more broad-brush. Take the thematic objective of capable and efficient public administration, where the ripple effects on national systems of EU integration are clearly in play. Regulation 1303/2013 speaks of a Member State response ranging from 'strategic planning of legal, organisational and/or procedural reform actions' to 'the development of quality management systems', and on through 'integrated actions for the simplification and rationalisation of administrative procedures' to 'the development of skills at all levels of the professional hierarchy'.[48]

Reinforcement of the rules on so-called 'macroeconomic conditionality', whereby structural funding is linked to a Member State's compliance with the demands of EU economic governance, has been hotly contested. It is after all the least developed regions that are liable to bear the brunt of central government failings. Acting via the Council, the net contributors to the EU budget have been firm however.[49] Under the 'preventive arm' of the policy, the Commission may request changes to programmes in accordance, for example, with Council recommendations on sound economic governance. If the Member State fails to take effective action, the Commission may ask the Council to suspend part or all of the payments for the programmes concerned. Under the 'corrective arm', the Commission must propose that the Council suspend part or all payments or financial commitments for programmes where the Member State has failed to take appropriate action to comply with the Union's strengthened rules on excessive deficits and macroeconomic imbalances.[50] Testimony to the many sensitivities, the legislation specifically requires that the scope and level of suspensions is 'proportionate' and respects 'equality of treatment between Member States'; it also establishes caps and mitigating factors, including a fall in GDP.[51] The European Parliament (EP) eventually won a role in the process; in making a proposal for suspension, the Commission must give due consideration to the Parliament's opinions expressed

[47] Ibid, Annex XI.
[48] Regulation 1303/2013, Annex XI, [11].
[49] See Conclusions of the European Council Meeting 7–8 February 2013, [7]–[8].
[50] Regulation 1303/2013, Art 23. See further, I Begg et al, *European Economic Governance and Cohesion Policy* (EP study, 2014).
[51] Regulation 1303/2013, Annex III.

through a special 'structured dialogue'.[52] The convoluted procedures underwrite the fact of a reserve mechanism, but the steering potential of Union *dominium* power exercised through the conditionality principle is highlighted.

ARTICLE OF FAITH: PARTNERSHIP

'Partnership' in cohesion policy has been visualised in two main ways.[53] Much of the administrative focus has been on intra-state partnerships, both vertically drawn between public authorities at national, regional and local levels, and horizontally constructed with the private and third sectors. Splendidly envisioned, the putative benefits include improved targeting through better understanding of needs and gaps; better coordination and more particularly mutual learning and pooling of resources; more effective implementation through local know-how and experience; local empowerment or mobilisation and 'ownership' of initiatives; and enhanced legitimacy via greater transparency and 'voice' in how the money is spent.[54] Legislatively, this conception has gained greater traction over the years, subject always to the need to accommodate the many shapes and sizes of sub-state government in Europe. Partially blurring the 'public–private' dichotomy in governmental arrangements, the framework has been made more inclusive. As well as requiring that each Member State in accordance with the domestic institutional and legal framework organises a partnership with regional and local authorities, Article 5 of Regulation 1303/2013 stipulates that the partnership should also include competent urban and other public authorities, economic and social partners and 'relevant bodies representing civil society' including environmental partners and bodies responsible for promoting social inclusion, gender equality and non-discrimination. The approach stretches across the whole programme cycle: 'in accordance with respect for the principles of multi-level governance', partners should be involved in 'the preparation, implementation, monitoring and evaluation'.[55]

Relations between the Commission and the national authorities have also been visualised in terms of a partnership. This is reflected in copious legislative reference to close cooperation and dialogue and the new legal and administrative tool of 'partnership agreements' (see below). Pointing up a chief source of tension however, this conception does not simply refer to central government, but may also connote governance-style relationships involving, as EU officials have historically been keen to promote,[56] the Commission and sub-state actors. It has

---

[52] Ibid, Art 23(9) and (15).
[53] P Craig, *EU Administrative Law*, 2nd edn (Oxford: OUP, 2012) 98–99.
[54] J Scott, 'Law, Legitimacy and EC Governance: Prospects for Partnership' (1998) 36 *Journal of Common Market Studies* 175; J Kelleher, S Batterbury and E Stern, *Thematic Evaluation of the Partnership Principle* (London: Tavistock Institute, 1999).
[55] Regulation 1303/2013, recital 11.
[56] I Bache, 'Partnership as an EU Policy Instrument: A Political History' (2010) 33 *West European Politics* 58.

been reflected in the make-up of the monitoring committees where, together with officials from the managing authorities, participation by intra-state partners is specifically guaranteed and the Commission is represented.[57] We touch here on the classic debate[58] between adherents of intergovernmentalism, which naturally places a premium on the 'gatekeeper role' of central government in controlling the access of other partners to the financial and administrative arrangements, and of multi-level governance, as predicated on the innately challenging idea of 'a breakthrough of the Community level to the subordinate levels of the Member States' administrations'.[59]

Rhetoric and Reality

Partnership arrangements have been here, there and everywhere in cohesion policy; to the extent, when enthusiastically adopted, of multiple local partnerships, multiple thematic partnerships and numerous strategic partnerships, in a single programme.[60] DG Regio is not slow to trumpet improvements to programme design in individual cases of joint and constructive partnership working.[61] Successive studies rightly warn however against conflating the simple fact of involvement with influence or empowerment or 'true' multi-level governance.[62] A Commission survey records that 'authorities in charge of programming tend to consider NGOs ... as the most problematic element in the partnership process ... while the NGOs tend to be frustrated when confronted with a narrow range of prescribed choices'.[63] Member State discretion to decide who represents what in civil society for the purposes of the legislation has been a flashpoint.[64]

A recurring theme is the 'wide differences across the Member States on application of the partnership principle, depending on national institutional set-ups and political cultures'.[65] One key variable is the extent to which the domestic politico-administrative system is decentralised or, conversely, how closely regional and/or

---

[57] Though today only in an advisory capacity: Regulation 1303/2013, Art 48.

[58] I Bache, *The Politics of European Union Regional Policy: Multi-Level Governance or Flexible Gatekeeping?* (Sheffield: UACES, 1998).

[59] Schondorf-Habold, 'Common European Administration', above (n 4) 30; and see, eg, CoR, *The future of EU cohesion policy as seen by regions and cities* (2012).

[60] R Rawlings, 'Law, Territory and Integration: A View from the Atlantic Shore' (2001) 67 *International Review of Administrative Sciences* 479.

[61] DG Regio, Partnership in the 2000–2006 programming period: analysis of the implementation of the partnership principle (2005).

[62] See, eg, A Allen, 'Cohesion Policy Pre and Post-enlargement' in M Baun and D Marek (eds), *EU Cohesion Policy after Enlargement* (Basingstoke: Palgrave Macmillan, 2008).

[63] EP, 'The Partnership Contracts – How to implement multilevel governance and to guarantee the flexibility of Cohesion Policy' (2012) 25.

[64] A Batory and A Cartwright, 'Revisiting the Partnership Principle in Cohesion Policy: The Role of Civil Society Organizations in Structural Funds Monitoring' (2011) 49 *Journal of Common Market Studies* 697.

[65] Commission, 'The Partnership Principle in the implementation of the Common Strategic Framework Funds – elements for a European Code of Conduct on Partnership' SWD (2012) 106 final, 3.

local government is constrained. The existence or otherwise of systems of fiscal equalisation is most relevant, defining as they do the financing capacity of each tier.[66] Attention is drawn to the importance of domestic traditions of consensual policymaking in securing the institutionalisation of partnership, though even here there may be problems of 'fit' (for NGOs) in the light of a strong official and/ or corporatist orientation.[67] The issue of administrative and technical capacity in lagging regions again looms large; so too, the fact of unequal distribution of private and third sector resources for engaging in partnership. Recent studies highlight the particular challenges for partnership in those countries where cohesion policy is now largely concentrated. Meaningful collaborative arrangements may develop over time, but a legacy of centralised decision-making and limited civic involvement in many E-12 States cannot be wished away.[68] Awkward questions are raised about the transferability of the partnership approach.

The contribution of the monitoring committees as the primary institutional expression of partnership in the delivery of programmes has been mixed at best. They require the managing authorities to justify priorities and actions through the course of a programming period and provide useful opportunities for lobbying and/or networking among the stipulated lists of stakeholders. All too often however, the committees have lacked the time and resources to reach near their potential as a sounding board and/or machinery for oversight. Procedures have commonly appeared formalistic: at worst, amounting to little more than a box-ticking exercise to meet legislative requirements. An inbuilt tension exists with the role and interlocking architecture of the managing authorities.[69]

A recent EP assessment of intra-state partnership was notably downbeat: inside national systems 'the impact so far is limited'. National authorities 'perceive partnership as more or less problematic . . . it is often seen as time consuming and requiring extra effort without adding value'. Such complaints are hardly new, but they have increased resonance at a time of financial retrenchment in the Enlarged Union. To anchor the partnership principle firmly in cohesion policy – after 25 years of trying – the report recommended 'a focus on capacity building within the administrations and a comprehensive communications strategy'.[70] Soft governance techniques of networking had already proved an attractive option for the Commission. Established and promoted with the help of DG Regio, the leading example in the 2007–13 programming period was the 'Community of Practice on Partnership in the ESF'. Comprised of management authorities and intermediary

[66] 'The Partnership Contracts', above (n 63) 9.
[67] I Bache and J Olsson, 'Legitimacy through Partnership? EU Policy Diffusion in Britain and Sweden' (2001) 24 *Scandinavian Political Studies* 215.
[68] M Baun and D Marek, 'EU Cohesion Policy and Sub-National Authorities in the New Member States' (2008) 2 *Contemporary European Studies* 5; M Dabrowski, 'EU Cohesion Policy, Horizontal Partnership and the Patterns of Sub-national Governance: Insights from Central and Eastern Europe' (2013) *European Urban and Regional Studies online*.
[69] S Piattoni, 'Informal Governance in Structural Policy' (2006) 7 *Perspectives on European Politics and Society* 56; A Batory and A Cartwright, 'Monitoring Committees in Cohesion Policy: Overseeing the Distribution of Structural Funds in Hungary and Slovakia' (2012) 34 *European Integration* 323.
[70] 'The Partnership Contracts', above (n 63) 9–10.

234   *Cohesion Policy*

bodies from five Member States, together with Commission representatives, this was a pilot project typically focused on information exchange, peer review and dissemination of best practice.[71]

As for the new programming period, the EP together with the CoR and the European Economic and Social Committee (EESC) once again demanded a strengthening of intra-state partnership in the face of serious reservations in the Council;[72] the Commission prioritised a 'more consistent application'.[73] Giving tangible expression to both visualisations, Regulation 1303/13 not only confirms the principle as an article of faith in cohesion policy, but also provides additional modalities.

Partnership Agreements

As a well attested technique of governance, more or less formally binding agreements can serve in the EU 'administrative space' as a way of modelling institutional relations (all those Memorandums of Understanding (MoUs)); as a source of administrative rules or vehicle for planning; as a 'tin opener' (allowing the Commission to delve inside national systems); and (carrying the threat of sanction) as a means of conditioning the transfer of resources.[74] Connoting a sense of Member State obligation and accountability, the novel 'partnership agreement' is expected to perform all these functions in the new programming period.

In fact, the partnership agreement gives the Union's more prescriptive approach much of its cutting edge. Replacing the NSRF, it 'sets out the Member State's strategy, priorities and arrangements for using the ESI Funds in an effective and efficient way so as to pursue the Union strategy for smart, sustainable and inclusive growth'.[75] Fleshing this out, Regulation 1303/13 stipulates that the content must include analysis of development needs with reference to the Common Strategic Framework and to Council recommendations on employment policies; ex ante evaluation justifying both the selection of thematic objectives and the indicative allocations of CSF funds; explanation of arrangements and mechanisms for an integrated approach to territorial development supported by the funds; information required for ex ante verification of additionality; explanation of how the applicable ex ante conditionalities are met or a schedule for meeting them; and performance targets and indicators.[76] Effectively designed to discipline the planning process through greater specificity, the potential scale of the 'tin opening' is remarkable.

[71] Community of Practice on Partnership in the ESF, Partnership Learning Manual (2012).
[72] EP, Resolution on good governance with regard to the EU regional policy, 14 December 2010 P7_TA(2010)0468; CoR, 'White Paper on Multilevel Governance' (2009); EESC, Opinion on efficient partnership in cohesion policy ECO 258 (2010).
[73] 'The Partnership Principle', above (n 65) 3.
[74] See C Harlow and R Rawlings, *Law and Administration*, 3rd edn (Cambridge: CUP, 2009) ch 8.
[75] Regulation 1303/2013, Art 2(2).
[76] Ibid, Art 15.

With an eye to sub-state mobilisation or buy-in, the Commission has set much store on the process of making an agreement.[77] Drawn up by the Member State in cooperation with domestic partners, the document is 'approved by the Commission following assessment and dialogue with the Member State'.[78] In view of the functional limits to contract-style 'presentation' (see chapter six), a welcome element of administrative flexibility – space for renegotiation – is factored in.[79] Time will tell how enthusiastic and resourceful the Commission is in pursuing alleged 'breaches' by exercising concomitant powers to suspend payments or impose financial corrections. But closer regulation by partnership agreement underwrites its broader responsibility to protect the EU's financial interests.

Code of Conduct

The Commission has aimed to give intra-state partnership a boost by means of a mini-code laying down minimum requirements.[80] The proposal was initially rejected by the Council and, in emphasising principles of subsidiarity and proportionality as well as multi-level governance, the eventual compromise up-plays Member State discretion over the ways in which partnership is organised.[81] In empowering the Commission to provide for the 'European Code of Conduct on Partnership' (ECCP), Article 5(3) of Regulation 1303/2013 yields some clues about the more problematic aspects of partnership in practice. It prescribes as elements of the Code: transparent procedures for identifying partners; forms of involvement of the different categories; rules of membership and internal procedures of monitoring committees; avoidance of conflicts of interest; and use of ESI funds to strengthen the institutional capacity of partners. Article 5(5) downplays the possibility of sanction however: infringement of the Code is not an irregularity founding a penalty or financial correction.

Established by delegated regulation,[82] the Code is a mix of statements of principle, basic conditions and relevant factors; accompanying it in a Commission document are 'inspiring examples of good practice'.[83] The treatment of consultation, where the Commission has read across some well-worn nostrums from its own soft law practices (see chapter five), makes plain the attempt to inculcate the WPEG-style principles of good governance. According to the Code, Member States 'shall take account of the need' for timely disclosure and easy access to

---

[77] See 'The Partnership Contracts', above (n 63).
[78] Regulation 1303/2013, Arts 2(20), 14. Adoption is via implementing acts: Art 16(2).
[79] Ibid, Art 16(4).
[80] Commission, 'The Partnership Principle in the implementation of the Common Strategic Framework Funds – elements for a European Code of Conduct on Partnership' SWD (2012) 106 final, 4.
[81] See EESC, Opinion on Code of Conduct on Partnership, ECO/330 (2012).
[82] Delegated Regulation 240/2014/EU on the European code of conduct in the framework of the European Structural and Investment Funds [2014] OJ L74/1.
[83] Commission, 'Best practices as regards implementation of the partnership principle in the European Structural and Investment Funds' programmes SWD (2013) 540 final, 2.

adequate information, sufficient time for analysis and comment on draft documents, and suitable channels for questions and feedback. Again, the Code recognises the importance of pre-emptive action in the fight against corruption; managing authorities 'shall take appropriate measures to avoid potential conflict of interest' where partners are involved in the preparation or assessment of proposals.[84] Based on the earlier pilot project, a 'cooperation mechanism' to facilitate mutual learning and capacity-building in true networking style is part of the package. The 'European Community of Practice on Partnership' will be open to interested Member States, managing authorities and organisations representing the partners at Union level.[85]

MANAGEMENT AND FINANCIAL SUPERVISION: AUDIT

Decentralised Management: Supervisory Growth

The logic of a decentralised system in which Member States are expressly made responsible for the operation and control of programmes is that managing authorities have to do most of the 'heavy lifting'.[86] But given the need for financial assurance at Union level, the arrangement has also engendered a growth industry of EU-shaped supervision; the more so, in view of recurring fraud and error. The Member State is made responsible 'in the first instance' for investigating irregularities, for making the requisite financial corrections and, under the shadow of liability for loss incurred as a result of its fault or negligence, for recovering monies wrongly paid out.[87] Commission leverage extends all the way from ex ante steering instructions and prompts to the ex post disciplines of default or secondary enforcement powers, via the classic bureaucratic routines of periodic accounting and reporting.[88]

Representing a mix of generic rules associated with the Financial Regulation, and specific requirements for the sector, the formal legal provision again abounds. Regulation 1303/2013 sets out the managing authority's responsibilities and functions under the three broad headings of (a) programme management; (b) selection of operations; and (c) financial management and control, where a series of front line and supervisory activities is specified. In addition to the general instruction to 'put in place effective and proportionate anti-fraud measures taking into account the risks identified', these include ensuring that beneficiaries maintain proper accounting systems, establishing documentary procedures to ensure adequate audit trails and, for the purpose of verifying compliance with the funding rules, on-the-spot

---

[84] Delegated Regulation 240/2014, Arts 4 and 13.
[85] Ibid, Art 18.
[86] Regulation 1303/2013, Art 125; also Art 72 on the general principles of management and control systems.
[87] Ibid, Art 143.
[88] As for de-commitment (where allocations have not been spent), see ibid, Arts 86–88, 136.

investigations. At one with the Financial Regulation, the managing authority is required to make a declaration of assurance on the functioning of management and control, as well as to report any weaknesses identified and any corrective action taken.[89] The day to day actions of managers in the national systems are then of critical importance; experience confirms that where managing authorities lack adequate institutional capacity, problems are likely to ensue.[90]

The legislation is similarly prescriptive about the functions of the certifying authority, a key piece in the jigsaw since Commission payments now largely take the form of reimbursements of actual expenditure, the regularity of which must be officially attested. ICT requirements feature strongly: from recording and storing the raw data for payment applications to maintaining accounting records of expenditure declared to the Commission.[91] In the case of the certifying authority the legislation duly specifies functional independence as an essential organisational prerequisite. But it again goes much further, effectively constituting a template for audit activity complete with references to 'appropriate' forms of sampling and 'internationally accepted audit standards'.[92]

Regulation 1303/2013 further highlights the Commission's ability to reach into the nooks and crannies of national administrative procedure through the creative use of executive legislation. As the Court of Auditors (ECA) has tartly observed, the matters covered by delegated acts, meant to cover non-essential elements of EU legislation (see chapter five), in fact deal with key elements of the cohesion policy framework.[93] They include the procedures for reporting irregularities and recovery of monies; the standards of national audit; the accreditation criteria for managing authorities and certifying authorities; and the criteria for determining financial corrections.[94] Meanwhile, the Commission's implementing powers extend in the realm of financial management and control to not insignificant technical or methodological issues such as the rules on exchange of information between beneficiaries and national authorities, the models for audit strategy and the rules concerning use of data collected during audits.[95] Dutifully listed on the DG's website, the preparatory work has involved a plethora of meetings under the aegis of the 'Expert Group on Delegated and Implementing Acts for the European Structural and Investment Funds'. Technical complexity likewise sees guidance piled on guidance.[96]

Pointing up the role of financial supervision at Union level, DG Regio currently has four audit units, including one devoted to coordination and relations with the

---

[89] Ibid, Art 125(4).
[90] Commission, 'Analysis of errors in cohesion policy for the years 2006–09' SEC (2011) 1179 final.
[91] Regulation 1303/2013, Art 126.
[92] Ibid, Art127.
[93] ECA, Opinion 7/2011 on the proposal for a Regulation laying down common provisions on the European Regional Development Fund et al, 8.
[94] See Regulation 1303/2013, Arts 149–50.
[95] Ibid, recitals 124–25.
[96] See, eg, Commission, Programming Period 2014–2020: Guidance on Monitoring and Evaluation (2013).

238   *Cohesion Policy*

EU anti-fraud body (OLAF) and the ECA. An impressive set of powers includes inspection by the Commission or a national authority at its request, and administrative sanctions applicable, for example, if significant deficiencies are identified in a Member State's management and control system.[97] Rightly, the Commission enforcement process is designed to ensure not only that past irregularities are corrected, but also that national systems are improved for the future: fire-watching as well as firefighting. So the Commission can request national authorities to implement financial corrections and if necessary impose them, request corrective actions so that expenditure not yet declared is properly processed and interrupt or suspend payments until appropriate corrections are completed.[98] A recent ECA report concluded that the Commission generally deals well with irregularities once they are discovered and is able in most cases to ensure that financial corrections are correctly applied. Notwithstanding the many declarations of cooperation, obtaining assurance that the deficiencies revealed in Member States' management and control systems are dealt with is more of a problem.[99]

Targeting?

Regulation 1303/2013 makes some significant changes in the financial management and control system. Reflecting demands both for streamlining and for increased controllability of projects and expenditure, these include an annual clearance of accounts regime designed to lighten the burden of document retention and avoid the risks associated with long drawn-out audit trails.[100] For similar reasons, if somewhat belatedly in the light of the ICT revolution, Member States must ensure that by the end of 2015 all exchanges of information between beneficiaries and managing authorities, certifying authorities, audit authorities and intermediate bodies can be carried out solely by electronic means.[101] The Commission has also come to recognise that requiring multiple separate agencies is itself burdensome and can blur responsibilities; Member States now have the option of merging the managing and certifying authorities.[102]

There is renewed emphasis on the better regulation principle of 'targeting'. As the Union legislature has evidently had to accept, some national and regional systems require more EU intervention than others to protect taxpayers' interests. The roots of the development lie in the 'Barroso road map' for improvements to

---

[97] Regulation 1303/2013, especially Art 75. The CJEU has been understandably protective of Commission sanctioning decisions in the name of probity: see, eg, Case C-500/99 P *Conserve Italia Soc Coop v Commission* [2002] ECR I-867; and Case C-330/01 *Hortiplant SAT v Commission* [2004] ECR I-1763.
[98] Ibid, especially Art 85.
[99] ECA, 'Special Report 3/2012, Structural Funds: Did the Commission successfully deal with deficiencies identified in the Member States' management and control systems?'
[100] COM (2011) 615 final, 11; Regulation 1303/2013, Arts 84, 138–39.
[101] Regulation 1303/2013, Art 122.
[102] Ibid, Art 123.

audit (see chapter two); and in particular the so-called 'contract of confidence', a soft law device that became enshrined in the 2007–13 programming vehicle, whereby those Member States able to demonstrate high quality systems could expect limited audit work by the Commission.[103] Under the legislative rubric of 'proportional control of operational programmes', the Commission now envisages 'full implementation of a risk-based audit methodology'.[104] Where the Commission judges a Member State to have strong, independent and well functioning audit authorities, it is only likely to audit operations where the DG's risk assessment identifies specific problems. Conversely, the Commission envisages focusing audit activities on 'high risk programmes' whereby expert resources can be used more efficiently and effectively. The political and administrative sensitivities are self-evident.

Blight on the System

Many of the reports into financial management of structural funds make unhappy reading, especially those from OLAF. The office has a very challenging role to play amid the billions of expenditure, the plethora of projects and the many levels of administration and supervision. Given that under the shared management system fraud investigations will usually be initiated by administrative or law enforcement agencies in Member States, the 'three Cs' of communication, cooperation and collaboration are central to OLAF's work. Bolstered by information exchange and cross-checks, coordination of forensic audits etc,[105] cases will often involve the long slog through false documentation to do with the costs of projects or the eligibility of beneficiaries, coupled perhaps with doses of official corruption.

According to the Commission's recent annual reports on the subject,[106] Italy, Bulgaria and Romania top the list for reported fraudulent irregularities in cohesion policy; big-spending Member States such as France and Spain continue to report very low numbers, an indication either of non-compliance with reporting principles or of the ability of national control systems to detect and deter fraud. The Commission estimates total annual financial losses of over €250 million, roughly two-thirds of the reported fraudulent irregularity in EU expenditure. Given the nature of the beast, it is reasonably hypothesised that the vast bulk of the fraud never sees the light of day.[107]

With resources stretched, OLAF has been very dependent on complaints. In 2012, it received 343 'incoming informations' relating to the structural funds:

[103] Regulation 1083/2006, Arts 62, 73.
[104] Regulation 1303/2013, Art 148; 'Analysis of errors in cohesion policy', [25].
[105] Now usefully underpinned by the revamped OLAF legislation: Regulation 883/2013/EU concerning investigations conducted by the European Anti-Fraud Office [2013] OJ L248/1.
[106] Commission, 'Protection of the European Union's financial interests – Fight against fraud' AR 2010 COM (2011) 595 final; AR 2011 COM (2012) 408 final; AR 2012 COM (2013) 548 final.
[107] See, eg, UK House of Lords EU Committee, *The Fight against Fraud on the EU's Finances*, 12th *Report of Session* (HL 2012–13) 158.

almost half the total. Most however came from private sources: the office considers that public bodies could do rather more.[108] Cohesion policy also accounts for the highest numbers of investigations (134); the amounts recommended for recovery (€63 million) and actually recovered (€33 million) appear modest however. The threat from organised crime is attested by several spectacular investigative results. Recently for example, assets worth €28 million were seized after the Italian authorities and OLAF jointly uncovered major fraud in an employment training scheme in Sicily.[109]

Structural funds have long been a prime concern of the ECA, as shown in a stream of special reports and opinions supplementing its core activity of auditing the final accounts settled by the Commission.[110] The ECA's formal assessment that projects are affected by a material level of error, and that both Member State and Commission control and supervisory systems are only partially effective in ensuring the legality and regularity of reimbursed expenditure, is an annual event. 'Non-fraudulent irregularity' in the sector far exceeds the official 2 per cent degree of tolerance in EU accounting. The best that can be said is that estimated levels of reimbursements erroneously made have reduced: from 11 to 12 per cent in 2006–07 to 6 to 7 per cent in 2011–12.[111] Commission analysis confirms that most of the administrative errors involve non-compliance either with the general eligibility criteria or – a telling finding in view of the complex sectoral regulation (see chapter six) – with the public procurement rules. Underscoring the case for regulatory targeting, very high concentrations of error have been identified in particular programmes in particular regions, especially in Spain and Italy.[112]

As recently as 2006, the Commission appeared in denial about the scale of the risks of fraud and error in the sector. In the light of additional control measures already taken, which included the development of financial corrections procedure, the good citizens of Europe should rest assured: the Commission required 'the very best systems', there were only 'isolated problems' and the monitoring committees in particular kept 'everyone on their toes'.[113] Under pressure from a parliament[114] demanding stricter enforcement and oversight in the light of continuing ECA criticism, the Commission has subsequently made considerable efforts to tackle financial mismanagement in the structural funds. A major new action plan in 2008[115] contained a litany of some 40 items where the Commission could do better, some of which, for example prompt action to suspend payments once serious weakness in a national control system is detected, or follow-up

---

[108] OLAF, AR 2012, [13]–[16].
[109] OLAF press release (April 2013).
[110] See, eg, ECA, 'Special Report 10/2001 Concerning the Financial Control of the Structural Funds'; 'Special Report 7/2003 On the Implementation of Assistance Programming for 2000–06'.
[111] ECA, AR 2011, 127–50; AR 2012, 133–63.
[112] SEC (2011) 1179 final, [9]–[13].
[113] D-G Regio, 'A Reformed Cohesion Policy for a Changing Europe' (2006), [3].
[114] See especially, EP Resolution of 19 February 2008 on Protection of the Communities' financial interests – Fight against fraud – Annual reports 2005 and 2006 (2006/2268(INI)).
[115] Commission, 'Action plan to strengthen the Commission's supervisory role under shared management of structural actions' COM (2008) 97 final.

enquiries on systemic errors identified by the ECA, are basic requirements of sound financial management under the Financial Regulation. An in-house evaluation in 2010 reported 'positive results' owing in part to sharper disciplines of compliance audit targeted on 'risk-prone areas'; however, Member State data on irregularities – long-criticised by the ECA for incompleteness and inaccuracy[116] – needed improvement.[117] The levels of financial correction implemented in the sector under shared management are sharply increased. In 2012 for example, they amounted to €3.1 billion, which was not that short of the total in the entire 2000–06 programming period (some €3.5 billion).[118] Meanwhile, some 200 decisions to interrupt or suspend payments were taken, involving over €5 billion.[119] The more the auditors look, the more irregularity they find.

In Search of Results

Yet the Commission must take care not to over prioritise compliance audit, whereby performance becomes defined largely in terms of legality and regularity to the exclusion of other good governance values and forms of accountability. Heightened tension between demands for simplification (less 'red tape') and, in the context of reform of the Financial Regulation, for tighter financial supervision, was also made apparent in the 2010 evaluation.[120] The ECA has many times highlighted the fact of a shared management system that is fundamentally input-based in the sense of being primarily concerned with the absorption of funding.[121] Effectively pointing up a hole in the heart of cohesion policy, the Commissioner for Regional and Urban Policy, Johannes Hahn, has pursued the argument, lamenting that 'up to now we have had a limited body of evidence on the question whether interventions make a real difference or not'.[122]

The talk in the new programming period is of 'reinforcing the performance orientation of the cohesion policy': more focus on 'result achievement'; and, more particularly, economic impact.[123] As the Commission puts it, 'citizens expect to know what has been achieved with public money and want to be sure that we run the best policy';[124] especially, it may be added, in a period of economic difficulty

---

[116] See, eg, 'Special Reports 10/2001 and 7/2003'.
[117] Commission, 'Impact of the action plan to strengthen the Commission's supervisory role under shared management of structural actions' COM (2010) 52 final, 3.
[118] Ibid, 2.
[119] AR 2012, 17–18.
[120] COM (2010) 52 final, 13; see also, C Mendez and J Bachtler, 'Administrative Reform and Unintended Consequences: An Assessment of the EU Cohesion Policy "Audit explosion"' (2011) 18 *Journal of European Public Policy* 746.
[121] See, eg, Opinion 7/2011, [9]–[10].
[122] Commissioner Hahn, speech 14 March 2013. The contribution of cohesion policy to the dynamics of economic development is much contested; for recent commentary, see T Farole, A Rodriguez-Pose and M Storper, 'Cohesion Policy in the European Union: Growth, Geography, Institutions' (2011) 49 *Journal of Common Market Studies* 1089.
[123] COM (2011) 615 final, 2.
[124] 'Programming Period 2014–2020', above (n 96) [1].

– high unemployment – in many parts of the enlarged Union. The development fits the strategic exercise of dominium power in the service of Union goals and hence the greater steering of poorer countries and regions via thematic concentration and conditionality. Emphasis is placed on improving monitoring and evaluation procedures and, in particular, on alternative forms of performance audit based on 'clear and measurable targets and outcome indicators'.[125] This feeds into the use, for example, of performance reserves (financial 'carrots' to reward progress towards objectives).[126]

The potential for a true 'audit explosion', whereby heavy use of evaluative techniques underwrites an expanded mode of Member State accountability that ranges far beyond rule compliance, is demonstrated. A dedicated governance infrastructure is already in place, centred on DG Regio's specialist evaluation unit. The Evaluation Network on Regional Policy draws together Member State officials in an epistemic community, while EVALSED is an online portal providing detailed guidance on evaluation methods and project assessment. The practical and technical difficulties should not be underestimated however. Officials concede that in the 'real world of socio-economic development we rarely have the time or resources to implement a comprehensive state of the art evaluation'.[127] Basic methodological problems rear their head, for example how to distinguish factors unrelated to a specific programme or how to assess possible long-term impacts.[128] A fixed list of result indicators was deemed inappropriate in the light of the diversity of regions and – a major concern with performance audit – the need not to suppress creativity and initiative.[129] More prosaically, the ECA confirms that national data requires 'significant improvements' for the expanded evaluation to be securely based.[130]

CONCLUSION

As job-sharing specifications go, planning, funding, managing, implementing and supervising myriad individual projects inside multiple Member State programmes is best described as challenging. While key administrative principles such as programming, concentration and additionality have stayed the course, successive policy periods show a continuous process of adaptation in which other principles such as proportionality and subsidiarity have come to the fore. Associated changes

---

[125] 'Fifth Cohesion Report', above (n 2) conclusions [2.4]; Council Regulation (EU) 1303/2013, Arts 54–57.
[126] Regulation 1303/2013, Art 20.
[127] DG Regio, 'EVALSED: The resource for the evaluation of Socio-Economic Development – Evaluation guide' (2012), [7].
[128] ECA Opinion 7/2011, [13]; and see further, J Hoerner and P Stephenson, 'Theoretical Perspectives on Approaches to Policy Evaluation in the EU: The Case of Cohesion Policy' (2012) 90 *Public Administration* 699.
[129] Commissioner Hahn, speech (14 March 2013).
[130] ECA Opinion 7/2011, [21].

in the administrative procedures have been driven by general EU developments such as Enlargement and reform of the Financial Regulation as well as by sectoral concerns about inadequate delivery and accounting. Sometimes appearing to creak under their own weight, the arrangements are characterised by a thick form of proceduralisation involving increased legislative provision.

Moving beyond the older intergovernmentalism versus multi-level governance debate, this chapter has examined the scope for steering of individual countries and regions through the many strings attached to structural funding. Operationalised through administrative procedures, this usage of the Union's huge dominium power in the form of novel partnership agreements, burgeoning types of conditionality and managerialist targets and measurements, is brought into sharp focus against a backdrop of economic recession and collective economic and industrial priorities. Standing for administrative and good governance values of cooperation, inclusion and voice, the partnership principle has enduring – and in this context, special – appeal. Typically involving both hard and soft law techniques, current attempts to breathe new life into intra-state partnerships in the light of divergent Member State practice also point up countervailing concerns about cost and effectiveness. The shared management system is seen as partly lacking in stability, with decentralised expenditure generating continuous pressure for greater supervision including at Union level. Notwithstanding attempts at more targeted supervision, the reworked framework of cohesion policy further serves to illustrate the extraordinary scale of EU penetration into domestic systems of public administration. Encompassing but ranging well beyond requirements of agency independence, the development is substantially driven by audit-style techniques directed to both financial accountability and evaluation of results.

Enough has been said to show the misleading countenance of elegant models of shared administration. They bear little relation to the complicated and sometimes poorly coordinated web of managerial, administrative and supervisory arrangements in cohesion policy. The better description is a veritable 'jungle' of intersecting bodies, powers and procedures where it can be very difficult to follow the money.

10

Agencies, Networks and Accountability: The Case of Europol

IN CHAPTER ONE, we focused on the Commission and its position as the main executive arm of the EU. We looked at its governance principles, its reform after a period of administrative crisis, the increasing trend to proceduralisation under the influence of a managerial ethos, the introduction of good governance values and the use of soft governance techniques for purposes of coordination and cooperation. We noted too the advancement of agencies as significant actors in the EU governance system and the speed with which, though theoretically barred by the non-delegation doctrine[1] from evolving into true regulatory agencies, EU agencies were beginning to acquire functions other than information gathering. We saw that EU agencies possess certain common characteristics: a limited mandate laid down in legislation; a standardised structure and administrative organisation based on a management board representative of Member States and an executive director elected by the management board. Staffed by EU officials, subject to the general EU staff and budget regulations, they are overseen by the Commission and subject to scrutiny by the Court of Auditors (ECA) and European Parliament (EP). In this chapter, we shall look more closely at these developments with a study of Europol, the European Police Office.

Our study comprises four main themes. Our first is the progression of Europol from an informal intergovernmental unit into a standard EU agency. Our second theme is Europol's role as a significant network actor both within and outside the EU. It is today a paradigm 'network organisation' and 'coordinator of networks', its objective being to act as a 'hub' for criminal information and support centre for law enforcement and law enforcement expertise. Europol's function as a criminal information hub leads on to our third theme of data processing procedures. Europol is formally authorised to collect, process, retain and exchange data on an unprecedented scale; it operates and is empowered to access extensive databanks. Highly specialised and specific data processing procedures are contained in the Europol Decision, which has been important in imposing a greater degree of control than is general in EU administration, where new, general data protection regulation is proving very difficult to agree. Our fourth theme is accountability. Europol

---

[1] See above, ch 1, p 32.

functions in areas of organised crime, terrorism and security often exempt in national systems from full transparency, accountability and control, a situation carried over into the third pillar of the EU. Our study shows how the position is changing, albeit slowly: the Commission and European Ombudsman (EO) have gained supervisory functions and, since Lisbon, the CJEU has jurisdiction.

EARLY DAYS AND EVOLUTION

Europol's origins lie in the arrangements for internal security cooperation among EC interior and justice ministers introduced at the Rome Summit in 1975 to counter terrorism and help coordinate policing, a Member State responsibility (the TREVI Group). The Group operated through five informal working groups, which played a substantial part in the secret planning that led ultimately to Europol. A second starting point was the European Drugs Unit,[2] a tiny information-gathering unit set up to assist police and other competent agencies with cross-border drugs offences. Ten years later, the Schengen agreement on open borders was signed on an intergovernmental basis by five of the then 10 Member States. This was the foundation for the Schengen Information System (SIS), a centrally administered database initially set up for purposes of border control and operated by the Commission. In 1999, when Europol became operational, it established an information exchange, which in 2002 transmuted into an information system; the Europol Information System (EIS), a data bank for which, as its name suggests, Europol was in charge.

At the 1991 Luxembourg Summit, the German Chancellor unexpectedly called for a 'European FBI' but the idea found no favour with other Member States, careful of their national sovereignty. Instead, Article K1 of the 1992 Maastricht Treaty authorised limited cooperation 'in connection with the organization of a Union-wide system for exchanging information within a European Police Office (Europol)' and Article K3 empowered Member States 'to cooperate for the purposes of preventing and combating terrorism, unlawful drug trafficking and other serious forms of international crime'. Not until 1995 was agreement secured for the agency, which became operational in 1999. The Conclusions of the 1999 Tampere Summit, which devoted much space to illegal immigration and cross-border crime, made specific mention of Europol's key role in supporting EU-wide crime prevention, agreed to the formation of Eurojust to facilitate coordination between police and prosecuting authorities and authorised the two agencies to cooperate.[3]

As we explained in Chapter one, in the third pillar, a process of informal lawmaking existed in which policy was developed by *ad hoc* groups of national experts and EU officials known as 'Friends of the Presidency', coordinated by the Council's General Secretariat. Policy was formalised in the legally ambiguous machinery of

[2] Joint action 95/73/JHA concerning the Europol Drugs Unit [1995] OJ L 62/1.
[3] Tampere Conclusions, [46].

Council joint action, joint positions, and conventions to which Member States could accede.[4] Proposals were discussed in secret in Council working parties and agreed at a meeting of Council home affairs ministers. Accountability measures were introduced only gradually, usually in response to great pressure and 'after professional and policy agendas ha[d] been implemented'.[5] In the manner that marked out third pillar policy-making, responsibility for preparing the Europol initiative was largely left to the K4 Coordinating Committee, a group of senior officials from national interior ministries reporting to the Council of Ministers.[6] The fact that composition varied from meeting to meeting according to subject matter made it hard to carry out its coordinating function effectively.[7] Supervision of Europol was attenuated, with oversight largely left to the K4 Committee; in the Council, to which Europol technically reported, oversight was provided by the rotating Council Presidency, whose representative chaired the Europol Management Board.

Europol came into being through an intergovernmental Convention, its status underlined by the fact that Member States were legally responsible for resourcing, albeit with an EU subvention. It then progressed to a Council Decision, which remains its present basis; at the time of writing an EU Regulation is proceeding through the legislative process somewhat less quickly than anticipated. In this sketchy framework, Europol advanced into a full-blown agency employing around 800 staff, hosting 145 Member State liaison officers and coordinating over 13,500 cross-border investigations annually – a progression that has involved a steady and secretive process of 'mission creep'. It was not the Commission but the Council of Ministers that authorised these irregular developments. Emphasising where the power lay, the Europol Convention provided for the Commission to have a single member on the Management Board with observer status.

MISSION CREEP: THE EUROPOL CONVENTION

The Europol Convention[8] established Europol as a body with legal personality, a Management Board (MB), Executive Director (ED), Financial Committee and Controller, thus starting it down the road to EU agency status. Article 2(1) of the Convention underlined Europol's networking function. Its objective would be

---

[4] See on the legal status of these instruments, S Peers, *EU Justice and Home Affairs Law*, 3rd edn (Oxford: OUP, 2011) 14–15.

[5] M Den Boer, 'Towards an Accountability Regime for an Emerging European Policing Governance' (2002) 12 *Policing and Society* 275, 277. And see N Walker, *Policing in a Changing Constitutional Order* (London: Sweet & Maxwell, 2000) 256.

[6] T Bunyan, 'Trevi, Europol and the European State' in T Bunyan (ed), *Statewatching the New Europe* (London: Statewatch, 1993).

[7] E Guild, 'The Constitutional Consequences of Lawmaking in the Third Pillar of the European Union' in P Craig and C Harlow (eds), *Lawmaking in the European Union* (Dordrecht: Kluwer Law International, 1998) 75–78.

[8] Council Act of 26 July 1995 [1995] OJ C316/1. The Convention came into force in 1998. See S Peers, 'Europol: The Final Step in the Creation of an "Investigative and Operational" European Police Force', Statewatch Analysis 2007.

to improve . . . the effectiveness and co-operation of the competent authorities in the Member States in preventing and combating terrorism, unlawful drug trafficking and other serious forms of international crime where there are factual indications that an organised criminal structure is involved and two or more Member States are affected by the forms of crime in question in such a way as to require a common approach by the Member States owing to the scale, significance and consequences of the offences concerned.

Article 2(1) was in many ways restrictive: it limited Europol's function to serious, organised, cross-border, international crime and provided that policy priorities were to be settled by the Council. In common with 'first wave' agencies, Europol's core tasks were information gathering, information exchange and information processing. It would gather, collate, manage and retain data and use it to provide 'strategic analyses' or 'risk assessments', designed to enable stakeholders to develop strategies for the prevention and inhibition of organised crime.[9] These innocuous sounding functions remain Europol's core functions today. The Convention dealt in some detail with maintenance of the database necessary for the performance of its main objectives and the persons able to access the information and a supervisory body was set up to ensure the adequacy of data protection. We look more closely at these important provisions below.

There were three Protocols to the Europol Convention, each of which expanded Europol's competence. Protocol 1 covered money laundering.[10] Protocol 2 was in some ways restrictive in that it curtailed a more ambitious Danish proposal to expand Europol's remit and to facilitate data transfer with third countries, in exchange for a minor extension of EP supervision. But it did give Europol competence to 'participate in a support capacity in joint investigation teams', to 'request Member States to start investigations and participate in joint investigation teams' and to cover the coordination, organisation and implementation of investigative and operational action carried out jointly with a Member State's competent authorities or in the context of joint investigation teams, where appropriate in liaison with European or third countries' bodies.[11] Its operational functions were increasing. There was steady 'mission creep', a process facilitated by the fact that new offences could simply be annexed to the Convention without the need for amendment (Article 43(3)).

The degree of mission creep was on this occasion slight enough to persuade a Select Committee of the UK House of Lords that Europol's support and advisory role would not be affected. But if, as had been advocated

> a fully operational role were proposed for Europol, this would be a very significant change, for which there should be a different legal basis, which could then be the subject of a major debate across the EU. It is important that Europol should not develop a

---

[9] J Parkin, 'EU Home Affairs Agencies and the Construction of EU Internal Security' (2012) CEPS Paper, Liberty and Security in Europe No 53.
[10] First Protocol to Europol Convention (powers re money laundering) [2000] OJ C358/1.
[11] Council Act [2002] OJ C312/1. JITs are set up in terms of the Convention on Mutual Assistance in Criminal Matters: Council Act [2000] OJ C197/3.

248 *Agencies: The Case of Europol*

major operational role simply as a result of a succession of relatively small changes to its remit.[12]

Protocol 3[13] exemplifies precisely the sort of 'mission creep' that had worried the House of Lords. There are substantial extensions of competence: cross-border public order policing, as at international football matches, would now be added to the mandate. Rights to access data were extended; wider access to the information system with greatly simplified access procedures was authorised. The House of Lords noted with disapproval that the Danish proposals for deeper parliamentary scrutiny had been significantly watered down in the process of negotiations; they raised 'important issues about the nature of Europol's accountability and the respective roles of the European Parliament and national parliaments' that merited wider consideration.[14] In the event, fairly extensive rule-making powers were offset only by a minimal grant to the EP of supervisory power, exercised through a special report on the work of Europol, which had to be forwarded annually to the EP by the Council Presidency. The EP also had to be consulted before the Convention was 'amended in any way'[15] yet the recitals to Protocol 3 state baldly that the Europol Convention needed to be amended 'in the light of the discussions within the Council on a proposal from the Management Board'. This was certainly not the major policy debate envisaged by the House of Lords in its critique of Protocol 2.

The Convention Model of Rule-Making

Before the Convention came into force, its provisions on data compilation were augmented by detailed provisions for data protection set out in four separate sets of rules. These were presented as establishing a regulatory framework for operational cooperation with third states and EU or non-EU bodies. As implementing measures, they did not suffer the inconvenience of being shown to any parliament, which did not deter the House of Lords EU Committee from making a retrospective scrutiny that noted with regret 'the defensive attitude of the Council'.[16] The committee suggested that the texts should have been more widely circulated with a view to eliminating ambiguities and infelicities in 'a number of not necessary compatible sets of rules'. It thought the Rules often badly integrated and that the drafting 'err[ed] too far on the side of trying to protect Europol and

---

[12] Select Committee on European Communities, *Europol: Joint Supervisory Body* (HL 1998–99, 71) para 31, scrutinising Council Framework Decision 2002/465/JHA of 13 June 2002 on joint investigation teams [2002] OJ L162/1.
[13] Council Act [2004] OJ C 2/1.
[14] UK House of Lords Select Committee on the European Union, *Europol's Role in Fighting Crime* (HL 2002–03, 43) paras 32–34.
[15] Art 34 of the Europol Convention.
[16] UK House of Lords Select Committee on European Communities, *Europol: Third Country Rules* (HL 1997–98, 135) para 92, discussing Art 4(4) of Europol 38.

its officials from criticism'. Provisions leaving wide discretion to Europol and its Director were possibly ultra vires the powers granted by the Convention – notably the Director's powers to supply data to third counties and non-EU bodies without any formal agreement and in circumstances that allowed for circumvention of the EU data protection rules.[17] One set of rules seemed to be incompatible with human rights law. The committee recommended that human rights clauses be inserted in all third-party agreements to 'give a clear indication of the standards expected by the EU of itself and its Members and of those with whom it deals'.[18] What the committee had pinpointed was that procedures resembling those used for implementing legislation were here being used for significant policy change for which legislation would be more appropriate.

Highlighting the function of rules in promoting good administration, a witness commented that the Council had

> done Europol a disservice by framing rules with what appear to be deliberate loopholes because without really rigorous rules to back them up, senior officials of Europol are going to find it hard to ensure that over-zealous or over-ambitious employees do not bend the rules unnecessarily.[19]

The UK Data Protection Registrar made a similar point concerning the role of administrative procedure in the protection of rights. She thought the Rules should provide *expressly* for information received from third-party states and bodies to be subject to the same controls and create the same rights as information transmitted within the EU because 'the Rules are going to be the working documents. The Rules are going to be what are used day-by-day by those who are handling the information, and who must make sure that the rights of individuals are protected'.[20]

Whether the new powers that Europol was steadily accumulating were 'executive' or merely 'operational' in character is perhaps immaterial;[21] the reality was that they were sufficiently substantial to raise serious questions as to whether the internal administrative arrangements were robust enough to support Europol's functions. (The ad hoc management arrangements were deplored in a further House of Lords report in 2007.)[22] Moreover, the questions of external accountability that had arisen in negotiations for amendment remained un-discussed and unsettled. By the time the amending protocols finally entered into force in 2007, however, the Commission had already expressed concern at the lack of

---

[17] Art 6 of Council Decision 2009/934 now expressly prohibits transfer of information in the absence of an agreement assuring confidentiality but Art 11 maintains the criticised exception.
[18] *Europol: Third Country Rules*, above (n 16) 135, paras 6, 86, 87.
[19] Ibid, para 69, citing evidence from Justice at QQ 166–68.
[20] HL, *Europol: Third Country Rules*, above (n 16) 135, para 17, QQ 137–38.
[21] Parkin, above (n 9) [3.1.1.2].
[22] UK House of Lords European Union Committee, *Europol: Coordinating the Fight against Serious and Organised Crime* (HL 2007–08), 183.

democratic accountability and had tabled a proposal to replace the Convention with a Council Decision.[23]

By now Europol had moved some way towards developing a major operational and policymaking role through a succession of relatively small changes to its remit that brought it closer to the model of a true regulatory agency, which combines executive functions and quasi-regulatory powers.[24] The institutional framework of third pillar operations had provided an opportunity for Europol to be not only 'on the receiving end of policy implementation', but indirectly to frame common responses to given policy issues.[25] This position had been achieved through the regular production of organised crime reports based on a methodology that enabled systematic assessment of crime and the threat of crime (the OCTA). Europol called the OCTA 'a new approach' and 'a first step towards a paradigm change in policing' that would provide a forward-looking and proactive approach to fighting organised crime.[26] Commentators remarked how, 'with Member States increasingly adhering to Europol's policy recommendations, Europol has expanded its (*de facto* not *de jure*) role in EU organised crime policy-making'.[27] From protocol to protocol, its transnational networking capacity had been greatly enhanced, enabling it to work through a combination of operational procedure and skilful networking. Critics were beginning to see the agency as a policymaking body with 'substantial responsibility to pinpoint the areas, activities or populations which represent the greatest threats and which should be given priority in the fight against crime'.[28] Europol's networking processes allowed it to draw on a wide range of information sources that were not necessarily robust. Moreover, the secrecy and absence of sturdy accountability machinery was putting its scientific output beyond the reach of evaluation and democratic controls.

THE EUROPOL DECISION: A SUBSTANTIVE TRANSFORMATION

In contrast to the Convention, the Council Decision, adopted in 2009 by the Justice and Home Affairs Council after a public hearing organised by the EP, was founded on a Commission consultation and proposal.[29] Its objectives were

---

[23] Commission, Proposal for a Council Decision establishing the European Police Office (Europol) COM (2006) 817 final. And see A De Moor and G Vermeulen, 'The Europol Council Decision: Transforming Europol into an Agency of the European Union' (2010) 47 *Common Market Law Review* 1089, 1093–94.

[24] See M Shapiro, 'The Problems of Independent Agencies in the United States and European Union' (1997) 4 *Journal of European Public Policy* 276.

[25] Parkin, above (n 9) [3.1.1.2].

[26] AR 2008 27.

[27] H Carrapico and F Trauner, 'Europol and its Influence on EU Policy-making on Organized Crime: Analyzing Governance Dynamics and Opportunities' (2013) 14 *Perspectives in European Politics and Society* 357, 362.

[28] Parkin, above (n 9) [3.1.1.2].

[29] Council Decision 2009/371/JHA of 6 April 2009 establishing the European Police Office (Europol) [2009] OJ L121/37. And see generally De Moor and Vermeulen, above (n 24).

expressed as being: (i) to enhance the role of the EP in the control of Europol through its involvement in the adoption of an EU budget and establishment plan; (ii) to subject Europol to standard EU financial procedures; and (iii) to subject Europol to 'the general rules and procedures applicable to similar Union entities'. This would ensure administrative simplification, allowing Europol to devote more of its resources to its core tasks. The Decision described Europol's objectives in terms of networking: it was to 'support and strengthen action by the competent authorities of the Member States and their mutual cooperation in preventing and combating organised crime, terrorism and other forms of serious crime affecting two or more Member States'. The expanded competences now covered organised crime, terrorism and 'other forms of serious crime . . . affecting two or more Member States in such a way as to require a common approach'; it extended also to 'related' or ancillary crimes. As 'principal tasks', Europol had the following:

- **Information and intelligence gathering,** carried out through the maintenance of extensive data banks to which its many partners were given access, with ancillary powers to prepare threat assessments, strategic analyses and general situation reports.
- **Communication** with 'the competent authorities' of Member States, through the circulation of assessments profiling the structure and operation of organised crime groups, the main types of organised crime affecting the EU and the state of the terrorist challenge across the EU.
- **Assistance** to national units in investigations and in policing 'major international events'.

Loyal Cooperation

Article 7(4) of the Decision placed familiar procedural obligations on Member States. It obliged them to supply Europol on their own initiative with the information and intelligence necessary for it to carry out its tasks and to respond to Europol's requests for information, intelligence and advice. They must also keep information and intelligence up to date, evaluate it in accordance with national law and transmit it to the relevant authorities, issue requests for advice, information, intelligence and analysis to Europol and supply Europol with information for storage in its databases. The reality was rather different, as the UK House of Lords learned in 1997. The 'vast majority' of information exchanges between liaison bureaux occurred outside the formal systems and over 80 per cent of exchanges were bilateral; more regrettably, Europol received only 10 per cent of the information on terrorism that Member States were obliged to supply.[30] Enlargement would accentuate the problem. In 2007, the Council's Multidisciplinary Group on Organized Crime reported that very few Member States were technically 'completely ready to operate the

---

[30] HL, *Europol: Third Country Rules*, above (n 16) 135, para 50 in reliance on evidence from Professor de Kerchove, the EU Counter-terrorism Coordinator (Q 210).

system'.[31] A year later, the High-Level Advisory Group stressed the need to reinforce Europol by integrating police file management and improving data transfers from Member States.[32]

In the context of a package of policies designed to strengthen law enforcement cooperation,[33] the Stockholm Programme (below) therefore stressed the need for integration, calling on Europol to 'become a hub for information exchange between the law enforcement authorities of the Member States, a service provider and a platform for law enforcement services'.[34] Europol talked in response of an increased role in European policing as the 'EU criminal information hub' and the need to undertake 'activities needed to ensure that Europol has the right capabilities to achieve its workflows'.[35] But the problem was recurrent. In 2012, a MB member told the Rand Survey that one of Europol's weaknesses was lack of commitment of the Member States; they did not share information with Europol in a timely way, especially in the field of terrorism.[36]

Europol as Rule-Maker

Europol was also gaining rule-making powers: its MB may make rules governing joint investigations and is empowered to conclude agreements and working arrangements both with EU institutions, bodies, offices and agencies and with international organisations and other public bodies, though only with authority from the Council after consultation with the EP. However, agreements concerning the exchange of operational, strategic or technical information need approval from the Council after consultation with the MB (unless access to personal data and classified information is involved when the Joint Supervisory Body (JSB) must be consulted). Thus, the Decision maintained substantial powers for Europol to shape procedural rules and to conclude significant international agreements, subject to the classic *Meroni* compromise that these must be at least rubber-stamped by the Council. It was authorised to 'establish and maintain cooperative relations with third bodies'. It could enter into operational cooperation agreements with third states and parties to become 'associates' and enter into 'cooperative relationships' with international institutions like the World Bank

---

[31] Council Doc 13321/2/07, 29.
[32] Report of the Informal High-Level Advisory Group on the Future of European Home Affairs Policy, *Freedom, Security, Privacy - European Home Affairs in an Open World*, Council Doc 11657/08.
[33] Implemented in Council Decisions 2008/615/JHA of 23 June 2008 [2008] OJ L210/12; 2008/616/JHA of 23 June 2008 [2008] OJ L210/12; 2008/617/JHA of 23 June 2008 [2008] OJ L210/73. And see Commission, 'Overview of information management in the area of freedom, security and justice' (Communication) COM (2010) 385.
[34] 'An Open and Secure Europe Serving and Protecting Citizens' [2010] OJ C115/1, [4.3.1].
[35] Europol Work Programme for 2013 (11 July 2012); Europol Strategy 2010–2014 (11 February 2010).
[36] Rand Europe, 'Evaluation of the implementation of the Europol Council Decision and of Europol's activities' (2012) (hereafter 'Rand', available on the Europol website) [4.1]; De Moor and Vermeulen, above (n 23) 1099.

and International Monetary Fund, both concerned with the recovery of criminal assets. Not only did Europol sign operational agreements, which permit the exchange of personal data, but also strategic agreements, which do not. The rules and agreements governing these arrangements are drawn up by the Europol MB, though they are formally made by the Council, which also settles the list of states with which agreements may be signed.[37] This is a cooperative form of rule-making notably prone to rubber-stamping. Agreements were proliferating and a complete overhaul of the Council's peremptory approach to rule-making was long overdue.

How far involvement of the EP acting through its LIBE Committee represented an extension of control and accountability is debateable in the light of an inter-institutional squabble that took place shortly before the Lisbon Treaty came into force. The Council sent to the EP four Europol proposals dealing with its core areas of activity: its analysis work files, rules on confidentiality, exchange of personal data with its partners and third country agreements. The EP adopted the advice of its LIBE Committee to reject the proposals, arguing that Europol rules should not be amended until the EP became a co-legislator in the area; they asked the Council to withdraw the proposals and table new proposals after the Lisbon Treaty had come into force. Instead, the General Secretariat, after considering the EP opinion, requested the Permanent Representatives Committee (Coreper) to put the draft Decision on the Council agenda as an A-item, which was duly adopted.[38]

Good Governance

The British House of Lords had criticised the internal management of Europol, stressing the need for continuity, with a chairman elected by the MB for at least two years.[39] The Europol Decision recognised the need for better governance, providing greater clarity and openness and simplified procedures, with the establishment of a 'common procedure for decision-making'. The Decision allocates decision-making responsibility clearly; it lists the responsibilities of the Director, who is appointed by the Council for three years from a list of at least three candidates presented by the MB, which must introduce regular appointment procedures. The MB is responsible for establishing the principles and limits under which data processing and storage systems shall operate and, acting on a proposal from the Director after consultation with the JSB, the MB can also set up new systems. New public management (NPM) style managerial measures are applied

---

[37] See Council Decision 2009/935/JHA of 30 November 2009 determining the list of third States and organisations with which Europol shall conclude agreements [2009] OJ L325/12.

[38] EP press release, 'MEPs criticise Council and demand democratic scrutiny' (November 2009); Council Inter-institutional File 2009/0808 (CNE); Council Decision 2009/934/JHA of 30 November 2009 adopting the implementing rules governing Europol's relations with partners, including the exchange of personal data and classified information [2009] OJ L325/6.

[39] The first Director resigned in 2004 and, after an interim period, the present Director, Rob Wainwright, was appointed in 2009 to oversee the reforms; in 2012, his appointment was renewed until 2017.

to the agency, including establishment of policy objectives, performance indicators, report and reporting and the standard EU budgetary procedures.

Thus, after the Decision Europol followed the standard Commission formula for a regulatory agency:[40] a statutory mandate set out in regulation; a representative management board with responsibility for laying down general guidelines and adopting work programmes within the terms of reference and priorities established by the Council; an executive director responsible for the programme of activities and proper management of the agency; a financial committee and scientific advisory committees; a staff of EU officials governed by the EU staff regulations. The Commission model also requires that regulatory agencies, although they require 'a certain degree of organisational and functional autonomy', must be accountable 'to the institutions, operators concerned and more generally the public'. Their activities therefore 'need to be fully transparent so that the various players concerned can effectively monitor their operations'.[41] This is perhaps a tall order for an agency whose core activity is the processing of sensitive data.

As already noted, the Decision enhanced control over Europol by the EP, though openness is still strictly limited; Europol presents only a redacted public report to the EP, although it presents an extended version in secret to the Council.[42] Curtin believes that the EP was at first slow to debate the Europol Annual Review or call in directors for questioning, though it later changed its ways.[43] The most complete evaluation of Europol's performance by Rand Europe records some unease among consultees that the EP might start to intervene in operations; it recommends the agency to develop a strategy to deal with possible future change to Europol accountability.[44] This is an important recommendation in the light of the fact that the stronger check on Europol activity currently provided by the JSB is to be wound up by the new legislation.

EUROPOL AND DATA PROTECTION

Mention has been made throughout this chapter of extensive data banks through which Europol carries out its information and intelligence gathering functions. In recent years these databases have proliferated until they form a confusing network. Europol's powers to collect and process data, operate and access extensive data banks, raise concerns over civil liberties and human rights. The problem is accentu-

---

[40] Commission, 'The operating framework for the European regulatory agencies' (Communication) COM (2002) 718 final. And see above, ch 1.

[41] Ibid, 5.

[42] D Curtin, 'Delegation to EU Non-majoritarian Agencies and Emerging Practices of Public Accountability' in D Gerardin et al (eds), *Regulation through Agencies in the EU. A New Paradigm of European Governance* (Cheltenham: Edward Elgar, 2005) 108.

[43] D Curtin, 'Holding (Quasi-)Autonomous EU Administrative Actors to Public Account: Beyond Delegation and Control' (2007) 13 *European Law Journal* 523, 536–37.

[44] Rand [11.6]. In Table 11.1 Rand records 11 visits by Europol staff to the EP in 2011.

ated by the multiplicity of agencies and databases, which are separately regulated, with overlapping functions and ever-wider access provisions that create a risk of unauthorised access. Thus Europol is directly responsible for the technical and operational aspects of the EIS, for oversight of the system and for deletion of inappropriate data. A Data Protection Officer ensures 'in an independent manner' the lawfulness of data transactions and compliance with the Europol Decision.[45] The EIS, 'a reference system' for offences, individuals involved and other related data based on information supplied by and accessible to Member States, Europol and its cooperation partners, incorporates the Secure Information Exchange Network Application (SIENA), an information exchange platform designed to enable swift, secure and user-friendly communication and exchange of operational and strategic crime-related information and intelligence between Europol, Member States and third parties. The Schengen Information System, today upgraded as SIS II, deals with the movement of people within the EU. SIS II is a database that can hold many millions of entries[46] and is accessible to Europol. SIS II is now operated by the EU Agency for Large-Scale IT Systems (EU-LISA), established in 2011, which also manages VIS (the EU database for visas) and EURODAC (the database of asylum-seekers' and irregular migrants' fingerprints).[47]

From its inception Europol has possessed a significant executive role in data processing. Article 10(1) of the Europol Decision authorised Europol to process information and intelligence, including personal data 'insofar as it is necessary for the achievement of its objectives' and to establish and maintain systems processing personal data. In addition, it has gradually accrued wide powers to transfer data to third countries, their public authorities and agencies and, although these agreements are formally authorised by the Council, control is relaxed under a concession allowing Europol to receive and use information (including personal data and classified information) *prior* to the conclusion of any agreement 'insofar as is necessary for the legitimate performance of its tasks'. These powers are exercisable after consultation with the JSB by the MB in conjunction with the Director. The English Information Commissioner sees this as a matter for concern, as third states do not always provide data protection equivalent to the requirements imposed on Europol.[48]

Although like all EU agencies Europol is authorised to formulate its own organisational procedures,[49] its specialised data processing procedures are not only regulated by but also specified in great detail in the founding Europol Decision. This specificity has been important in imposing a greater degree of control over data processing by Europol than has been the case in other policy areas where data

---

[45] See on the role of the DPO, Rand [7.5.1].
[46] Regulation (EC) 1987/2006 of 20 December 2006 on the establishment, operation and use of the second generation Schengen Information System (SIS II) [2006] OJ L381/4.
[47] Regulation (EU) 1077/2011 [2011] OJ L286/1.
[48] Evidence from the English IC to the House of Lords: HL, *Europol: Third Country Rules*, above (n 16) 135, paras 51–62.
[49] MB, Rules of Procedure [2010] OJ C46/8.

protection has so far remained largely a Member State responsibility. (It is currently, as we shall see later, in a transitional phase). Data protection within the Community is covered by the elderly EC Directive 95/46,[50] in need of urgent reform, and within the EU by a Council Framework Decision on data processing in criminal matters,[51] which followed the Prüm Convention (Schengen III) on DNA profiling and fingerprint databases.[52] Europol, Eurojust and the SIS were expressly excluded.

In contrast, the recitals to the Europol Decision explicitly state that Charter rights and the principle of public access to official documents are to be respected. The Decision requires Europol to guarantee a minimum level of data protection corresponding to the principles in the Council of Europe Convention on Data Protection as updated.[53] It is detailed and specific; what data may or may not be included in the EIS is closely regulated and only specified data, such as name and address, or criminal convictions, can be included. Data subjects are confined to persons who have committed, participated in or are likely to commit an offence in which Europol has competence, and inclusion must be based on 'factual indications' or reasonable suspicion. The right to input and retrieve data is reserved for the Europol Director, Deputy Directors and duly empowered staff, national units and liaison officers. Inputting parties must be clearly identifiable as the party responsible for overall legality of retention and retrieval and their particulars must be entered. National units and transactions between them are governed by national laws, as is access to the index function created by Europol for its analysis files, to be formulated in a specified format. Data is to be used by Europol only 'for the performance of its tasks' and can be used and transmitted only to prevent 'serious forms of crime'; it may be stored only so long as is necessary for these purposes and necessity must be reviewed triennially.

This is an area of shared responsibility; responsibility for the accuracy of information is strictly apportioned between Europol and the Member State concerned and it falls to Member States to ensure compliance with the law in every exchange of information between themselves and Europol. Where the data inputs do not tally, the parties concerned are to consult each other and reach agreement. Where a party not entitled to input data wishes to modify, correct or delete or supplement data, it must immediately inform the inputting party, which must examine such information without delay and if necessary modify, supplement, correct or delete the data immediately. If a Member State objects, it must give its reasons to

---

[50] Directive 95/46/EC on the protection of individuals with regard to the processing of personal data and on the free movement of such data [1995] OJ L281/31. Regulation (EC) 45/2001 ([2001] OJ L8/1) applies data protection law to Community institutions.

[51] Council Framework Decision 2008/977/JHA on the protection of personal data processed in the framework of police and judicial cooperation in criminal matters [2008] OJ L350/60.

[52] The Prüm Convention on the stepping up of cross border cooperation, particularly in combating terrorism, cross border crime and illegal migration was signed in 2005: see House of Lords European Union Committee, *Prüm: an effective weapon against terrorism and crime* (HL 2006–07, 90).

[53] Council of Europe Convention for the Protection of Individuals with regard to Automatic Processing of Personal Data (28 January 1981).

Europol, permitting evaluation of the ground for refusal in terms of the conditions of the Decision. Similar provisions cover Europol's analysis files, which must be indexed so as to allow interested parties to ascertain whether analysis files contain information pertinent to them. The procedures for the design of the index function, including conditions of access, are to be designed by the MB after obtaining advice from the JSB. These are specialised and highly technical provisions; how far they can be monitored and supervised by non-specialist bodies is very much open to question. There is heavy reliance in practice on the expertise of the JSB.

SUPERVISION AND CONTROL: THE JOINT SUPERVISORY BODY

The JSB is an independent body established under the Europol Decision to ensure rights to data protection. Made up of two members from national data supervisory bodies, whose own independence must be assured according to EU law,[54] the JSB combines firefighting and fire-watching activities. As firefighter, it handles requests from individuals to check, access or amend personal data records and appeals from refusals by Europol. A sub-committee examines the appeal and must 'cooperate closely' with the national supervisory body or competent judicial body in coming to a decision, which needs a two-thirds majority to overrule a national objection. Decisions, which must be implemented by Europol, can be taken only after Europol and Member States concerned have been heard; perhaps surprisingly, no due process rights for applicants are specified other than to be notified. The JSB calls this 'a simplified legal regime for citizens' rights'[55] and, for purposes of an ombudsman investigation, the JSB has been defined as an administrative body independent of Europol, a device that opens its practice to scrutiny by the EO.[56]

The supervisory or fire-watching activities of the JSB are more far-reaching and significant. To carry out its basic remit of protecting individual rights and monitoring Europol's use of personal data, the JSB works closely with the Europol Data Protection Officer and unit. It has rights to access all Europol premises, documents, files and data files and makes annual inspections. Moving outside Europol, the JSB has surveyed the Europol national units to see that data processing corresponded with Europol competences, recommending the introduction of guidelines and harmonised data input criteria.[57] It issues Opinions on rules, projects and policies and, as indicated earlier, in draft relationship agreements. Its Opinions are undoubtedly expert. Its participation in negotiations between Europol and the US was, for

[54] See Case C-518/07 *Commission v Germany* [2010] ECR I-1885; Case C-614/10 *Commission v Austria* (judgment of 16 October 2012).
[55] Fifth Activity Report 2008–2012, 8–9. In that period, Europol handled around 200 requests for access annually and the JSB received 13 requests to check and five appeals.
[56] Inv 111/2008/TS. The EO cannot investigate if a judicial remedy is open.
[57] JSB, 'Report on the conditions for Europol National Units in relation to data processing in Europol's Information System no 12-61' (2012).

example, welcomed by a House of Lords committee as 'potentially the best way to ensure satisfactory data protection provisions in such agreements', though it is significant too that the Committee also expressed disappointment that the JSB did not take a sufficiently independent approach.[58] The two Opinions from the JSB on the draft Europol Regulation (below) showed careful textual analysis and it aims at transparency. So far as possible JSB proceedings are public and accessible to the public in terms of Regulation 1049/2001.[59] Its reports are accessible and clear if highly technical and not wholly comprehensible to a non-expert reader. For this reason in particular, it is hard for a non-technical observer to assess how effective the JSB is, whether its procedures are fit for purpose and whether it constitutes adequate machinery for control or accountability.

The draft Europol Regulation (below) proposes abolition of the JSB and transfer of the role of independent external supervisory body to the European Data Protection Supervisor (EDPS) on the grounds that 'streamlined and consistent data protection supervision over all EU agencies by an EU data protection body could be seen as advantageous'.[60] This argument may seem a little disingenuous since data protection provisions are not being 'streamlined'. It may be significant too that the Commission's impact assessment (IA) weighed the well-established JSB record against its lack of enforcement powers and dependence on Europol for funding. Change has been welcomed by the EDPS as likely to ensure 'a strengthened and effective supervision of Europol'[61] yet the EDPS, in contrast to the JSB, has never had responsibility or experience in the criminal law and policing field. Perhaps naturally, its demise is strongly opposed by the JSB, which has rightly called for effective joint supervision through 'an independent and effective joint supervision structure with equal participation of each national DPA and the EDPS'.[62]

RE-ORDERING THE BLOCKS: THE EUROPOL REGULATION

Article 88 of the Lisbon Treaty called for a new legislative base for Europol, in the shape of regulations adopted by ordinary legislative procedure to 'determine Europol's structure, operation, field of action and tasks'. This call must be read against the background of the Stockholm Programme, which set the priorities for the area of justice, freedom and security.[63] Its outlook was apparently positive and coherent; it linked the idea of a Europe of rights and justice with the development

---

[58] HL, *Europol's Role in Fighting Crime*, above (n 14) 43, para 53.
[59] JSB, Rules of Procedure [2010] OJ C45.
[60] Commission Staff Working Document, SWD (2013) 98 final.
[61] EDPS, 'Opinion on the Data Reform Package'. But see Resolution of the Conference of European Data Protection Authorities on ensuring an adequate level of data protection at Europol (Lisbon, 16–17 May 2013), which suggests that the level of data protection will be diminished.
[62] JSB, Opinion 13/31 with respect to the proposal for a Regulation on Europol (10 June 2013) 10.
[63] European Council, 'The Stockholm Programme- An open and secure Europe serving and protecting citizens' [2010] OJ C115/1.

of an internal security strategy to 'enhance police and judicial cooperation in criminal matters'. At the same time, this was an era of mounting concern over misuse of data banks, the growth of a 'surveillance state' and consequential erosion of civil liberties.[64] Unusually, Article 8 of the European Charter of Fundamental Rights (ECFR) creates a right protecting personal data; it must be processed fairly for specified purposes either on the basis of consent or for 'some other legitimate basis laid down by law'. Everyone has a right to access data collected concerning them and to have it rectified with compliance guaranteed by an independent authority. Article 16 TFEU called for legislation to secure this right.

Echoing Stockholm, the Commission called on Europol to evolve and 'become a hub for information exchange between the law enforcement authorities of the Member States, a service provider and a platform for law enforcement services'.[65] ECFR Article 8 afforded an opportunity for the Commission to launch procedures designed to engrain a 'single shared approach to information exchange amongst EU Member States and authorities'.[66] Its proposal for a regulation – which is, at the time of writing, progressing slowly through the law-making process – was expansive; it watered down the definition of 'serious crime' and suggested a coordinating role in investigations. It also had an integrating objective, 'to place Europol as a **unique** centre where all law enforcement information falling within Europol's competence must be processed'.[67] This was to be achieved (with a sweetener of increased financial support) by the creation of an obligation on Member States to cooperate with Europol in the fulfilment of its tasks. In addition, national liaison units would become the first (and only?) point of contact with Europol. Enforcement of these provisions would be through the normal procedural mechanisms of report and supervision; national bodies would inform Europol, which would be under a correlative obligation to report not only to the EU institutions, but also to national parliaments on the 'extent to which individual Member States provide it with information'. This looks much like a takeover bid.

Management and Administration

The draft Regulation places responsibility for the administrative and managerial tasks of the agency, including planning and budgetary planning and implementation of the work programmes, on the ED, who is in turn accountable to the MB which appoints him together with Deputy Directors. The MB remains

[64] EDPS Inventory 2013, 'Data Protection is essential across all EU policy areas', EDPS/13/1 (18/01/2013).
[65] Commission, 'Proposal for a Regulation on the European Union Agency for Law Enforcement Cooperation and Training (Europol) and Repealing Decisions 2009/371/JHA and 2005/681/JHA' COM (2013) 173 final.
[66] Commission, 'Strengthening law enforcement cooperation in the EU: the European Information Exchange Model (EIXM)' (Communication) COM (2012) 735 final.
[67] JSB, Opinion 13/31, 6. Our high-lighting is significant.

representative of Member States and members must be appointed on the basis of their knowledge of law enforcement cooperation; there is one non-voting Commission member. The MB's functions are clearly delineated. It decides the budget and multi-annual and annual work programmes and has power to make procedural rules, including the rules for appointment of the Director. The MB may appoint a small Executive Board, with a Commission representative, with a view to reinforcing supervision of administrative and budgetary management, in particular on audit matters. Parliamentary control is marginally enhanced (below).

Whether the managerial structures and processes are adequate as a basis for Europol's rapidly expanding activities is debateable. In the last 10 years, its staff has expanded from around 300 to over 800, under the control of a Director, three deputies and a MB that meets twice yearly. As Busuioc discovered in her work on EU agencies, management boards are often a weak link in the accountability chain, usually due to agency design.[68] They are generally too large and members may be inappropriately selected, lacking managerial expertise or technical know-how. The Europol MB consists of 28 high-ranking, Member State representatives from interior ministries, national police forces and intelligence services, plus the Commission's Director General for Home Affairs. It meets biennially to settle the budget and discuss the work programme and a general report from the Director. Given the technicality and importance of the subject matter, this does not suggest an in-depth supervisory role.[69]

Further control is exercised by the JSB which, as indicated, takes its responsibilities seriously and by the EO, who has handled 13 complaints in relation to Europol. Although these have not revealed systemic maladministration, they exposed sufficient deficiencies in handling requests for information to warrant an Own-Initiative Investigation (OII).[70] Interpreting his firefighting functions quite expansively, the EO pinned a site visit to Europol to his OII. Criticising the lack of transparency, he stipulated that Europol procedures for access to documents[71] should be aligned with Regulation 1049/2001 and asked for a separate annual review of Europol's handling of public access to documents requests. The Director undertook to install a 'public access management functionality' and ensure the coordinated management of public access requests; a public access Internet website would be retroactively 'populated' with Europol's public documents and a Europol register of publicly accessible documents.[72]

[68] M Busuioc, *European Agencies, Law and Practices of Accountability* (Oxford: OUP, 2013) ch 5, para 5.5.
[69] See M Busuioc, 'Accountability, Control and Independence: The Case of European Agencies' (2009) 15 *European Law Journal* 599, 613.
[70] See explanatory letter winding up investigations in Inv 2166/2012/BEH; Inv 2167/2012/BEH; and Inv 2168/2012/BEH.
[71] Management Board Decision laying down the rules concerning access to Europol documents (8 July 2009).
[72] Report of the EO following his visit to the European Police Office (Europol) and Director's Response, OI/9/2012/OV.

Is all this sufficiently rigorous? The Europol Decision launched the agency as a networking body, whose success was 'conditional upon close cooperation' with a multiplicity of bodies, often with highly dubious credentials. By 2012, Europol had relationships with the 28 Member States and nine EU bodies, including OLAF and the two closely related agencies of Eurojust and Frontex. When the Europol–Eurojust agreement was modified in 2008, the JSB complained of haste and sloppy drafting: the agreement used terminology from the proposed Decision before it would come into force; this raised doubts about the legal basis for the data processing activity that the agreement supposedly covered.[73] The underlying awareness that the agreement would in fact be implemented underscored the JSB's lack of enforcement powers. Europol has negotiated around 40 agreements with states ranging from Australia to Russia. The JSB once criticised a potential agreement between Europol and Russia on the ground of insufficient evidence that data protection was adequately regulated in Russia or that the Russian data protection authority was, as was necessary for agreement, sufficiently independent of the Russian government. Emphasising that it understood the need for cooperation, the JSB nonetheless insisted that it must be 'in compliance with the data protection rules the Council has adopted for Europol' and asked for further analysis.[74] Again, Peers, an outside observer, critiquing a US–Europol agreement, called it 'highly deficient as regards data protection rights'.[75] There were worrying contradictions between the text of the agreement and 'an exchange of letters of ambiguous legal status', which were not referenced in the main text; this was 'clearly not a transparent or coherent way to draft treaties raising important civil liberties issues'. He added that only one of the treaties concluded by Europol had been published in the *Official Journal* and very few were contained in the Council register of documents; none were online on the Europol website and its press releases referred to only a small number of agreements. This is indeed worrying.

Peers also drew attention to a generally overlooked problem of enforcement and oversight; the JSB could hardly 'examine whether the other party upholds its obligations under the agreement' and only Europol fell within the competence of the EO. Yet 10 non-EU countries and organisations were working with Europol on the basis of cooperation agreements and it networks with US public bodies, including the Secret Service and FBI,[76] over which it has no control whatsoever. It hosts and supports numerous other bodies, such as the CARIN, an 'informal network' of judicial and law enforcement experts from over 50 states, jurisdictions and international organisations.[77] It is a member of the Cross-Border Surveillance Working Group, which exists to encourage international cooperation and provide a forum for the

---

[73] JSB, Opinion 08/56. Eurojust coordinates the work of EU prosecuting authorities; Frontex coordinates and develops European border management. Both agencies have substantial networking functions.
[74] JSB, Opinion 09/77.
[75] S Peers, 'The exchange of personal data between Europol and the USA', Statewatch analysis No 15 (undated).
[76] *AR 2012*.
[77] *AR 2012*, 22.

discussion and development of safe and effective law enforcement surveillance techniques for use against serious and organised crime.[78] And as a nodal point on a data processing network, Europol can access outside databanks. In addition to access rights to SIS II, CIS and VIS, it works with ENLETS, described as a secure environment for specialists from a variety of law enforcement areas to share 'knowledge, best practices and non-personal data on crime hosts'. ENLETS comprises over 2000 users.[79] How far are administrative procedures in place to control these bodies, and to what extent can they be adequately controlled?

Europol also provides a database and communication channels for secure communication and information exchange between participants in the ISLE project, a network managed by British, Belgian and German crime prevention agencies and funded by the EU to the extent of €115,614, to develop coordination, cooperation and 'mutual understanding' between law enforcement agencies using 'specialist techniques'. This might seem wholly in line with the core Europol function of information exchange, until we learn that 'specialist techniques' apparently include 'covert entry into premises or vehicles and the facilitation of covert searches of property, covert forensic capabilities and covertly installed technical devices'. At national level, such practices, which not only threaten civil liberties but may also violate the rule of law, would normally require authorisation from a representative parliament and be subject to judicial review. Yet the ISLE project came to light only incidentally through disclosures made by the NGO Statewatch, and through questions asked by members of the German Bundestag.[80]

Even without new legislation, new responsibilities are constantly being added to Europol's workload. As foreseen in the Stockholm action plan and roadmap,[81] a cybercrime alert platform at European level was inaugurated as a centre of specialised expertise and focal point in the fight against cybercrime in 2012.[82] Again after the EU–US agreement on the Terrorist Finance Tracking Programme (TFTP),[83] Europol was given the added function of requesting relevant data and verifying whether requests from the responsible US authorities were legally compliant. Europol set up a dedicated unit to handle requests. In an information note to the EP,[84] Europol claimed that it had 'discharged its responsibilities with great care and to a high professional standard' and to the satisfaction of the MB and Commissioner Malmström. The JSB and EP begged to differ; following an inspection, a JSB report to LIBE concluded that

[78] Europol Annual Review for 2009, Council Doc 10099/10 (31 May 2010).
[79] Information from the Europol website.
[80] 'Answer of the Federal Government to the Minor Interpellation tabled by the Members of the Bundestag' (31 May 2012), published in Statewatch News Online (23 August 2012).
[81] Commission, 'Action Plan Implementing the Stockholm Programme' (Communication) COM/2010/0171 final.
[82] See Rand Europe, *Feasibility Study for a European Cybercrime Centre* (2010).
[83] 'Agreement between the EU and US on the processing and transfer of Financial Messaging Data for the purposes of the Terrorist Finance Tracking Program' [2010] OJ 2010 L195/5.
[84] Europol Public Information, 'Europol Activities in Relation to the TFTP Agreement', File no 2566-566 (8 April 2011).

the written requests Europol received were not specific enough to allow it to decide whether to approve or deny them ... the US requests were too general and too abstract to allow proper evaluation of the necessity of the requested data transfers. Despite this, Europol approved each request it received.[85]

According to Amicelli, LIBE's reaction was one of 'dissatisfaction, unrest and discomfort'. And MEP Sophie In't Veld criticised Europol for granting requests 'orally over the telephone' as a 'complete violation of the term of the agreement'. For Amicelli, this was inherent in the absence of external accountability machinery: a judicial body would have focused on the legal criteria and a data protection body on data protection but Europol analysts assess US requests 'in the light of operational considerations and security needs'.[86] This underscores the need for strong accountability machinery, which will itself be heavily reliant on experts.

A Robust Data Protection Regime?

Data protection within the EU is in a transitional phase; a proposal for a *general* Data Protection Regulation[87] is, at the time of writing, awaiting a vote in plenary by the EP after substantial amendments were demanded by the LIBE Committee.[88] This raises the crucial question why the processing and transfer of personal data by Europol should receive separate treatment. The LIBE Committee rapporteur, Jan Phillip Albrecht – who is fortunately a lawyer specialising in privacy and data protection laws – commented unfavourably on the missed opportunity to coordinate and 'ensure consistency with the data protection package';[89] the JSB too thought it preferable at least to await the outcome of data protection legislation before legislating for Europol. The official view is, however, that greater detail in Europol data protection provisions is needed because of 'the particular nature, functions and competences of Europol'.[90] As the JSB concluded in its first Opinion, Europol's data processing procedures must be specific if the 'existing robust data protection regime, safeguarded by strict, tailor-made rules and effective supervisory arrangements' were to be maintained. Its 'legal basis must contain specific provisions for data processing and responsibilities in relation to

---

[85] JSB, First Inspection on the TFTP agreement (2 March 2011); EP Press Release, 20110314IPR15463.
[86] A Amicelle, 'The EU's Paradoxical Efforts at Tracking the Financing of Terrorism: From criticism to imitation of dataveillance' (2013) CEPS Paper, Liberty and Security in Europe No 56, 11.
[87] LIBE Report on the proposal for a General Data Protection Regulation (COM (2012) 0011 – C7-0025/2012–2012/0011 (COD).
[88] See COM (2012) 11/4 and Commission Report on the Framework Decision COM (2012) 12 final; Commission, 'Proposal for a Regulation on the protection of individuals with regard to the processing of personal data and on the free movement of such data' COM (2013) 228 final.
[89] LIBE Report 199; EDPS, Opinion on the Proposal [17]. And see for further comment C Kuner, 'The European Commission's Proposed Data Protection Regulation: A Copernican Revolution in European Data Protection Law' *Privacy and Security Law Report*, 11 PVLR 06, 4.
[90] Recitals to Europol Decision and Commission Communication, 'Safeguarding Privacy in a Connected World- A European Data Protection Framework for the 21st Century' COM (2012) 9/3; De Moor and Vermeulen, above (n 23) 1120.

each task and each data processing procedure'.[91] The JSB concluded that the proposed regulation fell well short of this. It joined the European data supervisors in asserting that the proposal would result in a weaker Europol data protection regime, a downgrading that would not only expose Europol to risk but would endanger individuals' rights.[92]

The data processing provisions are presented as a 'state-of-the-art' system designed to process data more quickly and efficiently and enable the IT architecture to be adapted to future challenges and the needs of EU law enforcement authorities. For the first time also the door is open to relations with the private sector; at present private parties cannot transmit data directly to Europol but the restriction is under consideration. The intention is expressed to ensure a 'robust data protection regime' for Europol under the supervision of 'a fully independent and effective' supervisory body and the provisions reflect a wish also to conform to accepted data protection principles as laid down from time to time by the EU and Council of Europe. Thus, data clearly obtained in breach of human rights may not be processed and data may be transferred only on the basis of an 'adequacy decision' by the Commission that the transferee ensures an adequate level of data protection or of an international or cooperation agreement made prior to the entry into force of the Regulation.

Detailed rules concerning processing, retention and access are provided, covering data subjects, purposes for which data can be processed, records and reports, logging and documentation, rectification, checking and erasure. Attempts have been made to clarify responsibilities. Thus, a 'principle of ownership' is introduced that allows Member States and Europol partners to determine the purpose for which their data is processed and to restrict access rights and responsibility for the accuracy of data and the legality of transfer remains with Member States. Effectively, however, this is a co-ownership principle, as Europol has to ensure fairness, legality and compliance with the stated objectives of the process and must keep extensive and detailed records; data is also to be assessed and labelled according to the reliability of its source. A data protection officer must be employed to monitor compliance, whose independent discretion must be assured.[93]

In its First Opinion, the JSB reported broadly on matters of principle. In contrast to the LIBE Report on the Regulation, which is largely amenable to integration and focused on augmenting the powers of the EP,[94] the JSB Second Opinion provides a detailed textual analysis of the data processing procedure.[95] It criticises variant terminology, failures to comply with legal requirements, restrictions on competence and failure to spell out and comply with Europol's objectives. OLAF,

[91] JSB, Opinion 13/31, 2.
[92] Ibid. And see Resolution of the Conference of European Data Protection Authorities, 16–17 May 2013.
[93] See on the role of the DPO, Rand [7.5.1].
[94] 'Report on the Proposal for a Regulation on Europol' COM (2013) 173 final PE513, C7-0094/2013-20130091 (COD).
[95] JSB, Opinion13/56.

for example, would in future have access to 'what is probably a huge amount of personal data that do not have any link with its tasks and competences'; it was important that access should be given only for data that fell within the tasks of the requesting organisation.[96]

In its two Opinions on the projected Europol Regulation, the JSB fastens on the essential feature of the EU governance system; *collaboration* between the Union and its Member States. In the case of Europol, it points to blurred responsibilities and lack of coordination between Europol and national authorities, whose interests are by implication being neglected. The Opinion also pinpoints the essential link between law and procedure. A clear description of Europol's objectives is necessary 'for embedding its activities in a framework'; without a sufficiently specific legal framework Europol will always be in danger of overstepping its boundaries.[97]

DEMOCRATIC ACCOUNTABILITY

The creation of Europol as an agency of the EU created a need for accountability machinery at Union level. But Peers suggests that it was not until the 1999–2004 session that the EP began to push for greater control over Europol,[98] expressing its displeasure in a series of hostile reports. In 2002, the LIBE rapporteur complained of Council 'offhandedness' in failing to provide an explanatory memorandum for an otherwise uncontroversial proposal on Europol personnel. He recommended rejection; the consultation was 'bogus'; no action had ever been taken by the Council on parliamentary recommendations and the Council would 'not take a blind bit of notice' of any amendments. Rejection would make a political point: 'It is not in the interests of Parliament, which has been no more than a legislative pygmy in such matters to date, to behave like a political pygmy too'.[99] A year later, the EP rejected a Danish proposal on Europol confidentiality on the ground that Europol had not yet adopted measures for access to documents. Again the rapporteur summarised the position on parliamentary accountability, saying:

> There has been since the creation of Europol a wide debate and repeated requests have been expressed on the necessity of **strengthening democratic control** of Europol through wider **parliamentary and judicial scrutiny**. Europol is in fact submitted to a fragmented and indirect control from national parliaments that are anyway not able to organise, individually, a sufficient parliamentary supervision of the Council in police affairs and of Europol.

---

[96] Ibid, 27.
[97] Ibid, 3 and 6.
[98] S Peers, 'Governance and the Third Pillar: The Accountability of Europol' in D Curtin and R Wessel (eds), *Good Governance and the European Union: Concept, Implications and Applications* (Antwerp: Intersentia, 2005).
[99] The Defrez Report, A5-0345/2002, PE 323-720, adopted by the EP 21 October 2002 [2003] OJ C300 E12.

Under the proposal the 'EP will keep its current role with regards to Europol: discussing without anybody listening and making reports without anybody implementing them'.[100]

At the time, the EP was asking for funding through the Community budget subject to Community budget procedure; involvement in the appointment and dismissal of Europol's Director and Deputy Directors; two elected representatives at MB meetings; agreed information and consultation rights on an extended range of subjects; and revision of the Europol Convention to comply with higher standards and methods of democratic and judicial control. In the proposed new Regulation, the majority of these demands have been conceded.[101] In addition, the Commission has suggested an inter-parliamentary forum made up from the committees responsible for police matters in the European and national parliaments to meet regularly and invite the Director of Europol to discuss questions relating to the agency's work.[102]

The basis for a strong parliamentary network that could hold Europol to account is provided by TFEU Article 53, which requires the Director and chair of the MB to appear at their request 'before the European Parliament, jointly with national parliaments' to discuss matters relating to Europol. In the absence of statutory machinery, the inter-parliamentary Speakers' Conference was chosen as an appropriate venue. Enter the LIBE Committee of the EP, which tabled an amendment to the Europol Regulation recommending transfer of scrutiny functions to a new inter-parliamentary scrutiny unit, which would meet at the EP and be convened by the chair of LIBE.[103] This centralising amendment provoked a strong reaction in the UK Parliament, where the European Scrutiny Committee recommended that the matter should be referred to the next Speakers' Conference and that no action should be taken prior to this. These highly negative views were transmitted 'in the spirit of political dialogue' to the Commission, Council and LIBE Committee.[104]

CONCLUSION

This chapter has traced the process of 'mission creep' whereby an EU agency can progress almost imperceptibly from inception as an informal group of national representatives working together informally to an EU agency fully regulated by an

---

[100] The Turco Report, EP 13875/2002 – C5-0553/2002 – 2002/0823 (CNS).

[101] See Commission, 'The procedures for the scrutiny of Europol's activities by the European Parliament, together with national Parliaments' (Communication) COM (2010) 776 final; Proposal for a Regulation, above, fn 88. The exceptions are parliamentary representation on the Management Board and a role in appointment: see Commission Communication above at [5.3].

[102] Communication [5.1]. The present Director, Rob Wainwright, already works closely with the UK House of Lords, which has published five reports on Europol.

[103] Draft Report on the Europol proposal (Rapporteur, A Díaz De Mera García Consuegra), LIBE_PR(2013)513116, 66.

[104] UK House of Commons European Scrutiny Committee, *Reforming Europol* (HC 2013–14, 83-iii) ch 1.

EU regulation, an outcome for which the Commission and EP have fought long and hard. We have observed the uses of agency structure in imperceptibly expanding EU competence. We have noted the transfer of rule-making and operational powers to Europol and watched the extension of supervisory power over national organisations. We have watched the usefulness of agency quasi-autonomy in network-building.

As we have been at pains to stress, accountability machinery forms a crucial element in good administrative procedure and Europol provides a paradigm example of the accountability problems created by the semi-autonomous status of agencies. Europol has accountability relationships with the Council, Commission and EP, national parliaments, the EDPS and the EO – institutions with conflicting interests, whose requirements may vary considerably: the classic problem of 'too many eyes'.[105] The lines of accountability are never sufficiently clear.

In her work on EU agencies, however, Busuioc finds it helpful to distinguish 'accountability' in the sense of explanations given to external bodies from 'control' in the sense of oversight and scrutiny.[106] Our study suggests that the JSB has achieved a measure of success in providing control in this semi-hierarchical sense. It points also to the beginnings of an 'accountability network' of a kind that the authors have elsewhere described as essential for proper control of multi-level decision-making and composite decisions.[107] We exemplified the European Network of Ombudsmen (see chapter 3) and the well-developed network of European auditors, best developed at the time we wrote. IPEX, the platform for EU Interparliamentary Exchange, was then in its initiatory stages. It has, however, evolved fairly rapidly since the Lisbon Treaty and is in the process of developing its own identity. These networks involve practitioners of particular forms of accountability, who come together to help provide accountability cover throughout European administrative space. The JSB and EDPS represent a variant on this theme in which national experts are brought together at Union level to create a centralised accountability body – the model incidentally desired in respect of parliamentary accountability by the LIBE committee of the European Parliament, resulting in the inter-parliamentary exchanges recorded above.

Though representative of Member States, sufficient independence can be given to a centralised scrutiny body of this type by ensuring autonomy at national level – as has indeed been done in the case of data protection supervisors.[108] In an area as technical as data processing, where democratic accountability can only be exercised through the control of experts, it is a pity that the 'independent and effective joint supervision structure' of the Europol JSB seems likely to be demolished.

---

[105] See M Bovens, 'Analysing and Assessing Public Accountability. A Conceptual Framework', in D Curtin and A Wille (eds), *Meaning and Practice of Accountability in the EU Multi-Level Context* (CONNEX Report Series Nr 07 (2008)).
[106] Busuioc, 'Accountability, Control and Independence', above (n 69).
[107] C Harlow and R Rawlings, 'Promoting Accountability in Multi-Level Governance: A Network Approach' (2007) 13 *European Law Journal* 542.
[108] See above, n 55.

11

Integration and Crisis: Financial Services Regulation

THE WORST FINANCIAL crisis since the 1930s has cast a long shadow over the writing of this book. In this chapter we look directly into the eye of the storm, focusing on major developments in EU financial services regulation before, during and after the recent market turmoil. If indeed we were asked to single out a field in which in the most recent period EU administrative procedure exhibits strong – even exponential – growth, it would be this one. Nor, emphatically, is the dynamic played out.

Major crises are proverbially the 'mother of invention'. The precise extent of the shift may be disputed, but it is clearly possible to distinguish two periods of regulatory reform with substantially different objectives.[1] At the beginning of the century, the overriding concern was completion of the internal market in financial services, as reflected in arguments about regulatory arbitrage where rules and standards differ between jurisdictions, and reduced global competitiveness by reason of underdeveloped capital markets.[2] Behind this lay a seemingly ever more dominant neo-liberal paradigm grounded in a strong belief in efficient market disciplines, one familiarly associated with the UK (and the City of London).[3] The focus then was structural regulation and greater uniformity of law and implementation, in practical terms the agglomeration of financial markets increasingly laced with 'light-touch' approaches to regulation.

Fast forward a decade or so and the official discourse is primarily about improving regulatory supervision and, more particularly, promoting or limiting the risks to financial stability.[4] This typically involves thickening extant regulation, widening EU regulation to encompass previously self-regulated activities and strengthening

---

[1] L Quaglia, 'The "Old" and "New" Politics of Financial Services Regulation in the EU' (2012) 17 *New Political Economy* 515; E Ferran, 'Crisis-Driven Regulatory Reform: Where in the World is the EU Going?' in E Ferran et al (eds), *The Regulatory Aftermath of the Global Financial Crisis* (Cambridge: CUP, 2012).

[2] Commission, 'Financial Services: Building a Framework for Action' (Communication) COM (1998) 625 final; 'Action Plan: Implementing the Framework for Financial Markets' (Communication) COM (1999) 232 final. And see N Moloney, *EC Securities Regulation*, 1st edn (Oxford: OUP, 2002).

[3] A Gamble, *The Spectre at the Feast: Capitalist Crisis and the Politics of Recession* (Basingstoke: Palgrave Macmillan, 2009); G Underhill, J Blom and D Mügge (eds), *Global Financial Integration Thirty Years On* (Cambridge: CUP, 2010).

[4] Commission, 'European Financial Supervision' (Communication) COM (2009) 252 final.

the institutional and administrative framework of financial services supervision. Opening a new chapter in Union history, the Commission has led the way in exploring fresh opportunities for financial and regulatory integration under the broad rubric of 'Banking Union'.[5] The fact that by stimulating more pan-European financial activity, greater concentration of firms and increased financial product innovation and complexity,[6] the previous round of unguarded reform helped sow the seeds of market contagion is largely glossed over.

We focus on three successive and related developments. The first is the 'Lamfalussy process'[7]; a template for legislative and regulatory coordination and convergence which dominated the field prior to the financial crisis. Lamfalussy process resembles a 'regulatory laboratory' demonstrating the then state of the art in expansive uses both of executive legislation and soft law, and in 'better regulation' and regulatory networks. The second development is the European System of Financial Supervision (ESFS), a formal network rapidly established following the market turmoil of 2008 and which partly – but not wholly – replaces Lamfalussy process. Of particular interest are the European Supervisory Authorities (ESAs) such as the European Banking Authority (EBA).[8] Equipped to play important roles in standard setting and supervision, they take Union level 'agencification' to new heights (see chapter two). Movement towards 'Banking Union' in the form of a Single Supervisory Mechanism (SSM) is the third main development. Representing a huge new dose of integration, but also reinforcing the notion of 'a multi-speed Europe',[9] it is very much a work in progress. Involving some highly intricate administrative procedures in the light of major political and legal constraints and concerns about national sovereignty, it sees a veritable 'big beast', the European Central Bank (ECB), tasked with risk regulation of 'big capital', the eurozone's 125 plus most important banks.

ELITE CONCEPTION

The Four-Level Model

Lamfalussy process stemmed from the Commission's 1999 Financial Services Action Plan (FSAP) outlining the steps necessary to complete the internal market in the sector, which included some 40 pieces of legislation. Once more invoking

---

[5] Commission, 'A Roadmap towards a Banking Union' COM (2012) 510 final.
[6] Commission, 'Review of the Lamfalussy Process: Strengthening Supervisory Convergence' (Communication) COM (2007) 727 final. Not that the process of market integration was ever uniform or complete; see E Grossman and P Leblond, 'European Financial Integration: Finally the Great Leap Forward?' (2011) 49 *Journal of Common Market Studies* 413.
[7] Lamfalussy Committee, Initial Report on the Regulation of European Securities Markets (November 2000); Final Report (February 2001).
[8] Regulation 1093/2010/EU establishing a European Supervisory Authority (European Banking Authority) [2010] OJ L331/12.
[9] Regulation 1024/2013/EU conferring specific tasks on the European Central Bank concerning policies relating to the prudential supervision of credit institutions [2013] OJ L287/63.

that determinedly elitist device in EU governance of 'a Committee of Wise Men', the Council sought advice about how this gargantuan task might be timeously achieved and how regulation of European securities markets might be adjusted accordingly. Chaired by economist/financier Baron Alexandre Lamfalussy and featuring leading bankers and regulators, the Committee made a carefully crafted case for major procedural reform, the general thesis not surprisingly being that regulation in this area should be more expert and market-driven and politically insulated. Premised on the principle of mutual recognition and minimum harmonisation, and with no agreed template for national regulatory supervision, the existing EU legislative framework had only 'begun to open previously closed markets'. What with globalisation, the euro and ICT, a strong dose of regulatory modernisation was necessary: the speed of change in the financial markets already was 'breathtaking and accelerating'. However, the Union's legislative process presented a 'main difficulty': it was 'too slow, too rigid . . . and over-reliant on primary legislation for determining detailed rules'; seeking a political consensus tended to produce 'too much ambiguity . . . resulting in inconsistent implementation'.[10] Garnering support from the Commission, the Council and, if more grudgingly in view of the implications for democratic control of greater use of executive legislation, the European Parliament (EP),[11] the Committee duly elaborated its famous four level model of Lamfalussy process. Conveniently, no treaty amendment was required for what would later be described as 'a dramatic change in the detail, regulatory sophistication, and the degree of intervention in Member States' systems of the EC securities and investments regime'.[12]

'Level 1' denoted framework legislation, which Lamfalussy defined in terms of 'the core political principles, the essential elements of each proposal'. Adopted via the key democratic safeguard of co-decision procedure, this would specify the nature and extent of 'the technical implementing measures' (TIMs) taken at 'level 2'.[13] Authority for adopting these regulatory 'details' would thus be delegated to the Commission, acting through the regulatory procedure of the comitology. Soon established on the basis of Commission decisions, two new bodies would assist the work of Directorate-General Internal Market and Services (DG Markt). Made up of representatives of the national supervisory authorities, the Committee of European Securities Regulators (CESR) would first operate as a technical advisory committee helping with the preparation and drafting of Commission proposals (so providing an additional element of 'buy-in').[14] Made up of high level representatives of the Member States, and chaired by the Commission, the European Securities Committee (ESC) would deliver opinions in comitology

[10] Lamfalussy Initial Report, above (n 7) 2, 15, 18–19.
[11] See D Alford, 'The Lamfalussy Process and European Bank Regulation: Preliminary Assessment and Future Prospects' (2006) 21 *Journal of Banking Law and Regulation* 59.
[12] N Moloney, 'The Lamfalussy Legislative Model: A New Era for the EC Securities and Investment Services Regime' (2003) 52 *International & Comparative Law Quarterly* 509, 509.
[13] Lamfalussy Final Report, above (n 7) 22–23.
[14] Ibid, 31; Commission Decision 2001/527/EC establishing the Committee of European Securities Regulators [2001] OJ L191/43, Arts 1–2.

mode and provide policy advice (and political weight).[15] In the abstract, there was nothing particularly novel about these twin proposals for increasing the speed and flexibility of EU regulation by rebalancing the formal rule-making function in favour of executive – Commission – power, and for a double deployment of committees to provide expertise and oversight in the rule-formulation. But they represented a significant change of approach in a policy domain long jealously guarded by Member States. In the long view, Lamfalussy can also be seen as anticipating the arrival of general powers to make delegated and implementing acts (see chapter four).

The real innovation lay in 'level 3', which stood for 'strengthened cooperation between regulators to improve implementation'. CESR, it was envisaged, would wear a second hat as 'a fully independent committee of national regulators' grounding 'a co-operative network'. More particularly, CESR would be responsible for building on the formal legal product of levels 1 and 2 through a variety of soft law means designed to promote greater uniformity in the application and supervision of EU measures. This would include administrative guidance on regulatory routines; common standards including perhaps in areas not covered by EU legislation; joint interpretative recommendations; and peer review. Non-binding yes, but the 'Wise Men' reckoned that 'it would carry considerable authority'.[16]

'Level 4' was about strengthening the enforcement of Community rules. The 'Wise Men' invoked that old friend the centralised infringement procedure (see chapter seven), saying that the Commission 'should be bolder' in holding Member States legally to account. In the context of a largely complaints-based system, these elite insiders spoke of 'a partnership approach' between the public and private sectors, placing particular emphasis on the responsibility of national regulators to alert the Commission.[17] In the event, the Commission again preferred soft techniques, the common round of guidelines, bilateral and multilateral meetings and scoreboards.[18]

As for outputs, four level 1 directives and 12 implementing level 2 measures were adopted in the securities sector in the first five years, including some major pieces of legislation such as the Market Abuse Directive and the sprawling Markets in Financial Instruments Directive (MIFID).[19] In the Commission's view, this would not have been possible without CESR's technical advice.[20] Meanwhile, the tentacles of Lamfalussy process had spread to include banking and insurance through the establishment in a further series of Commission Decisions of functionally equivalent committees: the European Banking Committee (EBC) and the

---

[15] Lamfalussy Final Report, above (n 7) 30; Commission Decision 2001/528/EC establishing the European Securities Committee [2001] OJ L191/45.
[16] Lamfalussy Final Report, above (n 7) 31, 37–39.
[17] Ibid, 40.
[18] COM (2007) 727 final, 6.
[19] Directive 2003/6/EC on Insider Dealing and Market Manipulation [2003] OJ L94/16; Directive 2004/39/EC on Markets in Financial Instruments [2004] OJ L145/1.
[20] COM (2007) 727 final, 3.

272   *Financial Services Regulation*

Committee of European Banking Supervisors (CEBS); the European Insurance and Occupational Pensions Committee (EIOPC) and the Committee of European Insurance and Occupational Pensions Supervisors (CEIOPS).[21] These too began to produce significant hard law and soft law outputs, though more slowly.[22] The 'Wise Men', it should be added, were not blind to the dynamic of increased integration of the markets increasing their exposure to common shocks; but they felt unable to evaluate such risks or make recommendations.[23] As the later market travails would brutally demonstrate, this left the entire regulatory system vulnerable.

Better Regulation

Lamfalussy process pioneered the Union's version of 'better regulation' (see chapter two). A Commission evaluation in 2007 was very positive, attributing to the openness and transparency of the process the minimisation of regulatory arbitrage and enhancement of the quality and predictability of the policymaking.[24] Consultation procedures for example had been a key part of the 'Wise Men's' prospectus in the form of 'early and institutionalised involvement of market practitioners and consumers', with 'particular weight given to those with knowledge and expertise of the subject in question'.[25] The techniques deployed quickly ranged through written and Internet consultations to the more or less formal devices of public hearings and roundtables; meanwhile multiple consultative working groups were formed involving market practitioners.[26] The Commission evaluation duly reported that 'systematic and transparent consultation has been strongly welcomed by stakeholders'. Echoing developments in competition (see chapter eight), the Commission commented that 'where alternatives are proposed they should be accompanied by sufficient and persuasive economic evidence, which is not the case today'.[27] Viewed through technocratic eyes, it clearly made sense so to raise the bar; yet this also raised the nagging question of who among the stakeholders has the power and resources to affect outcomes.

By 2007, all level 1 legislation was subject to impact assessment (IA) with a view both to evaluating the need for regulation and ensuring quality. In expansive even heroic fashion, the Commission thought to 'scope each issue and determine the most appropriate option' by reference to 'costs and benefits across the broad economic, social and environmental dimensions'. Also of the view that 'better

[21] Commission Decision 2004/10/EC establishing the European Banking Committee [2004] OJ L3/36; Commission Decision 2004/5/EC establishing the Committee of European Banking Supervisors [2004] OJ L3/28; Commission Decision 2004/9/EC establishing the European Insurance and Occupational Pensions Committee [2004] OJ L3/34; Commission Decision 2004/6/EC establishing the Committee of European Insurance and Occupational Pensions Supervisors [2004] OJ L3/30.
[22] COM (2007) 727 final, 3.
[23] Lamfalussy Final Report, above (n 7) 17.
[24] COM (2007) 727 final, 5.
[25] Lamfalussy Final Report, above (n 7) 21, 33.
[26] See for details, CESR's (final) *AR 2010*.
[27] COM (2007) 727 final, 5.

regulation is a holistic concept – all parties must work for the overall result to be optimal', the Commission already envisaged the mass deployment of IAs in a seemingly never-ending quest for evidence-based decision-making. The level 3 committees when advising the Commission, and the Council as well as the Parliament when making substantive amendments, were invited to accompany their proposals with comprehensive IAs; since TIMs could have significant impacts for particular stakeholders, DG Markt set about extending IAs to them.[28] Perhaps not surprisingly, no IA was attached covering the cost and delay of all this paper piled on paper.

A leading commentator detected 'greater willingness by the Commission to rely on market discipline and on internal firm mechanisms to address risks to the pan-EC marketplace'.[29] This fits with broader currents in (better) regulation theory, with much being heard in the world of financial services of alternative approaches to older forms of command and control regulation. Together with classic forms of self-regulation, fashionable nostrums of 'meta-regulation' or leverage of corporate control systems, of 'co-regulation' or mixed public–private responsibilities, and of 'decentred regulation' or 'regulation in many rooms', increasingly informed what the same commentator described as 'a more subtle approach to intervention in the post-FSAP period'.[30] For example, coerced forms of self-regulation and co-regulation – rule adoption by the industry in the shadow of threatened intervention – emerged as a leading policy option, as illustrated by codes of conduct for such important activities as credit rating and clearing and settlement.[31]

External Dimension

We touch here on the strong external dimension to policy and practice in this regulatory sphere. Although international cooperation and coordination would markedly expand in the wake of the worldwide credit crunch, the Commission had already prioritised this aspect in the context of the drive to complete the internal market. The touchstone is a 2005 White Paper on financial services policy, which drew attention to the way in which, grounded in the work of leading international bodies such as the Basel Committee on Banking Supervision, standards and best practices in the sector were increasingly set and defined at global level.[32] The Commission looked forward to 'an ambitious opening of global financial services

---

[28] Ibid, 5–6.
[29] N Moloney, 'Innovation and Risk in EC Financial Market Regulation: New Instruments of Financial Market Intervention and the Committee of European Securities Regulators' (2007) *European Law Review* 627, 632.
[30] Ibid; for discussion by the authors of these broad regulatory trends, see C Harlow and R Rawlings, *Law and Administration*, 3rd edn (Cambridge: CUP, 2009) ch 6.
[31] International Organisation of Securities Commissions (IOSCO), Code of Conduct for Credit Rating Agencies (2004); European Code of Conduct for Clearing and Settlement (2006).
[32] J Braithwaite and P Drahos, *Global Business Regulation* (Cambridge: CUP, 2000).

markets' especially through the World Trade Organization (WTO); the EU, it was said, must have a leading role in the standard setting by reason not only of the size of the internal market, but also of 'Europe's experience in pragmatically uniting the legitimate call for harmonised rules and the diverging needs of different markets/cultures/players'.[33] The Commission particularly urged closer European coordination, indeed 'precise European negotiating positions', in a range of less high profile but sector-significant transnational forums such as the International Organisation of Securities Commissions (IOSCO) and the International Association of Insurance Supervisors (IAIS), as well as UNIDROIT, the International Institute for the Unification of Private Law.

Attention is also drawn to the use of bilateral 'regulatory dialogues' with key economic partners. As high level forums for exchanging information, identifying potential problems (not least those of international regulatory arbitrage) and seeking mutually acceptable solutions, these had predictably begun with the United States and that formidable actor the Securities and Exchange Commission (SEC). At one with changing patterns of global power, the White Paper signalled the widening of dialogues on financial regulation with China, Japan, India and Russia.[34] Meanwhile, in the context of Lamfalussy process CESR had begun to take on a supplementary international role. A 2006 joint work plan with SEC spoke of 'close co-operation' between staff to promote such desiderata as high quality accounting standards, 'full consideration of international counterparts' positions regarding . . . enforcement', and avoidance of conflicting regulatory decisions.[35]

Regulatory Network

CESR was one of a new breed of essentially horizontal networks developing around the turn of the century.[36] Situated at the heart of the functioning economy in such sectors as telecommunications, energy and transport as well as securities, these 'European Regulatory Networks' (ERNs) would be given wide tasks and a broad national membership but few formal legal powers. As in the case of CESR, the development reflected, first, the rise of delegated governance ('the regulatory state') in many jurisdictions, and hence a special premium on coordination and cooperation between national supervisory bodies in the internal market; and, second, resistance among Member States to dedicated Union-level regulatory

---

[33] Commission, 'White Paper – Financial Services Policy 2005–2010' COM (2005) 629 final, 15–16. See further, G Bertezzolo, 'The European Union Facing the Global Arena: Standard-Setting Bodies and Financial Regulation' (2009) 34 *European Law Review* 257.

[34] COM (2005) 629 final, 16.

[35] CESR/SEC, Developing Cross Atlantic Financial Markets (2006) 1.

[36] D Coen and M Thatcher, 'Network Governance and Multi-level Delegation: European Networks of Regulatory Agencies' (2008) 28 *Journal of European Public Policy* 49; M Maggetti and F Gilardi, 'The Policy-making Structure of European Regulatory Networks and the Domestic Adoption of Standards' (2011) 18 *Journal of European Public Policy* 830.

machinery (a 'Euro SEC' for example)[37] in these economically strategic domains. In contrast to competition (large-scale decentralisation via the ECN (see chapter eight)), this particular model of network governance was largely a bottom-up development, one founded on extant supervision at the domestic level and, in the case of CESR, some limited attempt at cross-border cooperation and policy development.[38] As CESR's place in Lamfalussy process also shows, the ERNs would be highly dependent for impact on the effective exercise of influence and use of soft law.

A 'network constitution' in the form of a soft law Charter spoke boldly of CESR's determination to operate on the basis of consensus across the whole cycle of implementation: from fostering common and uniform transposition and application of Community legislation to consistent supervision and enforcement.[39] There would be an annual work programme and permanent and expert groups. For example, CESR-Pol, an in-house forum of senior surveillance and enforcement officials, would develop policy options and facilitate cooperation and exchange of information in market abuse investigations.[40] A review panel, officially described as a peer pressure group, would operate a 'comply or explain' approach to the reception of CESR guidelines, and establish benchmarks for collective and self-assessment and national supervisory practice.[41] Further, Lamfalussy process demanded cross-border colleges of supervisors to secure the oversight of big cross-border firms, and also arrangements for cooperation between the different level 3 committees over financial conglomerates.[42] Increasingly resembling a 'network of networks', CESR would go on expanding, eventually including a dozen standing committees supplemented by a range of task forces, panels and consultative groups for sub-sectors of the industry. Yet more formidable however was the great variety of more or less technical issues confronting this ERN under such general headings as 'corporate finance' or 'investor protection'. CESR was fated to grow in a desperate attempt to stay abreast.

Testimony to CESR's privileged and strategic position between the Commission and the markets, it was variously described as sitting 'at the centre of the institutional web', inhabiting 'a grey zone' and playing 'a pivotal role' out of proportion to its non-binding powers.[43] CESR's Charter made soothing noises about working

---

[37] See, eg, A Murray, 'Over but Far from Finished – The EU's Financial Services Action Plan' (London: Centre for European Reform, 2004).
[38] By the Forum of European Securities Commissions (FESCO); see further, L Quaglia, 'Committee Governance in the Financial Sector in the European Union' (2008) 33 *European Integration* 565.
[39] CESR Charter (original version, 2001) Arts 4–5.
[40] CESR, *AR 2010*, 28; CESR, Multilateral Memorandum of Understanding on the Exchange of Information and Surveillance of Securities Activities (1999).
[41] CESR, *AR 2010*, 27. CESR could in this way be visualised as providing internal network accountability: see above, ch 10.
[42] COM (2007) 727 final, 12.
[43] Moloney, 'Innovation and Risk', above (n 29) 11, 16; T Tridimas, 'EU Financial Regulation: Federalization, Crisis Management and Law Reform' in P Craig and G de Búrca (eds), *The Evolution of EU Law*, 2nd edn (Oxford: OUP, 2011) 787.

in a transparent manner, while also making clear that the committee would respect the national and EU legislation regarding secrecy and confidentiality. Particularly concerning was the evident lack of formal legal and political accountability; the most the Charter could offer was an annual report to the Commission and some periodic reporting to the EP.[44] As time went on, some effort was made to ameliorate the situation through better communication with the Parliament, but development was muted.

Before the Fall: Evaluation

Providing more comforting reading, the Commission's 2007 review concluded that Lamfalussy process had contributed significantly to the development of a more flexible European regulatory system; had made the overall decision-making process more efficient, inclusive and timeous; and had begun to pave the way for greater supervisory convergence and cooperation. 'Better regulation' was said to have done the trick by helping to create a dynamic framework whereby EU capital markets could develop and innovate.[45] The review suggested 'some practical, necessary and achievable improvements', some already mentioned. On levels 1 and 2, the most significant proposal was to avoid potential bottlenecks and improve legal coherence and understanding by working on the legislation and TIMs simultaneously. Neatly illustrating the close interplay between rule formulation and scrutiny, the Commission prayed in aid the 'regulatory procedure with scrutiny' (see chapter four) as sufficiently safeguarding institutional balance or democratic control. The report focused at level 4 on the transposition of directives and the need for those Member States 'repeatedly in the slow lane' to do better.[46] Passing reference was made to the possibility of developing the EU supervisory framework in order to secure financial stability.[47]

Level 3 presented some difficulty. The Commission clearly felt frustrated: results had not always met (its remarkably high) expectations of common regulatory solutions and consistent application on the ground. Despite the network growth, the review concluded that the committees were not fully equipped to perform their tasks; the Commission Decisions establishing the committees did 'not sufficiently reflect their importance' in an ever more integrated market. Rightly grasping the issue of accountability, the review pointed up the twin-hatted situation of the national supervisors, lamenting that, if there was conflict with their committee's soft law measures, 'supervisors will let national obligations prevail'. Yet the Commission clearly felt constrained: at this time major institutional

[44] CESR Charter, Arts 5–6.
[45] COM (2007) 727 final, 3–4. See likewise, Inter-institutional Monitoring Group, Monitoring the Lamfalussy Process: Final Report (2007).
[46] COM (2007) 727 final, 6.
[47] Ibid, 3; in the context of work in ECOFIN on common principles for cross-border financial crisis management: see Conclusions of the European Council Meeting (9 October 2007) [22]–[29].

changes were 'not feasible given . . . the lack of agreement among Member States and other stakeholders'. The main recommendation was a small dose of political accountability, whereby the committees would regularly report on progress in meeting a joint Council and EP statement of objectives.[48]

The Council reached similar conclusions in its evaluation: 'experience to date with the Lamfalussy process is positive', though the efficiency and effectiveness of the level 3 process of informal governance needed improvement. It adopted a modest roadmap for reform, which signalled greater resources for, and qualified majority voting in, CEBS, CEIOPS and CESR, while maintaining the legally non-binding nature of their product.[49] In short, had it not been for the dramatic events that followed, Lamfalussy process would likely have been the subject of incremental development and fine-tuning.

AGENCIFICATION: FOURTH WAVE

Market Turmoil: Re-Evaluation and Reform

The financial turmoil in 2008 shattered such complacency, prompting the EU institutions to re-evaluate Lamfalussy process with a view to coping with new market conditions. Tasked specifically with issues of financial stability – how supervision in Europe should best be organised to ensure the orderly functioning of markets and prudential soundness of institutions, and likewise how to strengthen European as well as international cooperation – another body of 'Wise Men' was hastily assembled, chaired by leading banker Jacques de Larosière. An essay in 'regulatory repair', the report spoke of 'quite fundamental failures in the assessment of risk, both by financial firms and by those who regulated and supervised them'.[50]

Separating supervision from rule-making, but also assigning it the broad objective of 'ensuring that the rules applicable . . . are adequately implemented',[51] the group duly concluded that the Lamfalussy level 3 arrangements needed urgent reform. First, stressing the need for supervision at the macro (market-wide) as well as the micro (individual institution) level, the report highlighted the obvious gap in the regulatory framework hitherto: a lack of 'big picture' analysis or focus on systemic risk. A new EU body to monitor macro-level trends and provide early warnings was thus recommended.[52] Second, drawing attention to the seeming inability of the underpowered and under-resourced level 3 committees to grapple with rapidly evolving market developments, de Larosière made the case for their replacement by a corresponding set of Union bodies with legal personality in the

---

[48] COM (2007) 727 final, 3, 6–8.
[49] Conclusions of the European Council Meeting (4 December 2007) [15]–[22].
[50] Report of the High-Level Group on Financial Supervision in the EU (2009) 8.
[51] Ibid, 13, 38.
[52] In the form of a 'European Systemic Risk Council': ibid, 39–46.

form of the ESAs. A model partly moulded by the previous soft and evolutionary development would thus break the mould of EU agencification (see chapter two). Importantly however, 'national supervisors . . . would continue to carry-out day-to-day supervision and preserve the majority of their present competences': they 'are closest to the markets and institutions they supervise'. In proposing the establishment of the ESFS, de Larosière thus envisaged a largely decentralised structure: 'an integrated network of European financial supervisors, working with enhanced level 3 committees ("Authorities")'.[53]

These 'Wise Men' understood that improvements in a supervisory framework cannot sensibly be considered in isolation from the rules which the supervisors have to apply.[54] Seizing the moment, de Larosière propounded a recipe for 'more Europe', justified by the familiar arguments about competitive distortion, regulatory arbitrage and cross-border inefficiencies. It was then a case of 'equipping Europe with . . . a harmonised set of core rules' based wherever possible on regulations or otherwise involving maximum harmonisation in directives. After all, in this integrationist perspective, Lamfalussy process carried the seeds of its own destruction. Since the (framework) directives at level 1 typically left a range of national options, it was 'unreasonable to expect the level 3 committees to be able to impose a single solution'.[55]

'Wise Men' again proved influential in determining the chief contours of reform. The Commission rapidly produced analysis to the effect of the level 3 committees having reached their functional limits and legislative proposals for changes to the European supervisory architecture along the lines advocated by de Larosière.[56] A not so technical impact assessment pitched high, elaborating the argument that because divergent national interpretations of supervisory rules remained a common problem, the new ESAs would need powers to create binding supervisory standards and take decisions regarding individual firms.[57] Arduous negotiations followed involving objections from Member States to practical steps bearing on their particular national interests.[58] In the light of the ongoing financial crisis, and with strong support from the EP, an expansive legislative formulation eventually won out, though with the scars of convoluted administrative procedure to show for it.

The Council[59] had also given its blessing to the idea of 'a single rule book' with the overarching aim of a more uniform regulatory framework grounded in high quality technical standards directly applicable throughout the EU. Behind this lay

[53] Report of the High-Level Group on Financial Supervision in the EU (2009) 47.
[54] Ibid, 48; and see J Black, 'Risk Based Regulation: Choices, Practices and Lessons Being Learned' in OECD (ed), *Risk and Regulatory Policy: Improving the Governance of Risk* (Paris, 2010).
[55] Report of the High-Level Group on Financial Supervision in the EU (2009) 27, 29.
[56] Commission, 'Driving European Recovery' (Communication) COM (2009) 114 final, 5–7; COM (2009) 252 final; and eg, Commission, 'Proposal for a Regulation establishing a European Banking Authority' (Communication) COM (2009) 501 final.
[57] Commission, Impact assessment accompanying COM (2009) 252 final.
[58] P Snowdon and S Lovegrove, 'The New European Supervisory Structure' (2011) 83 *Compliance Officer Bulletin* 1.
[59] Conclusions of the European Council Meeting (18–19 June 2009) [8].

a surge of legislative activity aimed at making the whole sector more robust, the scale of which is difficult to exaggerate.[60] Key pillars of reform such as stronger prudential requirements would be complemented by stricter rules on particular structures (hedge funds), particular practices ('short selling') and particular methodologies (credit ratings).[61]

Developments in banking regulation illustrate the interlocking nature of the process. We note first the reinforced international dimension promoted especially by the G20 group of major economies and its associated Financial Stability Board, which finds tangible expression in 'Basel III', the strengthened minimum standards on the adequacy of bank capital recently promulgated by the Basel Committee.[62] Second, we see those standards being elaborated in terms of capital, liquidity and leverage through a monumental EU legislative package on capital requirements appropriately described as 'the backbone' of the single rule book in this sector.[63] A highly prescriptive and detailed regulation now covers the key prudential elements banks need to respect, coupled with a directive coordinating national provisions on such matters as authorisation or access to the industry and corporate governance.[64] Third, following the launch of the ESFS in January 2011, we see the EBA both operating against the backdrop of increasingly thick legal provision and actively contributing to it through standard setting.

Formal Network

Marking the step change from Lamfalussy, the ESFS is today the epitome of a formal administrative EU network, with shared and mutually reinforcing responsibilities grounded in a welter of legislation. Consisting of the European Systemic Risk Board (ESRB), three ESAs and a joint committee, and the many national competent authorities (NCAs) with direct responsibility for financial markets supervision, the institutional arrangements take the classic form of 'hub-and-spoke'. As first launched in January 2011, the network architecture was uniformly designed across the different financial services sectors; as indicated however, we will see important modifications introduced by virtue of the move towards Banking Union.

Duly tasked with macro-prudential oversight, the ESRB shows the importance of the preventive or 'fire-watching' role. In seeking to combat systemic risk and 'avoid periods of widespread financial distress' the chief weapons in the armoury are warnings and recommendations for remedial action, though notably toughened by 'act

---

[60] See Commission Memorandum, 'A comprehensive EU response to the financial crisis' (July 2013) 4.
[61] See, eg, Regulation 462/2013/EU on credit rating agencies [2013] OJ L146/1.
[62] For a useful overview, see G Ferrarini, K Hopt and E Wymeersch (eds), *Rethinking Financial Regulation and Supervision in Times of Crisis* (Oxford: OUP, 2012).
[63] Commission Memorandum, 'A comprehensive EU response', above (n 60) 3.
[64] Regulation 575/2013/EU on prudential requirements for credit institutions and investment firms [2013] OJ L176/1; Directive 2013/36/EU on access to the activity of credit institutions and the prudential supervision of credit institutions and investment firms [2013] OJ L176/338.

280 *Financial Services Regulation*

or explain' procedures.[65] As the Commission delicately explains, the ESRB's 'performance is contingent on how well it manages relations with other stakeholders'.[66] Not only is the Board highly reliant on the ECB and the national central banks to mitigate the systemic risks that it identifies, assesses and prioritises, but it is also dependent on statistical authorities for its very lifeblood – voluminous and credible macroeconomic and micro-financial data from across the EU.[67] There is exceptionally close linkage between this formally independent body and the ECB, which leads and hosts it and provides the secretariat responsible for preparing the analysis and conducting the day to day business.[68] Questions are naturally raised about possible clashes of function in this context and also lines of accountability.

Following the de Larosière prescription, the day to day micro-prudential supervision remains in the hands of the designated NCAs. Institutional diversity is then a defining feature of the network, more especially in banking by reason of the domestic mix of central bank and/or agency supervisory models (to which the ECB is now added as part of the SSM (see below)). Further illustrating a major contemporary trend in EU governance, we see these frontline network actors themselves made subject to detailed legislative provision over and above the general principle of 'sincere cooperation'. Stipulating the tools of prudential supervision across the Single Market, the 2013 coordinating Directive on banking and investment represents the state-of-the art in harnessing and empowering decentralised supervisory authority. On the one hand, Member States are under a duty to ensure that, as parties to the ESFS, their competent authorities 'cooperate with trust and full mutual respect . . . make every effort to comply with guidelines and recommendations issued by EBA . . . and respond to the warnings and recommendations issued by the ESRB'.[69] On the other hand, the directive ranges through the requisite assessment, inspectorial and reporting powers for, and horizontal exchanges of information between, NCAs, and on to the obligation to have in the national regulatory armoury administrative penalties 'sufficiently high . . . to be dissuasive even to larger institutions'.[70] Optimistically perhaps, Member States should ensure 'the expertise, resources, operational capacity, powers and independence necessary' to carry out relevant functions.[71] The directive speaks of NCAs suitably versed in the collective EU interest, hence considering the effect of their decisions 'not only on the stability of the financial system in their jurisdiction but also in all other Member States concerned'.[72]

---

[65] Regulation 1092/2010/EU on European Union macro-prudential oversight of the financial system and establishing a European Systemic Risk Board [2010] OJ L331/1, Arts 3, 16–18.
[66] Commission, ESFS review: public consultation (2013) 10.
[67] Regulation 1092/2010, Art 15.
[68] Ibid, Arts 4–5.
[69] Directive 2013/36/EU, Art 6.
[70] Ibid, recital 36; and see Arts 49–72.
[71] Ibid, Art 4.
[72] Ibid, recital 50; and see Art 7 ('Union dimension of supervision').

ESA Template

What we call the ESA template was established by a series of virtually identical regulations substituting the EBA,[73] the European Insurance and Occupational Pensions Authority (EIOPA)[74] and the European Securities and Markets Authority (ESMA)[75] for the three Lamfalussy level 3 committees. Incorporating and expanding on previous intervention at Union level, the mandate ranges widely to encompass elements of rule-formulation, cooperation and coordination and, on the operational side, monitoring, evaluation and enforcement. ESA tasks thus include contributing to the establishment of high-quality common regulatory and supervisory standards; contributing to the consistent application of legally binding EU acts, in particular by promoting a common supervisory culture; assessing market developments and examining the resilience of financial institutions (stress-testing); promoting transparency, simplicity and fairness for consumers; and guarding against activities that threaten the orderly functioning of the markets or financial stability.[76]

The ESAs may be said to represent a fourth wave of agencification at Union level (see chapter one), with the founding legislation establishing a fresh high-water mark of powers.[77] Authority to develop draft 'regulatory technical standards' (RTs) and draft 'implementing technical standards' (ITs) and – typically in the form of default powers – to take individual decisions addressed to national supervisors and – in cases involving directly applicable EU law, to financial institutions, is the essence of this. Supplementary powers include issuing guidelines, recommendations and opinions; promoting cross-border colleges of supervisors; establishing common methodologies for testing financial processes and products; collecting information on financial institutions; peer review; and developing international links.[78] The legislation is once again voluminous.

The quid pro quo for more centralisation at Union level is entrenched influence for the frontline NCAs. The ESAs then are both constituted as a higher or secondary supervisory tier and effectively colonised by representatives of the lower or primary level. The touchstone of this bottom-up or 'club' conception is the role and composition of the board of supervisors established for each authority. Assigning them the key duties of appointing the chairperson, guiding the

---

[73] Regulation 1093/2010.
[74] Regulation 1094/2010/EU establishing a European Supervisory Authority (European Insurance and Occupational Pensions Authority) [2010] OJ L331/48.
[75] Regulation 1095/2010/EU establishing a European Supervisory Authority (European Securities and Markets Authority) OJ L331/84.
[76] eg, Regulation 1093/2010, Arts 8(1) and 9; for a useful overview, see E Wymeersch, 'The European Financial Supervisory Authorities or ESAs' in G Ferrarini, K Hopt and E Wymeersch (eds), *Rethinking Financial Regulation and Supervision in Times of Crisis* (Oxford: OUP, 2012).
[77] M Busuioc, 'Rule-Making by the European Financial Supervisory Authorities: Walking a Tight Rope' (2013) 19 *European Law Journal* 111; E Chiti, 'European Agencies' Rulemaking: Powers, Procedures and Assessment' (2013) 19 *European Law Journal* 93.
[78] See, eg, Regulation 1093/2010, Arts 8(2), 21–23, 29–35.

agency's work and adopting the opinions, recommendations and decisions,[79] the original ESA template envisaged the boards generally proceeding by simple or qualified majority.[80] They have as voting members all the heads of the national supervisory systems and as non-voting members representatives from the Commission, the ESRB and other ESAs, and, in the case of the EBA, the ECB. Of course the legislation says that all board members shall act independently and objectively in the sole interest of the Union as a whole.[81]

The template predictably includes a management board (elected by and from the voting members of the board of supervisors), and as full-time professionals both the chairperson (appointed subject to objection by the EP) and an executive director.[82] Silo mentality to the detriment of the ESFS network being an obvious danger, the legislation further provides for some joined-up governance at Union level. The joint committee of the ESAs is cast as a forum 'in which the [authorities] shall cooperate regularly and closely and ensure cross-sectorial consistency' in their work.[83] A joint board of appeal is established, comprised of independent members 'with a proven record of relevant knowledge and professional experience', to review ESA decisions addressed to a national supervisor or individual party.[84]

Standards and Guidelines

RTs and ITs correspond to delegated and implementing acts within the meaning of Articles 290–91 of the Treaty on the Functioning of the European Union (TFEU) (see chapter five).[85] However, dealt with in subtly different ways from other executive legislation adopted under Lamfalussy level 2, they constitute a new category of measures in the canon of EU regulation, a development which involves stretching the historically restrictive *Meroni* doctrine.[86] Whereas the label 'technical' is meant to denote measures that do 'not imply strategic decisions or policy choices',[87] experience teaches that, in a complex and sometimes arcane field like financial services regulation, such distinctions are apt to be blurred. Forefronting problems associated with agencification of control and accountability, there lurks behind the dull label considerable responsibility.

---

[79] Ibid, Art 43.
[80] Ibid, Art 44 as originally drafted; as explained below, the EBA now operates on a different basis in light of the SSM.
[81] Ibid, Arts 40 and 42.
[82] Ibid, Arts 45–53.
[83] Ibid, Arts 54–55.
[84] Ibid, Arts 58–60. Art 61 makes provision for actions before the CJEU.
[85] Ibid, Arts 10 and 15.
[86] See above, ch 1, p 32; and see, N Moloney, 'The European Securities and Markets Authority and Institutional Design for the EU Financial Market – A Tale of Two Competences: Part 1 – Rule-Making' (2011) 12 *European Business Organization Law Review* 41.
[87] Regulation 1093/2010, Art 10(1).

The power to endorse what are binding technical standards is formally delegated to the Commission,[88] but with the resounding legislative message of a high degree of autonomy for the ESAs in developing and promoting them. Draft RTs should be subject to amendment 'only in very restricted and extraordinary circumstances, since the Authority is the actor in close contact with and knowing best the daily functioning of financial markets'.[89] The ESAs' novel power to initiate the standard-setting process is then all the more significant; one leading commentator has characterised them as 'quasi-rule-makers'.[90] Other provisions chip away at the Commission's otherwise dominant position. Formal dialogue is envisaged should it be minded to reject or amend a draft standard; the legislation even contemplates the Council or EP summoning the warring parties to explain their differences.[91] The respective powers of those two institutions to veto RTs, and indeed to revoke the whole delegation,[92] provide a necessary safeguard, but ultimately, amid rapidly multiplying standard setting by the ESAs, only that.

The design also highlights the possibilities of soft law 'with sticks'. Taking forward the quest for consistent supervision and common application pursued by the Lamfalussy committees, guidelines and recommendations issued by the ESAs may be addressed both to NCAs and financial institutions. Although not classified as legally binding measures, and so avoiding input from the Council and EP, the Regulation commands that recipients 'shall make every effort to comply' with them.[93] Procedural disincentives are used to underwrite this: items in what is aptly described as 'the naming, blaming, and shaming toolkit of the ESA'.[94] Playing on the importance of market reputation, provision is made for a guideline or recommendation to require that financial institutions 'report, in a clear and detailed way', whether they comply with it.[95] Alternatively, reading across to the arena of institutional politics, not only is a NCA to comply or explain, but the ESA is also directed to advertise the fact of non-compliance and to report sinning members of the club to the big three EU institutions, outlining how it intends to ensure better behaviour in the future (perhaps through a binding decision).[96] As a way of fostering compliance, this hard-edged form of soft law is likely to cast a long shadow in the banking sector. Amending legislation passed for the purposes of the SSM mandates the EBA to draw up a 'single supervisory handbook' in consultation with the competent authorities.[97] Envisaged in terms of a common framework for the

---

[88] Ibid, Arts 10(1) and 15(1).
[89] Ibid, recital 23.
[90] Busuioc, above (n 77) 113.
[91] Regulation 1093/2010, Arts 10 and 14.
[92] Ibid, Arts 11–12.
[93] Ibid, Art 16.
[94] P Weismann, 'The European Financial Market Supervisory Authorities and their Power to Issue Binding Decisions' (2012) 27 *Journal of International Banking Law & Regulation* 495, 496.
[95] Regulation 1093/2010, Art 16(3).
[96] Ibid, Art 16(4).
[97] Regulation 1022/2013 EU amending Regulation 1093/2010 establishing the European Banking Authority as regards the conferral of specific tasks on the European Central Bank [2013] OJ L287/5, Art 1.

identification, measurement and analysis of risk, together with common guidance for supervisory intervention and corrective action across the Single Market,[98] it will not take the form of legally binding acts. But the recital is blunt: 'competent authorities should use the handbook'.[99]

The legislation factors in 'better regulation' as a source of legitimacy. When preparing technical standards, and likewise with guidelines and recommendations 'where appropriate', the ESAs – unlike in Commission practice (see chapter five) – are under a legal obligation to engage in open public consultation and cost–benefit analysis.[100] Enjoying privileged access, at the heart of this formal proceduralisation is a sector-specific equivalent of the European Economic and Social Committee (EESC) (see chapter four). Take the 'Banking Stakeholder Group' which the Regulation requires the EBA to appoint and give administrative resources, provide with all necessary information and consult.[101] The Group is empowered to submit opinions and advice to the agency on any matter, but with 'particular focus' on the hard and soft law aspects. The membership must include both industry and non-industry representatives; in practice, many of the members have been directly or indirectly involved in implementing EBA norms.[102] In terms of input values, such close engagement between public and private practitioners – a highly corporatist approach – scores well for expertise or market know-how in a highly complex area. Conversely however, it is not entirely surprising to learn of complaints to the EO about skewed representation, especially when it is discovered that the membership category 'users of bank services' has included audit firms, rating agencies and bank consultants.[103] 'Constructing a civil society', we recall, is a perilous task.

Decisions, Decisions

In their role of secondary supervisory tier, the ESAs' intervention powers can usefully help to shore up market confidence and mutual trust between Member States. Three main scenarios need to be covered: the day to day possibilities of poor supervision by NCAs and hence breaches of EU law; disputes between NCAs arising from time to time in the decentralised system; and the hopefully rare experience of severe and immediate threats to the markets. Again treading novel ground, the powers are intended to ensure that, via their representatives in the three ESA 'clubs', the first tier or front line supervisors may not only be encouraged, supported and acculturated, but also effectively cajoled. The better the cooperation through the instrumentality of the ESAs, the less often the formal administrative procedures will operate, or so the argument goes.

---

[98] EBA, *AR 2012*, 7.
[99] Regulation 1022/2013, recital 7.
[100] Regulation 1093/2010, Arts 10(1), 15(1), 16(2); subject to proportionality. And see EBA, Public Statement on Consultation Practices (2012).
[101] Ibid, Art 37.
[102] Banking Stakeholder Group, End of term report (2013) 5.
[103] Ibid, 6; EO, Inv 1966/2011/(EIS)LP.

Actual or apparent failure by a competent authority properly to apply binding rules or standards, 'in particular by failing to ensure that a financial institution satisfies the requirements', grounds a three-stage procedure.[104] The ESA can again initiate matters, being empowered to investigate with a view to addressing a recommendation to the front line supervisor. Should this not have the desired effect (in the light of more provision for 'naming and shaming'), the Commission can choose to step in through the medium of a formal opinion stipulating compliance. Should the competent authority still prove recalcitrant, then as the last resort in a situation where timely compliance is necessary to maintain neutral competitive conditions or orderly markets, the ESA may bypass it by addressing an individual decision to a financial institution requiring the necessary action.

The elongated nature of the decision-making chain bears testimony to the political and administrative sensitivities and especially the demand to tailor to *Meroni* by weaving in the common thread of Commission control. The framework of recommendation/formal opinion/individual decision also matches with the familiar idea in regulatory theory of escalated responses to non-compliance.[105] Even so, the elongated procedure is visualised as a fast track enforcement mechanism, operating alongside, and 'without prejudice to',[106] a general Commission infringement procedure famed for providing Member States with multiple opportunities to put things right (see chapter seven). In fact, neatly pointing up a growth in multiple tiers of supervision, this set of default powers not only operates in the shadow of, but may also by remedying infringements halt recourse to, the TFEU Article 258 mechanism. Attention is drawn to the qualitative difference between the two enforcement mechanisms: by ultimately targeting the financial institution, the one reaches parts the other cannot reach.

As for coordinating supervision, ESA powers to mediate and arbitrate between competent authorities operating in a transnational market place are the logical next step. Multiplying rules and standards in such a technically complex and fast-moving field are apt to produce genuine issues of interpretation and/or about the appropriate regulatory response. As and when an official dispute arises, an ESA panel may be tasked with brokering a consensual solution.[107] Should this 'conciliation phase' fail to produce results, the legislation envisages the ESA upping the ante: first, by a decision resolving the matter with binding effects for the authorities involved; and second, by another bypassing decision addressed to the market participant. By the standards of EU governance, these too are appropriately described as 'eye-catching powers'.[108]

---

[104] Regulation 1093/2010, Art 17.
[105] I Ayres and J Braithwaite, *Responsive Regulation: Transcending the Deregulation Debate* (Oxford: OUP, 1992).
[106] Regulation 1093/2010, Art 17(6).
[107] Ibid, Arts 19 and 41.
[108] N Moloney, 'The European Securities and Markets Authority and Institutional Design for the EU Financial Market – A Tale of Two Competences: Part 2 – Rules in Action' (2011) 12 *European Business Organization Law Review* 177, 202.

286 *Financial Services Regulation*

High level political involvement is called for in emergency situations. Power to declare one in view of adverse developments seriously jeopardising market integrity or the stability of all or part of the financial system is assigned to the Council, in practice operating on confidential recommendations from the ESFS network. The legislation then envisages the agencies, in those 'exceptional circumstances where coordinating action . . . is necessary', adopting individual decisions formally instructing the front line authorities to act, for example by prohibiting dealings in acutely high-risk financial products.[109] These default powers though are subject to especially close constraint. Not only is the subsequent option of targeting private parties put in terms of urgent cases where the competent authority is in manifest breach, but also a special constitutional safeguard applies, whereby ESA decisions impinging on Member States' fiscal responsibilities can be challenged in the Council.[110] Happily, as with the exercise of their other intervention powers, the ESAs have not yet found it necessary to take emergency action.[111]

Going On

The ESAs were operationalised through a so-called omnibus directive listing specific areas under existing financial services legislation where they might exercise powers.[112] Underwriting the qualitative shift from Lamfalussy-style advisory committees, this measure also paved the way for the ongoing accretion of ESA powers via subsequent legislative interventions. Organisationally speaking, there has typically been no clean break however. We read for example of 'CESR . . . transformed into ESMA', with the committee reviewing internal structures and designing future procedures and policies for the agency.[113] Following in the footsteps of their not so illustrious predecessors, the ESAs would soon be filling out, in the case of ESMA by a doubling of staff to over one hundred. Not large scale, but sufficient it appears for six divisions: three sub-sectoral ones – markets, investment and reporting and credit rating; and three cross-cutting ones – economic research, the tellingly titled 'legal, cooperation and convergence division' and operations. Once more drawing together expert officials from the front line competent authorities, much of ESMA's technical work is carried on in multiple standing committees, working groups, task forces and panels. There are strong echoes of CESR in a peer-pressurising review panel and in the work of 'ESMA-Pol' on market integrity.[114] The role of Union-level agencies in promoting horizontal cross-fertilisation among Member State administrations is clearly prioritised (see chapter one).

[109] Regulation 1093/2010, Art 18.
[110] As is also the case with arbitration decisions: ibid, Art 38.
[111] ESFS review: public consultation (2013) 4–5.
[112] Directive 78/2010/EU [2010] OJ L331/120 ('Omnibus I').
[113] CESR, *AR 2010*, 'Foreword'.
[114] ESMA, *AR 2012*, ch 3.

Early workings confirm the significance of the ESAs' standard-setting role. Take the EBA. In 2012, the agency conducted 23 public consultations on draft technical standards, 16 of which concerned 'possibly the most important area in which truly uniform standards are required', the definition of bank capital.[115] In true managerialist jargon, the 2014 work programme identifies a long list of 'regulatory products' requiring delivery under the capital requirements legislation; bearing such mysterious titles as 'countercyclical capital buffer', 'market risk internal models' and 'asset encumbrance', they include some 50 RTs and 25 ITs, as well as seven sets of guidelines.[116] An online 'single rule book Q&A' tool for the benefit of supervisors and supervisees has been launched. Designed with the aim of ensuring that the rule book 'embodies a "living" and evolving regulatory framework', there is however more to this than meets the eye. Soft governance and agency ambition combining, it is envisaged that peer pressure will be 'a driving force in ensuring adherence to and compliance with the responses provided in the Q&A process, even though they have no force in law'.[117]

Symptomatic of a never-ending swing of the pendulum, the Banking Stakeholder Group (BSG) has already expressed concerns about the prospect of over regulation. The talk is of 'excessive granulation' in the developing single rule book; of 'cumulative impact', or whether in strict cost–benefit terms the totality of the new regulation is proportionate; and of 'substantial detail' in some of the reporting requirements. Perhaps confusingly however, the BSG speaks both of 'lack of diversity as banks converge on similar business models and behaviour', and of the regulatory regime being applied in some areas 'in a particularly nationalistic way'.[118] Convergence, we are reminded, is a process not an event!

NEW FRONTIER

Testimony to the ongoing impact of the financial crisis on European integration, the ESFS would soon be officially characterised as necessary but insufficient. The ESA template certainly tested the constitutional parameters in EU governance, but what of more thoroughgoing institutional reform most obviously for the eurozone? In June 2012, the European Council agreed on a Banking Union to place matters on a sounder footing and restore confidence in the euro as part of a longer-term vision for economic and fiscal integration.[119] Underscoring the point that 'mere coordination' was too rickety a framework for securing stability in the context of a single currency, the Commission's road map presented the single supervisory mechanism, which entails the large-scale assumption at Union level

---

[115] EBA, *AR 2012*, 'Foreword'.
[116] EBA, Work Programme (2014) 11.
[117] Ibid, 6.
[118] BSG, 'End of term report', 21.
[119] Conclusions of European Council meeting (28–29 June 2012); Van Rompuy report, *Towards a Genuine Economic and Monetary Union* (December 2012).

of direct supervisory responsibilities previously exercised by Member States either in the eurozone or opting to participate, as 'a first important step'.[120] While the EBA would continue to lead work on the 'single rule book' in the context of the Single Market, the road map identified as other pillars of the Banking Union an integrated crisis management framework, more particularly a single mechanism to govern the resolution (winding-up) of failed banks, and a common system of deposit guarantees to protect customers.[121] At the time of writing, legislation is being carried forward on a single resolution mechanism and on bank shareholders and creditors taking losses.[122]

The SSM tackled two immediate sets of problems. Fostered by the financial crisis, and especially an evident propensity for 'home bias' (national authorities treating their domestic institutions more favourably), the first one is fragmentation of EU banking markets.[123] The second involves the vicious circle – of which people in southern Europe have been made grimly aware – where banks hold large quantities of sovereign debt and that debt loses value, banks become financially unstable and public assistance is required, which further degrades the value of the banks' holdings. The Commission is seen scrambling to promote the SSM since, under the Treaty creating the European Stability Mechanism, failing banks might then be recapitalised directly.[124]

The unhappy fact of over €4.5 trillion of taxpayers' money diverted to bank rescues has served not only to keep reform at the top of the agenda, but also to ensure close, high-level scrutiny. The original timetable of ECB supervision by mid-2013 always appeared optimistic however, given the many political, legal and administrative difficulties involved. The legislation was only finally approved in October 2013, together with an Inter-Institutional Agreement (IIA) centred on the Bank's accountability to the EP for its new supervisory role.[125] The ECB will operate the system from November 2014.

Architectural Issues

In one sense the policy-makers were fortunately placed because Article 127(6) TFEU, which envisages the ECB being delegated supervisory powers by means of

---

[120] COM (2012) 510 final, 3-4; and see T Beck (ed), *Banking Union for Europe: Risks and Challenges* (London: CEPR, 2012).

[121] COM (2012) 510 final, 4–9.

[122] Commission, 'Proposal for a Regulation establishing uniform rules and a uniform procedure for the resolution of credit institutions in the framework of a Single Resolution Mechanism and a Single Bank Resolution Fund' COM (2013) 520 final; Commission, 'Proposal for a Directive on establishing a framework for the recovery and resolution of credit institutions and investment firms' COM (2012) 280 final. Updated rules on guaranteed deposits are part of the package.

[123] COM (2012) 510 final, 3.

[124] Commission, 'Proposal for a Regulation conferring specific tasks on the European Central Bank concerning policies relating to the prudential supervision of credit institutions' COM (2012) 511 final, 2.

[125] EP and ECB, Inter-Institutional Agreement on the cooperation on procedures related to the Single Supervisory Mechanism (2013).

Council regulations, provided an obvious basis for the new legislative policy. Not only could the vicissitudes of further treaty amendment be avoided, but so too could the *Meroni* doctrine (which effectively precluded the alternative of an agency (the EBA) as hands-on supervisor). Conversely however, the precise wording of the Treaty caused difficulties. Creating a whole series of limitations, Article 127(6) is couched in terms of unanimity, of 'specific tasks' for the ECB, of prudential supervision (and not for example crisis management) and of banks or credit institutions (but not insurance undertakings). The resulting design is inevitably missing key elements of flexibility.

And then there was the multifaceted question of the SSM/Single Market relationship. Encouraging non-eurozone countries to participate sat comfortably with the goal of promoting financial stability, but another major problem of fit arose with such countries lacking voting rights in the ECB's Governing Council and in any case not being bound by ECB decisions.[126] Here, as elsewhere in the design, procedural contortions mark the way forward: a tribute to official ingenuity. Again, since non-eurozone countries – most notably the UK – could not be compelled to participate, the (competing) model of direct national supervision would still need to be accommodated in the Single Market: a multi-speed Europe writ large. Attention is drawn to the fault-line confronting the policymakers in the relationship between the ECB and EBA by reason both of their different geographical remits and their divided regulatory responsibility.

As a piece of terminology the 'single supervisory mechanism' sounds well, but what does it actually connote? The Commission initially put forward a centralised and all-embracing model in which the ECB would have direct supervisory responsibility for the over 6000 deposit-taking banks in the eurozone, with national eurozone institutions cast in the role of modest under-workers (doing preliminary tasks and providing information).[127] Member States led by Germany would not put up with this, including for good pragmatic reasons of overload or lack of targeting.[128] The resulting institutional architecture is a complex hybrid, a so-called single mechanism that involves several main overlapping tiers of supervisory authority: (a) general responsibility of the ECB 'for the effective and consistent functioning' of the system; (b) direct supervision by the ECB of banks deemed 'significant'; and (c) direct supervision of other banks by national institutions; as well as (d) certain shared forms of macro-prudential intervention.[129] Given the risk of failure by reason of continuing supervisory fragmentation, a high premium is placed on establishing effective collaborative procedures across the tiers – a challenging task. The way in which a qualitatively different role –

---

[126] TFEU, Arts 282–83; ECB Statute, Art 10(1).
[127] COM (2012) 511 final, 4–5.
[128] See D Howarth and L Quaglia, 'Banking Union as Holy Grail' (2013) 51 *Journal of Common Market Studies Annual Review* 103.
[129] Regulation 1024/2013, Arts 4–5. For further details, see E Ferran and V Babis, 'The European Single Supervisory Mechanism' (2013) 13 *Journal of Corporate Law Studies* 255; and S Verhelst, 'Assessing the Single Supervisory Mechanism: Passing the Point of No Return for Europe's Banking Union'(2013) Egmont Paper No 58.

involving close interaction with market actors – has been grafted on to the constitutional model of a determinedly independent central bank tasked with broad monetary responsibilities deserves special emphasis. Raising further questions of fit, the legislation thus sees many new modalities being incorporated in the institutional framework of the ECB: from internal separation of functions to investigative powers, and on through due process and accountability.

Inside the SSM: Tasks, Powers and Division of Labour

Regulation 1024/2013 provides the ECB with a long list of specific supervisory tasks, which include authorising credit institutions (and withdrawing authorisations); ensuring the adequacy of internal capital; supervising the credit operations of financial conglomerates; assessing mergers and acquisitions; and supervising governance arrangements.[130] The logic of the system is that much of this activity will concern compliance with the single rule book, premised in particular on regular stress tests of balance sheets and asset quality. Par for the course, the Bank's investigative armoury includes powers to request information from 'persons belonging to' any institution it regulates; to examine books and records; and conduct on-site inspections, with national authorities under an obligation to assist.[131]

The Bank's enforcement powers include requiring regulatees to take corrective measures when, or when likely to be, in breach of EU requirements; levying administrative sanctions for violations up to 10 per cent of annual turnover; and – potentially raising tricky problems of judicial review in a multi-level system – requiring Member State authorities to open proceedings for sanctions under national law.[132] Especially noteworthy is the power to require action whenever, within the framework of a supervisory review, the ECB determines that a bank's 'arrangements, strategies, processes and mechanisms' and 'funds and liquidity' do not ensure 'a sound management and coverage of its risks'. Regulation 1024/2013 proceeds to specify a whole range of obligations which the ECB can impose, for example that the institution uses net profits to strengthen funding, holds funds in excess of capital requirements laid down by EU law, restricts dividends to shareholders and removes delinquents from the management body. The ECB in short will have big teeth.

Article 6 of the Regulation deals with the division of supervisory labour under the pleasing title 'Cooperation within the SSM'. 'Less significant' banks, and hence the ambit of national control, should be identified by reference to size, economic significance for the Union or any participating Member State and significance of cross-border activities. More specific criteria (assets for example of over €30 billion) ensure however that all the big players will be in the care of the ECB. With a view to securing the credibility of the system, not only will banks in receipt of a

[130] Regulation 1024/2013, Art 4(1).
[131] Ibid, Arts 9–13.
[132] Ibid, Arts 16 and 18.

bail out automatically come under ECB supervision, but the ECB may also at any time take on the direct supervision of a bank 'when necessary to ensure consistent application of high supervisory standards'. Another fine illustration of steering, the ECB will issue regulations, guidelines and general instructions to national authorities on how to perform their parallel role. Supervisory tasks not covered by the Regulation and hence remaining at national level include consumer protection and prevention of money laundering and terrorist financing (see chapter twelve).

Article 6 follows the familiar path of specific provision building on the overarching principle of sincere cooperation (see chapter two). Both the Bank and NCAs 'shall be subject to a duty of cooperation in good faith, and an obligation to exchange information'. In case the message is not fully understood, subsequent paragraphs state that national authorities 'shall in particular' provide the ECB with 'all information necessary' for carrying out its supervisory tasks, and 'shall be responsible for assisting the ECB . . . with the preparation and implementation of any [supervisory] acts . . . including assistance with verification activities'. A significant rule-making power, the ECB has been tasked in consultation with national authorities with adopting and making public 'a framework to organise the practical arrangements for the implementation' of Article 6.[133] The subsequent SSM Framework Regulation[134] supplies a wide range of technical and procedural detail about practical workings: from the specific methodology for assessing a bank's economic importance[135] to organisational matters such as joint supervisory teams and colleges of supervisors[136] and to the use of administrative sanctions.[137]

Inside the Bank: Separation and Autonomy

In part reflecting German influence, the policymakers have aimed to keep the ECB's supervisory role separate from the monetary policy responsibilities in order to avoid any conflicts of interest between the two functions. The tasks conferred by the one 'shall neither interfere with, nor be determined by' the tasks relating to the other.[138] This approach has also served the EP well, effectively opening up the possibility of discrete democratic oversight in the face of a stern treaty provision enjoining protection of monetary policy activity from political interference.[139] The obvious administrative strategy is so-called 'Chinese walls'. Regulation 1024/2013 provides that ECB staff working on bank supervision must be organisationally

---

[133] Ibid, Art 6(7).
[134] Regulation 468/2014/EU of the European Central Bank establishing the framework for cooperation within the Single Supervisory Mechanism between the European Central Bank and national competent authorities and with national designated authorities [2014] OJ L141/1.
[135] Ibid, Arts 39–66.
[136] Ibid, Arts 3–6, 8–10.
[137] Ibid, Arts 120–37.
[138] Regulation 1024/2013, Art 25(2).
[139] TFEU, Art 130.

separated from monetary policy staff and must report through different hierarchies, and also requires published rules on professional secrecy and information exchanges between the two functional areas. The Bank must likewise ensure that 'the operation of the Governing Council is completely differentiated', including by 'strictly separated' meetings and agendas.[140] The practical reality of all this is open to question.

With a view to increasing the Bank's operational capacity, while underwriting functional separation and providing those non-eurozone countries desirous of supervision by the ECB with a forum, the legislation goes further, providing that the planning and execution of the ECB's supervisory tasks shall be 'fully undertaken' by a new Supervisory Board (SB).[141] Consisting of a chair, a vice-chair, four representatives of the ECB and, ensuring national numerical dominance, one representative from the competent authorities of each participating Member State, the Board may normally proceed by simple majority. The Commission had envisaged the Bank's Governing Council (GC) delegating specific tasks to the SB, but this approach was of doubtful validity by reason of the guaranteed constitutional position of the GC as the Bank's ultimate decision-making authority.[142] Hence circumlocution: formally speaking, the SB does not exercise supervisory decision-making powers; instead it will make 'draft decisions' for adoption by the GG, which will be deemed adopted unless the GC timeously objects.[143] If the GC intervenes, a national supervisor may seek assistance to resolve the matter from the national representatives who constitute the Bank's mediation panel.[144] In sum, given the scale of the ECB's new supervisory responsibilities and hence the likely large number of decisions, the SB resembles a 'de facto agency': one that is housed in the Bank but which will operate with a high degree of autonomy.

Variable Geometry

In face of the fact that non-eurozone countries cannot be full members of a Banking Union, the EU legislature has had to fall back on 'close cooperation' to accommodate their participation in the SSM. The opt-in state, in return for all its banks becoming part of the Mechanism, must undertake to provide all relevant regulatory information and to ensure that the NCA will abide by any ECB guidelines and – crucially – is obliged by national law to adopt any supervisory measures requested by the Bank.[145] The difficulty of ensuring mutual trust is illuminated by multiple provisions on suspension and termination. The opt-in state may end the arrangement with immediate effect if it disagrees with a draft decision, or after

---

[140] Regulation 1024/2013, Art 25.
[141] Ibid, Art 26.
[142] COM (2012) 511 final, 7; TFEU, Art 129(1) and ECB Statute Art 9(3).
[143] Regulation 1024/2013, Art 26(8); the procedure is akin to the reversed QMV model sometimes used in the Council of Ministers.
[144] Ibid, Art 25(5).
[145] Ibid, Art 7(2). See further, Arts 106–17 of the SSM Framework Regulation.

three years' membership, but this means no new deal for the next three years. The ECB may suspend or terminate 'close cooperation' where, for example, the opt-in state fails to heed a warning to comply with its undertakings or the NCA cavils at a requested supervisory measure.[146]

In practical terms, it is also appropriate to speak of a double supervisory mechanism in the Single Market. The UK, that most determined non-participant in the SSM, accounts through the City of London for almost 50 per cent of EU financial services business.[147] While the ECB and the Bank of England[148] will both have to hand the single rule book and supervisory handbook, there is clear scope for disagreement between these two behemoth institutions. Regulation 1024/2013 ventures soft law as the solution. Memorandums of Understanding (MoUs) linking the ECB and the NCAs of non-participating (non-eurozone) countries will make general provision for supervisory cooperation under EU law; supplementary MoUs will cover situations where the non-participant state (the UK) hosts a bank of global systemic importance.[149] Noteworthy in this context is the ringing legislative statement that the ECB should aim to ensure not only the soundness and stability of banks and participating financial systems, but also the unity and integrity of the Single Market, and in particular must take into account the principles of equality and non-discrimination.[150]

The new EBA Regulation not only strengthens the agency's role in general, but also, as was its original purpose as part of a package with Regulation 1024/2013,[151] reworks some key procedural modalities so as to forestall the perverse effect of the SSM fragmenting the Single Market in financial services. This again is a product of hard bargaining among Member States.[152] Take first the inter-organisational aspect, where the London-based agency is legally privileged over the Frankfurt-based institution. Through the expedient of the ECB being designated a 'competent authority', the pre-existing model of vertical relations between the EBA and national supervisory bodies has been read across to the Union level.[153] Glossing over the unlikelihood, the recital states that the EBA should be able to carry out its tasks in relation to the ECB 'in the same manner', with its extended powers of mediation and emergency action being adjusted accordingly to remain effective.[154] As for the second, intra-organisational aspect, the Commission had appeared to envisage the supervisors from SSM countries following agreed lines in EBA decision-making.[155] Non-eurozone countries have successfully demanded

---

[146] Regulation 1024/2013, Art 7(5)–(9); SSM Framework Regulation, Arts 118–19.
[147] See UK House of Lords EU Committee, *European Banking Union: Key Issues and Challenges* (HL 2012–13, 88).
[148] In the guise of its subsidiary, the Prudential Regulation Authority.
[149] Regulation 1024/2013, Art 3(6).
[150] Ibid, recital 30.
[151] Commission, 'Proposal for a Regulation amending Regulation 1093/2010' COM (2012) 512 final.
[152] See S Seyad, 'The Impact of the Proposed Banking Union on the Unity and Integrity of the European Union's Single Market' (2013) 28 *Journal of International Banking Law and Regulation* 99.
[153] Regulation 1022/2013, Art 1(2).
[154] Ibid, recital 12.
[155] COM (2012) 512 final, 4.

procedural protection in the guise of a double majority arrangement. Important decisions such as those on breaches of EU law or on technical standards, which were previously taken in the EBA's board of supervisors by simple or qualified majority, now also require simple majorities of both SSM and non-SSM states.[156] The collective interest of Member States in the Single Market is here prioritised over the collective interest of 'eurozone plus' countries in Banking Union – at the risk of delay, weak decision-making and/or stasis.

Due Process and Accountability

A striking feature of the Commission's original plans for ECB supervision was the scarce attention paid to the good governance values of due process and accountability.[157] Highlighting the role of institutional politics in the development of administrative procedure, both the Council and the EP sought to make good the deficiency, to the extent of EP delaying tactics with a view to squeezing concessions from the ECB. The affair further illustrates the inter-institutional agreement as a source of procedural provision (see chapter four).

Happily, Regulation 1024/2013 makes specific reference to the rights of the defence and reasoned decisions, procedural protection which is fleshed out in the SSM Framework Regulation.[158] It also establishes an administrative board of review tasked on request with procedural and substantive scrutiny of draft supervisory decisions.[159] Experts appointed by the Bank for a five-year term, board members are naturally required to 'act independently and in the public interest' and 'not be bound by any instructions'. Yet another convoluted procedure in the face of the Bank's entrenched constitutional position, the SB will consider the board's non-binding opinion and make a new draft decision abrogating, amending or restating the original one, subject to objection by the GC. Reflecting the Bank's new found engagement with market actors, the development is welcome nonetheless, especially given the delay and cost associated with proceedings in the Court of Justice of the European Union (CJEU).

As to accountability, the Regulation again contains much that is unexceptional: from annual reporting to public hearings in the EP, and on to 'sincere cooperation' with any parliamentary investigations. The Council jointly with the EP also has the rights to approve, and request the removal of, the chair and vice-chair of the SB. Reflecting the importance of the Bank's new role, special provision is made for ad hoc and confidential meetings involving the chair of the SB and the chair and vice-chairs of the competent EP committee.[160] National parliaments of

---

[156] Regulation 1022/2013, Art 1(24). Art 2 provides though for early review of the arrangement.
[157] See COM (2012) 511 final, 7.
[158] Regulation 1024/2013, Art 22; SSM Framework Regulation, Arts 31–33.
[159] Regulation 1024/2013, Art 24.
[160] Ibid, Arts 20 and 26.

participating states may 'invite' the SB 'to participate in an exchange of views' concerning supervision.[161]

In elaborating on their relationship the EP–ECB Inter-Institutional Agreement reminds its readers that 'any conferral of supervisory powers to the Union level should be balanced by appropriate accountability arrangements'.[162] That things are not so simple is shown by some hotly contested provision. Whereas MEPs naturally sought access to confidential information about the actual conduct of supervision, better to promote accountability, the ECB understandably resisted in light of the potentially damaging or destabilising effects of unnecessary disclosure. The eventual compromise sees the Bank not disclosing the minutes of meetings but agreeing instead to provide the parliamentary committee 'at least with a comprehensive and meaningful record of [SB] proceedings . . . that enables an understanding of the discussions, including an annotated list of decisions'. The IIA likewise states that discussion in the special confidential meetings 'shall follow the principle of openness and elaboration around the relevant circumstances' but that 'no minutes or any other recording . . . shall be taken', that no media statements shall be made, and that 'each participant . . . shall sign every time a solemn declaration not to divulge the content'.[163] Representing a very private form of public accountability, this arrangement is fated to be severely tested.

CONCLUSION

Financial services afford the most striking illustration of the evolution of EU administration this side of the millennium. Repeated and overlapping processes of moulding, remoulding and breaking the mould of administrative arrangements characterise the three main sets of developments discussed in this chapter. A standard visualisation would be movement from national control of markets to greater (though certainly not full) Union control. Closer examination however reveals a complicated set of institutional dynamics, not least by way of multilayered supervision, strong bottom-up elements, divided regulatory functions at Union level and variable geometry or a 'multi-speed' Europe. This short history of integration and crisis also serves to highlight the potential of, and problems associated with, reform of administrative procedure in a difficult climate. The patchily convincing efforts of 'Wise Men' give a veneer of calm and measured deliberation: events driven, the policymakers have often had to scrabble around in the face of fierce economic forces. Much energy and ingenuity has gone into the cycle of legislative and bureaucratic responses. On the other hand, there is a pervasive sense of the ad hoc and piecemeal or convoluted; and the more so in the light of intense Member State and institutional politicking in this vital area of the functioning economy.

[161] Ibid, Art 21.
[162] EP and ECB, Inter-Institutional Agreement, recital D.
[163] Ibid, 4.

Subsequent developments should not obscure the fact that just a decade ago Lamfalussy process was accounted 'gold standard' in EU governance. An administrative design of expansive Commission rule-making powers supported and supplemented by expert advisory committees sat comfortably with the chief aim of stimulating competition and innovation in ever more integrated markets. Framework legislation ('level 1') could suitably accommodate a preference for light-touch regulatory approaches; the ERN-type model of informal governance was relatively easy to assemble. True, the verdict on soft law techniques of supervisory convergence was 'could do better', but the matter was not deemed an urgent priority. Amid benevolent conditions in the market place, why do more than the papier mâché construction represented by the 'level 3' committees? Illuminating the mismatch whereby financial institutions increasingly operated across borders in the Single Market, while supervision remained essentially national in character, de Larosière gave the answer.

The resulting formal network – the ESFS – goes some but only some way to meeting the demand for a robust institutional and procedural framework. Designed to tackle issues of unevenness and limited coordination while helping to ward off wintry conditions, it puts a premium on the efficient and effective workings of the ESAs and more particularly on contributions from the front line supervisory tier, an aspect which neatly illustrates the need for a capacious definition of 'EU administration' (see chapter one). As a form of agencification in EU governance, the ESA template shows important strengths. The procedures for indirect or secondary supervision fit the need to preserve and foster administrative responsiveness on the front line; an active standard-setting role should go quite some way in promoting the quest for a coherent and technically advanced 'single rule book'. From the 'good governance' perspective, however, there are nagging problems of privileged access and opaque lines of authority and accountability. The potential for friction between Commission and agency, or by reason of double-hatted actors, cannot be wished away.

The SSM brings the ECB centre stage in EU administrative law. An often tortuous structural and procedural development evidences the need to render the Bank fit for purpose in its new supervisory and coordinating role. Looking forward, a reworked treaty provision is surely in prospect as and when Union leaders judge the moment propitious for major constitutional changes. Enough has been said to show that, as between the ECB and other competent authorities not only inside the SSM but also within the Single Market outside it, and further with the EBA under a reworked ESA template, cooperative procedures must bear a heavy load. Let us hope they do not snap.

12

Procedural Trading: An International Market

PREVIOUS CHAPTERS, WHICH track EU administrative procedures in a wide variety of operational contexts, have placed great emphasis on the Commission role as 'coordinator of networks'. We have observed Commission efforts at coordinating Member State public procurement procedure (chapter six), and the establishment of the network of competition authorities to coordinate competition procedure in the Member States (chapter eight). Much attention has been paid to the Commission's supervisory role. We have looked too at 'bottom-up' mechanisms by which procedures are exported from Member States to the Union and, perhaps more frequent, 'top-down' procedures, which transfer EU procedures to Member States;[1] at the 'Open Method of Coordination' and the use of 'soft governance' to encourage 'best practice' and bring together actors and bodies with common interests and policy goals and at committees, which act for this purpose as revolving doors. Sometimes a process involves a wider range of actors, as with structural funding policies, implemented through regional and local public authorities and with the help of civil society and the private sector (chapter nine). We emphasised the growing use of EU agencies for networking, looking closely at the case of Europol, and watched them emerge as important players in pan-European networks, bringing together public and private actors and promoting 'horizontal cross-fertilisation among national administrations'.[2]

There are hints too at wider relationships and networks involving actors external to the EU. In financial services regulation, for example, the EU works with the Basel Committee on Banking Supervision and submits to its regulatory consistency assessments. Again, EU agencies increasingly network at supranational level. The European Food Safety Authority (EFSA), interacts with the Codex Alimentarius Commission, established by the World Health Organization (WHO) and the Food and Agriculture Organization (FAO) to set and publish

---

[1] See E Chiti, 'The Administrative Implementation of European Union Law: A Taxonomy and its Implications' in H Hofmann and A Türk (eds), *Legal Challenges in EU Administrative Law: Towards an Integrated Administration* (Cheltenham: Edward Elgar, 2009).

[2] B Rittberger and A Wonka, 'Introduction: Agency Governance in the European Union' (2011) 18 *Journal of European Public Policy* 780, 781.

international food standards. The European Fisheries Control Agency (EFCA), works with campaign groups active in marine environment issues, with regional fisheries management organisations and advisory councils like the International Commission on the Northwest Atlantic Fisheries Organization (ICNAF). The International Convention for the Conservation of Atlantic Tunas has been transposed into EU law and a control and inspection programme set up by the Commission to monitor its implementation.[3]

Increasingly too, the EU is directly affiliated to international regimes. It became a member of the World Trade Organization (WTO) alongside its Member States in 1995 and is represented in the General Council by the Commission. This has had procedural implications. Famously, the WTO dispute panel has held that signatory states must respect due process procedures when engaging in rule-making or adjudicatory functions; it has also ruled that decisions should be formal and written.[4] Such rulings can impinge on EU administrative procedure both directly or indirectly through the dual membership of its Member States. The connection may affect inter-EU relationships; Denmark recently called on the WTO dispute resolution machinery to resolve a dispute with the EU Commission over fisheries.[5] The EU also works closely with the United Nations (UN) and its agencies. Both the short case studies in this chapter involve the UN.

Nearer home, the Commission cooperates closely with and attends the meetings of the Council of Europe – which has had an active public administration programme since 1977.[6] Significantly, the Council of Europe Convention on Access to Official Documents, which has been open for signature by all Member States and the EU since 2009, has been signed by only five and ratified by three Member States.[7] Under the Lisbon Treaty, the EU is empowered and mandated to seek accession to the European Convention on Human Rights (ECHR) (see chapter three). More directly connected to public administration, the EU collaborates with the Organisation for Economic Co-operation and Development (OECD) in the PUMA programme through which the OECD promotes good governance. Together they founded the SIGMA project, a joint initiative that supports improvement in governance and management. SIGMA provides expert assistance on public administration and probity, works with candidate and potential candidate countries as in the PHARE programme (chapter one) and, under the rubric of EuropeAid, with 'EU Neighbourhood countries'. In Kosovo, where the EU operates its rule of law mission (EULEX) under a UN mandate,[8] SIGMA is work-

---

[3] Regulation 302/2009/EC concerning a multiannual recovery plan for bluefin tuna [2009] OJ L 96/1, as amended.

[4] See Report of the Appellate Body, WT/DS587AB7RW (22 October 2001); J Scott, 'On Kith and Kine (and Crustaceans): Trade and Environment in the EU and WTO' in J Weiler (ed), *The EU, the WTO and the NAFTA. Towards A Common Law of International Trade* (Oxford, OUP, 2000).

[5] Document WT/DS469/1.

[6] See Resolution (77) 31 on the Protection of the Individual in Relation to the Acts of Administrative Authorities (28 September 1977); Council of Europe, *The Administration and You* (Council of Europe Publishing, 1996).

[7] Council of Europe Convention on Access to Official Documents CETS No 205 (18 June 2009).

[8] Established by Joint Action 2008/124/CFSP, [2008] OJ L 42/92 as updated.

ing to improve administrative procedures and drafting a General Administrative Procedure Law.

The EU is, in short, becoming an actor in several aspects of the globalised system of 'distributed public governance',[9] in which transnational and supranational bodies exercise public authority and carry out public functions. A growing number of international bodies now engage in rule-making and standard-setting or install compliance and dispute resolution machinery comparable to that of the WTO. Import of standards and principles from international bodies may enhance the procedural standards of national or transnational administrations like the EU and augment their systems of administrative law in much the same way as membership of the EU has sometimes done with Member State administrative law. Equally, it may, as Mendes fears, help to 'weaken or bypass procedural standards that would otherwise apply'.[10] It is not always a case, in other words, of levelling up. In chapter five we saw 'levelling down' in operation in the context of open government and access to documents in EU law; here we follow the process outside EU administration with two case studies that illustrate the import and export effects of multi-level decision-making where one of the actors is a creation of international law. Our first case study looks at the Aarhus Convention, designed to augment the degree of public participation in environmental decision-making. Our second looks at the impact of the UN 'smart sanctions' regime. We focus here on the role of the Luxembourg Courts as originators of administrative procedures – and perhaps as exporters of good governance principles to an embryonic system of global administrative law.

AARHUS: ENSCONCING ENVIRONMENTAL DEMOCRACY

First Steps: Walking Alone

Environmentalism crept on to the Community agenda surprisingly early. In 1972, the nine Member States declared at the Paris Summit that economic expansion was not an end in itself; attention should be given 'to intangible values and to protecting the environment'. The institutions were invited to establish an action programme accompanied by a precise timetable. Concern for the environment was at first closely linked to the Community's economic interests; environmental protection did not at that stage fall squarely within the Community competence, though an early Council Declaration suggested that 'improvement in the quality of life and the protection of the natural environment'[11] was a fundamental

---

[9] On its competence to do this, see M Cremona, 'External Relations and External Competence: The Emergence of an Integrated Policy' in P Craig and G de Búrca (eds), *The Evolution of EU Law* (Oxford: OUP, 1999).

[10] J Mendes, 'EU Law and Global Regulatory Regimes: Hollowing Out Procedural Standards?' (2012) 10 *International Journal of Constitutional Law* 988, 991.

[11] Council Declaration of 22 November 1973 on the action programme on the environment [1973] OJ C112.

Community task. The take-off point for EU environmental policy is generally seen to be the Single European Act of 1985, which added a separate Title (Articles 130R, 130S, 130T) to the EEC Treaty. Though the Single European Act did not specifically mention environmental protection, it was designed to foster cooperation between the levels, providing for reasoned notification of changes in policy, to be based on 'scientific facts'. Shortly afterwards Directive 85/377 (the 'Impact Assessment Directive') found its way on to the statute book.[12] The directive provided for Member States to make an environmental impact assessment (EIA) when considering planning permission for any project likely to have significant effects on the environment and laid down detailed provisions for content and method. Member State concern over these developments was reflected in the proviso that the Community should intervene in environmental matters only when this action could be attained better at Community than at Member State level (the standard subsidiarity formula).

Maastricht saw 'sustainable growth respecting the environment' installed as a Community policy; Amsterdam moved the objective to the front of the Treaties with new Articles, notably Article 3c, which provided for 'environmental protection requirements' to be integrated into Community policies and activities. Article 6 EC stated that 'Community policy on the environment shall aim at a high level of protection taking into account the diversity of situations in the various regions of the Community'. Declaration 12 attached to the Treaty of Amsterdam recorded that the Commission undertook to prepare EIAs for any of its proposals that might have significant environmental implications. In 2000, a new and more potent link between environmentalism and human rights then coming into being was reinforced by the European Charter of Fundamental Rights (ECFR); Article 37 reiterates that 'a high level of environmental protection and the improvement of the quality of the environment must be integrated into the policies of the Union and ensured in accordance with the principle of sustainable development'.[13] This underscored the emergent idea of quality of the environment as a matter of concern to individuals.

The first directives dealt with substance rather than procedure, covering, for example, protection of natural resources, nature conservation and waste management. The intention was 'to concentrate Community action on certain priority areas', including better access to environmental information.[14] This in practice meant: 'exchanges of technical information between the regional and national pollution surveillance and monitoring networks' with the twin objectives of setting up a Community information system, an agreement on a 'common methodology' for establishing 'quality objectives' and a 'decision-taking process'.

[12] Council Directive 85/337/ EEC [1985] OJ L175/40 as later amended by Directive 2003/35/EC of 26 May 2003 on the assessment of the effects of certain public and private projects on the environment [2003] OJ L156/17. At the time of writing, this Directive is in the course of replacement: see COM (2012) 628, 2012/0297/COD.

[13] ECFR, Art 37 [2000] OJ C364/8.

[14] See [1973] OJ C112; Council Resolution of 17 May 1977 [1977] OJ C139/1; Council Resolution of 19 October 1987 [1987] OJ C289/3.

In its Fourth Programme, the Commission promised to 'take the necessary steps' to ensure 'close cooperative action' in the implementation of environmental policy, to standardise and rationalise 'the general obligation to submit reports' and introduce an obligation to report on all proposed national environmental legislation. It undertook to see these obligations observed through infringement proceedings (see chapter seven). Not only does this replicate a standard pattern of EU administrative procedure familiar from earlier chapters, but it looks much like the agenda for early agencies, including that of the European Environment Agency (EEA). The mission of the EEA was to provide (in the words of its first Director) 'objective, reliable and comparable information for those concerned with framing and implementing European and national environmental policy, and for the public'.[15] The EEA had overt networking functions. Not only did it manage the European Environment Information and Observation Network (EIONET), but it was empowered by its governing regulation to cooperate with external bodies, including the OECD, the Council of Europe and the UN and its specialised agencies, more particularly the UN Environment Programme. This networking function carried the expectation that the EEA would 'carry out its functions in close cooperation with the existing national and international facilities' and 'promote the incorporation of European environmental information into international environment monitoring programmes such as those established by the United Nations and its specialized agencies'.[16]

By the early 1990s, the EU had moved far beyond its first, tentative concept of environmental protection as an adjunct of 'the accomplishment of the internal market'. It was now experimenting with three procedures that have emerged as central to environmental policymaking: impact assessment (IA), dissemination of environmental information and public participation. Directive 85/337 had added the procedural requirement that the 'public concerned' should have access to environmental information early in the decision-making process, defining this term widely to include both natural and legal persons and 'their' associations, organisations or groups. In addition, the Directive provided that 'non-governmental organisations promoting environmental protection and meeting any requirements under national law' should be 'deemed to have an interest' in environmental decision-making, a provision that might prove valuable in founding *locus standi* in the courts. The objective of Directive 90/313, addressed to the Member States, was 'to ensure freedom of access to and dissemination of information on the environment held by public authorities and to set out the basic

---

[15] D Jiménez-Beltrán, 'The European Environmental Agency' in A Kreher (ed), *The EC Agencies Between Community Institutions and Constituents: Autonomy, Control and Accountability* (Florence: EUI, 1997). The EEA was established by Council Regulation (EEC) 1210/90 of 7 May 1990 [1990] OJ L120/1.

[16] Regulation (EC) 401/2009 codifies Regulation 1210/90 and deals with the EIONET. Today the EIONET has 33 country members and six cooperating countries, working in all with about 350 bodies.

terms and conditions on which such information should be made available'.[17] It balanced a general public right to information against a restrained list of specified exceptions (see Article 3) but left final discretion to the authority whether to withhold information on these grounds. It contained too the familiar obligation to inform. The Strategic Environmental Assessment (SEA) Directive,[18] dealt with environmental assessment of 'plans and programmes' with significant effects on the environment of another Member State and provided for adequate arrangements for trans-boundary consultations, for which Member States would have responsibility.

Working with Friends

In moving towards this position, the Community was not working alone. Several Member States had significant green agendas and were active promoters of environmental protection and from its outset the Community environmental programme had had a wider international dimension. Soon after the Paris Summit, the Council not only declared its intention to 'follow with interest' the work of the numerous international bodies working in the area, but also to 'continue the very active cooperation which it has established in this field with most of the international bodies, particularly the OECD, the Council of Europe and the United Nations Organization'.[19] In 1991, UNECE held a conference on EIA in a transboundary context, to which the SEA made specific reference. In 1995, EU ministers participated in the important 'Environment for Europe' conference in Sofia, where guidelines were agreed for public participation in environmental decision-making. Sofia provided a stepping stone both for review of current EU legislation and negotiations leading up to the Aarhus Convention. Around the same time, the European Court of Human Rights (ECtHR) was also taking an interest, holding that failure to provide access to environmental information was a breach of human rights ancillary to ECHR Article 8 (the right to privacy and family life), which might, in severe cases of pollution, be infringed.[20]

Thus, the scene was set in advance for the Community, as well as its Member States to work towards and ultimately ratify the Convention on Access to Information, Public Participation in Decision-Making and Access to Justice in Environmental Matters (hereafter Aarhus). Aarhus is one of five environmental conventions sponsored by the UN Economic Commission for Europe (UNECE), set up in 1947 to promote pan-European economic integration. Unsurprisingly,

---

[17] Council Directive 90/313/EEC of 7 June 1990 on the freedom of access to information on the environment [1990] OJ L158/56.

[18] Directive 2001/42/EC on the assessment of the effects of certain plans and programmes on the environment [2001] OJ L197/30.

[19] See further P Compton et al (eds), *Environmental Management in Practice: Vol. 1: Instruments for Environmental Management* (London: Routledge, 2013) 405–07.

[20] See *Lopez Ostra v Spain* [1995] 20 EHRR 277; *Guerra v Italy* [1998] 26 EHRR 357.

UNECE's first efforts were aimed at economic development and its environmental programmes started with concern over cross-boundary industrial air pollution. It has become a paradigm networking organisation: today 56 countries, some outside Europe, and over 70 international organisations and NGOs 'dialogue and cooperate' under its aegis.

Among international signposts to Aarhus listed in the official *Implementation Guide*, the most significant is perhaps the pioneering Council of Europe Resolution on access to public authority information.[21] Two EEC Directives, Nos 85/337 and 90/313, are also listed as important.[22] Jendroska suggests that Community legislation became the 'benchmark' for procedural protection of environmental decision-making.[23] Ralph Hallo, who participated as expert adviser to the Netherlands delegation, states that the text of Directive 90/313 'strongly influenced' the drafting of the access to information provisions of Aarhus. This he attributes to the influence of the 'EcoCoalition', a grouping of environmental organisations, set up under the umbrella of the European Environmental Bureau (EEB) to work for full implementation of Directive 90/313 on expiry of the transposition date in 1993.[24] The EcoCoalition apparently put together a network of experts, which remained in place to help negotiate strong access to information and participation at Aarhus.[25] The EcoCoalition reflects the Commission's work in promoting 'peak associations' (see chapter four). The EEB, founded in 1974, works through its Brussels office to 'coordinate EU-oriented activities with EEB Members at national level around Europe'. Representing 140 member organisations from 31 countries, it receives substantial donations from the Directorate-General for the Environment (DG Environment).[26]

The EC signed Aarhus at a time when DG Environment was strongly favourable to citizen and NGO participation in environmental policymaking. Commentators suggest that it came too at a point when policymaking was shifting from formal, centrally-determined standards towards a 'bottom-up' approach consonant with Member State competence and the principle of subsidiarity.[27] This was a context in which proceduralisation was useful. As Lee and Abott saw matters, 'proceduralisation seems to be used as a mechanism to balance against

---

[21] Council of Europe Committee of Ministers, Recommendation No (81) 19 (25 November 1981).
[22] See J Ebbeson et al, *The Aarhus Convention: An Implementation Guide*, 2nd edn, 2013. This publication can be accessed as an e-book, through the UNECE website.
[23] J Jendroska, 'Public Participation in Environmental Decision-Making. Interactions Between the Convention and EU Law and other Key Legal Issues in its Implementation in the Light of the Opinions of the Aarhus Convention Compliance Committee' in M Pallemaerts (ed), *The Aarhus Convention at Ten* (Groningen: Europa Law Publishing, 2010) 58–59.
[24] R Hallo, 'Access to Environmental Information' in M Pallemaerts (ed), *The Aarhus Convention at Ten* above (n 24) 94. Hallo was at the time Senior Adviser to the Dutch *Stichting Natuur en Milieu* and an EEB Board member.
[25] Ibid, 62–63.
[26] In 2009, DG Environment contributed around €940,139 of a total income of €2,339,744; in 2010, the contribution was €898,912 of €2,218,526: EEB *AR 2010*.
[27] J Scott, 'Flexibility in the Implementation of EC Environmental Law' (2000) 1 *Yearbook of European Environmental Law* 56; R Macrory and S Turner, 'Participatory Rights, Transboundary Environmental Governance and EC Law' (2002) 39 *Common Market Law Review* 489, 495.

greater Member State independence on substantive environmental standards';[28] there was, to put this differently, trade-off between procedure and substance. EU legislation tended to follow the pattern of the key Integrated Pollution Prevention and Control Directive ('IPPC Directive')[29] in substituting for centralised standards 'a framework of objectives' with considerable Member State discretion as to implementation but combined with 'tightening of constraints on the procedures and processes associated with implementation'.[30] Presented by the Commission as an exercise in integrated control combined with 'as much freedom as possible' for the Member States in implementation,[31] it has been described by one leading commentator as

> a clear manifestation of the emerging generation of Community legislation on the environment which reflects the ethics of decentralisation and deregulation that are inherent in both the principles of subsidiarity and proportionality and the Community's more flexible approach to environmental regulation.[32]

This analysis is consonant with Hallo's view that Aarhus greatly influenced EU environmental policymaking. On his count, 17 Aarhus provisions and 30 recommendations from the EcoCoalition found their way into the text of Directive 2003/35[33] and 'lobbying for these recommendations was made vastly easier as a result of the Aarhus Convention, since the Convention already incorporated provisions addressing most of the major demands made'.[34]

Directive 2003/35 deals with EIA – often described as the basis for participation. It contains a duty for Member States to make information concerning new projects and development available to the public at an early stage and specifies in some detail what information (including the Decision and draft Decision) is to be supplied. Information supplied by the developer must be in an appropriate form. The public must be notified of the arrangements for participation in an appropriate fashion, with provision for interstate consultation where developments have trans-border implications. Member States must notify the Commission of any national law that exists in the field; it also provides for exchange of information between the Commission and Member States so that the Commission can if necessary submit additional proposals to the law makers, with a view to ensuring that the directive is applied in a sufficiently coordinated manner

---

[28] M Lee and C Abbot, 'The Usual Suspects? Public Participation under the Aarhus Convention' (2003) 66 *Modern Law Review* 80.

[29] Council Directive 96/61/EC of 24 September 1996 concerning integrated pollution prevention and control [1996] OJ L257/26. And see J Holder and M Lee, *Environmental Protection, Law and Policy*, 2nd edn (Cambridge: CUP, 2007) ch 9.

[30] Macrory and Turner, above (n 27) 497.

[31] Commission, '*Proposal for a Council Directive on integrated pollution prevention and control*' COM 93/423 final.

[32] R Macrory, *Regulation, Enforcement and Governance in Environment Law* (Oxford: Hart Publishing, 2010) 675.

[33] Directive 2003/35/EC, [2003] OJ L156/17.

[34] Hallo, above (n 24) 63.

The Aarhus Model

In three particular ways Aarhus departs from the standard model of multilateral agreements: (i) it deals not with inter-party obligations but with obligations owed to the wider public; in this respect UNECE claims that 'it is not only an environmental agreement, it is also a Convention about government accountability, transparency and responsiveness'; (ii) its provisions are procedural rather than substantive; (iii) it is enforceable in two main ways: first, through the administrative machinery of a compliance committee and second through the access to justice requirements of 'Pillar 3', below. Article 3 outlines the Convention's ambit: it requires signatories to ensure that 'officials and authorities assist and provide guidance to the public in seeking access to information, in facilitating participation in decision-making and in seeking access to justice in environmental matters'. Thus, Aarhus has three procedural pillars. Pillar 1 covers access to information relating to environmental matters (the subject of Directive 90/313). Articles 4 and 5 contain an obligation to make environmental information available to the public on request (subject to limited and specified exceptions). Pillar 2 (Articles 6–8) is designed to ensure public participation in environmental decision-making (the subject of Directive 2003/35). Pillar 3 underpins these rights by requiring enhanced access to justice in environmental cases. In practice, this has proved the most controversial and hard to implement, partly because of the impact on national legal orders and judicial procedure, partly because of the implications of Article 9(5), which requires signatories 'to consider the establishment of appropriate assistance mechanisms to remove or reduce financial and other barriers to access to justice' – an area, incidentally, where the EU has, or was thought to have, minimal competence. A proposal[35] presented by the Commission in 2003 was not progressed.

Since Aarhus provides a set of guiding principles theoretically applicable to all environmental decision-making, its influence is naturally traceable in sector-specific laws. The Water Framework Directive is notable for its 'soft governance' approach based on the prescription of specific procedural tools for decision-making coupled to the Common Implementation Strategy, which provides for cooperation between Member States, the Commission and other actors in detailed implementation.[36] Heyvaert suggests that Aarhus has had a wider impact, contributing to 'the burgeoning good governance discourse that has so dominated the last years of EU regulatory studies' but her study of the important REACH

---

[35] Commission, 'Proposal for a Directive on Access to Justice in Environmental Matters' COM (2003) 624 final.
[36] Directive 2000/60/EC of 23 October 2000 establishing a framework for Community action in the field of water policy [2000] OJ L327/1; M Lee, 'Law and Governance of Water Policy' in J Holder and M Lee, *Environmental Protection, Law and Policy*, 2nd edn (Cambridge: CUP, 2007). A full list of legislation is provided by D Obradovic, 'EU Rules on Public Participation in Environmental Decision-Making Operating at the European and National Levels' in M Pallemaerts (ed), above (n 23) 154–55.

provisions on toxic chemicals[37] provides little concrete evidence.[38] There is no mention of Aarhus in the 'White Paper on European Governance' (WPEG) and it finds no place either in the generally narrower provisions of Regulation 1049/2001 on access to information; indeed, the two sets of disparate provisions still await coordination.[39]

Implementation and Transposition

For the EU administration, implementation is a complex matter. EU Member States are in a dual relationship with Aarhus, owing double obligations: at national level, directly to implement Aarhus, to which they are all signatories; indirectly, through the EU, which is also a signatory. Further to complicate matters, much environmental and procedural law falls within the competence of Member States, jealous of the autonomy of their own systems. The raft of directives – mostly now updated – followed a familiar pattern. At Union level, the pattern was one of standard-setting and supervision. Three main directives were on the table in 2003 in preparation for ratification; two subsequently passed into law. Directive 2003/4[40] repealed Directive 90/313/EEC on public access to environmental information, on the ground that 'disparities' with Aarhus (with which EU legislation must be consistent) justified total replacement. Transparency demanded that 'interested parties should be provided with a single, clear and coherent legislative text'. The Directive applies to public authorities (widely defined)[41] and guarantees a right of access to environmental information (again widely defined). This right is specifically stated to create a general rule of disclosure, subject to specific and clearly defined exceptions, which must be 'interpreted in a restrictive way, taking into account for the particular case the public interest served by disclosure'.[42] In contrast, Directive 2003/35 merely amended previous EU legislation, while the SEA Directive (2001/42) remains in place. There are dangers in this approach, as the Court of Justice (CoJ) observed in the *Terre Wallonie* case,[43] where the complainants argued that the Region had failed to hold an EIA necessary in terms of

---

[37] Regulation (EC) 1907/2006 concerning the Registration, Evaluation, Authorisation and Restriction of Chemicals (REACH) [2007] OJ L136/3; J Scott, 'REACH: Combining Harmonization and Dynamism in the Regulation of Chemicals' in J Scott (ed), *Environmental Protection: European Law and Governance* (Florence: EUI, 2009).

[38] V Heyvaert, 'Aarhus to Helsinki: Participation in Environmental Decision-Making on Chemicals' in M Pallemaerts (ed), above (n 23) 211.

[39] Commission Green Paper, 'Public Access to Documents held by institutions of the European Community: A review' COM (2007) 185 final. And see ch 5.

[40] Directive 2003/4/EC of 28 January 2003 on public access to environmental information [2003] OJ L41/26.

[41] And see Case C-279/12 *Fish Legal, Emily Shirley v Information Commissioner and others* (judgment of 19 December 2013).

[42] Recital 16, virtually replicating Case C-321/96 *Mecklenburg v Kreiss Pinneberg der Landrat* [1998] ECR I-3809.

[43] Joined Cases C-105 and 110/09 *Terre Wallonie and Inter-Environment v Région Wallonie* [2010] ECR I-05611.

the directives. Criticising the failure to coordinate the legislation, the Court ended the anomaly by holding that a SEA should be held.

Directive 2003/35 opened by recognising public participation as a public good and asserting that organised participation by 'associations, organisations and groups, in particular non-governmental organisations promoting environmental protection' should be fostered. Input values predominated: effective public participation was said to enable the public to express, and the decision-maker to take account of, opinions and concerns relevant to decision-making.[44] 'Effective participation' meant 'early and effective opportunities to participate when all options are open' — a phrase interpreted widely by the CoJ in a recent case to mean the first stage of the planning process, when all relevant information must be made available to the public; these procedural rights must, moreover, be capable of enforcement through interim measures including the temporary suspension of a disputed planning permit.[45]

Marking the fact that Aarhus preceded the era of e-governance, Directive 2003/4 expressed the hope that environmental information would be progressively disseminated to the public 'by the use, in particular, of computer telecommunication and/or electronic technology'. Information to be made available and progressively disseminated electronically is listed, including 'policies, plans and programmes relating to the environment', EIAs and risk assessments. The directive went on to set out the basic terms and conditions of and practical arrangements for exercise of the right; Member States were placed under customary obligations to report regularly and give notice of 'imminent threats' to the environment; otherwise they were left with relatively wide discretion as to national legislation.

AARHUS AND ENFORCEABILITY

The *Aarhus Implementation Guide* contains the warning that 'effective implementation of the Convention depends on the Parties themselves and their willingness to implement its provisions fully and in a progressive manner'.[46] As indicated earlier, the EU (usually the Commission) is given supervisory powers. These powers can be followed through by infringement proceedings, as in *Commission v UK*,[47] where the Commission persuaded the CoJ that English procedure on costs violated the Aarhus requirement that legal proceedings in environmental cases should not be 'prohibitively expensive'. Enforcement is double-banked by the possibility of European Ombudsman (EO) investigations. Failure to take infringement proceedings in

---

[44] Recital 3 of Directive 2003/35/EC [2003] OJ L156/17, now reconfigured as Directive 2011/92/EU of 13 December 2011 on the assessment of the effects of certain public and private projects on the environment [2012] OJ L26/1.
[45] Case C-416/10 *Križan v Slovenská inšpekcia životného prostredia* (judgment of 15 January 2013).
[46] *Aarhus Implementation Guide*, above (n 22) 1.
[47] Case C-530/11 *Commission v United Kingdom* (judgment of 13 February 2014).

respect of impact assessment has been a source of regular complaint, culminating in the recent 'Vienna Airport affair'. The Commission had received complaints from 27 citizens' groups fighting the expansion of Vienna airport, that the obligatory EIA had not been held. The Commission then agreed with the Austrian authorities to carry out a retrospective EIA, which was duly done and reported to the Commission. The EIA was, however, criticised by the complainants on the grounds (i) that it had not been impartial and (ii) that they did not have access to a review procedure in terms of Directive 85/337. The EO closed this inquiry after a Commission assurance that file would remain open until it was satisfied that the Austrian authorities 'had taken the necessary steps'. When the complainants came back with a second complaint, the EO found from inspection of the Commission file that the Commission had taken no significant action; there was no correspondence with the Austrian authorities and the complainants' representations had not been discussed. Not unnaturally, the EO found maladministration and made a special report to the European Parliament (EP).[48] Tying this to both a proposed revision of the EIA Directive and the need for 'a general regulation on administrative procedure', the EP duly obliged with a confirmatory resolution.[49]

Aarhus handed a more potent weapon to environmentalists to use in national courts. Pillar 3 prescribes alternative remedies: there must either be access to justice that is not unduly expensive or a suitable administrative alternative. Because both the EU and its component Member States are signatories to Aarhus, this judicial remedy is again double-banked; in principle, litigation starts in national courts but through expansive interpretation of procedural requirements, the CoJ has availed itself of preliminary reference procedure to exercise a general harmonising effect.[50] In *Lesoochranárske zoskupenie*, an environmental group claimed standing rights in the Slovakian courts in terms of Aarhus. The CoJ ruled on preliminary reference that, although the Aarhus Convention did not have direct effect in EU law, rights could be created in EU law when the EU had legislated on the subject matter, as it had done in the instant case with the Habitats Directive.[51] It was then for the national court

> in order to ensure effective judicial protection in the fields covered by EU environmental law, to interpret its national law in a way which, to the fullest extent possible, is consistent with the objectives laid down in Article 9(3) of the Aarhus Convention.[52]

---

[48] Inv 2591/2010/GG. There have been eight similar complaints, starting with the early Newbury Bypass affair, Inv 132/21.9.95/AH/EN.

[49] See (2012/2264(INI)), PE496.315v01-00 6/12 PR\912517EN.doc; and for the Commission, 'Proposal amending Directive 2011/92/EU' COM (2012) 0628.

[50] See Case C-396/92 *Bund Naturschutz in Bayern v Freistaat Bayern* [1994] ECR I-3717, a case brought by an environmental group; *Commission v Germany* [1995] ECR I-02189; Case C-72/95 *Aannemersbedrijf PK Kraaijeveld BV v Gedeputeerde Staten van Zuid-Holland* [1996] ECR I-5403. And see J Maurici and R Moules, 'The Influence of the Aarhus Convention on EU Environmental Law: Part II' (2014) 2 *Journal of Planning & Environment Law* 181.

[51] Council Directive 92/43/EEC of 21 May 1992 on the conservation of natural habitats and of wild fauna and flora [1992] OJ L206/7, as amended by Council Directive 2006/105/EC, [2006] OJ L363.

[52] Case C-240/09 *Lesoochranárske zoskupenie VLK v Ministerstvo životného prostredia Slovenskej republiky* [2011] ECR I-01255, [50].

Again, in a reference from Germany concerning a permit for a coal fired power station in a conservation area, the CoJ ruled that an environmental group could rely on access rights conferred by Directive 85/337 to contest an alleged violation of national law based on the Habitats Directive, even though German procedural law did not permit this. Member States could not use their discretion under the directive 'to deprive environmental protection organisations which fulfil the conditions laid down in Article 1(2) of that directive of the opportunity of playing the role granted to them both by Directive 85/337 and by the Aarhus Convention'.[53] There is a hint of double standards in the case law. In both the *LPN* case, where an environmental NGO sought access to a Commission file on infringement proceedings, and in *ClientEarth*, where the Commission refused access to compliance-checking studies, the GC upheld the non-disclosure, ruling that the general presumption of non-disclosure for infringement proceedings applied.[54]

This highly integrative jurisprudence opened the door to a new Commission centralising initiative. As already indicated, the 2003 Commission proposal had not been progressed, as the Member States took the view that that the proposal impinged on traditional judicial systems, 'which vary significantly'. The policy was now taken out of wraps and made the subject of a public consultation and Commission roadmap, rationalized on the ground that the Lisbon Treaty and 'important recent case-law of the CJEU have substantially altered the legal context since 2003 and helped to bring about a tentative shift in the political climate as regards access to justice'.[55]

The Aarhus Convention Compliance Committee

At both levels, the judicial remedies are double-banked. The Aarhus Convention Compliance Committee (ACCC), made up of nine members of the governing body, who are not required to be legally qualified, is a non-judicial body for dispute resolution. It takes complaints directly from the public, posts a preliminary determination on the UNECE website and proceeds, after a formal hearing, to make recommendations to the full meeting of the Aarhus parties.[56] Both the EU

---

[53] Case C-115/09 *Bund für Umwelt und Naturschutz Deutschland, Landesverband Nordrhein-Westfalen eV v Bezirksregierung Arnsberg* [2011] ECR I-03673, [44].

[54] Respectively, Joined Cases C-514/11 P and 605/11 P *Liga para a Protecção da Natureza (LPN) and Finland v Commission* (judgment of 14 November 2013). Case T-111/11 *ClientEarth v Commission* (judgment of 13 September 2013). These cases are more fully discussed in ch 7.

[55] Commission initiative on Access to justice in environmental matters at Member State level in the field of EU environment policy (11/2013).

[56] See Decision 1/7 of the Meeting of the Parties (October, 2002). Seven EU Member States are currently members of the ACCC. See further, *Aarhus Implementation Guide*, above (n 22) 236–39 with a full list of ACCC findings at ix. And see, J Maurici and R Moules, 'The Influence of the Aarhus Convention on EU Environmental Law: Part I' (2013) *Journal of Planning & Environment Law* 1496, 1499–1511.

and its Member States have come before the ACCC on several occasions.[57] In its significant 'Crossrail Decision', which involved review of environmental decisions taken by legislative procedure, the ACCC ruled that British hybrid bill procedure fell outside the requirement because it was 'a process under Parliament, the body that traditionally manifests the legislative powers in a democratic state'. But, noting the existence of similar procedures elsewhere, it warned that although they were 'a reasonable way' to deal with large projects of significant national or transboundary impact, adequate opportunities for public participation must nonetheless be ensured.[58] The Committee does not always respect the rulings of the CJEU. In 'ClientEarth', for example, where the GC had ruled that Aarhus was not directly applicable, the ACCC commented very unfavourably on the 'examined jurisprudence' of the CJEU on standing – remarks that raise wider considerations of compatibility with ECHR Article 6(1) (see chapter three).[59] The primary target of complainants in the 'Irish Feed-In Tariffs' case[60] was Irish public authorities but they also attacked the Commission for failure to exercise its supervisory powers. As Ireland had yet to ratify Aarhus, Maurici and Moules rightly criticise the ACCC for 'using the EU institutions, and in particular, the Commission to enforce Aarhus obligations' where these have not been assumed. This raises 'potentially wider issues in relation to the Commission taking up, via infraction, issues raised by the Compliance Committee'.[61] As always, wider issues of subsidiarity arise.

The relationship of the EU and its Member States with Aarhus is by no means unequivocal. It has been said that, although they 'like to position themselves as champions of environmental democracy in global fora', commitment is 'not actually as strong as the political rhetoric of [their] institutions might have suggested'.[62] Several Member States, including Germany and Finland, were notably slow to ratify the Convention, and the EU legislated in respect of its own institutions only in 2006.[63] No EU legislation yet exists concerning the access to justice obligations under pillar 3 of Aarhus.[64] Both the EU and several Member States have been found in breach of their obligations.

The single most important lesson lies, however, in the complexity of the transnational relationships. There is a tangled web of implementing legislation, in which horizontal EU legislation (Regulation 1049/2001) conflicts with the sector-specific requirements of Regulation 1367/2006. Again, national implementation

[57] J Jendroska, 'Compliance by the European Union with the Aarhus Convention: Findings and Recommendations of the Aarhus Compliance Committee in case ACCC/C/2008/32 (Part I) with Explanatory Notes' (2011) 8 *Journal of European Environmental & Planning Law* 375.

[58] ACCC/C/2011/61 [53]–[56]. Compare the view of the CoJ in Joined Cases C-128/09, C-131, C-134, C-135/09 *Boxus and others v Région Wallonie* [2011] ECR I-09711, [53]–[56].

[59] ACCC/C/2008/32; T-111/11 *ClientEarth v Commission* above (n 54).

[60] ACCC/C/2010/54.

[61] Maurici and Moules, 'The Influence of the Aarhus Convention: Part I', above (n 54) 1596.

[62] M Pallemaerts, 'Introduction' in M Pallemaerts (ed), above (n 23) 5.

[63] Regulation (EC) 1367/2006 of 6 September 2006 on the application of the provisions of the Aarhus Convention on Access to Information, Public Participation in Decision-making and Access to Justice in Environmental Matters to Community institutions and bodies [2006] OJ L264/13.

[64] But see above, p 309. And see ACCC/C/2008/32.

of Aarhus may differ from that provided in EU law, which does not necessarily imply lower standards; arguably, neither the Commission's soft law provision for relationships with civil society[65] nor the standing rules of the CJEU measure up to Aarhus requirements. The consequence is confusion. Member States are under asymmetrical obligations as to implementation, leaving the CJEU to fill gaps, providing in this respect some justification for the present Commission initiative (above). On the other hand, any move to install common procedural standards in respect of Aarhus raises serious issues concerning subsidiarity at a time when there is much public disquiet and some resistance from Member States. It is fair to summarise the present position by saying that the Aarhus hope of promoting a citizen-oriented system of 'environmental democracy' has not taken root in the EU nor is there much sign that Aarhus has contributed to the debate at Union level on transparency and accountability.[66] The general effect of Aarhus has in short been less to forward a citizen-friendly 'environmental democracy' than to add substantially to regulation, procedural complexity – and litigation. A new field perhaps for Kelemen's 'Eurolegalism'.

CREATIVE COURTS: UN SANCTIONS AND DUE PROCESS

Courts and Due Process Again

In earlier chapters of this book the claims of the Luxembourg Courts as primary initiators of administrative procedure were disputed. Without denying their undeniably significant role in the development of EU administrative procedure, we saw the role of courts as generally interpretative. In other words, we see procedural principles as evolving from administrative practice fleshed out in detail as soft law or legislation, the function of courts being to interpret these rules. The right of public access to documents, for example, stems from the EC Treaty. It was first implemented through rules of procedure, later by legislation. A heavy task remained for the Courts: to interpret the parameters of the statutory framework and evaluate the compliance of administration with the statutory provisions. In the course of this process, a further function emerged: the Courts were able to introduce subsidiary rules that were highly significant, notably the administrative duty to examine each requested document separately and to make decisions in accordance with the principle of proportionality – incidentally, a judge-made principle. Similarly, the obligation to give reasons is a treaty right but in deciding whether 'sufficient' reasons have been given the Courts have been able to add the significant rider that the reasons must also be 'adequate', an important addendum, which has greatly strengthened their grip over administration. In a myriad of other ways

---

[65] Commission, 'Towards a Reinforced Culture of consultation and dialogue – General principles and minimum standards for consultation of interested parties by the Commission' (Communication) COM (2002) 704; see above, ch 3. And see Obradovic, above (n 36).
[66] Pallemaerts, above (n 62) 6.

courts have added substantially to procedural requirements, a role that clearly involves a measure of standard-setting. It remains the case, however, that cases like *Transocean Paint*,[67] where a court is able deliberately to select new procedural principles for a young legal system are exceptional. And it is this exceptional aspect of judicial process on which this section focuses.

It is generally accepted that, in the development of due process rules, the CJEU has played an unusually creative role. As we saw in chapter three, it first established due process as a right in administrative decision-making and then 'constitutionalised' the right as a general principle of EU law. This process of creating the 'first generation of participation rights'[68] occurred largely in the field of competition law and closely related subjects and was greatly stimulated by the activities of wealthy transnational corporations able to carry on 'litigation wars' – the practice of 'eurolegalism'.[69] Here, in the very different sphere of human rights law, we see the Luxembourg Courts at their most creative and, consonant with the import/export character of EU administrative procedure, we see their outward influence on the shape of counterterrorism procedures in the UN Sanctions Committee (SC).

Smart Sanctions and Asset Freezing

The asset-freezing procedures with which this section deals are 'smart sanctions' imposed on individuals who engage in or otherwise support or encourage terrorism; these targeted sanctions form a small part of UN counterterrorism strategy. They start with UN Resolution 1267 (1999), which called on all UN Member States – including for this purpose the EU which, as indicated earlier, is not a full UN member – to freeze funds and financial resources owned or controlled directly or indirectly by Osama bin Laden, Al-Qaida and the Taliban. States-signatories were required 'to act strictly in accordance with' the provisions of the Resolution and to cooperate fully with the Security Council (SecC) to bring proceedings against persons and entities within their jurisdiction violating its provisions and to impose appropriate penalties. UN Resolution 1373 (2001) was aimed at terrorism generally. It extended smart sanctions to the freezing of funds made available 'by any person or body with the intention that the funds should be used, or in the knowledge that they are to be used, in order to carry out terrorist acts' and required UN Member States to 'increase cooperation and fully implement the relevant international conventions and protocols relating to terrorism and [relevant] Security Council resolutions'. Procedurally, the two Resolutions differed: under Resolution 1267 the listing of suspects was to be carried out by the Sanctions

---

[67] Case 17/74 *Transocean Marine Paint Association v Commission* [1974] ECR 1063.
[68] F Bignami, 'Three Generations of Participation Rights before the European Commission' (2004) 68 *Law and Contemporary Problems* 61.
[69] D Kelemen, 'Suing for Europe: Adversarial Legalism and European Governance' (2006) 39 *Comparative Political Studies* 101', discussed above, p 78.

Committee (SC), a sub-committee of the SecC, composed of all its members; under Resolution 1373, it was left to states to conduct the listing process, with a 90-day period for all states to report to the SC on the steps taken to implement the Resolution.

From the outset, these Resolutions were procedurally contestable; they were said to raise 'numerous human rights issues which the [SC] could have addressed, in the interest of helping to ensure the resolution was effectively implemented at the national level'.[70] They were notably silent on the important question of due process rights. The only way to contest a listing at UN level was to seek help from one's Member State which could, if it wished, intervene on one's behalf, subject to the difficulty that decisions were taken by the SC on the basis of unanimity. There were no UN-level procedural protections limiting this arbitrary procedure until a 'focal point' was later established by the SecC as a sort of 'helpline'.[71]

The measures taken by the EU to implement the two UN Resolutions followed this UN pattern. Two disparate asset-freezing regimes came into being.[72] Resolution 1267 was implemented by Council Regulation 881/2002/EC, which authorised asset freezing within the Community 'further to a designation by the UN authorities'. In this regime, decisions were seen to be taken by the SC and transmitted to the EU authorities, which – or so they have consistently argued – have minimal discretion to reject them. The jurisdiction of the CJEU over this Community measure is uncontested. UN Resolution 1373 was, in contrast, implemented by Council Common Position (CP) 2001/931, a measure taken under the then Common Foreign and Security pillar[73] where judicial review was strictly limited.[74]

CP 2001/931 was applicable generally 'to persons, groups and entities involved in terrorist acts'[75] as defined and listed in the Annex. It provided for listing and delisting decisions to be taken directly by the Community and required the Council to review listed names at regular intervals and at least once every six months to ensure that there were grounds for keeping names on the list. Before listing, the Council should check the names of individuals, corporations and groups to lessen the chance of wrongful listings and listing should be based on

> precise information or material in the relevant file which indicates that a decision has been taken by a competent authority in respect of the persons, groups and entities concerned, irrespective of whether it concerns the instigation of investigations or prosecution for a

[70] E Flynn, 'The Security Council's Counter-Terrorism Committee and Human Rights' (2007) 7 *Human Rights Law Reports* 371.
[71] SecC Resolution 1730 (2006).
[72] Several other asset-freezing regimes are in place both at UN and EU level: see, eg, Council Regulation (EC) 560/2005[2005] OJ L95/1, directed specifically at the Côte d'Ivoire, which came before the CoJ in Case C-417/11P *Council v Bamba* (judgment of 15 November 2012).
[73] CP 2001/931/CFSP on the application of specific measures to combat terrorism [2001] OJ L344/93).
[74] See TEU, Art 35. TFEU, Arts 75 and 275 now specifically confer jurisdiction to review the legality of decisions 'providing for restrictive measures against natural or legal persons adopted by the Council'.
[75] Thus some listings cover terrorist activities by groups such as the Basque ETA movement (see Case C-355/04P *Segi, Izaga, Galarraga v Council* [2007] ECR I-1657) or alleged activists from the Philippines (see Case T-47/03 *Sison v Council* [2007] ECR II-73).

terrorist act, an attempt to perpetrate, participate in or facilitate such an act based on serious and credible evidence or clues, or condemnation for such deeds.[76]

The first lists were adopted by the Council acting in its legislative capacity by 'written procedure', a secretive process that minimised debate in the Council and almost ensured non-compliance with these provisions.

Judicial Intervention

In the first case to come before the CJEU under Regulation 881/2002/EC, the Court of First Instance (GC) complied rigidly with the UN requirement to act strictly in accordance with its resolutions. International law was paramount; the UN Resolutions must be implemented without question by Member States and the Community must be considered to be bound by the obligations. The GC had no jurisdiction to review the lawfulness of decisions of the SecC or its SC and no authority to call into question, even indirectly, their lawfulness in the light of Community law. More specifically, the GC ruled that due process rights were inapplicable, being trumped by 'the essential public interest in the maintenance of international peace and security in the face of a threat clearly identified by the Sanctions Committee in accordance with the Charter of the United Nations'.[77]

The significance of the CoJ judgment on appeal in *Kadi*,[78] with its constitutional assertion that respect for human rights is a 'condition of the lawfulness of Community acts', cannot be overstated. It opened the door to judicial control and oversight, effectively asserting the paramountcy of judicial review of *all* Community acts, including Community measures designed to give effect to UN Resolutions. The standard of review should in principle be 'full review' and the law applicable should include 'the fundamental rights forming an integral part of the general principles of Community law'.[79] The CoJ also confirmed the importance of due process rights. The listing procedure was invalid, being adopted

> without any guarantee being given as to the communication of the inculpatory evidence against [the appellants] or as to their being heard in that connection, so that it must be found in so far as it concerns the appellants that that regulation was adopted according to a procedure in which the appellants' rights of defence were not observed, which has

---

[76] CP 931, Arts 1(4) and 1(5).

[77] Case T-315/01 *Yassin Abdullah Kadi v Council and Commission* [2005] ECR II-3649. International lawyers divide on the rightness of this decision: compare C Tomuschat at (2006) 43 *Common Market Law Review* 537 and G De Búrca, 'The ECJ and the International Legal Order after Kadi' (2010) 51 *Harvard International Law Journal* 1 with M Nettesheim, 'UN Sanctions against Individuals – A Challenge to the Architecture of European Union Governance' (2007) 44 *Common Market Law Review* 567. And see T Tridimas and J Gutierrez-Fons, 'EU Law, International Law and EC Sanctions against Terrorism: The Judiciary in Distress?' (2009) 32 *Fordham International Law Journal* 660.

[78] Case C-402/05 *Kadi v Council and Commission* [2008] ECR I-6351.

[79] Ibid, [283]–[85] and [326].

had the further consequence that the principle of effective judicial protection has been infringed.[80]

This could hardly be the last word. As Tridimas observed, the exercise of finding a balance between the overriding interests of public security and the rights of the individual was just about to begin;[81] the GC, reviewing CP 931 procedure, had already begun to fashion appropriate due process principles.[82]

Intensity of Review

In chapter three, we looked at the standard of review applied by the Luxembourg Courts, noting that it was often limited to the narrow concept of 'manifest error of appreciation'. Unsurprisingly then, this is the standard of review for which the institutions have argued consistently in cases involving security. In *Sison*,[83] where a *minimum* standard of review had been adopted by the GC in a case involving access to information, the CoJ accepted the minimalist approach, ruling that the standard of review for legality could 'vary according to the matters under consideration'. In areas involving complex political, economic or social assessments, where the institutions possess 'a broad discretion', the Court would apply only its lowest standard of proportionality testing, intervening only where a measure is 'manifestly inappropriate having regard to the objective which the competent institution is seeking to pursue'. Thus, the Court was confined to verifying whether the procedural rules and duty to state reasons had been complied with, whether the facts had been accurately stated and whether there had been a 'manifest error of assessment or a misuse of powers'. It was perhaps surprising therefore to find the CJEU in *Kadi* using the term 'full review'.

It was left to the GC to flesh out these words, interpreting them generously:

> The Community judicature must not only establish whether the evidence relied on is factually accurate, reliable and consistent, but must also ascertain whether that evidence contains all the relevant information to be taken into account in order to assess the situation and whether it is capable of substantiating the conclusions drawn from it. However, when conducting such a review, it must not substitute its own assessment of what is appropriate for that of the Council.[84]

Not surprisingly, the Courts have been asked to revisit this ruling on many occasions and they found an opportunity to do so in a later instalment of the *Kadi* saga. The Commission and Council argued strenuously for the lowest standard of

---

[80] Ibid, [332].
[81] T Tridimas, 'Terrorism and the ECJ: Empowerment and Democracy in the EC Legal Order' (2009) 34 *European Law Review* 103, 126.
[82] Case T-228/02 *Organisation des Modjahedines des peoples d'Iran v Council* [2006] ECR II-4665.
[83] Joined Cases T-110, T-150 and T-405/03 *Sison v Council* [2005] ECR II-1429; Case C-266/05 P *Sison v Council* [2007] ECR I-1233, [32]–[34].
[84] Case T-256/07 *Organisation des Modjahedines des peuples d'Iran v Council* [2008] ECR II-3019, [154].

review – manifest error of assessment or misuse of power – on the ground that the EU institutions possessed only strictly limited discretion to reject the findings of the SC. To formulate this argument differently, the institutions were themselves confined to the lowest standard of assessment in implementation and this should be replicated in the Courts' adjudication. The GC firmly rejected this argument; if such a limitation were accepted, 'there would be no effective judicial review of the kind required by the Court of Justice but rather a simulacrum thereof'. Brushing aside the objection that it was effectively reviewing the Security Council and its SC, the GC declared its task to be to ensure 'the full review of the lawfulness of the contested regulation in the light of fundamental rights, without affording the regulation any immunity from jurisdiction on the ground that it gives effect to resolutions adopted by the Security Council'.[85]

An appeal in which the Council and Commission renewed their minimalist argument provided an occasion for the CoJ to settle the matter. Despite the AG's support for a strict standard of 'manifest error', the CoJ held firmly to 'full review'. Reiterating the fundamental principle that the Courts had the duty to determine whether the competent authority had complied with the statutory procedural safeguards, the CoJ said:

> The effectiveness of the judicial review guaranteed by Article 47 of the Charter also requires that, as part of the review of the lawfulness of the grounds which are the basis of the decision to list or to maintain the listing of a given person . . . the [EU] Courts are to ensure that that decision, which affects that person individually . . . is taken on a sufficiently solid factual basis . . . That entails a verification of the allegations factored in the summary of reasons underpinning that decision . . . with the consequence that judicial review cannot be restricted to an assessment of the cogency in the abstract of the reasons relied on, but must concern whether those reasons, or, at the very least, one of those reasons, deemed sufficient in itself to support that decision, is substantiated.[86]

Due Process Rights

Due process in EU law is organised around the constitutional principle of access to the court and the treaty right to reasons. In principle, a statement of reasons must enable effective judicial review; it must, in other words, be sufficient both to enable the party to defend his rights and for the court to evaluate the validity of the reasoning. In *OMPI*[87] therefore, the GC firmly rejected the argument that the statement of reasons could consist 'merely of a general stereotypical formulation'; it must indicate 'the actual and specific reasons' for either listing or delisting and must

---

[85] Case T-85/09 *Yassin Abdullah Kadi v Commission* [2010] ECR II-5177, [123], [126].

[86] Joined Cases C-584, 593 and 595/10P *Commission v Kadi* (judgment of 18 July 2013) [119]. But see Opinion of AG Bot. See also Joined Cases C-539 and 550/10 *Al-Aqsa v Council* (judgment of 15 November 2012) [68]; Case C-478/11 *Gbago and others v Council* (judgment of 19 December 2012) [56].

[87] Case T-228/02 *Organisation des Modjahedines des peuples d'Iran v Council* [2006] ECR II-4665.

disclose in a clear and unequivocal fashion the reasoning followed by the institution which adopted the measure in question in such a way as to enable the persons concerned to ascertain the reasons for the measure and to enable the competent court to exercise its power of review of the lawfulness thereof.[88]

This has become the standard formulation. There is, however, some latitude. The content of the statement must depend on the circumstances of each case: it is not necessary for the statement of reasons to specify all relevant matters of fact and law; it is open to the court to bear in mind the relationship of the authorities with the party concerned, previous statements made to him and his knowledge of the affair, together with the 'practical realities and the time and technical facilities available for making the decision'.[89] But the discretion is not unlimited: it remains subject to the Courts' powers of full review and the burden of proof falls on the institution to show that the evidence is sufficient to justify listing or relisting.

As expounded by the GC in *OMPI*,[90] the right to be heard in administrative proceedings consists of two elements: notification – the party concerned must be informed of the evidence adduced against him; and hearing – he must be afforded the opportunity effectively to make known his view of the evidence. Further and more specific procedural requirements have from time to time been grafted on to the fundamental principles by applying the standard case law of the two Courts.[91] Thus, while notice need not follow the general rule that it must *precede* the administrative action, the grounds for listing must be communicated 'at the very least, as swiftly as possible after that decision in order to enable those persons or entities to exercise, within the periods prescribed, their right to bring an action'.[92] Again, a statement of reasons must be given not only for the initial decision to freeze, but also for subsequent relisting. Reasons must refer not only to the statutory requirement of the existence of a national decision taken by a 'competent authority', but also contain 'the actual and specific reasons' for the asset-freezing measure; moreover, the EU Courts would scrutinise the quality of the national authority with some care.[93] Furthermore, where a statutory review under CP 931 is required before relisting, there is a duty to ensure that 'subsequent fund-freezing measures adopted after the annulling judgment and governing periods subsequent to that judgment are not vitiated by the same defects'.[94] Only exceptionally could 'security considerations' override both the right to receive notification and the right to

---

[88] Ibid [141]–[45].
[89] Case T-47/03 *Sison v Council* [2007] ECR II-73, [188].
[90] Case T-256/07 *OMPI*, [93].
[91] See C Eckes and J Mendes, 'The Right to be Heard in Composite Administrative Procedures: Lost in between Protection?' (2011) 36 *European Law Review* 651.
[92] Case C-402/05 *Kadi v Council and Commission*, [336], citing Case 222/86 *UNECTEF v Heylens* [1987] ECR 4097.
[93] Notably, Case T-256/07 *OMPI*, [170]–[79]; Case T-47/03 *Sison*; Case T-127/09 *Abdulrahim v Council and Commission* (judgment of 9 September 2010).
[94] Case T-256/07 *OMPI*, [61]–[62] citing Joined Cases 97, 99, 193, 215/86 *Asteris and Others v Commission* [1988] ECR 2181.

a hearing.[95] Relisting decisions must be preceded by 'review' of the situation not solely to establish whether the person concerned is still engaged in terrorist activity, but also to check whether continuing to include him in the list 'remains justified' on the basis of new information or evidence.[96] These requirements approximate to a duty of 'due diligence'.

We suggested in chapter three that the due process case law of the Courts was variable and indecisive; in the asset-freezing cases we find them in an assertive mood. In the face of considerable opposition, they have steadily pushed the EU authorities – most notably the Council – to assure the rights of individuals by establishing fair procedures. The Council has often responded negatively to the Courts' decisions. They have used a 'cat-and-mouse' technique of relisting successful applicants or sought to have them relisted at another level of the composite decision-making process, forcing the suspects back to court. In the final episode of the *Kadi* saga,[97] the Council, Commission and UK appealed the decision despite the fact that Sheikh Kadi had been delisted at UN level;[98] and seven Member States intervened in support of the Commission while 12 supported the Council. This gave an opportunity for the Grand Chamber of the CoJ to return to the subject of due process. Largely approving the approach of the GC, the Court explained in some detail the appropriate balance between openness and secrecy and the way in which evidence should be provided to and scrutinised by the Court.

Council and Commission have responded less negatively to general procedural pronouncements. Over the years, the Council has softened its position. A standing Council working party was installed in 2007 to monitor procedural safeguards. The contribution of the two Luxembourg Courts to this progression has been substantial; they have acted as the primary standard-setters in establishing the due process principles to be applied. Requirements on notification, a prescribed formula for the statement of reasons and a proper delisting procedure, all now in existence, are partly responses to an increasingly concerned judiciary, which has steadily ratcheted up the intensity of its review. Reforms also include the introduction of six-monthly reviews, stated requirements on notification, a prescribed formula for the statement of reasons and publication of the delisting procedure.[99] This is not to say that enough has been done to humanise a process once described by the GC as 'a particularly drastic measure . . . capable even of preventing [someone] from leading a normal social life and of making him wholly dependent on public assistance'.[100] But it is unquestionably a strong start.

---

[95] Case T-256/07 *OMPI*, [137]. And see Joined Cases T-37 and 323/07 *Mohamed El Morabit v Council* [2009] ECR II-131.

[96] Case T-256/07 *OMPI*, [81]–[82].

[97] Joined Cases C-584, 593, 595/10 P *Commission and Council v Kadi* (Judgment of 18 July 2013).

[98] SC, Decision taken following review of delisting request submitted through the Office of the Ombudsperson, SC/10785 (5 October 2012).

[99] See for a detailed account of the interplay between Courts and Council, M Eriksson, *In Search of a Due Process – Listing and Delisting Practices of the European Union* (Uppsala University SPITS Publications, 2006).

[100] Case T-49/04 *Hassan v Council and Commission* [2006] ECR II-32, [80]. And see Case T-253/02 *Ayadi v Council* [2006] ECR II-2139.

Conflicting Obligations: A Houdini Approach

In the case of *Hassan and Ayadi*,[101] the two applicants tried a different line of approach. They argued that:

1. The Council had infringed the principle of subsidiarity by requiring Member States to adopt measures under EU law that restricted their rights under international law – an argument that once more highlights the problems posed by double obligations.
2. The EU was not a member of the UN and was therefore not bound strictly to the letter of Resolution 1267, an argument that the CJEU had virtually accepted in *Kadi*.
3. There had been violations of ECHR Articles 3 (inhumane treatment), 8 (right to privacy and family life) and Article 1, Protocol 1 (right to property).

This brings us back to the starting point of this chapter: the export, import or interchange of procedural standards and procedures through international relationships. In asset-freezing cases, the EU and its courts were hemmed in by a set of differing obligations imposed by different participants in a composite decision-making network. The Courts have managed this predicament in subtly different ways. With respect to Member States, the Courts have accepted the logic of composite decisions with a two-level procedure, deferring so far as possible to the decisions of national authorities, as the GC did in *OMPI*. Their reasoning here is based on concepts of solidarity, mutual respect and cooperation, which have emerged in earlier chapters as key values of EU administrative law.

The relationship of the CoJ with the ECHR was, however, somewhat equivocal throughout the saga. In *Kadi*, the Court purported to draw its inspiration from

> the constitutional traditions common to the Member States and from the guidelines supplied by international instruments for the protection of human rights on which the Member States have collaborated or to which they are signatories. In that regard, the ECHR has special significance.[102]

But it was careful to claim ownership of the principles by asserting its duty to 'ensure the observance of the general principles of EU law of which fundamental rights form an integral part'.[103] The formulation in terms of EU law was significant; it allowed the CJEU to draw due process principles from home jurisprudence: from the treaty duty to give reasons (now TFEU Article 296) and the Charter right to 'a fair and public hearing within a reasonable time by an independent and impartial tribunal previously established by law' (ECFR Article 47). As developed in the Courts' jurisprudence therefore, due process is stated to be first and foremost 'a general principle of Community law stemming from the constitutional

---

[101] Joined Cases C-399 and 403/06 *Hassan and Ayadi* [2009] ECR I-11393 [93]–[98]. The arguments were unsuccessful.
[102] Joined Cases C-402 and C-415/05 P *Kadi*, [283].
[103] Ibid.

traditions common to the Member States', though one that reflects ECHR Articles 6 and 13 and is 'reaffirmed' by the Charter. For the Luxembourg Courts, export is apparently preferable to import.

Much less kindly is their relationship with the SecC, progenitor of the contested procedure. As suggested earlier, by 2006, the SecC had modified its procedures by installing a 'focal point' to help with delisting. Member states were 'encouraged' when seeking listing to provide a detailed statement of the case and as much relevant information as possible, which should be enough properly to identify the potential subject.[104] The SC was directed to publish on its website a narrative summary of reasons for listing. An executive directorate, mandated to liaise with the Office of the UN High Commissioner for Human Rights and other human rights organisations in matters related to counterterrorism,[105] issued procedural guidelines.[106] Yet in the seminal *Kadi* judgment, AG Maduro strongly criticised UN delisting procedure on the ground that it was 'purely a matter of inter-governmental consultation'. There was only minimal access to the information on which the decision was based and no right to be heard: 'Procedural safeguards at the administrative level can never remove the need for subsequent judicial review. Yet, the absence of such administrative safeguards has significant adverse affects on the appellant's right to effective judicial protection'.[107] Shortly afterwards, an ombudsperson was installed at UN level,[108] tasked with examining requests for delisting and submitting recommendations to the SC supporting the requested delisting.

This step was not enough to prevent the GC from expressing its sense of the superiority of EU practice, where a two-tier system of justice guaranteed the rights of the defence. These were not only effectively safeguarded by national and EU procedures, including review by the national courts, but this could be followed up where necessary by review in the Luxembourg Courts and ultimately, if necessary, there was recourse to the ECtHR.[109] In contrast, the SC was willing to accept 'a number of general, unsubstantiated, vague and unparticularised allegations' unsupported by evidence; fair hearing and the rights of the defence had been observed only 'in the most formal and superficial sense'. In short, 'the creation of the focal point and the Office of the Ombudsperson cannot be equated with the provision of an effective judicial procedure for review of decisions of the Sanctions Committee'.[110] There the matter for the time being must rest.

[104] UN Resolutions 1730 (2006); 1735 (2006); 1822 (2008).
[105] UN Resolution 1535 (2004).
[106] SC, *Counter-terrorism Best Practice* (2003 text as updated).
[107] Case C-402/05, *Kadi v Council*, Opinion of AG Maduro [51]. Admittedly, adverse comment was fairly general: see Note from the Office of the HCHR to the Chair of the Counter-Terrorism Committee: A Human Rights Perspective on Counter-Terrorist Measures (23 September 2002) and The Watson Institute Targeted Sanctions Project, 'Strengthening Targeted Sanctions through Fair and Clear Procedures' (2006).
[108] By SC Resolution 1904 (2009).
[109] Case T-85/09 *Yassin Abdullah Kadi v Commission*, [186].
[110] Ibid, [128]. But see to the contrary, C Harlow, 'Composite Decision-making and Accountability Networks: Some Deductions from a Saga' (2013) 1 *Yearbook of European Law* 11–12.

CONCLUSION

In discussions of EU administrative law and public administration, there is typically much talk of convergence and Europeanisation. This has to a certain extent been our focus in earlier chapters, where we have looked at the function of administrative procedure as 'super glue', focusing on the principle of cooperation and the raft of supervisory procedures used to coordinate the implementation of EU law. Up to a point this chapter follows a similar pattern, most notably when the jurisprudence of the CoJ is considered. In overseeing the implementation of Aarhus by national courts, the CoJ has undoubtedly favoured Europeanisation while its asset-freezing jurisprudence reveals an equivalent tendency to internalise characteristic of its general attitude to human rights (see chapter three). But the chapter contains a further dimension and highlights a further source for administrative procedures. In the last epoch of the twentieth century, good governance has tended to assume the character of a universal value and to become an established part of the conceptual vocabulary of liberal, democratic societies.[111] The EU and its Member States have played a substantial role in the global quest for good governance: for example, as drafters and signatories of the Aarhus Convention, through cooperation with the OECD Puma and Sigma programmes and through the mouthpiece of their powerful and respected courts. This chapter has explored a small corner of that participation. It shows the EU as an enthusiastic advocate for and exporter of its brand of administrative procedure but as a somewhat reluctant importer.

---

[111] C Harlow, 'Global Administrative Law: The Quest for Principles and Values' (2006) 17 *European Journal of International Law* 187, 198–200.

13

Conclusion: A Regulatory Bureaucracy

IN THE INTRODUCTION, we described this book as a functionalist study of EU administrative process and procedure. Our main objective has been to provide an overview of the subject and to examine procedural developments in a variety of contexts. Our first two chapters looked at the changing structural context of the EU in which its administrative procedures developed. They traced the evolution of the EU administrative system from a relatively simple structure, in which Community institutions and six Member States engaged – supposedly – in 'direct', 'indirect and 'shared' administration. The first task at the start of the Community was to set in place the framework for an effective administration with the Commission at its hub. Thus, chapter one referred to the formal 'Community method' of operation and the formal structures and methods used in financial regulation and staff governance. In today's much more complex system of multi-level governance, where much of the decision-making is 'concerted' or 'composite', there is greater emphasis on cooperation and coordination. Chapter two outlined 'the toolkit' or set of administrative principles and practices with which the administration operates. There was a heavy emphasis on rules and rule-making, the core technique of modern administration, but we also noted an apparent growth, partly due to Enlargement, of 'soft law' and 'soft' methods of governance. We looked too at the means by which administration is delivered, emphasising the heavy reliance of the EU on information technology.

Introducing a distinction between 'horizontal' and 'vertical' administration, we looked at two horizontal, Union-level procedures. Chapter four dealt with the many complexities of executive law-making in the EU, driven by a succession of inter-institutional power struggles. In chapter five, we turned to the fight for access to information, where we identified a serious clash of values. The public procurement and Commission infringement procedures discussed in chapters six and seven are both horizontal and vertical. Both are aimed at Member States rather than the Union; on the other hand, both are horizontal in the sense that they apply across the board to all public contracts (with specified exceptions) and all types of infringements of EU law.

The remaining chapters, which are sector-specific, were chosen to illustrate different aspects of EU administration. Chapter eight deals with competition, once the paradigm example of direct EU administration, latterly reconfigured in terms of the European Competition Network, a Union–Member State network under the overarching control of the Commission. In chapter nine, cohesion policy shows the Commission in both cooperative and supervisory mode but with its practices and procedures under considerable strain from Enlargement. Chapter ten considers the recent but fast developing practice of 'agencification'. Our case study of Europol focuses particularly on Europol's aspirations to emerge as the EU 'information hub' in the area of serious crime and terrorism and its role in stimulating cross-border cooperation. The study of financial services regulation in chapter eleven moves us into a different administrative era; gone are the generous attitudes of late twentieth-century integration to be replaced in the bleak financial climate of the twenty-first century with a mindset of control and coordination. Finally, we turn in chapter twelve to the EU as an international actor. In the context of international treaty making and conventions, we look at the impact of globalisation.

THE 'THREE CS' OF EU ADMINISTRATION

When the Community came into being, the administrative structures that underpinned the new regime were weaker and less centralised than might have been expected. As no strong federal-type, central administration was put in place, the Commission, a relatively small agency endowed with important regulatory and supervisory functions, was in practice heavily dependent for implementation on national administrative systems. Their administrative practices and procedures were sheltered (at least in principle) by the doctrine of national procedural autonomy. The primary task for the Union public service was to fashion an effective administration and, in working towards this objective, the Commission had to work largely through negotiation and cooperation. As a direct consequence, a trio of three basic principles – cooperation, coordination and communication – emerged as key values of EU administration. These three principles overlap and are mutually reinforcing. We see them as the 'hidden wiring' of the EU administrative system – or even perhaps as the 'super glue' that holds an essentially piecemeal structure in place.

Cooperation was always a functional necessity and, as Schmidt-Aßerman so pertinently observed,[1] must therefore stand as the guiding principle at the apex of EU administration. The most original principles of EU administrative law are those that foster cooperation, such as the duty of fidelity or loyal cooperation based on TEC Article 10, ex EC Article 5, on which the Court of Justice (CoJ) could fall back in the absence of specific procedural provisions. For many years too enforcement was achieved primarily through cooperation, mediated through a conciliatory and highly discretionary set of judicially approved procedures, which operated behind the scenes through negotiation (see chapter seven). More important still, the EU legal order was itself not only founded on the principle of

[1] E Schmidt-Aßmann, 'Introduction' in O Jansen and B Schöndorf-Haubold (eds), *The European Composite Administration* (Antwerp: Intersentia, 2011).

'effective judicial protection', but the cooperation of national courts in the joint enterprise was imperative.

Cooperation was always closely linked to coordination. Underpinned by the twin concepts of equal treatment and of the 'level playing field' was the feeling that outcomes across the EU should not vary too greatly. Sometimes the Commission aimed for harmonisation; more often, as chapter nine vividly illustrates, it had either to make do with approximation or work through soft governance methods to encourage an acceptable minimum of convergence. We would argue that Enlargement, with the financial instability of recent years, has brought a change of emphasis. There is less concern for the softer values of cooperation and, especially via expanded disciplines of supervision, greater stress on coordination and 'steering'. This is particularly noticeable in the way the conditionality doctrine has been used expansively to shape administration in the E-12, a point we will pick up later in the context of Enlargement.

Communication and E-Governance

Cooperation placed a premium on communication. Information gathering and reporting procedures have always been central to EU administration, with the onus falling largely on national administration to gather, record and report. The crucial function of information gathering in enabling cooperation highlights the often overlooked linguistic problems of EU administration, justifying the large sums expended on translation. Early experiments with ICT were limited in scope and designed for the provision of technical information to provide an evidential basis necessary for policymaking. This remains a core element of the important 'Better Regulation' programme, a process rendered more efficient by the establishment of a European statistical office (Eurostat), intended at first for the improvement of quality.

The EUROPA ICT system installed in 1995 was the start of a drive towards an information society. The initiative was designed for 'top-down' communication, its avowed purpose being to 'provide people in Europe and elsewhere with clear, comprehensive and up-to-date information on the objectives, institutions and policies of the European Union'.[2] Relations with citizens and citizen-oriented administrative processes such as public consultation exercises or complaints handling were carried out online in the name of efficiency. Key components of the EU administrative process, such as data gathering, were increasingly carried out via sophisticated forms of ICT management. Ominously, a growing number of undisclosed and lightly regulated databanks stored a growing amount of data. This was significant, as information was seen as essentially the property of Member States and EU institutions. Before it became the subject of general EU legislation (see chapter five), transparency was a neglected value, as also was data

[2] Commission Press Release, IP/95/172 (23 February1995).

protection, which remained a Member State responsibility. Public access to documents was subject to institutional rules of procedure or Member State discretion. Document registers (if they existed), agendas and minutes of committees and even of the Council were not widely available to the public. Concern about these matters and measures taken to resolve them is documented and discussed in chapters five and ten.

In recent years there has, however, been a sea change in the attitude to information sharing. The linguistic diversity of the EU has been formally recognised in the European Charter of Fundamental Rights in terms of a right to good administration (ECFR Article 41). ICT systems are increasingly citizen-oriented and user-friendly; online administrative processes, especially public consultation exercises, are often interactive. These changes to administrative attitudes and practice are all made feasible by EUROPA. Handling complaints has become much easier now that the European Ombudsman (EO), the European Network of Ombudsmen and the SOLVIT complaints procedure are all accessible online. Thus, on the one hand, EUROPA has had the beneficial effect of enabling a more user-friendly and accessible administration; on the other, these developments do not mean that the need for greater openness and public participation, recognised in the Commission White Paper on European Governance, has been achieved.

ADMINISTRATION UNDER LAW

In placing our 'three Cs' at the top of the objectives for EU administration, we are not to be read as underrating principles enunciated in the Treaties or established as general principles of EU law. A number of highly significant foundational values are laid down in the Treaties, starting with a commitment to the process of European integration, to the 'four freedoms' and to 'the universal values of the inviolable and inalienable rights of the human person, freedom, democracy, equality and the rule of law'. From our standpoint as administrative lawyers, we would single out the rule of law doctrine, as concretised in the all-important administrative law principle of legality, as standing at one and the same time as the foundation stone of good administration and of control by judicial review. It is to the Treaties that we must look also for the indispensable obligation to give reasons, applicable to all EU institutions and bodies and all forms of decision-making, which we regard as the cornerstone of good administration. At the doctrinal level, reason-giving epitomises a commitment to rational administration; more pragmatically, it provides the underpinning for the protection of individual rights through a rational system of judicial review.

We have seen too that the commitment to human rights – which, over the last half-century, have achieved the status of the benchmark against which democratic government is measured – has also grown in importance. All Member States have ratified the European Convention on Human Rights (ECHR), most have domestic bills of rights or charters and many have powerful constitutional courts with a human rights jurisdiction. The influence on the CJEU has been considerable. The EU is currently negotiating accession to the ECHR (see chapter three). In one respect too, the EU is an undoubted leader: it was the first European polity to incorporate in its Charter of Fundamental Rights a right to good administration (ECFR Article 41). In chapter three, we discussed the symbolism of the right to good administration, using this term in its two opposing senses. On the credit side, Article 41 installs citizens at the heart of EU administration at Union level, providing them with a base on which to found claims to good governance and alerting officials to the need to take citizens seriously. On the debit side, we described it as narrowly drafted and too court-oriented in its emphasis on a limited number of due process rights enunciated by the CJEU. The right to good administration makes no mention of principles such as transparency, participation and accountability associated with contemporary popular democracy, which we see as fundamental to good governance.[3] In this context, we are intrigued by the unwillingness of the Court of Justice (CoJ) to allow development of an umbrella principle of sound administration, comparing its hesitancy with the very different approach of the EO. Article 41 might serve as a significant starting point for such a development and might then come in time to be something more than a symbol. That point has, however, not as yet been reached.

Narrow legalism of this type is one reason why this book has focused less on general administrative law principles and more on administrative practice. It is not that we underrate the need for principle; indeed, we address the issue directly in chapter three. But rather than focusing narrowly on a particular set of judicial values embodied in the jurisprudence of the CJEU, we have tried to be pluralistic. A recurrent theme of the book is the rich mix of administrative, legal and political values, beliefs, tenets and even ideology that we see as shaping EU administrative processes. Thus, in chapter three we compare and contrast the general principles of EU administrative law established by and enforceable in the CJEU with the good governance principles championed by the EO in his soft law 'Code of Good Administrative Behaviour'. Chapter two focuses on the Commission's good governance values as promoted in its 'White Paper on European Governance', and on other tenets dear to administrators, such as the principles of objectivity and equal treatment.

Doctrinal debate over legal principle has not been central to this study, while legal procedure lies outside its parameters; in chapter twelve, for example, we dealt only peripherally with the access to justice requirements of the Aarhus Convention. But although we hold strongly to the view expressed in our introduction that courts should not be seen as the sole or primary source of procedural principle, we certainly would not want to underrate their substantial contribution. We have taken very seriously the essential mission of the CJEU to ensure that 'in the interpretation and application of the Treaties the law is observed' (TEU

---

[3] C Harlow, 'Accountability as a Value for Global Governance and Global Administrative Law' in G Anthony et al (eds), *Values in Global Administrative Law* (Oxford: Hart Publishing, 2011).

Article 19(1)). We applaud the role played by the CoJ in preserving the structure and institutional balance of the Treaties, as it did in *Meroni*[4] by limiting the practice of sub-delegation. This decision in our view made an important contribution to accountability by nipping in the bud a trend towards unconsidered delegation to agencies. Similarly, by refusing to acknowledge an inherent power to make delegated legislation,[5] the Court helped, in a further contribution to accountability not only to maintain the 'institutional balance' inherent in the Treaties, but also to boost the authority of the representative European Parliament (EP). In general, however, we have deliberately chosen to focus on those judge-made principles that have the strongest connection with, and most direct impact on, administrative procedure, notably the proportionality test – the benchmark against which the legality and propriety of EU administrative action is now routinely measured – and the due process principles, first established by the Court of Justice in competition cases (see chapter eight) and later reformulated as 'fundamental rights' in a wider, more global context.

Our stance has often been critical. We have expressed our lack of sympathy in particular with the marked judicial failure to engage with the subsidiarity principle, which we believe to be a fundamental principle of EU administration; we see this indeed as a failure to preserve and protect the structure and institutional balance of the Treaties. We accept the mission statement of the CJEU as a partial justification for the marked judicial bias towards integration, once described by a judge of the CoJ as 'a genetic code transmitted to the Court of Justice by the founding fathers'.[6] On the other hand, we look unfavourably on that Court's often heavy-handed impact on the administrative systems of Member States. Some of the case law on access to documents or concerning implementation of the Aarhus Convention[7] can be read as an unwarranted incursion into the procedural autonomy of Member States and an impingement on Member State sovereignty in the matter of national administration. The CoJ is often guilty of double standards; it frequently imposes burdens on Member States from which the Union and its institutions would be absolved – a point made forcefully by Tridimas in describing the differential application of the proportionality principle to the Union and Member States.[8] The Commission is similarly guilty, arguing strongly for its own administrative discretion in infringement proceedings, resisting judicial enforcement of the Transparency Register, opposing a European Administrative Procedure Law – but promoting burdensome regulation on Member States.

---

[4] See above, ch 1, p 32.
[5] See above, ch 4, p 95.
[6] F Mancini and D Keeling, 'Democracy and the European Court of Justice' (1994) 57 *Modern Law Review* 175, 186.
[7] See above, ch 12, p 307.
[8] See above, ch 3, p 70.

CLASHING VALUES

Political scientists have engaged very fully in debate over EU public administration and we owe a considerable debt to their contribution. We have grounded much of our evaluation on the concepts of output and input function used by political sociologists to distinguish performance-oriented government functions of policymaking and decision-making from communicative, citizen-oriented functions of interest representation and political aggregation.[9] We drew on this vocabulary in chapter four, to express the clash of values between (output) values of efficiency and effectiveness and (input) values of representation and citizen participation within the process of executive rule-making. In a recent extension of the accepted terminology, Schmidt introduces the notion of the 'throughput' of governance to cover the process-oriented functions of government. She argues that 'the quality of the governance processes, and not only the effectiveness of the outcomes and the participation of the citizenry',[10] is of importance in establishing the legitimacy of a governance system. With this conclusion we entirely agree. Indeed, one way to interpret the arrival of good administration as a Charter right is as symbolic of its important new legitimation function.

We should not, however, read Schmidt's new terminology as suggesting a bias towards output values of efficiency and effectiveness in evaluating EU administration. To put this differently, throughput functions are not simply an element in or facet of output legitimacy. The EU has travelled far from its small start as regulator of a common market, in which it was entirely logical to ground legitimacy in the efficiency of its output. In the last decade, demand has grown for an administration imbued with input values of representative democracy and affording machinery for citizen participation. The 'throughput of government' has therefore to be measured in terms of both output and input values. This book has tracked the procedural consequences of demand for citizen input and considered the effectiveness of machinery introduced to meet it, notably through enhanced opportunities for consultation. Our conclusion is that neither the success of the movement nor the justification for it is as yet any way assured; perhaps, indeed, its culmination – even its zenith – lies in the sketchy arrangements for the Citizens' Initiative described in chapter four. Our own assessment largely corresponds with the pessimistic assessment of Beatrice Kohler-Koch that, at least currently, support for participatory input values is in decline.[11] We shall return to the recurrent clash between output and input values in discussing the case for a codifying Administrative Procedure Act.

---

[9] D Easton, *A Systems Analysis of Political Life* (New York: Wiley, 1965); F Scharpf, *Governing in Europe. Effective and Democratic?* (Oxford: OUP, 1999).

[10] V Schmidt, 'Democracy and Legitimacy in the European Union Revisited: Input, Output *and* "Throughput"' (2013) 61 *Political Studies* 2.

[11] See B Kohler-Koch and V Buth, 'The Balancing Act of European Civil Society; Between Professionalism and Grass Roots' in B Kohler-Koch and C Quittkat (eds), *De-Mystification of Participatory Democracy. EU Governance and Civil Society* (Oxford: OUP, 2013).

The influence of politics on administrative procedure is direct and substantial and we have not attempted to avoid it; it forms a dimension of every chapter, surfacing from time to time in a particularly blatant fashion. Chapter four, for example, follows at some length an inter-institutional power struggle between Council, Commission and EP to exert control over executive law-making. Chapter five revealed deep divisions between Member States over transparency, as the Scandinavian states, motivated by the need to protect their constitutional rights and cultural values, joined with the Netherlands to spearhead a campaign for open government at Union level. Again, in highlighting the importance of subsidiarity as a general principle of EU administrative law we have touched on another recurrent clash of values. This is the central difference of opinion between those who work continuously for convergence and integration and those who, like ourselves, favour acceptance of diversity.

As we have been at pains to emphasise, however, our primary interest lies in what goes on behind the curtain of the policymaking executive familiar from the work of political scientists. We have been fortunate in having at our disposal a growing body of empirical research, for example, on the way agencies function. The behaviour and performance of the comitology is no longer a secret; the Commission itself is much more open. In chapter seven, we were able to look in some detail at problems that face the Commission in ensuring the implementation of laws decided at Union level in the very different circumstances of the various Member States. We considered enforcement from three different standpoints: that of the Commission, as it devises administrative procedures that will best serve to bring about implementation of EU law; that of the CoJ, seeking to establish the authority of its notionally binding judgments; and that of the EO, acting as the 'citizen's advocate', who has tried to make space in the infringement process for complainants.

EVOLVING STRUCTURES, CHANGING GOVERNANCE MODES

It could be said of EU governance that its most significant feature is structural fluidity. Over its short life, it has undergone an almost continuous process of structural modification. It started life as a regulatory trade regime but (briefly to recapitulate what is writ large in other chapters) the Council and European Council at a succession of European summits and intergovernmental conferences added new functions to the portfolio in a piecemeal fashion – often, it must be said, with the deliberate intention of evading constitutional accountability machinery by working through intergovernmental cooperation. In this respect the Maastricht Treaty marked a step change. It installed the new EU with a clutch of new competences, unsupported by an appropriate constitutional framework, floating free from national accountability procedures and untrammelled by those of the Union. The EU became, in Curtin's celebrated metaphor, a 'Europe of bits-and-pieces'[12]

---

[12] D Curtin, 'The Constitutional Structure of the Union: A Europe of Bits and Pieces' (1993) 30 *Common Market Law Review* 17.

administered pragmatically and coordinated by a complex network of committees and powerful working groups advisory to the Commission and Council (see chapter one). Integration by formal law – the classical Community method – was supplemented by extralegal 'soft governance'.

As the EU grew, it was transmuting. Community administrative governance had firm foundations. It was rooted in the national administrative systems of its Member States. But as Majone's regulatory agency model[13] – if not the regulatory function – was outgrown and with it, the two-tier conceptual vocabulary of 'direct' and 'indirect' administration, this limiting terminology gave way to the amorphous concept of a 'European administrative space' in which administration was conceived as 'mixed' 'shared' or 'concerted', and 'composite' decisions were taken.[14] The EU followed the path of late twentieth-century governance, in which authority was increasingly devolved at national level downwards to regions, sideways to experts, agencies, regulators and the private sector and upwards to supranational regimes. The EU also followed the fashion for agencification. A new wave of EU agencies burst out of the simple, information-gathering model role to emerge as EU regulatory agencies with embryonic executive and rule-making functions. The solid institutional hub of the Community was surrounded by disparate policy networks engaged in common cooperative enterprises of policy-making and regulation; in short, the EU had become a supranational administrative governance system. It was also engaging in supranational relationships: EU agencies played the role of network hubs, linking the EU into the globalised world of 'distributed public governance'.

Enlargement: Problem or Opportunity?

The two major Enlargements that took place in 2004 and 2007 in the course of which the EU grew from 15 to 27 Member States was a second step change. The geographical changes in size and scale were enormous; the central EU administration had to reach further and do more. Even more significant was the new administrative and cultural diversity. Previous enlargements had been smaller and gentler and had, with one or two exceptions, brought into the EU states that were 'closer to the existing EU in terms of economic development and professionalism of national administrations'.[15] The administrative structures of the E-12 were essentially non-equivalent; many states had, for example, newly emerged from soviet-style *dirigisme* and had little experience of democratic governance – a sine qua non of EU membership. The cultural shock was not confined to Member State level; new entrants came into the Commission with a demonstrably different ethos, allegedly making it more difficult to coordinate.[16] The effect on the way that

[13] See above, ch 1, p 10.
[14] H Hofmann, 'Mapping the European Administrative Space' (2008) 31 *West European Politics* 662.
[15] H Kassim et al, The European Commission of the Twenty-First Century (Oxford: OUP, 2013) 249.
[16] Ibid.

the EU was administered was profound. The candidate states were required to familiarise themselves with EU objectives and procedures, and to generate sufficient administrative capacity to implement the EU *acquis communitaire*, which was made a condition of entry, implemented through the doctrine of conditionality, or the requirement that EU 'partners' must meet certain conditions or standards in order to access and/or retain full funding.

Enlargement on such a scale was necessarily problematic. Unprecedented supervisory powers were handed to the Commission to ensure coordination and oversee compliance.[17] All this involved the Commission in long periods of pre-entry training – conducted in practice in conjunction with the Organisation for Economic Co-operation and Development (OECD) –and, with the cooperation of national and sub-national partners, there were innovative administrative experiments with practices such as 'twinning'.[18] Soft governance methods helped the 'levelling-up' process. The need to shore up some of the institutions of administration is reflected in TFEU Article 197, which authorises the Union for the first time to support Member States' efforts 'to improve their administrative capacity to implement Union law' through measures such as exchange of information and personnel and provision of training schemes.

By bringing into the EU new Member States with different administrative methods and cultures, Enlargement should have provided an opportunity for greater pluralism. Harmonisation ought to have involved a two-way process based on participation, exchange and acceptance of diversity; indeed, the very scale of Enlargement rendered divergence a necessity. Instead, Enlargement was a largely 'top-down' process with a displacement of cooperation from the apex of the 'three Cs' and its replacement by coordination. Soft governance experienced a hardening process, being reshaped around concepts of standardisation and regulation and around structures of supervision and control.

PROCEDURAL CODIFICATION?

This book has looked in some detail at the use of rules in contemporary EU administration. In chapter two, we considered the positive side of rules. Rules and procedures contribute greatly to rational administration in promoting uniformity and consistency in decision-making. Rules satisfy public expectations that policy will be adhered to and that administration can be relied on. They define the boundaries of the administrative process and structure the use of administrative discretion. They contribute to transparency, enabling citizens to know the basis on which public power is exercised and check that there is lawful authority for what has been done. It is this liberal and positive *Rechtsstaat* vision of a public administration in which rules stand for orderliness, coherence, objectivity and

[17] E Heidbreder, *The Impact of Expansion on EU Institutions: The Eastern Touch on Brussels* (Basingstoke: Palgrave Macmillan, 2011) 4.
[18] See above, ch 1, p 17.

rationality that underlies the call for a generalised Administrative Procedure Act (APA).

The idea of codifying EU administrative procedures is by no means new; it has been on the agenda since the mid-1990s.[19] In 2004, the Swedish Government called for an EU Administrative Procedure Law and took action by commissioning a survey of administrative procedure in Member States.[20] This produced the information that 17 of the 25 Member States surveyed had a general APA, usually in a default format, which gave way to sector-specific legislation when that specified more detailed procedures. Most of the respondent Member States recognised the 10 core values of good administration selected in the survey; the devil lay in the detail, where very substantial divergences appeared. In part this was stylistic: some laws allowed a wide measure of administrative discretion, leaving the parameters to be judicially defined; others tried to list the most essential procedures.[21] This divergence is not entirely helpful in agreeing a common approach.

Further action became realistic only when the Lisbon Treaty introduced provisions on which a codification could be based. TFEU Article 298 provided that 'the institutions, bodies, offices and agencies of the Union shall have the support of an open, efficient and independent European administration' and described the implementation of EU law as a matter of 'common interest'. It mandated the EU legislator to act in the matter 'in compliance with the Staff Regulations and conditions of employment'. As indicated earlier, TFEU Article 197 authorises Union support for Member State administration. Article 197(2) provides, however, that no Member State shall be obliged to avail itself of such support and excludes specifically any attempt at 'harmonisation of Member State law and regulation'. Experts differ as to the scope and meaning of these ambiguous provisions. The most restrictive reading would confine EU competence in public administration to (i) matters closely connected with the EU public service and (ii) non-intrusive backup of Member States' public services when engaged in the implementation of EU law. Widely interpreted, the provisions might extend to an overall codification of EU administrative procedure, provided only that no direct attempt at 'harmonisation' was undertaken.[22]

---

[19] C Harlow, 'Codification of EC Administrative Procedures? Fitting the Foot to the Shoe or the Shoe to the Foot' (1996) 2 *European Law Journal* 3. The EP's Resolution of 6 September 2001 (Resolution C5-0438/2000-2000/2212 (COS)) approving the EO's 'Code of Good Administrative Behaviour' called on the Commission to present a proposal for a Regulation on the subject based on TEC Art 308. This was never done.

[20] Statskontoret, *Principles of Good Administration in the Member States of the European Union* (2005). The principles included in the survey were lawfulness, non-discrimination, proportionality, the right of access to documents and the right to be heard.

[21] Ibid, [3.1]–[3.3].

[22] The EP commissioned papers that rehearse the various arguments: see D Papadopolou, *Towards an EU Regulation on Administrative Procedure?* (EP Policy Department C, 2010); O Mir Puigpelat, 'Arguments in favour of a general codification of the procedure applicable to EU Administration', PE 432.776, See also M Chiti, 'Towards an EU Regulation on Administrative Procedure?' (2011) 21 *Rivista Italiana di diritto pubblico comunitario* 1; J Schwarze, 'European Administrative Law in the Light of the Treaty of Lisbon' (2012) 18 *European Public Law* 285.

The EP, which has so far spearheaded the codification initiative, has taken a cautious stance. It starts from the citizen-oriented premise of a 'fundamental' right to good administration and the difficulties facing citizens who need to know their rights. It points to the wide variety of sources – from rights embedded in the Treaties or Charter to sector-specific codes of procedure and soft law administrative codes. The coverage, it is said, is spotty, difficult to access and leaves obvious gaps. The EP has therefore called on the Commission to meet the need for a coherent and comprehensive set of rules by submitting a proposal for a European Law of Administrative Procedure that will

> codify the fundamental principles of good administration and should regulate the procedure to be followed by the Union's administration when handling individual cases to which a natural or legal person is a party, and other situations where an individual has direct or personal contact with the Union's administration.[23]

There are few surprises in the list of principles on which the EP wants legislation to be based. Lawfulness, non-discrimination and equal treatment, proportionality, consistency and legitimate expectation, privacy, fairness and transparency all make an appearance. Public servants must be independent; they should always act in the Union's interest and for the public good and not be guided either by personal, financial or family interests or by national interest or political pressures. In short, like ECFR Article 41, the EP has drawn heavily on EU sources; these are all received values and well-understood practices – even if they are not always followed. Again like Article 41, the proposal suggests a narrow mandate, essentially directed to individual decision-making. Moreover, the legislation would be residual; it should lay down *de minimis* standards that will give way to sector-specific legislation unless the latter falls below the *de minimis* standards.

Such minimalist legislation, in some ways narrower than the existing 'Code of Good Administrative Behaviour', fills few gaps. It will hardly resolve the type of problem in which there is a clash of values, as in the *Bavarian Lager* case,[24] where a choice had to be made between access to information and privacy or data protection – both, incidentally, protected Charter rights. Nor will it resolve the issue of 'composite decision-making', as described in chapter twelve, where decision-makers operating in a shared decision-making process are proceeding according to different standards of administrative behaviour. It is therefore unlikely to satisfy the main proponents of codification, prompting the question whether legislation would really be worthwhile. The response from the Commission has so far been muted; it has held a colloquium and announced (yet another) in-depth analysis into the way administrative rights are protected across EU administration.[25] This is hardly an enthusiastic response.

---

[23] Resolution of 15 January 2013 with recommendations to the Commission on a Law of Administrative Procedure of the European Union (2012/2024(INI) P7_TA-PROV(2013) 0004, adopting the Berlinguer Report to JURI, A7-9999/2012 PE492.584v02-00 (12 November 2012).
[24] See above, ch 5, p 131.
[25] Maroš Šefčovič, Speech to Seminar on EU Administrative Law (21 February 2014).

Ziller has made the case for a comprehensive APA at Union level, arguing that 'soft law instruments would miss the purpose of providing for sufficient homogeneity across institutions, bodies, offices and agencies and establishing default rules to fill the gaps in existing and future sector specific regulations'. Such legislation could cover 'not only single decision-making but also rule-making (the use of regulatory powers) as well as the adoption and management of contracts and agreements, and all the issues linked with information management'.[26] He admits, however, that the degree of detail would be a difficult issue, a point that emerges very clearly from a draft under consideration by the ReNEUAL project, sponsored by a group of academics of whom Ziller is one; this draft is framed as six separate books.

This 'hard law' approach to codification leaves out of account the phenomenon of 'eurolegalism' - Kelemen's term for steady juridification of the governance process.[27] Eurolegalism involves a governance cycle in which policies are expressed as rules and their implementation is governed by procedures that are constantly referred to courts for interpretation. We have met this process in the area of competition policy, where Nehl describes the case law of the CJEU as a transmutation of administrative procedure from a tool for efficient policy implementation to a vehicle for the advancement of individual interest.[28] Similar concerns underlie the warning of Maroš Šefčovič, the Commissioner for Inter-Institutional Relations and Administration, in a speech to the Commission colloquium.[29] At Union level, he reminds us, all parts of the EU administration are already subject to a very extensive framework of legislation and guidelines, governing all aspects of their activities and relations with the general public. This developed over decades and was the subject of an extensive case law; care must be taken not to destroy well-established practices 'in sometimes economically extremely sensitive areas'. The contemporary tendency, he continued, was to respond to problems by rewriting the rules; 'too often new rules are preached as the answer to a problem whereas it would be much more efficient to solve the problem immediately by determined action under existing rules'; good administration is as much about culture and behaviour as about rules.

A softer package could be patterned on the US concept of Restatements, the approach actually taken by the ReNEUAL group, whose six books are described as a set of Model Rules. This soft approach has advantages. Not only does it take into account the complex existing pattern of procedural regulation, but it allows for a measure of necessary flexibility. A Model Code could establish general requirements at Union level that could 'foster the evolution of national administrative

---

[26] J Ziller, 'Alternatives in Drafting an EU Administrative Procedure Law', PE 462.417 (2011), paper for the ReNEUAL project, available on the ReNEUAL website at: http://www.reneual.eu/ Ziller has also made the case for a soft law restatement: see J Ziller, 'Towards Restatements and Best Practice Guidelines on EU Administrative Procedural Law', PE 425.652 (2010), available on the ReNEUAL website.

[27] D Kelemen, *Eurolegalism: The Transformation of Law and Regulation in the European Union* (Cambridge MA: Harvard University Press, 2011).

[28] H-P Nehl, *Principles of Administrative Procedure in EC Law* (Oxford: Hart Publishing, 1999).

[29] Maroš Šefčovič, Speech to Seminar on EU Administrative Law (21 February 2014).

law in the direction of bridging gaps between EU and national administrative law methods'.[30] From a Member State standpoint, it is non-binding, leaving choices to be made as to compatibility with their own established practices. But there are weasel words in the proviso added by George Bermann: 'provided the efficacy of EU law and policy is not threatened'. This gives a green light to the CJEU to indulge in 'levelling up'.

Essentially, the choice to codify is, like the selection of administrative procedures, a question of politics and values. Integrationists hope for an overarching, hard law codification to push the EU towards the forbidden goal of harmonisation; supporters of pluralism and diversity will oppose such moves. A further step on the road to voluntary convergence, the Model Code is undoubtedly seen by some as a step on the way to legislation. To move further or faster would, in the authors' view, be undesirable. At one level, there is a serious danger of undercutting or weakening established administrative procedures tailored to political understandings and cultural values in the Member States. At another level, the deadening effect of too much standardisation should be firmly resisted. These are points that the authors have made elsewhere and which we wish to reiterate.[31]

A REGULATORY BUREAUCRACY

A helpful insight into EU governance is Lindseth's picture of the EU system as premised on a twentieth-century model of the 'administrative state'.[32] Although it is not a state, the EU has many of the qualities of an administrative state, including powers of autonomous law-making and a formidable combination of executive powers blocked up in a single institution – the Commission. The key function of the EU, however, remains regulation: government contracting, environmental protection, policing, financial regulation – all now come within its expanded portfolio. We live in a 'risk society' in which risk management is 'a model of organisation in its own right'[33] and much of the work of risk regulation has now been delegated upwards to the Union level. A by-product of Lindseth's administrative state is an extensive and reliable bureaucracy, essential for the accomplishment of the regulatory cycle of rule-making, implementation and supervision and enforcement. This is why we see EU administration in terms of 'regulatory bureaucracy'.

---

[30] G Bermann, 'A Restatement of European Administrative Law: Problems and Prospects' in S Rose-Ackerman and P Lindseth (eds), *Comparative Administrative Law* (Cheltenham: Edward Elgar, 2010).

[31] C Harlow and R Rawlings, 'National Administrative Procedures in a European Perspective: Pathways to a Slow Convergence?' (2010) 2 *Italian Journal of Public Law* 215; C Harlow, 'Voices of Difference in a Plural Community' (2002) 50 *American Journal of Comparative Law* 339. See similarly C Timmermans, 'Developing Administrative Law in Europe: Natural Convergence or Imposed Uniformity?' Speech to the Raad van State (29 November 2013); Chiti, above (n 22).

[32] P Lindseth, *Power and Legitimacy: Reconciling Europe and the Nation-State* (Oxford: OUP, 2010).

[33] M Power, *The Risk Management of Everything* (London: Demos, 2004) 10–11.

We have depicted policymaking processes enmeshed in a tangled web of regulation, in which laws, delegated and implementing regulations, and softer forms of bureaucratic rule-making all find a place. Soft law instruments such as recommendations or guidelines are used routinely by the Commission for purposes of communication and to carry out its manifold supervisory functions. This so-called soft law may sometimes possess near-binding force; it may even occasionally modify the operation of hard law, as with the inter-institutional agreements used to shape the comitology process.[34] It may be given a hard edge by administrative practice. The Commission Communication[35] that indicated a 'new approach' to the use of penalty payments in infringement procedure is, for example, technically soft law but the indication that the Commission will proceed in this manner lends it the appearance of a rule. Other soft law, as in the Open Method of Coordination (OMC), relies less on enforcement mechanisms and more on behavioural practice for its observance.[36] Too often the picture is one of uncoordinated muddle.

In chapter four, we dealt at length with formal executive law-making, noting the complexity and formality of the process. The Commission plays a lead role in the EU law-making process and has powers to make both delegated and implementing regulations. The extended powers of executive law-making, together with its procedural complexity, owe much to the technical nature of EU regulation. This encourages dependence on expert committees and promotes the notion of 'evidence-based legislation' and the pseudo-scientific procedures on which this is based. We noted in this context the extent to which other Union bodies are increasingly engaged in rule-making. Agencies and committees such as the European Economic and Social Committee (EESC) or Committee of the Regions (CoR) govern their own procedure and make their own procedural rules, though always in accordance with Commission templates. The social partners make rules in the field of social policy and technical standard-setting is often delegated to private bodies with technical expertise. In a significant development, agencies in the area of financial services are well on the way to possessing formal rule-making powers.

We noted too the extent to which Commission policy initiatives are increasingly standardised. Governed by and based on managerial procedure, policy objectives, road maps, communications, impact assessment and consultation procedures, all designed by officials, are a recurrent theme. Here the internal reforms of the Commission, introduced in response to the 1999 Report of the Committee of Independent Experts,[37] have been highly influential in promoting an audit-style, managerial ethos. The Experts' investigation revealed only too clearly the extent to which the Commission, as the central administration of the Communities, had failed to keep pace with its growing responsibilities.

[34] See above, ch 4, p 98.
[35] See above, ch 7, p 193.
[36] See above, ch 2, p 54.
[37] See above, ch 1, p 22.

The reforms that followed focused on audit. A total overhaul of existing financial procedures imposed stricter control over the disbursement of funds and strengthened accountability structures through internal audit units and EP budgetary committees. A new Financial Regulation standardised procedure for managing decentralised and contracted-out administration. The Court of Auditors gained substantially in influence through the introduction of 'value for money' (VFM) audit, which is now a routine practice. The same reforms drew heavily on managerial doctrines, which had swept through the world of public administration in the 1980s under the rubric of 'new public management' (NPM).[38] NPM or managerialism swung the throughput functions of government heavily towards output values. Focusing on economy, efficiency and effectiveness, its main objectives were to slim down the apparatus of the burgeoning 'administrative state', to refocus its endeavours and modernise administration. NPM borrowed quantitative audit procedures and set them in a framework of market-style transparency. It worked through the model of planned policy initiatives, targeted goals, performance indicators, repeated impact assessment, evaluation, supervision and oversight.

We see the Commission as bureaucratic in the double sense that its management style is in equal measure managerial and structured by rules. There is a preference for operating by a rule book in which procedures are elaborated and pinned down. The Commission is an 'audit society', governed by a 'targets culture',[39] with a highly managerial style based (to reiterate) on processes of data collection, information gathering, recording, performance indicators, impact assessment and quantifying whatever is (said to be) quantifiable. This audit-based package has become the centrepiece of Union-level administrative procedure with assessment and evaluation as its central tool. It forms the pattern for the standardised Commission framework for agencies,[40] which the Commission is busily introducing to agencies such as Europol previously under the sketchy supervision of the Council. It infuses an important new policy brief for financial services regulation, redolent of the managerial jargon of 'coordination', 'supervision' and 'risk assessment' and based on the key managerial principles of transparency, responsibility, supervision and crisis prevention, and management centred on a standardising 'single rule book'.[41] The theme runs through many of our case studies, extending from the partnership agreements used to manage the new cohesion policy programme (see chapter nine) to the management of Enlargement through conditionality (see chapter two). Managerial practice infuses the 'Better' or 'Smart' Regulation agenda, which relies on a standard mixture of procedures such as regulatory impact assessment, cost–benefit and risk-based analysis, selective consultation and (possibly) post-legislative impact evaluation. Throughput governance functions – administration and administrative procedure – have become a policy objective in their own right.

---

[38] See above, ch 1, p 23.
[39] M Power, *The Audit Explosion* (London: Demos, 1994).
[40] See above, ch 1, p 35.
[41] See above, ch 11, p 278.

In chapter nine, we questioned the way EU financial procedures operate in practice, suggesting that they are unduly complex. While there has been much talk about 'simplification' in cohesion policy, and elsewhere, the over-proceduralisation of the oversight machinery makes it unduly hard to pursue new programmes while the scope for corruption has certainly not been eliminated. Audit procedures are contributing to bureaucracy in the derogatory sense used by Crozier to signify 'the slowness, the ponderousness, the routine, the complication of procedures, and the maladapted responses of "bureaucratic" organisations to the needs which they should satisfy, and the frustrations which their members, clients or subjects consequently endure'.[42] Much the same can be said of excessive rulemaking – and, indeed, of proceduralisation more generally. Audit-based administrative procedure is certainly orderly. It is useful in familiarising officials with an administrative process or for purposes of coordination, whether hierarchically or in networks. Its negative side is the production of a 'tick-box' mentality, which treats rule-making as a substitute for implementation and the filling in of forms as a substitute for action. Tickbox administration is bureaucratic rather than dynamic. Initially introduced as a counterweight to a bureaucratic public service ethos, managerialism is steadily transforming EU administration into a regulated, regulatory bureaucracy.

Essentially then, EU administration is a world dominated by experts and by output values, with which the input values of citizen participation are unlikely to be able to compete. We have little time for the top-down methods in place to 'organise' European civil society and provide for citizen input. And civil society organisations are not well placed – other than in the exceptional case of access to documents – to mount legal challenges based on participation rights in the CJEU.[43] Bureaucratic administrative procedures such as the need to register on the Transparency Register or restrictive criteria for the European Citizens' Initiative pose obstacles to citizen participation. It is in our view questionable whether civil society ought to be 'organised'. Can popular democracy be built on administrative procedure - or indeed accommodated in a transnational governance system?[44] We suspect that it cannot.

We remain concerned that accountability structures, which we regard as an essential element in democratic governance, are so weak at Union level.[45] We are concerned too that so little attempt has been made to construct or install appropriate accountability machinery, as instanced in the argument over the Joint Supervisory Board of Europol.[46] We are concerned by the generally weak position of national parliaments notwithstanding the reinforcements introduced by the Lisbon Treaty. We are concerned too that so little fire-watching effort has been made to counter the detrimental effects of composite decision-making and multi-

---

[42] M Crozier, *The Bureaucratic Phenomenon* (Chicago: University of Chicago Press, 1963) 3.
[43] See above, ch 4, p 114.
[44] See P Cerny, 'Globalization and the End of Democracy' (1999) 36 *European Journal of Political Research* 1.
[45] C Harlow, *Accountability in the European Union* (Oxford: OUP) 2002.
[46] See above, ch 10, p 258.

level governance, leaving too much to sporadic firefighting efforts in the historically integrationist CJEU. We see both Courts and Commission as again guilty of double standards, expecting of Member States a greater degree of even-handedness and sincere cooperation than they are willing to accept at Union level.

In the course of our journey we have learned to respect the work of the EU officials who execute its policies in the framework of a set of haphazard and incoherent governance structures. They have worked hard to systematise the structures and processes of EU governance. Their style is orderly and rational. By and large they respect their treaty obligation to give reasons. Our metaphor of administrative procedure as 'super glue' holding in place the fragments of an unwieldy governance system is, in short, essentially justified. Nonetheless, we detect an unwelcome trend to standardisation for the sake of standardisation and a tendency to micro-manage. Good administration should not extend to the regulation of every comma. Diversity and pluralism are valuable EU assets that should not lightly be dismantled. 'Super glue' is a useful product but it should be thinly applied.

Index

Aarhus Convention, 299
  Aarhus Convention Compliance Committee (ACCC), 309–11
  access to information, 303, 305, 306
  citizen participation, 112, 299, 301, 305, 307
  enforceability:
    EO investigations, 307–08
    infringement proceedings, 307
  enhanced access to justice, 305, 308–09
  environmental policy, 299, 302–04
    pre-Aarhus developments, 299–302
  implementation, 309–11
  obligations owed to public, 127, 305, 306
  proceduralisation, 303–04
  transnational relationships, 310
access to documents, 26, 120, 338
  Aarhus Convention, 302–03, 305–06, 327
  ECHR, 132
  EO investigations, 81–83, 135–39
  establishment of the right, 123–24, 127–28, 311
  Europol procedures, 260, 265
  infringement procedure, 131, 185–87
  see also freedom of information; transparency
accountability, 1–2, 34, 64, 241–42, 244–45, 250, 276–77, 338–39
  committees, 29–31
  competition law, 209–20
  conditionality principle, 46–47
  data processing and retention, 26
  ECB, 294–95
  EO, 64–65
  EP, 190–91
  Europol, 248, 254, 265–66
  expert groups, 29–30
  LIBE Committee, 253
  NPM, 23
  partnership agreements, 234
  soft governance, 53
  subsidiarity, 43–44
  WPEG, 45–46
  see also Aarhus Convention; transparency
administrative procedures, 1, 8, 38–63, 326–27
  administrators' toolkit, 60–62
  citizen participation, 112–13
  codes of conduct, 123–27
  codification, 331–35
  cohesion policy, 223, 227, 242–43
  competition law, 196, 204, 220
  courts, 311–12
  development, 1–37
  EU external relations and, 14–15, 298–99
  judges' role, 184–85
  principles and standards, 38–48
  process distinguished, 2
  public procurement, 142–44, 149–51
  transparency, 117–18, 119–41
agencies, 6, 31, 244–45
  accountability, 244–45, 260, 263, 266–67
  'agencification', 34–36
  ECN, 197
  Europol, 244–67
  information gathering, 32
  Meroni doctrine, 95
  networking, 33–34, 96–97, 112, 297
  promoting horizontal cross-fertilisation, 33, 286, 297
  regulation, 49
  role, 32
  rule-making powers, 96, 244–45, 330, 334, 336
  structure, 33
  WPEG, 96
  see also Europol
agencification, 3, 10, 31, 34–36, 269, 277–87, 296, 323, 330
  Common Approach, 35
alternative dispute resolution (ADR), 161
  SOLVIT, 84–85, 172
  WPEG, 181
arm's-length public bodies, see agencies
audit, 22–24, 38, 48–51, 61–62
  accountability, 48
  cohesion policy, 221–24
    decentralised management, 236–38, 239, 241–42
  constitutional oversight, 49
  ECA, 49, 240–41
  Financial Regulation, 49–50
  Prodi-Kinnock reforms, 48
  public procurement, 157
  rationalisation of internal procedures, 48–49
  reform, 337–38
  soft governance, 50–51
  structural funds, 240
  VFM audits, 58

Banking Union, 177, 279, 287–88, 294
  single supervisory mechanism, 269, 288
Basel Committee on Banking Supervision, 273, 297
'Better Regulation', 6, 10, 19, 55–56, 93, 324
  consultation 112, 117

Index

'Better Regulation' *cont.*
  financial services regulation, 272–73, 276, 284
  impact assessment, 117
  targeting, 238–39
bilateral cooperation agreements, 47, 208
bureaucratic culture, 8, 63, 109
  Commission, 24–26, 112–13, 236–37
  public service, 20–22
  regulatory bureaucracy, 335–39

Chief Competition Economist, 203
citizen participation, 12–13, 21–22, 112, 62, 338
  conflict, 328–29
  environmental policy, 299, 301, 305, 307
  European Citizens' Initiative, 116
civil society, 106–08, 117–18, 338
  cohesion policy:
    partnership, 231–32
  Commission's relationship with, 108–09, 111, 112, 311
  Lisbon Treaty and, 116–17
  participation, 28, 45, 94
    open consultations, 112–13
  see also Non-Government Organisations (NGOs)
codes of conduct, 123–26
  classification and secrecy, 126–27
cohesion policy, 241–43, 323
  'additionality', 227, 242
  Committee of the Regions (CoR), 205
  community regional policy, 224–25
  'concentration', 226–27, 242
  European Regional Development Fund (ERDF), 225
  European Social Fund (ESF), 225
  partnerships, 231–34
    codes of conduct, 235–36
    partnership agreements, 234–35
  policy development and implementation, 226
  priorities, 226
  'programming', 224–31, 242
  proportionality, 227–28
  subsidiarity, 225, 227–28
  structural funds, 221–24
  see also structural funds
Comitology 1, 97
Comitology 2, 98, 101–02
Comitology 3, 99–101
comitology procedure, 27, 57, 97, 270–71, 329
  advisory committee procedure, 97
  Comitology Register, 30, 105
  consultation procedures, 112
  guidance, 98
  management committee procedure, 97, 98
    regulatory committee procedure distinguished, 99
  regulatory committee procedure, 97

  management committee procedure distinguished, 99
  scrutiny, 99
  reforms, 103–05
  risk regulation, 75
  safeguarding procedure, 98
  transparency, 101–02, 132, 140
  see also Comitology 1; Comitology 2; Comitology 3
Commission, *see* European Commission
Commission Impact Assessment Board, 70
Committee of European Banking Supervisors (CEBS), 272, 277
Committee of European Insurance and Occupational Pensions Supervisors (CEIOPS), 272, 277
Committee of European Securities Regulators (CESR), 270, 271, 274–76, 277, 286
Committee on Civil Liberties, Justice and Home Affairs, *see* LIBE Committee
committees, 2, 6–7, 36
  independence, 28
  law-making, 97–102
  network governance, 10–11, 15, 18, 27–29
  quality, 28
  transparency, 29–31
  use of experts, 28–29
  see also comitology procedure
Common Agricultural Policy (CAP), 11, 48
Common Approach, 35
  impact assessment, 35
Common Strategic Framework, 228, 234
'communication, cooperation and coordination', 10, 36–37, 52, 60, 197, 239, 323–25
competition law, 196–98, 220, 322–33
  cartels, 211
  CJEU, 198–99, 202–04
    judicial standards, 204
  cooperation:
    networks, 205–06
  enforcement, 210–11
    decision-making, 213–14
    investigations, 212–13
  fundamental rights, 217–19
  good governance, 209–10
  modernisation, 197
    CJEU and, 202–04
  reform, 198–202
    block exemptions, 199
    consumer welfare, 201–02
    de minimis, 199
    Merger Regulation, 201
    Modernisation Regulation, 200–01
  sanctions, 216–17
complaints handling, 61, 324
  ENO, 85–86, 92
  EO, 65, 84–86
  SOLVIT, 84–85, 109

Index

compliance, 173–79
  Aarhus, 305
    Aarhus Convention Compliance
      Committee, 309–11
  agencies, 33
  cohesion policy, 222–23
  competition law, 200
  compliance theory, 174
  compliance-promoting tools, 175–79
    correlation tables, 177–78
    effectiveness, 178
    inspection authorities, 176
    legislation, 176
    transposition and implementation plans
      (TIPS), 178
  contract compliance, 152–53, 156, 158–60,
    163, 168–69
  ECB, 290
  EU Pilot project, 182–84
  human rights, 84–85
  national parliaments, 170–71
    subsidiarity principle, 43
  transparency, 138–40, 150
  see also infringement
composite administration, 11, 13, 40, 61
composite decision-making, 6, 8, 11, 52, 65, 267,
  318–19, 333, 338
conditionality principle, 17, 39, 46–48, 62, 208,
  224, 324337
  accountability, 46–47
  Eurozone crisis, 47–48
  structural funds, 229–31
    macro-economic conditionality, 230
consultation procedures, 6, 10, 56, 94, 112
  comitology, 112
  enforcement, 113–14
  judicial abstention, 114–16
  open consultations, 112–13
  written consultations, 112
control, 1–2, 64
  Joint Supervisory Body, 257–58
  see also accountability
convergence, 3, 5, 9, 14, 51
  competition, 220
  Lamfalussy process, 269, 276
  Open Method of Coordination, 53–54
cooperation, 323–24
  bilateral cooperation agreements, 208
  competition law, 205–06
  see also sincere cooperation
Coreper, 18, 97, 105, 106, 253
Council, 5, 18–19
  committees and, 28, 30, 97–98
  delegation, 95
  EO and, 135–39
  executive law-making, 95, 97–100
  OMC, 53–54
  openness, 46, 83, 128–31

  EO and, 135–39
  regulatory procedure, 99
  right of scrutiny, 104
  transparency, 140
    codes of conduct, 123–26
    freedom of information, 121–23
courts, 6–7, 64
  due process, 15, 74–75, 311–12
  ECB, 294
    technical regulation, 96
  functions, 65–68
  general principles of market integration, 149
  individual rights versus public interest, 65
  intensity of review, 71–78
  protection of fundamental freedoms, 149
  standard of procedural review, 78
  see also judicial decision-making

data processing and retention, 26
  Europol, 255–56
data protection, 30, 60, 71, 131–32, 139, 244–45,
  247–49
  Europol, 254–57, 261, 263–64
  JSB, 257–58
  see also freedom of information
delegation, 22, 49, 117
  CJEU and, 95
  experts, 96–97
  justification, 96
  law-making and, 94–95
  Meroni doctrine, 32, 36, 95
  regulatory agencies, 32
  scientific regulation, 96–97
  technical regulation, 96–97
Diamandorous, N, 79, 83, 122, 139
  infringement procedure, 188–89
direct administration, 5, 11, 15, 48
  competition law, 196–98
dispute resolution, 1–2
  see also alternative dispute resolution
double accountability, 172–73
due diligence, 318
  right to good administration, 88, 188
due process, 7–8, 15, 65, 67, 311–12, 327, 316–18
  conflicting obligations, 319–20
  ECB, 290
    accountability and, 294–95
  ECHR, 90–91
  public security v rights of the individual,
    313–15, 318
  rights:
    access to court, 316, 317
    right to reasons, 74–75, 316, 317–18
    standard of review, 315–16
    technical regulation, 96

e-Commission, 26
e-governance, 25–26, 60, 307, 324–25

e-governance *cont.*
  access to documents, 26
  concerns, 26
enforcement policy, 172, 175, 178
  constitutional parameters:
    Commission actions against infringement, 171
    division of labour, 170
    mutual responsibility, 170–71
    private actors as enforcers, 171
  see also fire-watching
enlargement, 16–17, 27, 322–24, 330–31
  competition, 197, 200
  economic assistance, 17
  enforcement issues, 172
  EU law and, 330–31
  influences, 14–16
  national procedural autonomy, 13–14
  see also cohesion policy
environmental impact assessments, 15, 55, 81, 300
environmental policy:
  Aarhus Convention, 299, 302–04
  citizen participation, 299, 301, 305, 307
  development, 299–301
    close cooperation, 301
    infringement proceedings, 301
    EEA, 301
  dissemination of information, 301
  impact assessment, 301
  national green agendas, 302
  origins, 299
  proceduralisation, 303–04
  see also Aarhus Convention
EU Emissions Trading System (ETS), 44, 96
EU law:
  due process, 74
  evolution, 329–30
    enlargement, 330–31
  general principles, 64–65, 325
  infringement, 81
  proportionality testing, 68, 70
EU Network for the Implementation and Enforcement of Environmental Law (IMPEL), 34, 176
EU Pilot project, 179, 180, 182–84, 189
'Eurolegalism', 78, 149–50, 171, 220, 311–12, 334
Europe 2020, 47
  cohesion policy, 228, 229
  OMC, 53
  public procurement, 146, 161, 166–67
European Anti-Fraud Office (OLAF), 49, 50, 81, 238, 239–40, 261, 264
European Banking Authority (EBA), 269, 279–82, 283–84, 293–94, 296
European Banking Committee (EBC), 271–72
European Central Bank (ECB), 269, 280, 282, 288–90
  accountability, 294–95
  cooperation:
    national competition authorities, 291
    SSM, 290
  due process, 294
  enforcement powers, 290
  EP-ECB Inter-institutional Agreement, 295
  good governance, 294
  non-eurozone countries and, 292–94
  separation of powers:
    monetary policy role, 291–92
    supervisory role, 290–92
  sincere cooperation, 291
  SSM and, 290–91, 296
European Charter of Fundamental Rights, 21, 67, 197–98
  access to information, 136, 256
    protection of personal data, 259
  complaints handling, 85, 87–89
  due process, 319–20
  good administration, 87–91, 92, 325–26, 328, 333
  quality of the environment, 300
European Citizens Advisory Service, 109, 112, 114, 122, 136
European Commission:
  administrative reform:
    new public management, 23
  agencies, 6
  'Better Regulation' agenda, 19, 272–73
  bureaucratic culture, 21
  civil society:
    CONCORD, 109–10
    consultation, 112–17
    European Citizens Advisory Service, 109
    European Transparency Initiative, 108
    public interest, 108–09
    voluntary sector relationships, 108–09
  classification of infringements, 173–74
  committees, 27–29
  competition law:
    in-house checks, 214–16
    role of Hearing Officers, 215–16
  cooperation, 27
  EC central administration, 3
  functions, 3–4, 18–19
    policymaking, 18
    workaday public service, 19
  good governance, 45–46
  information sharing, 19
  monitoring, 19
  NGOs:
    registration, 110–11
    representativity, 111
    status, 110
  oversight, 19
  procedural inadequacies, 22–23
  structural funds, 221–24

Index   345

structural inadequacies, 22–23
supervisory role, 19
see also agencies; 'Better Regulation'; New Public Management (NPM)
European Committee for Electrotechnical Standardization (CENELEC), 96
European Committee for Standardization (CEN), 96
European Community:
executive federalism, 13
national cultural influences, 14–16
France, 14–15
Germany, 15
open government, 15
Rechtsstaat, 15
Scandinavia, 15
UK, 15
European Competition Network (ECN), 197
enforcement, 205–06
judicial cooperation with, 208
model leniency programme, 207
policy development, 206–07
European Confederation of Relief and Development (CONCORD), 109–10
European Convention on Human Rights, 182, 197–98, 325–26
access to documents, 132
due process, 90–91
European Cooperation Group on Undercover Activities, 30
European Court of Auditors (ECA), 22, 49
structural funds, 237, 240–41
value for money auditing, 49–50
European Court of Justice (CJEU), 1, 10
Aarhus and, 310–11
competition, 198–99, 202–04, 216
delegation and, 95
due process, 312, 326–27
firefighting functions, 68–76, 91–92
powers of constitutional review, 66–68
procedural rulings:
competences, 67
public procurement:
scope of legislative framework, 151–52
transparency, 150–51
wrongful application of rules, 150
European Economic and Monetary Union (EMU), 47, 225
OMC, 53–54
European Economic and Social Committee (EESC), 27, 106–08, 110, 234, 284, 336
corporate consultation, 112
European Environment Agency (EEA), 32, 301
network functions, 33–34
European Environment Information and Observation Network (EIONET), 34, 301
European Fisheries Control Agency (EFCA), 34, 298

European Food Safety Authority (EFSA), 96, 105, 297
European Investment Bank (EIB), 71, 223
proportionality, 71
European Insurance and Occupational Pensions Committee (EIOPC), 272
European Network of Heads of Nature Conservation, 34
European Network of Law Enforcement Technology Services (ENLETS), 16, 262
European Network of Ombudsmen (ENO), 65, 267, 325
complaints handling, 85–86
European Ombudsman (EO), 1, 64–65
Code of Good Administrative Behaviour, 83–84, 87, 138–39, 333
proportionality, 71
competences, 79–80
complaints handling, 135–37
ENO, 85–86
problem-solving, 84–85
SOLVIT, 84–85, 172
creation, 79
due diligence, 188–89
EU Pilot project, 184
function, 79–82
good governance, 7, 81, 83–84, 92
impact on administrative procedure, 80
implementation of recommendations, 81
infringement procedure, 187–90
investigations, 80, 81, 84
open government:
complaints, 135–37
own-initiative investigations, 137–39
own-initiative investigations, 137–39
principles, 82–84
reform, 81–82
right to good administration, 87–91, 92, 188–89
due diligence, 88, 188–89
duty of care, 88
EU Charter of Fundamental Rights, 87–89
role, 79
transparency, 15, 122
values, 82–84
European Parliament (EP), 5
comitology and, 97–100, 101, 103
data protection, 263
inter-parliamentary scrutiny unit, 266
Europol and, 265–66
executive law-making, 97–100
infringement procedure, 190–91
legislative principles, 333
procedural codification, 333
transparency, 122
see also LIBE Committee
European Regional Development Fund (ERDF), 225, 226, 228

346   Index

European Regulatory Networks (ERNs), 274–75
European Securities and Markets Authority, 35–36, 66–67, 103, 281
European Social Fund (ESF), 225, 228, 233
European Stability Mechanism (ESM), 288
   conditionality principle, 47
European Supervisory Authorities (ESAs), 269, 282–84, 286–87
   ESA template, 281–82
   intervention powers, 284
      emergency situations, 285
      mediation and arbitration, 284
   see also Banking Union
European System of Financial Supervision (ESFS), 269, 278–79
   ESA template, 281–82
   role, 279–80
European Union (EU), 9–13
   convergency, 5, 9
   Council of Europe and, 298
   external relations, 297–99, 323
      conflicting obligations, 319–20
   procedural approximation, 5
   procedural concerns, 8
'Europeanisation', 5, 14, 47–48, 54, 220, 321
Europol, 244–45, 323
   accountability, 265–66, 267
   cooperation of member states, 251–52
   data protection, 254–57
      accuracy of information 256
      European Data Protection Supervisor (EDPS), 258
      Europol Regulation, 263–65
      principle of public access, 256
   establishment, 245–46
   Europol Convention, 246–47
      regulatory framework, 248–50
   Europol Decision, 250–51
   Europol Regulation, 258–59
      data protection, 263–65
      management and administration, 259–63
   good governance, 253–54
   Joint Supervisory Body
      abolition (proposed), 258
      role, 257–58
   mission creep, 266–67
   origins, 245
   role:
      assistance to national units in investigations and policing, 251
      communication with competent authorities, 251
      information and intelligence gathering, 251
      rule-making powers, 252–53
Eurostat, 25, 132, 226, 324
Eurozone crisis, 27, 52, 145–46
   conditionality principle, 47–48
Executive law-making, 93–94

committee law-making and, 97–102
delegation, 94–97
   CJEU recognition, 95
   delegated legislation and implemented legislation, 94
   Lisbon Treaty reforms, 102–06

Financial Regulation, 17, 221–22
   EU budget, 48
   managing authority, 236–37
   reform, 50, 224, 241, 243
   sound financial management, 222, 241
   supervisory procedure, 49
Financial Services Action Plan (FSAP), 269
financial services regulation, 268–69, 295–96, 323
   ESFS, 279, 296
      ESA template, 281–82
      role, 279–80
   Lamfalussy process, 296
      'better regulation', 272–73
      evaluation, 276–77
      external policy and practice, 273–74
      four level model, 270–72
      origins, 269
      outputs, 271–72
      regulatory networks, 274–76
   single supervisory mechanism, 288, 296
      ECB and, 290–91
      non-eurozone countries, 292–94
      see also European Central Bank (ECB)
'firefighting', 214
   CJEU, 66–68, 91, 339
   EO, 92, 260
   Joint Supervisory Board, 257–58
'fire-watching', 64–65, 91, 195
   alternative dispute resolution, 181
   Commission fire-watching, 173–79, 180, 198
   composite decision-making, 338–39
   EO functions, 79–84, 92
      complaints handling, 84–86
   ESRB, 279–80
   Joint Supervisory Board, 257–58
   judicial decision-making, 64–65
   see also enforcement policy
Food and Agriculture Organization (FAO), 297–98
freedom of information, 60, 120–21, 133
   EO interventions, 8, 92
   information laws, 133–34
   political right, 121–23
   statutory procedures, 134–35
   see also access to documents
Frontex, 85, 99–100, 261
functionalism:
   administrative procedure, 1–8
fundamental rights, 9
   competition law, 217–19

data processing and retention, 26
openness, 121–22
right to good administration, 87–89
  procedure as a human right, 89–91
transparency, 120–21
  freedom of information, 121–23

'guarding the guardian', 172–73
General Court (GC), 1
  comitology, 102
  freedom of information, 121
  infringement proceedings, 177
  scrutiny of Commission, 199
  see also European Court of Justice (CJEU)
good governance, 62, 305, 321
  Better Regulation, 56
  competition, 209–10
  cooperation, 224, 243
  EO and, 92, 326
  Europol Decision, 253–54
  EU external relations, 298–99
  partnership, 224
  transparency, 119
  WPEG principles, 38, 45–46, 209–10, 235
  participation, 112
  see also transparency
governance, 1–3, 9–10
  committee, by, 27–28
  conditionality, 47
  democratic principles, 9
  e-governance, 25–26
  multi-level governance, 12–13
  network governance, 6, 12
  soft governance, 5, 16, 27, 38, 50, 287, 331
    Aarhus model, 305
    complaints handling network, 92
    Lisbon presidency, 53–55, 226
    OMC, 51–53, 60, 63, 297
    SOLVIT, 85
  WPEG, 38, 45
  see also good governance

Hearing Officers:
  competition, 214–16
human rights:
  asset-freezing, 312–14
  CJEU and, 326
  commitment to, 325–26
  see also fundamental rights

impact assessment:
  Common Approach, 35
  financial regulation, 38, 50–51
  Impact Assessment Guidelines, 56–57
  smart regulation, 56–58
    proportionality principle, 56, 58
    subsidiarity principle, 56
  subsidiarity, 43, 56

indirect administration, 5, 11, 15, 34
  e-governance, 25–26
  regulatory steering, 25
information and communications technology,
      197, 270
  audit processes, 237
  e-governance, 25–26, 324–25
  infringement procedure, 174, 175
  see also data processing and retention; data
      protection
infringement, 170–71, 195
  access to documents, 185–87
  Commission classification, 173–74
  compliance-promoting tools, 175–79
  compliance theory, 174
  elongated decision-making chain, 179–80
  enforcement policy and, 170–73
  EO, 187–90
  EP and, 190–91
  EU Pilot, 182–84
  judicial policy, 184–85
  priorities, 181–82
  sanctions procedures, 171, 174–75, 191–95
  serious infringement, 181
  see also compliance theory; sanctions
      procedure
integration:
  Banking Union, 177
  'bottom-up' mechanisms, 11
  cohesion policy and, 225
  financial and regulatory integration, 268–96
  'top-down' mechanisms, 11
International Association of Insurance
      Supervisors (IAIS), 274
International Competition Network, 209
International Organisation of Securities
      Commissions (IOSCO), 274

judicial decision-making, 65–68
  administrative procedure, 68
  due process rights, 74–75
  proportionality testing, 68–71
  rationality, 74
  reason-giving, 73–74
judicial review, 1–2, 36, 65–66, 78, 204, 320, 325
  administrative procedure and, 100, 158, 202
  financial services regulation, 290
  firefighting function, 64
  primacy of human rights, 314–16
  reason-giving, 73, 316
Justice and Home Affairs (JHA), 15, 18, 90, 122,
      250

Kadi case, 7, 85, 314, 315, 318–20
Kelemen, D
  'Eurolegalism', 78, 311, 334
Kinnock, N, 23
  Prodi-Kinnock reforms, 48

348 *Index*

Lamfalussy process:
  'better regulation', 272
    co-regulation, 273
    impact assessment, 272–73
    self-regulation, 273
  evaluation, 276–77
  external policy and practice, 273–74
    bilateral regulatory dialogues, 274
    international cooperation and coordination, 273
  four level model:
    cooperation, 271
    enforcement, 271
    legislative framework, 270
    outputs, 271–72
    technical implementing measures, 270–71
  Lamfalussy, A, 270
  origins, 269
  outputs, 271–72
  re-evaluation, 277–79
  regulatory networks:
    CESR, 274–76
    ERNs, 274–75
  see also European System of Financial Supervision
LIBE Committee, 140, 253, 262 – 67
limitations, 144–45, 154, 163
  judicial procedures, 8
  legislative and administrative process distinguished, 6
  separation of powers, 6
Lisbon Strategy, 228
  OMC, 53–55
  soft governance, 53–54
Lisbon Treaty, 94–95
  centralised enforcement, 182
  citizen participation, 89
  civil society, 116
    European citizens' initiative, 94, 116–17
  delegated legislation, 103–04
  ECHR, 91, 182, 298
  Europol, 258–59
  implementing procedure, 104–06
  national procedural autonomy versus 'common interest', 14
    competition law, 205–06, 210
  reforms, 102–03, 140
    appeals, 105
    comitology, 102–06
    delegated legislation, 103–04
    implementing procedure, 104–06
  right to good administration, 67

Maastricht Treaty, 300, 329
  Common and Foreign Security Policy (CFSP), 18
  EMU, 225
  Justice and Home Affairs (JHA), 15, 18

  NGOs, 108–09
  Office of the EO, 79
  subsidiarity, 42–43
  transparency, 120–21
Majone, G
  regulatory agency model, 10, 19, 330
managerialism, 15, 48–51, 338
  Commission reform, 23–25
  financial regulation 50–51
managing authorities:
  code of conduct, 235–36
  financial supervision, 236–38
  partnership and, 232, 233
  sanctions, 238
Meroni case, 32, 36, 95, 252, 282, 285, 289, 327
multi-level governance, 12–13, 222
  complaints handling, 85
  partnership, 224–25, 231–32, 235

national procedural autonomy, 13–14, 160
  competition law, 205–06, 210
national sovereignty, 13, 269
  internal security, 245
  subsidiarity and, 43–44
Nehl, H-P, 7, 73, 75, 88, 334
network governance, 6, 10–12, 27–29, 36, 60, 297
  accountability, 50
    ombudsmen network, 65
  agencies, 31–34, 35, 267
    Europol, 246, 250–51, 261–62, 266
  agencification, 279–80, 282
  citizen participation, 112
  committees, 27–29, 330
  competition, 197, 205–06
  complaints handling, 84, 92
    ENO, 85–86
    SOLVIT, 84–85
  cooperation, 205–09
    good governance, 209–10
  development of formal network system, 279–80, 282
  environmental policy, 301, 303
  NGOs, 108–10
  regulatory networks, 274–76
  soft law, 52–53, 93, 96–97
New Public Management, 38
  administrative reform of Commission, 23, 24–25
  conditionality and, 46–47
  financial regulation, 50–51
  OMC and, 54
Non-Government Organisations (NGOs), 108–10
  registration, 110–11
  representativity, 111
  status, 110
  transparency, 122

Office for Harmonization in the Internal Market (OHIM), 32, 137
open government, 15, 127–28
  EO, 135–39
  exemptions, 129
  public access to law-making process, 128–33
  regulation and, 127–28
    freedom of information, 133–34
    law-making, 128–33
  transparency, 119–21, 122
  see also freedom of information; transparency
Open Method of Coordination (OMC), 38, 63
  close cooperation, 54
  consent, 54
  Lisbon Strategy, 53–55
  NPC and, 54
  performance, 54–55
  soft governance, 53–55, 336
Organisation for Economic Cooperation and Development (OECD), 46, 55, 65, 209, 298, 301, 302, 331

partnerships, 224
  application of partnership principle, 232–33
  cohesion policy, 231–34
    codes of conduct, 235–36
    partnership agreements, 234–35
  intra-state partnerships, 233–34
    codes of conduct, 235–36
PHARE programme, 17, 25, 52, 298
precautionary principle, 76–78
privacy, 26, 128, 131, 319, 333
  see also data processing and retention; data protection
privilege, 136
  legal professional privilege, 129, 212, 216
  self-discrimination, 212, 215
proceduralisation, 3, 36, 104–05, 243, 248, 338
  consultation procedures, 94
  soft governance and, 53, 85, 220
  subsidiarity and, 303–04
  see also managerialism
Prodi, R, 23
  Prodi-Kinnock reforms, 48
proportionality principle, 15, 43, 61, 68–69, 90
  CJEU proportionality testing, 69–71, 75, 125, 327
  cohesion policy, 227–28, 242–43
  courts and, 311, 315, 327
  decision-making, 212
  'Europeanising effect', 70
  impact assessment, 56, 58
  individual versus public interest, 65
  public procurement, 164–65
Prum Convention (Schengen III), 30, 256
public participation, *see* citizen participation
public procurement, 142–46, 168–69

CJEU:
  scope of legislative framework, 151–52
  transparency, 150–51
compulsory competitive tendering, 143
conceptual model, 154–58
  competitive dialogue, 155
  negotiated procedure, 155
  open procedure, 155
  restricted procedure, 155
contract compliance, 152–53
contract theory, 145
contracting out, 143
disclosure of private interests, 166
flexibility, 165
governance, 167–68
green procurement, 153
invitations to tender, 155–56
legislation, 146–48
monitoring, 158
national procedures, 144–45, 166
outsourcing, 143
procedures, 148–49
process, 154–58
proportionality, 164
reform, 161–62
  impact assessment, 162–63
  simplification, 163–64
remedies:
  effectiveness principle, 159
  pre-contractual remedies, 159–60
review procedures, 158
  national systems, 160–61
  remedies, 159–61
revised public sector and utilities directives, 161
scope of regulatory regime, 164–65
Public Procurement Network (PPN), 161
public service:
  Staff Regulations, 20–21

rationality, 120
  bounded rationality, 39
  discretionary powers and, 186
  reason-giving, 39, 73–74
  reasoned decision-making, 39–40
  risk assessment, 75–78
reason-giving, 39
  judicial decision-making, 73–74
  judicial review, 73, 316
  rationality, 39, 73–74
Rechtsstaat, 15, 39–40, 143, 150, 199, 331–32
recovery of monies, 237
sincere cooperation, 41–42
regulation:
  'Better Regulation', 6, 10, 19, 55–56, 93, 324
    consultation 112, 117
    financial services regulation, 272–73, 276, 284

regulation *cont.*
    impact assessment, 117
    targeting, 238–39
  impact assessment, 38, 50
    proportionality principle, 56, 58
    subsidiarity principle, 56
  open government, 127–40
  smart regulation, 38, 55–56
    impact assessment, 56–58
    REFIT, 58–60
Regulatory Fitness and Performance Programme (REFIT), 58–60, 179, 223
risk assessment, 57, 75, 337
  audit and, 239
  environment, 307
  Europol, 247
  lack of expert knowledge, 76
  precautionary principle, 76–78
  rationality principle, 75–78

sanctions, 61–62, 174
  cartels, 211
  Commission toolkit, 216–17
  ECB and, 290–91
  enforcement model, 212
  financial sanctions, 171, 172, 179–80, 185, 193–94
  procedure:
    CJEU, 193
    Commission, 191–93
    fast-tracking, 193–94
  right to make representations, 115
  see also smart sanctions
Scientific Committee on Consumer Safety (SCCS), 29
Scientific Committee on Emerging and Newly Identified Health Risks (SCENIHR), 29
Scientific Committee on Health and Environmental Risks (SCHER), 29
Secretariat-General, 24, 63
Securities and Exchange Commission (SEC) (US), 274
separation of powers, 6, 66
sincere cooperation, 40–41, 137, 170
  ECB and national competition authorities, 208, 280, 291
  mutual assistance, 41–42
  subsidiarity principle and, 206
  tax administrations, 41–42
single supervisory mechanism, 41, 269, 287–88
  non-eurozone countries, 292–94
  role, 290–91
smart regulation, 38, 55–56, 337
  impact assessment, 56–58, 337
    proportionality principle, 56, 58
    subsidiarity principle, 56
  REFIT, 58–60

smart sanctions:
  asset-freezing, 312–14
Söderman, J, 15, 82–84, 139, 188, 191
  own-initiative investigations, 137
  right to good administration, 87
  transparency, 122, 135
soft governance, 3, 16, 63
  audit, 50–51
  benchmarking, 52
  concerns, 53
  definition, 51
  instruments, 51
  respect for diversity and pluralism, 51–53
  see also Open Method of Coordination (OMC)
sovereignty, *see* national sovereignty
split-level analysis, 10–12
  horizontal and vertical procedures, 4
  national procedural autonomy, 13–14
Standing Committee on the Food Chain and Animal Health (SCFCAH), 29
Statewatch, 110–11, 122, 135–37, 140, 262
Strategic Environmental Assessment (SEA) Directive, 302
structural funds, 61, 110, 114, 221–24
  'additionality', 227
  administrative procedure, 226–28
  budgetary restraint, 228
  central and eastern Europe, 225
  community regional policy, 224–25
  'concentration', 226–27
  conditionality, 229–31
    implementation of EU law, 229–30
    macro-economic conditionality, 230–31
  ECA, 240–41
  European Regional Development Fund (ERDF), 225
  European Social Fund (ESF), 225
  financial management, 239
  fraud, 239–41
  OLAF, 239–40
  see also cohesion policy
subsidiarity, 14, 38, 42–45, 62, 89, 225, 227–28, 235, 242
  accountability and, 43–44
  added value test, 42–43
  cohesion policy, 225
  environmental policy, 303–04, 311
  impact assessment, 43, 56
  necessity test, 42–43
  sincere cooperation and, 206
  smart regulation, 56, 59
Subsidiarity Monitoring Network (SMN), 44

technological research and development, 16, 146, 165, 226
transparency, 62, 119, 140–41, 331

CJEU, 150–51
codes of conduct, 123–26
  classification and secrecy, 126–27
  European Council, 124
comitology, 101–02
committees, 29–31, 101–02
competition law, 209–10
freedom of information, 121–23
market transparency, 119–21
reform, 139–40
see also freedom of information; open government
Treaty on European Union (TEU):
  accession to ECHR, 91
  added value, 43
  CJEU mandate, 66, 170, 326–27
  consultation, 116
  law enforcement, 171
  necessity, 43
  proportionality, 43, 68
  sincere cooperation, 40
  subsidiarity, 43
  transparency, 120, 124
  universal values, 9, 39
Treaty on the Functioning of the European Union (TFEU), 14, 212, 331–32
  CJEU review of procedures, 66–67
  due process, 319
  cohesion policy, 221
  competition, 196, 198
  compliance:
    financial sanctions, 171, 174, 193
  delegation, 95, 103–04, 282–84, 288
  EO's role, 79
  Europol, 266

harmonisation measures:
  subsidiarity, 45
  implementation, 104–06, 115, 153, 282–84
  infringement procedure, 181, 191, 216–17
  precautionary principle, 76
  reasoned decision-making, 40
  reason-giving, 73

UN Conference on Trade and Development (UNCTAD), 209
UN Economic Commission for Europe (UNECE), 302–03, 305
  see also Aarhus Convention
UNIDROIT, 274
United Nations (UN), 5
  cooperation, 298, 302
  environment monitoring programmes, 301

value for money auditing, 23, 49–50, 145, 224, 337

White Paper on European Governance (WPEG), 99
  accountability, 45–46
  ADR, 181
  agencies, 32–33, 96
  conditionality and, 46–47
  delegation, 96
  enforcement priorities, 181
  good governance principles, 38, 45–46
    competition, 209–10
  participation, 112
World Health Organization, 297–98
World Trade Organization (WTO), 5, 151, 209, 274, 298